Collectors' Information Bureau's

DIRECTORY TO LIMITED EDITION COLLECTIBLE STORES

Diane Carnevale Jones

Collectors' Information Bureau
2420 Burton S.E.
Grand Rapids, Michigan 49546
(616) 942-6898

Acknowledgments

Whenever the Collectors' Information Bureau can offer more quality information to collectors, we accept the challenge! The premier issue of this book required a high level of cooperation between all parties involved. The Collectors' Information Bureau extends its deep gratitude to the more than 1,000 participants, who have provided valuable information for this book. May these dedicated and knowledgeable individuals gain many new customers and friends, as they educate collectors about their hobby.

The Collectors' Information Bureau would like to thank the following persons who contributed to the creation of this book: Dave Goodwin, Wm. C. Brown & Co.; Diane Bower, Linda L. Joswick, Laurie Schaut, Dave Stafford, and Joy Versluys all with Trade Typographers, Inc.

Teamwork is the key to any successful project. The executive director wishes to thank her staff who contributed countless hours to the creation of this book: Betsy Bindley, Emily Eldersveld, Jessica Hybarger, Sue Knappen, Bethany Kuiper, Courtney Lawrence, Debi Ley, Carol VanElderen and Cindy Zagumny.

A special thank you is also extended to the Collectors' Information Bureau's Board of Directors who were very supportive of this new venture: Karen Feil, The Bradford Exchange; Bruce Kollath, John Hine Studios; Ron Jedlinski, Roman, Inc; Heio W. Reich, Reco International; James P. Smith, Jr., The Hamilton Collection; and Susan K. Jones, Special Consultant.

Copyright 1993 by Collectors' Information Bureau
Library of Congress Catalog Number: 92-50455
All rights reserved. No part of this book may be reproduced or used in any forms or by any means — graphics, electronic or mechanical, including photocopying or information storage and retrieval systems — without written permission from the copyright holder.

Although all editorial listings have been checked for accuracy, neither the editor nor publisher are responsible for any errors that may occur, nor for any losses that may be incurred through the use of this book.

Printed in the United States of America

ISBN: 0-930785-14-2   Collectors' Information Bureau

IBSN: 0-87069-701-3   Distributed by Wallace-Homestead, a division of Chilton Book Company

CREDITS:

Book design and graphics: Laurie Schaut, Trade Typographers, Inc., Grand Rapids, Michigan

Cover design: Bethany Kuiper

Contents

Acknowledgments ii
A Warm Welcome from the Collectors' Information Bureau v
How to Use This National Dealer Directory vii
Key to Manufacturer and Other Abbreviations ix
Retail Listings... 1
Subject Index 261
Contest Information: Shoot 'N Smile Collector Style! 290
Order Form for CIB Books.. 293

A Warm Welcome from The Collectors' Information Bureau

by Diane Carnevale Jones
Executive Director

In 1982, 14 collectible manufacturers became charter members of the Collectors' Information Bureau (CIB), which was formed to increase the public's awareness of the collectibles industry, an industry which has experienced extraordinary growth and collector enthusiasm in recent years. Today, the Collectors' Information Bureau is recognized as an authoritative source within the industry, providing the most accurate and up-to-date information on limited edition plates, figurines, bells, graphics, ornaments, dolls and steins. This not-for-profit trade organization has 80 member companies and reaches out to thousands of collectors across the country and around the world!

Books! Books! Books!

Collectors who enjoy reading about their hobby will enjoy the variety of books published by the Collectors' Information Bureau.

The Collectibles Market Guide & Price Index offers collectors nearly 600 pages of compre-

The Collectibles Market Guide & Price Index

Collectibles Price Guide

Directory to Secondary Market Retailers

Directory to Limited Edition Collectibles Stores

hensive information about most every aspect of collecting. Illustrated feature articles, a secondary market Price Index, manufacturer profiles, artist biographies and a complete listing of collector clubs are among the many topics covered in this ever-expanding edition. Rich color abounds on the cover and within the book, making this annual guide a 'must' for every collector.

The *Collectibles Price Guide*, published mid-year, features a Price Index listing over 30,000 active market prices based upon constant communication with a panel of expert retailers throughout North America, who buy and sell retired collectibles. Collectors who insure their artwork against theft and breakage, find this price guide an invaluable document, as well as hobbyists who buy and sell retired collectibles on the secondary market.

The Collectors' Information Bureau headquarters receives hundreds of phone calls from collectors who are interested in participating in the secondary market, yet need more information about the mechanics behind this venture. In an effort to educate collectors about this area, the Bureau makes available the *Directory to Secondary Market Retailers: Buying and Selling Limited Edition Artwork*. This book features a comprehensive listing of today's most respected secondary market dealers and exchanges nationwide, in addition to a practical guide outlining the basics of secondary market trading.

This exciting companion book to the *Directory to Limited Edition Secondary Market Retailers* was introduced in July 1993. Entitled *Directory to Limited Edition Collectible Stores*, this national dealer directory features over 1,000 collectible stores, making it easier for collectors to locate stores while vacationing. Collectors who live in small towns without collectible shops will now be able to locate sources for their favorite collectibles. We hope you will enjoy this premiere edition and meet many friends along the way! Don't forget to read about the photo promotion. By making use of this directory *you* could be one of the lucky collectors to win beautiful collectibles *or* the grand prize—a trip for two to the 1995 South Bend Collectibles Exposition.

Operation "Collector Hotline"

The Collectors' Information Bureau offers a hotline number to assist collectors with their difficult-to-answer questions. By calling (616) 942-9'CIB', collectors receive personal assistance in locating information on their favorite artists, phone numbers of manufacturers or perhaps values for their collectibles. Any questions that cannot be answered by phone are then directed to the research staff, who mail responses to collectors, once the information has been located.

```
COLLECTIBLES HOTLINE
CALL (616) 942-9 "CIB"
```

```
THE SOURCE FOR LIMITED EDITION
COLLECTIBLE INFORMATION:
Plates, Figurines, Bells, Graphics,
Christmas Ornaments, Dolls, Steins

Collectors' Information Bureau, 2420 Burton S.E.
Grand Rapids, MI 49546, Fax (616) 942-8594
```

Media Blitz

The Collectors' Information Bureau is actively involved in the media, both in supplying collectibles information to the top 500 daily newspapers, in addition to writing several magazine columns for collectible publications. Executive Director Diane Carnevale Jones has also appeared on cable television and has participated in numerous radio talk shows on the subject of collecting.

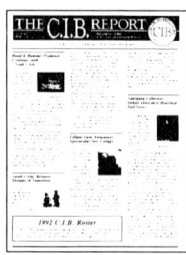

Newsletters, Collector Conventions and Seminars

The "C.I.B. Report" newsletter, published three times annually, contains the latest collectibles news, including recent product introductions, collector club activities, artist open houses, product retirement announcements

The Collectors' Information Bureau's booth at the International Collectible Exposition was staffed by (L to R) Diane Carnevale Jones, Sue Knappen and Cindy Zagumny. This show, held each July in South Bend, Indiana and one other collector show held in the Spring on either the East or West Coast, is managed by McRand International, Ltd. of Lake Forest, Illinois.

and convention news. These 40-page color newsletters are distributed at national collector conventions, through retailers and directly to collectors who purchase CIB books.

The Collectors' Information Bureau, along with scores of manufacturers, exhibits at annual national collector conventions on the east and west coasts, as well as in South Bend, Indiana. Thousands of collectors attend these events, strolling through exhibition halls viewing recent product introductions, meeting the artists who create these products and attending seminars. The Collectors' Information Bureau is on hand to distribute newsletters, answer collectors' secondary market questions and to present seminars on this same topic.

The Collectors' Information Bureau looks to new opportunities and challenges as the organization continues to expand its services, offering accurate, up-to-date and educational information to collectors, retailers, manufacturers and the media. We remain "**the** source for limited edition collectibles information!"

How To Use This National Dealer Directory

The Collectors' Information Bureau receives telephone calls daily from collectors wondering where they can locate their favorite collectibles. It was evident that a handy directory would be used and appreciated by collectors nationwide. Therefore the CIB staff contacted retailers from every state (and Canada too!), inviting them to be a part of this first-ever directory! The response was tremendous. Never before has so much information been presented in a book for collectors of contemporary limited edition collectibles. The style is easy-to-read. The collectible lines are indexed in the back of the book for handy reference.

Who should read the Directory to Limited Edition Collectible Stores?

- Collectors who travel across the country, who wish to visit collectible stores enroute to and from their final destinations. Every state is represented, affording collectors the opportunity to sample a taste of America! The variety of stores is outstanding. Some are located in the hearts of big cities, while others are nestled in the countryside (one even serves tea and oatmeal cookies every day!). No matter where you travel, you will experience a wonderful shoppers' haven,

with collectibles in abundance. Many stores carry other products and often feature the artwork of local artists.
- Collectors living in small towns may not have a collectibles store nearby. Perhaps you regularly read collectible magazines and have seen collectibles you wish to own. Consider this book your passport to adventure. Retailers invite you to simply call them to place your orders. You will automatically be placed on mailing lists and receive information on the availability of future issues.

What type of information is available in each retail editorial listing?

- Name of retail store
- Address
- Phone and fax number (look for several 800 numbers!)
- Store hours (remember which time zone you are calling!)
- A list of manufacturer lines featured in the store
- Information about credit cards accepted, and shipping and layaway availability
- Catalog and trade organization affiliation
- Collector Club Redemption Centers
- And more!

Should you contact these retailers for strictly limited items?

Most retailers have a local following in their own hometown and feel strongly about offering strictly limited edition pieces to their loyal customers first, and rightly so. Please use good judgment when contacting retailers about collectibles you are seeking.

How should the subject index be used?

If you are looking for a particular manufacturer's line and will be traveling to a specific state(s), simply look the name up in the index. Several page numbers will be listed, including a key as to the state in which they are located.

How can I win a trip for two to the 1995 South Bend Collectibles Exposition?

If you are the adventuresome sort and like to take photographs, please read on! Have you ever attended a national collectibles exposition, where the top manufacturers exhibit their collectibles and the top artists in the field are on hand to meet collectors? You could be the lucky winner of this grand prize to the 1995 South Bend Collectibles Exposition or one of several others. Simply turn to the back of this book and read the contest rules. By visiting stores featured in this book and taking photos, you can not only enter this photo contest, but meet many friends along the way. Get those cameras ready and begin clicking!

....

The Collectors' Information Bureau is always on hand to answer your questions. Should you have any questions about collectibles or need further information about the contents of this book, we welcome each of your calls. The CIB staff is exceptionally courteous and knowledgeable and looks forward to speaking to anyone who calls.

Key To Manufacturers And Other Abbreviations

In an effort to list as many manufacturers in each editorial feature as possible, abbreviations are often used. The following is the key to those abbreviations:

All God's Children	AGC
Bing & Grondahl	B&G
Cherished Teddies	CT
Duncan Royale	DR
Distinguished Service Retailer	DSR
David Winter	DW
Emmett Kelly, Jr.	EKJ
Emmett Kelly, Sr.	EKS
Gifts Creation Concepts	GCC
Kurt S. Adler	KSA
Memories of Yesterday	MOY
National Assn. of Limited Edition Dealers	NALED
Original Appalachian Artwork	OAA
Precious Moments	PM
Royal Copenhagen	RC
Sports Impressions	SI
Wee Forest Folk	WFF

ALABAMA

CLASSIC COLLECTION

2314 First St. N.E.
Birmingham, AL 35215

PHONE: (205)854-1701

Monday-Friday: 10:00-5:30
Saturday: 10:00-5:00

Dept. 56 Showcase Dealer: All Villages, Snowbabies, Merry Makers, All Through the House, Winter Silhouette, Precious Moments, Memories Of Yesterday, Cherished Teddies, Calico Kittens, Maud Humphrey, Enesco Musicals, Tom Clark Gnomes, Lladro, Walt Disney Classics Collection, Swarovski, David Winter, Roman Fontanini, Dreamsicles, Byers' Choice, Andrea by Sadek, Maruri, and M.I. Hummel.

All major credit cards accepted. Layaway. Shipping. Free gift wrapping.

Second Location: 105 Third St. North, Oneonta. Phone:(205)274-8663.

GIFTWICK SHOP

240 Century Plaza Mall
Birmingham, AL 35210

PHONE: (205)592-3190

Open Daily: 10:00-9:00

All God's Children, Dept. 56, Swarovski Crystal, Memories of Yesterday, David Winter Cottages, Maud Humphrey, Golden Memories, Cairn Gnomes, Hallmark Ornaments, Raikes Bears, Laura's Attic, Hummel, Precious Moments, Dreamsicles, Fenton, Shelia's and PenDelfin.

Other location: 3401 Bel Air Mall, Mobile, AL 36606. Phone: (205)471-6973.

(Some lines not available at Mobile store.)

THE CRYSTAL CORNER

P.O. Box 756
Boaz, AL 35957

PHONE: (205)593-6169

Monday-Saturday: 9:00-5:00

Precious Moments, Miss Martha's, All God's Children, Hummels, Sarah's Attic, Maud Humphrey, Jan Hagara, Emmett Kelly, Cairn Studios: Lee Sievers, Tim Wolfe, Tom Clark Gnomes. Snow Village, Snowbabies, Ashton-Drake, Bradford Exchange Plates, Lowell Davis, Laura's Attic, Positive Images, Storybook Collection, Claire Craft (Nutcases), Raikes Bears, North American Bears, Effanbee dolls, Gorham Dolls, Middleton, Sandra Kuck, collector plates, Daniel Monfort, Largo, Michael Garman, Frumps, and Austin figurines.

All major credit cards accepted. Layaway and shipping available. Gift wrapping. Matching service for discontinued china, crystal and stainless.

THE TREASURE CHEST

111 St. Joseph Ave.
Brewton, AL 36426

PHONE: (205)867-9757
FAX: (205)867-4662

Open Daily: 9:00-5:30

David Winter, Swarovski, Waterford, Possible Dreams, Byers' Choice, Precious Moments, Ron Lee, Walt Disney/Schmid, Middleton, Gorham Inc., Kirk Stieff, Reed & Barton, John Hine Studios Inc.

NALED member. Secondary Market Service.

ALABAMA

THE OLD COUNTRY STORE

3025 E. Meighan Blvd.
Gadsden, AL 35903

PHONE: (205)492-7659

Monday-Saturday: 9:00-5:00

All God's Children, Tom Clark Gnomes, Dept 56 Villages, Maud Humphrey Bogart, Bradford Exchange Plates, Ashton-Drake Dolls, Sports Impressions, David Winter, Fenton Glass, Cherished Teddies, Laura's Attic, Dreamsicles, Snowbabies, Top Cats, Sarah's Attic, Melody In Motion, Miss Martha's Collection, Emmett Kelly, Jr., Sports Impressions, Duncan Royale, Possible Dreams, and Dave Grossman.

All major credit cards. NALED member. Layaway. Toll Free order line 1-800-852-1297.

COLLECTIBLE COTTAGE

439 New Fieldstown Rd.
Gardendale, AL 35071

PHONE: (205)631-2413
FAX: (205)631-0511

Open Daily: 10:00-5:30

Dept. 56 Showcase Dealer, Bradford Plate Dealer, Swarovski, Byers' Choice, Tom Clark Gnomes, David Winter Cottages, Lilliput Lane, LEGENDS, North American Bear, Lladro, Precious Moments, Cat's Meow, Shelia's, All God's Children, Hummel, Walt Disney Classics, Robert Olszewski Miniatures, and Madame Alexander Dolls.

Second Location: 141 Lorna Brook Village, Birmingham, AL 35216. Phone: (205)988-8551.

NALED member. All major credit cards accepted. Layaway-extended terms on Dept. 56.

MONTEREY GIFTS & COLLECTIBLES

900 Bob Wallace Ave. Ste. 106
Huntsville, AL 35801

PHONE: (205)539-0809

Monday-Saturday: 10:00-5:30

Monterey Gifts and Collectibles is an award winning Swarovski retailer with a tremendous inventory of Silver Crystal as well as the exclusive Swarovski Selection line. Specialists in fine collectibles with a large selection of each collectible line. Authorized Redemption Center for all lines carried. They emphasize friendly service.

Swarovski Silver Crystal, Swarovski Selection, Lladro, Lladro Goyescas, Chilmark, M.I. Hummel, LEGENDS, Lilliput Lane, Maud Humphrey, Dept. 56 Snowbabies, Armani, Iris Arc.

Visa, MC, American Express accepted. Layaway. Shipping. Free gift wrapping. Secondary Market Dealer.

ROBERT MOORE & CO.- INC CHRISTMAS TOWN /VILLAGE

4213 Halls Mill Rd.
Mobile, AL 36693

PHONE: (205)661-3608
(205)661-3693

Monday-Saturday: 10-6 Sunday: 1-6
Extended Holiday Hours

Enchantica, Hummel, Lowell Davis, Krystonia, ANRI, Boehm, Armani, John Hine Studios (all collections), Lilliput Lane (all collections), Andrea, Maruri, Sports Impressions, Precious Moments, Cherished Teddies, Enesco, Duncan Royale, Royal Doulton, Schmid, Disney Collection (an anchor store), Possible Dream Santas, Swarovski, Egg Fantasies, Annalee, Margaret Furlong, Steinbach, Ulbricht, Zuber, Dept. 56 (all lines), Fontanini, Cybis, Ispanky, Rohn Sculptures, Kaiser, Dresden, and Meissen. Dolls: Collectables, Gorham, S. Wakeen, Mde. Alexander, Jerri Dolls, Lee Middleton.

ALABAMA/ALASKA

HOMEMADE HEAVEN COLLECTIBLES & GIFTS

1206 Woodward Ave.
Muscle Shoals, AL 35661

PHONE: (205)383-0182
FAX: (205)383-0182

Monday-Saturday: 9:30-5:30
Nov-Dec Open Sundays: 1:00-5:00

Largest collectible store in the area. Tom Clark Gnomes, Lee Sievers and Tim Wolfe by Cairn Studios, Dept. 56, Walt Disney Classics Collection, Precious Moments, Bradford Exchange, Cherished Teddies, Sports Impressions, Beatrix Potter, Lowell Davis, Hummels, Frumps, Lilliput Lane, Fenton, Madame Alexander, Emmett Kelly Jr., Duncan Royale, Fontanini, German beer steins, Dave Grossman, Krystonia, Dragon Keep, Kitty Cucumber, Hidden Kingdom, Laura's Attic, Miss Martha's, Byers' Choice and Swarovski America Ltd.

GCC Dealer. Visa, Mastercard, and Discover accepted. Layaway available.

HELEN'S ANTICS

Midtown Shopping Center
721 E. Main St.
Prattville, AL 36067

PHONE: (205)365-0788

Monday-Saturday: 10:00-5:00

A collector's paradise! Serving the area for 14 years with dolls, bears, and collectibles. Madame Alexander, Alice Darling, Himstedt, GADCO, Heidi Ott, Effanbee, Ginny, Georgetown, Dynasty, World Doll, Gotz, The Doll Maker, Susan Wakeen, Zook, Barbie, Original Cabbage Patch and more. All God's Children, Miss Martha's Originals, Sarah's Attic, Duncan Royale, Tom Clark, Jan Hagara, Laura's Attic, Maud Humphrey, Cherished Teddies, Lowell Davis, Precious Moments, Dreamsicles, Lilliput Lane, Muffy & Family, Raikes Bears, and Alexander Bear.

Doll Repairs. Major credit cards accepted. Layaway and gift wrapping.

OLDE POST OFFICE

226 Main St.
Trussville, AL 35173

PHONE: (205)655-7292

Monday-Saturday: 10:00-5:30
Sunday: 1:00-5:00

Dept. 56, Snowbabies, David Winter, Lladro, Hummel, Armani, Swarovski, Vaillancourt, Precious Moments, Bradford plates, Nutcrackers, Santas, Maud Humphrey, Lowell Davis, Miss Martha's Originals, Duncan Royale, Hudson Pewter, Shelia's, and Muffy VanderBears.

Second largest dealer in Alabama for Snowbabies. Big secondary on Dept. 56. Bradford Dealer. All major credit cards accepted. Free shipping. Layaway. NALED member.

STEPHAN FINE ARTS

600 W. 6th Ave.
Anchorage, AK 99501

PHONE: (800)544-0779
(907)274-5009
FAX: (907)274-2292

Call 24 Hours A Day

Alaska's Art Source!....Stephan Fine Arts is Alaska's premier art gallery and publisher of fine art and collectibles. Featuring Chilmark collectibles and Alaska's largest collection of Caithness fine crystal. Publishers of Charles Gause, renowned wildlife and scenic artist. As well as many fine images of Mt. Denali and The Northern Lights . Also featured is the dramatic Ilfochrome prints by nature photographer Johnny Johnson. Unique moose antler carvings by Wes Lancaster. A full-service dealer for Greenwich, Millpond, and Hadley House.

To receive a wholesale catalog just call or write. Shipping: Federal Express.

ARIZONA

RUTH'S HALLMARK

1100 Hwy. 260 Suite D-5
Cottonwood, AZ 86326

PHONE: (602)634-8050

Monday-Saturday: 8:00-6:00
Sunday: 12:00-5:00

Large selection of LEGENDS, Tom Clark Gnomes, Tim Wolfe, Dept. 56, Disney, Raikes, David Winter, Lilliput Lane, Sadek, DeGrazia, Precious Moments, Duncan Royale, Shoemaker's Dream, Miniature Hummel, M.I. Hummel, Lowell Davis, Memories of Yesterday, Maud Humphrey Bogart, Miss Martha, Jan Hagara, Laura's Attic, Sarah's Attic, P. Buckley Moss, Iris Arc, Madame Alexander, J.H. Boone, Mill Creek, PenniBears, Maruri, Cherished Teddies, Windy Meadows, and others.

NALED Dealer. All major credit cards accepted. All club redemptions. Layaways welcome. Service oriented. UPS shipping.

THE ARTISAN

1430 W. Southern Ave. #C3
Mesa, AZ 85202

PHONE: (602)833-0495
(800)942-9961

Monday-Saturday: 10:00-6:00
Thursday: 10:00-8:00

The Largest Collectors Gallery in the Phoenix area, in business for over 15 years. The Artisan carries: DeGrazia plates and figurines. M.I. Hummel plates and figurines: A large selection of older trade marks (Crown thru Current), Club Member and retired items in stock at all times.

David Winter and Lilliput Lane Cottages, Chilmark and LEGENDS Pewter, Lladro, Tom Clark Gnomes, Tim Wolfe Animals, and The Walt Disney Classics Collection. Many limited edition plates by many well-known artists.

Redemption Center for all major collectors clubs. Bradford Exchange Dealer. Visa and Mastercard accepted. Layaway available.

CAROUSEL GIFTS

542 East Monroe
Phoenix, AZ 85004

PHONE: (602)253-0377
(800)788-2324

Monday-Saturday: 10:00-5:00
Sunday: 11:00-5:00

At The Mercado. Here, all the warmth and charm of an authentic Mexican Village. Austin, Tom Clark Gnomes, Precious Moments, Swarovski Crystal, David Winter, Jan Hagara, Hummel, Wee Forest Folk, LEGENDS, Duncan Royale, Krystonia, Plates, Dolls, Sarah's Attic, Armani, DeGrazia, Dept. 56, Lladro, Miss Martha's, Lilliput Lane, Little Cheesers, WACO, and Perillo.

Free shipping!

COLLECTORS PARADISE

Metro Marketplace
9005 N. 29th Ave. #4
Phoenix, AZ 85051

PHONE: (602)943-8005

Monday-Friday: 10:00-6:00
Saturday 10:00-5:00

Limited Edition Plates, Hummels, Precious Moments Figurines, Tom Clark Gnomes, Krystonia, Jan Hagara, Lilliput Lane, Cherished Teddies, Maud Humphrey, Lowell Davis, Little Cheesers, Hidden Kingdom, Laura's Attic, Miss Martha, Sarah's Attic, Beatrix Potter, United Design, Fontanini, Perillo, DeGrazia, dolls, teddy bears, etc.

Visa, Mastercard, American Express and Discover accepted.

ARIZONA

EXPRESSIONS COLLECTIBLES, INC.

Paradise Valley Mall
4568 E. Cactus Rd.
Phoenix, AZ 85032

PHONE: (602)996-8610
FAX: (602)443-9602

Open Daily: 10:00-9:00

Lladro, G. Armani, Dept. 56, M.I. Hummel, DeGrazia, Swarovski, Chilmark, Walt Disney Classics Collection, Lilliput Lane, German Nutcrackers, Sandicast, David Winter, Ron Lee Clowns, Maruri, Andrea by Sadek, Snowbabies, Precious Moments, Byers' Choice, LEGENDS, Caithness, and many others.

Other locations in Flagstaff, Tucson, Phoenix, Mesa and Scottsdale.

Visa, Mastercard, American Express and Discover accepted. Layaway available. Secondary Market Dealer!

HOUSE OF DENT

10720 W. Indian School Rd. #22
Phoenix, AZ 85039-2330

PHONE: (602)877-8401

Tuesday-Saturday: 9:00-6:00

Thomas Kinkade, Lilliput Lane, David Winter, Jon Herbert, Tom Clark, Tim Wolfe, Land of Legends, Maruri, Sarah's Attic, Miss Martha, Maud Humphrey, Raikes Bears, Snowbabies, Precious Moments, Fontanini, steins, artist plates, Cherished Teddies, Calico Kittens, Nutcrackers, Lance Pewter.

DOLLS: Hamilton, Georgetown, Seymour Mann, Gorham, Dynasty, Mattel, Timeless Creations, Gotz, Engel-Puppen, Lissi, Lexington Hall, Corolle, Wakeen, Dolls by Pauline, Dolls by Jerri, European Artist, and Effanbee.

Visa and Mastercard accepted.

MILLIE'S HALLMARK

5027 E. Elliot Rd.
Phoenix, AZ 85044

PHONE: (602)893-3777
FAX: (602)598-1946

Monday-Friday: 9-8; Saturday: 9-6
Sunday: 12-5
Holiday Hours After Thanksgiving:
Monday-Saturday: 9-9; Sunday: 12-5

Precious Moments (DSR), Cherished Teddies, Calico Kittens, Enesco Musicals, Memories of Yesterday, Lilliput Lane, DeGrazia, Lladro, Dreamsicles, David Winter, Iris Arc, Dept. 56 Showcase Dealer (Snow Village and Heritage Village) Snowbabies, Precious Moments Dolls, Hallmark Ornaments, M.I. Hummel, Walt Disney Classics Collection, Sports Impressions, Miss Martha's Originals. Featuring a large gift line.

Visa, Mastercard, Discover, and American Express. GCC Dealer. Shipping available. Complimentary gift wrapping.

CLEMONS-EICKEN FINE EUROPEAN IMPORTS

6166 N. Scottsdale Rd. Suite 204
Scottsdale, AZ 85253

PHONE: (602)998-9042

Monday-Saturday: 10:00-5:30

Specialists in fine porcelain, crystal and collectibles since 1981. Largest Boehm and Cybis dealer in Arizona. Armani, Connoisseur, David Winter, DeGrazia, Hibel, Lalique, LEGENDS, Lladro, Maruri, Mats Jonasson, Royal Doulton and Swarovski.

Sponsor of "Best Friends", Arizona's only local chapter of the Lladro Collector's Society.

Secondary Market service. Happily accept all club redemptions, phone orders, and major credit cards. Layaway and shipping available.

ARIZONA

FOX'S GIFTS & COLLECTABLES

7030 5th Ave.
Scottsdale, AZ 85251
**PHONE: (602)947-0560
(800)592-2555**

Monday-Saturday: 10:00-5:00

Bradford Dealer, DeGrazia, Bing & Grondahl, Royal Copenhagen, Cairn Gnomes, Jan Hagara, Hummel, Lladro, Dept. 56 Villages, ANRI, Cat's Meow, Lilliput Lane, Precious Moments, Edna Hibel, P. Buckley Moss, Ashton-Drake dolls, Simple Wonders, Perillo, Royal Doulton, Brambley Hedge, Beatrix Potter, Delft, Fred Stone, fox plates and figurines and custom plate frames.

Newsletters! Layaway and gift wrapping available. Visa, Mastercard, American Express and Discover accepted.

MISTY'S GIFT GALLERY

228 W. Fry Blvd.
Sierra Vista, AZ 85635
**PHONE: (800)528-4846
(602)458-7208**

Tuesday-Friday: 10:00-6:00
Saturday: 10:00-5:00

Specializing in collectibles since 1971. Bradford Dealer, Precious Moments (DSR), DeGrazia, Swarovski, Perillo, Annalee, Cross Gallery, M.I. Hummel, David Winter, Krystonia, Enchantica, Legends, Thomas Kinkade lithographs, Ashton-Drake dolls, Possible Dreams, Goebel Miniatures, Cherished Teddies, Sarah's Attic, Rick Cain, and Neil Rose.

Redemption Center for most collector clubs. Visa, Mastercard and Discover accepted. Mail order and layaway available.

PRESTIGE COLLECTIONS

10001 W. Bell Rd. #128
Sun City, AZ 85351
**PHONE: (602)977-9947
FAX: (602)815-0385**

Monday-Saturday: 9:00-5:00

Fine gifts and collectibles. David Winter, Swarovski, Lladro, Hummel, Armani, De Grazia, Tom Clark, Lilliput, Dept. 56, Precious Moments, Marty Bell, Olszewski Miniatures, Snowbabies, Raikes, Memories Of Yesterday, Hagara, Maud Humphrey, Disney Classic Collection, Laura's Attic, Miss Martha, Duncan Royale, Ron Lee, Emmett Kelly, Jr., Melody In Motion, Granget, Margaret Furlong Designs, Harbour Lights, Swarovski Selection, Maruri USA, and Sports Impressions. Redemption center for all collector clubs.

Visa, Mastercard, American Express, Discover accepted. Layaway. UPS shipping. Call 1-800-457-3595.

LORI'S COLLECTIBLES

6121 E. Broadway #134
Tucson, AZ 85711
PHONE: (602)790-6668

Tuesday-Friday: 10-6; Saturday: 10-5
Closed Sunday and Monday

Bradford plates, Lladro, M.I. Hummel, Lowell Davis, ANRI, Dept. 56, including Snowbabies, Royal Doulton, Precious Moments, David Winter, Olaf Wieghorst lithographs, Zolan lithographs, Lilliput Lane, Chilmark, LEGENDS, Bossons, Wideman, Disney Collection, DeGrazia, Krystonia, Memories of Yesterday, Ashton-Drake, Gartlan USA, Rockwell, Gorham, Goebel Miniatures, Tom Clark, Fontanini, Swarovski, Sports Impressions, Cairn Gnomes, Royal Copenhagen/Bing & Grondahl, and Sarah's Attic.

Secondary Market on all lines listed.

ARIZONA/ARKANSAS

MARYLYN'S COLLECTIBLES

7401 N. La Cholla Blvd. #171
Tucson, AZ 85741
PHONE: (602)742-1501

Monday-Friday: 10:00-9:00
Saturday: 10:00-6:00; Sunday: Noon-5:00

Armani, Byers' Choice, Cairn, Caithness, Cat's Meow Village, David Winter, DeGrazia, Dept. 56, Disney Classics, Emmett Kelly Jr., Enesco Musicals, Goebel Miniatures, Hummels, LEGENDS, Lilliput Lane, Lladro, Marty Bell, Maud Humphrey, Miss Martha, Memories of Yesterday, P. Buckley Moss, Precious Moments, Ron Lee, Sarah's Attic, Swarovski, Lightpost/Thomas Kinkade, Willitts Amish Collection, and Wee Forest Folk.

All major credit cards accepted. NALED member.

BROWN'S COUNTRY STORE INC.

18718 I-30 Exit 118
Benton, AR 72015
PHONE: (501)778-5033
FAX: (501)778-0825

Daily: 6:30am-8:30pm

"Shipping all over U.S." In business for 20 years. Large selection of All God's Children, Miss Martha's Originals, Sarah's Attic, Cairn Studios, J.H. Boone, LEGENDS, Colonial Village, Daddy's Long Legs, Jan Hagara, Mill Creek, Red Mill, Seymour Mann dolls, United Design, Little People, Fenton Art Glass, Glynda Turley Limited Edition Prints, Marty Sculptures, Mayflower Glass Ships, Hootchoo Collection.

Visa, Mastercard, and Discover accepted. Offering everything from Lye soap and coonskin caps to the finest collectibles. "In the Heart of Arkansas."

BRASS HATCH

50 Spring St.
Eureka Springs, AR 72632
PHONE: (501)253-9391
(800)554-9391

Monday-Sunday: 10:00-5:00

Serving the collector for 8 years. Located one hour south of Bronson, MO. Bradford plates, Hamilton, Reco, Hollywood, David Winter, Lilliput, Precious Moments, Emmett Kelly Jr. and Sr., Hummel plates, bells and figurines, All God's Children, Miss Martha, PenniBears, Enesco, Wee Forest Folk, Disney, United Design Santas, North Pole Village, Anheuser and German steins, Perillo plates, Duncan Royale, NAO by Lladro, Goebel Miniatures, Hudson and Gallo pewter, Ron Lee, Maruri, Lowell Davis, Laura's Attic, Cherished Teddies, Maud Humphrey, Michael Garman, professional figurines, teacups and saucers. Club Redemption Center. Layaway and shipping. All credit cards.

HOUSE & GARDEN

460 Southwest Dr.
Jonesboro, AR 72401
PHONE: (501)932-1580

Monday-Saturday: 9:30-5:30

Gifts-Bridal Registry-Collectibles! ANRI, Belleek, Byers' Choice Carolers, Tom Clark Gnomes, Cybis Porcelain, Dept. 56: Snow Village, Dickens Village, Christmas in the City, and North Pole--Lalique Crystal, David Winter, Hibel, Hummels, Maud Humphrey, Miss Martha's Originals, Sports Impressions, United Design Santas. Royal Copenhagen, Bing & Grondahl, and Lenox collector plates. Maruri, Andrea by Sadek figurines, Sabino Glass, Goebel bells and eggs, Cherished Teddies and much more.

Major credit cards accepted. Layaway available. Redemption Center.

ARKANSAS/CALIFORNIA

PETTY'S HALLMARK SHOP

143 Indian Mall
Jonesboro, AR 72401

PHONE: (501)932-7821

Monday-Saturday: 10:00-9:00
Sunday: 1:00-5:00

Dept 56, Precious Moments (DSR), All God's Children, Miss Martha's Originals, Lladro, M.I. Hummel, Sarah's Attic, David Winter, Lilliput Lane, Harbour Lights, Cherished Teddies, Emmett Kelly, Jr., Maud Humphrey, Castagna, Krystonia, Sports Collectibles, United Design.

Visa, Mastercard, Discover, American Express.

THE BAMBOO TREE

2921 Lakewood Village Dr.
North Little Rock, AR 72116

PHONE: (501)753-1966

Monday-Saturday: 10:00-8:00

David Winter, Tom Clark, Swarovski, Precious Moments, Boehm, Kaiser, Lowell Davis, Hummel, All God's Children, LEGENDS, Chilmark, Dept. 56.

All major credit cards accepted. Layaway available. Redemption center. Satellite store for David Winter.

VICTORIA'S COTTAGE

5801 Kanan Rd.
Agoura Hills, CA 91301

PHONE: (805)252-5653

Monday-Saturday: 10:00-7:00
Sunday: 11:00-5:00

Thomas Kinkade, Marty Bell, Alan Maley, Dennis Lewan, Corinne Layton, Lena Liu, Annalee, Dept. 56, Fitz and Floyd, Lilliput Lane, Lladro's Golden Memories, Hummel, Sarah's Attic, Schmid, Daddy's Long Legs, Lizzie High, Attic Babies, Colonial Village, Sandra Kuck, June McKenna, Wee Forest Folk, and Bradford Dealer.

Secondary Market Service. All major credit cards accepted. Layaways welcome.

Second Location:

19347 Soledad Canyon Rd.
Canyon Country, CA 91351

LIEBERGS

101 E. Main St.
Alhambra, CA 91801

PHONE: (818)282-8454

Tues. Wed. Thurs. Sat: 10:00-6:00
Monday and Friday: 10-9; Sunday: 11-5

In business since 1911. Specializing in Disney Animation. Disney, Hummel, Lladro, Bradford Dealer, Precious Moments, LEGENDS, Chilmark, David Winter, Lilliput Lane, Leo Smith, Cherished Teddies, Sarah's Attic, Miss Martha, Royal Doulton, Beatrix Potter, Snowbabies, Dept. 56 Villages, Colonial Village, Melody In Motion, Enesco Small World of Music, Norman Rockwell, Ashton-Drake, Hallmark and Enesco Ornaments, Lenox, Sandicast, Dreamsicles, Ron Lee, Gartlan USA, Sports Impressions, Dynasty.

Redemption Center. NALED member. Free appraisals. Price/ repair/ replace/ satisfaction program. Layaway. Free shipping in the US. Visa and MC accepted.

CALIFORNIA

DISNEYLAND

1313 Harbor Blvd.
Anaheim, CA 92803

PHONE: (714)999-4212
FAX: (714)999-4325

Call Guest Relations For Park Operating Hours at (714)999-4565

When visiting Disneyland, stop in the following stores to purchase these collectibles:

Main Street-China Closet: Lladro, M.I. Hummel, Precious Moments, Ron Lee, PJ's Carousels, Fitz & Floyd and Walt Disney Classics Collection.

Main Street Disneyana: M.I. Hummel and Walt Disney Classics Collection.

Fantasyland-Tinker Bell Toy Shoppe and Critter Country-Crocodile Mercantile: Collectible dolls and teddy bears.

Or call the Mail Order Dept. at (800)362-4533 to order. Mail order's fax number is (714)999-4236.

CHRISTINE'S GIFTS & COLLECTIBLES

1 West Duarte Rd. #C
Arcadia, CA 91006

PHONE: (818)447-7564

Monday-Saturday: 10:00-7:00
Sunday: 10:00-4:00

Lladro, Precious Moments, Hummels, Dept. 56, Swarovski, Jan Hagara, Tom Clark, Memories of Yesterday, Krystonia, David Winter, Maud Humphrey, Armani, Snowbabies, Lilliput Lane, Donald Zolan, Miss Martha's, Cast Art, DeGrazia, Harbour Lights, Beatrix Potter, Sandicast, Sports Impressions, Collector dolls and plates. Authorized Bradford Dealer.

Personal checks, Visa, Mastercard, American Express and Discover accepted. 60 day layaway. UPS shipping always available.

THE ELEGANT TOUCH

Santa Anita Fashion Park
400 S. Baldwin Ave. #328
Arcadia, CA 91007

PHONE: (818)445-8868
FAX: (818)445-7258

Monday-Friday: 10:00-9:00
Saturday: 10:00-6:00; Sunday: 11:00-6:00
Extended Holiday Hours

Specializing in Lladro, Swarovski (including select crystal line), Lalique, Lilliput Lane, Hummels, PM, Memories of Yesterday, Armani, Caithness, Sarah's Attic, Snowbabies, Maruri, Cherished Teddies, Duncan Royale, Royal Doulton, Laura's Attic, Rick Cain, Andrea by Sadek, Maud Humphrey, Cybis, and Ron Lee.

Major credit cards accepted. NALED Member. Layaways. Free shipping on orders over $100. Complimentary gift wrap.

Inside shopping mall next to Santa Anita Race Track, by JC Penney's.

GALLERY DECOR

Santa Anita Fashion Park
400 S. Baldwin
Arcadia, CA 91007

PHONE: (800)995-6005

Open everyday, except Christmas

Gallery Decor has been caring for your collectibles since 1973. Dept. 56 Showcase Dealer and premier dealer for Enesco's Treasury ornaments and Small World Of Music. World's finest collectibles including Lladro, Swarovski, Hummel, Lilliput Lane, DW, Sarah's Attic, Lowell Davis, DeGrazia, PM, Ashton-Drake, Ardleigh and Elliott Musicals, Belleek, Waterford, Wedgwood, WFF, Perillo, MOY, Hibel, Walt Disney Classics, Jan Hagara, Goebel Miniatures, Miss Martha's, CT, Rockwell, Cast Art, sports collectibles, Krystonia, Emmett Kelly, Jr., Lenox, Beatrix Potter and Tom Clark. Authorized Bradford Dealer. Secondary Market. All major credit cards accepted.

CALIFORNIA

CAROL'S GIFT SHOP

17601 S. Pioneer Blvd.
Artesia, CA 90701

PHONE: (310)924-6335
FAX: (310)924-2677

Monday-Saturday: 9:30-5:30
Friday: 9:30-7:00

Established in 1958! Dept. 56 Villages and Snowbabies, Precious Moments, Sarah's Attic, All God's Children, Swarovski, Hummels, Royal Doulton, David Winter, Lilliput, Bradford Exchange, Fenton, Wee Forest Folk, Sterling Ornaments: Hand & Hammer, Reed & Barton, Gorham and Buccellati. Ashton-Drake, Lladro, B&G/ RC, Goebel Miniatures, Marty Bell, Thomas Kinkade, V.F. Fine Art, Past Impressions, Lowell Davis, Armani, Perillo, Rockwell, Enesco Musicals, plates and accessories.

Club redemption center. Secondary Market Specialist. NALED member. All major credit cards. Insured shipping. Layaway. Custom gift wrap.

FORGET-ME-NOT-SHOP

882 Lincoln Way
Auburn, CA 95603

PHONE: (916)885-5127

Monday-Friday: 9:30-6:00
Saturday: 10:00-5:30

Bradford Exchange, Ashton-Drake, Lilliput Lane, Tom Clark, Bergsma, and German beer steins. Nutcrackers: Holzkunst, Christian Ulbricht, Erzgebirgische, original Erzgebirge, Herrdrosselmeyer, Votkskunst, and others. Dreamsicles and Tobin Fraley. Secondary Market on plates.

Club Redemption Center. Visa and Mastercard accepted. Layaway. Shipping available. Free gift wrapping.

JJ'S CARDS-N-GIFTS

13390 Lincoln Way
Auburn, CA 95603

PHONE: (916)885-9276

Monday-Friday: 9:00-7:00;
Saturday: 9:00-6:00; Sunday: 10:00-4:00

Precious Moments, Cherished Teddies, Memories of Yesterday, Calico Kittens, Enesco Treasury Ornaments, Dreamsicles, Bessie Pease Gutmann, Beatrix Potter, Carlton Ornaments, Raikes Bears, Fenton Art Glass, M.A. Hadley Stoneware, United Design, Walt Disney, Legacies, Sandicast.

Also featuring cards, Christian books and gifts, plush and candy. CreataCard, crystal, picture frames, Enesco birthday girls, complete line of wedding and baby gifts. Glass miniatures.

Visa, Mastercard, Discover, and American Express accepted. Layaway and shipping available. Free gift wrapping.

THE GIFT HORSE

2926 Domingo Ave.
Berkeley, CA 94705

PHONE: (510)843-7264
FAX: (510)843-3176

Monday-Saturday: 10:00-5:00
Sunday 10:00-4:00

The Gift Horse carries an extensive line of Christopher Radko ornaments and figurines as well as other fine gift items from Possible Dreams, Midwest Importers, Towle Silversmiths and Dept. 56.

Visa and Mastercard are accepted. Layaways welcome.

CALIFORNIA

DER WEIHNACHTS MARKT

P.O. Box 802
652 Pine Knot
Big Bear Lake, CA 92315

PHONE: (909)866-8468
FAX: (909)866-8976

Saturday: 9:00-9:00
Sunday-Friday: 10:00-5:00

Dept. 56, Lladro, Hummel, Armani, Possible Dreams, Disney, Swarovski, Bradford, Hamilton, Duncan Royale, Steins, Nutcrackers, Smokers, Cuckoo Clocks, Maurice Wideman, Rick Cain, Chilmark, Maruri, and Kurt Adler.

Layaway. UPS Shipping. Christmas year round!

VIRGINIA'S GIFT SHOP

At Knott's Berry Farm
8039 Beach Blvd.
Buena Park, CA 90620

PHONE: (714)220-5323
FAX: (714)220-5321

Open Daily: 9:00-9:00

Serving the collector for 40 years. Thomas Kinkade, Marty Bell, Patrick Lewan, Duncan Royale, Lowell Davis, Jan Hagara, Lilliput Lane, Swarovski, M.I. Hummel, All God's Children, Ron Lee, Precious Moments, Miss Martha's Originals, Goebel Miniatures, Armani, Lladro, Fenton Glass, Tom Clark and more!

Major credit cards accepted. Layaway available. Free gift wrap (with purchase over $5.00).

THE DANA DRUG STORE & BOUTIQUE

317 North Pass Ave.
Burbank, CA 91505

PHONE: (818)562-1177
FAX: (818)953-5120

Monday-Friday: 9:00-9:00
Saturday: 9:00-7:00; Sunday: 9:00-6:00

Located near Universal and Warner Bros. Studios. Tom Clark Gnomes, Dept. 56 Villages and Snowbabies, David Winter, Enesco Musicals, Cherished Teddies, PM, MOY, Maud Humphrey, Miss Martha, Calico Kittens, Enesco Treasury Ornaments, Sports Impressions, Possible Dreams, M.I. Hummel, Krystonia, Lilliput Lane, Lladro, AGC, Swarovski, Caithness, Cat's Meow, Royal Doulton, Dreamsicles.

Visa, Mastercard, American Express and Discover accepted. Layaway. Free gift wrapping. Shipping available.

T & J COLLECTABLES

917 West Olive Ave.
Burbank, CA 91506

PHONE: (818)841-2270

Monday-Thursday: 8:00-5:00
Saturday: 10:00-4:00

Authorized Bradford Dealer. Limited edition plates and plate accessories by Zolan, Fred Stone, and P. Buckley Moss. Ashton-Drake Dolls.

Payment by cash or check only. Layaway available. A secondary market dealer.

CALIFORNIA

SIMPLE PLEASURES

4210 Bridge St. #1
Cambria, CA 93428

PHONE: (805)927-4793
FAX: (805)927-4497

Monday-Saturday: 10:00-6:00
Sunday: 10:00-4:00

Wonderful displays of santas, angels, nutcrackers, Christopher Radko, All God's Children, Old World Christmas, Le Fever's World Of Sinterklaas, Vaillancourt Folk Art, Department 56, Byers' Choice and Jody Bergsma.

Major credit cards accepted. Layaway and shipping.

ARMIK'S SEA LIFE BOUTIQUE

18279 Soledad Canyon
Canyon Country, CA 91351

PHONE: (805)252-0994

Tuesday-Friday: 11:30-8:00
Saturday: 10:30-7:00

LEGENDS, Chilmark, J.H. Boone, Mill Creek, Perth Pewter, Gallo Pewter, Rawcliffe Pewter, Golden Memories, Mark Hopkins Bronzes, Lee Middleton and Bradley dolls, seashells and corals.

Visa, Mastercard, and Discover accepted. Layaway. ASAP orders, dated orders and open bookings. Catalog sales. Secondary Market Dealer. Redemption Center for LEGENDS and Chilmark. Artist shows.

Second Location: 6701 Variel Ave., Woodland Hills, CA 91351 (818)702-6794. Friday, Saturday, Sunday: 10:00-6:00.

FRIENDS COLLECTIBLES

27239 Camp Plenty Rd.
Canyon Country, CA 91351

PHONE: (805)298-2232

Monday-Saturday: 10:00-5:00
Thursday: 10:00-8:00; Sunday: 11:00-4:00

Your "Personal" Service in Collectibles. Authorized Bradford Exchange Dealer. Ashton-Drake dolls, Cherished Teddies, *David Winter, *Enchantica, Hamilton Collection, *Hummel, *Jan Hagara, *Lilliput Lane, *Maud Humphrey Bogart, *Memories of Yesterday, Rockwell, *Swarovski Silver Crystal, *Walt Disney Classics Collection, Wyland, Zolan Trading Center (*Redemption Center). Accessories by Lynette, Bard's, Oak Originals, Tripar, Van Hygan & Smythe and more. Certified picture framer on staff. Artwork by Burke, Burns, J. Kramer Cole, Cat Corcilius, Ray Day, Fernandez, Frace, Kinkade, Kuck, Kurz, Liu, Luce, Redlin, F. Stone, D. Zolan and many more. All cards welcome.

FERRARI FLORIST/GIFTS

1408 41st Ave.
Capitola, CA 95010

PHONE: (408)479-7666
(408)479-7889

Monday-Friday: 8:30-6:00
Saturday: 8:30-5:00; Sunday: 12:00-5:00

Located on Monterey Bay next to Santa Cruz. In business since 1946, and serving the experienced collector for 15 years. Lines include: Dept. 56 Dickens, Christmas in the City, Snow Village, North Pole, Snowbabies and accessories, David Winter, Michael's Limited, Krystonia, Midwest Importers Cottontale Lane Villages and accessories, Dreamsicles, Andrea by Sadek figurines, Precious Moments figurines previous to 1992, Armani, Enesco Small World of Music, and older Willitts carousel horses.

Redemption Center for David Winter. All major credit cards accepted. UPS shipping and layaway available. Free gift wrapping.

CALIFORNIA

EVERY LITTLE THING

P.O. Box 4055
San Carlos At Ocean
Carmel, CA 93921

PHONE: (408)625-1723

Daily: 9:30-6:00

Featuring: Goebel Miniatures, Hudson Pewter, Tiny People by Elayne, Little Cheesers, Linda Archer's Mixed Blessings, Cherished Teddies, Brian Baker's Deja Vu Collection, Adorables, Thumb Print Teddys, Large selection of thimbles and Raggedy Anns.

Visa, Mastercard and American Express accepted. Shipping anywhere in the U. S.

THOMAS KINKADE STUDIO GALLERIES OF CARMEL

P.O. Box 4378 Ocean Ave.
Between Lincoln and Dolores
Carmel, CA 93921

PHONE: (408)626-1927

Open 7 Days A Week: 10:00-6:00

On California Central Coast. Thomas Kinkade's two studio galleries may be found amidst flourishing gardens. "The Authority" on primary and secondary market pieces, one may find the largest inventory of this luminist's work.

Resale, dealer and client consignment, with current up-to-date pricing information. The customer service department will arrange for safe delivery of your Thomas Kinkade treasure anywhere in the world.

Second Location: At the Barnyard, 3738 The Barnyard. Phone:(408)622-0939.

CHATSWORTH PHARMACY & GIFT BOUTIQUE

21501 Devonshire St.
Chatsworth, CA 91311

PHONE: (818)341-4600
FAX: (818)341-0540

Monday-Friday: 9:00-7:00
Saturday: 9:00-6:00; Closed Sundays

Dept. 56: all Villages, Snowbabies, All Through the House, Merry Makers, Lilliput Lane, Cherished Teddies, Precious Moments, Jan Hagara, Dreamsicles, Cast Art, J.H. Boone Sculptures, Leo R. Smith/Midwest, Enesco Musicals, plates by Marty Bell, Sandra Kuck, Russian Fairy Tales, plates and steins by Villeroy & Boch, Anheuser-Busch Steins, Attic Babies, Sports Impressions, and Little Souls Dolls.

Shipping and Layaway. All major credit cards accepted. Custom gift baskets and free complimentary gift wrapping.

MAR-CHER PLATES

5486 Riverside Dr.
Chino, CA 91710

PHONE: (909)628-3381

Monday-Friday: 10:00-5:00
Saturday: 10:30-4:00; Sunday: 10:00-2:00

Specialists in collectible plates since 1981. Bradford Dealer, primary and secondary market service. Ashton-Drake, Barbie Dolls, Hamilton Dolls, Georgetown Dolls, Cherished Teddies, Precious Moments, Hummel, Jan Hagara, Sports Impressions, Lowell Davis, Hadley House, H & G Studios, Gartlan USA Inc., Dave Grossman Creations, Michael's Limited, Kuck and Zolan prints and plates.

Redemption center for collector clubs. Visa and Mastercard accepted. Secondary Market. Layaway. Free shipping in the U.S.

CALIFORNIA

MARY'S HALLMARK

12845 Mountain Ave.
Chino, CA 91710

PHONE: (909)591-5184
FAX: (909)591-8827

Monday-Friday: 10:00-6:00
Saturday: 9:30-5:30

Large collection of fine gifts and collectibles. Precious Moments (DSR), Dept. 56, Lladro, David Winter, Lilliput Lane, Sarah's Attic, All God's Children, Wee Forest Folk, Maud Humphrey, Laura's Attic, Memories of Yesterday, Jan Hagara, Swarovski, Tom Clark Gnomes, Krystonia, Hamilton Gifts, J.H. Boone, Maruri, United Design, Hummel and Byers' Choice.

Visa, Mastercard, and American Express. All club redemptions accepted. Shipping anywhere in the continental U.S.

Call today for fast friendly service. There is always a reason to shop at Mary's.

FOUNTAIN SQUARE

7115 Greenback Lane
Citrus Heights, CA 95621

PHONE: (916)969-6666

Open Daily: 9:00-6:00

Fountain Square is a collection of specialty shops nestled within a living landscape of exotic plants and bubbling fountains.

Lines include: Annalee Mobilitee Dolls Inc., Christopher Radko, Dept. 56, Edna Hibel, Fitz & Floyd, Goebel Inc., Goebel Miniatures, Kirk Stieff, Kurt S. Adler, Lladro Collectors Society, Maruri USA, Old World, Schmid, and Swarovski America Ltd.

From August to January, an exciting Christmas Shop is in place, with 75 beautifully decorated trees featured.

THE TINDER BOX

6144 Sunrise Mall
Citrus Heights, CA 95610

PHONE: (916)725-3231

Monday-Saturday: 10:00-9:00
Sunday: 11:00-6:00

Cairn: Tom Clark, Sievers, Wolfe. Artaffects: Perillo, Enesco, Miss Martha, Flambro, Emmett Kelly, Michael Garman, M. Cornell, and Polland. Gorham, Goebel and Hamilton plates. Daniel Monfort, Willitts Designs, Bossons, Steinbach Crystal, Norwegian Good Luck Trolls (3" to 3'), German beer steins, chess sets, and Smokers gifts.

Engraving services available. Special Orders and Layaways welcome. Shipping anywhere.

MARY CONKLIN COLLECTIBLES

623 N. Main D7
Corona, CA 91720

PHONE: (909)272-4040

Monday-Friday: 10:00-6:30
Saturday: 10:00-5:00

Bradford Dealer, Ashton-Drake Dolls, Maud Humphrey, MOY, Armani, Ron Lee, Laura's Attic, The Collectables, Enesco Musicals, Possible Dreams, Miss Martha's, Little Cheesers, Colonial Village, Dolls by Pauline, Raikes, Bearly People, Cherished Teddies, Hamilton Dolls, Louis Icart, Treasured Memories, Rockwell, Miss Martha's, Lexington Dolls by Gustave and Gretchen Wolff, VickiLane, Sports Impressions, Calico Kittens, Bessie P. Gutmann, EKJ, Superman, Looney Tunes, Hawthorne Cottages, Corinne Layton and custom silk arrangements.

Visa, Mastercard and American Express accepted. Free Shipping.

CALIFORNIA

PM COLLECTABLES

10893 N. Wolfe Rd.
Cupertino, CA 95014

PHONE: (408)725-8858

Monday-Wednesday: 10:00-6:00
Thursday: 10:00-8:00
Friday & Saturday: 10:00-5:30
Last Sunday of Month: 9:00-4:00

Collectibles for every collector. If you want it, it is in stock. If not try their locator service. Authorized dealer for Wee Forest Folk, Tom Clark, Showcase Dept. 56, Chilmark, Lilliput, Kurt S. Adler, Anheuser-Busch, Annalee, Enesco, Hudson Pewter, Mark Hopkins, Castagna, Bosson Heads, PM (DSR), Pocket Dragons. Dolls: Ashton-Drake, Shackleford, Victoria Impex, Hamilton, Good-Kruger, Dolls by Jerri, Georgetown and others.

Visa and Mastercard. Layaway. UPS shipping anywhere. Special order. Open houses and artist appearances. NALED. Club redemption center. Bradford Dealer.

ENCORE CARDS & GIFTS

10191 Valley View
Cypress, CA 90630

PHONE: (714)761-1266
FAX: (714)761-5052

Monday-Friday: 10:00-8:00
Saturday: 10:00-6:00; Sunday: 12:00-5:00

Full line dealer and redemption center. Precious Moments (DSR), MOY Heritage, Miss Martha's, Sarah's Attic, Lilliput, Jon Herbert, David Winter, Maud Humphrey, Ashton-Drake, Gartlan, Calico Kittens, Sports Impressions, Dept. 56 Showcase Dealer, Iris Arc, Cherished Teddies, PenniBears, Byers' Choice, Krystonia, J.H. Boone, Little Cheesers, Shelia's, Roman, Cast Art, Daddy's Long Legs, Mayflower, Michael Garman, Hamilton, Artaffects, Hadley House, Winston Roland, and others.

NALED and GCC Member. Bradford Dealer. All major credit cards accepted. Free Shipping over $100. Layaway for 90 days.

JOE KOSMO'S LABEL LINE

5663 Lincoln Ave. Suite B
Cypress, CA 90630

PHONE: (714)527-5663
(800)541-8834

Monday-Saturday: 10:00-5:00

Established in 1970, Joe's lines include Budweiser, Michelob, Busch, Coors, Miller, Stroh's mugs and steins, collector plates, Christmas ornaments, watches, AB truck banks, mini cars and trucks and other related beer logo collectibles. Will purchase complete collections. Visit the store when in South California where many items, both old and new are on display.

Mastercard and Visa accepted. Many Secondary Market Lines.

REFLECTIONS AT BLACKHAWK

3616 Blackhawk Plaza Circle
Danville, CA 94506

PHONE: (510)736-9050

Open 7 Days A Week: Hours Vary

Dept. 56: All Villages, accessories, All Through the House, Winter Silhouette, Snowbabies. Lilliput Lane, David Winter, Armani, Lladro, Swarovski, Hummel, Maud Humphrey, Sports Impressions, Tom Clark Gnomes, Precious Moments, Sugar Town, Cherished Teddies, Krystonia, PenDelfin, Fontanini, Fraser Creations, Ashton-Drake Dolls, Annalee Dolls, plates and many more.

Bradford Dealer. NALED Member. Redemption Center. All major credit cards are accepted. Shipping available. Mail and phone orders taken.

CALIFORNIA

CRYSTAL PALACE

435 Parkway Plaza
El Cajon, CA 92020

PHONE: (619)593-9303
FAX: (619)232-7289

Monday-Friday: 10:00-9:00
Weekends: 10:00-6:00

All God's Children, Dept. 56, Snowbabies, Limited Edition Collector Plates, Disney Classic Collection, Hummel, Lladro, Swarovski, Waterford, Chilmark, Golden Memories, Little Cheesers.

Dolls: Ashton-Drake, Hamilton, Seymour Mann, Lexington, Dynasty.

Crystal Palace has something for everyone! Redemption center for above collector clubs. All major credit cards accepted.

WILLOW GLEN

5050 Laguna Blvd. #115
Elk Grove, CA 95758

PHONE: (916)684-7885

Monday-Friday: 10:00-7:00
Saturday: 10:00-6:00; Sunday: 11:00-5:00

Located 15 miles south of Sacramento in Laguna Creek Town Center. Lines include: Avonlea Traditions-Anne of Green Gables, Bunnies by the Bay, Lizzie High, Attic Babies, Thomas Kinkade, Marty Bell, Schmid, Beatrix Potter, Hummel figurines, Corinne Layton, Ayshford, Fenton Art Glass, Dept. 56 novelties, Gorham dolls, Bessie Pease Gutmann, Midwest Importers, Reco, and United Design.

Layaway and shipping available. Visa, Mastercard, American Express and Discover accepted.

JASMINE GIFTS & TOBACCO

3741 B San Pablo Dam Rd.
El Sobrante, CA 94803

PHONE: (510)223-4470

Monday-Friday: 10:00-7:00
Sunday: 11:00-5:00

LEGENDS, Chilmark, Ron Lee, Lilliput Lane, Gartlan USA, Enesco, Sports Impressions, Hamilton Plates, Bradford Exchange Dealer, Miss Martha, Bubble Fairies, Crystal By Happy World, Maruri, Enchantica.

Most major credit cards accepted. Layaway and shipping available. Redemption Center for Chilmark, Gartlan, Sports Impressions, Lilliput Lane and LEGENDS.

HOWELL'S GIFT GALLERY

162 S. Rancho Sante Fe Rd.
Suite E-40
Encinitas, CA 92024

PHONE: (619)634-2442
FAX: (619)634-2442

Monday-Saturday: 10:00-5:30

Lladro, Boehm, Cybis, Armani, Hummel, Disney Classics, Krystonia, Swarovski, Lalique, Daum, David Winter Cottages, Dept. 56, LEGENDS, Chilmark, Hopkins, Edna Hibel, P. Buckley Moss plates, Ron Lee, Emmett Kelly, ANNA-PERENNA, Kosta Boda, ANRI, Lowell Davis, many retired and limited edition pieces.

Redemption Center for all of the above. Shipping anywhere in the continental USA. NALED member. Most major credit cards accepted. Limited Secondary Market.

CALIFORNIA

SUTTER STREET EMPORIUM

731 Sutter St.
Folsom, CA 95630

**PHONE: (916)985-4647
(800)255-6243(OUTSIDE CA)**

Daily: 10:30-5:00

"The Collectors' Paradise". Largest selection of limited edition collector dolls in Northern California. Also plates, musicals, thimbles and limited edition figurines.

Club Redemption center for Cairn Studios, Enchantica, MOY, PM, All God's Children, Lilliput Lane, Pocket Dragons, Enesco Treasury of Ornaments, Enesco Musical Society, Krystonia, Jan Hagara, Perillo, Lowell Davis, Melody In Motion, Dolls by Jerri, and Wendy Lawton Dolls.

Member of the National Association of Limited Edition Dealers and National Doll Retailers Association. Generous layaway program. Visa, Mastercard, Discover and American Express accepted.

GIFT CAROUSEL

39197 Farwell Dr.
Fremont, CA 94538

PHONE: (510)794-0333

Monday-Wednesday: 10:00-7:00
Thursday and Friday: 10:00-8:00
Saturday: 10:00-6:00; Sunday: 12:00-5:00

Lines: Sarah's Attic, Maud Humphrey, Jan Hagara, Dept. 56 Heritage Village. Dolls: Annalee, Lee Middleton, Turner, Annette Himstedt, GADCO, United Design Santas, Ladie and Friends, Johanna Zook, Muffy VanderBears and more.

Extensive gift selections. Shipping available. Major credit cards accepted. Layaways welcome.

WILSON GALLERIES

Fig Garden Village
5080 N. Palm Ave.
Fresno, CA 93704-2201

PHONE: (209)224-2223

Monday-Friday: 10:00-6:00
Thursday: 10:00-9:00

Marty Bell, Red Skelton, Thomas Kinkade, P. Buckley Moss, Alan Maley, Sandra Kuck, Bradford Exchange Plate Dealer, Reco, Ron Lee, Edna Hibel, Hummel, Lilliput Lane, Gartlan USA sports figurines and plates, Terry Redlin, Perillo, and Zolan. Older pieces include Bateman, G. Harvey, and Olaf Weighorst Western Art Prints.

NALED Member. Secondary Market Service on some lines. Mail order and layway available.

HEIRLOOMS OF TOMORROW

106 W. Wilshire Ave.
Fullerton, CA 92632

PHONE: (714)525-1522

Tuesday-Saturday: 10:00-6:00

David Winter, Marty Bell, Jan Hagara, Snowbabies, Gartlan, Lowell Davis, Krystonia, Armani, Thomas Kinkade, all Dept. 56 Villages, Sandra Kuck, All God's Children, Little Cheesers, Byers' Choice Carolers, Swarovski, LEGENDS, Disney Classics Collection, Olszewski Miniatures, Lladro, PenniBears, Tom Clark Gnomes, Memories of Yesterday, Gorham dolls, Pocket Dragons, P. Buckley Moss, Sarah's Attic, Maud Humphrey, Laura's Attic, Hummel Miniatures, Hibel, Dreamsicles, Bradford Dealer.

All major credit cards accepted. Shipping anywhere in the Continental U.S.

CALIFORNIA

COLLECTORS WORLD

2249 Honolulu Ave.
Glendale/Montrose, CA 91020
PHONE: (800)366-7890
(818)248-9451
FAX: (818)248-0439

Monday-Saturday: 10:00-5:30

Thomas Kinkade, Lladro, Hummel, Tom Clark, David Winter, Lilliput Lane, LEGENDS and Chilmark Pewter, Duncan Royale, Lowell Davis, Wee Forest Folk, ANRI, Maud Humphrey, Memories of Yesterday, Jan Hagara, All God's Children, Olszewski, Disney Classics Collection and much, much more...the finest collectible shop in the L.A. area.

Specializing in retired and discontinued pieces from all the lines listed above. Extensive contacts throughout Europe and the U.S. Active Buy/Sell listings.

OWL ANTIQUES & COLLECTIBLES

160-I North Glendora Ave.
Glendora, CA 91741
PHONE: (818)963-5616

Tuesday-Saturday: 10:00-5:00

Specializing in collector plates both primary and secondary since 1978. Figurines, lithos, frames and dolls by: Jan Hagara, Sandra Kuck, Donald Zolan, Fred Stone, Krystonia, M.I. Hummel, Miss Martha, Maud Humphrey, Memories Of Yesterday, Thomas Kinkade, Marty Bell, Norman Rockwell, Perillo, Ashton-Drake and others too numerous to list.

Authorized Bradford Dealer. Redemption Center for most clubs. Major credit cards accepted. Layaways welcome.

ROSSMYER'S

1200 E. Alosta Suite 110
Glendora, CA 91740
PHONE: (818)914-1611

Monday-Friday: 10:00-6:00
Saturday: 10:00-4:00

David Winter, Swarovski, Hummel, Lladro, All God's Children, Cherished Teddies, Maud Humphrey, Jan Hagara, Bradford Dealer, collector plates and frames.

Lithos include Thomas Kinkade, Stone, Maija, Sandra Kuck, and Terri Redlin.

Dolls include Ashton-Drake, A. Himstedt, Barbie, Hamilton and Georgetown.

Courtesy gift wrapping. Layaways welcome.

JEWELLS

111 Mill St.
Grass Valley, CA 95945
PHONE: (916)272-3769
(800)432-8940

Open 7 Days A Week

Joyce Barbour, an avid collector herself for 35 years, invites collectors to visit Jewells.

Lladro, Hummel, Miss Martha's, Lilliput, Michael Garman, Ron Lee, Emmett Kelly, Tom Clark, Chilmark, DeGrazia, Perillo, Hibel, Rockwell, Bradford Dealer, Crystal World, Maud Humphrey, Jan Hagara, Sandra Kuck, Laura's Attic, Kewpie dolls, Ashton-Drake, Victoria Ashlea, Gorham and Kaiser dolls, Lone Star Bears.

Gallery of Red Skelton, Mario Fernandez, Lena Liu, Corinne Layton. Bossons, Rick Cain, Southwestern/Indian art, jewelry, rug, pottery, collectible plates and dolls.

Visa, Mastercard, Discover and American Express accepted. Shipping available.

CALIFORNIA

THE LOUVRE GALLERY

760 S. Auburn
Grass Valley, CA 95945

PHONE: (916)272-3733

Monday-Thursday: 9:00-5:30
Friday and Saturday: 9:00-6:00
Sunday: 11:00-5:00

Collector Limited Edition Prints: Doolittle, Robert Bateman, Steve Lyman, James Gurney, James Christiansen, Rod Fredericks, Fred Stone, Terpning, Thomas Kinkade, Assaro, Bogle, Frace, McCarthy and many more. Original Indian artwork: Zuni, Pueblo, Hopi, handwoven rugs, jewelry, pottery and sculptures. Original wildlife bronze sculptures. The Gentle Giant (Drafthorse) Bronze Sculpture, some select, and original books.

Visa and Mastercard accepted. Layaway and UPS shipping available. Secondary Market Dealer.

GINGERBREAD BARN

755 Main St. P.O. Box 69
Half Moon Bay, CA 94019

PHONE: (415)726-6996
FAX: (415)879-0020

Monday-Saturday: 10:00-5:00
Sunday: 11:00-4:00

Specializing in Ladie and Friends, Sarah's Attic Collector Center, Byers' Choice, P. Buckley Moss Plates, Thomas Kinkade, Daddy's Long Legs, Thumb Print Bears, Mama's Babies, Dennis Lewan, Windy Meadows Pottery, Shelia's Collectibles, Designs by Milford, Gail Laura, Attic Babies, and Cat's Meow. Send self-addressed stamped envelope for list of retired pieces.

Visa and Mastercard accepted. Layaways welcome. UPS shipping.

CLASSY COLLECTIBLES

7561 Center Ave #4
Huntington Beach, CA 92647

PHONE: (714)897-2229

Monday-Sunday: 11:00-6:00
Other Times By Appointment

Beer steins, all brands, new and secondary market. Frances Hook figurines, Disney memorabilia, Coca-Cola-Disney World 15th Anniversary 60 pin set (mounted and framed), Budweiser, Ski Country, Wild Turkey, breweriana and Ertl Metal Banks and Cars. Secondary market lines: Liquor decanters, Jim Beam, Ezra Brooks, Canadian Mist, Cutty Sark, Cyrus Noble, Dug's Nevada brothels, Famous First, Grenadier, Hawaiian Distillers, Hoffman, Laurel and Hardy, Lionstone, McCormick, John Wayne, Old Commonwealth, Pacesetter, Pancho Villa, Raintree Clowns, Ski Country, Wild Turkey, etc.

Visa, Mastercard and Discover accepted. UPS shipping.

JOLLY HOLIDAY GIFTS

7561 Center Ave. Unit 8
Huntington Beach, CA 92647

PHONE: (714)895-5366
(800)866-8498
FAX: (714)895-5366

Monday-Saturday: 10:00-6:00
Sunday: 12:00-5:00; Closed Wednesday
Additional Seasonal Hours

Jolly Holiday Gifts is primarily a collectible Christmas Store year round. Featuring Christopher Radko, collectible ornaments, Barbara Paul Bunnies and collectible dolls, elegant eggs, hand carved Christmas and Easter collectible goose eggs, Fitz and Floyd Holiday Hamlet and Halloween Don Post Masks. Other collectible lines include Seymour Mann Dolls, Lynn West, Lynn Haney, Tilly Collectibles, Mark Klaus Christmas Collection, and Russian Alexander Nevesky Collection.

Visa, Mastercard and American Express accepted.

CALIFORNIA

NANCY'S GIFTS & COLLECTIBLES

7561 Center Ave. #6
Huntington Beach, CA 92647

PHONE: (714)895-1906

Wednesday-Friday: 11:00-5:00
Saturday-Sunday: 12:00-5:00

Bradford Dealer, Ashton-Drake, Hamilton plates, Jan Hagara, Donald Zolan Trading Center, MOY, DeGrazia, Marty Bell, Hibel plates and figurines, Perillo dolls, Dave Grossman Gone with the Wind, B&G/RC ornaments and plates, Lowell Davis, Precious Moments, Hummel.

All major credit cards. Shipping and layaway available.

Nancy's Gifts was established in 1977 and specializes in collector plates, back issues and obtaining them for you at affordable prices. Secondary market specialists for the lines listed above as well as others. All inquiries welcome.

TRIMS & TREASURES

33 Main St.
Jackson, CA 95642

PHONE: (209)223-3453
FAX: (209)223-3948

Monday-Saturday: 10:00-5:00
Sunday: 11:00-4:00; Extended Fall Hours

Dept. 56 Showcase Dealer: Dickens Village, Christmas in the City, New England Village, North Pole, Alpine Village, Little Town of Bethlehem, Snow Village, Snowbabies, Winter Silhouette, Merry Makers, All Thru the House, General Store, and Holiday Trim. Enesco Treasury Ornaments, C. Radko, Dreamsicles, Possible Dreams Santas, House of Hatten, Designs Americana Pencil Santas, Fontanini Nativity figures, and collectible Santas and ornaments from around the world. Christmas year round!

All major credit cards. Shipping available throughout the continental U.S. Secondary brokerage for Dept. 56 collectibles.

MEMORIES N' GIFTS

30100 Town Center Dr. Suite B-1
Laguna Niguel, CA 92656

PHONE: (714)363-5595

Open Daily: Monday-Saturday
Extended Holiday Hours

Thomas Kinkade, Dennis Patrick Lewan, Sandicast, Enesco Music Boxes. Dolls: Hamilton, Barbara Paul, Gustave Wolff, Ashton-Drake, Zook, The Collectables, Lawton, Gorham, Annalee, Himstedt, Seymour Mann, Jan Hagara, Bradley, Effanbee and others. Lowell Davis, Maud Humphrey, Beatrix Potter, Laura's Attic, Precious Moments. Boyd's Bears. Bradford Dealer.

Most major credit cards. Layaway and shipping available. Redemption Center. Free gift wrapping. Many unique items. Great gifts for all occassions. Specializing in Holiday Fanfare.

MAC KINNONS STATIONERY

305 E. LaHabra Blvd.
LaHabra, CA 90631

PHONE: (714)879-5850
(310)697-8210
FAX: (310)694-0506

Monday-Friday: 8:30-6:00
Saturday: 9:00-5:30

Lladro, Dept. 56, Krystonia, Laura's Attic, Enesco Memories of Yesterday, Byers' Choice Ltd., Tom Clark Gnomes, Annalee, Hallmark, Jan Hagara, Sarah's Attic, Precious Moments, Sports Impressions, Walt Disney Classics Collection, M. I. Hummel, Swarovski, Lilliput Lane, Miss Martha's, Little Cheesers, Knot Knoggins, and Cherished Teddies.

NALED member. Distinguished Service Retailer. All major credit cards accepted. *Swap and Sell the second Sunday of March, July and November.

CALIFORNIA

VILLAGE PEDDLER

2021 W. LaHabra Blvd.
LaHabra, CA 90631

PHONE: (310)694-6111

Monday-Saturday: 10:00-5:30

Bradford and Ashton-Drake Dealer. Lilliput Lane, Colonial Village, Muffy and Raikes Bears, Cherished Teddies, Calico Kittens, Perillo, Laura's Attic, Sandicast, Castagna, Marty Sculptures, United Design, Sarah's Attic, Lowell Davis, Novelino, Lucy & Me, Kinka, Michael Garman, Maruri U.S.A., Fenton Glass, Precious Moments Dolls and a wide selection of musicals, dolls, plates, frames, cases, stands and tea pots.

Liberal layaway policy. Shipping available. NALED Member.

LOUISE MARIE'S FINE GIFTS

1550 Railroad Ave.
Livermore, CA 94550

PHONE: (510)449-5757

Monday-Saturday: 10-6
Sunday By Appointment Only

Dept. 56, P. Buckley Moss, Madame Alexander, Lilliput Lane, David Winter, Tom Clark Gnomes, Thomas Kinkade, Sports Impressions, Gartlan, Heritage Village plates and frames, Hummels, dolls, Lee Middleton, All God's Children, Perillo, and Hibel.

Good service. Open by appointment anytime. NALED member. All major credit cards accepted. Secondary Market in Snow Village and Heritage. Layaways available. Shipping anywhere.

NYBORG CASTLE GIFTS & COLLECTIBLES

Virginia Hills Shopping Center
6662 Alhambra Ave.
Martinez, CA 94553-0888

PHONE: (510)930-0200
(800)995-5603
FAX: (510)930-7588

Monday-Friday: 10:00-6:00
Saturday: 10:00-5:30
Open Sunday November and December

All Dept. 56 Villages and Snowbabies, Cat's Meow, Precious Moments, David Winter, Lilliput Lane, Cherished Teddies, Wee Forest Folk, collector plates, Hummels, All God's Children, Lucy & Me, Byers' Choice, Lizzie High, Swarovski, Annalee, Krystonia, MOY, Sarah's Attic.

Free gift wrapping on items over $10.00. Shipping available in continental U.S. Charter NALED member. Serving collectors since 1972. Visa and Mastercard accepted. Layaways available.

RUMMEL'S VILLAGE GUILD

1859 Montebello Town Center
Montebello, CA 90640

PHONE: (213)722-2691

Monday-Friday: 10:00-9:00
Saturday: 10:00-7:00; Sunday: 11:00-6:00

Lladro, Hummel (including secondary), Disney Classics, Cherished Teddies, Precious Moments, Snowbabies, Dept. 56 (all villages), Wee Forest Folk, Jan Hagara, Maud Humphrey, Swarovski, David Winter, plates, dolls, frames, Ron Lee, Annalee, Krystonia, Dreamsicles, Rawcliffe pewter, Miss Martha's Originals, Armani, Marty Bell lithos and plates, Neil Rose sculptures, DeGrazia, Sandicast, Lowell Davis, P. Buckley Moss, Rockwell, PenniBears, Lilliput Lane, and Bing & Grondahl/Royal Copenhagen.

GCC and NALED Member. All credit cards accepted. UPS shipping and layaway available.

CALIFORNIA

DOLLS N' THINGS

2330 Atlantic Blvd.
Monterey Park, CA 91754

PHONE: (213)721-6679

Monday-Saturday: 11:00-6:00
Or By Appointment

Artist Collectibles, Ashton-Drake, The Collectables, Daddy's Long Legs, Dolls by Jerri, Ellenbrooke, Enesco, GADCO, Good-Kruger, Dave Grossman, Hamilton, Zook, Himstedt, Knowles, Seymour Mann, Middleton, Georgetown, Precious Heirloom (FayZah Spanos), Pauline, Mattel Porcelain Barbies, Virginia Turner, Gotz, United Design. Bears: North American, Raikes, CT. Bradford Dealer and Hamilton Plates. Originals by Kathy Kiss (sculpted and cloth). Full line of wizards, fairies, and mermaids, many one-of-a-kinds.

Doll club and free shipping on orders over $50. Free 3 month layaway. Secondary Market Dealer. All major credit cards. Special order. Private parties.

TOWNSEND'S CARD ATTACK

12125 Day St. Suite H-303
Moreno Valley, CA 92557

PHONE: (909)788-3989

Monday-Saturday: 10:00-8:00
Sunday: 11:00-6:00

Primary Lines: Bradford Exchange and Hamilton Plates, Ashton-Drake and Hamilton Dolls, Cherished Teddies, MOY, Sarah's Attic, All God's Children, Miss Martha's, Krystonia, Pocket Dragons, Raikes Bears, Roosevelt Bears, Iris Arc Crystal, Daddy's Long Legs, LEGENDS, Calico Kittens, Lewan Lithographs, Sandra Kuck, Lena Liu, Little Cheesers, Kewpies, P. Buckley Moss, and Seymour Mann Dolls.

Secondary Market Service. Shipping available. Layaways.

HERRITT'S FLOWERS & GIFTS

1546 First St.
Napa, CA 94559

PHONE: (707)224-8381

Mon-Fri: 8:30-6:00; Saturday: 9:00-5:30

One stop collectible shop and more in the heart of the Napa Valley in downtown Napa. Dept. 56, Sarah's Attic, Annalee Mobilitee Dolls, Possible Dreams, Westland, Andrea by Sadek, CT, Armani, United Design, Midwest Importers, Schmid, Roman, Christopher Radko, Old World Imports, Gorham, Tilly's Collectibles, Miss Martha, Clay Art, Bunnies by the Bay, Attic Babies, Ashton-Drake, Bradley Dolls, Sports Impressions, Hollywood, Reco, Bradford Dealer, Glynda Turley, Donna Barton, Thomas Kinkade, and Hadley House. Redemption Center for Lilliput Lane, Hummel, Armani, Sarah's Attic, Marty Bell. All major credit cards. Layaway and shipping available.

TORCH WORK GIFTS

2033 New Park Mall
Newark, CA 94560

PHONE: (510)793-0716

Monday-Saturday: 10:00-9:00
Sunday: 11:00-6:00

Tom Clark, Sarah's Attic, Krystonia, David Winter, Armani, Timothy Wolfe, Chilmark, Perth Pewter, Sabino, lead crystal figurines, paperweights, perfume bottles, hand-blown glass sculpture, glass wedding cake tops, glass engraving. Also featuring sterling silver jewelry, quartz crystals, mineral speciman and American Indian artwork.

Mastercard and Visa accepted. Layaway and shipping available. Secondary Market Dealer for Tom Clark, Sarah's Attic and Krystonia. Golden Heart Store for Sarah's Attic.

CALIFORNIA

BURT'S PHARMACY & GIFT SHOPPE

2333 Borchard Rd.
Newbury Park, CA 91320
PHONE: (805)498-1591
FAX: (805)498-8017

Monday-Saturday: 10:00-8:00
Sunday: 11:00-5:00

Annalee, Bradford Exchange Dealer, *Cherished Teddies, *Cast Art Dreamsicles, *David Winter, Dept. 56 Villages and Snowbabies, Enesco Premier Ornament Center, Hamilton Plates, *Iris Arc Crystal, J.H. Boone, *Jan Hagara, Laura's Attic, *Lilliput Lane, Marty Bell plates, Maud Humphrey, *Memories of Yesterday, Miss Martha's, Precious Moments (DSR), Raikes Bears, Sports Impressions, *Tom Clark Gnomes, Tim Wolfe. *Redemption Center.

GCC member. All major credit cards accepted. 90 day layaway with 20% down. UPS shipping. Free gift wrapping.

PAGLIACCI

3432-105 Via Oporto
Newport Beach, CA 92663
PHONE: (714)673-6292
FAX: (714)673-6293

Daily: 11:00-5:00; Friday: 11:00-6:00
Saturday: 11:00-9:00

Established in 1978. Home of Red Skelton Art and Collectibles. From plates and porcelain plaques to photos and books published by Mr. Skelton. Collector Center for Armani, Ron Lee, Hummel, WACO Melody in Motion, Lladro, Emmett Kelly Sr. and Jr., and all types of clown and porcelain pierrot dolls.

All major credit cards accepted. Shipping worldwide.

GIFT GALLERY NORTHRIDGE PHARMACY

9167 Reseda Blvd.
Northridge, CA 91324
PHONE: (818)349-7000
FAX: (818)349-0344

Monday-Friday: 9:00-10:00pm
Sunday: 9:00-9:00

Dept. 56 (all villages), Lladro, Lilliput Lane, David Winter, All God's Children, Sarah's Attic, Precious Moments, Maud Humphrey Bogart, Memories of Yesterday, Daddy's Long Legs, Swarovski, Sports Impressions, Hummel, Krystonia, Maruri, Lenox, LEGENDS, Rick Cain, Cherished Teddies, Cat's Meow and Caithness.

All major credit cards accepted. GCC member. Layaway available. Dept. 56 Secondary Market.

HERMAN'S STATIONERS

11018 E. Rosecrans
Norwalk, CA 90650
PHONE: (310)864-8494
(310)864-7735
FAX: (310)863-9226

Monday-Saturday: 9:00-7:30
Sunday: 10:00-5:30

GCC Member. Located East of I-605 and North of I-91. Lines include: PM (DSR), MOY (Heritage), Preferred dealer for Ron Lee, Disney, DW, Lilliput, Gartlan, Maud Humphrey, Sports Impressions, Hummel, Armani, Hallmark Galleries, EKJ, WACO and Enesco Musicals, Tobin Fraley, Krystonia, Miss Martha's, CT, Cain, LEGENDS, Neil Rose, Iris Arc, Dreamsicles, Colonial Village, Dept. 56 Villages, accessories, and Snowbabies, Lucy and Me, Duncan Royale, Kurt Adler Santas, Mark Klaus, Laura's Attic, Sarah's Attic, PenniBears, Raikes, Little Cheesers, Hidden Kingdom, Hallmark Ornaments, Enesco Ornaments and Beatrix Potter.

CALIFORNIA

IT'S CHRISTMAS

1013 2nd. St.
Old Sacramento, CA 95814

PHONE: (916)444-0428

Daily Monday-Sunday

A complete line of Dept. 56 Collectibles, The Heritage Village Collection (Dickens Village, Christmas in the City, New England, North Pole Collection, Alpine, and Little Town of Bethlehem), The Original Snow Village, Snowbabies, Winter Silhouette, Merry Makers, All Thru the House, General Store, and Holiday Trim. Enesco Treasury of Christmas Ornaments, C. Radko, Blown Glass Collection, Cast Art Dreamsicles, Possible Dreams Santas, House of Hatten, Designs Americana Pencil Santas, Fontanini nativity figures, and collectible Santas and ornaments from around the world. Christmas year round!

Major credit cards. Shipping available throughout continental U.S.

COLLECTIBLES OUTLET II

1100 W. Chapman
Orange, CA 92668

PHONE: (714)639-3200
FAX: (714)744-0907

Monday-Friday: 10:00-6:00
Saturday: 10:00-5:00; Sunday: 12:00-5:00

Lladro, Hummels, Dept. 56, Precious Moments, David Winter, Lilliput Lane Cottages, Treasured Memories, Swarovski, Lenox, Waterford, Madame Alexander Dolls, Maruri, Sadek, Jan Hagara, Krystonia, Maud Humphrey, Cherished Teddies, All God's Children, Miss Martha's, Beatrix Potter, Lalique, Baccarat.

Second Location: 1899 W. San Carlos, San Jose CA 95128. (408)288-6027.

JULIET'S COLLECTIBLES

Eldorado Center
342 N. Tustin Ave.
Orange, CA 92666

PHONE: (714)633-GIFT

Tuesday-Sunday: 10:30-5:30

All God's Children, All Bradford Lines, Wee Forest Folk, David Winter, decorative display hangers and stands. Lithos by Corinne Layton, Thomas Kinkade, Terry Redlin, Zolan and Ozz Franca.

Custom framing available. Will ship all over the world. Mastercard and Visa accepted. 90 day layaway plan. All secondary market.

RUANN'S GIFTS & COLLECTIBLES

1330 N. Glassel at Katella
Orange, CA 92667

PHONE: (714)771-3003

Monday-Friday: 10:00-6:00
Saturday: 10:00-5:00
Sunday By Appointment Only

Collectibles store since 1974! Thomas Kinkade art, Alan Maley, Marty Bell, Alan Murray Austin Sculptures, Heritage Lace, and over 500 collectors plates, plate frames, fine gifts and many more collectibles.

Secondary Market on Kinkade and Marty Bell. Visa and Mastercard accepted. Layaway on all merchandise.

CALIFORNIA

MARY ANNE'S HALLMARK

Acorn Plaza
4869 S. Bradley Rd.
Orcutt, CA 93455

PHONE: (805)937-0800

Monday-Friday: 9:30-7:00
Saturday: 9:30-6:00; Sunday: 12:00-5:00

In addition to a complete selection of Hallmark cards, lines also include Precious Moments, Lowell Davis, Dickens Village, Lilliput Lane, All Dept. 56 Houses, Hummel, Maud Humphrey, Jan Hagara, David Winter, Duncan Royale, and Hallmark Ornaments.

Second location: The Adobe Plaza, 7357 El Camino Real, Atascadero CA 93422. Phone: (805)466-8868.

Gold Crown Plus Store. Club redemption center. Layaway. All major credit cards. Shipping and gift wrapping available.

COLLECTIBLE CORNER

1213 East Imperial Hwy.
Placentia, CA 92670

PHONE: (714)528-3079

Tuesday-Saturday: 10:00-6:00

Precious Moments, David Winter, Thomas Kinkade, Jan Hagara, Snowbabies, Hummel, Maud Humphrey, Memories of Yesterday, DeGrazia, Disney, frames and accessories.

All major credit cards accepted. Layaway and shipping availabale. Gift wrapping. NALED Member. Bradford Exchange. Secondary Market Dealer. Redemption Center for all of the above. They carry most collectibles, if they don't have it-- they'll find it.

THOMAS KINKADE GALLERY

262 Main St.
(Above The Cottage Shop)
Placerville, CA 95667

PHONE: (916)621-4453

Monday-Saturday: 9:30-5:30
Sunday: 12:00-5:00

The world's largest distributor of Thomas Kinkade Fine Art. Exclusive Thomas Kinkade Works--all plates, prints (both canvas and paper), and three dimensional cottages.

Bradford Dealer. Secondary Market Dealer. Custom Framing. Layaway plan. Most major credit cards accepted.

EVA MARIE, DRY GROCER

1915 S. Catalina Ave.
Redondo Beach, CA 90277

PHONE: (310)375-8422

Monday-Saturday: 10:00-6:00

Some inventory is 20 years old. Old and new collectible plates and figurines. If it is collectible, it is probably in stock. Precious Moments, Memories of Yesterday, Hummel, Martha Holcombe, All God's Children, Tom Clark Gnomes, Lowell Davis.

NALED member. Bradford Dealer. Visa, American Express, and Mastercard accepted. Phone orders also accepted.

CALIFORNIA

GALLERIA GIFTS

1049 G Street
Reedley, CA 93654

PHONE: (209)638-4060

Monday-Friday: 9:30-5:30
Saturday: 9:30-5:00

Walt Disney Classics Collection, David Winter, All God's Children, Dept. 56, LEGENDS, Marty Bell, Thomas Kinkade, Lilliput, Lladro, Tom Clark Gnomes, Sarah's Attic, Hummels, Swarovski, Maud Humphrey, Byers' Choice Carolers, Raikes Bears, Goebel Miniatures, Duncan Royale, Miss Martha, Annalee, Cherished Teddies, Jan Hagara, Lizzie High, MOY, Sports Impressions, Sandra Kuck, PenniBears, Perillo, Tim Wolfe, Laura's Attic, Dreamsicles, and Little Cheesers. Authorized Bradford Dealer.

All major credit cards accepted. NALED member. UPS daily.

BREWSTERS

6052 Magnolia Ave.
Riverside, CA 92506

PHONE: (909) 686-1979

Monday-Friday: 9:00-8:00
Saturday and Sunday: 10:00-6:00

Collector Redemption Center: Lladro, Hummel, Disney Classics, Enesco Musicals, David Winter Cottages, Precious Moments, Lalique and Swarovski Crystal.

Waterford, Baccarat, Orrefors, Crystal World, Boehm, Cybis, Andrea birds, Jon Herbert Shoehouses, Artesania Rinconada, and Lenox giftware.

In depth selection: candle shop, Hallmark Cards, kitchen and sporting knives, fine jewelry.

Available: Courtesy giftwrap. Gift Certificates. Interest-free layaway and Brewsters Advantage Card. Mastercard, Visa and American Express accepted. Brewsters collectible auction in June.

DISCOVERIES AND DADSON GALLERIES

3567 Main St.
Riverside, CA 92501

PHONE: (909)787-8862

Tuesday-Friday: 10:00-6:00
Saturday: 11:00-6:00

Edna Hibel, Penni Anne Cross, Dennis Lewan, Thomas Kinkade, Marty Bell, Alan Maley, Ozz Franca, Robert Bateman, Terry Redlin, Steve Hanks, Lee Bogle, Pati Bannister, Fred Stone, Sandra Kuck, Michael Ward, Charles Frace, Julie Kramer Cole, G. Harvey, Zolan, Vargas.

Jan Hagara, Lowell Davis, Maud Humphrey, Rick Albee, Rick Cain, Neil Rose, Icart, Fraser Cottages, Shoemakers Dream, Duncan Royale, Golden Memories, Kaleidoscopes.

Gift Shop and Art Gallery. Mastercard, Visa, American Express accepted. Layaway and shipping available. Gift wrap.

TOMORROW'S TREASURES

11498 Pierce St. Suite A
Riverside, CA 92505-3308

PHONE: (909)354-5731

Monday-Friday: 10:00-5:30
Thursday: 10:00-7:00; Sunday: 11:00-5:00

Ron Lee, Imhoff, Laura's Attic, Hummel, Lilliput Lane, Lowell Davis, Maud Humphrey, Memories of Yesterday, Jan Hagara, Wee Forest Folk, Maruri, Disney Classics Collection, Annalee, Little Cheesers, Willitts, Cherished Teddies, Enesco, Possible Dreams, Bradford, Hollywood, Ashton-Drake, Royal Doulton, VIB Bears, Muffy Vanderbears, Iris Arc, Hagen Renaker, Frumps, Kitty Cucumber, Cecile's, United Design, DeGrazia, Perillo, Dept. 56, Harbour Lights, Fitz & Floyd, PenniBears, and Goebel Miniatures.

All major credit cards accepted. Club dealer for all the collectible lines carried.

CALIFORNIA

ELLIS IN WONDERLAND

2533 Fair Oaks Blvd.
Sacramento, CA 95825

PHONE: (916)485-2295

Monday-Friday: 10:00-6:00
Saturday: 11:00-6:00; Sunday: 12:00-3:00

Specializing in fine collectibles and featuring artist appearances and other in-store events. Chilmark, Lladro, Swarovski, All God's Children, Lilliput Lane, David Winter, LEGENDS, Hudson, Mark Hopkins bronzes, Armani, Tom Clark, Caithness, Sarah's Attic, Maruri, Tim Wolfe, Marty Bell, Little Cheesers, Bossons, fantasy and mythical figurines.

Redemption center for lines listed. Major credit cards accepted. Layaway and shippping available.

KAREN'S HALLMARK

2527 Fair Oaks Blvd.
Sacramento, CA 95825

PHONE: (916)489-5700
FAX: (916)758-4415

Monday,Tuesday, Friday, Saturday: 1-6
Wednesday and Thursday: 10-8
Sunday: 12-5

Gold Crown Hallmark with Galleries, *Precious Moments (DSR), Kinka, *Memories of Yesterday, Laura's Attic, North Pole Village, NAO, United Designs, Bluebird of Happiness, *Krystonia, *Small World of Music Action Musicals, *M.I. Hummel, *Walt Disney Classics Collection. *Premier Dealer for Enesco Treasury Ornaments, Cherished Teddies, Dept. 56- Snow Village, Flambro Imports, Hallmark Keepsake Ornaments, Lefton Village, Roman Inc., Willitts Designs.

Mastercard, Visa, American Express and Discover accepted. Shipping available.

*Club Memberships available.

DESIGNERS CENTER

302 B Tanforan Park
San Bruno, CA 94066

PHONE: (800)328-4849
FAX: (415)349-9293

Monday-Friday: 10:00-9:00
Saturday: 10:00-7:00; Sunday: 11:00-6:00

All God's Children, Armani, Dept. 56, Gartlan, Hummel, Lladro, Lilliput, Miss Martha, Maud Humphrey, Enesco Musical Society, Tom Clark, David Winter, Swarovski, Sports Impressions, Precious Moments, Snowbabies, Goyesca and Disney Classics Collection.

Free gift wrapping and shipping with mention of Collectors' Information Bureau. All major credit cards accepted. Free layaway. GCC member. Minutes from San Francisco Airport.

THE FAMILY AFFAIR

13330 Paseo Del Verano Norte
San Diego, CA 92128

PHONE: (619)485-5850
FAX: (619)485-7208

Tuesday-Saturday: 10:00-5:00
Sunday: 11:00-5:00

Marty Bell, Thomas Kinkade, Zolan, DeGrazia, Jan Hagara, Sandra Kuck, Rockwell, Maud Humphrey, Moss, Perillo, Hibel, Precious Moments, Hummel, Lilliput Lane, Ashton-Drake, Hamilton Dolls, and frames and accessories.

Many back issues. Good selection of graphics, plates and figurines.

Major club redemptions.

Authorized Bradford Exchange Dealer.

Visa, Mastercard and Discover accepted.

CALIFORNIA

LE CADEAU

Seaport Village
837 West Harbor Dr. Suite B
San Diego, CA 92101

PHONE: (619)232-0228

Open 7 Days A Week: 10:00-9:00/10:00

Thrill to many one-of-a kind creations crafted by talented local and world renown artists. Wall decor in the form of metal flowers, three dimensional houses, carousel horses and miniature etchings are among the treasures to be found. Choose from a large selection of Michael's Houses, Harbour Lights, John Hine Studios, Sarah's Attic, Cairn Studio, Daddy's Long Legs, Ron Lee Clowns, Roberta and Jody Bergsma prints, Rotraut Schrott and Lee Middleton dolls.

Visa and Mastercard accepted. Layaway and shipping. Redemption Center.

THE TINDER BOX

4465 La Jolla Village Dr. H3-8
San Diego, CA 92122

PHONE: (619)452-9444

Monday-Friday: 10:00-9:00
Saturday: 10:00-7:00; Sunday: 11:00-6:00

Melody in Motion, Incolay, Fables, Bossons, Linden Clocks, Armani, Colibri, Zippo, DuPont, Tom Taber decoys, Comoys of London, Tom Clark Gnomes, Tim Wolfe, Enchantica, David Winter, Chilmark, LEGENDS, Windstone, Dragon Keep, Krystonia, Enchanted Kingdom, Sandicast, fancy pewter figurines, Livingstone. The top cigar store in San Diego County with unique gifts from around the world.

Major credit cards accepted. Layaway and shipping available. Free gift wrapping.

VILLAGE HANDMAIDEN

981 Arrow Hwy.
San Dimas, CA 91773

PHONE: (714)592-0373

Monday-Saturday: 10:00-6:00

All God's Children, Byers' Choice Carolers, Wee Forest Folk, Lizzie High Dolls, Attic Babies, Little Cheesers, and PenniBears.

Most major credit cards accepted. Layaway and shipping available. Redemption Center.

"Specializing in that country feeling!"

SIDERS COLLECTIBLES & FINE GIFTS

4626 Meridian Ave.
San Jose, CA 95124

**PHONE: (800)846-6545
(408)264-6545**

Monday-Saturday: 10:00-7:00
Sunday: 1:00-4:00

Your primary and secondary collectibles specialists. Bradford Plates, Lladro, Armani, Swarovski, Wee Forest Folk, Hummel, P. Buckley Moss plates, Maud Humphrey, Annalee, Marty Bell Lithos, Walt Disney Collection, David Winter, Lilliput Lane, Precious Moments, PenniBears, ANRI, Golden Memories, dolls, and sports collectibles.

All Club redemption. All major credit cards. Layaway and shipping available.

CALIFORNIA

BURLWOOD GALLERY
SAUSALITO/SAN FRANCISCO
& COLLECTORS GALLERY

721 Bridgeway
Sausalito, CA 94965

PHONE: (415)332-6550
FAX: (415)332-7589

Open Daily: 10:00-6:00

Lladro, Armani, M.I. Hummel, LEGENDS, Chilmark, Ron Lee, Capodimonte, Mark Hopkins, selected glass sculptures by different artists, water sculptures, redwood furniture, Tiffany Lamps, and much more.

All major credit cards accepted. Free shipping and gift wrapping. Club Redemption Center.

SPYGLASS TRADING CO.

2665 Shell Beach Rd.
Shell Beach, CA 93449

PHONE: (805)773-1309
FAX: (805)773-1849

Monday-Thursday: 9:00-8:00
Friday and Saturday: 9:00-9:00
Sunday: 10:00-8:00

Dept. 56, Hummel, Precious Moments, Plates include P. Buckley Moss, S. Kuck, Marty Bell, Hamilton, Hollywood, and Lowell Davis. Annalee Mobilitee Dolls, Dreamsicles, Cherished Teddies, Incolay Stone, and Fontanini by Roman.

Visa, Mastercard, American Express accepted. 30 day layaway plan. Post office and UPS shipping available. Some secondary market. Club redemption center for Precious Moments, M.I. Hummel, Fontanini, and Dreamsicles.

THE DOLL SHOPPE

13759 Ventura Blvd.
Sherman Oaks, CA 91423

PHONE: (818)784-3655

Antique dolls: Armand Marseille, Eden Bebe, Handwerck, Heubach, K & R, Kestner, Kewpie, Lenci, Schoenhut, Simon & Halbig, S.F.B.J., Half Dolls and others.

Contemporary Dolls: Madame Alexander, Effanbee, Ideal, Voque, Mann, Dynasty Dan, Duck House, Lissi, Fiba, Naber Kid, Woods, Crees and others.

Buy-Sell-Repair. Layaways. Shipping available. Doll locator service. Visa and Mastercard accepted.

Doll books, display furniture, doll display cases, miniatures and doll stands!

Member of DOLLNET.

LITTLE STUGA

50 W. Sierra Madre Blvd.
Sierra Madre, CA 91024

PHONE: (818)355-9113

Monday-Friday: 9:30-5:30
Saturday: 9:30-9:00

All God's Children, Cat's Meow, Little Cheesers, Thomas Kinkade, Rowe Pottery, Muffy VanderBear, United Design, and Ginny Dolls.

All major credit cards accepted. UPS shipping and layaway available.

CALIFORNIA

SANTA'S VILLAGE

P.O. Box 638
Skyforest, CA 92385
PHONE: (909)336-3661

Open Seasonally 10:00-5:00
Call for Schedule

Christmas Decorations: Chistopher Radko, Old World, Whitehurst, Enesco, Possible Dreams, Kurt Adler, Silvestri, Roman. Dolls: Madame Alexander, Gorham, Pauline, Effanbee, Ginny, Porcelain. Gifts: Cairn Gnomes, Lefton Colonial Village, Enesco Music Boxes, Raikes Bears, Maud Humphrey, Clay Art, Hopkins Shop, Red Mill.

Unique Toys. 13 Fun Filled Rides and much more.

Bring this book to Santa's Village for one free Adult admission (one time only), Validated at Entrance.

THE MOLE HOLE OF SOLVANG

1603 Copenhagen Dr.
Solvang, CA 93463
PHONE: (805)688-7669

Open Daily: 9:30-5:30

Premier dealer for: Christopher Radko, Wee Forest Folk, Lladro, Swarovski Crystal, LEGENDS, Caithness, Lilliput Lane, Thomas Kinkade, Marty Bell, David Winter, Byers' Choice, Armani, Dept. 56 Villages and Snowbabies, Vaillancourt, Limoge boxes, Corre' figurines, Old World, Christmas nutcrackers, unusual one-of-a-kind items, and collector dolls and gifts from around the world.

Visa, Mastercard and American Express accepted. Free gift wrapping available. Will ship anywhere in the U.S.

THE UGLY DUCKLING

1557 Mission Dr.
Solvang, CA 93463
PHONE: (805)688-6640
(805)688-7533

Monday-Saturday: 8:30-5:30
Sunday: 9:00-5:00

Serving the collector since 1960. A full-line of Dept. 56: Dickens, Alpine, New England, Christmas in the City, North Pole, Snow Village, accessories, Snowbabies, and All Through the House. Tom Clark Gnomes, current and retired, Tim Wolfe's Wildlife, Robert Olszewski's Miniatures, M.I. Hummel Miniatures and figurines, Krystonia and collectible plates.

Visa, Mastercard, and Discover accepted. Layaway and mail order available. Secondary Market Dealer. Redemption Center for Hummel, Krystonia and Tom Clark.

PARDINI'S

302 Lincoln Center
Stockton, CA 95207
PHONE: (209)957-2414
FAX: (209)957-2417

Monday-Friday: 10:00-5:30
Saturday: 10:00-5:00

Bradford Dealer, David Winter, Dept. 56, Precious Moments, Lowell Davis, Swarovski, Lladro, Hummel, Tom Clark Gnomes, Madame Alexander Dolls, Ashton-Drake Dolls, ANRI Figurines, Armani, Cybis, Walt Disney Classics Collection, Memories of Yesterday, Possible Dreams, Sports Impressions and Gartlan USA.

Doll and figurine cases made to order. Visa, Mastercard and American Express accepted.

CALIFORNIA

KAE'S & RICK'S HALLMARK SHOP

10493 Sunland Blvd.
Sunland, CA 91040
PHONE: (818)353-1891
FAX: (818)352-0672

Monday-Friday: 10:00-9:00
Saturday: 10:00-6:00; Sunday: 11:00-5:00

Dept. 56: Dicken's Village, Christmas in the City, North Pole and Snowbabies; Hallmark Galleries, Keepsake Ornaments, Krystonia, Jan Hagara, Precious Moments, Hopkins House, Daddy's Long Legs, Napoleon, United Design, Willitts Designs.

Gold Crown Store. A Designated Leadership Guide. Receive all special product introductions, especially relating to Keepsake Ornaments.

American Express, Visa and Mastercard accepted. Layaway.

ROSTAND FINE JEWELERS

8349 Foothill Blvd.
Sunland, CA 91040
PHONE: (800)222-9208
(818)352-7814
FAX: (818)352-3792

Monday-Friday: 9:30-6:00;
Saturday: 9:30-5:30
Closed Sundays except in December

Lladro, Waterford, Baccarat, Lalique, Armani, Chilmark, LEGENDS, Hummel, Ron Lee, Golden Memories, Gorham, Walt Disney Classics Collection, David Winter, Harbour Lights, Andrea Birds, Maruri, Capodimonte, Swarovski, Wedgwood, and Rolex watches.

Free gift wrapping. Layaway. In business for 33 years. Recognized by the Lladro organization to be the "pioneer of the Lladro Secondary Market."

DARVA JEWELERS

18410 Ventura Blvd.
Tarzana, CA 91356
PHONE: (818)881-4653
FAX: (818)881-3494

Monday-Friday: 9:30-5:30
Saturday: 10:00-5:00

Lladro, Lalique, Baccarat, Swarovski, Waterford, Judith Leiber Purses, and Fine Jewelry.

Extensive line of Swiss watches including Ebel, Concord, Omega, Breitling, Movado, TAG Heuer, Raymond Weil, Rado, Baume & Mercier, Vacheron Constantin and Swatch.

Secondary Market Dealer for crystal, and antique jewelry and watches.

FRAME OF MIND ARTS & GIFTS

20021 Valley Blvd. Suite B
Tehachapi, CA 93561
PHONE: (805)822-1698
FAX: (805)822-8100

Monday-Saturday: 9:30-5:30

Art Gallery featuring Marty Bell, Thomas Kinkade, Dennis P. Lewan and LEGENDS Sculptures. Authorized Bradford Exchange Dealer. Lilliput Lane Cottages, Duncan Royale Santas and Ebony Collections, Emmett Kelly Clowns, Miss Martha's Collection, Lladro figurines, Maruri Elephants, Hummingbirds, Birds of Song, Maud Humphrey Bogart and Sandra Kuck figurines.

CALIFORNIA

CAMEO FINE GIFTS & COLLECTIBLES

Town Center-Near Target
27540 Ynez Rd. Suite J3
Temecula, CA 92591

PHONE: (909)676-1635

Monday-Saturday: 10:00-5:30

Dept. 56 Showcase, Lladro, Precious Moments (DSR), Lilliput Lane, David Winter, Wee Forest Folk, Ashton-Drake and Madame Alexander Dolls, Hummel, Lowell Davis, Tom Clark Gnomes, Snowbabies, Jan Hagara, Cherished Teddies, Armani, Swarovski, Raikes, Miss Martha, Sarah's Attic, and Maud Humphrey.

All major credit cards accepted. NALED member. Layaway. Authorized Bradford Exchange Dealer. Club redemption center.

ROSE COTTAGE

235 North Moorpark Rd.
Thousand Oaks, CA 91360

PHONE: (805)497-0901

Monday-Saturday: 10:00-6:00
Sunday: 11:00-5:00

Wee Forest Folk, Lilliput Lane, Byers' Choice, Possible Dreams, Sarah's Attic, All God's Children, Cherished Teddies, Vaillancourt, Tattered Rabbit, Barbara Bourgeau Richards, Heritage Collection by Midwest Importers, June McKenna Santas, Glynda Turley. Bears by Wendy Brent and Muffy Bears. Margaret Furlong Designs, Enesco Treasury Ornaments, Ladie and Friends, Cat's Meow and Annalee dolls.

This country gift shop also features pine furniture, greeting cards, American Folk Art, handcarved decoys, tin, pewter, Yankee Candles, and gourmet candy and coffee.

Visa and Mastercard accepted. Layaway and shipping available.

THE SECRET DRAWER

1341 E. Thousand Oaks Blvd.
Suite 100
Thousand Oaks, CA 91362

PHONE: (805)497-1121

Monday-Saturday: 10:30-6:00

Authorized Bradford Dealer. Thomas Kinkade Fine Art and plates, Snowbabies, Maud Humphrey, Miss Martha's Collection by Enesco, Wee Forest Folk, Byers' Choice, Annalee, David Winter, Jan Hagara, Sandra Kuck, P. Buckley Moss, Corinne Layton, Donald Zolan, Fred Stone, Muffy Vanderbear, Marty Bell plates, Duncan Royale Ebony Collection, Lawton Dolls, Ashton-Drake, Alexander, Dolls by Jerri, Steiff, Gund, Raikes and English Paddington Bears.

Credit cards accepted. Secondary Market. Club redemptions.

COUNTRY CONNECTION

3902 Pacific Coast Hwy.
Torrance, CA 90505

PHONE: (310)375-8106
FAX: (310)378-5065

Monday-Wednesday, Saturday: 10-6
Thursday-Friday: 10-8; Sunday: 12-5

Specializing in the finest country oak furniture and accessories in the South Bay. A vast selection includes such famous artists as Marty Bell, Thomas Kinkade, and Dennis Patrick Lewan, to only name a few. Also featuring the wonderful world of Daddy's Long Legs, Duncan Royale, Attic Babies, and Schmid. Country furniture manufacturers include Richardson Bros. Dino of California, People Loungers, Trend Manor, and of course, everything is made in America.

Remember "Nancy's Deals" are always the best deals in town. Let them help you make your house a home.

MC/Visa/Disc. Financing O.A.C. Layaway.

CALIFORNIA

MARGIE'S GIFTS & COLLECTIBLES

24536 Hawthorne Blvd.
Torrance, CA 90505

PHONE: (310)378-2526
(310)378-8134

Monday-Saturday: 10:00-5:30

"A Collector's Delight," serving the South Bay since 1971. Fine gifts and collectibles featuring All God's Children, ANRI, Armani, Byers' Choice, Calico Kittens, Cherished Teddies, Lowell Davis, Walt Disney Classics, DeGrazia, Hummel, Maud Humphrey, Kuck, Kinkade, Krystonia, Lilliput Lane, Little Cheesers, Lladro, Miss Martha, Moss, Muffy Bears, Olszewski Miniatures, Pocket Dragons, PM, PenniBears, Raikes Bears, Sarah's Attic, Swarovski, David Winter and more!

Serving over 20 collector clubs. Secondary Market service. Mail orders and layaway available. Bradford/NALED dealer. Friendly staff ready to serve all your needs.

THE YELLOW DOLLHOUSE & MINIATURES

3774 Pacific Coast Hwy.
Torrance, CA 90505

PHONE: (310)378-9665

Monday-Saturday: 10:00-5:00
Closed Tuesday and Sunday

The largest doll shop in the Los Angeles area with Lawtons, Dolls by Jerri, The Collectables, Ruth Treffeisen, Janet Ness, Brenda Burke, Good-Kruger, Edna Dali, as well as doll accessories. Doll house kits and assembled shells. Whickerville miniatures by Marie Terrones. 1" to 1/2" scale miniatures. Other lines include: Kingdom of Knoch, Hidden Kingdom, Wee Forest Folk, Little Cheesers, Goebel Miniatures, Hummel, PenniBears, and Maud Humphrey.

Redemption Center for Hummel, PenniBears and Maud Humphrey. Layaway on dolls. Mail order. Major credit cards.

JUSTIN PORTERFIELD, LTD.

17350 E. Seventeenth St.
Tustin, CA 92680

PHONE: (714)544-5223
FAX: (714)544-7649

Monday-Friday: 10:00-5:30
Saturday: 10:00-5:00; Sunday: 12:00-4:00

Armani, Byers' Choice, Thomas Kinkade, David Winter, small Madame Alexander dolls, Alan Maley prints, Francis Jerome prints, extensive collection of English enamel boxes and French limoges, and local ceramic artists.

High-end home decor, gifts and collectibles. Specializes in unique and specialty items, such as prints and canvas transfers. Serves a delightful afternoon high English tea in the loft-turned tearoom.

GALLERIA OF PRECIOUS MEMORIES

403-A N. Central Ave.
Upland, CA 91786

PHONE: (714)946-7346
FAX: (714)946-5416

Monday-Saturday: 9:00-6:00

Lladro, Dept. 56, Snowbabies, Laura's Attic, Sarah's Attic, Maud Humphrey, Jan Hagara, Chilmark, Little Cheesers, Cherished Teddies, PM, David Winter, Lilliput Lane, Annalee, Goebel Miniatures, Iris Arc, Mobex, Maruri, Lowell Davis, Thomas Kinkade, Alan Murray, Lena Liu, Sandra Kuck, Alan Maley, Corinne Layton, Dennis P. Lewan, Erlene Moses, Liliana Frasca, Perillo, Disney Classics, P. Buckley Moss, Boehm, Byers' Choice, Duncan Royale, Incolay, Sports Impressions, and PenniBears. Bradford Dealer.

All major credit cards accepted. Layaway. Shipping available.

CALIFORNIA

THE COBBLESTONE COTTAGE

24335 W. Magic Mountain Pkwy.
Valencia, CA 91355

PHONE: (805)253-0209
FAX: (805)255-0669

Monday-Saturday: 10:00-6:00
Sunday: 12:30-4:30

Located at River Oaks. Lines featured: Lladro, David Winter, Lilliput Lane, Marty Bell Lithos, Swarovski, Byers' Choice Carolers, Dept. 56 Heritage Villages, June McKenna, Royal Doulton, Wee Forest Folk, Fitz & Floyd, Alan Maley Lithos, Michael Garman and Dennis Patrick Lewan Lithos.

All major credit cards accepted. Layaway plan available. The Cobblestone Cottage is the largest collectible store in the Santa Clarita Valley. Serving the collectible market since 1987.

KACEE'S GIFTS, ART & ANTIQUES

23417 Lyons
Valencia, CA 91355

PHONE: (805)254-4499

Monday-Friday: 10:00-8:00
Saturday: 10:00-6:00; Sunday: 11:00-5:00

A blend of the old and new! Featuring the artwork of Thomas Kinkade, Dennis Patrick Lewan, Lena Liu, Alan Maley and Alan Murray. Maud Humphrey, Hagara, Enesco Musicals, Sports Impressions, Cherished Teddies, Miss Martha Originals, Coca-Cola Collectibles, H & G Studios, WACO Melodies In Motion, Fenton Art Glass, Hamilton Collection, Harbour Lights, Bradford plates, Windstone Editions. Antique furniture.

Mastercard, Visa, American Express and Discover accepted. Layaway. Free shipping in the U.S. Gift wrapping available.

BLEVINS PLATES 'N' THINGS

301 Georgia St.
Vallejo, CA 94590

PHONE: (707)552-9345
(800)523-5511

Monday-Friday: 10:00-6:00
Saturday: 9:00-5:00

Bradford Exchange, Hamilton, Van Hygen and Smythe, Ashton-Drake, John Hine, Lilliput, Cairn, Hummel, Rockwell, Goebel Miniatures, DeGrazia, Perillo, Penni Ann Cross, Jan Hagara, Lucie Atwell, Maud Humphrey Bogart, All God's Children, Sarah's Attic, PM, Lowell Davis, Wee Forest Folk, Disney, Sports, Duncan Royale, Swarovski, Madame Alexander, Mattel, Good-Kruger, Raikes, Middleton, Hadley House, Lena Liu, Lawton Dolls, B&G/RC, GADCO and Sandra Kuck.

NALED member. Secondary Market. Special orders. 90 day layaway. Credit cards accepted. Shipping available.

ALL-STAR CELEBRITY COLLECTIBLES

248 E. Main St.
Ventura, CA 93001

PHONE: (805)643-9224
(800)634-FANS

Open Daily: 11:00-5:30

Gartlan USA, Salvino Inc., Sports Impressions, Pro-Sport Creations, Sports Collectors Warehouse, Hollywood Limited Editions, Windstone Editions, Hopkins Shop, Lynette Decor, Hackett American and Armstrong plates.

Visa, Mastercard, American Express and Discover accepted. Layaway and shipping available. Secondary Market Dealer. Redemption Center for Gartlan, Salvino, and Sports Impressions. Free estimates on figurine repair service.

CALIFORNIA

EASTLAND HALLMARK

1449 S. Victoria Ave.
Ventura, CA 93003

PHONE: (805)654-8818
FAX: (805)654-0415

Monday-Thursday: 9:30-7:00
Friday: 9:30-6:30; Saturday: 9:30-5:30
Sunday: 12:00-4:00
Extended Holiday Hours

Dept. 56: Dickens Village, Christmas in the City, New England Village, North Pole and Snowbabies; Precious Moments, Lilliput Lane, Sarah's Attic, Miss Martha, Maud Humphrey, Beatrix Potter, Golden Memories, Neil Rose, Jan Hagara, Sandra Kuck plates, Perillo plates, crystals and more.

Visa, American Express, and Mastercard accepted. 30-day layaway plan. Will ship out of town.

THE GIFT GALLERY

3338 S. Mooney Blvd.
Visalia, CA 93277

PHONE: (209)733-2511

Monday-Saturday: 10:00-5:30

Lines include: All God's Children, Lladro, David Winter, Swarovski, Byers' Choice, Dept. 56, Precious Moments, Memories of Yesterday, Miss Martha's, Lizzie High, Cat's Meow, Hummel, Maud Humphrey, Krystonia, Little Cheesers, Annalee, Midwest, Alexander Doll Co., Dreamsicles, Cherished Teddies, Maruri, VickiLane Designs, Willitts and Roman.

Credit cards and phone orders accepted. Shipping and layaway available.

CLARK'S COLLECTION

21022 E. Colima Rd.
Walnut, CA 91789

PHONE: (909)598-8123

Mon-Fri: 10-7; Sat: 10-6; Sun: 11-5

Specializing in friendly personal service, serving the Diamond Bar/Walnut and surrounding area for 12 years. Located at the junction of the 57(Orange) and 60 (Pomona) freeways.

Bradford Dealer, Premier Dealer for Thomas Kinkade, Marty Bell, David Winter, Lladro, Dept. 56 (Dickens Village, North Pole, Christmas in the City, Snowbabies), Maruri, Cherished Teddies, Sarah's Attic, Memories of Yesterday, Sandicast, Precious Moments, Krystonia, Calico Kittens, Jan Hagara, Raikes, Hummels, Muffy Vanderbear, PenniBears, Ashton-Drake, Tobin Fraley, and Jon Herbert.

Club Redemption Center for most lines carried. All major credit cards. Layaway and free gift wrapping.

OLD WORLD CRYSTAL

3673 Thousand Oaks Blvd.
Westlake Village, CA 91362

PHONE: (805)496-6411

Monday-Friday: 10:00-6:00
Saturday: 10:00-5:00

Specializing in collectibles and different crystal lines. Located in the Evergreen Shopping Center, off Ventura Freeway. Lines include: Lladro, Armani, Swarovski, David Winter, Lilliput Lane, Sandicast, Little Cheesers, Mats Jonasson Crystal, Ron Lee, Old World Ornaments, Lalique, Waterford, Orrefors, Baccarat, Gallway Crystal, Limoge Boxes, Michael's Limited, Capodimonte, Glass Eye Crystal, Murano Clowns, Star Collection, and Enesco Musicals.

Club Redemption. Secondary Market Service in figurines, crystal, and cottages. Layaway. Visa, Mastercard and Discover. Shipping. Free Gift Wrapping.

CALIFORNIA

BLUE HILLS NURSERY AND GIFT SHOP
16440 E. Whittier Blvd.
Whittier, CA 90603
PHONE: (310)947-2013
FAX: (310)943-0620

Open Daily: 9:00-5:00; Closed Tuesday

Serving the community for 45 years. Byers' Choice Ltd., Department 56, David Winter Cottages, Jon Herbert Shoes and Clocks, Enesco Musicals, Wee Forest Folk, Muffy VanderBear with Family & Friends, Lladro, Lladro Collectors Society, Royal Albert, Beatrix Potter, Royal Doulton, Brambly Hedge, Bunnykins, Rick Cain Studio, Fitz & Floyd, Omnibus, Cast Art Dreamsicles, Possible Dreams, Schmid, and Boyds.

Layaways welcome. Personalized Service. All major credit cards accepted.

SHARI'S HALLMARK
15015 E. Whittier Blvd.
Whittier, CA 90603
PHONE: (310)698-0491

Monday-Friday: 10:00-7:00
Saturday: 10:00-6:00; Sunday: 12:00-5:00

Located 20 minutes from Knotts Berry Farm and 30 minutes from Disneyland. Hallmark Ornaments, Dept. 56, Precious Moments, Enesco Treasury Ornaments, Enesco Musicals, Laura's Attic, Memories of Yesterday, Midwest Importers Santas, Sisters and Best Friends, Cherished Teddies, Dreamsicles, Walt Disney Classics Collection and more.

Visa, Mastercard and American Express accepted. Layaway. Complimentary gift wrapping.

DODIE'S FINE GIFTS & COLLECTIBLES
1264 E. Gibson Rd.
Woodland, CA 95776
PHONE: (916)668-1909
FAX: (916)661-6116

Monday-Friday: 10:00-9:00
Saturday: 10:00-6:00; Sunday: 11:00-6:00

David Winter, Lilliput Lane, Bradford Exchange, Ashton-Drake, M.I. Hummel, Enchantica, Jan Hagara, Maud Humphrey, Swarovski Crystal, PenDelfin, PenniBears, Willitts Designs, Cherished Teddies, Walt Disney, Lefton Village, Little Cheesers, WACO Melody In Motion, Reco, Princeton Gallery and All God's Children.

NALED member. Visa and Mastercard accepted. UPS Shipping. Secondary Market.

COLLECTIONS *UNLIMITED*
4867-1/2 Topanga Canyon Blvd.
Woodland Hills, CA 91364
PHONE: (818)713-9390
FAX: (818)703-6173

Tuesday-Saturday: Noon-5:30pm

Dept. 56, Duncan Royale, CT, Calico Kittens, dolls, Sports Impressions, 1,000+ Collector plates, Hibel, Lilliput Lane, DeGrazia, Perillo, F. Stone Graphics, D. Zolan, S. Kuck, Wildlife, Cat Collectibles, Rockwell figurines and plates, Maud Humphrey, J. Hagara, Enesco, Cottage Prints, lithographs by O. Franca, D. Lewan T. Redlin, P. Bannister, L. Liu, Maija, Disney Ornaments, Throws and more. Club Redemption Service for many. Raikes Bear trader. Star Trek items. Frames, Display Accessories and Cabinets for every need.

NALED Member. Nationwide Delivery. Secondary Market Specialist. Credit cards accepted. "Serving Collectors Nationwide Since 1977." Largest selection in the area.

CALIFORNIA/COLORADO

MARY ANN'S CARDS, GIFTS & COLLECTIBLES

20467 Yorba Linda Blvd.
Yorba Linda, CA 92686

PHONE: (714)777-0999

Monday-Thursday: 10:00-7:00
Friday: 10:00-8:00; Saturday: 10:00-6:00
Sunday: 11:00-5:00

Dept. 56: All Villages and Snowbabies, Enesco Musical Society, Lilliput Lane, Byers' Choice Carolers, Cherished Teddies, Raikes Bears, Duncan Royale, Krystonia, Windy Meadows, Maud Humphrey, Steinbach Nutcrackers, Calico Kittens, Sisters and Best Friends, North American Bear, Hummel, some Precious Moments, Carlton Ornaments, Dreamsicles, Napoleon Capodimonte, and collector plates.

All major credit cards accepted. NALED Member. UPS shipping anywhere in US. Collector Clubs for most lines. Layaways and phone orders welcome!

GRECO COLLECTIBLES

3186-D S. Parker Rd.
Aurora, CO 80014

PHONE: (303)755-6048

Monday-Friday: 10:00-7:00
Saturday: 10:00-6:00; Sunday: 12:00-4:00

Personalized attention to every order. Free shipping with mention of this listing. Lines include Lilliput Lane, Pocket Dragons, Ray Day prints and cottages, Premier Dealer Of Enesco Treasury of Ornaments, Musical Showcase, Precious Moments, Laura's Attic, North Pole Village, Cherished Teddies, Calico Kittens, Chilmark and Hudson Pewter, Sarah's Attic, Frumps, Harbour Lights, Fraser Creations, and Sports Impressions.

Secondary Exchange and Club Redemptions. UPS shipping every day. Layaway available. All major credit cards accepted. Senior discount.

SWISS MISS GIFT SHOP

8455 Hwy 24 West.
Cascade, CO 80809

PHONE: (719)684-9679
FAX: (719)684-9824

Daily: 9:30-5:00

Dept. 56, PM (DSR), Hummel, Swarovski, David Winter, Lladro, Tom Clark Gnomes, All God's Children, Olszewski, Marty Bell, Thomas Kinkade, Raikes, Lilliput Lane, Silver Deer, Lowell Davis, Wee Forest Folk, Bradford Exchange Plate Dealer, ANRI, EKJ, Krystonia, Enchantica, Ashton-Drake Dolls, Walt Disney Classics, Steinbach, Milford Nutcrackers, Duncan Royale, Maruri, WACO, Melody In Motion, Bossons, Charles Sadek, Maud Humphrey, Chilmark, Alexander Doll, Enesco Musicals, Cherished Teddies, Little Cheesers, Armani, Dreamsicles.

All major credit cards accepted. NALED member. Layaway. Mail orders & shipping. Redemption center for all collectibles.

KINGS GALLERY OF COLLECTIBLES

2428 W. Colorado Ave.
Colorado Springs, CO 80904

PHONE: (719)636-2228

Open Daily: 9:00-5:00
Sunday: 12:00-5:00

A Collectors Haven! Your Bradford and NALED Dealer, Miss Martha, Lighthouses, Lilliput Lane, David Winter, Precious Moments, Hummels, Lladro, Dept. 56, Maud Humphrey, Perillo, Tom Clark Gnomes, Snowbabies, Penni Anne Cross.

All major credit cards accepted. Layaway. Shipping. Gift wrapping. Redemption Center for most major collectibles.

COLORADO

A LAVENDER COTTAGE, INC.

5172 N. Academy Blvd.
Colorado Springs, CO 80918

PHONE: (719)598-0988

Monday-Friday: 10:00-6:00
Saturday: 10:00-5:00

Thomas Kinkade Limited Edition canvas prints, United Design limited editions, Lilliput Lane Cottages, Enesco Small World of Music Showcase dealer, Dept. 56 Snowbabies and Winter Silhouette, Raikes Bears, Dolls by Annette Himstedt, Gustave and Gretchen Wolfe, Pauline, Jeckle-Jansen, Esche, and Fontanini Collectible Creches.

Collector Clubs: Lilliput Lane, Fontanini, Thomas Kinkade, dolls and bears.

Visa, Mastercard and Discover accepted. Layaway available. Many Secondary Market dolls and collectible lines. Registry for special needs.

THE KENT COLLECTION

3401 S. Lincoln St.
Englewood, CO 80110

PHONE: (303)761-0059

Tuesday-Saturday: 10:00-5:00
Open 7 Days In December

One of the first appointed Bradford dealers. Collector plate accessories, Bing & Grondahl, Memories of Yesterday, Maud Humphrey, Terry Redlin, DeGrazia, Gregory Perillo, Summerhill Crystal, Sandra Kuck, Lowell Davis, P. Buckley Moss, Cherished Teddies, Norman Rockwell, Hummel, Colorado Rockies memorabilia, Sports Impressions, and greeting cards and gifts. Always updating lines carried in the store!

NALED member (former member of the board). Will help customers locate Secondary Market pieces. Free gift wrapping. UPS shipping to anywhere. Layaway available. Visa and Mastercard accepted.

INTRIGUE GIFT SHOP

P.O. Box 2147
112 E. Elkhorn Ave.
Estes Park, CO 80517

PHONE: (303)586-4217

Nestled in the heart of the majestic Colorado Rockies, just minutes from the Rocky Mountain National Park, lies the quaint village of Estes Park, Colorado. Established in 1969, serving the collectors: Chilmark, LEGENDS, Don Polland, Tom Clark Gnomes, Lladro, All God's Children, Armani, Lowell Davis, The Disney Collection, Wee Forest Folk, David Winter, Lilliput Lane, Mill Creek Sculpture, Cherished Teddies, and collectible dolls.

Shop hosts numerous artist appearances throughout the year. Layaway. Visa, Mastercard and Discover accepted. Shipping available. Intrigue Gift Shop promises to take care of your collectible needs.

LITTLE COUNTRY CUPBOARD

125 West Elkhorn-P.O. Box 3989
Estes Park, CO 80517

PHONE: (303)586-6760

Open Daily: 10:00-6:00 (May-Dec)
Friday-Sunday: 11:00-4:00 (Jan-April)

Featuring Swarovski, Hummel, DeGrazia, Lomonosov Russian Porcelain figurines, Andrean Porcelain figurines, Lomonosov Russian cups and saucers, bells, and paperweights, Spoontique Pewter, United Designs Legends of Santa Claus, Mats Jonasson Swedish Crystal, and Bovano of Cheshire.

Even though it's small, it's worth the trip to see many unique collectibles. Visa and Mastercard accepted. Shipping available.

COLORADO

PLATES 'N' MORE

3307 S. College, #102B
Fort Collins, CO 80525

PHONE: (303)226-0568

Monday-Saturday: 10:00-6:00

Bradford Exchange Plates, Ashton-Drake Dolls, Rockwell, Perillo, Bing & Grondahl, Royal Copenhagen, Silver Deer, Memories of Yesterday, Miss Martha's Collection, and Rick Cain. Year Round Christmas, plate and doll display accessories.

BETTY BLUE'S

215 E. Foothills Pkwy.
Foothills Fashion Mall
Ft. Collins, CO 80525

PHONE: (303)223-1883

Monday-Friday: 10:00-9:00
Saturday: 10:00-6:00; Sunday: 12:00-5:00

All God's Children, Miss Martha's Originals, Cherished Teddies, Lilliput Lane, David Winter, Wee Forest Folk, M.I. Hummel, Laura's Attic, G. Armani, Shoemaker's Dream, Lowell Davis, Snowbabies, Harbour Lights, Willitts Designs, Memories of Yesterday, Thomas Kinkade, Marty Bell, LEGENDS, collectible display cases, Enesco Treasury Ornaments.

Layaways welcome. Mastercard, American Express, Discover and Visa accepted. Shipping available.

THE TOBACCO LEAF

Villa Italia Mall
7200 West Alameda Ave.
Lakewood, CO 80226

**PHONE: (303)935-8188(STORE)
(800)523-6746**

Monday- Friday: 10:00-9:00
Saturday: 10:00-6:00; Sunday: 11:00-5:00

All God's Children, Armani, Bosson Wall Heads, Rick Cain, Chilmark Pewter, Tom Clark Gnomes, Lowell Davis, DeGrazia, Hudson Pewter, Hummel Figurines, Krystonia Fantasy Figurines, Ron Lee Clowns, Lilliput Lane Cottages, Perth Pewter, Neil Rose Sculptures, Sandicast, Disney Classics, Cast Art, Amish Heritage Collection, Memories of Yesterday, Miss Martha's Collection, WACO Melody In Motion.

Mail orders. Layaway welcome. Visa, Mastercard, American Express and Discover accepted.

MULBERRY CREEK TRADING CO.

Northglenn Mall
10566 Melody Dr.
Northglenn, CO 80234

PHONE: (303)451-7706

Monday-Friday: 10:00-9:00
Saturday: 10:00-7:00; Sunday: 11:00-6:00

The largest collectible store in Northern Denver. Cairn Studios, Precious Moments, Memories of Yesterday, PenniBears, David Winter, Sarah's Attic, United Designs, Legends of Santa Claus, Hopkins Shop, Snowbabies, Lizzie High Dolls, Shoemakers Dream, Emmett Kelly Jr., Dreamsicles, Martha Carey's Dragon Keep, The Herd, Pocket Dragons, Cherished Teddies, Bradley Dolls, Napoleon.

Most major credit cards accepted. Layaway and shipping available. Redemption center.

CONNECTICUT

THE CHRISTMAS SHOP IN BETHLEHEM

18 East St.
Bethlehem, CT 06751

PHONE: (203)266-7048

Open 7 Days A Week: 10:00-6:00

Celebrating their 15th year in 1993, the Christmas Shop is housed in a 200-year-old New England barn in the tiny historic district of Bethlehem. Lines carried: Dept. 56 Showcase Dealer (villages and Snowbabies), Byers' Choice, Old World Christmas mouth-blown glass ornaments, Fontanini, Cat's Meow, Duncan Royale, Cast Art Dreamsicles, David Winter Cottages, Beatrix Potter, Lizzie High dolls, German Nutcrackers, Smokers and collectibles (Steinbach, Ulbricht), Lynn Haney Santas, and "many more!"

Visa, Mastercard, and Discover accepted. Layaway available. Newsletter. "Cache Club" for valued customers. Many special events throughout the year.

PASSAGES GALLERY

16C Mountain Ave.
Bloomfield, CT 06002

**PHONE: (203)286-9501
(800)742-5071**

Tuesday-Wednesday: 9:30-5:30
Thursday: 9:30-8:00
Friday-Saturday: 9:30-6:00

Art, framing and collectibles. Dealer center for wide selection. All God's Children, Miss Martha's Collection, Blackberry Bonnett Collection, Duncan Royale Ebony Collection, Daddy's Long Legs, Sarah's Attic, African-American: Figurines, dolls, clowns, sculptures and Black memorablia.

Club redemption center for collectibles listed above. UPS shipping nationwide. Gift wrapping and gift register. Visa and Mastercard accepted. Secondary Market.

JOY'S HALLMARK

White Turkey Shopping Plaza
Brookfield, CT 06804

**PHONE: (203)775-6363
FAX: (203)775-4800**

Monday-Saturday: 9:30-9:00
Sunday: 11:00-5:00

Swarovski, Lladro, complete line of Dept. 56, Snowbabies, Lowell Davis, Tom Clark Gnomes, Maud Humphrey, Precious Moments, Chilmark, Hallmark Galleries, Cherished Teddies, Emmett Kelly, Norman Rockwell figurines, United Design, Lenox, Duncan Royale, Sports Impressions, Collectible Santas, Cat's Meow, Harbour Lights, Royal Copenhagen, Belleek.

Most major credit cards accepted. Shipping available. Gift wrapping. Layaway. Secondary Market Dealer. Redemption Center for all major collectibles.

Second Location: 228 S. Main St., New Town, CT 06470. Phone:(203)426-1234

MAHAIWE JEWELERS

25 Railroad St.
Canaan, CT 06018

**PHONE: (203)824-7516
FAX: (203)824-7949**

Monday-Saturday: 9:00-5:30

Schmid, Hummel, Goebel, Rockwell, ANRI, Sebastian, Maud Humphrey, Perillo, Lowell Davis, Lenox, Reco, David Winter, Malcom Cooper, Lilliput Lane, Iris Arc, Ron Lee Clowns, Co-Boys, dolls and Sports Impressions.

Mail order available. Major credit cards accepted.

CONNECTICUT

LINEHAN HALLMARK

Danbury Fair Mall
Danbury, CT 06810

PHONE: (203)798-7515

Daily: 10:00-9:30; Sunday: 11:00-6:00

Dept. 56 Showcase Dealer, Heritage Village, Snow Village, Christmas in the City, Snowbabies, Precious Moments (DSR), Hummel, Cast Art Dreamsicles, David Winter Cottages, Cherished Teddies.

Seasonal lines include Possible Dreams Santas, Designs Americana Pencil Santas, Margaret Furlong Ornaments, Christopher Radko.

All major credit cards accepted. Redemption Center for Precious Moments, Hummel, Krystonia, David Winter, and Cast Art.

MELISSA'S HALLMARK

1100 Village Walk
Guilford, CT 06437

PHONE: (203)453-4631
FAX: (203)453-0505

Monday-Friday: 9:30-6:00
Saturday: 9:30-5:30; Sunday: 11:00-5:00

Dept. 56 Villages and Snowbabies, Annalee, Beatrix Potter musicals and Collectibles, Cat's Meow, Cherished Teddies, Harbour Lights, Lilliput Lane, Precious Moments, Maud Humphrey, Sandicast, Enesco and Schmid Music Boxes, Hallmark and Enesco Ornaments, Calico Kittens, Sisters & Best Friends, Margaret Furlong Designs, Midwest Importers.

Visa and Mastercard accepted. Layaway. Shipping. A Hallmark Gold Crown account.

Largest gift and collectible store along the shoreline.

CARD & GIFTWORKS

2300 Dixwell Ave.
Hamden, CT 06514

PHONE: (203)288-4344
FAX: (203)288-0615

Monday- Friday: 10:00-9:00
Saturday: 10:00-6:00; Sunday: 11:00-5:00

M.I. Hummel, Precious Moments, Lladro, Miss Martha's Originals, David Winter, Swarovski, Armani, Wee Forest Folk, Sports Impressions, Memories of Yesterday, Krystonia, Enchantica, Cherished Teddies, Byers' Choice, Department 56, Annalee, WACO Musicals.

Layaway and shipping available. Free gift wrapping.

RAY COYLE GALLERY

749 Boston Post Rd.
Madison, CT 06443

PHONE: (203)245-4458

Monday- Friday: 10:00-5:30
Saturday: 10:00-5:00

Lilliput Lane Cottages, Jan Hagara figurines, Edna Hibel Prints and Lithos, Caithness Paperweights, Mats Jonassen Crystal Sculpture, Harbour Lights, Marty animals, Maruri Porcelain, Nutcrackers, David Winter Cottages, Belsnickle Santas, KSA/Rubel Santas, Crummels Enamel boxes, Hagen-Renaker miniatures, Schmid, Margaret Furlong, Lance Corporation, Dept. 56, Summerhill Crystal, Classical Creamware, and Port Meirion.

Visa, Mastercard, and American Express accepted.

CONNECTICUT

THE TAYLOR'D TOUCH

P.O. Box 27 Route 66
Marlborough, CT 06447

PHONE: (203)295-9377

Monday-Saturday: 9:30-9; Sunday: 12-5

Open since 1984, specializing in that unique customer service throughout their 3,600 square feet store. Lines include Lilliput Lane, Walt Disney Collection, M.I. Hummel, Tom Clark Gnomes, Krystonia, All God's Children, Miss Martha, P. Buckley Moss plates and figurines, Duncan Royale, Dept. 56 Villages, Snowbabies, Annalee Mobilitee, Precious Moments, Sandicast, Enesco Treasury ornaments, Hudson Pewter, Lee Middleton Dolls, Kurt Adler, Maruri, Midwest Importers, Roman, Silvestri, Brambly Hedge, Schmid, Silver Deer, and Melodies In Motion.

Club Redemption Center for most collectibles listed. Layaways. NALED member. Visa, Mastercard and Discover. UPS shipping available.

R.A. GEORGETTI & COMPANY

Olde Mistick Village
Mystic, CT 06355

PHONE: (203)536-2964
(800)243-3176
FAX: (203)536-9974

Monday-Saturday: 10-6; Sunday: 12-5

Fine gifts and collectibles for 15 years. Paperweights by major studios and individual artists--featuring Caithness, Perthshire, Lundberg and Banford. Paperweight artist appearances throughout the year. Herend Porcelain, Lladro, Armani, Swarovski, Walt Disney Classics Collection, Swarovski Selection, Baccarat, Dooney & Bourke Leather, Wee Forest Folk, PenDelfin, Halcyon Days, Lilliput Lane and others.

Their selection and service excel and they don't discount*. A visit to their store is a treat--the next best thing is opening a package from them delivered UPS. *Loyal customers get special consideration.

THE THREE CHEERS COMPANIES

1231 East Main St. (Ames Plaza)
Meriden, CT 06450

Comprised of retail stores in Connecticut and two mail order divisions, The Three Cheers Companies provide a great opportunity for collectors far and wide.

THE ORNAMENT RETAILER
(800)524-6123

This mail order division specializes in Christmas ornaments with particular emphasis on the complete Hallmark collectible lines. Call for information and free literature on Merry Miniatures, Tender Touches, Kiddie Car Classics, Hallmark Galleries, and all Gold Crown Collectibles. Layaways, "Early Buy" previews, free literature, and helpful friendly service are a phone call away...

THE THREE CHEERS COMPANIES

COLLECTIBLES ON CALL

(800)622-4114

The second mail order division offers a similar program on many collectible lines. Madame Alexander, Annalee Doll, Ashton-Drake, David Winter, Tom Clark Gnomes, all Dept. 56 lines, Byers' Choice, Swarovski, All God's Children, Precious Moments, Maud Humphrey, June McKenna, Krystonia and lots more. Call today!

THREE CHEERS HALLMARK
(203)634-7509
Monday-Saturday: 9-9; Sunday: 10-5

The Flagship store is right off Interstate 91 between Hartford and New Haven. Come check out their huge store, meet their great staff and get the best in collector information and the best in collector customer service.

CONNECTICUT

MYSTIC PEWTER SHOP

Olde Mistick Village
Mystic, CT 06355

PHONE: (203)536-7643
FAX: (203)536-9974

Monday-Saturday: 10:00-6:00
Sunday: 12:00-5:00

Specializing in Pewter since 1975. "Master Showcase" Dealer of Chilmark Pewter figurines. Many other collectible pewter lines including Hudson, Fort, Pewter Port and Collectors Case. Also Pewter giftware items from Woodbury, Preisner, Connecticut House and others. Cranberry Glass and ceramic steins with sports and historical motifs. A treat to visit.

UPS Shipping.

FIFTH AVENUE
CARD COLLECTIBLES & GIFTS

New London Mall
New London, CT 06320

PHONE: (203)443-8546
FAX: (203)447-9627

Monday-Saturday: 10-9; Sunday: 12-5

Your one stop Collectible Shop! Dept. 56 Showcase Dealer, Precious Moments (DSR), Memories of Yesterday Heritage Dealer, David Winter Cottages, Shoemaker's Dream, EKJ, Sports Impressions, Maud Humphrey, Swarovski, Krystonia, United Design, Sandicast, Castagna and Livingstone animal figurines, Miss Martha's, Cherished Teddies, Calico Kittens, Laura's Attic, Hallmark Ornaments, Enesco Treasury Ornaments, Tobin Fraley, J.H. Boone Indian figurines and artifacts, Anheuser-Busch and Dramtree steins and Snowbabies.

All major credit cards accepted. Layaway available. Shipping anywhere in the US.

MAURICE NASSER

New London Shopping Center
New London, CT 06320

PHONE: (203)443-6523
(800)243-0895

One of the largest collectible stores in Connecticut, specializing in plates and figurines. Serving the collectible industry since 1975 and in business over 50 years. Lines include: Hummel plates and figurines, Goebel Olszewski Miniatures, Swarovski Silver Crystal, Anri Ferrandiz and Sarah Kay woodcarvings, Lilliput Lane, Norman Rockwell, Hibel, Hagara, DeGrazia, Perillo, Kuck, Moss, Red Skelton, Gartlan, MOY, Bradford Dealer, Ashton-Drake dolls, Gorham, Lowell Davis, Lenox, Sports Impressions, Bing & Grondahl, Royal Copenhagen, Royal Doulton, and Sebastian.

Club Redemption Center. Charter member of NALED. Visa, Mastercard and Discover accepted. Shipping available.

MADE TO BE LOVED DOLL HOSPITAL AND SHOP

289 Main St.
Niantic, CT 06357

PHONE: (203)739-7756

Monday-Friday: 10:00-5:30
Saturday: 10:00-5:00

Robin Woods, Lenci, Artist Collectibles, Virginia Keith, Jeckle & Jansen, Corolle, Sarah's Attic, stuffed animals: North American Bear and Herman. Antique Dolls.

Both new and antique dolls as well as stuffed animals repaired at the on-site Hospital.

Mail order. Visa, Mastercard and American Express accepted. Layaway and shipping available. Free gift wrapping.

CONNECTICUT

THE SILVER SKATE CHRISTMAS SHOP

488 Main St. Exit 74 Ct. Tpke.
Niantic, CT 06357

PHONE: (203)443-0592

Open Mid-June to Dec. 24
Daily: 11:00-5:00

Almost 4,000 square feet of collectibles. Including Dept. 56, Kurt S. Adler, Annalee, Byers' Choice, Constance Collection, Hummel, June McKenna, Midwest Importers, Possible Dreams, Lizzie High Dolls, Christopher Radko, nutcrackers, Cherished Teddies, country and Christmas presents, Simpich figurines, Roman Inc., Schmid, Vaillancourt Folk Art.

In business for 27 years. Layaways and credit cards accepted.

CRICKET'S HALLMARK

Waldbaum's Plaza
57 Washington Ave.
North Haven, CT 06473

PHONE: (203)239-0135

Monday-Saturday: 9:30-9:00
Sunday: 10:00-5:00

Enjoy diverse collectible lines: Dept. 56 Villages and Snowbabies, Precious Moments, Enesco Small World of Music, Miss Martha's Originals, Maud Humphrey, Sports Impressions, Cherished Teddies, Annalee Dolls, M.I. Hummel, Dreamsicles, Anheuser-Busch Steins, Summerhill Crystal, David Winter Cottages, Lladro, Lilliput Lane Cottages, United Design, Memories of Yesterday, Little Cheesers, Cat's Meow, and Hallmark Keepsake Ornaments.

Redemption center for major clubs. Layaway and Secondary Market service. All major credit cards accepted.

THE WINDSOR SHOPPE

117 Washington Ave.
North Haven, CT 06473

**PHONE: (203)239-4644
(800)676-4644
FAX: (203)234-1882**

Mon.- Wed.: 10-6; Thurs.- Fri.: 10-9
Sat.: 10-6; Extended Hours Begin Nov. 15

Educating collectors for 25 years. Dept. 56 Showcase Dealer, Precious Moments (DSR), Lladro, Swarovski, Hummel, David Winter, Lilliput, Krystonia, Snowbabies, PenDelfin, MOY, Miss Martha's Originals, All God's Children, Emmett Kelly, Jr., Rockwell, Lowell Davis, Annalee, Madame Alexander, Byers' Choice, Armani, Cherished Teddies, Disney Classic, Melody In Motion, Goebel Miniatures, Harbour Lights, Sarah's Attic, Maud Humphrey, Merry Monks, All Thru The House, Willitts, Fontanini and many more.

Member GCC and NALED. Layaway. UPS shipping. Free gift wrapping. All major credit cards accepted.

THE ENGRAVING STORE

205 Main Ave.
Norwalk, CT 06851

**PHONE: (203)847-1234
FAX: (203)847-1944**

Tuesday and Wednesday: 9:30-6:00
Thursday and Friday:9:30-8:00
Saturday: 9:30-5:00

Specializing in engravable goods and giftware. Many lines of gifts, including Oneida, Reed & Barton, Royal Crystal Rock, AT Cross and Mont Blanc, Wilton Armetale, among others. Collectible lines include Lilliput Lane cottages and literature, Hudson and Lance Pewter pieces, Linden music boxes, and Beatrix Potter porcelain figures.

Visa, Mastercard, and American Express accepted. Layaway. Shipping service available in U.S.

CONNECTICUT

McDERMOTT JEWELERS

Norwichtown Mall
Norwich, CT 06360

PHONE: (203)887-0887

Monday-Friday: 10:00-8:45
Saturday: 10:00-5:45; Sunday: 11:00-3:45

Adagio, All God's Children, Beatrix Potter, Cased Crystal, Cedar Mesa Products, Margaret Furlong, Glass Eye, Ron Lee, LEGENDS, Lilliput Lane, Linden Jewelry Boxes, Lladro Collector's Society, Maruri U.S.A., Mill Creek Studios, Nova, Perth Pewter, Pocket Dragons, Royal Doulton, Schmid and Swarovski America Ltd. Specializing in Indian Pottery and Jewelry, including Hopi Kachina Dolls, Zuni jewelry and pottery, and Navajo sand paintings.

There is a large selection of frames, mirrors, etc. from local crafts people. UPS shipping if you need a particular item.

ADAR PEWTER COMPANY

280 Ethan Allen Hwy.
Ridgefield, CT 06877

PHONE: (203)438-7107
FAX: (203)438-9321

Monday-Friday: 9:30-6:00
Saturday: 9:00-5:00

Located 8 miles from I-84 South, 12 miles from Merritt/Route 15 North on Route 7.

Chilmark, Perth Pewter, Hudson, Spoontiques, Rawcliffe, Pewter Port, Seagull Pewter, Woodbury Pewter, Kirk Stieff, Preisner Pewter, Colonial Casting Pewter.

Specializing in custom designs for corporate or sporting event.

There is a full-service repair for pewter, silver, gold and brass on the premises. Engraving available. Custom awards and gifts. Mastercard and Visa accepted.

EXCLUSIVELY YOURS GIFTS & COLLECTIBLES

996 Wilcoxson Ave.
Stratford, CT 06497-2497

PHONE: (203)377-4344

Monday-Saturday: 10:00-5:30

Plates: Bradford Exchange, Artaffects, Reco, American Artists, Pemberton & Oakes, and Hamilton.

Lithos: Kinkade, Perillo, Sandra Kuck, Zolan, Lowell Davis, Jan Hagara, and Hibel.

Figurines: Maud Humphrey, Lowell Davis, ANRI, Duncan Royale, Sarah's Attic, Constance, Chilmark, Jan Hagara, Rockwell, Sports Impressions, PenDelfin, Perillo, Mill Creek and DeGrazia.

Dolls, art glass, musicals, and display accessories.

Visa, Mastercard and American Express accepted. Secondary Market Service. Club Redemptions.

EXPRESSIONS

29 Main St.
Torrington, CT 06790

PHONE: (203)496-0389

Daily: 10:00-5:30; Thursday: 10:00-8:00
Sunday: 11:00-4:00

Dept. 56, Annalee Dolls, David Winter, Lilliput Lane, Pocket Dragons, Precious Moments, Memories of Yesterday, All God's Children, Miss Martha's Originals, Cherished Teddies, Jan Hagara, Calico Kittens, M.I. Hummel, Cat's Meow, Laura's Attic, Sarah's Attic, Krystonia, Norman Rockwell, Beatrix Potter, Emmett Kelly, Maud Humphrey, Shoemaker's Dream, Byers' Choice, Tom Clark, Chilmark and Hudson Pewter, Ron Lee, PenDelfin, Sebastian Miniatures, June McKenna, Snowbabies, and Silver Deer.

Redemption Center for most collectibles. All major credit cards accepted. Layaway and shipping available. Secondary Market.

CONNECTICUT/DELAWARE

PERIWINKLE

435 Hartford Turnpike
Vernon, CT 06066

PHONE: (203)872-2904
FAX: (203)872-4759

Monday-Friday: 10:00-9:00
Saturday: 10:00-6:00; Sunday: 12:00-5:00

Dept. 56 Showcase Dealer including Villages, Snowbabies, Merry Makers, All Thru the House and accessories, Precious Moments, Maud Humphrey, Krystonia, All God's Children, PenDelfin, David Winter, Shoemaker's Dream, Tom Clark Gnomes, Calico Cats, Cherished Teddies, M.I. Hummel, Cat's Meow Village, Emmett Kelly Jr., Harbour Lights, Dreamsicles, Willitts Designs, and J.H. Boone.

Redemption Center. NALED and Gift Creations Concepts Member. Layaway and shipping available. All major credit cards.

VINNY'S GARDEN CENTER

1076 S. Colony Rd.
Wallingford, CT 06492

PHONE:(203)265-9309

Monday-Saturday: 9:00-8:00
Sunday: 9:00-5:00

Vinny's Gift Shop is very unique, filled with many "Hidden Treasures." Included collectibles are Christopher Radko, Precious Moments, Byers' Choice, Snow Village, Snowbabies by Dept. 56, Lilliput Lane, Daddy's Long Legs, Memories of Yesterday, Maud Humphrey, Little Souls, Annalee, Seymour Mann, Lee Middleton Dolls, Steinbach Nutcrackers, Shelia's Collectibles, Cat's Meow Village, Laura's Attic, John Hine Studios, Fitz & Floyd, Cherished Teddies, Sisters & Best Friends, Enesco Small World of Music, Jan Hagara, and Miss Martha.

Free gift wrap. Mail order available. Visa and Mastercard accepted. Showcase dealer for many lines.

WASHINGTON SQ. LTD.

605 Christiana Mall
Newark, DE 19702

PHONE: (302)453-1776
FAX: (302)453-1784

Monday-Friday: 10-9:30; Sunday: 11-6

Area's largest collectible store. Precious Moments(DSR), Dept. 56 Showcase Dealer, M.I Hummel, David Winter, Memories of Yesterday, Duncan Royale, Enesco Music Boxes, Treasury of Christmas Ornaments, All God's Children, Miss Martha's Collection, Lladro, Armani, Swarovski, Krystonia, Jan Hagara, Bradford Plates, Ashton-Drake Dolls, Emmett Kelly, Jr., Lowell Davis, Castagna, United Design, Moss Prints and Plates, Wee Forest Folk, Lilliput Lane, Cherished Teddies, Thomas Kinkade, Byers' Choice.

Redemption Center for all collector clubs, many instant club redemptions. All major credit cards accepted. Layaway and shipping available.

TULL'S HOME & GARDEN CENTER

1408 Stein Hwy.
Seaford, DE 19973

PHONE: (302)629-3071
FAX: (302)629-3775

Monday-Saturday: 8:00-5:30
(Extended Hours November-December)

Dept. 56 (Showcase Dealer), June McKenna, Precious Moments, Byers' Choice, Hummel, David Winter, Annalee Dolls, Enesco Musicals, Shelia's Houses, Harbour Lights Lighthouses, United Design, Cast Art, Gail Laura, Ladie and Friends, Little Cheesers, Midwest Importers, and Red Mill Mfg.

FLORIDA

THE CHRISTMAS COLLECTION

749 W. Hwy 436
Altamonte Springs, FL 32714
PHONE: (407)862-5383
FAX: (407)862-2717

Monday-Friday: 9-6; Saturday: 9-5

Dept. 56 Showcase Dealer and Secondary Market, Snowbabies, Maud Humphrey, Annalee, Middleton, Susan Wakeen and Phyllis Parkins Dolls, David Winter, Lilliput Lane, Jan Hagara, June McKenna, Lowell Davis, Duncan Royal Santas, Wee Forest Folk, Byers' Choice Carolers, Memories of Yesterday, United Design, Lladro, Swarovski, Miss Martha, Cherished Teddies, Christopher Radko, Precious Moments, Ladie and Friends, Possible Dreams, Roman, and many more.

NALED member. Secondary Market. Layaway (except secondary). Club redemptions. Visa, Mastercard and Discover accepted.

THE LOOKING GLASS

Altamonte Mall
451 E. Altamonte Dr. #445
Altamonte Springs, FL 32701
PHONE: (800)546-3349
FAX: (407)331-3349

Open since 1973! Anri, Armani, Artesania Rinconada, Beasties of the Kingdom, Bubble Fairies, Castagna, David Winter, Hibel, Emmett Kelly, Golden Memories, Jon Herbert's Shoemaker's Dream, John Hopkins Castles, Hagara, Harbour Lights, Hummels, Iris Arc, Kaiser, Krystonia, Laura's Attic, LEGENDS, Lilliput Lane, Little Cheesers, Lladro, Maruri, Michael Garman, Mats Jonasson Crystal, Memories of Yesterday, Reco plates, Ron Lee Clowns, Sandicast, Sarah's Attic, Silver Deer Crystal, Snowbabies, Waterford Crystal, Disney Classics, Swarovski, Swarovski Selection, Sports Impressions, Wetherbee Studios, and Windy Meadows Houses. Free insured shipping. No out of state tax. Club dues paid!

JAX OF FLORIDA INC.

1707 First St. East Ste. B-C
Bradenton, FL 34208
PHONE: (813)746-0267
(800)741-4438

Tuesday-Sunday: 9:00-4:00

David Winter, Swarovski, Iris Arc, Goebel Miniatures, Sandicast, Marty Sculptures: The Herd, Dragon Keep, Bear Foot, Whiskers, Purfect Pet, Snow Makers, Bergsma, Little Cheesers, Hudson Pewter, Stone Critters, Maud Humphrey, Miss Martha, Jan Hagara, Ron Lee, Disney Treasures, Enesco Musicals, Cherished Teddies, Calico Kittens, Krystonia, Lilliput Lane, Pocket Dragons, Bubble Fairies, Shoemaker's Dream, Father Time Clock, Westland Carousels, Mickey's Carousels by Willitts, Michael Garman, Glass Eye, Glass Barons, Bovano of Chesire, Southwest Pottery. All major credit cards accepted. Layaway. Mail order. Behind Plaza with flea markets on Wednesday, Saturday and Sunday.

THE CALICO CAT

716 West Lumsden Rd.
Brandon, FL 33511
PHONE: (813)684-2072
FAX: (813)681-3821

Monday-Saturday: 10:00-6:00
Thursday: 10:00-8:00; Sunday: 12:30-5:00

Duncan Royale, June McKenna, Sarah's Attic, Vaillancourt Folk Art, Byers' Choice, Maud Humphrey, Possible Dreams, Miss Martha's Collection, All God's Children, Cherished Teddies, Dept. 56: Dickens, New England, Alpine, Christmas in the City, North Pole Villages, Snowbabies, All Thru the House; and Lizzie High.

All major credit cards accepted. Layaways welcome. Monthly newsletter.

FLORIDA

VILLAGE PLATE COLLECTOR

120 Forrest Ave.
Cocoa, FL 32922

**PHONE: (800)PLATES-1
(407)636-6914**

Monday-Saturday: 10:00-6:00

Caithness, Dept. 56, Disney Classics, Mark Hopkins, Bradford, Armani, Ashton-Drake, Olszewski, M.I. Hummel, Lance, LEGENDS, Lilliput Lane, Lladro, Reco, Roman, Royal Copenhagen, Bing & Grondahl, Schmid, Swarovski, Sabino, Steinbach Crystal, Marty Bell, Hibel, Dolfi, Memories of Yesterday, Precious Moments, Ardleigh Elliott, V.F. Fine Arts, Pat Buckley Moss plates and figurines, Mats Jonasson, Toby Maude Originals.

Charter member of NALED. Secondary Market dealer. Visa, Mastercard and Discover accepted. Ship UPS insured.

TISKETS N' TASKETS INC.

241 Miracle Mile
Coral Gables, FL 33134

PHONE: (305)443-4806

Open Monday-Saturday: 10:00-6:00
Friday: Until 7:30

David Winter, Lilliput Lane, Brian Baker's Deja Vu, Hanford Heirlooms, Shelia's, Silver Deer, Altona collectible clocks, Cast Art Dreamsicles, Anheuser-Busch. Also carries Crabtree and Evelyn, and Seagull Pewter.

A complete gift shop for babies, weddings, men's and women's gifts, and decorative accessories. Something for everyone.

All major credit cards available. Layaway and shipping available. Limited Secondary Market. Redemption Center. Complimentary gift wrapping.

CROWN COLLECTIBLE & GIFTS

8192 Wiles Rd.
Coral Springs, FL 33067

PHONE: (305)344-2666

Monday-Friday: 10:00-7:00
Saturday: 10:00-6:00; Sunday: 11:00-4:00

Krystonia, Hummel, Silver Deer, Precious Moments, Memories of Yesterday, David Winter, Dept. 56 Villages: Dickens, Snow Village, Christmas in the City, North Pole, New England and Snowbabies, Walt Disney Classics Collection, Emmett Kelly Jr., Cherished Teddies, Calico Kittens, Enesco Musicals, Dreamsicles, Tom Clark Gnomes, Budweiser Steins, Laura's Attic, Willitts Carousels, Rawcliffe Pewter, Star Trek, Maruri, and John Hine Studios.

All major credit cards accepted. Layaway. Free gift wrapping. Shipping. GCC Member.

ELLIE'S HALLMARK

4731 S. University Dr.
Davie, FL 33328

PHONE: (305)434-2807

Monday-Friday: 9:30-9:00
Saturday: 9:30-6:00; Sunday: 12:00-5:00

Dept. 56 Showcase Dealer, Precious Moments, Miss Martha, Cherished Teddies, M.I. Hummel, Lladro, Emmett Kelly, Jr., Perillo, sports collectibles, Krystonia, Enchantica, Hallmark Keepsake Ornaments, J.H. Boone, Iris Arc Crystal, Michael's Ltd., Roman, Cast Art, Calico Kittens and Holiday Hamlet by Fitz & Floyd.

All club redemptions. Large selection of Native American collectibles and giftware. Major credit cards accepted. Layaway available. Will ship anywhere.

Specialize in Secondary Dept. 56 and Precious Moments markets.

FLORIDA

CARDS N' GIFTS GALORE

Volusia Point Shopping Center
1808 Volusia Ave. (Rt. #92)
Daytona Beach, FL 32114

PHONE: (904)255-6624

Monday-Friday: 10:00-6:00
Saturday: 10:00-5:30

Precious Moments (DSR), Sarah's Attic Golden Heart Store, Swarovski, Dept. 56, Lladro, Tom Clark, Lilliput Lane, M.I. Hummel, Dreamsicles, Memories of Yesterday, All God's Children, David Winter Cottages, PenniBears, Cherished Teddies, Krystonia, Annalee, and Snowbabies.

Redemption Center for all collector clubs. Mastercard and Visa accepted. Layaway and shipping available.

CLASSIC CARGO

5494 E. Hwy 98 #32
Destin, FL 32541

PHONE: (904)837-8171
FAX: (904)837-3933

Open 7 Days A Week: 10:00-9:00

Swarovski, Lladro, Armani, David Winter, Lilliput Lane, Tom Clark Gnomes, All God's Children, LEGENDS, Chilmark, Precious Moments, Cherished Teddies, Hummel, Waterford, Walt Disney Classics, Lowell Davis, Maud Humphrey, Sports Impressions, Emmett Kelly Jr., Caithness Glass, Fenton Art Glass, Hallmark Keepsake Ornaments, Ron Lee Clowns, United Design, Possible Dreams and Duncan Royale.

A 2,400 square feet store in a large resort area, since 1981. All major credit cards accepted. NALED member. Layaway available. Secondary Market on lines listed.

Second location: Panama City Mall, Panama City, FL. Phone: (904)785-1968

BELLEVUE FLORIST & GIFTS

208 Moody Blvd.
P.O. Box 1177
Flagler Beach, FL 32136

PHONE: (904)439-2841
(800)771-6640

Monday-Saturday: 9:00-5:00

In business since 1977! Located 20 miles North of Daytona Beach.

New and retired plates: Bing & Grondahl, Norman Rockwell, Royal Copenhagen, Kaiser, Fred Stone, Hamilton, Pemberton & Oakes. Also specializing in custom fresh and silk floral arrangements. Large in-stock selection of Secondary Market plates.

All major credit cards accepted. Layaway and shipping available. Free gift wrapping.

Able to acquire anything Viking Import House or Hollywood Limited Edition Inc. offers.

CROSS STITCH CUPBOARD

1600 N.E. 26th St.
Ft. Lauderdale, FL 33305

PHONE: (305)563-6363

Monday-Saturday: 10:00-5:30
Tuesday: 10:00-8:00

Walt Disney Classics Collection, Dept. 56 Dickens, Christmas in the City, New England and North Pole Houses, Muffy Bear, Ladie and Friends, Byers' Choice, Snowbabies, Cat's Meow, Carriage House, Leo Smith Santas, Duncan Royale, and Vaillancourt.

Secondary Market. Redemption Center for all collector clubs. Layaway and shipping available. Also the best cross stitch inventory and decorative accessories in the South.

FLORIDA

MINDY'S HALLMARK

80 W. Oakland Park Blvd.
Ft. Lauderdale, FL 33311
PHONE: (305)565-5828

Monday-Friday: 9:30-8:45
Saturday: 9:30-6:00; Sunday: 10:00-4:00

Collectible lines include: David Winter, Lilliput Lane, Dept. 56, Precious Moments (DSR), Colonial Village, Snowbabies, Sarah's Attic, Cast Art, Miss Martha's by Enesco, Hummel, Sandicast, Cherished Teddies, and Enesco Musical Showcase. Heritage Dealer for Memories of Yesterday and a Collection Center for Emmett Kelly Jr. Largest collection of All God's Children in the area.

All major credit cards accepted. Redemption center for all lines listed. Layaway available. Will ship anywhere.

P.G.'S ENCHANTED DOLLS & THE DOLL HOSPITAL

4360 W. Oakland Park Blvd.
Ft. Lauderdale, FL 33313
**PHONE: (305)739-9030
(800)783-1235**

Monday-Saturday: 10:00-5:00

Mde. Alexander, Gunzel, Alice Darling (Robin Woods), Heidi Ott, Lawton, Robert Tonner, Ashton-Drake, Georgetown, Ginny, Barbies, Boyds Bears, Muffy's, Zook, Wakeen, Good-Kruger, GADCO, Janet Ness: Elizabeth Exclusive, Marilyn Bolden, Alice Lester, Middleton, Himstedt, Helen Kish and many more. Playmobile: Victorian Doll Houses; Tin Toys, Britains, Bryer Horses, books, paper dolls and magazines. Doll dishes, chairs, carriages, trunks, wardrobes and supplies. Vinyl, cloth, porcelain, and compo repairs.

A full-service collectible doll shop. Buy-Sell-Trade-Special Order-Doll Club. Discover, MC, AE and Visa accepted.

THE PORCELAIN COLLECTION

1410 S.E. 17th St.
Ft. Lauderdale, FL 33316
**PHONE: (800)624-1155
(305)764-1185**

Monday-Friday: 9:00-5:30
Saturday: 9:30-5:00

Specialist in primary and secondary collectibles. Bradford plates and dolls. Precious Moments, Cherished Teddies, Calico Kittens and Enesco Musicals and Ornaments. Lilliput Lane, David Winter, Shoemaker's Dreams and Memory Lane Cottages. Largo Sculptures. Leroy Black Figurines. Sandicast Animals, M.I. Hummel, Royal Doulton and Kaiser. Swarovski, Annalee Dolls, Royal Doulton, Hamilton Collection. Edna Hibel, P. Buckley Moss, Greg Perillo, Sandra Kuck and Lowell Davis, Royal Copenhagen, Bing & Grondahl, Sports Impressions.

Redemption Center for most clubs. All major credit cards. Free shipping.

SEA RANCH CARD & GIFT SHOP

4741 N. Ocean Blvd.
Ft. Lauderdale, FL 33308
**PHONE: (800)741-0869
(305)942-0869**

Monday-Saturday: 9:00-5:30

Large quantity of quality collectibles. Over 400 different Lladro. Over 300 different Hummels. Over 200 different Precious Moments. Large quantities of Swarovski, Dept. 56 (Cottages and Snowbabies), David Winter, Armani, and Disney Collection.

Personalized service in collectibles including gift wrapping and shipping. All major credit cards accepted. Free freight for all purchases over $100.

FLORIDA

THE FEATHERED NEST

6600 Midway Rd.
Ft. Pierce, FL 34986

PHONE: (407)468-2998
FAX: (407)465-6820

Monday-Friday: 10:00-5:30
Saturday: 10:00-3:00

Annalee Mobilitee, The Cat's Meow, Hanford Heirlooms, Muffy VanderBear, Celebration Quilts, Bunnies by the Bay, and Cast Art Dreamsicles.

Visa, Mastercard and Discover accepted. Shipping and layaway available.

WORLD TRADE GALLERIES

Oaks Mall
6329 W. Newberry Rd.
Gainesville, FL 32607

PHONE: (904)331-7246

Monday-Saturday: 10:00-9:00
Sunday: 12:00-6:00

Primary lines carried: LEGENDS, Rick Cain, J.H. Boone, Enchantica, Caithness, Lowell Davis, Schmid Hidden Kingdom, Ron Lee, Emmett Kelly, Star Trek, Chilmark, Limited Edition Plates: Bradford Exchange, Hamilton, Reco and others; Enesco, Goebel Miniatures, Westland Music Boxes, Munro, Authentic Native American goods, and Russian Boxes. Limited Edition Collectibles.

All major credit cards accepted. Layaway available. Special orders. Shipping worldwide. Personalized customer service. Locally owned and operated. Unique gifts from around the world.

GREAT GIFTS!

204 N.E. 1st Ave.
Hallandale, FL 33009

PHONE: (305)454-9911
(800)445-9911

Monday-Saturday: 9:30-4:30

Swarovski, Lladro, Precious Moments, Armani, Dept. 56, Snowbabies, Laura's Attic, Memories of Yesterday, Sports Impressions, Golden Memories, John Hine Studios: David Winter; Sisters and Best Friends, Cherished Teddies, Steiff, Dreamsicles, Flambro Imports, J.H. Boone, Iris Arc Crystal, Precious Art, Stanton Arts and Ron Lee.

All major credit cards accepted. Layaway. Redemption Center. GCC Dealer.

JORDAN'S GIFT SHOP

1715 E. Young Circle
Hollywood, FL 33020

PHONE: (305)921-0515
(800)484-8574 EXT 0515
FAX: (305)922-0072

Monday-Friday: 9:00-9:00
Saturday: 9:00-6:00; Sunday: 12:00-5:00

All God's Children*, Precious Moments*, Muffy VanderBear*, Department 56: Dickens, Christmas in the City, North Pole, Snow Village, All Through the House, Merry Makers, Snowbabies. Byers' Choice*, Lizzie High*, Cherished Teddies, Calico Kittens, Sisters & Best Friends, Annalee Dolls, Lilliput Lane*, David Winter*, Bearly People, Hallmark Ornaments*, VickiLane*, Cast Art* (Dreamsicles), Cat's Meow*, Attic Babies, Forma Vitrum "Vitraville": lighted stained glass houses.

Major credit cards accepted. Layaway. Free shipping. *Redemption Center.

FLORIDA

SUN ROSE GIFTS

265 E. Eau Gallie Blvd.
Indian Harbour Beach, FL 32937

PHONE: (407)773-0550
FAX: (407)779-1901

Monday-Saturday: 9:00-7:00
Sunday: 11:00-5:00

Precious Moments, Memories of Yesterday, David Winter, Lilliput Lane, Tom Clark Gnomes, Dept. 56 Lighted Houses, Snowbabies, Annalee, Cherished Teddies, Dreamsicles, Calico Cats.

Secondary Market: Precious Moments, Dept. 56, and Tom Clark.

Visa and Mastercard accepted. Layaway.
NALED member.

THE ENTERTAINER

314 Regency Square
Arlington Expressway
Jacksonville, FL 32225

PHONE: (904)725-1166
(800)982-7390

Mon-Sat: 10:00-9:00; Sun: 12:30-5:30
Extended Holiday Hours

Your primary and secondary market specialists. Large Cairn Studio selections. PM (DSR), Dept. 56 Showcase Dealer, Bradford Exchange Dealer, Lilliput Lane, Caithness, Walt Disney Classics, Hummel, Maruri, Lowell Davis, All God's Children, Krystonia, Andrea, Miss Martha's, CT, Laura's Attic, Emmett Kelly, Jr., Enesco, Norman Rockwell, Lladro, Snowbabies, Byers' Choice, Bossons, Possible Dreams, LEGENDS, Fontanini, Cat's Meow, Year round Christmas, angels, and santas.

NALED member. Layaway. Major credit cards accepted. Collector Club Redemption Center. Wrapping and shipping available.

PRECIOUS CARGO

9972 Baymeadows
Jacksonville, FL 32256

PHONE: (800)749-1414

Monday-Saturday: 10-6; Sunday: 12-4

Dept. 56: Snow Village, Dickens, Christmas in the City, Alpine, North Pole, New England, Snowbabies, All Through The House; Byers' Choice, All God's Children, Emmett Kelly Jr., David Winter, Swarovski, Walt Disney Classics, Lladro, Cat's Meow, Cherished Teddies, Precious Moments, LEGENDS, Hummel, Goebel Miniatures, Tom Clark, Krystonia, Madame Alexander dolls, Muffy VanderBear, Annalee, Edna Hibel, Sheila's, Enesco Elf Village, Calico Kittens, Maud Humphrey and Laura's Attic, Sports Impressions, Old World Christmas, Fontanini Nativity, C. Radko, Fitz & Floyd Holiday Hamlet.

Layaway. Free freight over $50 orders. All major credit cards. Redemption Center for most lines. Some Secondary Market.

ROBERTA'S PLACE INC.

4972 N. Pine Island Rd.
Lauderhill, FL 33351

PHONE: (305)749-2612

Monday, Wednesday, Friday: 10:00-9:00
Tuesday, Thursday, Saturday: 10:00-6:00
Sunday: 10:00-5:00

Located in The Atrium Plaza near Ft. Lauderdale. Lines include: The largest selection of G. Armani in Florida. As well as Walt Disney Classics Collection, Emmett Kelly Jr., M.I. Hummel, Maud Humphrey, Icart, Lladro, Precious Moments, Swarovski, E. Tezza, Golden Memories, Enesco and WACO Musicals.

In business for 5 years, established in 1988. Redemption center for above lines. Secondary Market Service. All major credit cards accepted. Ship daily. Mail orders and layways welcome.

FLORIDA

THE BRONZE LADY

12957 Gulf Blvd. East
Madeira Beach, FL 33708

PHONE: (813)398-5994

Open Daily: 10:00-5:30

American Artists, Armani, Armstrong's, Jody Bergsma, Rick Cain, Calico Kittens, Cast Art Dreamsicles, Cherished Teddies, Tom Clark Gnomes, Daddy's Long Legs, The Herd, Annette Himstedt Dolls, Hummels, Jeckle-Jansen Dolls, Emmett Kelly Sr. and Jr. figurines and paintings, Ron Lee, LEGENDS, Lladro, Memories of Yesterday, Lee Middleton Dolls, Miss Martha's Originals, Robert Olszewski, Norman Rockwell, Sarah's Attic, Red Skelton, Snowbabies, Sports Impressions, David Winter.

Major credit cards accepted. Layaway. Secondary Market Service. Up to date newsletter available. Shipping anywhere.

The Most Gifted Store in Florida.

SWEETSER'S

Santa Rosa Mall
Mary Esther, FL 32569

PHONE: (904)243-2973

Monday-Saturday: 10:00-9:00
Sunday: 12:00-5:00

Gunther Granget, Lladro Golden Memories, Boehm, Armani, Perillo, Cybis, Emmett Kelly, Austin, Ron Lee, WACO, Walt Disney Classics, Duncan Royale, Goebel Miniatures, Hummels, Gorham, Maud Humphrey, Irene Spencer, Francis Hook, Jan Hagara, Gone With the Wind figurines, ANRI, Kitty Cucumber, David Winter, Swarovski Classics, Kaiser, Chilmark Pewter, LEGENDS Pewter, Lance, Polland, Caithness, Vandermark Merrit Glass, Lowell Davis, Beatrix Potter, Roman, Maruri, PenDelfin, and Michael Garman.

In business for 22 years! All major credit cards accepted. Layaway available. Secondary Market service.

THE DOLL GALLERY

7911 72nd Ave. Suite 106
Medley, FL 33166

**PHONE: (305)882-0086
(800)882-DOLL**

Monday-Friday: 10:00-5:00
Saturday: 12:00-5:00

Ashton-Drake, Barbie, Bearly People, Berjusa, Carla Thompson, Corolle, Daddy's Long Legs, Dolls by Jerri, Dynasty, Frederica, GADCO, Georgetown, Jennie, Good-Kruger, Gunzel, Hamilton, Hartmann, Helen Kish, Himstedt, Jeckle-Jansen, Kay McKee, Kingstate, Louise Tierney, Madame Alexander, Maggy Maid, Matie's Originals, Middleton, North American Bears, Pauline, Phyllis Parkins, Raikes, Sabine Esche, Sandicast, Seymour Mann, Shoemaker, Spanos, Treffeisen, Turner, Wakeen, Zanini, Zambelli, Zook and more!

Mastercard and Visa accepted. Shipping. Layaway. Ask about repeat customer discount.

CHRISTMAS COTTAGE & GIFT SHOPPE

1002 E. New Haven Ave.
Melbourne, FL 32901

**PHONE: (407)725-0270
(800)635-NOEL (6635)**

Showcase Dealer for Dept. 56 carrying all Villages. Other collectibles include Annalee Dolls, Byers' Choice, Hummels, Walt Disney Classics Collection, Cherished Teddies, Calico Kittens, Laura's Attic, David Winter, Swarovski, Shoemaker's Dream, Lee Middleton Dolls, Maud Humphrey, Steinbach Nutcrackers, United Design, Possible Dreams, Christopher Radko, Iris Arc Crystal, Krystonia.

Visa, Mastercard and Discover accepted. Layaway available.

FLORIDA

ALL THAT GLITTERS

8823 S.W. 107th Ave.
Miami, FL 33176

PHONE: (305)279-2531

Tuesday-Friday: 10:00-6:00
Saturday: 10:00-5:30
Closed Sunday and Monday

A collectible and jewelry store! Hummel, North American Bears, Boyd's Bears, Ginny dolls, Seagull Pewter, Mattel, Annette Himstedt dolls, Barbie dolls, Gallo Pewter, Comstock Pewter, Rawcliffe Pewter, T.Y. stuffed toys, Raikes bears, and collector plates. One of the largest Ginny doll dealers in Miami.

Member of JBT and DNB. Visa, Mastercard, and Discover accepted. Phone orders welcome. Secondary Market on plates. Can special order almost any collectible.

THE CHRISTMAS SHOPPE

14711 S. Dixie Hwy.
Miami, FL 33176

PHONE: (305)255-5414
FAX: (305)255-5625

Monday-Saturday: 9:00-6:00
Sunday: 12:00-5:00
September: Open Until 8

Precious Moments (DSR), MOY, Dept. 56 Showcase Dealer, Ladie and Friends, Byers' Choice, Swarovski, Iris Arc, DW, Lilliput Lane, CT, United Design Santas, Gorham, Victoria Ashlea, C. Radko, Enesco Ornaments and Musicals, Old World Christmas, Michael's Ltd., ANRI, Possible Dreams, Dreamsicles, Krystonia, Lladro, Walt Disney, Hummels, Miss Martha, Shelia's, Maurice Wideman, Jon Herbert, Calico Kittens, Cat's Meow, Sarah's Attic, Snowbabies, Fontanini, AGC, Annalee.

All major credit cards accepted. Shipping available. NALED and GCC member. Layaways. Free gift wrapping.

EVETS COLLECTIBLES

5254 NW 94th Doral Place
Miami, FL 33178

PHONE: (305)592-5701

24 Hour Answering Machine
Hours By Appointment Only

Located in Northwest Miami, 8 miles from the airport. The showroom features over 250 steins and mugs including Budweiser, Anheuser-Busch, Miller's, Strohs, Coors, C.U.I./Dramtree and others.

Member of the National Association of Breweriana Advertising (NABA) and the American Breweriana Association (ABA). Very active in Secondary Market for Brewery Beer Steins. Mail order service. A 90 day layaway plan and shipping are available. American Express accepted. Special introductory prices on all new lines.

GAIL'S HALLMARK

7449 Dadeland Mall
Miami, FL 33156

PHONE: (305)666-6038
FAX: (305)665-8790

Monday-Saturday: 10:00-9:00
Sunday: 12:00-5:30

Precious Moments, Memories of Yesterday, David Winter, Royal Doulton, Shelia's, Lladro, Hummels, Dept. 56, Annalee, Wee Forest Folk, Lowell Davis, PenniBears, All God's Children, Krystonia, Michael's Ltd., Harbour Lights, Sarah's Attic, Hidden Kingdom, Windy Meadows, Enesco ornaments, Hallmark ornaments, Iris Arc, Cherished Teddies, Sarah's Attic, Laura's Attic, ANNA-PERENNA, Cairn Studio, Dreamsicles, Miss Martha's Originals, PenDelfin, Roman, and Stanton Arts.

All major credit cards accepted. NALED member.

FLORIDA

COUNTRY PINE NEWTIQUES OF FLORIDA

130 Fifth Ave. West
Mt. Dora, FL 32757

PHONE: (904)735-2394
(800)637-2394

Monday-Thursday: 10:00-5:30
Friday & Saturday: 10:00-6:00

Mount Dora's largest gift and collectibles store offers a variety of unique and unusual items. Showcasing Dept. 56...All Villages and Snowbabies. Other collectibles include: Tom Clark, Tim Wolfe, Precious Moments and Memories of Yesterday by Enesco, Wee Forest Folk, Armani, Swarovski, Cherished Teddies, Byers' Choice, Sports Impressions, All God's Children, Miss Martha's Originals, Budweiser Steins, June McKenna Santas, and Michael Garman Western Sculptures.

All major credit cards accepted. Layaway and free shipping available.

THALHEIMER'S

2095 E. Tamiami Trail
Naples, FL 33962

PHONE: (813)774-4666
(800)729-8994
FAX: (813)774-3315

Monday-Saturday: Seasonal Hours
Call For Information

Lladro, Connoisseur, Boehm, Cybis, Royal Doulton, Lalique, Dresden, Meissen, Hand-Cut Crystal, Ivory, Cloisonne.

Yearly winter auction featuring an extensive collection of retired Lladro figurines only. Also hold weekly auctions.

Visa, Mastercard and Discover accepted. Shipping anywhere. Secondary Market Dealer. Redemption Center.

HEIRLOOMS OF TOMORROW

750 N.E. 125th St.
North Miami, FL 33161

PHONE: (305)899-0920

Monday-Wednesday, Friday: 9:30-6:00
Thursday: 9:30-8:00; Saturday: 9:00-5:00

David Winter Cottages, Lilliput Lane, ANRI, Hibel Gallery, Lladro, Goebel, M.I. Hummel, Armani, Swarovski, Dept. 56, Wee Forest, Olszewski, Cabbage Patch Adoption, Memories of Yesterday, LEGENDS, Golden Memories, Disney Classics, Chilmark, Precious Moments, Napoleon Capodimonte, Howard Miller Curios, Magic Glass Curios and Showcases. Dolls and Teddy Bears: Ashton-Drake, Madame Alexander, Gund, North American Bears and others.

All major credit cards accepted. NALED member. Bradford Dealer. Layaway program. Secondary Market Listings.

DEBORAH'S HALLMARK & GIFTS

5154 S. Conway Rd.
(Corner of Hoffner & S. Conway)
Orlando, FL 32812

PHONE: (407)851-6526

Monday-Friday: 10:30-7:30
Saturday: 10:00-6:00; Sunday: 1:00-5:00

David Winter, Dept. 56, Jan Hagara, Fenton, Maruri, Cat's Meow, Shelia's, PenniBears, Cherished Teddies, Precious Moments, Maud Humphrey, Lowell Davis, Hummel, Hallmark Ornaments, Star Trek, Dreamsicles, Annalee Dolls, Emmett Kelly Jr., Memories of Yesterday, Lilliput Lane, Shoemaker's Dream, Raikes, various plates, Laura's Attic, Enesco Music Boxes, Little Cheesers.

Visa, Discover, American Express and Mastercard accepted. Special orders. Layaway. Access to secondary pieces for David Winter and Jan Hagara.

FLORIDA

FIBBER MaGEE'S KOUNTRY SHOPPE & CHRISTMAS KOTTAGE

11247 E. Colonial Dr.
Orlando, FL 32817
PHONE: (407)277-7480
FAX: (407)277-9981

Monday-Saturday: 9:30-5:30
Sunday: 12:00-5:00

Dept. 56 Showcase Dealer (Dickens Village, North Pole, Christmas in the City, New England, Alpine, Snow Village, Snowbabies, Merry Makers, All Thru the House), Byers' Choice, Tom Clark, Lizzie High, David Winter, Margaret Furlong, Possible Dreams, Enesco Musicals, PM, Cat's Meow, Cherished Teddies, Sarah's Attic, J.H. Boone, Midwest Importers, Dreamsicles, and Attic Babies.

Dept. 56 Secondary Market and collector club available. Layaway and shipping available. Visa, Mastercard and Discover.

REEF HALLMARK

Greenwood Shopping Center
1694 S. Congress Ave.
Palm Springs, FL 33461
The Palm Beaches
PHONE: (800)537-7890 (ORDERS)
(407)967-9999
FAX: (407)967-1704

Monday-Saturday: 9:30-9:00
Sunday: 10:00-5:00

Established in 1959.

Cherished Teddies, all Dept. 56 including Snowbabies, David Winter, Disney Classics Collection, Dreamsicles, Enesco Treasury Ornaments, Fontanini, Hallmark Ornaments, Hummel, Memories of Yesterday, Precious Moments, Sports Impressions, and Swarovski.

GCC Member. Mastercard, Visa and Discover accepted. Free shipping over $50.00. Florida residents add 6% sales tax.

Specialize in Precious Moments, Dept. 56, and Walt Disney Classics.

CORNER GIFTS

1665 N. Hiatus Rd.
Pembroke Pines, FL 33026
PHONE: (305)432-3739

Monday-Friday: 10:00-6:00
Saturday: 10:00-5:30

South Florida's largest selection of limited edition collectibles. Bradford Exchange Dealer. NALED member. Specializing in primary and secondary market plates. Dolls by Ashton-Drake, Hamilton, Dept. 56, Snow Village and Snowbabies, Krystonia, Sarah's Attic, Emmett Kelly, Sr., Beatrix Potter, Norman Rockwell, Hibel, Sandra Kuck, Perillo, Donald Zolan etc., PM, CT, Heritage Dealer for Memories of Yesterday, Laura's Attic, Treasured Memories, Miss Martha's, Enesco Musical Showcase Dealer, Maud Humphrey, SI, Armani, Artaffects, Cast Art, Calico Kittens, Dave Grossman Creations, Hadley House, Little Cheesers and Lilliput Lane.

Many more lines. Call for information.

SIMPLY COUNTRY

2114 Jim Redman Parkway
Plant City, FL 33566
PHONE: (813)754-5683
FAX: (813)754-5683

Monday-Saturday: 10-6; Closed Sunday

Dept. 56: Snow Village, Dickens, New England, Alpine, Snowbabies, All Thru the House, North Pole, Christmas in the City, Merry Makers, Dickens China, Winter Silhouette. Roman, Sarah's Attic, All God's Children, Lizzie High, Cat's Meow, Enesco, Hamilton, Cherished Teddies, United Design, Lee Middleton Dolls, Sandra Kuck, David Winter, Memories of Yesterday, Tom Clark, Sheilas, Aus-Ben Studios, Schmid, Treasured Memories, Sports Impressions, Lincoln County Garden Club, Carriage House Studio, Dreamsicles, Maruri, June McKenna, Midwest Importers, PJ's Carousels, VickiLane, and Ann Taylor.

Mastercard and Visa honored. Layaway available. Secondary Market service.

FLORIDA

THE SILVER SLEIGH

1319 E. Sample Rd.
Pompano Beach, FL 33064
PHONE: (305)943-4388

Monday-Saturday: 10:00-5:00

Open all year for all your holiday needs. A unique holiday shop featuring Christmas, flowers and gifts. Eight to ten theme trees. Holiday music played year round! One-of-a-kind wreaths and centerpieces.

Featuring Department 56, Byers' Choice, Lilliput Lane Cottages, Roman Fontanini Nativities, Christopher Radko, Old World, Kurt S. Adler, Midwest Importers, Margaret Furlong Designs.

American Express, Visa and Mastercard accepted. Layaway and shipping available. Secondary market dealer. Quality customer service.

THE CHRISTMAS SHOPPEE

2805 Proctor Rd.
Sarasota, FL 34231
PHONE: (813)923-6084

Open Daily: 10:00-5:00
Nov. 1-Dec. 31: Daily: 10:00-8:00
Sunday: 12:00-5:00

Dept. 56: Snow Village, Heritage Village, North Pole Collection, Snowbabies, and all ornament and decorative lines; Annalee, Byers' Choice Carolers, Christopher Radko and Old World Christmas Ornaments, Duncan Royale, Fontanini, Lowell Davis, Vaillancourt, Caspari, Haut Papier paper products, Schmid Music Boxes, and Silvestri Midwest Ornaments. Also featuring silk ribbons, floral arrangements, trees and wreaths.

Visa, Mastercard, and Discover accepted. Layaway. Shipping. Limited Secondary Market. Redemption Center for Fontanini, Old World and Byers' Choice.

LEE'S OF ST. ARMANDS, INC.

27 N. Blvd. of Presidents
Sarasota, FL 34236
PHONE: (813)388-1336

Monday-Saturday: 9:30-5:00

Walt Disney Classics Collection, Byers' Choice Carolers, Sterling Silver ornaments including Hand & Hammer and Cazenovia Abroad, Baccarat Crystal animals, Royal Crown Derby paperweights, Margaret Furlong Designs (Carriage House), 1940's issues of original Varga Calendars (and some Petty), Georg Jensen, Royal Copenhagen and Bing & Grondahl plates.

Special Ordering. All major credit cards accepted. Free gift wrapping. Shipping available.

PIPER'S COLLECTIBLES

7350 S. Tamiami Trail
Sarasota, FL 34231
PHONE: (813)923-5237

Monday-Friday: 9-5; Saturday: 9-4

Over 3,000 square feet to service any collector. Preferred LEGENDS Dealer. Showcase Dealer for Chilmark, L. Davis, DW, Wideman, Anheuser-Busch, Lilliput, Royal Doulton, SI, EKJ, Disney, Hummel and Expressions of Youth. Also PM, MOY, Maud Humphrey, B.P. Gutmann, Bossons, Tom Clark, Bradford Exchange, Dept. 56 Villages, accessories and Snowbabies, Goebel Miniatures, CT, Calico Kittens, Laura's Attic, Miss Martha, Lucy and Me, Sisters, The Herd, DeGrazia, Hibel, DR, P.B. Moss, B&G/RC plates, Perillo plates and figurines, Beatrix Potter, Ashton-Drake, Hamilton, Gorham, and Middleton.

Redemption Center. Specializing in Secondary Market for plates, figurines and dolls. Layaway, charges and shipping.

FLORIDA

CAROL'S CORNER

138 Mariner Blvd.
Spring Hill, FL 34609

PHONE: (904)683-9304

Monday-Saturday: 9:30-5:30

Authorized Bradford Dealer. Large selection of collector plates, past and current issues. One of Florida's largest dealers. If they don't have the plate you want, they will buy it for you on Secondary Market. Ashton-Drake Dolls, Van Hygen and Smythe frames and doll cases, Ardleigh Elliott, Rockwell, Hummels, Sebastians, ANRI, Lowell Davis, Frances Hook, DeGrazia, Hagara, Perillo, Lilliput and more.

Club Redemption Center for lines carried. Supreme service. Layaway welcome. Mastercard and Visa accepted. Celebrating their 15th year March 1993.

CASA ITALIA

12 Cathedral Place
St. Augustine, FL 32084

PHONE: (904)824-1961
FAX: (904)797-5508

Monday-Friday: 10:00-6:00
Saturday-Sunday: 12:00-6:00

In business for 10 years. Dolls and clowns by: Gorham, Dynasty, Lee Middleton, Goebel, Legacy, Kingstate, Seymour Mann, Pauline, Georgetown Collection, Vickie Walker, unique hand-crafted dolls from India. Also Raikes Bears, music boxes, Spanish hand made fans and ships, Italian porcelain figurines and Burago cars, antique doll postcards and doll furniture.

Layaway and shipping available. All major credit cards and personal checks accepted.

THE CHRISTMAS SHOP/ TEPEETOWN, INC.

12 Castillo Dr.
St. Augustine, FL 32084

PHONE: (904)824-9898 (E.S.T.)
FAX: (904)829-8555

Open Daily: 9:30-6:00

M.I. Hummel, Lladro, Precious Moments, Department 56, Chilmark, Duncan Royale, David Winter, Lilliput Lane, Lowell Davis, Perillo, DeGrazia, Goebel, Alexander dolls, Cairn Studios (Tom Clark), Artists of the World, Cherished Teddies, Emmett Kelly Sr., Emmett Kelly Jr., Enesco, J.H. Boone, John Hine Studios, Maruri USA, Polland Studios, Roman, Sarah's Attic, and Silver Deer.

Secondary Market Service. Buy outright-- paid in cash or merchandise.

J & C COLLECTIBLES

4446 S.E. Federal Hwy
Stuart, FL 34997

PHONE: (407)286-8717
(800)833-8717

Monday-Saturday: 10:00-5:00

American Artists, Artaffects, Ashton-Drake, B&G/RC, Bradford Exchange, CT, Steiff, Muffy and Raikes Bears, Campbell Kids, Phyllis Parkins, Hibel, Effanbee, Emmett Kelly Jr., Enesco, Flambro Imports, Goebel, Georgetown, Gorham, H & G Studios, Hamilton Collection, Hummel, Fred Stone, Lilliput Cottages, Incolay, Hadley House, Jan Hagara, Edwin Knowles, Land of Legend, Lilliput, Maruri, Middleton, Rockwell, Schmid, Precious Art, Reco, Roman, Sports Impressions, Villeroy & Boch. Dolls, plates, figurines, lithographs and more!

Authorized Dealer for Limited Edition Collectibles. Free shipping on orders over $50. Visa, Mastercard, and American Express.

FLORIDA

THE CALICO CAT

5101 E. Busch Blvd.
Tampa, FL 33617

PHONE: (813)988-0481
FAX: (813)622-7505

Monday-Saturday: 10:00-6:00
Thursday: 10:00-8:00; Sunday: 12:30-5:00

Duncan Royale, June McKenna, Sarah's Attic, Vaillancourt Folk Art, Byers' Choice, Maud Humphrey, Possible Dreams, Miss Martha's Collection, Cherished Teddies, Dept. 56: (Dickens, New England, Alpine, Christmas in the City, and North Pole Villages), Snowbabies, All Thru the House and Lizzie High.

All major credit cards accepted. Layaways welcome. Monthly newsletter.

THE CALICO CAT

14434 N. Dale Mabry Hwy.
Tampa, FL 33624

PHONE: (813)962-3583
FAX: (813)960-1495

Monday-Saturday: 10:00-6:00
Thursday: 10:00-8:00; Sunday: 12:30-5:00

Duncan Royale, June McKenna, Sarah's Attic, Vaillancourt Folk Art, Byers' Choice, Maud Humphrey, Possible Dreams, Miss Martha's Collection, All God's Children, Cherished Teddies, Dept. 56: (Dickens, New England, Alpine, Christmas in the City, and North Pole Villages) Snowbabies, All Thru the House and Lizzie High.

All major credit cards accepted. Layaways welcome. Monthly newsletter.

TOPAZ COLLECTIBLES & JEWELRY

4008 W. Linebaugh Ave.
Tampa, FL 33624

PHONE: (813)969-1063 (Office)
FAX: (813)969-1365

Monday-Saturday: 10:00-9:00
Sunday: 12:00-6:00

Swarovski Crystal, Lladro Porcelain, Precious Moments, David Winter, Cherished Teddies, Sports Impressions, Maud Humphrey, Southern Heritage, Wee Forest Folk, Andrea by Sadek, Sandicast, and United Design.

Several locations in Tampa/Lakeland area: Westshore Plaza-Tampa (813)286-8528; University Mall-Tampa (813)971-4573; Tampa Bay Center-Tampa (813)876-3378; Eastlake Mall-Tampa (813)626-3684; Lakeland Square-Lakeland (813)859-3030.

All major credit cards accepted. Layaway available. Shipping and special orders.

GOODNER'S HALLMARK

Tequesta Shoppes
123 N. US Hwy. #1
Tequesta, FL 33469

PHONE: (407)746-7904
FAX: (407)746-4551

Monday-Saturday: 9:00-8:00
Sunday: 10:00-4:00

All God's Children, Precious Moments, Memories of Yesterday, Tom Clark Gnomes, Dept. 56 Cottages, Enesco Ornaments, Cherished Teddies, Lilliput Lane, Snowbabies, Hallmark Ornaments, and Possible Dreams Santas.

Mastercard, Visa, Discover. Free gift wrapping. Shipping.

FLORIDA

CINDY'S HALLMARK AND GIFTS

Miracle City Mall
Titusville, FL 32780

PHONE: (407)269-4774

Daily: 9:30-9:00
Sunday: 12:00-5:00

Your collectible headquarters for David Winter Cottages, Hummels, Tom Clark, Precious Moments, Golden Memories by Lladro, Iris Arc Crystal, Cherished Teddies, Miss Martha's Collection, Calico Kittens, Sports Impressions, Maruri figurines, Andrea by Sadek and Hallmark Galleries.

Layaways welcome. Visa and Mastercard accepted.

LOTS-A-STUFF

122 Miracle Strip Pkwy. S.E.
Walton Beach, FL 32548

PHONE: (904)243-4402

Monday-Saturday: 9:00-6:00
Sunday: 12:00-5:00
Summer and Christmas Hours 9:00-9:00

Lines include Bradford Exchange, Ashton-Drake dolls, Sandicast, Precious Moments, Memories of Yesterday, All God's Children, Miss Martha's Originals, Maud Humphrey, Sarah's Attic, Cherished Teddies, Gregory Perillo, Calico Kittens, Raikes Bears, Fontanini and Sports Impressions.

Secondary Market Service for Precious Moments and plates. All major credit cards honored. Ship for exact amount of shipping cost, never over.

SOUTHERN TRADITIONS

1609 South Wickham Rd.
West Melbourne, FL 32904

PHONE: (407)951-8810

Monday-Saturday: 10:00-6:00

Cat's Meow, All God's Children, Lilliput Lane, Edna Hibel, Lizzie High, Sarah's Attic, Little Cheesers, Cherished Teddies, Raikes Bears, Steiff and Muffy Bears, and Katherine Grunefeld prints.

Mail orders welcomed. Mastercard and Visa accepted.

SUE'S HALLMARK

851 Village Boulevard #503
West Palm Beach, FL 33409

PHONE: (407)683-8300
FAX: (407)624-9446

Monday-Saturday: 9:30-9:00
Sunday: 12:00-5:00

Sue's Hallmark is new in the business and would appreciate your patronage! One of the largest selections of Precious Moments in South Florida. A complete selection of Dept. 56 (Dickens Village, Christmas in the City, Snowbabies). If you're an animal lover, Sue's carries Cherished Teddies, Calico Kittens, Partners in Crime, and Sandicast originals. Hallmark and Enesco Ornaments premiere dealer. Sports collectibles. And lets not forget Cast Art cherubs! Ever increasing collectible lines. Call for an update. Prompt redemptions. Mastercard, Visa, Discover. Layaways. Free shipping on all orders over $100.00. Prompt, courteous service.

FLORIDA/GEORGIA

PARTIN'S COLLECTIBLES, INC

1188 Havendale Blvd.
Winter Haven, FL 33881

PHONE: (813)294-1211

Monday-Friday: 9:30-6:00
Saturday: 9:30-5:00

Personal Service! Walt Disney Classics, Harbour Lights, Lowell Davis, LEGENDS, Swarovski, David Winter, Lilliput, All God's Children, Chilmark, Lladro, Wee Forest Folk, Annalee, PenniBears, Byers' Carolers, Tom Clark Gnomes, Maud Humphrey, Emmett Kelly, Memories of Yesterday, Vaillancourt, PenDelfin, and Little Cheesers.

Redemption Center for all lines with collector societies. Layaway and shipping available.

"Serving The Collector With Integrity"

THE BASKET PLACE

Winter Park Mall
500 N. Orlando Ave.
Winter Park, FL 32789

PHONE: (407)629-9005

Monday-Saturday: 10:00-9:00
Sunday: 12:00-5:30

David Winter Cottages, Cat's Meow, Brian Baker's Deja Vu and Summer Breeze, Dept. 56 Snowbabies bisque and pewter miniatures, Maud Humphrey Bogart figurines, Cherished Teddies, Dreamsicles, Harbour Lights, Fontanini, Roman, Constance Collection, Shelia's, and Dave Grossman's Gone With the Wind figurines.

Also featuring gift items, wicker furniture and home accessories.

Visa, Mastercard, Discover, and American Express accepted. Phone orders gladly taken.

Second location: Longwood Village, Longwood, FL. Phone: (407)260-5568.

THE CENTER STREET GALLERY

136 Park Ave. South
Winter Park, FL 32789

PHONE: (407)644-1545

Monday-Saturday: 9:30-5:30

For over forty years The Center Street Gallery has been offering gifts and decorative accessories for any occasion, and exhibits important contemporary artists. Dept. 56 Showcase Dealer, David Winter, Swarovski, Christopher Radko, ANRI nativity figures, Duncan Royale, Byers' Choice, Silver Deer, Enesco Musicals, Castagna animals.

Visa, Mastercard and American Express accepted.

BIT O' THE SOUTH

North Point Mall
1108 N. Point Circle
Alpharetta, GA 30202

PHONE: (404)518-1445

Monday-Saturday: 10:00-9:00
Sunday: 12:00-5:00

Dept. 56, Hummels, Maud Humphrey, Jan Hagara, Miss Martha's Originals, Duncan Royale, Lilliput Lane, Cherished Teddies, Possible Dreams, Enesco Ornaments and Musicals, World Doll, Harbour Lights, Laura's Attic, Emmett Kelly, Dave Grossman's Southern Memorabilia.

Mastercard and Visa accepted.

GEORGIA

OAK TOWNE

3000 Old Alabama Rd.
Alpharetta, GA 30202

PHONE: (404)664-4946

Monday-Saturday: 10:00-6:00

Oak Towne has been in service for three years. Specializing in Sarah's Attic, Lilliput Lane, United Design, Michael Garman, and Kaiser Porcelain.

Oak Towne is located 25 miles outside of Atlanta. All major credit cards accepted. A three month layaway plan available.

GALLERY II

Georgia Antique Center-Shop 13
6624 N.E. Expressway (I-85)
Atlanta, GA 30093

PHONE: (404)448-2448 (Shop)
(404)872-7272 (Office)

Wednesday-Saturday: 11-6; Sunday: 12-6
Office Phone Answered Daily: 9:30-5:30

Dept. 56 Villages, Snowbabies, EKJ, AGC, R. Doulton, D. Winter, M. Humphrey, Hummels, PM, Enesco NP Village, Miss Martha, CT, PenDelfin, WFF, Little Cheesers, L. Davis, J. Hagara, Lilliput Lane, Dreamsicles, MOY, Krystonia, DeGrazia, PenniBears, D. Royale. Plates: Bradford, Hamilton, Rockwell, F. Stone, Hibel, Kuck, Perillo, Zolan, P. Buckley Moss, B&G, RC, Red Skelton. Dolls: Ashton-Drake, Mde. Alexander, Barbie, Lee Middleton, GWTW, Annalee and more!

Visa, Mastercard and Discover. Layaway. Authorized Club Redemption Ctr. NALED member. Active secondary market dealer.

CREATIVE GIFTS

3299 Peach Orchard Rd.
Augusta, GA 30906

PHONE: (706)796-8794

Monday-Thursday: 9:30-5:30
Fri.: 9:30-6:30; Open Sat. before Holidays

Bradford Dealer. Dept.56, T. Clark, AGC, Miss Martha's, Schmid, L. Davis, B. Potter, Calico Kittens, Red Mill, Maruri, Hummel, OAA, Lladro: Golden Memories, DW, SI, Rockwell, J. Herbert, M. Humphrey, MOY, Laura's Attic, Sisters & Friends, Ashton-Drake, Effanbee, Gorham, United Design, Duncan Royale, Ebony Collection, Positive Image, Dreamsicles, Angel Babies, Cairn, Via Vermont, Russ, Applause, Raikes, Josef, Tripi, Sandicast, Land of Legend, Legend of Little People, Poortvliet, US Stamps, PM, Lefton Colonial Village, Ron Lee, EKJ, EKS, Enesco, Fenton, Flambro, Cast Art, Roman, clowns, gnomes, music boxes, plates, figurines, sculptures, dolls, gold, silver, flowers, crystal, and brass.

GIFTS & SUCH

3626 Walton Way Ext.
Augusta, GA 30909

PHONE: (800)828-3445
(706)738-4574

Monday-Friday: 10:00-5:30
Saturday: 10-4/ Extended Holiday Hours

"Augusta's most complete collectibles store." Located in mid-Eastern Georgia on the South Carolina Border. Featuring Disney Classics, Dept. 56, PM, Byers' Choice, Tom Clark, David Winter, All God's Children, Wee Forest Folk, Bradford, Ashton-Drake, Duncan Royale, Lilliput, Lizzie High, Sarah's Attic, Hummel plates and figurines, Goebel Miniatures, Lladro, Laura's Attic, Maud Humphrey, Cherished Teddies, Calico Cats, Enesco Musicals, Rockwell, Lowell Davis, and Storybook.

NALED member. Secondary Market Service in cottages and figurines. Redemption Center. Layaway and shipping available. All major credit cards accepted.

GEORGIA

EASTERLING'S COLLECTIBLES

River Rd. and Appalachian Hwy.
P.O. Box 656
Blairsville, GA 30512

PHONE: (800)448-4271
(706)745-3946
FAX: (706)745-7974

Monday-Saturday: 10:00-5:30
And Most Sunday Afternoons

"A must stop for discriminating collectors." Antiques, furniture and accessories, glassware, figurines, dolls, collector plates, Tom Clark Gnomes, Miss Martha Original Inc. (All God's Children), Precious Moments, Maud Humphrey, and David Winter Cottages.

Easterling's Collectibles specializes in antique restoration and refinishing. Visa, Mastercard, American Express and Discover accepted. Phone and mail orders. Shipping available. Gift wrapping.

SPECIAL EFFECTS GIFTS & COLLECTIBLES

102 Valley Village Shopping Ctr.
Blue Ridge, GA 30513

PHONE: (706)632-6950

Tuesday-Saturday: 10:00-5:30

All God's Children, Ashton-Drake Dolls, Bradford Exchange plates, Byers' Choice Carolers, Case knives, Cat's Meow, Cherished Teddies, Colonial Village by Lefton, David Winter, Dept. 56 Snowbabies, All Through the House, Disney Classics, Duncan Royale, Emmett Kelly Jr., Hamilton dolls and plates, Hummel, Krystonia, LEGENDS, Lilliput Lane, Maud Humphrey, Memories of Yesterday, Precious Moments figurines and dolls, Shelia's, and Wee Forest Folk.

Visa and Mastercard accepted. Layaway. UPS shipping available. NALED member. Redemption Center for most lines.

CHAMBERHOUSE

131 W. Main St.
Canton, GA 30114

PHONE: (800)477-9115
(404)479-9115

Monday-Friday: 9:30-5:30
Saturday: 9:30-5:00

17,000 square feet of shopping pleasure, featuring fine gifts, collectibles and limited editions. Dept. 56 (All Villages, accessories, Snowbabies, All Thru the House and Winter Silhouette), Precious Moments, Miss Martha's Collection, All God's Children, Memories of Yesterday, Maud Humphrey, David Winter, Lilliput Lane, Tom Clark, Cherished Teddies, Bradford Dealer, Anheuser and Dramtree Steins. Dolls by Alexander, Gorham, Barbies, Ashton-Drake, and more.

Redemption Center for most collectibles listed. Credit cards, layaway and shipping available. NALED member. Secondary Market Dealer.

MARTHA JANES GIFTS & COLLECTIBLES

18 Broad St.
Cave Spring, GA 30124

PHONE: (706)777-3608

Monday-Saturday: 10:00-5:30
Sunday: 1:00-5:30

Dept. 56 Showcase Dealer, Bradford Exchange Dealer, Miss Martha, David Winter, Vaillancourt Folk Art, Swarovski, PenniBears, LEGENDS, P. Buckley Moss plates and figurines, June McKenna, and santas.

This shop including giftware, homemade fudge, and gourmet food items, is located in a small village 16 miles SW of Rome, GA. Located in an old 1850's building. Featuring arts and crafts shows the second weekend in June and last in Sept. Local artists making unique santas, bronze sculptures, baskets, and pottery. NALED Member. Major credit cards. Layaways.

GEORGIA

PARSONS

525 Lakeland Plaza
Cumming, GA 30130

PHONE: (404)887-9991

Monday-Saturday: 10:00-7:00
Friday Open Until 9:00

Lladro, Swarovski, Hummel, Dept. 56, Duncan Royale, David Winter, John Hine Studios, Tom Clark, Maud Humphrey, Jan Hagara, Madame Alexander, All God's Children, Bradford Exchange, Golden Memories, Hallmark, Byers' Choice, Precious Moments, Gone With the Wind, Michael Garman, Shelia's, J.H. Boone, Fontanini, Sierra Brook, Cherished Teddies, London by Gaslight, Dreamsicles, Margaret Furlong, and others.

All major credit cards accepted.

In business since 1925. GCC Member.

MOUNTAIN CHRISTMAS/ MOUNTAIN MEMORIES

P.O. Box 2092 Town Square
Dahlonega, GA 30533

**PHONE: (706)864-9115
(800)535-2641**

Monday-Friday:10-5; Saturday: 10-6
Sunday:11:00-5:00

Dept. 56, David Winter, Swarovski, Madame Alexander, LEGENDS, EKJ, Jan Hagara, United Design, Christopher Radko, M. Garman, Monfort, Marty Bell, Thomas Kinkade, Terry Redlin, Lilliput Lane, steins, Bergsma, PM, Armani, Bradford Exchange, Dreamsicles, WFF and All God's Children.

Located in William P. Price Building which is listed in the National Historic Register. Dahlonega is the sight of the first major gold rush in the U.S.

NALED member. Visa, Mastercard and Discover accepted. Layaway. Free shipping for orders over $100.

HEART OF COUNTRY

"On the Square"
123 Stonewall Ave.
Fayetteville, GA 30214

PHONE: (404)460-0337

Monday-Saturday: 10:00-6:00
Sunday: 1:00-5:00

All Dept. 56 lighted houses including Snow Village and Snowbabies, Emmett Kelly, Jr., Jan Hagara, Miss Martha, PenDelfin, Laura's Attic, Sports Impressions, David Winter Cottages, Memories of Yesterday, Norman Rockwell, Duncan Royale, Cat's Meow, Sarah's Attic, Maud Humphrey, Gone With the Wind, LEGENDS, Sandra Kuck, Lilliput Lane, Cherished Teddies, Lowell Davis, Bradford Exchange Dealer.

All major credit cards accepted. Layaway. Free shipping. Free gift wrapping. Redemption Center for collectibles.

PAM'S HALLMARK SHOP

39 Hudson Plaza
Fayetteville, GA 30214

PHONE: (404)461-3041

Monday-Thursday: 10:00-7:00
Friday and Saturday: 10:00-6:00

Dept. 56, PM, Walt Disney Collection, David Winter, Lilliput Lane, Byers' Choice, Hummel, L.Davis, Lizzie High, Cat's Meow, J. Hagara, Duncan Royale, Maud Humphrey, Laura's Attic, CT, Calico Kittens, Enesco Musical Showcase, MOY, Hallmark Galleries, PJ's Carousels, Willitts, WFF, Dreamsicles, Miss Martha's, Michael Garman, Hallmark ornaments, SI, Dave Grossman Creations, Ron Lee clowns, J.H. Boone, Steiff, WACO, and Beatrix Potter.

Most major credit cards. Layaway. Shipping. NALED member. Redemption Center.

Two other locations: Stockbridge, GA (404)389-3188; Peachtree City, GA (404)487-2776.

GEORGIA

KAREN'S HALLMARK

128 Parkway Center
Ft. Oglethorpe, GA 30742

PHONE: (706)861-4035

Monday-Saturday: 10:00-9:00
Sunday: 1:00-6:00

Precious Moments (DSR), Memories of Yesterday Heritage Dealer, Dept. 56, David Winter, Calico Kittens, Cherished Teddies, Michael Garman, Sports Impressions, Tom Clark, Designs Americana, Dreamsicles, Emmett Kelly Jr., Maruri, Sandicast Blue Ribbon Dealer, Miss Martha's Originals, Byers' Choice, Sarah's Attic, and Maud Humphrey.

Major credit cards accepted. Layaways welcome. Personal service. Redemption Center. Free gift wrap.

Other location: Karen's Hallmark, 805 Market St., Downtown Chattanooga, TN 37402. Phone (615)267-9685.

THE SUPPLY COMPANY

214 S. Main St.
Glennville, GA 30427

PHONE: (912)654-3082
FAX: (912)654-3080

Monday-Friday: 8:00-6:00
Saturday: 8:00-1:00

Lilliput Lane, Laura's Attic, Norman Rockwell, Shirley Temple, Maud Humphrey Bogart, Jan Hagara, Roman, Sports Impressions, Noritake Eggs, Cherished Teddies, Dept. 56 Dickens' Village, Snowbabies, North Pole, and New England Village, and Byers' Choice Carolers.

All major credit cards accepted. Secondary Market Dealer.

BECKY'S SMALL WONDERS

P.O. Box 575 N. Main St.
Helen, GA 30545

PHONE: (800)762-6129 (ORDERS)
(706)878-3108

Open Daily: 10:00-6:00

All God's Children, Bing & Grondahl, Byers' Choice Carolers, Castagna, Decoy Ducks, Dept. 56 Villages and Snowbabies, Deja Vu and Summer Breeze by Michael's Ltd., Duncan Royale, Glassmasters, Glynda Turley Prints, Hudson Pewter, M.I. Hummel, Lilliput Lane, Lowell Davis, Lynn Haney Santas, miniatures, North Pole Village, Precious Moments, sports collectibles, Texas Stamps, United Design Santas and angels and wildlife sculptures.

NALED member. Major credit cards accepted. Layaways and shipping available.

WESSON'S

P.O. Box 460 Main St.
Helen, GA 30545

PHONE:(800)643-4438

Daily: 11:00-5:00; Closed Tuesday

Hummel, Lladro, Chilmark, LEGENDS, David Winter, Lilliput Lane, PenDelfin, Maruri, Michael Garman, The Herd, Anheuser-Busch Steins, Black Forest Cuckoo Clocks, Landstrom's Black Hills Gold, Kaiser Porcelain, Swiss Army Brands, Carolina Collection Steins, M. Cornell Steins, Little Cheesers, J.H. Boone, and Kevin Francis.

Redemption Center for items listed. All major credit cards accepted. No shipping charge on purchases over $100. NALED member. Try them for retired pieces.

GEORGIA

TRIFLES & TREASURES, INC. GIFT SHOPPE

131 N. Main St.
Jonesboro, GA 30236

PHONE: (404)471-1725

Monday-Friday: 10:00-6:00
Saturday: 10:00-5:00

All God's Children, Miss Martha's, Maud Humphrey Bogart, Tom Clark Gnomes, David Winter Cottages, Hummel, Cat's Meow Village, Byers' Choice Carolers, Lizzie High Dolls, Beatrix Potter, Jan Hagara, Cherished Teddies, Raikes Bears, Cast Art Dreamsicles, Josef, Sarah's Attic, Gone With the Wind Memorabilia. Wide assortment, unique gifts, and Georgia products.

Most major credit cards accepted. Layaway and shipping available. Secondary Market Dealer. Redemption Center.

DIAMOND

800 Ernest Barrett Pkwy.
Cobb Place #5
Kennesaw, GA 30144

PHONE: (404)428-6170
FAX: (404)514-1020

Monday-Saturday: 10-6; Sunday: 1-6

Bradford Plate Dealer, Ashton-Drake Dolls, Wee Forest Folk, David Winter, Dept. 56, dolls, Krystonia, Miss Martha, Lladro, Muffy Bears, Little Cheesers, Precious Moments, Madame Alexander, Ray Day, Thomas Kinkade, Emmett Kelly Sr., Enesco, Good-Kruger, Dolls by Jerri, Elke Hutchens Originals, Hamilton Dolls, Ellenbrooke Dolls, The Collectables, GWTW Collectibles, All God's Children, Cat's Meow, Sheila's Houses, Yolanda Bello Dolls, Cherished Teddies, Christopher Radko, and Swarovski.

Secondary Market. All major credit cards accepted. We ship UPS daily. Layaway plan available.

COTTAGE GARDEN

2368 Ingleside Ave.
Macon, GA 31204

PHONE: (912)743-9897
(800)800-1559

Monday-Friday: 10:00-5:30
Saturday: 10:00-5:00

Dept. 56 Villages, Snowbabies, Wee Forest Folk, Swarovski, Bradford, All God's Children, Sarah's Attic, Disney Classics, Cat's Meow, Shelia's, Emmett Kelly, Lilliput Lane, David Winter, Gone With The Wind, Iris Arc, Neil Rose, Thomas Kinkade, Marty Bell, Lowell Davis, Maud Humphrey, Ashton-Drake, Hawthorne, Hamilton plates and dolls.

NALED member. Free shipping for purchases over $100. Layaway program. All major credit cards accepted. Located just off I-75.

GULLEDGE TWO

7550 Hawkinsville Rd.
Highway 247
Macon, GA 31206

PHONE: (912)781-4346

Monday-Friday: 10:00-5:00
Saturday: 10:00-6:00

38 original artist line dolls including Ashton-Drake, Hamilton, Georgetown Collection, Dolls by Jerri, Good-Kruger, Ellenbrook, Middleton, The Collectables, Seymour Mann, Precious Heirlooms by FayZah Spanos, McGuffey, Hartman, Artist Collectibles, Rotraut Schrott, Nahrgang, Thelma Resch, The Dollmaker, World Dolls, Lissi, Hofer, The Ultimate Collection, GADCO. Plates: Bradford Exchange, Reco and Hamilton. Music boxes, figurines and other collectibles. Limited Edition Angels and Santas are an addition to their lines.

All major credit cards. Free shipping continental US. Layaway. Secondary Market. Collector Club savings plan.

GEORGIA

KATHY'S HALLMARK SHOP

"On The Square"
33 W. Park Square
Marietta, GA 30060

PHONE: (404)424-6552

Monday-Friday: 10:00-6:00
Saturday: 10:00-5:00
Evenings & Sundays During Christmas

Every Dept. 56 collectible line, All God's Children, Byers' Choice Carolers, Snowbabies, Annalee Dolls, Lizzie High Dolls, Cat's Meow Houses, Shelia's Houses, Lincoln County Garden Club, Duncan Royale, Margaret Furlong, Jody Bergsma, Thumbprint Teddies, Atlanta's largest Russian Nesting doll selection, German Nutcrackers, current and retired Hallmark Ornaments, Merry Miniatures, Cherished Teddies, Dreamsicles and Austin Sculptures.

All major credit cards. Secondary Market participant. Shipping and layaway available.

RAINBOW'S END

901 Milford Church Rd. Suite G
Marietta, GA 30060

PHONE: (404)431-0950

Monday-Friday: 10:30-6:00
Saturday: 10:00-5:00

All God's Children, Jarrett Studios-Blackberry Bonnet, Original Appalachian Artwork, Madame Alexander Dolls, Raikes Bears, Middleton, Muffy Bears, Daddy's Long Legs and Naber Kids.

Redemption Center for many of the above. Jean Wallace was a doll collector who happened to meet Cabbage Patch trademark creator, Xavier Roberts, when he was just entering the doll market. In order to open an official adoption center, Jean was able to work out an agreement with a friend in an art gallery--which she took over in 1979. Jean's dolls are all displayed in realistic settings.

Visa, Mastercard, Discover. Layaway. Secondary Market sales.

SUE-ANNE'S DOLL SHOPPE, INC.

915 Carroll St.
Perry, GA 31069

PHONE: (912)987-2823

Monday-Friday: 10:00-6:00
Saturday: 10:00-5:00

I-75 Exit 42 or Exit 43 in Downtown Perry. Lines include: Dolls by Jerri, Gorham, Susan Wakeen, Lee Middleton, Barbie, Pauline, The Collectables, Zook, Seymour Mann, Ginny, World Dolls, The Doll Maker, Berjusa, Robin Woods, Lissi, MJC International, Greenleaf, Real Good Toys, Artply, DuraCraft, and Walmer Dollhouse Kits. Miniature furniture and accessories, construction material, lighting kits, dollhouse wallpaper and carpet. Plush by Dakin, Gund, Applause, Steiff and North American Bear and "Muffy" Headquarters.

All major credit cards accepted. Shipping available!

ROCKMART FLORIST & GIFT SHOP

303 West Elm St.
Rockmart, GA 30153

PHONE: (404)684-4711
(404)684-5712

Monday-Saturday: 9:00-6:00

Dept. 56: Villages, Snowbabies, All Through the House, Merry Makers. Sarah's Attic, Annalee, Debbie's Southern Heritage, Melody In Motion, Positive Image, Wood Carvings by Lee Simpkins, Santas in Slate by Candace McManus. Full service florist. A large selection of silks.

All major credit cards accepted. Guaranteed one day shipping.

GEORGIA

PIKE'S PICKS FINE GIFTS

10800 Alpharetta St. Suite 198
Roswell, GA 30076

PHONE: (404)998-7828
FAX: (404)993-5021

Monday-Friday: 10:00-6:00
Saturday: 10:00-5:00
(Open Sunday November-December)

David Winter, Wee Forest Folk, Swarovski, Tom Clark, All God's Children, Precious Moments, Cherished Teddies, Byers' Choice, LEGENDS, Maud Humphrey, Chilmark, Krystonia, Lladro, Jan Hagara, Lilliput Lane, Hummel, Lowell Davis, Calico Kittens, Lincoln County Garden Club, and all Department 56 lines--including Dickens, Snowbabies, All Through the House, Merry Makers, and all Villages.

NALED and GCC Member. All major credit cards accepted. Free shipping over $100. Layaway and gift wrapping. Secondary market service.

THE CHRISTMAS SHOP

18 Bishop Ct.
Savannah, GA 31401

PHONE: (912)234-5343

Monday-Saturday: 10:00-5:30
Sunday: 12:00-3:00

Christopher Radko, Starlite Dealer, Dept. 56 Showcase Dealer, Lynn West Santas and Fairies, Milford Nutcrackers, Margaret Furlong's Carriage House, The Vaillancourt Collection, Leo Smith Collection, House of Hatten, Old World, German Cottage, Industry, June McKenna, Midwest Importers, Wee Forest Folk, Whitley Bay, Harbour Lights, Shelia's, Dept. 56, and Enesco North Pole Village.

Visa, Mastercard, Discover and American Express accepted. Layaway and Secondary Market.

CHRISTMAS HOUSE OF STONE MOUNTAIN

987 Main St.
Stone Mountain, GA 30083

PHONE: (404)498-9887

Monday-Saturday: 10:00-5:00
Sunday: 1:00-5:00

Dept. 56 Showcase Dealer, M.I. Hummel, Precious Moments, United Design, June McKenna, Annalee, Fontanini, Dreamsicles, Cherished Teddies, Coca-Cola, Disney, Steinbach and Ulbricht Nutcrackers and Smokers, Enesco ornaments, Debby's Southern Heritage, Kitty Cucumber, Maurice Wideman, Whitley Bay Santas, and Yankee Candles.

Open year round. Visa, Mastercard and Discover accepted. Secondary Market Retailers. Collector Clubs. Shipping available. Newsletter.

SWAN GALLERIES

1525 E. Park Place Blvd.
Stone Mountain, GA 30087

PHONE: (404)498-1324

Monday-Saturday: 10:00-6:00

All Dept. 56, Walt Disney Classics Collection, Swarovski, Wee Forest Folk, Lilliput Lane, David Winter, Harbour Lights, Hummel, Toby Maude, Cherished Teddies, Duncan Royale, Lladro, LEGENDS, Chilmark, Emmett Kelly, Jr., Miss Martha's Collection, Lowell Davis, Dave Grossman, Shoemaker's Dream, Hidden Kingdom, Little Havens, Constance Collection, Imhoff's Homestead Life, Texas Stamps, Maruri, Michael Garman, Fraser Creations, Mill Creek Studios, and Indian Territory.

NALED member. Secondary Market in Dept. 56, Lilliput Lane, Swarovski, David Winter, and Wee Forest Folk.

All major credit cards accepted.

GEORGIA

TARA HALLMARK

308 South Church St.
Thomaston, GA 30286

PHONE:(706)647-3611
FAX:(706)647-3611

Monday-Saturday: 9:30-6:00

Dept. 56 Showcase Dealer, Snowbabies, Precious Moments, Miss Martha's Originals, Sarah's Attic, Byers' Choice, Cherished Teddies, Maud Humphrey, Gallery Dealer, Hallmark ornaments and santas, Sports Impressions, and Largo.

Layaways welcome. All major credit cards accepted. Secondary Market service. Shipping available.

GLASS ETC.

4135 Lavista Rd. #110
Tucker, GA 30084

PHONE:(404)493-7936

Monday-Friday: 10-8; Saturday: 10-6
Sunday: 1:00-5:00

Atlanta's most complete collectible store. Just inside the I-285 perimeter. Dealer in primary and secondary markets featuring: David Winter, PM (DSR), Dept. 56 (Showcase Dealer), Snowbabies, Lladro, Chilmark, LEGENDS, EK Sr., Hudson Pewter, Kitty Cucumber, Margaret Furlong, Swarovski, Wee Forest Folk, Lowell Davis, Byers' Choice, Hummels, Maud Humphrey, United Design, Enesco, Armani, Hagara, Krystonia, MOY, Olszewski, Rockwell, Miss Martha's, Old South Collectibles, Caithness Paperweights, PenDelfin, PenniBears, Sandicast, steins, Duncan Royale, Christopher Radko, Cherished Teddies, Sarah's Attic, Daniel Montfort and Michael Garman.

THE PLUM TREE

3983 LaVista Rd. Suite 192
Tucker, GA 30084

PHONE: (404)491-9433

Monday-Saturday: 10:30-8:00
Sunday: 1-5

Look what you can find under The Plum Tree: Tom Clark Gnomes and Woodspirits, Tim Wolfe's Tracks, Lee Sievers Good Life, Lilliput, AGC, LEGENDS, MOY, Duncan Royale, June McKenna, John Sandridge's Luvlife, Norman Hughes Positive Images, Blackberry Bonnet Collection, Little Cheesers, Rick Cain, Neil Rose, Original Russian Art, Daddy's Long Legs, Michael Garman, Toby Maude Originals, Artesania Rinconada, John Perry, Windstone Editions, United Design, Pocket Dragons, Kevin Francis, Fraser Creations, Harbour Lights, Kaiser Porcelain, Glassmasters, Toby Jugs, Spanglers Realm.

Most major credit cards. NALED Member. Many retired items. Shipping available.

SACKS ROUTE 1

Broad St. P.O. Box 677
Warm Springs, GA 31830

PHONE: (706)655-9093
(800)452-6778
FAX: (706)655-9093

Monday-Saturday: 10:00-6:00
Sunday: 1:00-5:00

LEGENDS, Disney Classics, Hummels, Precious Moments, Lilliput, Bradford Exchange, Hamilton, Ashton-Drake, Cherished Teddies, Colonial Village, P. Buckley Moss, Mill Creek, Memories of Yesterday, Raikes, David Winter, London by Gaslight, Marty Bell, Thomas Kinkade, Artaffects Ltd., J.H. Boone and Bonita Bears.

Located in historic Warm Springs, home of F.D.R.'s Little White House. Mastercard and Visa accepted. Free shipping on orders over $100.

GEORGIA/HAWAII/IDAHO

WHIMSEY MANOR

115 Russel Pkwy.
Warner Robins, GA 31088
PHONE: (912)328-2500

Monday-Saturday: 10:00-6:00

Dept. 56, Michael Garman, Iris Arc, Lilliput Lane, Andrea by Sadek, Maruri, Virginia Metal Crafters, Bradford Exchange, United Design, Anheuser-Busch, Enchantica, Largo, LEGENDS, Goebel Miniatures, Marty, Fontanini, Duncan Royale, Sarah's Attic, Emmett Kelly, Jan Hagara, Ron Wall Miniatures, Kitty Cucumber, Ray Day Prints and Cottages, Enesco Musicals, David Grossman, Schmid, Byers' Choice, London by Gaslight, Harbour Lights, and Precious Art Panton.

NALED member. Layaway available. Secondary Market service. Visa and Mastercard accepted.

KRIS KRINGLE'S DEN

The Ward Warehouse
1050 Ala Moana Blvd.
Honolulu, HI 96814
PHONE: (808)531-4050

Monday-Friday: 10:00-9:00
Saturday: 10:00- 5:00; Sunday: 11:00-4:00

Dept. 56, Precious Moments, Lladro, Hummel, Lilliput Lane, Tom Clark, Byers' Choice, Miss Martha's Collection, Steinbach, Duncan Royale, Collectible Dolls and Nutcrackers: Dolls by Jerri, Nahrgang, Annette Himstedt, Lee Middleton, Midwest Importers and Steinbach Nutcrackers, Swarovski, Memories of Yesterday, Royal Doulton, Walt Disney Classics Collection, WACO Musicals, and Maud Humphrey.

Visa, MC, AE, Discover, and Diners Club accepted. Shipping available. Free gift wrapping.

A COUNTRY TREASURE

315 Uluniu St.
Kailua, HI 96734
PHONE: (808)262-4344
FAX: (808)262-4344

Monday-Friday: 9:30-5:00
Saturday: 9:00-4:00; Sunday: 9:00-1:00

Daddy's Long Legs, Lizzie High Dolls, Windy Meadows Cottages, Faye's Cats, Attic Babies. Lines also include Amish quilts, country dolls and animals, baskets, handwoven rugs, many handpainted items, and decorative wall items by Karla's Kreations.

Mastercard and Visa accepted. Shipping available. Redemption Center for Daddy's Long Legs and Lizzie High.

THREE C'S GIFT GALLERY

350 N. Milwaukee
Boise, ID 83788
PHONE: (208)376-1945
(800)847-3302

Monday-Friday: 10-9; Saturday: 10-7
Sunday: 11:00-6:00

In business for 7 years, specializing in Chilmark, LEGENDS, David Winter, Lilliput Lane and Walt Disney Classics. Other lines include Perillo, Hummel, Armani, Hadley House. Prints by Herman Adams, Gary Canter, and Donna Jacobson. United Design, PenniBears, Maruri, Second Nature Wildlife Sculptures, Schmid, Hudson Pewter, Kaiser, Polland, Little Cheesers, Maurice Wideman, Marty Elephants, J.H. Boone, Rick Cain, Mark Hopkins and Shoehouses by Jon Herbert.

Club Redemption Center for most collectible lines. Visa, Mastercard and Discover accepted. Layaway program welcome. Shipping anywhere.

IDAHO/ILLINOIS

OWL SOUTHWAY PHARMACY

720 16th Ave.
Lewiston, ID 83501

PHONE: (208)743-5528

Monday-Friday: 8:00-7:00
Saturday: 9:00-6:00; Sunday: 11:00-6:00

Precious Moments, Dept. 56, Cherished Teddies, Memories of Yesterday, Snowbabies, Raikes, Miss Martha, Maud Humphrey, Dreamsicles, Fenton Art Glass, Hallmark Keepsake Ornaments, Midwest Importers, Roman Inc., United Design, and Enesco Ornaments.

Free Home Delivery. Visa and Mastercard accepted. Layaway available. Redemption Center. Free gift wrapping.

NANCY ANN'S LTD.

Karcher Mall
Nampa, ID 83651

PHONE: (208)467-2921

Monday-Friday: 10:00-9:00
Saturday: 10:00-6:00; Sunday: 12:00-5:00

David Winter, Lilliput Lane, Krystonia, Iris Arc, Bradford Exchange, Ashton-Drake, Seymor Mann Dolls, Sports Impressions, Tom Clark Gnomes, Tim Wolfe figurines, Hummels, Cherished Teddies, Sarah's Attic, Laura's Attic, Anheuser-Busch, Artaffects, Sandra Kuck, Donald Zolan, Hadley House artists: Terry Redlin, Steve Hanks. All Enesco collectible lines including Enesco Musicals, Precious Moments, Memories of Yesterday, Cherished Teddies, and Calico Kittens.

Visa, Mastercard, Discover and American Express accepted. Free gift wrapping. Secondary Market Dealer. Layaway and shipping available.

CINNAMON TREE GIFT SHOP

1015 E. Young St.
Pocatello, ID 83201

**PHONE: (208)232-6371
(800)543-4888**

Monday-Saturday: 10:00-5:30

Complete Collectors Gallery. Limited edition plates, Dept. 56, Precious Moments, Lladro, Hummel, David Winter, Wee Forest Folk, Swarovski, Chilmark, LEGENDS, Walt Disney Classics Collection, Tom Clark Gnomes, Mill Pond Press prints, Greenwich Workshop, All God's Children.

Mail Order Specialists. Major credit cards accepted. Layaways.

RANDALL DRUG & GIFTS

1455 W. Sullivan Rd.
Aurora, IL 60506

**PHONE: (708)907-8700
(800)448-4496
FAX: (708)907-8793**

Daily: 9:00-9:00; Sunday: 10:00-6:00

Hallmark Gold Crown Store, Precious Moments (DSR), M.I. Hummel, Disney Classics Collection, Lilliput, David Winter, Snowbabies, Lowell Davis, Laura's Attic, Maud Humphrey, Memories of Yesterday (Heritage), Cat's Meow Village, All God's Children, Sarah's Attic, Miss Martha's, Daddy's Long Legs, Lucy & Me Bears, Cherished Teddies, Artina Gnomes, Pocket Dragons, Sports Impressions and other sports collectibles, Enesco Small World Musicals, Tobin Fraley carousels, Annalee dolls, Hallmark and Enesco Ornaments, Cast Art, and Anheuser-Busch steins.

All club redemptions. Major credit cards accepted. Free layaway and shipping.

ILLINOIS

BARRINGTON SWEET TOOTH GIFTS AND COLLECTIBLES

113 W. Northwest Hwy.
Barrington, IL 60010

PHONE: (708)381-2855

Monday-Friday: 10:00-6:00
Saturday: 10:00-5:00

Specializing in fine collectibles. M.I. Hummel, Golden Memories by Lladro, Lilliput Lane, Hudson Pewter, Maud Humphrey, Cherished Teddies, Summerhill Crystal, Colonial Village, Raikes Bears, Sports Collectibles, Precious Moments, Sisters & Best Friends, Pocket Dragons, Dreamsicles, and Sarah's Attic.

Redemption Center for collector clubs. Visa and Mastercard accepted. Layaways available.

AUNT MARY'S PARLOR

310 East Main St.
Belleville, IL 62220

PHONE: (618)233-5551

Monday-Friday: 9:00-8:00
Saturday: 9:00-5:00; Sunday: 12:00-4:00

David Winter Cottages, Dept. 56, Lowell Davis, Tom Clark Gnomes, Hummel, Wee Forest Folk, Snowbabies, Christopher Radko, All God's Children, Jan Hagara, Beatrix Potter, Maud Humphrey, Royal Copenhagen, Memories of Yesterday, Cat's Meow Village, Iris Arc Crystal, Old World Ornaments, Byers' Choice Carolers, Cherished Teddies, Hamilton Gifts, Lance Corp., Michael's Ltd., Miss Martha's Originals, Possible Dreams, Roman, Royal Doulton, Schmid, United Design, and Lilliput Lane.

All major credit cards accepted. UPS shipping available.

EAGLE COLLECTIBLES, INC.

6600 West Main- Rear
Belleville, IL 62223

PHONE: (618)397-1BUD

Specializing in Anheuser-Busch Steins, both primary and secondary market steins. Gift shop items include jackets, shirts, sweatshirts, caps, glassware, clocks, memorabilia, breweriana items, mirrors, golf bags, gold plated golf clubs, neons, AB truck banks plus much more.

BCCA Member. Mastercard and Visa accepted. Store is located 20 minutes from St. Louis, MO.

Also visit the Anheuser-Busch Memorabilia Museum. The museum includes: Pre-Pro Specialties, complete sets of steins, possibly one of the largest displayed A-B Beer Can Collections in the United States. Many rare items all displayed for the Anheuser-Busch collector to view.

Not affiliated with Anheuser-Busch Inc.

COVE GIFTS

318-120 Army Trails Rd.
Bloomingdale, IL 60108

PHONE: (708)980-9020

Monday-Friday: 10:00-9:00
Saturday: 10:00-5:00; Sunday: 11:00-5:00

Serving the collector with a wide selection of: Lladro, Hummel, Armani, Dept. 56 (All Villages, Accessories, Snowbabies and All Thru the House), David Winter, Lilliput, DeGrazia, PM, Cherished Teddies, EKJ, Disney Classics Collection, Hamilton and Ashton-Drake dolls, Bradford plates, Norman Rockwell, Maruri, Krystonia, Enesco Musicals, Lena Liu lithos, Possible Dreams, Steinbach Nutcrackers, plate frames and rails, and Egyptian artwork.

NALED member. Secondary Market Service for plates. Layaway and shipping available. All major credit cards accepted.

ILLINOIS

POTPOURRI CARD & GIFT

251 S. Bolingbrook Dr.
Bolingbrook, IL 60440

PHONE: (708)759-8222

Monday-Friday: 9:30-9:00
Saturday and Sunday: 9:30-6:00

Precious Moments, Annalee dolls, Hummels, Cherished Teddies, Silver Deer Crystal, Cat's Meow, Sheila's Houses, Enesco ornaments, Carlton ornaments, Thomas Kinkade, Sarah's Attic, Sports Impressions, Little Cheesers, Calico Kittens, Bergsma's, Michael's Ltd., Neil J. Rose, Hadley House, Dreamsicles, Lee Middleton dolls, PenniBears, Ashton-Drake, Bradford Exchange, Hamilton, J.H. Boone, Possible Dreams Santas, Midwest Importers, and Roman.

Layaway available. All major credit cards accepted. Open on holidays until 2:00.

DANA'S HALLMARK

8803 S. Harlem
Southfield Shoppping Center
Bridgeview, IL 60455

PHONE: (708)598-6674
FAX: (708)388-0920

Monday-Friday: 9:00-9:00
Saturday: 9:00-5:30; Sunday: 10:00-3:00

11 Dana's Hallmarks across the Chicago South Suburbs. Precious Moments (DSR-Bridgeview), MOY, Sarah's Attic, Miss Martha's, Sports Impressions, All God's Children, Hummel, Enesco Small World Musicals, and Cherished Teddies.

Mastercard, Visa, Discover and personal checks accepted. Layaways welcome. UPS shipping to your home. Secondary market service offered.

Second Location: 462 Orland Square Mall, Orland Park IL. Phone: (708)460-1999. Fax: (708)388-0920. Mon-Fri: 10:00-9:00. Sat: 10:00-6:00. Sun: 11:00-5:00.

BETHANY'S COLLECTIBLE SHOPPE

762 E. Chestnut
Canton, IL 61520

PHONE: (309)647-4010
(800)445-8745
FAX: (309)668-2795

Monday-Saturday: 10:00-5:00

"If it is not in stock...Bethany's Collectible Shoppe will try to find it for you, ASAP." Specializing in Precious Moments, Bradford Exchange Plates, Cherished Teddies, Imhoff's, Gorham, Dreamsicles, Calico Cats, Knot Knoggins, MOY, AGC, Hallmark, Enesco, Lowell Davis, Sisters, Glynda Turley Prints, Laura's Attic, VickiLane and many "older" pieces of other lines. Specializing in Secondary Market Price Guides for Precious Moments, Hallmark, Merry Miniatures, Cookie Cutters and Lowell Davis. Join our "Collectible Clubs" free. Come visit on your next trip to Illinois or call now!

WHYDE'S HAUS

123 N. Main-Fulton Square Mall
Canton, IL 61520

PHONE: (309)647-8823

Monday-Friday: 9:00-6:00
Saturday: 9:00-5:00

Hummels, Precious Moments, Memories of Yesterday, Miss Martha's Collection, All God's Children, Stone Critters, Jan Hagara, Maud Humphrey Bogart, David Winter Cottages, Raikes Bears, Kitty Cucumber, Calico Kittens, Cherished Teddies, Enesco Treasury Ornaments, Enesco Musicals, PenniBears, Lowell Davis, Laura's Attic, Dolls by Pauline, and Partners in Crime.

Mastercard, Visa and Discover accepted. NALED member. Layaway plan available.

Large selection of old and retired secondary market figurines for Hummel and Precious Moments.

ILLINOIS

JBJ'S

723 S. Neil St.
Champaign, IL 61820

PHONE: (217)352-9610
(800)331-3229

Monday-Friday: 9-8; Saturday: 9-7
Sunday: 12:00-5:00

Largest collectible shop in Mid-Illinois! Dept. 56 Showcase Dealer, Precious Moments (DSR), Bradford plates, Ashton-Drake and Hamilton dolls, Mm. Alexander, Hummel, All God's Children, Royal Doulton, David Winter, Caithness paperweights, Lowell Davis, Lilliput, Wee Forest Folk, Steinbach Nutcrackers, ANRI, DeGrazia, Marty Bell, Maruri, Possible Dreams, Emmett Kelly, MOY, Laura's Attic, United Design, Fenton Glass, LEGENDS, Sports Impressions, Cherished Teddies. Christmas shop all year! NALED member. Major credit cards accepted. Redemption Center for most clubs. Layaway, shipping and gift wrapping. Preferred customer program. JBJ's Gnome and P.M. clubs.

GIGI'S DOLLS & SHERRY'S TEDDY BEARS INC.

7550 N. Milwaukee Ave.
Chicago, IL 60631

PHONE: (312)594-1540
FAX: (312)594-1710

Mon., Tues., Wed., Sat: 10:00-5:00
Thursday-Friday: 10:00-9:00
Sunday: 12:00-5:00

Specializing in collectors dolls, teddy bears, miniatures, and music boxes. Stop by or call for complete selection of Ashton-Drake and a large collection of Enesco music boxes, Kewpies, Laura's Attic, Cherished Teddies, Georgetown Collectibles, Annette Himstedt, Lawton's, Alexander, Daddy's Long Legs, Good-Kruger, Miss Martha's Originals, Susan Wakeen, Seymour Mann and many others.

All major credit cards accepted. Secondary Market for Ashton-Drake, Himstedts, Lawtons and Alexanders.

THE TINDER BOX

Water Tower Place
835 N. Michigan Ave.
Chicago, IL 60611

PHONE: (312)943-4475

Monday-Friday: 10:00-7:00
Saturday: 10:00-6:00; Sunday: 12:00-6:00

Lladro, Golden Memories, Precious Moments, Hummel, All God's Children, Sarah's Attic, David Winter, Lilliput Lane, Tom Clark Gnomes, Emmett Kelly, Jr., Ron Lee, Bossons, Cat's Meow Village, Reuge Music Boxes, Snowbabies, Carousel horses, Silver Deer Crystal.

All major credit cards accepted. Mail order and layaways welcome. Ship U.P.S.

JUST DUCKY

7511 Lemont Rd.
Darien, IL 60561

PHONE: (708)985-1250
(708)985-8443
FAX: (708)985-1251

Monday-Friday: 10:00-9:00
Saturday: 10:00-5:00; Sunday: 11:00-5:00

Specializing in gifts, home accessories and collectibles: Thomas Kinkade lithos, Marty Bell lithographs, Daddy's Long Legs, Miss Martha's Originals, Sarah's Attic, Ladie and Friends, Michael's Summer Breeze, Lilliput Lane, David Winter, Cat's Meow, Byers' Choice Carolers, Cherished Teddies, Muffy VanderBears, Shelia's, Dreamsicles, Possible Dreams, Christopher Radko Ornaments.

Major credit cards accepted. UPS and layaway available. Redemption Center for above lines.

ILLINOIS

THE ROUND CORNER

404 Gurler St.
DeKalb, IL 60115

PHONE: (815)756-1838

Summer: Monday-Saturday: 10:00-5:00
Winter: Monday-Saturday: 10:00-4:00
Or By Appointment

Lowell Davis, Memories Of Yesterday, Laura's Attic, Maud Humphrey, Miss Martha, Cherished Teddies, Calico Kittens, plates and lithographs by Terry Redlin, Limited Edition collector plates, and collectible dolls.

Layaway and shipping available. Redemption Center for Sandra Kuck, Lowell Davis, Memories of Yesterday and Maud Humphrey.

PAM'S HALLMARK

Dixon Plaza N.
Dixon, IL 61021

PHONE: (815)288-6600

Monday-Thursday: 9:00-8:00
Friday: 9:00-9:00
Saturday: 9:00-6:00; Sunday: 10:00-5:00

Precious Moments, Memories of Yesterday, David Winter, Small World of Music by Enesco, Treasured Memories, Dickens Village, Byers' Choice, Sports Collectibles, Cherished Teddies, Dreamsicles, Dept. 56: Snowbabies, Snow Village, and Heritage Village. Also Fanny May Candies.

Most major credit cards accepted. Layaway and shipping available. Redemption Center.

TRICIA'S TREASURES

525 Lincoln Hwy.
Fairview Hts., IL 62208

PHONE: (618)624-6334

Monday-Friday: 10:00-8:00
Saturday: 10:00-5:00; Sunday: 12:00-6:00

Department 56, Lladro, Hummels, David Winter, Lilliput Lane, Swarovski, Cat's Meow, Precious Moments, Tom Clark Gnomes, All God's Children, Lizzie High Dolls, Krystonia, Cherished Teddies, Ashton-Drake Dolls, Byers' Choice Carolers, Lucy & Me, Bradford Dealer, and Jan Hagara.

Mastercard, Visa, Discover and American Express accepted. Shipping and layaway available.

THE BLOSSOM SHOP COLLECTIBLES

112 N. Main St.
Farmer City, IL 61842

**PHONE: (800)842-2593
(309)928-3222**

Monday-Wednesday and Friday: 8:00-4:00
Thursday and Saturday: 8:00-12:00

Sebastian Miniature Figurines.

One of the country's foremost experts on the Sebastian Miniature Line. Matches buyers and sellers who collect these pieces. A Redemption Center for the Sebastian Miniature Collectors Society. Offers an appraisal service to collectors. Sponsor of Midwest Sebastian Fair held each October which features many activities, including look alike contest and premier auctions of rare miniatures.

ILLINOIS

KAREN'S NEAT STUFF

209 South Main
Galena, IL 61036

PHONE: (815)777-0911
FAX: (815)777-8113

Monday-Sunday: 9:00-5:00

Come visit Karen's in "the town time forgot." Dept. 56 Showcase Dealer, Byers' Choice, Roman Fontanini. Santas: Lynn Haney, Possible Dreams, Heritage Santa Collection/ Midwest, A. Costanza, Santas by Wood World, Merrytymes (made from antique quilts), House of Hatten, Sadler Teapots, Swarovski, Michael Bonne Copper, Angela Tripi, Leo R. Smith III, John Hine Studios including David Winter, Lilliput Lane, PM, CT, Calico Kittens, Attic Babies, Basement Babies, Lizzie High, Bunnies by the Bay, North American Bear, Steiff, Rockwell, Dreamsicles, Beatrix Potter. Collector's club information. Mail and phone orders. Layaway and shipping available. All major credit cards accepted.

GRETCHEN'S HALLMARK

2202 Bloomingdale Rd.
Glendale, IL 60139

PHONE: (708)894-3441
(800)953-3322
FAX: (708)894-3707

Monday-Friday: 9:30-9:00
Saturday: 9:30-6:00; Sunday: 10:00-5:00

Hummel, Enesco Ornaments and Musicals, Precious Moments, MOY, Cherished Teddies, Maud Humphrey, Sisters & Best Friends, Bradford Exchange plates, Hamilton plates, Hollywood, Emmett Kelly Jr., Sandicast, Krystonia, United Design, Calico Kittens, Fanikins, Dept. 56: Snowbabies, Christmas in the City, Dickens, Snow Village; Growing Up Girls, Josef, Lilliput Lane.

Personalized, friendly, efficient service is their motto!

Major credit cards accepted. Free gift wrapping. Shipping and Layaway available. Secondary market on PM and Dept. 56.

BLUE BIRD OF GLENWOOD

159 Main St.
Glenwood, IL 60425

PHONE: (708)758-6060

Tuesday-Saturday: 10:00-5:00

Blue Bird, an oasis of gifts, is located 30 miles south of Chicago Loop off all major highways. With 37 years experience serving the collector, they have seven beautiful rooms of collectibles and unique gifts. Their lines feature Lladro and ANRI, both primary and secondary, Swarovski, All God's Children, Hummel plates and figurines, Lowell Davis, Cherished Teddies, Lilliput, Byers' Choice, and Possible Dreams.

Redemption Center and free club membership offered (call for details). Layaway and free UPS shipping anywhere in U.S. available. Free gift wrapping. Visa and Mastercard accepted.

THE GLASS IMPRESSION

34014 Barron Blvd. (Rt 83)
Grayslake, IL 60030

PHONE: (708)223-0555

Monday-Thursday: 10:00-6:00
Saturday: 10:00-5:30; Sunday: 11:00-4:00

Many lines of collectibles including Swarovski, Hummel, Enchantica, Lilliput Lane, Artaffects, Royal Doulton, Summerhill Glass, Victoria Ashlea Dolls, Norman Rockwell, Walt Disney Classics Collection, Emmett Kelly, Bossons, Bing & Grondahl, Dear-Belcari, Paperweights, Crystal Jewelry by Savvy and Swarovski, Napoleon Capodimonte, and Bovano.

Specializing in cut crystal! Free layaway and gift packaging. Visa, Mastercard and Discover accepted.

ILLINOIS

C.A. JENSEN, JEWELERS

709 First St.
LaSalle, IL 61301

PHONE: (815)223-0377
FAX: (815)224-2338

Monday-Friday: 9:30-5:30
Saturday: 9:30-5:00

Plates: Sandra Kuck, Terry Redlin, McClelland, Lena Liu, Zolan, Blackshear, Disney, Gutmann, P. Buckley Moss, Lynn Kaatz, Perillo and many others.

Plates and Figurines: DeGrazia, Lowell Davis, Bing and Grondahl, and Royal Copenhagen.

Figurines: Goebel, Hummel, ANRI, Cybis, Ispanky, Boehm, Lladro, Belleek, Jan Hagara, Malcolm Moran, Kazmar, Lilliput Lane, Hudson Pewter, Burgues, and Royal Crown Derby.

Over 3,000 different collector plates in stock. Visa, Mastercard and Discover accepted. Downtown La Salle since 1919.

STRAWBERRY HOUSE

507 N. Milwaukee Ave.
Libertyville, IL 60048

PHONE: (708)816-6129

Mon., Tues., Wed., Fri.: 10:00-5:30
Thurs.: 10:00-8:00; Sat.: 10:00-5:00

Bradford Dealer, Schmid, Hummel, ANRI, PenniBears, Precious Moments, Dept. 56, Sarah's Attic, Memories Of Yesterday, Maud Humphrey, Iris Arc, and Cherished Teddies.

Dolls: Yolanda Bello, Amelia, Storybook Dolls, Ashton-Drake Gallery, and Precious Moments Dolls.

Secondary Market information service. NALED member. ANRI, Hummel, Precious Moments, Memories of Yesterday, and Maud Humphrey Collector Clubs. Layaway program available.

GIFTIQUE OF LONG GROVE INC.

120 Old McHenry Rd.
Long Grove, IL 60047

PHONE: (708)634-9171

Monday-Saturday: 10:00-5:00
Sunday: 12:00-5:00

Precious Moments (DSR), Lowell Davis, Sarah's Attic, All God's Children, PenniBears, Jan Hagara, Maud Humphrey, Enesco Musical Showcase Dealer, Annalee, Brambly Hedge, Beatrix Potter, Hummels, ANRI, Memories of Yesterday, Cherished Teddies, Little Cheesers, Lefton Villages, Possible Dreams, Lucy & Me, Sports Impressions, Harbour Lights, Enesco North Pole Village and more.

Visa, Mastercard, Discover, and American Express accepted. Free shipping in USA. Preferred customer savings card. NALED member. Phone orders. Redemption Center.

PINE CONE CHRISTMAS SHOP

210 Robert Parker Coffin Rd.
Long Grove, IL 60047-9539

PHONE: (708)634-0890

Open 7 Days A Week: 9:30-5:00

Dept. 56, Snowbabies, Steinbach, Zuber, Erzgebirge, Ulbricht Nutcrackers, Possible Dreams, Clothtique Santas, and a wide variety of German glass ornaments.

Most major credit cards. Shipping. Friendly, knowledgeable service.

ILLINOIS

HALL JEWELERS AND GIFTS LTD.

230 S. Main
Moweaqua, IL 62550

PHONE: (217)768-4990
(217)768-3859
FAX: (217)768-3859

Monday-Saturday: 9:00-5:30
Friday: 9:00-8:30

NALED Dealer--Swarovski, Dept. 56 Snowbabies, M.I. Hummel including miniatures, Precious Moments, Noah's Ark, Sugar Town, Memories Of Yesterday, Maud Humphrey Bogart, Cherished Teddies, Lilliput Lane, Lowell Davis, Golden Memories by Lladro, Waterford, Maruri, Andrea by Sadek, Hudson Pewter, Jan Hagara, Emmett Kelly Jr., Fort Pewter, United Design, Melody In Motion, Fenton Art Glass, and Napoleon Capodimonte.

Redemption Center. Visa, Mastercard. Layaway. Free gift wrapping. Shipping.

MARCY'S CARDS & GIFTS

1738 W. Golf Rd.
Mt. Prospect, IL 60056

PHONE: (708)398-6370
FAX: (708)398-0460

Monday-Saturday: 9:30-7:00
Sunday: 10:00-4:00

Precious Moments, Lilliput Lane, Laura's Attic, Memories of Yesterday, Cherished Teddies, Calico Kittens, Enesco Musicals, Enesco Treasury Ornaments, Carlton Ornaments, Fontanini, Sports Impressions, and Dreamsicles.

Visa, Mastercard, Discover, and American Express accepted. Layaway and Shipping available. Free gift wrapping.

INTERNATIONAL HOUSE

2827 W. Aurora Ave.
Naperville, IL 60540

PHONE: (708)717-5002
(800)332-6333

Mon.-Fri.: 10-9; Sat.: 10-6; Sun.: 11-5

Lines include: Walt Disney Classics Collection, Lladro, Hummel, Sarah's Attic, Miss Martha's, PM, Enesco Musical Society, Dept. 56, Swarovski, dolls and bears, North American Bear, Tom Clark Gnomes, MOY, Lilliput Lane, David Winter, Annalee, Emmett Kelly Jr., Sports Impressions, Armani, and much more.

Redemption Center for all major clubs. Phone and mail orders welcome. All major credit cards accepted. Shipping available anywhere in continental U.S. Free shipping when CIB is mentioned. Gift wrapping upon request. Chicagoland's most complete fine gift and collectible stores!

Second Location: 15802 LaGrange Rd. Orland Park, IL 60462. (708)349-3366.

TOENNIGES JEWELERS, INC.

33 W. Jefferson
Naperville, IL 60540

PHONE: (708)355-1321

Mon., Tues., Wed., Fri.: 9:00-5:30
Thursday: 9:00-9:00; Saturday: 9:00-5:00

Hummel, ANRI, Bing & Grondahl, Royal Copenhagen, P. Buckley Moss, Hibel, Schmid, Lowell Davis, DeGrazia, Goebel, and Bradford Exchange plates.

All major credit cards accepted. In business for 45 years. Established in 1948.

ILLINOIS

BITS OF GOLD JEWELRY & GIFTS

121 West St. Louis St.
Nashville, IL 62263

PHONE: (618)327-4261

Monday-Saturday: 8:30-5:00
Friday: Open Until 7:00
Or By Appointment

Hummel, Swarovski, Memories of Yesterday, Walt Disney Classics Collection, Maud Humphrey, Sports Impressions, Gartlan USA. Dolls: Ashton-Drake, Kathy Hippensteel, Gorham and Hamilton. Enesco Musicals, Silver Deer, Fenton glassware, Cherished Teddies, Calico Kittens, Artaffects, Bradford plate dealer, David Winter, Lilliput Lane, Belleek, Maruri, Golden Memories and more. Many retired collectibles.

Visa, Mastercard and Discover accepted. Layaway and shipping. Redemption Center for most collectibles.

EUROPEAN IMPORTS & GIFTS

Oak Mill Mall
7900 N. Milwaukee Ave.
Niles, IL 60648

**PHONE: (708)967-5253
(800)227-8670**

Monday-Friday: 10:00-8:00
Saturday: 10:00-5:30; Sunday: 12:00-5:00

In business since 1967. One of the largest collectible showcases in the US. Annalee, ANRI, Armani, Artaffects, Ashton-Drake, Bradford plates, Maud Humphrey, Byers' Choice, Tom Clark, Chilmark, Lowell Davis, Dept. 56 including Snowbabies, Duncan Royale, Goebel Miniatures, Gorham, Jan Hagara, Hamilton dolls and plates, Lizzie High, Hummel, Kaiser, EKJ, Krystonia, S. Kuck, LEGENDS, Lenox, Lilliput, Lladro, MOY, AGC, Rockwell, PM, Royal Doulton, Sandicast, Sebastian, SI, Steiff, Swarovski, WFF, M. Wideman, DW, Whitley Bay, Enesco, United Design, WACO.

THE CAT'S MEOW!

4141 W. Dundee
Northbrook, IL 60062

PHONE: (708)564-1180

Mon. and Thurs.: 10-8; Saturday: 10-5:30
Tues., Wed., and Fri.: 10-6; Sunday: 11-5

Complete selection of Precious Moments (DSR). Enesco North Pole Village and buildings. Enesco Musical Showcase Dealer. Also MOY, Sugartown, Laura's Attic, Cherished Teddies, and Calico Kittens. Lilliput Lane, Pocket Dragons, Ron Lee, ANRI, Lowell Davis, crystal, Hallmark Merry Miniatures, Growing Up Girls, Josef Originals, and Dreamsicles. Happy to take orders on current Lilliput, Pocket Dragons, and ANRI with deposit. In season, 40 foot display of Enesco Treasury, Hallmark, Carlton, PM, and Christopher Radko Ornaments. Wish lists for ornaments prior to shipments. Send wants for current items with charge number or will confirm and request a check prior to shipping.

LA ROSA'S FLOWERS & GIFTS

114 East State St.
O'Fallon, IL 62269

**PHONE: (618)632-7441
(800)944-7441**

Monday-Friday: 9:00-6:00
Saturday: 9:00-4:00

Miss Martha, Lowell Davis, Louis Icart, Memories of Yesterday, Maud Humphrey Bogart, Sports Impressions, Collectible dolls, Collectible Christmas ornaments, Harbour Lights, Silver Deer's Ark, Harrison Fisher's Gold Coast, Laura's Attic, All That Jazz, Bessie Pease Gutman, My American Dream, Cherished Teddies, Calico Kittens, Sisters, Civil War figures, aircraft figures, silk and dried florals, Mrs. Baker's scented candles.

All major credit cards accepted. Next day shipping. Layaway. Redemption Center. Free gift wrapping. Established in 1962.

ILLINOIS

THE PAINTED PLATE LIMITED EDITIONS

220 E. State St.
O'Fallon, IL 62269

PHONE: (618)624-6987

Monday-Friday: 9:30-5:30
Saturday: 9:30-4:00; Sunday: Call First

Major lines include: Bradford Dealer, Ashton-Drake dolls, Lilliput Lane Cottages, Sarah's Attic, Royal Doulton, Winston-Roland, Little Cheesers, Maud Humphrey, Sandra Kuck, Bing and Grondahl, Royal Copenhagen, Belsnickle Santas, Brian Baker's Deja Vu, Johanna Zook, and more.

Secondary Dealer for Ashton-Drake dolls, limited edition plates, Lilliput Lane Cottages, and Sarah's Attic Black Heritage.

Bradford Exchange and NALED member. Wide range of accessories--frames, stands, hangers etc. Shipping worldwide. Layaway available. Visa, Mastercard and Discover accepted.

THE KOZY SHOPPE

218 East Hicks Place
Palatine, IL 60067

PHONE: (708)359-5900

Tuesday-Saturday: 10:00-5:00

You will find three rooms filled with collectibles. Featuring Lizzie High dolls by Ladie and Friends, North American Bear, The VanderBear Family: Muffy, Hoppy, Fuzzy, Fluffy, Alice and Cornelius with extra outfits. Also by North American Bear Co the VIB bear. Lines also include: Sarah's Attic, Attic Babies, Little Cheesers by Ganz Co., Colonial Village Collection by Lefton and Dreamsicles. Many handmade gifts for all occasions.

The Kozy Shoppe will mail gifts out of town after charge card approval. Visa and Mastercard accepted. Layaways. Gift wrapping.

VILLAGE PLANTATION

Sheridan Village
4125 N. Sheridan Rd.
Peoria, IL 61614

PHONE: (309)686-0057
FAX: (309)688-2586

Monday-Saturday: 10:00-9:00
Sunday: 12:00-5:00

Village Plantation, the largest Dept. 56 Showcase Dealer in central Illinois. Serving collectors with two great locations.

Showcase Dealer for Dept. 56 including All Villages, Accessories and Snowbabies, North American Bears, Cat's Meow, Byers' Choice, Lizzie High, Annalee, Sandicast, Cherished Teddies and Dreamsicles.

Club Redemption Center. Ideation Catalog. Layaway. Visa, Mastercard, American Express and Discover. Shipping anywhere in the US. Free gift wrapping.

Second Location: Northwoods Mall. Peoria, IL 61615. Phone: (309)685)4697.

KIEFER'S GALLERY, INC.

23347 W. Lincoln Hwy. (Rt 30)
Plainfield, IL 60544

PHONE: (815)436-5444

Mon., Tues., Wed., Sat.: 10:00-6:00
Thurs. and Fri.: 10:00-8:00
Sunday Hours During Christmas Holiday

Hummel figurines, Maud Humphrey, Precious Moments (DSR), Dept. 56 Showcase Dealer, Lladro, Swarovski, Armani, Rockwell plates and figurines, DeGrazia, Perillo, David Winter, Lilliput Lane, Memories of Yesterday, Cherished Teddies, Emmett Kelly Jr., a large selection of collector dolls including Ashton-Drake, Mde. Alexander and many other lines. Redemption Center for Sandra Kuck, Jan Hagara, Hummel, Precious Moments, MOY, David Winter, Swarovski, Lilliput Lane, Duncan Royale, and Armani.

NALED member. All major credit cards accepted. Layaways welcome. Secondary Market Dealer. Bradford member.

ILLINOIS

THE VILLAGE PEDDLER

330 E. Main
Plano, IL 60545

PHONE: (708)552-9005
FAX: (708)552-4119

Tuesday, Thursday, Friday: 9:30-5:30
Wednesday: 9:30-8:00
Saturday: 9:30-5:00

Hummels, Lilliput Lane, Jan Hagara, Maud Humphrey, Bessie Pease Gutmann, Cherished Teddies, Memories of Yesterday, Terry Redlin, Zook Dolls, Bradford, Folk Art from around the country, antiques, country home decorating accessories, and furnishings.

Mastercard and Visa accepted. Layaway. Club Redemptions.

KIRLIN'S HALLMARK SHOPS

P.O. Box 3097
Quincy, IL 62305

HEADQUARTERS
PHONE: (217)224-8953
FAX: (217)224-9400

Specialist in collectibles, gifts, Hallmark cards and fine candies since 1948. Serving loyal collectors with 36 Precious Moments Distinguished Service Retailer locations, and the following collectible lines: Willitts, Cairn Studios, Andrea by Sadek, Precious Moments, Cherished Teddies, Memories of Yesterday, Sisters & Best Friends, Calico Kittens, Small World of Music Musicals, Flambro, Hummels, Iris Arc, David Winter, Lilliput Lane, Swarovski, Dept. 56, Cast Art, Anheuser-Busch Steins and Possible Dreams! Redemption Center for all collector clubs.

83 stores located in 10 Midwestern states: IL, MO, IA, IN, OH, WI, MI, KY, TN, OK. Call to find the Kirlin store nearest you!

SOMETHING SO SPECIAL

Edgebrook Center
1617 N. Alpine Rd.
Rockford, IL 61107

PHONE: (815)226-1331

Mon.-Fri.: 10:00-8:30; Sat.: 10:00-5:00
Sunday: 12:00-4:00 (Nov.-Dec.)

Chilmark, David Winter, Dept. 56 Villages and Snowbabies, Lilliput Lane, Lladro, Precious Moments (DSR), Swarovski, Tom Clark Gnomes and Wee Forest Folk.

Authorized Bradford Exchange Dealer, Artesania Rinconada, Cherished Teddies, collector ornaments and music boxes, Emmett Kelly, Fontanini, Hummels, J.H. Boone, Krystonia, Lowell Davis, Old World Ornaments, Penni Cross Lithos, Royal Doulton, Sandicast, Steinbach Nutcrackers

Ask how to receive free collectibles with their collector card. Mastercard and Visa. Layaway. Special Orders. NALED and Collector Showcase member. In business since 1980. Secondary Market Dealer.

STONE'S HALLMARK SHOPS

2508 S. Alpine
Rockford, IL 61108

PHONE: (815)399-4481
FAX: (815)399-0167

Monday-Friday: 9:00-9:00
Saturday: 9:00-5:30; Sunday: 11:30-5:00

Dept. 56 Showcase Dealer (complete line), PM (DSR), Miss Martha's, Annalee, Tom Clark, Lowell Davis, David Winter, Lilliput, Hallmark ornaments, Enesco Premier ornament Dealer, Ashton-Drake, Madame Alexander Dolls, Hamilton, Georgetown, Hummel, Hallmark Galleries, Disney, Cherished Teddies, Calico Cats, Enesco Musical, MOY, Krystonia, Bradford, collector plates, Raikes Bears, Armani, PenniBears, Iris Arc, and Sandicast.

Dept. 56 Club (800)829-6406/Inquiries only. Redemption center. NALED and GCC Member (free catalog). Layaway. Credit cards. Free shipping with $60.00 orders.

ILLINOIS

MC HUGH'S

3522 14th Ave.
Rock Island, IL 61201
PHONE: (309)788-9525

Monday-Friday: 9:00-6:00
Saturday: 9:00-5:00

McHugh's has been carrying fine gifts and collectibles for approximately 12 years. Primary lines include Disney Classics Collection, ANRI, Lowell Davis, Hummels, Swarovski, Cairn Gnomes, Lladro, Precious Moments (DSR), Jan Hagara, Dolls, Collector Plates: Bradford, Sandra Kuck, Sport Impressions, Perillo, Fred Stone. Cat's Meow, Snowbabies, Dept. 56 Showcase Dealer, Lilliput Lane, Lizzie High, David Winter, Emmett Kelly, Rick Cain, Byers' Choice, Cherished Teddies, Calico Kittens, Memories of Yesterday, and Dreamsicles.

Mastercard, Visa and Discover accepted. NALED member. Layaway available. Redemption Center.

HOADLEY'S HALLMARK

265 Railroad St.
Sandwich, IL 60548
PHONE: (815)786-8076
FAX: (815)892-2147

Mon.-Sat.: 9:00-6:00; Fri.: 9:00-7:00
Sunday: 12:00-4:00

Precious Moments (DSR), Memories of Yesterday Heritage dealer, Dept. 56, Hallmark Ornaments, Hallmark Galleries, Laura's Attic, Krystonia, Cherished Teddies, Calico Kittens, Enesco Musicals, Lilliput Lane (Montgomery), David Winter (Sandwich), J.H. Boone, Indians, Miss Martha's Collection, Dreamsicles, and Tobin Fraley.

All major credit cards accepted. Layaways and shipping available.

Second Location: 1850 Douglas Rd., Montgomery IL 60538. (708)892-2002.

Hours: Monday-Friday: 9:30-9:00; Saturday: 9:30-6:00; Sunday: 10:00-5:00.

STROHL'S

118 N. Morgan
Shelbyville, IL 62565
PHONE: (217)774-5222
(800)643-4007

Monday-Saturday: 9:00-5:00

Everything in fine collectibles and gifts. Features Dept. 56, Precious Moments, Swarovski, Golden Memories, Cherished Teddies, Calico Kittens, Lowell Davis, Lilliput Lane, David Winter, DeGrazia figurines, Perillo, Sisters & Best Friends, Hummel, Ashton-Drake and Hamilton Dolls, and Collectors Plates: Bradford, Hamilton, DeGrazia, Perillo, Redlin, Hummel, Schmid, Bing & Grondahl, and Royal Copenhagen. Secondary Market lines include Dept. 56 and Precious Moments.

A NALED and Bradford Dealer member. Visa, Mastercard and Discover accepted. Four month layaway available. 12 years of distinguished service.

TINY TREASURES INC.

939B Clocktower Drive
Springfield, IL 62704
PHONE: (217)787-6500

Monday-Friday: 10:00-6:00
Saturday: 10:00-5:00; Sunday: 12:00-5:00

Limited Edition plates, figurines, bells, and thimbles. Emmett Kelly, Melody In Motion, Constance Collection, Marty Sculptures, Ardleigh Elliott, Norman Rockwell Gallery, Rhodes Studios, Ashton-Drake dolls, Dave Grossman Creations, Flambro Imports, plate cases by Talsco. John Hopkins Castlettes, Dreamsicles, and Discovery candles and music boxes. Offering a large selection of plate frames and accessories.

Authorized Bradford Dealer. Always free gift wrap. Shipping available. Donald Zolan trading center.

ILLINOIS

TOMORROW'S TREASURES

625 N. Grand Ave. East
Springfield, IL 62702
PHONE: (217)753-0466

Tuesday-Friday: 10:00-5:00
Saturday: 10:00-3:00

Bradford Exchange Dealer, Hamilton, Reco, Artaffects, Ashton-Drake Dealer, Madame Alexander, Lee Middleton, Hamilton Dolls, Jan Hagara, Maud Humphrey Collectibles and many more.

Redemption Center for Jan Hagara and Maud Humphrey.

Visa, Mastercard, American Express, and Discover accepted. Layaways welcome.

JOHNSON'S PHARMACY & GIFTS

203 E. St. Paul St.
Spring Valley, IL 61362
PHONE: (815)664-5050

Mon.-Fri.: 8:00-7:00; Sat: 8:00-4:30

Wall to wall collectibles! Master Showcase Dealer for Chilmark, Hudson Pewter, Jan Hagara, Reco Plates, Lefton products including entire Colonial Village and figurines. Enesco including Precious Moments, Schmid, M.I. Hummel Figurines, Plates, Bells, Memories of Yesterday, Duncan Royale, Holly Hobbie, Flambro, Cherished Teddies, ANRI, Beam Decanters, Sports Impressions, Frances Hook, Capodimonte, American Greetings, Cast Art, Dreamsicles, Museum Collections Inc., Red Mill, Roman, Sebastian Miniatures, Ducks Unlimited Steins, Westmoreland Glass and Goebel Miniatures.

Redemption Center for Collector Clubs. Layaway available. One stop shop!

GRIMM'S HALLMARK WEST

1519 W. Main St.
St. Charles, IL 60174
PHONE: (708)513-7008

Monday-Friday: 9:00-9:00
Saturday: 9:00-6:00; Sunday: 12:00-5:00

In business for 103 years. Gold Crown Hallmark. Collectibles are Precious Moments, Memories of Yesterday, Laura's Attic, Maud Humphrey Bogart, David Winter, Rawcliffe, Myth & Magic, Hummels, Margaret Furlong, Enesco Musicals, Cherished Teddies, Lucy & Me, Hallmark Ornaments, Merry Miniatures, Tender Touches, Winter Silhouettes, Snowbabies, Dreamsicles, Sports Impressions and Beatrix Potter.

Visa, Mastercard, American Express, and Discover accepted. NALED member. Layaway available.

CINDY'S COLLECTABLES

20 East 33rd Place
Steger, IL 60475
PHONE: (708)755-3333

Tuesday-Friday: 10:00-6:00
Saturday: 10:00-5:00

North American Bear: Muffy VanderBear & Family, V.I.B., Raikes, Cooperstown and Merry Thought Bears. Enesco Musicals, Precious Moments Dolls, Cherished Teddies, Precious Moments, Lizzie High, Norman Rockwell, Memories of Yesterday, Calico Kittens, Emmett Kelly Jr., Golden Memories/Lladro, Lilliput Lane, Dreamsicles, Anheuser-Busch Steins. Gifts for everyone in every price range, including The Glass Eye ornaments, vases, perfume bottles, crystal, framed stamps and Flavia.

Visa and Mastercard accepted. Mail orders welcome. Layaway and shipping available. Free gift wrapping.

ILLINOIS

CHRIS' FLOWER SHOP, INC.

Westgate Plaza
P.O. Box 942
Streator, IL 61364-0942

PHONE: (815)672-0404
FAX: (815)672-0873

Monday-Friday: 10:00-4:00
Or By Appointment

Large selection of Collectibles. Precious Moments, M.I. Hummel, Rockwell, Goebel, DeGrazia, and Memories of Yesterday. Dolls: Ashton-Drake, Middleton, Madame Alexander, Zook, and Himstedt.

Authorized Bradford Exchange Dealer.

All major credit cards accepted.

COOPER'S JEWELRY LTD.

303 W. State St.
Sycamore, IL 60178

PHONE: (815)895-3377
FAX: (815)895-3342

Mon., Wed., Thurs.: 9:00-5:30
Friday: 9:00-8:30; Saturday: 9:00-4:00
Tuesday: Answering Service

Celebrating 40 years of business, specializing in the collectible ornament business. Mail order catalogs available.

Lines include: Gorham, Lunt, Kirk-Stieff, Reed and Barton, Sculpture Workshop Design, Towle, Wallace, M.I. Hummel plates and figurines, Byers' Choice, and Possible Dreams.

Club Redemption Center. Strong Secondary Market service in silver Christmas ornaments. American Gem Society Member. Layaway and shipping available. All major credit cards accepted.

CRYSTAL CASTLE

17601 S. Oak Park Ave.
Tinley Park, IL 60477

PHONE: (708)429-1313

Monday-Wednesday: 10:00-5:00
Thursday and Friday: 10:00-8:00
Saturday: 10:00-4:00; Sunday: 11:00-3:00

Swarovski, Armani, M.I. Hummel, Cherished Teddies, Maud Humphrey, Dreamsicles, Reco plates, Sandra Kuck, David Winter, Michael Garman, Napoleon Capodimonte, Roman Fontanini, Emmett Kelly Jr., Edna Hibel, Krystonia. Dolls: Lee Middleton, Gloria Vanderbilt. V.F. Fine Arts, Maruri, Hadley House graphics and plates. Goebel Miniatures, Hamilton plates, Pemberton & Oakes plates. Also featuring other crystal such as lamps, water pitchers decanters, vases, candlesticks and Bulova miniature clocks.

Visa and Mastercard accepted. Layaway. Shipping. Free gift wrapping.

MARY'S COLLECTIBLES

1880 Washington Rd.
Washington, IL 61571

PHONE: (309)444-8511

Monday-Friday: 8:00-8:00
Saturday: 8:00-5:00; Sunday: 10:00-4:00

Prints include Terry Redlin, Thomas Kinkade, Franca, Steve Hanks, all Hadley House, Jesse Barnes, Charles Peterson, Sandra Kuck, Robert Sissel, and many other artists. Steve Hanks posters, Richard Sloan, United Design figurines, Bradford Exchange dealer, Rockwell, Emmett Kelly Jr. and Sr., Jan Hagara, Laura's Attic, Ed Schaefer, domes, and plate frames and accessories.

Visa, Mastercard, and American Express accepted. Layaway and shipping available. Secondary Market for prints and plates.

ILLINOIS

SENTIMENTAL JOURNEY

123 Washington Square
Washington, IL 61571
PHONE: (309)444-7355

Monday-Saturday: 9:00-5:00
Sunday: 12:00-4:00

Specializing in collectibles: Swarovski Crystal, Precious Moments (DSR), Memories of Yesterday, Heritage Dealer, Lilliput Lane, David Winter, Cherished Teddies, Calico Cats, Byers' Choice Carolers, Dept. 56, Snowbabies, All God's Children, Sarah's Attic, Lowell Davis, Maud Humphrey Bogart, Annalee, music boxes, Cat's Meow, Lizzie High, Dreamsicles, Margaret Furlong, and Possible Dreams.

Instant gratification kits for most collectibles. Redemption Center for all collector clubs. NALED member. Visa Mastercard and Discover accepted. Layaway available.

POTPOURRI CARD & GIFT

3042 Wolf Rd.
Westchester, IL 60154
PHONE: (708)562-1440
FAX: (708)562-6011

Monday-Friday: 9:30-9:00
Saturday and Sunday: 9:30-6:00

Precious Moments, Annalee dolls, Hummels, Cherished Teddies, Lilliput Lane, Silver Deer Crystal, Cat's Meow, Shelia's Houses, Enesco ornaments, Carlton ornaments, Thomas Kinkade, Sarah's Attic, Sports Impressions, Lizzie High, Little Cheesers, Calico Kittens, J. Bergsma, Michael's Ltd., Neil J. Rose, Hadley House, Dreamsicles, Lee Middleton dolls, PenniBears, Hamilton, Artaffects, J.H. Boone, Possible Dreams Santas, Midwest Importers, Roman, VickiLane Designs, and United Designs.

Layaways available. All major credit cards accepted. Open on holidays until 2:00.

GATZ COLLECTIBLES

971 North Milwaukee Ave.
Wheeling, IL 60090
PHONE: (708)541-4033

Tuesday-Sunday: 10:00-5:00

Bradford dealer, Hamilton, Sports Impressions, Edna Hibel, Goebel Miniatures, extensive selection of Norman Rockwell, Lowell Davis, Emmett Kelly Jr., DeGrazia, Greg Perillo plates and figurines, Lilliput Lane, Hawthorne Register, Ardleigh Elliott music boxes and eggs, Schmid Disney. Lithos: Terry Redlin, Donald Zolan, Edna Hibel, Sandra Kuck, Greg Perillo.

Visa, Mastercard and Discover accepted. Layaway. Free UPS shipping in the continental US.

MAY HALLMARK

1001 E. 75th St.
Woodridge, IL 60517
PHONE: (708)985-1008

Monday-Friday: 10:00-9:00
Saturday: 9:30-5:30; Sunday: 11:00-5:00

Bradford Dealer, Precious Moments, David Winter, Lilliput Lane, DeGrazia, Perillo, Krystonia, Pocket Dragons, Memories of Yesterday, Tom Clark Gnomes, Snowbabies, Colonial Village, Hallmark Galleries and ornaments, Iris Arc Crystal (Showcase Dealer) Enesco Musical Showcase, North Pole Village, and Cherished Teddies.

NALED member. All major credit cards accepted. A six week layaway program available. UPS shipping.

INDIANA

CAROUSEL COTTAGE

108 East Main St.
Albion, IN 46701
PHONE: (219)636-2614
FAX: (219)636-2936

Monday-Friday: 10:00-5:30
Saturday: 10:00-4:00

Bradford Exchange, Ashton-Drake, Hamilton Collection, Georgetown, Willitts Carousel Lines, Artaffects, Seymour Mann, Kingstate, Dynasty Dolls, Ginny Dolls, Dolls by Jerri, The Collectables, Iris Arc, Sandra Kuck, Lowell Davis, Laura's Attic, Reco, Hadley House, Marty Bell, Jan Hagara, Glynda Turley, Corinne Layton, Donald Zolan, Perillo, Enesco, Hamilton Gifts, John Hine Studios, The Ultimate Collection, H. Gunzel and many more.

Visa, Discover and Mastercard. Bradford Exchange Secondary Market. Redemption Center for Iris Arc, Hagara, Kuck, Davis, Bell, Tobin Fraley, The Collectables, Dolls by Jerri, and Sports Impressions.

SEASONS OF THE HEART GIFT SHOPPE

975 East 400 South
Anderson, IN 46013
PHONE: (317)642-0502

Monday-Saturday: 10:00-5:00; Thursday: 10:00-7:00; Sunday: 12:00-4:00

Offering the complete source for enduring Handcrafted Folk Art and Contemporary Country Trends. An exceptional collection of the best loved looks of American Country including Victorian and Primitive. Cat's Meow, Sarah's Attic, Maud Humphrey, Bessie Pease Gutmann, Miss Martha's Collection, Cherished Teddies, Calico Kittens, Frumps, Zook dolls, Creative Carvings, Don Parks Carved Bears, and Glynda Turley prints.

Mastercard, Visa and Discover accepted. Layaways available.

Location: From I-69, exit 26 and 1/2 mile south.

TURNER DOLL SHOP

4743 St. Rd. 46 East
Bloomington, IN 47401
PHONE: (812)336-5210
(812)336-5239

Monday-Saturday: 10:30-5:30

Southern Indiana's largest! At Turner Doll Shop you will find an excellent variety of dolls for the most discriminating collector. In their shop you will find dolls by: Virginia Turner, Yolanda Bello, Vickie Walker, Dolls by Jerri, Phyllis Parkins, Annette Himstedt, Rotraut Shrout, Zook, Hildegard Gunzel, Pat Thompson, Patricia Rose, Faith Wick, Hoffman, Julie Good-Kruger, Blythe and Snodgrass, and Wendy Lawton. They also carry Barbie, Corolle, Gotz, Berjusa, Madame Alexander, and Ginny. Animals from Steiff, Wendy Brendt, Dakin, Boyds, and North American Bear. A nice assortment of doll carriages, hanging basket swings, wicker and wood furniture. Come in and visit their shop. It's worth it!

MARKER'S

P.O. Box 66
603 W. South St.
Bremen, IN 46506
PHONE: (219)546-3111

Open Daily: 10:00-6:00

Specializing in rare, crown mark and variation Hummel figurines. Many pre-1970's vintage Hummels in stock. Buy or sell. Want a special Hummel figurine? It is either in stock or they can locate the desired collectible.

"Catering to the advanced Hummel figurine collector!"

Hummel figurines!!!

INDIANA

NANA'S STITCHIN' STATION
223 South Broadway
Bulter, IN 46721
PHONE: (219)868-5634

Mon., Tues., Thur., Fri.: 9:00-5:30
Wednesday and Saturday: 9:00-3:00

Precious Moments, All God's Children, Snowbabies, Lilliput Lane, David Winter, Sarah's Attic, Cherished Teddies, Laura's Attic, Jan Hagara, Maud Humphrey Bogart, P. Buckley Moss plates, ornaments, and figurines, PenniBears, United Design, Possible Dreams, Terry Redlin plates and prints, Sports Impressions, Memories of Yesterday.

Small Community Service with large selections.

NALED Member. Layaway. Mastercard and Visa accepted. Shipping available.

GNOME CROSSING
12564 Gray Rd.
Carmel, IN 46033
PHONE: (317)846-5577
FAX: (317)846-1528

Monday-Saturday: 10:00-6:00

David Winter Cottages, Lilliput Lane Cottages, LEGENDS Pewter, DeGrazia, Dept. 56 Cottages and Snowbabies, Hummels, Sarah's Attic, Miss Martha's Originals, Raikes Bears, Tom Clark Gnomes and Woodspirits, Enesco, Emmett Kelly Clowns, Duncan Royale Santas, Cherished Teddies, Maud Humphrey, Walt Disney Classics Collection, Lowell Davis and ANRI.

NALED member. Visa, Mastercard and Discover accepted. Secondary Market Dealer. UPS shipping everyday.

OUR COMPLIMENTS GIFT & FLORAL SHOP
232 W. Van Buren St.
Columbia City, IN 46725
PHONE: (219)244-6120

Monday-Thursday: 9:00-6:00;
Friday: 9:00-8:00; Saturday: 9:00-5:00

Your Collectible Headquarters! Plates, Dolls, Figurines--Precious Moments, Memories of Yesterday, Miss Martha's Originals, Maud Humphrey, Jan Hagara, Snowbabies, Norman Rockwell, Cherished Teddies, Dreamsicles, Sports Impressions, Lowell Davis, Castagna, Laura's Attic, Lilliput Lane Cottages, Ashton-Drake, Hamilton, Gorham, and Georgetown Dolls. Bradford Dealer.

Redemption Center for Club Memberships. Mastercard, Visa, and Discover accepted. Layaway. UPS shipping. Primary and Secondary Market.

THE CHRISTMAS GOOSE
203 N. Capitol Ave.
Corydon, IN 47112
PHONE: (812)738-7250

Monday-Saturday: 10:00-5:30
Sunday: 12:00-5:30

Tom Clark Gnomes, Dept. 56, LEGENDS, June McKenna, Seymour Mann, Ashton-Drake, Georgetown Collection, Zook Originals, Lee Middleton, Wimbleton, All God's Children, Sarah's Attic, WACO, Flambro, Mill Creek, J.H. Boone, Annalee, Raikes Bears, Possible Dreams, Christopher Radko, Steinbach, Enesco and German Steins, Cornell Imports, Anheuser-Busch, Emmett Kelly Jr., Cherished Teddies, United Design, Shelia's, Silvestri, Kurt S. Adler, Midwest Importers, Nutcrackers and Smokers.

Mastercard, Visa and Discover accepted.

INDIANA

ANTIQUE AND MODERN DOLL SHOP
136 N. 2nd St.
Decatur, IN 46733
PHONE: (219)728-2377

Monday-Saturday: 9:00-5:00

Specializing in one of a kind artist original dolls and limited editions since 1981: Anna Avigail Brahms, Kristy Hall, Vicki Gunnell, Gail Lackey, Monika, Pat Thompson, Carol Trobe, Kimberly Lasher and Karin Schmeling. Also Wendy Lawton, Jan Hagara, Collectables, Sonja Hartmann, Heidi Ott Originals, Kathe Kruse, Virginia Turner, Carin Lossnitzer, Gotz, Alexanders, Ginnys, Sandi McAslan, Miss Martha's, All God's Children (large selection), Muffy and accessories. Antique dolls. Located in the heart of Downtown Decatur. Three shops in one building: Doll Shop, Antique Shop and Soda Fountain. Many antique malls and antique shops in Decatur.

COLLECTORS' DELIGHT
2104 Station Ct.
Elkhart, IN 46517
**PHONE: (219)293-1163
(800)892-0443**

Tuesday-Saturday: 10:00-5:30

Open the door to their shop for Figurines: All God's Children, Jan Hagara, Memories of Yesterday, Tom Clark, Lil' Doll Collection, Miss Martha's, Calico Kittens, Salvino Sports, Amish Heritage Collection, Cherished Teddies. Dolls: Bradley, Resch, Victoria Ashlea, Gorham, GADCO, Gotz, Bradley, Dolls by Pauline, Jan Nahrgang, Himstedt, Dolls by Jerri, Sandra Kuck, Jan Hagara, Father Christmas by Judy Freske. Teddy Bears: Muffy and VanderBears, VIB's, Raikes, Steiff, Canterbury, Signature by Gund, Bonita, Merrythought, and Cooperstown.

30 day layaway plan available. Visa, Discover and Mastercard accepted. UPS Shipping available.

ROSE MARIE'S
1119 Lincoln Ave.
Evansville, IN 47714
PHONE: (800)637-5734

Monday-Thursday: 10:00-5:00;
Friday: 10:00-7:00; Saturday: 10:00-5:00

Rose Marie's will pay your club dues. Ask for details. Dept. 56 Showcase Dealer, Walt Disney Classics Collection, Precious Moments (DSR), MOY Heritage Dealer, ANRI, Hummel, Lladro, Swarovski, David Winter, Armani, Iris Arc, Fontanini, Duncan Royale, All God's Children, Sarah's Attic, Cherished Teddies, Maud Humphrey, Tom Clark, Lowell Davis, Emmett Kelly, Perillo, DeGrazia, Bubble Fairies, Miss Martha's, Krystonia, Byers' Choice, Steinbach, Sports Impressions, Bing & Grondahl, Royal Copenhagen, and many more!

NALED and GCC Member. Dept. 56 Secondary Market. Layaway available. UPS shipment daily, orders over $100 ship free. Visa, Mastercard and American Express.

GALLERY OF JORGENSENS
6226 Covington Rd.
Fort Wayne, IN 46804
**PHONE: (219)432-5519
FAX: (219)436-3950**

Mon., Tues., Thurs.: 9:00-5:30
Wed. and Fri.: 9:00-7:00; Sat.: 9:00-5:00

Located one mile from Hwy I 69 at Hwy 14. Serving the collector in all areas of collectibles for 17 years.

LEGENDS Premier Dealer, Chilmark, Mark Hopkins, Baldwin Brass, Lalique, Lladro, Duncan Royale, Steinbach Nutcrakers, David Winter, ANRI, M. Wideman, Fitz and Floyd, Disney Classics, Royal Doulton Bunnykins and Beatrix Potter, Hummel, Goebel Miniatures, Staffordshire, Maruri, Crummels, Limoges, Thomas Kinkade, Midwest Importers, Possible Dreams, Mayflower Glass and ANNA-PERENNA.

Club Redemption Center. Layaway and shipping. Mastercard, Visa and American Express accepted.

INDIANA

JUDD DRUGS

502 W. Pike St.
Goshen, IN 46526

PHONE: (219)533-2685
FAX: (219)534-0349

Monday-Saturday: 8:00-9:00
Sunday: 8:00-5:00

David Winter, Precious Moments, All God's Children, Dept. 56, Kurt S. Adler Nutcrackers and Santas, Reco plates, Dreamsicles, Cherished Teddies, Calico Kittens, Sisters, Willitts Designs, United Designs, J.H. Boone, Hallmark Keepsake Ornaments.

All major credit cards accepted. Layaway and shipping available. Redemption Center for Precious Moments. Gift wrapping available.

CYNTHIA'S HALLMARK SHOP

1560-A N. State St.
Greenfield, IN 46140

PHONE: (317)462-6749

Monday-Saturday: 9:00-8:30
Sunday: 11:30-5:00

Anheuser-Busch, Byers' Choice Ltd., Cast Art, Calico Kittens, Cat's Meow, CT, Christopher Collection, Dept. 56 (Heritage Village), Dreamsicles, EKJ, Enesco, Fenton, Flambro, Hallmark Ornaments, Hamilton Gifts, Harbour Lights, John Hine, Jan Hagara, Maud Humphrey, Josef, Kitty Cucumber, Ladie and Friends, Lance, MOY, Middleton Dolls, Midwest Importers, Miss Martha, Novelino, Partners in Crime, Possible Dreams, PM, Raikes Bears, Roman, Schmid, Shelia's, United Design, Willitts, IU, PU, Coca-Cola, Star Trek.

Layaway available. Shipping UPS anywhere in the US. All major credit cards accepted. Redemption Center for many of the above.

TERESA'S HALLMARK SHOP

520 N. State Rd. 135
Greenwood, IN 46142

PHONE: (317)888-1206

Monday-Friday: 10:00-8:00
Saturday: 10:00-6:00; Sunday: 12:00-5:00

Precious Moments, Lilliput, Cherished Teddies, Maud Humphrey, Calico Kittens, Memories of Yesterday, Snowbabies, Dept. 56 Snow Village, Fenton, Shelia's, Cat's Meow, Laura's Attic, Dreamsicles, plus an extensive selection of qualilty gifts.

Free gift wrapping. All major credit cards accepted. Shipping and layaway available.

CARD & GIFT GALLERY

Southern Plaza Shopping Center
4200 South U.S. 31
Indianapolis, IN 46227

PHONE: (317)783-1555
FAX: (317)784-8600

Monday-Saturday: 10:00-9:00
Sunday: 12:00-5:00

Specializing in collectibles and fine gifts. In business for 25 years. Precious Moments Distinguished Service Retailer, M.I. Hummel, Dept. 56, Tom Clark Gnomes, Emmett Kelly, Jr., David Winter Cottages, Lilliput Lane, Snowbabies, Walt Disney Classics, Memories of Yesterday, Cherished Teddies, Cast Art Dreamsicles, Miss Martha's, Pleasantville 1893, Forest Gnomes, Melody In Motion, Sports Impressions, Michael Garman Master Dealer, Neil Rose and Anheuser-Busch.

Redemption Center for all collectors clubs. All major credit cards accepted. Layaway and shipping available.

INDIANA

GRAHAM'S CRACKERS

5981 E. 86th St.
Indianapolis, IN 46250

**PHONE: (317)842-5727
(800)442-5727**

Mon.-Sat.: 10:00-9:00; Sun.: 12:00-5:00

Large selection of collectibles and festive atmosphere at this store! Over 400 different nutcrackers and smokers, along with hundreds of Russian nesting dolls. Lines: Dept. 56 Villages, Merry Makers, Snowbabies, All Thru The House, Tom Clark, Lilliput Lane, David Winter, Lizzie High, CT, Michael Garman, Maud Humphrey, Iris Arc, Enesco Musical Showcase Dealer, M.I. Hummel, Disney Classics, Byers' Choice, Steinbach, Sarah's Attic, PM, Miss Martha's, Christian Ulbricht Nutcrackers, Possible Dreams, and Dreamsicles.

Secondary Market Service in cottages and figurines. Layaway, charges and shipping available. Club Redemption Center.

KITS & KABOODLE

8701 Keystone Crossing
Indianapolis, IN 46240

**PHONE: (317)574-3333
(800)252-TOYS (Orders)**

Monday-Friday: 10:00-8:30
Saturday: 10:00-6:00; Sunday: 12:00-5:00

Dolls: R. John Wright, Jeckle-Jansen, Lenci, Sue & Jim Parker, Brigitte Deval, M. Iacona, A. Himstedt, Edna Dali, K. Lesher, Lawton's, Corolle, J. Shackleford Originals, S. Esche, Madame Alexander, J. Reuger, R. Schrott and Steiff.

Bears: Steiff, C. Kinser, B. Sixby, C. Levy, W. Brent, Beaver Valley, H. Hulen, VanderBears, V.I.B's, Gund and many more!

All major credit cards accepted. Layaway. Shipping. Free gift wrapping.

TINDER BOX

Castleton Square
6020 East 82nd St.
Indianapolis, IN 46250

**PHONE: (317)845-0806
(800)777-7240**

Monday-Saturday: 10:00-9:00
Sunday: 12:00-5:30

David Winter Cottages, Possible Dreams Santas, Chilmark Pewter, Sarah's Attic, Norman Rockwell, Bradford Exchange plate dealer, collectible teapots, Emmett Kelly Jr., Maruri porcelain, Marty's Herd, German Steins, and Harbour Lights Lighthouses.

The finest in pipes, tobaccos and cigars.

Major credit cards accepted. UPS shipping. Layaways available.

Second location is in the Washington Sq. 10202 E. Washington St. (317)899-2811.

THE LANDMARK GIFTS & ANTIQUES

1503 East Morgan St.
Kokomo, IN 46901

PHONE: (317)456-3488

Monday-Saturday: 10:00-5:00
Or By Appointment
24 Hour Answering Service

Specializing in the collectible business for 14 years. Featuring: Hummel, David Winter, Lowell Davis, Emmett Kelly Jr., Lilliput Lane, MOY, Maud Humphrey, All God's Children, Rick Cain Studios, Amish Heritage, Calico Kittens, Cherished Teddies, Laura's Attic, Precious Moments, Stamps of Elegance, Dreamsicles, Iris Arc, Possible Dreams, Pencil Santas by Designs Americana, Star Trek, and Toby Mugs.

Redemption Center for most collectible clubs. Major credit cards accepted. NALED member. Layaway available. Free shipping. Secondary Market Service for Hummels.

INDIANA

FRAN'S HALLMARK

8211 Broadway
Merrillville, IN 46410
PHONE: (219)738-2554
FAX: (219)738-2054

Monday-Saturday: 10:00-9:00
Sunday: 11:00-5:00
Extended Holiday Hours

Hallmark Galleries, Precious Moments, Memories Of Yesterday, Maud Humphrey Bogart, Cherished Teddies, Sports Impressions, Krystonia, Lilliput Lane, Dept. 56 Snow and Heritage Villages, Snowbabies, Dreamsicles, Byers' Choice Carolers, Spoontique.

Most major credit cards accepted. Layaway available. Redemption Center for the above lines. Free club membership renewal program.

THE CHRISTMAS HAUS

801-4 W. Wayne
Heritage Square
Middlebury, IN 46540
PHONE: (219)825-2883

January 1- May 1: 10:00-5:00 Daily
May-December 31: 9:00-8:00 Daily

Byers' Choice-Complete Selection, Roman Waterglobes and related Roman products. Fontanini, Gail Laura, Snowbabies. Communicorp: Coca-Cola ornaments, village and related accessories. Enesco Music Boxes, Clothtique Santas: Kurt Adler's Heritage Collection and Possible Dreams. Lefton Colonial Village, Imported German Nutcrackers. Premier Enesco Dealer-Treasury Ornaments including many retired pieces from 1988. Precious Moments dolls and accessory items. Cherished Teddies.

Visa, Mastercard and Discover accepted, as well as personal checks.

SMUCKER DRUGS INC.

108 S. Main St.-P.O. Box 66
Middlebury, IN 46540
PHONE: (219)825-2485
FAX: (219)825-7839

Mon.-Fri.: 8:00-8:00; Sat.: 8:00-6:00

Bradford plates. Ashton-Drake, Precious Moments (DSR), Cherished Teddies, Lladro, Lowell Davis, David Winter, Lilliput Lane, Dreamsicles, Golden Memories, Hummels, Hallmark Keepsake Ornaments, Laura's Attic, Miss Martha's, Shelia's, J.H. Boone, Maud Humphrey, Sports Impressions, Napoleon, Melody In Motion, Stanton Art: Emmett Kelly. Partners In Crime, United Design, Swarovski, Dave Grossman, Marty's Sculptures: The Herd. Dept. 56 (Snow Village, Heritage Village, Snowbabies), and Enesco Musicals.

Visa, Mastercard and Discover. NALED member and Bradford Dealer. Layaway. Free gift wrapping. Club Redemption Center.

PRINCESS FLOWER & GIFT SHOP

703 W. McKinley
Mishawaka, IN 46545
PHONE: (219)259-7474
(800)659-7473

Monday-Friday: 9:00-5:30
Saturday: 9:00-5:00

Featuring a large collection of collectibles! Lladro, Maud Humphrey, M.I. Hummel, Cherished Teddies, Calico Kittens, Bessie Pease Gutmann, Kitty Cucumber, V.F. Fine Art (Sandra Kuck), Possible Dreams, Anheuser-Busch, Sports Impressions, Sanidcast, bells, music boxes.

Older collectible pieces include ANRI, Charlotte BYI Redheads, Sebastian and Ispanky. Dolls: Susan Wakeen, Lee Middleton, Effanbee, Delton.

All major credit cards accepted. Layaway. Shipping. Collector club redemption center. In business since 1957.

INDIANA

BETTY'S CORNER

107 N. Main St.
Monticello, IN 47960

PHONE: (219)583-4025

Monday-Saturday: 9:00-5:00

Major doll lines: Naber Kids, Mattel, Barbie, Himstedt, Jeckle-Jansen, Mason, Gunzel, Georgetown, Goetz, GADCO, Ellenbrooke, Dolls by Jerri, Wakeen, Robin Woods, World, Middleton, Seymour Mann, Dynasty Dolls, Kuck dolls and plates, Perillo dolls, figurines and plates. Silver Deer, Castagna figurines, McClelland figurines, Raikes Bears, Steinbach nutcrackers and smokers.

Visa, Mastercard, and Discover accepted. Layaway program available.

NORWAY GARDENS

306 Walleston St.
Monticello, IN 47960

PHONE: (219)583-3811

Monday-Friday: 9:00-5:30
Saturday: 9:00-5:00; Sunday: 10:00-4:00
Extended Hours May and December

In business for 23 years. Dept. 56 Showcase Dealer, Precious Moments, Lincoln County Garden Club Collection, United Design Antique Santas, Cherished Teddies, Kurt S. Adler Santas and Byers' Choice Carolers.

Yankee candles, a garden center specializing in herbs and perennials, complete Christmas shop from mid-October through December.

Visa and Mastercard accepted. Shipping and layaway available. Specializes in gourmet food packs and fruit baskets for holiday giving. Display gardens during Summer.

CAROL'S CRAFTS

125 S. Van Buren
P.O. Box 960
Nashville, IN 47448

**PHONE: (800)345-6388
(812)988-6388**

Open 7 Days A Week: 10:00-5:00

Goebel Miniatures, ANRI, Lilliput Lane, Chilmark, Sarah's Attic, Snowbabies, Miss Martha's, Memories of Yesterday, Winter Silhouette, Lowell Davis, Enesco's Small World Musicals, Walt Disney Classics Collection and Possible Dreams.

American Express, Visa and Mastercard accepted. Shipping is available. Newletters published to keep collectors informed.

WATSON'S

135 E. Michigan St.
P.O. Box 29
New Carlisle, IN 46552

**PHONE: (800)348-2530
(219)654-3550
FAX: (219)654-3969**

Monday-Saturday: 9:00-6:00

Outstanding display of collectible plates, figurines and limited edition prints since 1970. All God's Children, Armani, Ashton-Drake dolls, Byers' Choice Carolers, Lowell Davis, Ray Day, David Winter Cottages, Dept. 56 Showcase Dealer, Duncan Royale, Hagara, Hibel, Hummel, Thomas Kinkade Premier Dealer, Kuck, Lilliput Lane Cottages, Lladro, P. Buckley Moss plates and prints, Terry Redlin, Perillo, Precious Moments, Sarah's Attic, and Swarovski.

An Authorized Bradford Exchange Dealer. NALED member.

INDIANA

R. HOPPE JEWELERS & GIFTS

900 Promenade
Richmond, IN 47374

PHONE: (317)935-2488

Monday-Saturday: 9:30-5:00
Friday: 9:30-8:00

Dept. 56 Showcase Dealer, Precious Moments (DSR), EKJ, Hummel, ANRI, Duncan Royale, Lladro, Waterford, Chilmark, Cain Studios, J.H. Boone, Disney, Raikes Bears, Melody In Motion, Enesco Musicals, David Winter, MOY, Anheuser, Steinbach, Calico Kittens, CT, Sarah's Attic, Miss Martha, Gorham Dolls, Dynasty, Rockwell, Anheuser-Busch.

GCC Member. Redemption Center. Secondary Market in cottages. Layaway. In-House and major credit cards accepted. UPS shipping and free gift wrapping.

Second Location: Richmond Square Mall, Richmond IN 47374. (317)962-7411.

THE BOOK STORE

826 Main St.
Rochester, IN 46975

PHONE: (219)223-3817
FAX: (219)223-6369

Monday-Friday: 8:00-5:00
Saturday: 9:00-5:00

Selling collectibles for 14 years. This 125 year-old business originally sold school books, but is now primarily a collectible store and art gallery.

Tom Clark Gnomes, Jan Hagara, Hadley House, Ray Day plates, Lilliput, Raikes Bears, EKJ, Enesco and Hamilton Dealer, Hamilton Gifts, Sarah's Attic, Cherished Teddies, Dept. 56 Snow Villages and Snowbabies, LEGENDS, Anheuser-Busch, Krystonia, Lowell Davis, Lizzie High, Thomas Kinkade, Rockwell, Roman Classic Brides and Melody In Motion.

Redemption Center. Bradford Dealer. Layaway. Major credit cards. Shipping available. Secondary Market Service.

ALWAYS CHRISTMAS

State Road 5N P.O. Box 655
Shipshewana, IN 46565

PHONE: (219)768-7236

Monday-Saturday: 9:00-5:00

Always Christmas--a unique Christmas store! Featuring Byers' Choice, Duncan Royale Santas, Lefton, United Design Santas and Angels, Enesco: Treasury of Ornaments, Angels and Nativities; Laura's Attic, Old World Christmas Ornaments and Nutcrackers, Christopher Radko, Vaillancourt, and Cherished Teddies. An extensive selection of handmade santas and ornaments!

Visa and Mastercard accepted. Layaway and shipping available. Secondary market and free gift wrapping!

THE TOWN SHOP

115 N. Morton St.
Shipshewana, IN 46565

PHONE: (800)435-4442

Monday-Saturday: 9:00-5:00
Closed Sunday

The Town Shop is located in the heart of Northern Indiana's Amish Country. The area's largest Dept. 56 Dealer including: Heritage Village, Snow Village and the entire Snowbabies Collection! Also carrying the Possible Dreams Santa Collection featuring all the new releases. The Town Shop is the "Santa Claus Network" connection. Looking for Seymour Mann limited edition dolls? The complete line is in stock. Also featuring "The Bennett Collection" of limited edition lithographs by Linda Bennett, noted Northern Indiana Artist. Linda's work is primarily rich Amish Heritage scenes in soft pastels.

Visa and Mastercard. Layaway and shipping! Call or write for brochure.

INDIANA

ALLEANS COLLECTABLES

Thieves Market
Corner of Ironwood and Edison
South Bend, IN 46635
PHONE: (219)233-9820

Saturday and Sunday: 10:00-6:00

Housed in an interesting antique mall setting, Allean's Collectibles boasts a large collection of Bradford plates and Ashton-Drake dolls. They also carry: Hummels, Precious Moments, ANRI Woodcarvings, Jan Hagara, Maud Humphrey, Lowell Davis, and Cherished Teddies.

Secondary Market Service on lines listed. Layaway available. Visa and Mastercard accepted.

THE GOOD IDEAS CO.

407 Dixieway North
South Bend, IN 46637
PHONE: (219)277-6184
FAX: (219)277-6204

Monday-Wednesday: 10:00-6:00
Thursday and Friday: 10:00-7:00
Saturday: 10:00-6:00

Dolls: Kewpies, Constance Collection, Madame Alexander, Ginny's, Seymour Mann, Zook, Annette Himstedt, Hildegard Gunzel, Robin Woods, Gotz, Artist Collectables, Val Shelton Originals, Daddy's Long Legs. Bears: Herman, Steiff, VanderBears, PenniBears, Tide-Rider, Gund. Also: Laura's Attic, Miss Martha, Bennett's Brush Strokes, Jan Hagara, Wee Forest Folk, handmade quilts, Celebration quilts, Detweiler Wood Quilts, and retired Longaberger baskets (new baskets by order only).

Mastercard and Visa accepted. Layaway available. Secondary Market.

KAGEL'S DOLLS, GALLERY & GIFTS

602 N. Michigan
South Bend, IN 46601
PHONE: (219)233-2232

Monday-Friday: 9:00-5:30
Saturday: 10:00-2:00

Edna Hibel: lithos, prints and plates. Madame Alexander-largest selection in the mid-west, Bradford Exchange Dealer, Ashton-Drake, M. Martiros-world renowned artist, Lawton, Annette Himstedt, Good-Kruger, Fred Stone, Hadley House prints-Franca and Redlin, Lladro Golden Memories Collection.

Most major credit cards accepted. Layaway plan. Shipping throughout the U.S. Redemption Center for Hibel.

MAJEREK'S HALLMARK

North Village Mall
52565 U.S. 31 North
South Bend, IN 46637
PHONE: (219)277-1282

Daily: 9:00-9:00; Sunday: 12:00-5:00

Plates: Bing & Grondahl, Reco, Hamilton, Bradford. Dept. 56: All Villages, Snowbabies, Accessories, Merry Makers, All Thru the House. Precious Moments, Enesco Musicals, Cherished Teddies, Calico Kittens, Sisters and Best Friends, Tom Clark, Byers' Choice, Laura's Attic, Maud Humphrey, Lladro, David Winter, Sports Impressions, Hummels and Hallmark Ornaments. Also Crabtree & Evelyn.

Visa, Mastercard and American Express. Layaway. Shipping. GCC Member. 19 other locations throughout Northern Indiana and Southwest Michigan. For additional store information call the corporate office at (616)684-5115.

INDIANA/IOWA

PHILIPS GIFT GALLERY

3100 North Calumet
Valparaiso, IN 46383

PHONE: (219)464-8687
FAX: (219)465-1231

Monday-Friday: 8:00-8:00
Saturday: 8:00-5:00; Sunday: 9:00-4:00

Red Skelton originals, oil transfers/ books/ figurines/ plates!!

Walt Disney Classics Collection.

Swarovski, Department 56, Bradford Dealer, United Design, Emmett Kelly, Jr., Hummel, Precious Moments, Southwest lithographs.

Serving their customers for 14 years. Secondary Market service. Personal service in collectibles. Major credit cards accepted. Layaway available.

TEMPTATIONS COLLECTIBLES & GIFTS

13 Lincolnway
Valparaiso, IN 46383

PHONE: (219)462-1000

Monday-Saturday: 10:00-5:00

Collectibles and unique gifts can be found in this gift shop located in Downtown Valparaiso. Dept. 56, David Winter, Lilliput Lane, Precious Moments, Hummels, Lowell Davis, Memories of Yesterday, Goebel, Sports Impressions, Cherished Teddies, Perillo, Dreamsicles, Maud Humphrey, Krystonia, and other figurines, plates, dolls and collectibles that will remain in the family for generations.

Browse in their gift shop where you will receive service with a smile.

NALED member. Layaways welcome. Secondary Market service. All major credit cards honored.

HAWK HOLLOW

106 S. Riverview
Bellevue, IA 52031

PHONE: (319)872-5467

Open 7 Days A Week: 9:00-5:00

Disney Classics Collection, Lladro, PM, Lowell Davis, Armani, Hummel, all Dept. 56 Villages, Snow Village, Dickens Village, Bradford, Madame Alexander, Gorham, Raikes, Lilliput Lane, David Winter, Sarah's Attic, Emmett Kelly, Rockwell, Good-Kruger, DeGrazia, P. Buckley Moss, Sandra Kuck, Tom Clark, Memories of Yesterday, Snowbabies, ANRI, Ashton-Drake dolls, Maud Humphrey, Maruri, Possible Dreams, Bing & Grondahl, Perillo and Willitts.

Second location is at: 103 S. Main St., Galena, IL 61036. Phone (815)777-3616.

Mastercard and Visa accepted. NALED member. Layaway and shipping available. Free gift wrapping.

C & H WORLD OF PLATES

2726 Matthew Dr. S.W.
Cedar Rapids, IA 52404

PHONE: (319)390-3319

Tuesday-Friday: 10:00-4:00
Sunday: 12:00-4:00

Plates, Frames, Stands, Zolan Lithographs and Plaques. Zolan trading center. Most collector plates available.

Terry Redlin, Sandra Kuck, Greg Perillo, Red Skelton, and Hamilton.

Large Secondary Market. Phone answered 24 hours a day--leave a message.

Shipping available. Layaway.

IOWA

COUNTRY 'N MORE

Mall of the Bluffs
1751 Madison Ave.
Council Bluffs, IA 51501

PHONE: (712)322-6640
FAX: (712)322-7017

Monday-Saturday: 10-9; Sunday: 12-6

All Dept. 56 Villages, Snowbabies and All Through the House, Coca-Cola Collectibles by Communicorp International, MOY, All God's Children, Miss Martha's Originals, Jan Hagara, David Winter, Maud Humphrey, Calico Kittens, Sisters & Best Friends, Willitts Carousels, P. Buckley Moss plates and sculptures, Richard Zolan plates and miniature pictures, Raikes, Amish Heritage Collection, Fontanini, Possible Dreams, Kurt Adler Santas, Enesco Treasury of Christmas Ornaments.

Visa, Mastercard and Discover accepted. Layaway. Shipping. Redemption Center. Always adding new collectibles.

All calls welcome!

GIFTIQUE

1235 Merle Hay Mall
Des Moines, IA 50310

PHONE: (515)278-5730

Monday-Saturday: 10:00-9:00
Sunday: 11:00-6:00

Precious Moments, Memories of Yesterday, Dept. 56 Showcase Dealer, David Winter, Emmett Kelly, Jr., Hummels, Jan Hagara, Cherished Teddies, Krystonia, Dreamsicles, Lowell Davis, ANRI, Tom Clark, All God's Children, Lladro, LEGENDS, Fenton Art Glass, Pewter, Swarovski Crystal, Norman Rockwell plates, wedding and anniversary items, fine gifts and music boxes for all occasions. Preferred doll dealer for Precious Moments Company.

Layaways and phone orders are available. Visa, Mastercard and Discover accepted. Redemption Center for major collector clubs. Free shipping and free gift wrapping.

GIFTED, LTD.

100 Old Capitol Center
Iowa City, IA 52240

PHONE: (319)338-4123

Monday-Friday: 10:00-9:00
Saturday: 10:00-6:00; Sunday: 12:00-5:00

Byers' Choice, Possible Dreams Santas, Precious Moments, Dept. 56, Lladro figurines, Swarovski Crystal, Gorham Crystal, Austin & Alva Museum Replicas, Emmett Kelly Clowns, Sandicast Animals, Norman Rockwell figurines, Stannard & Woodstock Wind Chimes, Virginia Metalcrafters brass, Capodimonte flowers, Isabel Bloom garden sculptures, and Hummel figurines.

UPS shippng and free gift wrapping. Gift certificates and layaway available. All major credit cards accepted.

COMMEMORATIVE IMPORTS GALLERY

4140 Eagle Ave.
Ireton, IA 51027

PHONE: (712)278-2024

Monday-Sunday: 10:00-7:00

Wild Wing figurines, lithographs, plates and accessories, Reco, Sandra Kuck, Ray Day, Steiner Prints, Hollywood Limited Edition Plates including Bradford, Elvis by Delphi. Precious Moments Gold Cards, John Hine Studio Inc., Zolan and Canadian Plates.

Some back listings of plates and prints. Check or cash accepted. Shipping by UPS available.

IOWA

HICKORY HOUSE

819 North Court
Ottumwa, IA 52501
**PHONE: (515)682-8391
(800)247-1075**

Monday-Saturday: 9:00-5:00

Enesco: Precious Moments, Cherished Teddies, Calico Kittens, Partners in Crime, Sisters & Best Friends, Enesco Musicals, MOY, Miss Martha, Treasury Ornaments, Maud Humphrey, B.P. Gutmann. Lladro Golden Memories, M.I. Hummel, Dept. 56: All Villages, Snowbabies, All Thru the House, Merry Makers, B & G/RC, DeGrazia, Lowell Davis, Fenton and Gorham crystal, Dreamsicles, Krystonia, Midwest Importers, Roman, Fontanini, Andrea by Sadek, Flambro, Dave Grossman, Maruri, Napoleon Capodimonte, PM dolls and much more.

All major credit cards accepted. Layaway. Mail order. Free gift wrapping. Fall catalogs from GCC and Retail Resources.

BRENDLEE'S HALLMARK
FINE GIFTS & COLLECTIBLES

516 Grand Ave.
Spencer, IA 51301
**PHONE: (712)262-4145
(800)285-4145**

Monday-Saturday: 9:30-5:30

All Dept. 56 Collectibles including Villages, Snowbabies, All Through the House and Merry Makers, Tom Clark Gnomes, Precious Moments, Memories of Yesterday, David Winter Cottages, Lilliput Lane, Beatrix Potter, Possible Dreams Santas, Nutcrackers, Rock Santas, Hallmark Christmas Ornaments, Cherished Teddies, Calico Kittens, Dreamsicles, Reco collectors plate (Sandra Kuck, Jody Bergsma), and Napoleon Capodimonte.

Secondary market dealer in Tom Clark Gnomes. Some retired Dept. 56 pieces are available. Visa, Mastercard and Discover are accepted. Layaways available. Will ship UPS nationwide.

CHRISTMAS STOCKING

619 Elm Ave.
Story City, IA 50248
PHONE: (515)733-4145

Monday-Saturday: 9:30-5:00

Possible Dreams, Dept. 56, Dickens, New England, North Pole Villages, Snowbabies lighthouses and accessories, Winter Silhouettes, Memories of Yesterday, Hummel, Enesco Ornaments, Raikes Bears, Muffy VanderBear and accessories, Calico Kittens, Old World Christmas Ornaments, Christopher Radko, Byers' Choice Carolers, Fitz & Floyd, The Collectables, June McKenna, Porsgrund, Sebastian, Nutcrackers, Collectible Santas, Cornhusk dolls by Nan.

Mastercard and Visa accepted. Layaway and shipping available. Redemption Center.

Located in Scandia Centre.

HOMESTEAD HOUSE

2118 Kimball Ave.
Waterloo, IA 50702
PHONE: (319)233-4404

Monday-Friday: 9:00-8:00; Saturday: 9-5
Sunday: 12:30-5:00

Lladro, Lalique, Armani, Hummels, Isabel Bloom, ANRI, Golden Memories, Francis Hook, Flambro (Emmett Kelly), Memories of Yesterday, Maud Humphrey, Sarah's Attic, Cat's Meow, Jan Hagara, Lowell Davis, Bing & Grondahl, Chilmark, Fenton Eggs, Royal Copenhagen, Raikes, Maruri, Dept. 56 Houses and Snowbabies, David Winter, Rockwells, Duncan Royale, Russian plates and boxes, Moussali, Bradley dolls, Austin Sculptures, Cherished Teddies, Dolphi (Lisi Martin), Hallmark ornaments, Enesco ornaments, Beatrix Potter, Kitty Cucumber, Anheuser-Busch, P. Buckley Moss plates, Bradford Exchange, Miss Martha Originals, Possible Dreams, WACO, and Roman Inc..

IOWA/KANSAS

BRODERICKS

1551 Valley West Dr. #281
West Des Moines, IA 50266

PHONE: (515)225-3764

Monday-Saturday: 10:00-9:00
Sunday: 12:00-5:30

Dept. 56 Villages, Snowbabies, Precious Moments, Byers' Choice, Swarovski, Cairn Studio, Hummels, Lladro, P. Buckley Moss, ANRI, Lowell Davis, Walt Disney Classic Collection, All God's Children, Maud Humphrey, Jan Hagara, Artaffects Ltd., Artists of the World, Bing & Grondahl, Cast Art, Cherished Teddies, Daddy's Long Legs, Flambro Imports, J.H. Boone, Lailique, Middleton Dolls, and Possible Dreams. Music boxes, dolls, and anniversary plates also in stock.

Visa, Mastercard, and Discover accepted.
GCC Member.

RURAL ROOSTER

Rural Route #1 Box 172
McPherson, KS 67460

**PHONE: (316)241-1959
(800)864-1086**

Monday-Saturday: 9:00-5:00

Tom Clark Gnomes, Tim Wolfe, Dolls by Jerri, Lowell Davis, Maud Humphrey, LEGENDS, Muffy VanderBear, Hummels, Sarah's Attic, All God's Children, Raikes, Annalee, Jan Hagara's Complete line of dolls, bears, wall decor, etc., Memories of Yesterday, Armani, Marty Bell, Ashton-Drake dolls, Laura's Attic, Cherished Teddies, Gartlan USA, Sports Impressions, Roosevelt Bears, P. Buckley Moss, Dreamsicles, Possible Dreams, United Design, Duncan Royale, Frumps, Briercroft, Bavarian Wax and other santas.

Secondary Market on all my lines. Redemption Center. Layaways.

"You have to see it to believe it!"

CAROL'S CARDS & GIFTS

5285 West 95th St.
Overland Park, KS 66207

**PHONE: (913)642-8850
FAX: (913)642-5482**

Weekdays: 9:00-5:30
Saturday: 9:30-5:00

Precious Moments, Enesco Musicals, Memories of Yesterday, Miss Martha's, Cherished Teddies, Calico Kittens, PenDelfin, Snowbabies, Swarovski, Laura's Attic, and Shelia's Houses.

Mastercard and Visa accepted. Secondary Market Selection. Free gift wrapping and shipping.

GIFTS & ACCENTS

Metcalf South Mall
9611 Metcalf Ave.
Overland Park, KS 66212

PHONE: (800)822-8856

Monday-Saturday: 10:00-9:00
Sunday: 12:00-5:30

Precious Moments (DSR), Hummels, Memories of Yesterday, Dept. 56, David Winter, Lilliput Lane, Disney Classics, Lowell Davis, Goebel Miniatures, DeGrazia, Enesco Musicals, Jan Hagara, Tom Clark Gnomes, Sports Impressions, Gartlan, Bradford plates, Ashton-Drake dolls, collectible plates by Reco, Artaffects, and Hamilton, All God's Children, Sarah's Attic, Swarovski, Krystonia, Emmett Kelly, Madame Alexander dolls, Gotz dolls, Norman Rockwell, Fenton Glass and Sandicast.

Visa, Mastercard and Discover accepted. Layaway and shipping available.

KANSAS

CHURCHILL'S

West Ridge Mall
1801 S.W. Wanamaker
Topeka, KS 66604

PHONE: (913)273-0102
FAX: (913)272-6099

Monday-Saturday: 10:00-9:00
Sunday: 12:00-6:00

Chilmark, LEGENDS, Tom Clark Gnomes, David Winter, Swarovski Lead Crystal, collectible knives, Emmett Kelly Jr., Summerhill Crystal, and Michael Garman Sculptures. Churchill's also carries custom blended tobaccos, imported cigars, and collectible pipes, available by mail order.

Visa, Mastercard and American Express accepted. Layaways welcome.

COPPERFIELD

West Ridge Mall
1801 S.W. Wanamaker
Topeka, KS 66604

PHONE: (913)273-0085
FAX: (913)272-6099

Monday-Saturday: 10:00-9:00
Sunday: 12:00-6:00

Dept. 56 Dickens Village, Krystonia, Hallmark Galleries, Precious Moments, Lilliput Lane, Possible Dreams, Memories of Yesterday, Lowell Davis, Rick Cain Studios Inc., Cherished Teddies, Clay Art, Enesco Treasury of Christmas Ornaments, Enesco Small World of Musicals, Hallmark Keepsake Ornaments, Sandicast, United Design, Walt Disney Collectibles and Sabino Art Glass.

Visa, Mastercard and American Express accepted. Layaway available.

THE HOURGLASS

4600 W. Kellogg Towne West Sq.
Wichita, KS 67209

PHONE: (316)942-0562
(800)874-7564
FAX: (316)942-3657

Monday-Saturday: 10:00-9:00
Sunday: 12:30-5:30

Swarovski, Steiff, Hummel, David Winter, Lowell Davis, Lladro, Krystonia, Precious Moments, Cherished Teddies, Byers' Choice, Memories of Yesterday, Bossons, Snowbabies, Ashton-Drake Dolls, and Bradford Exchange.

NALED Member. Free gift wrapping.

LANCELOT'S

1700 E. Douglas
Wichita, KS 67214

PHONE: (316)267-3206
FAX: (316)267-3738

Monday-Saturday: 9:30-5:30
Sunday: 1:00-5:00 November-December

Hummel, Lladro, Duncan Royale, Flambro, Emmett Kelly Jr., Lilliput Lane, David Winter, Dept. 56, All God's Children, Precious Moments, Tom Clark Gnomes, Armani, Disney, Annalee, Iris Arc, Laura's Attic, Possible Dreams, Sarah's Attic, Roman, Royal Copenhagen, LEGENDS, Stanton Arts, Bing & Grondahl, Toby Maude, and Harbour Lights.

All on the Secondary and Primary Markets.

No consignments. Buy outright.

KANSAS/KENTUCKY

SEVEN SEAS

920 S. Oliver
Wichita, KS 67218

PHONE: (316)682-4981

Monday-Saturday: 10:00-5:30

Precious Moments, Hummel, Lowell Davis, the largest dealer of ANRI in Kansas, Michael Garman, Chilmark, Disney Classics, Memories of Yesterday, Cairn Studios, Dept. 56, Annalee, Jan Hagara, Sarah's Attic, Miss Martha's, Bessie Pease Gutmann, Limoge boxes, jewelry, a large collection of Victorian supplies.

Visa and Mastercard accepted. Layaway and shipping available. Secondary Market Service available for Chilmark and Precious Moments.

BRASS LANTERN RESTAURANT AND GIFTS

Hwy. 68
Aurora, KY 42048

PHONE: (502)474-2773
FAX: (502)474-2777

Open at 5:00PM Everyday in Summer
Closed Mon. and Tues. in Spring and Fall
Closed in Winter
(Open anytime by Appointment)

Shop and dine in rustic elegant atmosphere. Gifts, jewelry and decorative accessories. Collectibles include Byers' Choice, Michaels Ltd./Brian Baker, Lizzie High, Dept. 56/ Snowbabies, Vaillancourt Folk Art, Leo R. Smith III, Possible Dreams, and Duncan Royale.

In business for over 20 years. Located near Kentucky Lake. All major credit cards accepted. Shipping available.

BETSY'S HALLMARK

408 E 12TH St.
Benton, KY 42025

PHONE: (502)527-1848

Monday-Saturday: 9:00-6:00
Sunday: 1:00-5:00

Precious Moments, Dept. 56, David Winter, Hummels, Cherished Teddies, Snowbabies, All God's Children, Emmett Kelly, Jr., Lowell Davis, Maud Humphrey Bogart, Goebel, Duncan Royale, Hallmark ornaments, Lizzie High dolls, Reed and Barton, Krystonia, Iris Arc, Dreamsicles, Dave Grossman Creations, Hallmark Keepsake Ornaments, J.H. Boone, Lefton Colonial Villages, Possible Dreams, Spode, and Wedgwood.

Visa and Mastercard accepted. Layaway available. 1-800-974-1848 (In the 502 area code only). UPS shipping.

1890'S GIFT SHOP

307 3rd St.
Henderson, KY 42420

PHONE: (502)826-2198

Open Daily: 9:00-5:30

Located in a twelve room Victorian Home. Lines include: Hummel, Lladro, Waterford, Bing & Grondahl, Henford Heirlooms, Sarah's Attic, Sadek Birds, Lowell Davis, Possible Dreams Santas, Tom Clark Gnomes, Boyd's Bears, Rowe Pottery, Fitz and Floyd, VanderBear, Fontanini, Beatrix Potter figurines.

Visa and Mastercard accepted. Layaway and shipping available. Redemption Center. Free gift wrapping.

KENTUCKY/LOUISIANA

ANN'S

2909 Richmond Rd.
Lexington, KY 40509

PHONE: (606)266-9101
FAX: (703)989-6640

Monday-Friday: 10-9; Sunday: 12-5

Dept. 56, Precious Moments, Memories of Yesterday, Tom Clark Gnomes, Hummel, David Winter Cottages, Lilliput Lane, Lowell Davis, Cat's Meow, Shelia's, Fontanini, Annalee Mobilitee.

Stores also located at: 3355 Tates Creek, Lexington, KY 40502. Phone: (606)266-7302.

1082 Florence Mall, Florence, KY 41042. Phone: (606)525-7007.

6268 Glenway Ave., Western Woods Center, Cincinnati, OH 45211 Phone: (513)662-2021.

NALED member. All major credit cards accepted. Layaway available. Gold Crown frequent shopper card accepted.

YE OLE COUNTRY PEDDLER

1255 Natural Bridge Rd.
Slade, KY 40376

PHONE: (606)663-2683
(606)668-6256
(606)668-3596

Open Daily: 9:30-9:00

Dept. 56: All Villages, Snowbabies, All Through the House, Merry Makers, and regular Dept. 56 gift lines. John Hine Studios, David Winter Cottages, Maurice Wideman, Shoemaker's Dream, Anheuser-Busch Steins, Fenton Art Glass, Daniel Monfort Cowboys and Indians, Knot Knoggins, Spirit of the Redman by Mill Creek Studio, Calico Cottage Fudge, Dreamsicles, Enesco Calico Kittens, Nightwatch Lamps, Yankee Candle Co., and Emmett Kelly Jr.

Visa, Mastercard, and Discover accepted.

PLATES AND THINGS

14032 Jefferson Hwy.
Baton Rouge, LA 70817

PHONE: (504)753-2885
ORDERS: (800)345-1259

Monday-Saturday: 10:00-5:00

Stop by and enjoy browsing through a large selection of limited edition (current and secondary) plates, figurines, music boxes, etc. Lines include: Ashton-Drake Dolls. Works by Artaffects, Bradford Exchange, Bing & Grondahl, W.S. George, Dave Grossman, Hamilton, Edwin M. Knowles, Ardleigh Elliott, Hawthorne, Pemberton & Oakes, V.F. Fine Arts, Frames by Lynette Decor and Van Hygan and Smythe. A large selection by Lowell Davis, Fred Stone, and other artists. Authorized Bradford Dealer.

SOMETHING SPECIAL GIFTS

11831 Coursey Blvd.
Baton Rouge, LA 70816

PHONE: (504)292-2035

Monday-Friday: 9:30-6:00; Saturday: 10-3

Goebel Miniatures, Maud Humphrey, Sports Impressions, Sandicast, Precious Moments, P. Buckley Moss, Thomas Kinkade, Fenton Art Glass, Mark Hopkins Bronze, Sabino Crystal, Colonial Village by Lefton, Duncan Royale, Fontanini, Hudson Pewter, Steinbach Crystal, Steinbach Steins, Steinbach Nutcrackers, Sarah's Attic, Memories of Yesterday, Cherished Teddies, Emmett Kelly Jr., Fraser Creations, Gorham Dolls, Lilliput Lane, Dave Grossman Creations, Iris Arc Crystal, Jan Hagara, Ron Lee Clowns, PenDelfin, Reco, Red Mill Mfg., Roman, United Design, VickiLane Designs, Willitts Designs, Bradley Dolls, Creart, Napoleon, Armani, and American Greetings.

LOUISIANA

COLLECTOR'S WORLD

Heart O' Bossier
Shopping Center #19
1701 Old Minden Rd.
Bossier City, LA 71111

PHONE: (318)746-3053

Monday-Friday: 10:00-5:00
Saturday: 10:00-4:00

ANRI, Lowell Davis, M.I. Hummel, Sandra Kuck, Sebastian Miniatures, Sports Impressions, Sandicast, Greenwich Workshop, Mill Pond Press, John Stobart, Maruri, Bradford Exchange, Fred Stone, Hadley House, Ron Lee, Reco International and United Design.

Secondary market print service. Hummel Club Redemption Center. Custom framing. Visa and Mastercard accepted. Shipping available.

ROSE MARIE'S GIFTS

1307 N. Parkerson
Crowley, LA 70526

PHONE: (318)783-1324

Monday-Friday: 9:30-5:00
Saturday: 10:00-3:00

Nestled in a 75-year-old quaint cottage. Serving the collectors for 12 years. Located just off Highway 13 on Parkerson Ave.

Dept. 56 including Dickens Village, Snow Village, North Pole, Christmas in the City, New England, accessories, Snowbabies, All Through the House, Merry Makers and Winter Silhouette, Kurt S. Adler Santas, United Design, All God's Children, Cast Art, Reco plates and Edna Hibel Collection.

Club Redemption Center. Layaway. All major credit cards accepted. Tax free for international visitors. Shipping and free gift wrapping.

LA TIENDA

4000 Johnston St.
Lafayette, LA 70503

PHONE: (318)984-5920

Open Daily: 9:30-5:30

Armani, Bradford, Dept. 56 Showcase Dealer, Duncan Royale, Hummel, Lilliput Lane, Maruri, United Design, Schmid, Roman, Krystonia, Sarah's Attic, Maud Humphrey, Sebastian, Hibel, Sandra Kuck, Corinne Layton, Hamilton Collection, Sports Impressions, Jan Hagara, Lowell Davis, Thomas Kinkade, Reco, Cherished Teddies, Walt Disney, MOY, Marty Bell, Glynda Turley, Patti Bannister, Brenda Burke, and Dreamsicles.

The collection acquired reflects 25 years in business. All major credit cards accepted. NALED and GCC member. Layaway plan available. Secondary Market.

GALILEAN COLLECTIBLES & GIFTS

1804 C South 5th Street
Leesville, LA 71446

PHONE: (318)239-6248
(800)264-6248

Monday-Saturday: 10:00-7:00

Bradford Dealer, David Winter, M.I. Hummel, PenDelfin, Leroy, Miss Martha, Laura's Attic, Memories of Yesterday, Maud Humphrey, Jan Hagara, Lowell Davis, Sports Impressions, Gartlan, Pro-Sport, Sarah's Attic, Precious Moments, Emmett Kelley Jr., Chilmark, Maruri, Napoleon, Shoemaker's Dream, Wideman, Colonial Village, Norman Rockwell, Hollywood plates, Muffy Bear, Sandicast, and Dreamsicles.

NALED member. All major credit cards accepted. Ship UPS anywhere. Free shipping over $50. Layaway. Free gift wrap. Personal attention.

LOUISIANA

AD LIB

Lakeside Shopping Center
Metairie, LA 70002

PHONE: (504)835-8755

Monday-Saturday: 10:00-9:00
Sunday: 12:00-6:00

David Winter, Lilliput Lane, M.I. Hummel, Maud Humphrey, Dept. 56: Snow Village, Dickens and Snowbabies. Miss Martha's Originals, Lowell Davis, Cherished Teddies, Jan Hagara, Laura's Attic, Precious Moments, and Treasured Memories.

In business for 27 years. All major credit cards accepted. Layaway plan with no charge and no time limit. UPS Shipping.

THE PARTRIDGE CHRISTMAS SHOP

105 Riverwalk, 1 Poydras St.
New Orleans, LA 70130

**PHONE: (504)566-0149
(504)892-4477
(SHIPPING ORDERS)
FAX: (504)893-3777**

Monday-Saturday: 9:30-5:30

Personal service specialists in lighted villages and collectibles. Dept. 56 Showcase Dealer, Fontanini Dealer's Guild, Sarah's Attic Golden Heart Dealer, Byers' Choice, Cat's Meow, Duncan Royale, Lizzie High, Midwest Importers, Kurt Adler Fabriche, Possible Dreams, Steinbach and Christian Ulbricht Nutcrackers and Smokers and United Designs.

Additional locations in Covington, LA and Key West, FL.

NALED member. Layaways. Shipping worldwide. Secondary Market service.

PONTALBA COLLECTIBLES

517 St. Ann St.
New Orleans, LA 70116

**PHONE: (504)524-8068
(800)626-9306**

Open 7 Days A Week: 9:00-5:30

All God's Children, Armani, Bossons, Bradford Exchange, Calico Kittens, Cherished Teddies, Chilmark, David Winter, Emmett Kelly Jr., LEGENDS, Lee Sievers, Lilliput, Limoge, Lowell Davis, Maud Humphrey, Memories of Yesterday, Michael Garman, Michael's Limited, PenniBears, Precious Moments, Ron Wall, Sebastian, Snowbabies, Spoontiques, Tim Wolfe, Tom Clark, United Design, Walt Disney Classics, Wee Forest Folk, and Enesco Music Boxes.

Mastercard, Visa, Discover accepted. Secondary Market Service. Layaways welcome. NALED Member.

SERENDIPITY

1133 St. Vincent Ave. #140
Shreveport, LA 71104-4146

**PHONE: (318)226-1324
(800)259-1686**

Monday-Saturday: 10:00-10:00
Sunday: 1:00-5:00

With two locations, they carry a large selection of fine collectibles including: Cairn, Lladro, David Winter, LEGENDS, Sarah's Attic, Lilliput Lane, Enesco, Precious Moments, Homestead Country Folks, United Design, and Glass Baron.

Offering Secondary Market service for Lladro, LEGENDS, Cairn and others. Visa, Mastercard and Discover accepted. Layaway and shipping available. All shipping costs paid on orders of $100 or more.

Second store is located in The South Park Mall. Phone: (318)686-7414.

LOUISIANA/MAINE

THE CABBAGE PATCH GIFT SHOP

1311 Horridge St.
Vinton, LA 70668

PHONE: (318)589-2256

Monday-Friday: 9:00-5:00
Saturday: 9:00-12:00

Celebrating 15 years of service to the collectors. Located one mile off I-10 and seven miles from the Texas border. Specializing in Precious Moments for primary and secondary market. Enesco, Fenton Art Glass, Roman, Memories of Yesterday, Lefton Colonial Villages and accessories, Attic Babies by Maschino, Storybook Collection.

Redemption Center. Layaway plan welcome. Visa and Mastercard accepted. Shipping available

THE GOOSEBERRY BARN

359 Minot Ave.
Rt. 121 & 11
Auburn, ME 04210

**PHONE: (207)782-8964
(800)846-9627**

Open Daily: 9:00-5:00

National Award Winning Gift Shop!

Dept. 56: Heritage Village, North Pole, Snow Village, Snowbabies, All Through the House, Merry Makers, Winter Silhouette. Bears: Raikes, Muffy, Boyd's, Beaver Valley. Also featuring Tom Clark Gnomes, Lee Sievers, Tim Wolfe, Byers' Choice, Cat's Meow. Santas: June McKenna, Possible Dreams. A. Tripi, Designs Americana, Bossons, Krystonia, Fenton, Michael Garman, Dreamsicles, C. Radko, Neil Rose, Lizzie High, Little Souls, Sarah's Attic, German Nutcrackers, Sports Impressions, music boxes, Melody In Motion, Hibel.

Secondary Market Dealer.

THE CHRISTMAS SHOPPE BY PICTURE & GIFT

263 Main St.
Bangor, ME 04401

PHONE: (207)945-0805

Jan-June: Wednesday-Sunday: 10:00-5:00
July-Dec: Open 7 Days A Week: 10:00-5:00
October-December: Seasonal Hours

Over 24 decorated trees with 10,000 ornaments, life-like trees 6" to 10'. Dept. 56, Snowbabies, Tom Clark Gnomes, Hallmark Keepsake Ornaments, Fontanini Nativities, Shelia's, Old World German Glass Ornaments, Possible Dreams, PM, Steinbach Nutcrackers, Maud Humphrey, Krystonia, and Sandicast pets.

Free gift with coupon. Major credit cards accepted. Layaway and gift certificates. NALED member. Secondary Market Dealer. Redemption Center. Mail order. Ample parking for RV's. Bus and tour groups welcome. Handicap accessible.

THE CUBBY HOLE

25 Eden St.
Bar Harbor, ME 04609

**PHONE: (207)288-4294
(207) 288-4001**

May 1-October 9 Open Daily: 9:00-9:00

Cairn Studio, Tom Clark, Walt Disney, M.I. Hummel, Lilliput Lane, David Winter, Sarah's Attic, L. Davis, Hagara, Simpich, Walter Brockman, Cain Studio, Neil Rose Indian Heads, Bossons, Mill Creek, United Design: Legend of Santa, Angels, Legend of the Little People. Krystonia, Robarts Mice, Duncan Royale, Shoemaker's Dream, Hudson Villagers, Fort Perth, Hudson, Gallo Pewter, Frumps, Maud Humphrey, Little Cheesers, Flambro, Lynn Haney, Merry Tymes, Pocket Dragons, The Herd and Dragon Keep by Marty, Bubble Fairies, Clare Craft, Donna Green, Jody Bergsma, Adorables, WACO, Ron Lee.

Redemption Center for most collectibles. Major credit cards. Shipping available.

MAINE

KNOCK ON WOOD

Route 1
Baring, ME 04694
**PHONE: (207)454-7136
(800)336-7136**

Open 7 Days A Week: 9:00-5:00
Friday: Open Until 8:00

Open 360 days a year. Knock on Wood is the one-stop gift shop for Maine. As well as being a showcase dealer for Dept. 56 Heritage Village, they also specialize in Snowbabies, Byers' Choice Carolers, Cat's Meow Villages, Sarah's Attic Figurines, Lizzie High Dolls, Gund Plush Toys, Fontanini, Possible Dreams Santas, Glynda Turley Prints, Bradley Dolls, Clay Art, Dreamsicles, Fenton Art Glass, Kurt Adler, Ladie and Friends, Midwest Importers, Possible Dreams, Rockwell, Silver Deer, United Design and Porcelain dolls.

Layaways and shipping available. All major credit cards are welcome. Maine and Atlantic provinces: call (800)336-7136.

COUNTRY COLLECTIBLES

112 Bennett Dr.
Caribou, ME 04736
PHONE: (207)498-3936

Monday-Saturday: 9:00-5:00
Friday Open Until 7:00

Department 56, Walt Disney Classics Collection, David Winter, Snowbabies, Sarah's Attic, Lizzie High, Byers' Choice Ltd., Cast Art, M.I. Hummel, Jan Hagara, John Hine Studios, June McKenna, Midwest Importers, Possible Dreams, Schmid, Cat's Meow, Madame Alexander Dolls, Steiff, Cherished Teddies, Duncan Royale, Ginny Dolls, Tom Clark Gnomes, Raikes Bears, Dreamsicles, gourmet coffee and cocoa, Yankee candles, and Maine made products.

All major credit cards accepted. Will gladly ship anywhere. 30-day layaway. Club redemption center.

HERITAGE CHRISTMAS CANDLE & GIFT SHOP

Route 23 South Libby Hill
Oakland, ME 04963
PHONE: (207)465-3910

Monday-Sunday: 10:00-8:00

Two great locations serving the collectors, Pemaquid on the coast of Maine and Oakland in Delgrade Lake Region. Showcase Dealer for Dept. 56, Byers' Choice, Hummel, PM, MOY, Annalee, Roman/Fontanini, Armani, Miss Martha, Enesco Musicals, L. Davis, LEGENDS, United Design, Possible Dreams, DeGrazia, Gund, Steiff Bears, Hidden Kingdom and Belsnickle Santas.

NALED member/catalog. Layaway. Visa, MC and Discover. Shipping. Free gift wrapping.

Second Location: Pemaquid Point, Pemaquid, ME. Phone (207)677-2742. Hours:(May-Dec.) Mon.-Sat.: 10:00-6:00.

PORTER EMPORIUM

Route 25 P.O. Box 5
Porter, ME 04068
**PHONE: (207)625-8989
(800)486-1921**

Open 7 Days A Week: 10:00-5:30

Ashton-Drake, Georgetown, Hamilton, Cherished Teddies, Sarah's Attic, United Design, Maud Humphrey Bogart, Himstedt, Lawton, Mattel, Good-Kruger, Roman, GADCO, Gunzel, specializing in Limited Edition Dolls.

Visa, Mastercard and Discover accepted. Layaway. Free shipping over $100.

MARYLAND

CHERISHED MOMENTS LTD.

24 West Bel Air Ave.
Aberdeen, MD 21001

PHONE: (410)273-7361

Monday-Friday: 9:00-5:30
Saturday: 9:00-5:00

LEGENDS, Chilmark, Hudson, Harbour Lights, Memories of Yesterday, David Winter, Maud Humphrey, beer steins, including Anheuser-Busch and German steins, Maruri, Fenton Art Glass, Jan Hagara, Sarah's Attic, Sports Impressions, Cherished Teddies, Enesco Musicals, Louis Icart, Hadley House, Guildhall, Paragon Pictures, Rawcliffe Pewter.

Mastercard and Visa accepted. Layaway and shipping available. Free gift wrapping.

THE GOLDEN GULL

110 Dock St.
Annapolis, MD 21401

PHONE: (410)263-0663
(301)261-2329

Open 7 Days A Week: 10:00-6:00

Armani, The Walt Disney Classics Collection, Goebel, John Hine Studios, M.I. Hummel, Lance/Chilmark Showcase, LEGENDS, Lilliput Lane Ltd., Lladro Collectors Society, Maruri USA, Royal Copenhagen/Bing & Grondahl, Royal Doulton, Schmid, Swarovski, Lowell Davis, Harbour Lights, Andrea by Sadek, Hudson, Sebastian, Mark Hopkins Bronze, Rick Cain, and Herend.

Major credit cards accepted. Free gift wrapping. Ship via UPS. Secondary Market (some products).

BODZER'S COLLECTIBLES

White Marsh Mall
8200 Perry Hall Blvd.
Baltimore, MD 21236

PHONE: (410)931-9222
FAX: (410)661-1948

Monday-Saturday: 10:00-9:30
Sunday: 12:00-6:00

Maryland's largest Bradford plate dealer! Dept. 56, All God's Children, LEGENDS, M.I. Hummel, Lladro, Norman Rockwell, David Winter, Perillo, Krystonia, Emmett Kelly, Armani, Maud Humphrey and Harbour Lights. Dolls: Ashton-Drake, Wendy Lawton, Hamilton, Paradise Gallery, Lexington Hall, Gorham, Madame Alexander, Barbie, Mary Ann Oldenburg, Roman, and Sandra Kuck.

Always a full line of accessories. All major credit cards accepted. Layaway plan. Secondary Market.

ELLEN'S HALLMARK

Harford Mall
668 Bel Air Rd.
Bel Air, MD 21014

PHONE: (410)838-0284

Monday-Saturday: 10:00-9:30
Sunday: 12:00-5:00

Enesco: Cherished Teddies, Precious Moments, Calico Kittens, Sisters & Best Friends, Sugartown, Enesco Musicals, Sports Impressions. Ornaments: Hallmark, Enesco Treasury. Dept. 56 Villages, Snowbabies, Swarovski, David Winter, Miss Martha, Hamilton Gifts (Maud Humphrey Bogart), and Willitts (Star Trek collectibles). Retired figurines.

All major credit cards accepted. Redemption center for all collector clubs.

MARYLAND

PJ'S HALLMARK

Kent Plaza
Chestertown, MD 21620
PHONE: (410)778-5100

Monday-Thursday: 9:30-8:00
Friday: 9:30-9:00; Saturday: 9:30-6:00
Sunday: 10:00-4:00

Hallmark Ornaments, Snowbabies, Cat's Meow, Cherished Teddies, Calico Kittens, Dreamsicles, Precious Moments. Specializing in Yankee Candles and personalized Rowe Pottery, and custom-made gourmet baskets.

Mastercard and Visa accepted. Shipping available.

CAROLINE'S HALLMARK SHOP

36 Denton Plaza
Denton, MD 21629
PHONE: (410)479-1467

Monday-Friday: 9:30-8:00
Saturday: 9:30-7:00; Sunday: 10:00-4:00

Hallmark Ornaments, Snowbabies, Cat's Meow, Cherished Teddies, Calico Kittens, Dreamsicles, Memories of Yesterday. Also featuring Yankee Candles, personalized Rowe Pottery, and custom-made gourmet baskets.

Mastercard and Visa accepted. Shipping available.

PRECIOUS GIFTS

Historical District
8098 Main St.
Ellicott City, MD 21043
PHONE: (410)461-6813

Tuesday-Sunday: 11:00-6:00

Armani, Lladro, Swarovski, Walt Disney Classics, Hummels, David Winter, Lilliput Lane, Precious Moments, Memories of Yesterday, All God's Children, Beatrix Potter, Bunnykins, Calico Kittens, Cherished Teddies, Snowbabies, Pocket Dragons and fine Jewelry.

Precious Gifts is located in the Banker's Galleria "Mini Mall". Ellicott City was founded in 1772 and now, with its many shops and restaurants, has become the "Jewel" of Maryland's tourist attractions. Come visit us and enjoy the magic of historical Ellicott City.

All major credit cards accepted. Layaway and shipping available. Secondary Market.

CHERRY TREE CARDS & GIFTS

11200 Scaggsville Rd.
Routes 29 & 216
Laurel, MD 20723
PHONE: (301)498-8528

Monday-Friday: 10-9; Saturday: 12-6

Greeting cards, albums, balloons, calligraphy prints, and gift wrap. Specializing in collectibles, Precious Moments: over 500 current and retired figurines and 30 dolls on display; Cat's Meow, Tom Clark Gnomes, Lucy & Me, David Winter Cottages, Lilliput Lane, Enesco Musical Showcase, Growing Up Girls, Miss Martha's, Memories of Yesterday, Maud Humphrey Bogart, Melody In Motion, Sarah's Attic, Anheuser-Busch Steins, Ginny Dolls, Brian Baker Deja Vu, Marty Bell Prints and Stationery.

Visa and Mastercard accepted. NALED member. 90 day layaway.

MARYLAND

RD POOLS & CHRISTMAS

916 National Hwy.
LaVale, MD 21502

PHONE: (301)729-6977

Monday-Saturday: 10:00-6:00
Extended Holiday Hours

Norman Rockwell, Dept. 56 Snowbabies and All Through the House, German Nutcrackers: Steinbach and Christian Ulbricht. Lionel Ornaments and Village, Enesco Treasury Ornaments, Enesco Musicals, Enesco North Pole Village, Overly-Raker Santa Collection, Roman Fontanini, Sports Impressions, Today-Tomorrow, Midwest Importers Heritage Santa Collection, Possible Dreams, Silvestri, Miniature ornaments, and commercial decorations.

Visa and Mastercard accepted. Layaway and shipping available. Free gift wrapping.

EDWARD'S

1 North Division St.
P.O. Box 310
Ocean City, MD 21842

PHONE: (410)289-7000
FAX: (410)289-3199

Open Daily: 9:00am-11:00pm (Apr.-Sept.)

Swarovski, Hummel, Lladro, Chilmark, Precious Moments, Dept. 56, LEGENDS, Cherished Teddies, Laura's Attic, Miss Martha's Collection, Maud Humphrey Bogart, Sports Impressions, Norman Rockwell, Emmett Kelly Jr., Hudson Pewter, and Fenton Glass.

All major credit cards accepted. NALED member. Bradford Exchange.

THE PENN DEN

13015 9TH St.
Old Town Bowie, MD 20720

PHONE: (301)262-2430

Open 7 Days A Week: 11:00-5:00

Authorized Bradford and NALED Dealer. Primary and secondary dealer in all the major collectible lines. Over 800 plates and 500 dolls and figurines on display including; Annalee, Dept. 56, Enesco: Precious Moments, Musical Showcase, and Christmas ornaments. All God's Children, Swarovski, Lladro, Armani, David Winter, Lilliput Lane, Byers' Choice, Belleek, Emmett Kelly, Hummel, Madame Alexander, Hamilton, Ashton-Drake, Georgetown dolls, Willitts, Krystonia, Sports Impressions, Pocket Dragons, Lowell Davis Farm Club and Walt Disney Classics Collection.

Music boxes, beer steins and much more. Layaways and credit cards welcome.

KEEPSAKES & COLLECTIBLES

Owings Mills Mall
Owings Mills, MD 21117

PHONE: (410)356-3578
(800)695-5337

Monday-Saturday: 10:00-9:00
Sunday: 12:00-6:00

Specializing in Music Boxes with over 200 interchangeable music in stock.

Club redemption center for: AGC, Armani, Cat's Meow, Daddy's Long Legs, Disney Classics, Hibel, Hummel, Iris Arc, EKJ, Kinkade, Krystonia, Kuck, Melody in Motion, MOY, Miss Martha's, Sarah's Attic, Swarovski, Ashton-Drake, Bradford plates, Enesco Musical Society, Sports Impressions. Dept. 56 Showcase Dealer, Snowbabies, All Thru the House. Free catalogs and newsletter available. Daily UPS shipping. Gift wrapping.

Second Location: The Music Box, Inner Harbor, MD 21202. Phone:(410)727-0444.

MARYLAND

THE CHRISTMAS GOOSE LTD.

4624 Ocean Gateway
Queenstown, MD 21658

PHONE: (410) 827-5252

Monday-Saturday: 10:00-6:00
Sunday: 10:00-5:00
Extended Holiday Hours

Dept. 56 Villages, Snowbabies, Merry Makers, All Through The House, Annalee, Byers' Choice Carolers, David Winter Cottages, Cat's Meow, Shelia's, Matryoshka Russian Nesting Dolls, Fontanini Nativities, Steinbach Nutcrackers and Smokers, Christopher Radko, Old World Ornaments, one of a kind Chesapeake Santas, Possible Dreams Clothtique Santas.

Visa, Mastercard, and Discover accepted. Layaway and shipping available. Redemption Center for David Winter, Shelia's, Cat's Meow, Byers' Choice, and Possible Dreams.

MIXED EMOTION

7218 Muncaster Mill Rd.
Rockville, MD 20855

PHONE: (301)963-0877
(800)345-6955

Monday-Saturday: 9:00-9:00
Sunday: 11:00-5:00

Your primary collectible store since 1983. Located 25 minutes from Washington DC. Showcase Dealer for Dept. 56 (complete line), Possible Dreams, Cat's Meow, Fenton, PenDelfin, Laura's Attic, Anheuser-Busch, Precious Moments, Cherished Teddies, Calico Kittens, Precious Moments Dolls, Dreamsicles, Krystonia, Lizzie High, Annalee, Emmett Kelly Jr., Shoemaker's Dreams, United Design, Miss Martha's, Thomas Kinkade, Takahashi Boxes, Fenton.

Club Redemption Center. Secondary Market for Hummels. Layaway. All major credit cards. Shipping and gift wrapping available.

MINDY'S COUNTRY HOUSE

Park Plaza Shopping Center
558B Ritchie Highway
Severna Park, MD 21146

PHONE: (410)647-4840

Mon.-Tues., Sat.:10:00-6:00
Wed.-Fri.: 10:00-8:00; Sun. 12:00-4:00

Charming gift store that has been established for over 40 years. Specializing in premium collectibles including M.I. Hummel, Schmid, June McKenna Collectibles, Midwest Importers, Hamilton Gifts, Maud Humphrey, Bessie Pease Gutmann, Goebel, Possible Dreams, Royal Copenhagen, and Constance Collection. They are a registered M.I. Hummel, Lilliput Lane and Maud Humphrey/Bessie Pease Gutmann Collectibles Club Dealer. Other major lines represented are: Baldwin Brass, Virginia Metalcrafters, Colonial Candle with many other gift selections.

Cash, personal checks, Visa and Mastercard. Layaway and special orders.

THE GRAHAM COLLECTION

9915 Sutherland Rd.
Silver Spring, MD 20901

PHONE: (301)681-8979

By Appointment or Mail Orders Only

Duncan Royale, Constance Collection, Blackberry Bonnett Collection, Enesco's All That Jazz and On Cue, Luvlife Collectibles, Morini's Black Desire Series, Gail Laura Collectibles, Crafthouse's Positive Images, Viking Imports Leroy Series and many others.

Visa, Mastercard and American Express accepted. Layaway available.

MARYLAND

ALBERT S. SMYTH CO., INC.

29 Greenmeadow Drive
Timonium, MD 21093

PHONE: (800)638-3333
FAX: (410)252-2355

Monday-Saturday: 9:00-5:00
Thursday: 9:00-9:00

Lladro, David Winter, Lilliput Lane, Royal Copenhagen, Limoges Boxes, Crummles English Enamels, Swarovski, M.I. Hummel, Waterford, Noritake, Royal Doulton, Lenox, Fitz & Floyd, Kirk-Stieff, Wallace, Gorham, Lunt, Reed & Barton, Towle, Virginia Metal Crafters, Baldwin Brass.

For over 80 years Maryland's favorite store for collectors.

Shipping anywhere in the US. Layaway available. All major credit cards accepted. Most items shipped same day. Free Catalog.

GREETINGS & READINGS

809 Taylor Ave.
Towson, MD 21286

PHONE: (410)825-4225

Open 7 Days A Week

Established in 1969. Baltimore's premier gift store. Authorized Dealer for Alexander Dolls, All God's Children, Ardleigh Elliott, Ashton-Drake, Armani, Beatrix Potter, Maud Humphrey, Precious Moments, Bradford Exchange, Byers' Choice, Cat's Meow, Castagna, Cherished Teddies, Chilmark, Dept. 56, Walt Disney, Dreamsicles, Enesco Musicals, Fitz & Floyd, Glass Baron, Goebel, Gorham, Jan Hagara, Hallmark, Hawthorne, Hudson Pewter, Hummel, Emmett Kelly Jr., Lance, Lenox, Lilliput Lane, Lladro, June McKenna, Michaels Ltd, Otagiri, Portmeirion, Raikes Bears, Rockwell, Royal Doulton, Sadek, Sandicast, Sarah's Attic, Shelia's, Kirk-Stieff, Swarovski, Waterford, Wedgwood, and David Winter.

MAIN STREET MEMORIES

14801 Main St.
Upper Marlboro, MD 20772

PHONE: (301)627-8962

Monday-Saturday: 9:30-5:00
Sunday or Evenings by Appointment

Sarah's Attic, KVK Daddy's Long Legs, Pig Lady, Harbour Lights, Lincoln County Garden Club, Cat's Meow, Duncan Royale Ebony Collection, Maurice Wideman American Collection, Lefton's Colonial Village, Rowe Pottery, Possible Dreams, Emmett Kelly Jr. Clowns, Byers' Choice Carolers, Baldwin Brass, Goodwin Weavers Afghans, Capel Rugs, Miss Martha's collection, and Sisters and Best Friends.

Visa, Mastercard, and Discover accepted. Layaway. Phone orders. 200 Sarah's Attic retired pieces. Owner operated. Knowledge and service is the best product.

TIARA GIFTS

Wheaton Plaza
Wheaton, MD 20902

PHONE: (301)949-0210
(800)457-9911

Monday-Saturday: 10:00-9:30
Sunday: 12:00-6:00

Lladro, Chilmark, David Winter, Armani, Swarovski, Goebel Miniatures, Sarah's Attic, All God's Children, Waterford, Herend, Baccarat, Precious Moments, Hummel, Dept. 56, Walt Disney Classics.

One of America's leading collectible dealers.

Special orders and phone orders are welcome. Shipping throughout the country available. Major credit cards accepted.

Major Redemption Center for all major collector lines.

Think of Tiara first for Collectibles!

MASSACHUSETTS

SYLVIA'S GALLERY

27 Park St.
Adams, MA 01220
PHONE: (413)743-9250

Wed.: 10-7; Thurs: 10-9; Fri.: 10-7; Sat.: 10-5; Sun.: 12-5 Open by appt.

Located in Berkshire County. A cultural based area a short distance from Norman Rockwell and Grandma Moses Museum. Close to Tanglewood Concert, Jacobs Pillow (Dance) and Williamstown Theater Festival.

Lines include: Limited edition, original pieces and very collectible works by Sandra Kuck, Donald Zolan, Greg Perillo, Carol Roeda, Mago, Emmett Kelly, John McClelland, Lena Liu, Dave Grossman, Rockwell, Earl Roberts. Hamilton plates and dolls, Legends of the Little People and Native American pottery. Lithographs, figurines, original paintings, bronze sculptures and over 150 plates on display. Artist signings and personal appearances.

THE FARMERS DAUGHTER

At Hillcrest Farm
153 Millbury St.
Auburn, MA 01501
PHONE: (508)832-2995

Daily: 9:00-6:00; Extended Holiday Hours

Annalee Mobilitee, Lizzie High, Cheryl Spencer Collin New England Villages and Lighthouses, Dept. 56 Heritage Village: Dickens Village, New England Village, Christmas in the City, North Pole; Snow Village, Snowbabies. Lilliput Lane Cottages, Fontanini Creche, United Design-Legend of Santa, June McKenna Santas, Sebastian, Cat's Meow, Shelia's, Duncan Royale Santas, Enesco: Treasured Memories and Laura's Attic and Possible Dreams. Extensive line of Christmas Ornaments: Annalee, Snowbabies, Sebastian, Midwest, Roman, Adler. Visa and Mastercard accepted. Layaway. Gift Registry. NALED Member. GAA, Chamber of Commerce and Rotary Club.

LINDA'S ORIGINALS AND THE YANKEE CRAFTSMEN

220 Rt 6A
Brewster, MA 02631
PHONE: (508)385-4758
(508)385-2285

Summer: 9:00-8:00 Seven Days
Winter: 9:00-5:00 Seven Days

Located on Cape Cod. Features two stores in one location with over 500 craftsmen and collectible items. One of the largest collections of Byers' Choice is also displayed as well as Dept. 56, Possible Dreams, Lilliput Lane, David Winter and many more. Rowe Pottery, Lizzie High Dolls, Cat's Meow Villages, Snowbabies, Rockwell and Limited Glynda Turley Prints. Sandra Kuck, Annalee Dolls, Sarah's Attic, Emmett Kelly Jr., Enesco Musicals and MOY. PM, Artaffects, Lee Middleton, Midwest Importers and Swarovski. Credit cards. Layaway. Shipping. Collectors club. NALED member.

KOTLIAR'S CARDS & COLLECTIBLES

Cambridgeside Galleria
100 Cambridgeside Place
Cambridge, MA 02141
PHONE: (617)494-4733

Monday-Saturday: 10:00-9:30
Sunday: 12:00-6:00

Precious Moments, Lladro, Hummel, Armani, Dept. 56, David Winter, Lenox, Austin, Sadek, Michael's Ltd., Maruri, Krystonia, Fantasy and Gallo Pewter, United Design, Chokin, Dreamsicles, Mikasa, Justin's Vases, Treasure Masters, Roman, Flambro, Melody In Motion, Hopkins, Reco, and Enesco, MOY, Cherished Teddies, Calico Kittens, Sports Impressions, Sisters and Best Friends. Items not available in all stores.

Other Location: Greendale Mall, 7 Neponset St., Worcester, MA 01606. Phone: (508)856-0691.

MASSACHUSETTS

STACY'S GIFTS & COLLECTIBLES

The Mall at Walpole Route 1
East Walpole, MA 02032-1511

PHONE: (508)668-4212
(800)STACYS-1
FAX: (508)668-7553

Monday-Saturday: 10-9:30; Sunday: 12-6

Your primary and secondary collectible specialists. All God's Children, ANRI, Bosson Heads, Byers' Choice, Cherished Teddies, Chilmark and Hudson Pewter, Clowns by Emmett Kelly Jr., David Winter, Dedham Pottery Repro. Dept. 56 Houses, Ashton-Drake, Hibel, Frances Hook, Goebel Minis, Hummels, Jan Hagara, Thomas Kinkade, Lilliput Lane, Lladro, Lowell Davis, Melody In Motion, Miss Martha, Memories of Yesterday, PenDelfin, Perillo, Plates by Bradford, Hamilton, P. Buckley Moss, Precious Moments, Sebastians, Sports plates and figurines, Walt Disney Classics Collection, WFF, and Swarovski.

THE CRYSTAL PINEAPPLE

1582 Rt. 132
Hyannis, MA 02601

PHONE: (800)437-7760

Open Daily: 9:00am-8:00pm

Lines include: Walt Disney Classics Collection, Tom Clark, Dept. 56, All God's Children, Swarovski, David Winter, Cherished Teddies, Calico Kittens, Hummel, Lladro, Steinbach Nutcrackers, Lowell Davis, Gartlan, Iris Arc, Mark Klaus, Wee Forest Folk and Sports Impressions.

Layaway program available. All major credit cards accepted.

Second Location: 1540 Rt. 6A, West Barnstable, MA, 02668. Phone:(800)462-4009.

STANLEY'S HALLMARK

222F East Main St.
Marlboro, MA 01752

PHONE: (508)481-0097

Monday-Friday: 10:00-9:00
Saturday: 9:30-5:30; Sunday: 12:00-5:00

Dept. 56 Showcase Dealer, Enesco: Precious Moments, Cherished Teddies, Maud Humphrey, Sports Impressions. Snowbabies, Lladro, Hummels, David Winter, Krystonia, All God's Children, Ashton-Drake, and PenDelfin.

Major credit cards accepted. Layaway and shipping available.

WARDS

70 High St.
Medford, MA 02155

PHONE: (617)395-2420

Monday-Saturday: 9:00-5:30
Thursday: 9:00-8:30

Dept. 56, Hummel, Lladro, David Winter, Lilliput Lane, Wee Forest Folk, Precious Moments, Memories Of Yesterday, Lowell Davis, Disney Classics, Swarovski, Ashton-Drake dolls, Bradford Exchange, Sarah's Attic, Miss Martha's, Waterford Crystal, Royal Doulton, Sports Impressions, Cherished Teddies, Ron Lee, Annalee, Hallmark, PenDelfin, Krystonia, All God's Children, Hibel, Emmett Kelly Jr., Bing & Grondahl, Royal Copenhagen, Norman Rockwell and Laura's Attic.

All major credit cards. NALED member. Layaway.

MASSACHUSETTS

CHEERIOS

Emerald Square Mall
999 S. Washington St.
N. Attleboro, MA 02760
**PHONE: (800)374-1174
(508)643-1174**

Byers' Choice, Dept. 56, Swarovski, Krystonia, David Winter, Precious Moments, Hummels, Lladro, Emmett Kelly Jr., Lowell Davis, Lilliput Lane, Tom Clark Gnomes, All God's Children, Walt Disney Classics Collection, Chilmark, Wee Forest Folk, PenDelfin, Memories of Yesterday, Sports Impressions, Golden Memories by Lladro, and Armani.

Visa, Mastercard, American Express and Discover accepted. Free shipping! Layaway. Secondary Market Service.

GIFT BARN

Rt. 6 Box 5044
N. Eastham, MA 02651-5044
**PHONE: (508)255-7000
FAX: (508)240-2622**

Open April 1- Christmas

Bradford Exchange Dealer (plates, dolls and figurines), Dept. 56 Villages and accessories (Dickens Village, New England, Snow Village, North Pole, Christmas in the City, Snowbabies), Annalee Dolls, Gift Link (Lilliput Lane and Pocket Dragons), Precious Art (Krystonia), Wee Forest Folk, Lowell Davis, Sebastian, Sarah's Attic, Flambro (Emmett Kelly Jr.) Little Cheesers, Cheryl Spencer Light Houses, Windstone, Mill Creek, Jan Hagara, Precious Moments and more.

Shipping anywhere in continental US. Mastercard, Visa and Discover honored. NALED Member. Club Redemptions on all collectible lines listed.

COLLECTOR'S CABINET

946 Great Plain Ave.
Needham, MA 02192
**PHONE: (800)84-PLATE
(617)449-4550
FAX: (617)449-5315**

Monday-Wednesday and Saturday: 10-6
Thursday and Friday: 10-8

Specializing in current and secondary market plates, dolls, figurines and lithos. Authorized Bradford Exchange and Ashton-Drake Dealer. Disney Classics, M.I. Hummel, Goebel Miniatures, Lowell Davis, David Winter, Gartlan, Sports Impressions, Chilmark, Hudson and Perth Pewter. Emmett Kelly Jr. and Sr., Perillo, Kuck, Hibel, Fred Stone, P.B. Moss, DeGrazia, Rockwell, Maud Humphrey, Bing & Grondahl-Royal Copenhagen, Maruri. Display cases, frames for plates and accessories. Retail and mail order.

Redemption Center for most collector's Clubs. Major credit cards.

SNOW GOOSE GIFT & CHRISTMAS SHOPS

8 Spring Lane
Plymouth, MA 02360
PHONE: (508)747-2650

Open 7 Days Year Round: 10:00-5:00

Uniquely beautiful shops on the historic walking trail, a refreshing place to browse and shop. Lines include Harbour Lights, All God's Children, Cat's Meow, Byers' Choice, Dept. 56 Villages, All Through The House, Merry Makers, Snowbabies, nutcrackers, Margaret Furlong, Santas by Possible Dreams, Midwest Importers, and Kurt S. Adler, pottery, Fontanini, music boxes, Royal Doulton, Austin, David Winter, Crabtree and Evelyn, C. Radko, and Old World.

All major credit cards accepted. Layaway. Shipping nationwide. Free gift wrapping.

Second Location: 5 Mechants Square, Sandwich, MA 02563.

MASSACHUSETTS

STONED ELEPHANT OF SALEM, INC.
43 Wharf St.
Salem, MA 01970
PHONE: (508)744-4370
(800)662-XMAS (9627)
FAX: (508)744-4370

Monday-Saturday: 10:00-9:00
Sunday: 11:00-6:00

Dept. 56 Showcase Dealer, Lilliput Lane, David Winter, Cat's Meow, Shelia's Houses, Hummel, All God's Children, Tom Clark Gnomes, Jan Hagara, German Nutcrackers, Annalee Dolls, Precious Moments, June McKenna Santas, Duncan Royale Santas, United Design, and Possible Dreams Santas.

All major credit cards accepted. Layaway. Shipping. Redemption Center for Hummel, Jan Hagara, Annalee, and Lilliput Lane.

DIVIDED HOUSE OF GIFTS
255 Elm St. Route 110
Salisbury, MA 01952
PHONE: (508)462-8423

Tuesday-Saturday: 10:00-6:00
Sunday: 12:00-4:00
Oct.-Dec.: Open 7 Days A Week

Dept. 56 Snowbabies and Villages, Santas, Dreamsicles, Fontanini, Enesco Precious Moments and Musicals, Enesco Treasury Ornaments, Cairn Studio, Steiff, Sebastians, Krystonia, Emmett Kelly Jr., Hummels, C. Spencer Lighthouses, Cat's Meow, The Collectables, Himstedt Dolls, J.H. Boone, John Hine Studios, WACO products, miniatures, custom dollhouses made on the premises, and much more.

Visa, Mastercard and Discover accepted. G.C.C. member. Shipping available.

CUTIES BEARS & STUFFIES
1387 Fall River Ave.-Rt. 6
Seekonk, MASS 02771
PHONE: (508)336-7868
(800)336-7871
FAX: (508) 336-5777

Tuesday-Saturday: 10-5:30; Sunday: 12-4
Closed Sunday June-August

Centrally located near the Seaport City of Newport and Providence RI for 10 years. Bears: Steiff, Raikes, Muffy, Gund. Dolls: Ashton-Drake, Hamilton, Georgetown, Paradise Galleries and limited edition artist dolls and companies. PM, Cherished Teddies, AGC, Tom Clark Gnomes, Miss Martha's Originals, Calico Kittens, Krystonia, SI (plates and figurines), Sandicast, Rawcliffe Fairies, Daze Mortensen clay figures, Swarovski. Reco, Hamilton, and Bradford plates. Secondary Market dealer. Collector clubs and redemption center. All major credit cards accepted. "We know you have a choice. Thank you for choosing us."

THE LEONARD GALLERY
1067 E. Columbus Ave.
Springfield, MA 01105
PHONE: (413)733-9492

Monday-Saturday: 9-5; Thursday: 9-7

Your collectible source for plates, figurines, dolls, and lithos. Serving you for over 50 years! Ashton-Drake, Bing & Grondahl, Bradford Exchange, Calico Kittens, Cherished Teddies, David Winter, Walt Disney Classics Collection, Emmett Kelly Jr., Hibel, Hummel, Krystonia, Knowles, Lowell Davis, MOY, Maud Humphrey, Miss Marthas, PM, Ron Lee, Rockwell, Sports Impressions, Swarovski, Wee Forest Folk, Willitts Design, Melody In Motion, Dreamsicles and more.

Mastercard, Visa and Discover accepted. Layaway and shipping available. NALED member. Secondary Market Dealer. Redemption Center for all collectible lines. Picture framing and display accessories. Greenwich Workshop Dealer.

MASSACHUSETTS/MICHIGAN

HONEYCOMB GIFT SHOPPE

384 Main St.
Wakefield, MA 01880
**PHONE: (617)245-2448
(800)3BUSYBEE**

Monday-Thursday: 9:00-5:30
Friday: 9:00-7:30; Saturday: 9:00-5:00

Specialists in collectibles since 1974. Premier dealer for ANRI, PenniBears, Laura's Attic, Wee Forest Folk, PM, All God's Children, Lowell Davis, Ashton-Drake, Bradford Exchange, Tom Clark, Krystonia, Swarovski, Lilliput Lane, David Winter, Bossons, PenDelfin, Chilmark, Hudson, Perth, Steinbach Nutcrackers and Smokers, Emmett Kelly, Ron Lee, Memories of Yesterday, Lucy & Me, Kitty Cucumber, Rockwell, Byers' Choice, Disney, Cherished Teddies, Armani, Sports Impressions, Gartlan, lithos, Kuck, Fred Stone, Ferrandiz, Hibel plus many more. Secondary Market. Redemption center. All major credit cards. NALED member. Layaways available.

GIFT GALLERY

505 S. Main St.
P.O. Box 442
Webster, MA 01570
**PHONE: (508)943-4402
FAX: (508)943-1846**

Monday-Thursday: 10:00-6:00
Friday: 10:00-8:00; Saturday: 10:00-6:00

Dept. 56 Showcase Dealer (All Villages, accessories, Snowbabies, All Through the House, Merry Makers), David Winter, Lladro, Hummel, Byers' Choice, Swarovski, Annalee, Tom Clark, Tim Wolfe, Cat's Meow, Precious Moments, Lizzie High, Maud Humphrey, Cherished Teddies, Krystonia, Lilliput Lane, Walt Disney Classics, June McKenna, Calico Kittens, Frances Hook, Lowell Davis, Dreamsicles, Sports Impressions.

NALED member. Redemption Center. Layaway. All major credit cards accepted. Free shipping.

MERRY CHRISTMAS SHOPPE

785 Bedford St.
Whitman, MA 02382
**PHONE: (800)447-6677
(617)447-6677
FAX: (617)447-1387**

Monday-Saturday: 10:00-6:00
Thursday: Until 9:00; Sunday: 12:00-5:00

Your source for fine collectibles and dolls. Over 1,000 dolls on display. Dept. 56 Showcase Dealer-primary and secondary market. Snowbabies, Merry Makers, All Through The House, Byers' Choice Carolers, Enesco Musicals, Cherished Teddies, Precious Moments, Swarovski, Thomas Kinkade, Lladro, Hibel, Sports Impressions, David Winter, Lilliput Lane, Armani, Hummel, Emmett Kelly, and Krystonia.

NALED member. Free shipping with $100 orders. Special orders and layaways welcome. All major credit cards accepted.

HAPPY HOUSE GIFT SHOP

Westgate Shopping Center
2521 Jackson Rd.
Ann Arbor, MI 48103
**PHONE: (313)662-9635
FAX: (313)665-3607**

Monday-Friday: 9:30-8:00
Saturday: 9:30-6:00; Sunday: 12:00-5:00

Dept. 56 Showcase Dealer, Precious Moments, Memories of Yesterday, Cherished Teddies, Sarah's Attic, Lowell Davis, Lilliput Lane, David Winter, M.I. Hummel, Miss Martha's, Byers' Choice, Krystonia, Tom Clark, Hallmark Keepsake Ornaments, United Design, J.H. Boone.

Member Gift Creations Concepts. All major credit cards accepted. Redemption Center for most collectibles. Shipping available.

MICHIGAN

LAKEVIEW CARD & GIFT SHOP

632 Capital Ave. S.W.
Battle Creek, MI 49015
PHONE: (616)962-0650
FAX: (616)962-7374

Monday-Saturday: 9:00-5:30

Precious Moments (DSR), M.I. Hummel, Dept. 56, Lowell Davis, Lilliput Lane, retired Hallmark ornaments, Memories of Yesterday, Sarah's Attic, PenDelfin, Miss Martha's Originals, Cherished Teddies, Marty's Sculptures: The Herd. Emmett Kelly Jr., Flambro, Goebel Miniatures, Ispanky, Town Square Collection and Dreamsicles.

NALED member. Visa, Discover and Mastercard accepted. Layaway and UPS shipping available.

RUGGLES GIFT SHOP

727 Capital Ave. S.W.
Battle Creek, MI 49015
PHONE: (616)964-7534
FAX: (616)965-3428

Monday-Friday: 10:00-5:30
Saturday: 9:30-3:00

Lladro, David Winter, Walt Disney Classics Collection, Wee Forest Folk, Jan Hagara, Maud Humphrey, Krystonia, Hummel, Music Boxes, Staffordshire Enamel Boxes, Harbour Lights, and Lexington Hall dolls.

All major credit cards accepted. Layaway and shipping available. GCC Member. Redemption center for Hummel, David Winter and Disney. Gift wrapping available.

MIKKI'S HALLMARK

132 N. Main
Brooklyn, MI 49230
PHONE: (517)592-3354
FAX: (517)592-3354 (CALL 1ST)

Monday-Saturday: 10:00-6:00
Sunday: 12:00-5:00

Located in the beautiful Irish Hills just North of Michigan International Speedway.

Over 2,000 lines. Primary and Secondary Market specialists for Sarah's Attic, Jan Hagara, Hadley House including Terry Redlin, Steiff, Longaberger Baskets, North American Bear, Precious Moments, Memories of Yesterday, Cat's Meow, Maud Humphrey, Reco, Bennett's Brush Strokes. Also artist bears and estate jewelry. Hundreds of retired Sarah's Attic in stock.

Second location: Irish Hills Touch O' Country, 9947 N. Brooklyn Rd., Brooklyn, MI 49230. Phone: (517)592-3384.

Visa, Mastercard and American Express. Layaway and UPS shipping available.

BONNIE'S HALLMARK

110 N. Mitchell St.
Cadillac, MI 49601
PHONE: (616)775-4282
FAX: (616)775-7499

Monday-Saturday: 8:30-9:00
Sundays and Holidays: 10:00-6:00

Tom Clark Gnomes, Sarah's Attic, Precious Moments, Memories of Yesterday, Hallmark ornaments, Dept. 56, Golden Memories by Lladro, All God's Children, Miss Martha's Originals, Cherished Teddies, Jan Hagara, Lilliput Lane, Laura's Attic, Tobin Fraley Carousel Horses, Raikes Bears, Silver Deer, Fontanini, Sports Impressions, Lefton Village, Margaret Furlong, and Duncan Royale.

Secondary Market on Hallmark ornaments and Tom Clark Gnomes. Layaways welcome. Visa, Mastercard and Discover accepted. UPS shipping is available.

MICHIGAN

REME COLLECTIBLES

42839 Ford Rd.
Canton, MI 48187

**PHONE: (313)981-7500
(800)55-DOLLS**

Monday-Saturday: 10-8; Sunday: 12-5

Specialist in collectibles since 1988. Dolls, plates, figurines, prints and much more. Alexander Dolls, Barbie, Cast Art, Paul Crees, Dept. 56, Daddy's Long Legs, Edna Dali, Effanbee, Enchantica, Enesco, European Artist, Dynasty, GADCO, Georgetown, Jan Hagara, Hamilton, Annette Himstedt, Maud Humphrey, Jeckle-Jansen, Dolls by Jerri, EKJ, Good-Kruger, Sandra Kuck, Lilliput Lane, Marty Bell, Mattel, Lee Middleton, Monika, Heidi Otts, Phyllis Parkins, Michael and Lynn Roche, G. Schmidt, Swarovski, Roth Trefferson, Vlasta, Susan Wakeen, David Winter, D. Zolan, Zook, and much more. Redemption Center for collector clubs.

Major credit cards. Free layaway. Shipping.

EVERTS HALLMARK SHOP

192 N. State
Caro, MI 48723

PHONE: (517)673-2800

Monday-Saturday: 9:00-5:30
Friday: 9:00-8:00; Sunday: 12:00-4:00

David Winter Cottages, Dept. 56: Snowbabies, Heritage Village Collection, Snow Village. Precious Moments, Memories Of Yesterday, Dreamsicles, Possible Dreams, Cherished Teddies, Calico Kittens, Sports Impressions, Hallmark Keepsake Ornaments, Tender Touches, and Enesco Musicals.

30 minutes east of I-75 on M-81. Layaways welcome. Major credit cards accepted.

DIAMOND CONNECTION

6740 E. Ten Mile Rd.
Centerline, MI 48015

PHONE: (313)759-2520

Monday-Friday: 11:00-7:30
Saturday: 10:00-6:00

One of Gartlan U.S.A.'s top dealers. The Diamond Connection blends a strong sports backround with today's sports collectible explosion. In addition to the Gartlan product line, the Diamond Connection carries Sports Impressions, Salvino Sports Legends and D.H. Ussher plates. The Diamond Connection is also the producer of the "Legends of Hockey" postcard art series featuring Doug West.

Visa and Mastercard. The Diamond Connection offers a layaway program and is very active on the secondary market. Significant player in the sports artwork category including products from Simon Art, Legends in Lithographs, Michael J. Taylor and other prominent artists.

DAYSPRING GIFTS

115 South Main
Chelsea, MI 48118

PHONE: (313)475-7501

Monday-Wednesday: 9:00-6:00
Thursday-Saturday: 9:00-8:00
Sunday: 12:00-5:00

Gold Crown Hallmark Store in business since 1977. Hallmark Keepsake Ornaments, Dept. 56: All Villages, accessories, Snowbabies, All Through The House, and Dickens Brass. Enesco Musicals, Cherished Teddies, Calico Kittens, Precious Moments, Sports Impressions, Hummels, Cat's Meow, Hallmark Galleries, Fontanini, David Winter, The Doll Maker, Baldwin Brass, Thomas Kinkade prints, Possible Dreams, Dreamsicles, Silver Deer, United Design, Hallmark and Morley Candy. Made in Michigan gifts, and designer jewelry.

Club Redemption. Free gift wrapping. Layaway. Major credit cards accepted.

MICHIGAN

JEANIE'S VICTORIAN HEIRLOOMS

3568 N. Alamando Rd.
Coleman, MI 48618

PHONE: (517)465-6633

Thursday-Saturday: 10:00-5:00
By Appointment Anytime

"Treasured heirlooms for the collector." Located 3 miles east of Coleman Old US 10, 1/2 mile south on Alamando. Limited Porcelain dolls and bears by Dolls by Jerri, Seymour Mann, The Collectables, Bearly People, Mary Meyer, and Tree Top Angels. Secondary Market: Wendy Lawton, Turner Dolls, Gorham, Madame Alexander, Antique Porcelain. 50's and 60's vinyl dolls, doll furniture and buggies. Roman, Inc. Complete wedding accessories, specializing in photo albums. Decorate with a flair with dried flowers and crafts. "Designed for you, handmade by me!"

Visa and Mastercard accepted. Layaways. Secondary Market. Gift certificates.

AUNTIE M'S

510 W. Flint St.(Davison Rd.)
Davidson, MI 48423

PHONE: (313)653-1757

Monday-Saturday: 10:00-5:30
Closed Tuesday and Sunday

Bears:.Raikes and Bonita. David Winter, Sarah's Attic, Sandicast, and Lilliput Lane. Dolls: Goetz, Effanbee, Good-Kruger, Georgetown, Dolls by Jerri, Zook, Lee Middleton, Mattel, Victoria, Dolls by Pauline, Bradley Dolls, Edna Hibel, Kingstate, Precious Moments, and books.

Visa, Mastercard, Discover. Layaway, shipping. Collector club redemption center.

ADRAY'S

20219 Carlysle
Dearborn, MI 48124

PHONE: (313)274-9500
FAX: (313)274-6874

Monday-Saturday: 10:00-9:00

Serving the community since 1955. Impressive display of cottages from Lilliput Lane and David Winter. Also featuring Gorham, Lee Middleton, Sadek, Harbour Lights, Maud Humphrey Bogart, Waterford, Emmett Kelly, Bulova Mini-Clocks, American Music Box, Lladro, Lowell Davis, Crystal World, Cherished Teddies, Little Cheesers, Maruri USA, Armani, Sandra Kuck and Seiko, Citizen, Bulova, Longines-Wittnauer, Noblia and Lassale watches. A complete line of 14kt gold jewelry.

Club redemptions for Lilliput Lane, David Winter and Maud Humphrey Bogart. Layaways welcome. Major credit cards accepted.

CARD & GIFT CENTER

37061 Grand River
Farmington, MI 48335

PHONE: (313)471-5187
FAX: (313)471-1310

Monday-Saturday: 10:00-9:00
Sunday: 12:00-5:00

Precious Moments, Dept. 56, Memories of Yesterday, Annalee, David Winter, Hudson Pewter, Lilliput Lane, Sports Impressions, John Hine, Cat's Meow, Ron Lee Clowns, Bradford plates, Fontanini, Hallmark Onaments, Possible Dreams, Raikes Bears, Snowbabies, and Sandicast.

Most major credit cards accepted. Layaway and shipping available. Redemption Center for above. Other store locations in Rochester, Troy, Belleville, Livonia and Flint, Michigan.

MICHIGAN

THE 1/2 OFF CARD SHOP
PRESENTS
FOR COLLECTORS ONLY

31077 Orchard Lake Rd.
Farmington Hills, MI 48334

PHONE: (313)851-8580
FAX: (313)851-8581

Monday-Saturday: 9:30-9:00
Sunday: 10:00-5:00

LEGENDS, Tom Clark, Enesco Musicals, Ron Lee, Krystonia, Iris Arc, Crystal World, Gartlan, Sports Impressions, Possible Dreams, United Design, Lilliput Lane, Sarah's Attic, David Winter, and Michael Garman.

All major credit cards accepted. Layaways welcome.

CARAVAN GIFTS & COLLECTIBLES

610 Fenton Square
Fenton, MI 48430

PHONE: (313)629-4212

Monday-Saturday: 10:00-5:30

Hummels, PM, ANRI, Belleek, Lilliput Lane, Royal Copenhagen, Bing & Grondahl, David Winter, Lladro, Royal Doulton, Walt Disney, Dept. 56, Possible Dreams, Snowbabies, Castagna Animals, Sarah's Attic, Maud Humphrey, Madame Alexander dolls, Memories of Yesterday, Cherished Teddies, Ashton-Drake dolls, collector plates by Bradford, Hollywood, Hamilton, and many others. Dolls by Hamilton and Alexander. Bells by PM, Hummel, and Fenton. Iris Arc crystal and Baldwin Brass.

Visa, Mastercard and Discover accepted. NALED Member. Bradford. Secondary Market Service. Free gift wrapping. Layaways and shipping available.

THE 1/2 OFF CARD SHOP
PRESENTS
FOR COLLECTORS ONLY

G-3577 Miller Rd.
Flint, MI 48507

PHONE: (313)230-2420
FAX: (313)230-0131

Monday-Saturday: 10:00-9:00
Sunday: 12:00-5:00

Various lines include: Precious Moments, Sarah's Attic, Reco, Maruri, Memories of Yesterday, Maud Humphrey, Cherished Teddies, Snowbabies, Gartlan, Roman Inc., and United Design. Bradford Exchange Dealer.

For convenience, a layaway plan is available. Visa, Mastercard and Discover accepted.

UNDERHILLS ACCENTS

3253 Linden Rd.
Genesee Valley Center
Flint, MI 48507

PHONE: (313)230-1131

Monday-Saturday: 10:00-9:00
Sunday: 12:00-6:00

Unique! One stop collectible shop. Lines include: Dept. 56, Hummel, Swarovski, David Winter, Lladro, Snowbabies, Tom Clark, WFF, Sarah's Attic, Byers' Choice, Krystonia, All God's Children, Iris Arc, Armani, MOY, Sports Impressions, Hagara, Disney, Emmett Kelly Jr. and Sr., Lilliput Lane, Dolls: Hamilton, Madame Alexander, Ashton-Drake, Middleton, Wimbledon, The Dollmaker, and Pauline. Plates: Hamilton, Bradford and Reco. Santas: Possible Dreams, Midwest Importers, and KSA. Decorative accessories and more.

All major credit cards. Redemption Center. Both layaway and shipping are available.

MICHIGAN

BRONNER'S CHRISTmas WONDERLAND

25 Christmas Lane P.O. Box 176
Frankenmuth, MI 48734-0176

PHONE: (517)652-9931
FAX: (517)652-3466

Jan-May: Mon.-Thurs. and Sat.: 9-5:30
Friday: 9-9 Sunday: 12-5:30
June-Dec.: Mon.-Sat.: 9-9; Sun.: 12-7

Since 1945. World's largest Christmas store. Over 50,000 trims and gifts. Open 361 days. See collection of over 600 Hummels and complete collection of Precious Moments. Over 50 collectible lines including Annalee, Anri, Belleek, Byers' Choice, Cairn, Cherished Teddies, Lowell Davis, DeGrazia, Dept. 56 Showcase Dealer, Fontanini, Hallmark, Laura's Attic, Lladro, Lucy & Me, Hummel, MOY, Miss Martha, Possible Dreams, PM (DSR), and Disney. Redemption Center for many clubs. $5 coupon for club figurine redemption. Major credit cards. Shipping.

COVERED BRIDGE GIFT SHOP

775 S. Main St.
Frankenmuth, MI 48734

PHONE: (517)652-2902

Winter Hours
Sunday-Thursday: 9:30-6:00
Friday and Saturday: 9:30-9:00
Summer Hours
Open Daily: 9:00am-10:00pm

Precious Moments (DSR), Memories of Yesterday, Emmett Kelly Jr., Lowell Davis, Walt Disney Classics Collection, Hummels, Maud Humphrey, Cherished Teddies, Krystonia, Iris Arc Crystal, Sports Impressions, Miss Martha's Collection, Enesco Treasury Ornaments (Premier Dealer), Dept. 56: Snow Village, Heritage Village, Snow Babies, All Thru The House. Possible Dreams Santas.

10 month layaway plan. Visa, Mastercard, and Discover accepted. Gift Creations Concepts Member. Shipping available anywhere in the US.

THE CURIOSITY SHOP

P.O. Box 243
618 S. Main St.
Frankenmuth, MI 48734

PHONE: (517)652-8258
FAX: (517)652-9401

Open 7 Days A Week

Specializing in Kurt Adler/Santa's World including Christian Steinbach nutcrackers. Marina's Russian Collection including nested Russian art dolls. Midwest Importers including Christian Ulbricht nutcrackers, Leo Smith Collection and Heritage Santa. Possible Dreams, Traditions 'N' Stone by Artline, and Old World Christmas.

Mail orders. Visa, Mastercard and American Express accepted.

THE FRANKENMUTH BAVARIAN INN DOLL & TOY FACTORY

713 S. Main St.
Frankenmuth, MI 48734

PHONE: (800)BAVARIA
FAX: (517)652-3481

Summer: Open Daily: 9:00-9:30
Winter: Open Daily: 10:00-9:00

Same location since 1888. Featuring VanderBear Collection-Muffy and Family, V.I.P Bear by North American Bear, Thomas Tank Collectibles, Porcelain Doll-Bundles of Joy by Mary Ellen Hadden, Frankenmuth Freund Vinyl Dolls by Bavarian Inn, Depression glass doll dishes, Little Folk Dolls by Bavarian Inn, Bearly People Bears and Collector Scale Model Cars.

All major credit cards, Travelers checks, and Canadian currency accepted. Layaway and special orders available. Shipping.

MICHIGAN

THE FRANKENMUTH BAVARIAN INN GIFT SHOP

713 S. Main St.
Frankenmuth, MI 48734

PHONE: (517)652-6731
(800)BAVARIA
FAX: (517)652-3481

Summer: Open Daily: 9:00-9:30
Winter: Open Daily: 10:00-9:00

Same location since 1888. Featuring Andrea by Sadek birds, Armani, Napoleon Capodimonte, Kaiser Porcelain, United Design, Melody in Motion, David Winter, Animal Antics, Maurice Wideman, Father Time, Maud Humphrey Bogart, Hummel, Michael's Ltd., Royal Albert, Glass Baron, Swarovski, Savvy, Dreamsicles, German Nutcrackers, German Steins, European Crystal, and Fenton Glass Art.

All major credit cards, Travelers checks, and Canadian currency accepted. Layaway and special orders available. Shipping.

FRANKENMUTH GALLERY

568 S. Main
Frankenmuth, MI 48734

PHONE: (800)344-2917
FAX: (517)652-2005

Open 7 Days A Week: 10:00-9:00

Your collectibles store for the 90's. The largest Emmett Kelly Jr. Dealer, with annual appearance by Emmett.

Lines also include: Armani porcelains, Maruri porcelains, Thomas Kinkade, Terry Redlin, Sandra Kuck, Pleasantville 1893, David Winter Cottages, Don Rust, German Steins. Also featuring gift items, thousands of original oil paintings and frames and Limited Edition framed prints.

Home of "Emmett's friends." Call: (800)344-2917.

THE PEWTER KINGDOM

School Haus Square
245 S. Main
Frankenmuth, MI 48734

PHONE: (517)652-8622

Jan.-May: Monday-Saturday: 10:00-6:00
Sunday: 11:30-5:00
June-Dec.: Monday-Thursday: 10:00-6:00
Friday-Saturday: 10:00-8:00
Sunday: 11:00-6:00

LEGENDS. Chilmark. Other lines include Mill Creek, Emmett Kelly Sr., Hudson, Disney, Crystal World, Seagull, Duncan Royale, Looney Tunes, Fort, Rawcliffe, Tudor Mint, and Collector Case.

All 5 major credit cards accepted. Layaway and shipping available.

THE GINGERBREAD HOUSE

3735 Old 27 South
Gaylord, MI 49735

PHONE: (517)732-4135
FAX: (517)732-6962

Monday-Saturday: 10:00-5:30
Sunday: 11:00-4:00

Byers' Choice Carolers, Lizzie High, Shelia's, Kurt S. Adler Nutcrackers, Steinbach and Zuber, Sarah's Attic, Westminister Graphics, WACO, Tilly, Bunnies By the Bay, Victoria's Buttons, Legacy Dolls, Vitro-Dissney, Windy Meadow Pottery Ltd. (Hand Built Cottages), Annalee, retired pieces.

Visa and Mastercard accepted. Layaway and shipping available. Limited Secondary Market. Redemption center for Sarah's Attic.

MICHIGAN

TINA'S GIFTS & COLLECTIBLES

2583 South Old 27
Gaylord, MI 49735

PHONE: (517)732-7649

Open 7 Days A Week: 9:00-9:00

Northern Michigan's largest Bradford Exchange Representative. Lines include: Ashton-Drake dolls, plate frames and holders. Figurines by Emmett Kelly, Jr., Cherished Teddies, Perillo, M.I. Hummel, Norman Rockwell, and Donald Zolan. Also available are lithographs, Spoontique pewter miniatures, and dolls by Johannes Zook, Middleton, Susan Wakeen, Bradley, and many more.

Shipping available anywhere. Layaways welcome. Visa and Mastercard accepted.

LAKESHORE FLORAL & GIFTS

915 Washington Ave.
Grand Haven, MI 49417

PHONE: (616)842-4340

Monday-Saturday: 9:00-5:30

Located in the beautiful tourist area in SW Michigan on Lake Michigan, just East of US-31 on Washington St. Visit our 3500 square feet showroom displaying collectibles and seasonal gifts, with 15 theme trees at Christmas time. Featuring Dept. 56: Snow Village, Dickens, Christmas in the City, North Pole, New England, Snowbabies, All Thru the House, accessories, and Merry Makers. Chartered Precious Moments Dealer, Possible Dreams, beautiful Porcelin Dolls by local artists, Dreamsicles by Cast Art, Fontanini.

A Tri-Cities business for over 115 years. Redemption Center for Precious Moments and Possible Dreams. Layaway. House Accounts. All major credit cards accepted. UPS shipping anywhere.

FOUR SEASONS GIFT SHOP

218 S. Bridge
Grand Ledge, MI 48837

PHONE: (517)627-7469
FAX: (517)321-2515

Monday-Saturday: 10:00-5:00

Showcase Dealer for Chilmark, Byers' Choice Ltd., Sarah's Attic, PenDelfin, Lilliput Lane, Precious Moments, Hibel plates, P. Buckley Moss plates and figurines, Sandra Kuck plates, lithographs and figurines, Donald Zolan plates, Duncan Royale Santas, Cherished Teddies, Castagna, Calico Kittens, Enesco Musicals, WACO, Maruri eagles, and Enesco Treasury Ornaments.

Visa and Mastercard accepted. Layaway and shipping available. NALED member.

EASTERN FLORAL AND GIFTS

2836 Broadmoor S.E.
Grand Rapids, MI 49512

PHONE: (616)949-2200
FAX: (616)949-9009

Monday and Friday: 8:00-9:00
Tuesday-Thursday: 8:00-6:00
Saturday: 8:00-5:30; Closed Sunday
Summer Schedule Subject To Change

Dreamsicles, Dept. 56, M.I. Hummel, Tom Clark Gnomes, David Winter, Precious Moments, Byers' Choice Carolers, Lizzie High, Shoemaker's Dream by John Hine, Clay Art, Iris Arc Crystal, Fenton, Napoleon Capodimonte, Old World Christmas, Roman Inc., and United Design.

All major credit cards accepted. Layaway terms available. Club Redemptions.

MICHIGAN

FOX'S JEWELERS

Woodland Mall
Grand Rapids, MI 49508

PHONE: (616)956-7995
(616)459-6271
(FOR STORE LOCATION)
FAX: (616)956-9034

Monday-Saturday: 10:00-9:00
Sunday: 12:00-5:00

43 other locations throughout the Midwest: Michigan, Indiana, Illinois, Wisconsin and Iowa. Call for addresses and phone numbers.

Lines include: Swarovski, Lladro, Walt Disney Classics Collection, Hummel, and Waterford.

Visa, Mastercard, American Express, and Fox Charge accepted. Club Redemption Center. Layaway and shipping available. Free gift wrapping.

THE GIFT BASKET

2034 Lake Michigan Dr. N.W.
Grand Rapids, MI 49504

PHONE: (616)791-1800
FAX: (616)791-8810

Monday-Friday: 9:30-8:00
Saturday: 9:00-5:00

Year-round Christmas room! Located off I-96 at Lake Michigan Dr. and Covell in Edison Plaza. Lines include: Thomas Kinkade, Glynda Turley, Margaret Furlong, Fontanini, Cherished Teddies, Possible Dreams, Mill Creek, Sandicast, United Design, Artesania Rinconada, Clay Art Masks, Baldwin Brass, Dreamsicles. They also carry rubber stamps, toiletries, Yankee Candles, gourmet food and coffee, over 30 lines of greeting cards, and a large selection of quality jewelry.

Free gift wrapping. UPS shipping. Layaway available. Mastercard, Visa, and Discover accepted.

GIFTS FROM THE HEART

Eastbrook Mall
Grand Rapids, MI 49512

PHONE: (616)957-5009
FAX: (616)457-7395

Monday-Saturday: 10:00-9:00
Sunday: 12:00-5:00

Cat's Meow, Cherished Teddies, Country Cousins, Dreamsicles, Josef Angels, Lucy & Me, Old World Ornaments, Kitty Cucumber, Gail Laura Collectibles, Precious Moments, Raikes Bears, Sarah's Attic, Snowbabies, Stone Critter Animals.

Visa, MC and Discover accepted. Layaway and shipping available. Free gift wrapping available. Redemption center for Precious Moments, Sarah's Attic and Cat's Meow.

Second Location: Grand Village Mall, Grandville, MI 49418. (616)531-4221. Monday-Saturday: 10:00-9:00.

MARJ'S DOLL SANCTUARY

5238 Plainfield Ave. N.E.
Grand Rapids, MI 49505

PHONE: (616)361-0054
FAX: (616)361-0232

Monday-Saturday: 10:00-6:00

Over 150 collectable doll and bear lines including Alexander, Bearly There, Bello, Bryer, Barbie, Berjusa, The Collectables, Dakin, Effanbee, GADCO, Georgetown, Ginny, Good-Kruger, Gotz, Gund, Gunzel, Jan Hagara, Heath, Evie Hendrick, Herman Bears, Annette Himstedt, Dolls by Jerri, Julie Jones, Kish, Krey, Lawtons, Little Souls, Merrythought, Middleton, Naber Kids, Netterer, North American Bear Company, Oldenburg Originals, Pauline, Raikes, Roche, Rueger, Steiff, Shelton, Tilly, Toridan, Turner, Susan Wakeen, Robin Woods, and much more!

Mail orders and layaways are welcome. Mastercard, Visa, and Discover accepted.

Knowledgeable and friendly!

MICHIGAN

ROBINETTE'S GIFT BARN

3142 Four Mile Rd. N.E.
Grand Rapids, MI 49505

**PHONE: (800) GFT-BARN
(616)361-7180
FAX: (616)361-6445**

Monday-Saturday: 10:00-5:00
Open Sundays Sept.-Jan.

Dept. 56 Showcase Dealer including all villages, Snowbabies, Merry Makers, Winter Silhouette, and All Through the House, Possible Dreams, Margaret Furlong, Byers' Choice, Annalee, Lilliput Lane, Sarah's Attic, Daddy's Long Legs, Lizzie High, LEGENDS, Walt Disney Classics Collection, Thomas Kinkade, Cat's Meow, Harbour Lights, Texas Stamp, J.H. Boone, Beatrix Potter, CT, Calico Kittens, Shelia's, Band Creations, Zolan and Sandra Kuck plates, and Roosevelt Bears. Secondary Market. Club redemption center. Visa, Mastercard and Discover accepted. Layaway plan, call for details. Shipping. Free gift wrapping.

STANDALE COUNTRY HOUSE

365 Cummings N.W.
Grand Rapids, MI 49504

PHONE: (616)453-7298

Monday-Thursday: 10:00-5:30
Friday: 10:00-9:00
Saturday: 10:00-5:30

Located in a quaint English Tudor Cottage. Dept. 56 including all villages, accessories, Snowbabies and Winter Silhouette, Old World Ornaments, Midwest Importers, Leo Smith, Heritage, Snowbabies, Cat's Meow, Byers' Choice Carolers, Ladie and Friends-Lizzie High Dolls, Sarah's Attic, and Possible Dreams Santas. Antiques from lace to furniture.

Visa, Mastercard and Discover accepted. Layaways welcome. Shipping available. Free gift wrapping.

CHAPTER III GIFT SHOP

300 S. Lafayette
Greenville, MI 48838

**PHONE: (616)754-3289
FAX: (616)754-3904**

Monday-Thursday: 9:00-6:00
Friday: 9:00-7:00; Saturday: 9:00-5:30

Serving collectors for over 25 years. Chapter III Gift Shop is a Dept. 56 Showcase Dealer and a Precious Moments Distinguished Service Retailer. The store also carries the Miss Martha Collection (Enesco), David Winter, June McKenna Santas, Sarah's Attic, Cat's Meow, Zook Dolls, North American Muffy Bear. Secondary Market in Lowell Davis, Lilliput Lane, Dept. 56, Anheuser-Busch, Cairn Studios, Cherished Teddies, Dreamsicles, Hallmark Keepsake Ornaments, and Harbour Lights.

All major credit cards accepted. Layaway and UPS shipping available. GCC member.

THE PAPER PLACE & DOLL PLACE

212 S. River
Holland, MI 49423

**PHONE: (616)392-7776
FAX: (616)392-2499**

Monday, Thursday, Friday: 9:30-9:00
Tuesday, Wednesday, Saturday: 9:30-6:00

Steiff, Hermann, Artist Bears, Grizzly, Gund including Canterbury. Dolls include Hildegard Gunzel, Madame Alexander, Susan Wakeen, Wendy Lawton, Dolls by Jerri, Gorham, Ginny, Gertz, Robin Woods, Sonja Hartmann, Vlasta, Lee Middleton, Phyllis Parkins and many more.

Mastercard and Visa accepted. Layaway. Shipping available. NALED member. Redemption Center. Many hard to locate items.

Second location: 118 Washington, Grand Haven, MI 49417. Phone: (616)846-6280. Mon.-Sat.: 9:30-6:00; Fri.: 9:30-9:00.

MICHIGAN

WEEPING WILLOW

1 East 8th St.
Holland, MI 49423

PHONE: (616)396-6086
FAX: (517)546-1459

Monday-Friday: 10:00-5:30
Monday & Friday: Open again 7pm-9pm
Saturday: 10:00-5:00; Closed Tuesday

This collectors paradise store is small in size but large in selection. You must see it to believe it. Located in SW MI. Showcase Dealer for Dept. 56 (All Villages, Snowbabies, All Thru the House, Merry Makers and accessories), Old World and Christopher Radko, Lilliput, DW, Hummels, Kitty Cucumber, Tom Clark, Lowell Davis, Maud Humphrey, Jan Hagara, Bradford plates, Ashton-Drake, EKJ, Cherished Teddies, Zolan, Byers' Choice, Vaillancourt Santas, Matreshka Nesting Dolls, Steiff, Hermann, and Merry Thought Bears, Beatrix Potter, Cat's Meow, collectible santas, angels, bunnies and other animals.

COLLECTOR'S UNLIMITED

2164 Argentine Rd.
Howell, MI 48843

PHONE: (517)548-0564
FAX: (517)546-1459

Store Hours By Appointment Only

Featuring a very large selection of Emmett Kelly Jr. (plates, figurines, ornaments), Lowell Davis, Duncan Royale, a large inventory of Norman Rockwell figurines, plates and ornaments, Hibel dolls and plates, Belsnickles, John Hine (Sandra Kuck, Maurice Wideman, Shoehouses), Hidden Kingdom, Tom Clark Gnomes, Dolls by Jerri, Hamilton dolls, Lexington dolls, Limited Edition Fenton, Lenox Collectibles, Maud Humphrey, Spanos Dolls, Goebel and many more. Please call!

Visa and Mastercard accepted. Secondary Market Retailer. Layaway and shipping anywhere are available.

SANTINI GIFT & COLLECTIBLES
ELLE STEVENS JEWELERS

135 E. Aurora St.
Ironwood, MI 49938

PHONE: (906)932-5679

Mon.-Sat.: 9:00-5:00; Fri.: 9:00-6:00

Collectible Specialists! Figurines, plates, dolls, limited edition prints. Precious Moments (DSR), Dept. 56, Bradford plates, Swarovski, M.I. Hummel, Lladro, David Winter, Tom Clark, MOY, Ashton-Drake Dolls, Sports Collectibles, Miss Martha's Originals, Maud Humphrey, Cherished Teddies, Dreamsicles, Lilliput Lane, Willitts Designs, Terry Redlin plates and prints, Wildlife Art Gallery, fine jewelry, diamonds, 14K gold and custom designed jewelry.

NALED member. All major credit cards accepted. Layaway. Shipping anywhere in the USA. Phone calls welcome.

JACOBSON'S

Jackson, MI 49201

PHONE: (800)635-4770

Shop at Jacobson's and you will find fine collectibles from:

Lenox, Waterford, Reed and Barton, Gorham, Lunt, Wedgwood, Herend, Royal Doulton, Lladro, Faberge, Rick Cain Sculptures, Baccarat, Richard Lamson Sculptures, Orrefors, Hoya, Royal Copenhagen, Chase, Kirk Stieff, Fitz and Floyd, Towle, Mottahedeh, Wallace, Lalique and more.

Michigan, Indiana, Ohio and Florida. Call for the Jacobson's location nearest you.

MICHIGAN

KNIBLOE GIFT CORNER

1600 E. Michigan Ave.
Jackson, MI 49202

PHONE: (517)782-6846
FAX: (517)782-6668

Monday-Saturday: 9:00-5:30
Holiday Hours: Monday-Thursday and Saturday: 9:00-5:30
Friday: 9:00-8:00; Sunday: 12:00-5:00

Special collectible dolls and plates, Lladro, David Winter, Precious Moments (DSR), Memories of Yesterday, Hummel, Emmett Kelly Jr., Swarovski crystal, Dept. 56, Byers' Choice, Armani, Duncan Royale, Tom Clark, Cherished Teddies, Fontanini, Krystonia, Perillo, DeGrazia, Miss Martha's, All God's Children, Lowell Davis, Raikes Bears, Jan Hagara, Melody In Motion, Bosson Heads, Chilmark, Dreamsicles, Margaret Furlong, Walt Disney Classics Collection and Annalee.

All major credit cards accepted. NALED member. Bradford Dealer.

THE MOLE HOLE

300 S. Kalamazoo Mall
Kalamazoo, MI 49007

PHONE: (616)344-9000
FAX: (616)344-6623

Monday-Friday: 10:00-6:00
Saturday: 10:00-5:00; Sunday: 12:00-5:00

Dept. 56 Showcase Dealer, Villages and accessories, Snowbabies, All Thru The House, and Merry Makers. Swarovski, Showcase Dealer for Chilmark, Sarah's Attic, Iris Arc, Lilliput Lane, Hudson Pewter, Krystonia, Rick Cain, Roman, Fontinini, Byers' Choice, Duncan Royale Diamond Dealer, Wee Forest Folk, Crabtree and Evelyn, and Baldwin Brass.

Redemption Center for collectibles listed. All major credit cards accepted. Shipping available. Secondary Market Service. Cottages and figurines.

BREWHAUS GIFT SHOP

2622 N. East St.
Lansing, MI 48906

PHONE: (517)484-4417
(800)359-3414
FAX: (517)484-5212

Monday-Friday: 10:00-6:00
Saturday: 10:00-5:00

Anheuser-Busch collectibles, CUI, Henry Cornell Importers, Coca-Cola memorabilia, "breweriana." Retail licensed brewery logo items.

The collectors connection club which includes 4 newsletters 3 photo albums, featuring in total over 1,000 colored pictures of brewery collectibles and steins. Call for further information.

Visa, Mastercard and Discover accepted. A Secondary Market Dealer.

HADDAD'S GIFTS

Logan Square Shopping Center
3222 S. Logan
Lansing, MI 48910

PHONE: (517)882-8334
FAX: (517)882-1216

Mon.-Fri.: 9:30-9:00; Sat.: 9:30-6:00

"One of Michigan's Largest Gift and Collectable Stores!" Continually adding new lines to the ever growing collectible department: Memories Of Yesterday, Cherished Teddies, PM, Ashton-Drake Dolls, Bradford Exchange, Hamilton, Georgetown, Lowell Davis, Hummel, Hagara, R. Olszewski Miniatures, Melody in Motion, Sarah's Attic, Enesco Musicals, Raikes Bears, Walt Disney Classics, EKJ, Hook, Rockwell, Daddy's Long Legs, All God's Children, Hallmark Ornaments, Anheuser-Busch, Dept. 56, Duncan Royale, Tom Clark, Iris Arc, Krystonia, Fred Stone. Redemption Center for all clubs. Layaway. Shipping.

MICHIGAN

COUNTRY CLASSIC COLLECTIBLES

323 W. Nepessing
Lapeer, MI 48446

PHONE: (313)667-4080

Monday-Saturday: 10:00-5:00

Collector plates and dolls from the Bradford Exchange, Hamilton, Ashton-Drake Galleries, Disney Classics Collection, John Hine Studios featuring David Winter, American Collection and Shoehouses, Jan Hagara, Sarah's Attic Golden Heart Dealer, Cherished Teddies, Dreamsicles, Sports Impressions and Gartlan, Maruri, United Design, Rockwell Studios, American Artists, Cole Fine Art, Hadley House, Schmid (Disney, Beatrix Potter, and Hidden Kingdom), Designs Americana, and Mill Creek. Plate frames. NALED member. Visa, Mastercard and Discover. Special orders. Layaways. Secondary Market Service.

GWINN'S TRUE VALUE

66 W. Nepessing
Lapeer, MI 48446

PHONE: (313)664-3662
FAX: (313)664-3670

Monday-Thursday: 8:30-6:00
Friday: 8:30-8:00; Saturday: 8:30-5:30
Sunday: 12:00-4:00

Krystonia, Dreamsicles, Raikes Bears, Breyer Horses, Enesco Showcase Dealer for Small World of Music, Premier Dealer Enesco Treasury of Christmas, Fenton Art Glass, Hamilton Collection of Heritage Dolls, Sports Impressions, Bearly People Cherished Teddies, Enesco's My American Dream, Cherished Teddies, Calico Kittens and Laura's Attic.

Layaway and shipping are both available. Visa, Mastercard and Discover accepted.

MARION'S COLLECTIBLES

30206 Plymouth Rd.
Livonia, MI 48150

PHONE: (313)522-8620

Monday-Saturday: 10:00-6:00
Seasonal Hours

Bradford Exchange, Lilliput Lane, Precious Moments, Hibel, Golden Memories from Lladro, Chilmark, Hudson, MOY, Thomas Kinkade, Snowbabies, Sarah's Attic, David Winter, Miss Martha's, Emmett Kelly, Wee Forest Folk, Ashton-Drake dolls, Sandicast, Iris Arc, Krystonia, Enchantica, Enesco ornaments, Cairn Studio, Hamilton, Dreamsicles, Jan Hagara, Possible Dreams, Stanton Arts, Hummels, and collector plates and frames.

Special orders. NALED member. Some Secondary Market. All major credit cards accepted. Will ship nationwide.

LASTING IMPRESSIONS

514 S. Huron P.O. Box 399
Mackinaw City, MI 49701

PHONE: (616)436-7310
(616)436-7011

Open 7 Days A Week
May-October: 10:00-10:00
Nov.-Dec.: 10:00-5:00 On Friday-Sunday

Sarah's Attic, Precious Moments, Cherished Teddies, Laura's Attic, Jan Hagara, Jan Shackleford Dolls, Lee Middleton Dolls, Little Cheesers, Indian Quill Boxes, Michael's Limited, United Design, Cast Art Dreamsicles, Enesco Corp., Fenton Art Glass, Iris Arc Crystal and Roman.

All major credit cards accepted. Free gift wrapping.

MICHIGAN

THE 1/2 OFF CARD SHOP
PRESENTS
FOR COLLECTORS ONLY

32011 John R
Madison Heights, MI 48071

PHONE: (313)585-2444
FAX: (313)585-2245

Monday-Saturday: 10:00-9:00
Sunday: 12:00-5:00

Featuring a large selection of Cherished Teddies, David Winter, Snowbabies, The Herd, Precious Moments, Krystonia, Sarah's Attic, Reco, Maruri, Hudson, United Design, Jan Hagara, and Emmett Kelly, Jr. Bradford Exchange Dealer.

For convenience, a layaway plan is available. Visa, Mastercard and Discover accepted.

MC CANDLESS HALLMARK

219 E. Main
Midland, MI 48640

PHONE: (800)942-7908

Monday-Friday: 10:00-8:00
Saturday: 10:00-5:30

Precious Moments, Dept. 56, Hummel, Cairn's Gnomes, Swarovski, PenniBears, Goebel Miniatures, Lilliput Lane, Lowell Davis, Castagna, Lladro, Windy Meadows, Memories of Yesterday, Krystonia, Maud Humphrey, Miss Martha, Laura's Attic, Snowbabies, Duncan Royale, Emmett Kelly, Maruri, Treasured Memories, Enesco Musicals, Sports Impressions, David Winter, Cherished Teddies, Sandra Kuck, J.H. Boone, and WACO Musicals.

All major credit cards accepted. Free UPS shipping.

POST PHARMACY AND GIFT GALLERY

799 S. Mission
Mt. Pleasant, MI 48858

PHONE: (517)772-1566
(517)773-9407
FAX: (517)773-6437

Monday-Friday: 9:00-9:00
Saturday: 9:00-6:00; Sunday: 10:00-3:00

Department 56, Precious Moments, David Winter, Lilliput Lane, Memories of Yesterday, Hummel, Cast Art, Cherished Teddies, United Design, Silver Deer, and Hallmark Keepsake Ornaments.

Club redemption center. Visa, Mastercard, Discover and American Express accepted. Layaway and shipping. Free gift wrap.

CHURCHILLS

Twelve Oaks Mall
27470 Novi Rd.
Novi, MI 48377

PHONE: (313)348-9230
(800)388-1141

Monday-Saturday: 10:00-9:00
Sunday: 12:00-6:00

Bosson Heads, Cairn: Tom Clark Gnomes, Lee Sievers "Good Life" and Tim Wolfe "Tracks"; David Winter, Dreamsicles, Emmett Kelly Jr., Herd, Krystonia, Lilliput Lane, LEGENDS, Monfort Originals, Neil Rose, Rick Cain, Sarah's Attic, Swarovski, and Walt Disney Classics Collection.

All Club Redemptions. All major credit cards accepted. Layaway and free shipping available.

MICHIGAN

SCHULTZ GIFT GALLERY

219 Kaiser St.-Box 598
Pinconning, MI 48650

**PHONE: (517)879-3110
(800)223-8895 (ORDERS)**

Monday-Friday: 9:00-7:00
Saturday: 9:00-6:00

Collector plates, Miss Martha's, Kinka, Maud Humphrey, David Winter/John Hine, Lilliput Lane, Russian Collectibles, Bing & Grondahl, Hummel, Possible Dreams, Fontanini, Dept. 56/Snowbabies, Precious Moments, Memories of Yesterday, Lowell Davis, Iris Arc, Music Boxes, Emmett Kelly, Jr., Grossman, Disney Classics, Ashton-Drake Dolls, and Lladro Golden Moments.

NALED member and Bradford Dealer. Offering Secondary Market Service. Visa, Mastercard, and Discover accepted. Daily UPS shipping.

COUNTRY CHARM

322 S. Main
Plymouth, MI 48170

**PHONE: (800)288-5699
(313)454-9370
FAX: (313)454-3612**

Mon., Tues., Wed., Sat.: 10:00-6:00
Thursday and Friday: 10:00-9:00

Michigan's #1 dealer for Cat's Meow which includes primary and secondary pieces. Other lines include Sarah's Attic, June McKenna santas and ornaments, Margaret Furlong, Doris Morgan prints, home furnishings and accessories, hand crafted furniture, Rowe Pottery, and much more.

Club Redemption center for collectibles listed. Secondary Market Service available. Layaway and shipping. Visa, Mastercard, and Discover accepted.

GEORGIA'S GIFT GALLERY

575 Forest
Plymouth, MI 48170

**PHONE: (313)453-7733
(800)562-3655
FAX: (313)453-1596**

Monday-Wednesday: 10:00-7:00
Thurs.-Fri.: 10:00-8:00; Sat.: 10:00-6:00
Sunday: 12:00-5:00

Ashton-Drake Authorized Doll Dealer, access to all secondary dolls. Bradford Exchange Dealer, Disney Classics, Dept. 56 Showcase Dealer, Lladro, David Winter, Lilliput Lane, Hummel, PM, Sandra Kuck, T. Kinkade, Donald Zolan, Hamilton dolls, secondary plates, Ardleigh and Elliott, Van Hygan & Smythe frames, doll cases, curios and accessories; Norman Rockwell Gallery figurines, prints, waterglobes and Hawthorne figurines. Redemption center.

All major credit cards accepted. Layaway. Free giftwrap and shipping in the continental US. NALED member.

MURIEL'S DOLL HOUSE

824 Penniman
Plymouth, MI 48170

PHONE: (313)455-8110

Monday-Saturday: 10:00-5:00
Sunday: 12:00-5:00
Extended Hours September-December

A very unique doll and miniature store. Alexander, Himstedt, R. John Wright, Deval, Lynn and Michael Roche, Esche, Treffeisen, Gunzel, Christine Heath-Orange, Susan Krey, Good-Kruger, V. Turner, Janet Ness, Bello Creations, Marilyn Bolden, Nahrgang, Nancy Spain, The Collectables, Kathe Kruse, Middleton, Uta Browser, Sonja Hartmann, Robert Tonner, Julia Rueger. Bears by Steiff, Hermann, Bearcraft, Linda Spiegal-Lohr, Beary Special Friend-Laura March Originals.

Layaway. Shipping. Free stand. All major credit cards accepted. Gift wrapping.

MICHIGAN

KEEPSAKE GIFTS

Lapeer Rd.
Port Huron/Kimball, MI 48074

PHONE: (313)985-5855

Monday-Saturday: 10:00-6:00
Sundays Seasonal

Located 10 minutes from the Blue Water Bridge in Port Huron. Premier Dealer for LEGENDS, Cherished Teddies, Calico Kittens, Laura's Attic, Enesco Musical Showcase, Bradford Exchange, Hamilton, Ashton-Drake, Sports Impressions, Sarah's Attic, MOY, PM, Dept. 56 (Villages, accessories, Snowbabies, Merry Makers, All Through the House), Maruri, D. Winter, Lilliput, Maud Humphrey, Miss Martha, Bessie Pease Gutmann, Hummel, Krystonia. Georgetown, The Collectables, Zook, Middleton, Good-Kruger, Possible Dreams.

Club Redemptions. NALED member. Secondary Market. Layaway. MC, Visa and Discover. Shipping. Free gift wrapping.

VAGABOND GIFT CENTER

511 Fort St.
Port Huron, MI 48060

PHONE: (313)987-3300
(Area code 810 after December 1993)

Monday-Friday: 11:00-7:00
Saturday: 12:00-10:00
Sunday: 12:00-7:00

Swarovski, M.I. Hummel, Belleek, Sebastian Miniatures, Lladro, Hibel, David Winter, Norman Rockwell, Baldwin, Kaiser, Maruri, P.M. Craftsman, Snowbabies, GATCO, Incolay, Silver Deer, plates, figurines, and dolls.

Most club redemptions. All major credit cards accepted. Secondary Market. Free gift wrapping. UPS shipping service.

TOMORROW'S KEEPSAKES

3558 Pine Grove Ave.
Port Huron, MI 48060

PHONE: (313)985-4438
(Area code 810 after December 1993)

Mon.-Thurs.: 10:00-5:00; Fri.: 10:00-7:00
Sat.: 10:00-5:00; Sun.: 12:00-5:00

Bradford, Dept. 56, Royal Doulton, P.M. Craftsman, Jan Hagara, Lilliput Lane, Swarovski, M.I. Hummel, Chilmark, Lladro, Hibel, Maud Humphrey, Tom Clark, Ashton-Drake, Cairn, DeGrazia, Sports Impressions, Thomas Kinkade, Snowbabies, Marty Bell, Maruri, Bergsma, Walt Disney Classics Collection, GATCO, Roman, Sandra Kuck, Artaffects, Wolford, Kaiser, Reco, Michael Garman, Lee Middleton, Turner, Dynasty, Norman Rockwell, and collector dolls.

Club Redemptions. Layaway. Secondary Market. Free gift wrapping. UPS shipping available.

ROSEMARY'S COLLECTIBLES

19036 Fort St.
Riverview, MI 48192

PHONE: (313)479-0494

Monday-Friday: 9:30-9:00
Saturday: 10:00-6:00; Sunday: 12:00-4:00

Lines include: Lladro, Precious Moments, Hummel, David Winter, Lilliput Lane, Tom Clark, Lawton, Madame Alexander, Ashton-Drake, Gotz, Wee Forest Folk, Emmett Kelly Jr., Krystonia, Enchantica, Dept. 56 Showcase, Snowbabies, Memories of Yesterday, All God's Children, Sarah's Attic, Olszewski, Ozz Franca and Thomas Kinkade lithographs, crystal and giftware.

Visa, Mastercard and Discover accepted. Layaways and shipping available. Some Secondary Market Service.

MICHIGAN

PLAIN & FANCY GIFT SHOP

323 Main St.
Rochester, MI 48307

PHONE: (313)651-5188

Monday-Friday: 10:00-5:30
Saturday: 10:00-5:00
Additional Seasonal Hours

Lines: Annalee, Dept. 56 Showcase Dealer, Christopher Radko, Old World Christmas Ornaments, Byers' Choice Carolers, Tom Clark Gnomes, Mary Hadley Pottery, Dedham Pottery, Enesco Ornaments, German Nutcrackers and Smokers including Ulbricht, and Wee Forest Folks.

After Labor Day stop in and see the extensive collection of Christmas giftware and collectibles.

Visa and Mastercard accepted.

AMERICAN BUSINESS CONCEPTS AND GIFT GALLERY

University Square Mall
3038 Walton Blvd.
Rochester Hills, MI 48309

PHONE: (313)375-2515
FAX: (313)375-1367

Mon.-Thurs.: 9:00-9:00; Fri.: 9:00-7:00
Open Saturday and Sunday

Specializing in unique collectibles. Edna Hibel: Originals, Stone Lithographs, Reproductions and accessories; Showcase Dealer for Chilmark Pewter, Marty Bell, Sandra Kuck, LEGENDS, Silver Deer, Cherished Teddies, Laura's Attic, Duncan Royale, Dept. 56, unique one-of-a-kind Santas, custom framing, Miss Martha's, Enesco Musicals, Snowbabies, EKJ, Krystonia, Calico Kittens, Gnomes, Roman, Fontanini, Maruri, Rick Cain, Possible Dreams, Ron Lee Clowns and Stanton Arts.

BURLAP 'N RAGS/ THE CANDLE SHOP

Of Squires Street Square
52 Courtland
Rockford, MI 49341

PHONE: (616)866-4260

Monday-Saturday: 11:00-5:00
Open Sunday: 1:00-5:00 July-December

David Winter Cottages, Cat's Meow Houses, Sandicast Dogs, United Design Figurines, Thimbles, Spoontiques Pewter, Castagna Figurines, Dreamsicles, Personal Stamp Exchange, and Santas. Also available are kits and supplies for traditional rug hooking.

Discover the charm of Squires Street Square in Rockford, a unique remnant of the past with its many crafts and specialty shops.

Redemption Center. Mastercard, Visa, and Discover accepted. Layaways available.

CHRISTMAS FANTASY

67360 Van Dyke
Romeo, MI 48095

PHONE: (313)752-5003

Monday-Saturday: 10:00-6:00
Sunday: 11:00-6:00

Open 361 days a year!

Lines include: Dept. 56 Snowbabies, All Through the House and Winter Silhouette. Collectible santas by Possible Dreams, Lynn Haney, Midwest Importers, Silvestri, June McKenna, Leo R. Smith, and many others. Annalee Dolls, Byers' Choice Carolers, Cast Art, Duncan Royale, Fenton Art Glass, Old World, Fontanini, Sarah's Attic.

Also visit their other store, Fantasy Dolls and Bears, which features collectible dolls and bears. Located behind Christmas Fantasy.

Layaway available. Visa, Mastercard and Discover honored. Gift wrapping.

MICHIGAN

TUCK'S OF SAUGATUCK

249 Culver St. P.O. Box 689
Saugatuck, MI 49453-0689

PHONE: (616)857-4594

January-March: Sat. and Sun.: 12:00-5:00
April-December: Open 7 Days A Week
(Extended Hours During Summer)
24 Hour Answering Service

Year round Christmas shop located on Lake Michigan in the resort town of Saugatuck in Southwest Michigan.

Lines include Dept. 56 Showcase Dealer including all villages and accessories, Snowbabies, Merry Makers, and All Thru the House. Enesco Treasury Premier Dealer and Showcase Dealer for Enesco Musicals, Annalee Dolls, DeGrazia, Duncan Royale, Harbour Lights, Old World and Christopher Radko ornaments, Kurt S. Adler Santas and Steinbach Nutcrackers.

Secondary Market in cottages. Layaway and shipping. Visa and Mastercard accepted.

A DICKENS OF A PLACE
THE TWELVE MONTHS OF CHRISTMAS STORE

22210 Harper Ave.
St. Clair Shores, MI 48080

PHONE: (313)772-3620

Monday-Saturday: 9:00-6:00
Sunday: 12:00-5:00
Extended Holiday Hours:
Monday-Saturday: 9:00-9:00

Dept. 56: Snowbabies, Dickens Village and accessories. Annalee, Roman Fontanini. Excellent selection of Christmas items. Specializing in Victorian greeting cards and Victorian picture "scraps." Custom silk floral arrangements for all occasions. Christmas trims and gifts designed by Don Josef.

Visa and Mastercard accepted. Layaway and shipping available. Secondary Market Dealer for Dept. 56 and Annalee.

EMILY'S GIFTS, DOLLS & COLLECTIBLES

25414 Harper Ave.
St. Clair Shores, MI 48081

PHONE: (313)777-5250

Monday-Saturday: 10:00-7:00
Sunday: 11:00-5:00

Lilliput Lane, Hummel, Hidden Kingdom, T. Kinkade, Tom Clark Gnomes, L. Davis, PM (new and retired), Hamilton, Perillo, Kuck, Maud Humphrey, Rockwell, Hibel, Corinne Layton, Georgetown, Madame Alexander, Seymour Mann, Studio Editions by Dynasty, Mattel Barbies, Himstedt, Goetz, Maruri, Kaiser Porcelain, Hudson Pewter, Bergsma, P. Buckley Moss, Constance Collection, EKJ, Princeton Gallery, Fontanini, Colonial Village, Yankee Candles, Muffy VanderBear, Raikes Bears, Crystal, MOY, CT, Sports Impressions, The Collectables. Mastercard, Visa and Discover accepted. Free shipping.

EDGEWATER GIFTS

315 State St.
St. Joseph, MI 49085

PHONE: (616)983-2454

Monday-Saturday: 9:30-6:00
Memorial Day-Labor Day:
Thursday and Friday Until 9:00
Sunday: 12:00-5:00
Extended Holiday Hours

Lines include Dept. 56 Villages and Snowbabies, Constance Collection, United Design Stone Critters, Cast Art Dreamsicles, North American Bears, Muffy VanderBear, Cat's Meow Villages, Daddy's Long Legs, and Midwest Importers Santas. Steinbach and Erzgebirgische Nutcrackers. Christmas ornaments by Dept. 56 and Midwest Importers.

Phone orders accepted. Will ship immediately. Visa and Mastercard accepted. Layaways welcome. Special orders are gladly taken.

MICHIGAN

SPECIAL THINGS

43727 Van Dyke
Sterling Heights, MI 48314

PHONE: (313)739-4030

Monday-Wednesday, Saturday: 10:00-6:00
Thursday-Friday: 10:00-8:00
Sunday: 12:00-5:00

Specializing in primary and secondary collectibles. MOY Heritage Dealer, Maud Humphrey Gallery, Precious Moments, Ashton-Drake and Hamilton Dolls, Cherished Teddies, Calico Kittens, Sports Impressions, Miss Martha's, Laura's Attic, Jan Hagara, Sandra Kuck, Perillo, Tom Clark, Tim Wolfe, Raikes, David Winter, Lilliput Lane, Krystonia, Emmett Kelly, Jr., Maruri, Dreamsicles. Collector plates. Plate frames and accessories.

Bradford and NALED member. All major credit cards accepted. Layaway and shipping available. Most Club Redemptions.

HALLMARK HOUSE OF CARDS & GIFTS

104-106 W. Chicago Rd.
Sturgis, MI 49091

PHONE: (616)651-6011
FAX: (616)651-8982

Monday-Friday: 9:00-8:00
Saturday: 9:00-5:00; Sunday: 11:00-4:00

Dept. 56, Precious Moments, Memories of Yesterday, Sarah's Attic, Hummels, Emmett Kelly, Maud Humphrey Bogart, Miss Martha's Originals, Raikes Bears, David Winter Cottages and other John Hine collectibles, Possible Dreams Santas, Norman Rockwell, and Hallmark Gallery collectibles.

For friendly and knowledgeable service, stop by.

All Club Redemptions. All major credit cards accepted. Shipping anywhere in the continental U.S. Layaways welcome.

THE 1/2 OFF CARD SHOP
Presents
FOR COLLECTORS ONLY

14528 Racho Rd.
Off Eureka Rd.
Taylor, MI 48180

PHONE: (313)374-2450
FAX: (313)374-2209

Monday-Saturday: 10:00-9:00
Sunday: 12:00-5:00

Cherished Teddies, Sarah's Attic, Snowbabies, Krystonia, Reco, United Design, Maud Humphrey, Bessie P. Gutmann, David Winter, Emmett Kelly Jr., Jan Hagara, Hudson, and Gartlan. Bradford Exchange Dealer.

Discover, Visa and Mastercard accepted. Layaway plan available.

PETERTYL DRUG CO. INC.

111 East Front St.
Traverse City, MI 49684

PHONE: (616)946-4830
FAX: (616)946-7847

Monday-Saturday: 9:00-6:00
Open Sundays: Summer and Christmas

In the Collectible business since 1978! Inventory features Ashton-Drake Dolls, Sarah's Attic, Memories of Yesterday, Precious Moments, DeGrazia, Norman Rockwell, Maruri, Roman Fontanini, Enesco, Carlton ornaments, Brambly Hedge and Ardleigh Elliott music boxes. Bradford Plates on request.

Visa, Mastercard and Discover accepted. Shipping is available.

MICHIGAN

GENNA'S

29092 Van Dyke
Warren, MI 48093

**PHONE: (313)573-4542
(800)535-2111**

Monday-Saturday: 10:00-9:00
Sunday: 12:00-5:00

Swarovski, Hummel, Precious Moments, Walt Disney Classics Collection, Red Skelton, Waterford Crystal, Wee Forest Folk, Tom Clark, David Winter, Dept. 56, Norman Rockwell, Lilliput Lane, EKJ, Armani, Lladro, Memories Of Yesterday, Maud Humphrey, Duncan Royale, Thomas Kinkade, Cherished Teddies, Calico Kittens, Lenox, Miss Martha, Sandicast, Bradford Exchange, Lance, LEGENDS. Dolls by Hamilton, Alexander, Gunzel, Himstedt, Lawton, Middleton, Wakeen, The Collectables, Sabine Esche, Muffy Bears.

Redemption Center for major clubs. Most major credit cards accepted. Layaway available. Secondary Market Dealer.

GIFTS GALORE

Universal Mall
28428 DeQuindre
Warren, MI 48092

PHONE: (313)751-3500

Monday-Saturday: 10-9; Sunday: 12-5

Established in 1966. Precious Moments, EKJ., Dept. 56, Snowbabies, Ron Lee, Maud Humphrey, Iris Arc, Spoontiques, Andrea by Sadek, David Winter, Armani, Sandicast, Mikasa, Budweiser. Clocks: Howard Miller, Sligh and Ridgeway, Linden, and Cuckoo clocks. Westland Carousels, Pulaski Furniture, Robinson Rocking Chairs. Dolls: Seymour Mann, Dynasty, Zook, Pauline, Doll Makers of America, Kingstate, Mdme. Alexander, Precious Moments, Lexington Hall, Royal Doulton, Victoria Impex. Raikes Bears. Custom glass doll cases.

Layaway available. Visa, Mastercard, Discover and American Express accepted. Redemption Center for the above.

JACQUELYN'S GIFTS & COLLECTABLES

13828 14 Mile Rd.
Warren, MI 48093

PHONE: (313)296-9211

Monday-Friday: 10:00-8:00
Saturday: 10:00-6:00; Sunday: 12:00-3:00

Precious Moments, Dept. 56, Lladro, Memories of Yesterday, Laura's Attic, Cherished Teddies, M.I. Hummel, Emmett Kelly, Hudson Pewter, Jan Hagara, Armani, Krystonia, Silver Deer Crystal, and Bradford collector plates.

NALED member. Layaways available. All major credit cards accepted.

SALLY ANN'S COLLECTIBLES

5655 Dixie Hwy.
Waterford, MI 48329

PHONE: (313)623-6441

Mon, Tues, Wed, Fri: 10:00-6:00
Thurs: 10:00-8:00; Sat: 10:00-5:00

Ashton-Drake and Bradford Dealer. Other lines include: Hummel, Hibel, David Winter, Hagara, ANRI, Memories Of Yesterday, EKJ, Tom Clark, Lladro, Lowell Davis, Swarovski, Maud Humphrey, Lilliput, Dept. 56, Goebel Miniatures, LEGENDS, Chilmark, Kaiser, Sports Impressions, Marty Bell, Krystonia, Enchantica, Fontanini, Zook, Middleton, Miss Martha, Cherished Teddies, Dreamsicles, Sandicast, Thomas Kinkade, Rockwell, Raikes, Roman, Firelight Glass. Perillo, Hamilton, and Winston-Roland plates. A complete line of plate frames and accessories. Club Redemption Center. All major credit cards accepted. Layaway and shipping available.

MICHIGAN

LEO'S JEWELRY & GIFTS

34900 Michigan Ave.
Wayne, MI 48184

PHONE: (313)721-4311
FAX: (313)721-3010

Monday-Saturday: 9:00-6:00
Friday: Open Until 9:00

Calico Kittens, Cherished Teddies, David Winter, Dept. 56, Emmett Kelly, Harbour Lights, Hummel, LEGENDS, Lladro, Maud Humphrey, Maruri, Memories Of Yesterday, Precious Moments, Andrea by Sadek, Sisters & Best Friends, Swarovski, The Walt Disney Classics Collection.

All major credit cards accepted. Layaway. No shipping charges. Precious Moments Secondary Market Dealer. GCC member. Collector incentive program. Call for details.

TRADITIONAL TREASURES

100 E. Grand River
Williamston, MI 48895

PHONE: (517)655-3284

Monday-Saturday: 9:30-6:00
Friday: 9:30-8:00; Sunday: 12:00-5:00

Call or visit for that special active or retired collectible. Bradford Dealer, complete line of Dept. 56, Memories of Yesterday, Maud Humphrey, Duncan Royale, Lilliput Lane, M.I. Hummel, PenniBears, Armani, Byers' Choice Carolers, Tom Clark, LEGENDS, Lladro, United Design, Enesco, Emmett Kelly Jr., Ladie & Friends, Michael Garman, Lance, Middleton Dolls, and June McKenna Collection.

Visa, Mastercard and Discover accepted. Layaways welcome. Redemption Center. Secondary Market Service. Special orders welcome.

JOSIE'S HALLMARK

1057 Rogers Plaza
Wyoming , MI 49509

PHONE: (616)534-6370

Monday-Saturday: 10:00-9:00
Sunday: 12:00-5:00

Hallmark Gold Crown Store. In business since 1984. Dept. 56: All Villages (except Alpine), accessories, Snowbabies, and All Thru the House. Precious Moments figurines and accessories, Cherished Teddies, Calico Kittens, Dreamsicles, M.I. Hummel, Lilliput Lane, Emmett Kelly Jr. Miniatures, and United Design.

Club Redemption Center. Member of Parade of Gifts Catalog. Layaway. Visa, Mastercard, and Discover accepted. Shipping available.

ROGERS DEPARTMENT STORE

1001 W. 28th St.
Wyoming /Grand Rapids
MI 49509

PHONE: (616)538-6000
(800)727-7643
FAX: (616)538-0613

Monday-Saturday: 9:00-9:00

Goebel Dolls (Victoria Ashlea, Karen Kennedy, Bette Ball), Dolls by Gene Schooley, Artist Collectibles, Mill Creek, Baldwin Brass, Woodbury Pewter, Hanford Stamps, Goebel crystal, Napoleon Capodimonte, Possible Dreams, Old World Christmas, Silvestri, Midwest, Dept. 56 Snowbabies and ornaments, Seagull Pewter, L.S. Collection, Fenton. Artaffects, Nahrgang dolls, Hallmark Ornaments.

All major credit cards and Rogers' card. Layaway, shipping. Free gift wrapping.

West Michigan's largest apparel store.

MINNESOTA

NORTHPARK

424 Bridge Ave.
Albert Lea, MN 56007

PHONE: (507)373-3935

Monday-Friday: 8:30-6; Thursday: 8:30-8
Saturday: 8:30-5:00

Your source for collectibles. Precious Moments, MOY, Cherished Teddies, Sports Impressions, Maud Humphrey, Little Cheesers, Lilliput Lane, Pocket Dragons, Krystonia, Tom Clark, Perillo, ANRI, Swarovski, Hummel, DeGrazia, Sandicast, Snowbabies, WACO, P. Buckley Moss, Jody Bergsma, Fontanini, Jan Hagara, Emmett Kelly, Rockwell, Hallmark Authorized Bradford Dealer, Limited Edition Prints, Royal Copenhagen and Bing & Grondahl, Lance Corporation Pewter, Elsia, Maruri, Mill Creek, Iris Arc, Land of Legends, Schmid, and dolls.

Club Redemptions. Layaway. UPS shipping. Visa, Mastercard, Discover and Northpark Preferred Charge accepted.

ANDERSEN'S HALLMARK

216 S. Broadway
Albert Lea, MN 56007

**PHONE: (507)373-0996
(507)377-2440**

Monday-Friday: 10:00-9:00
Saturday: 10:00-5:00
Sunday: 12:00-5:00

Precious Moments Collector Center, Dept. 56 Showcase Dealer, Enesco Keepsake Ornaments, Hallmark Gold Crown, Jan Hagara, Maud Humphrey, Lowell Davis, Memories of Yesterday, Snowbabies, United Design, Lance/Hudson Pewter, North American Bears, Duncan Royale Santas, Roman, Cast Art Dreamsicles, Margaret Furlong Designs, Cherished Teddies, and All God's Children.

NALED member. Visa and Mastercard accepted. Free gift wrapping.

FROM THE HEART

522 Broadway
Alexandria, MN 56308

PHONE: (612)762-1754

Mon.-Sat.: 9:00-5:30; Thurs. Evenings
Seasonal Extended Hours

Located in the heart of downtown Alexandria in Central Minnesota's beautiful resort area. Lines include: Hummel, ANRI, Lladro, Royal Copenhagen, Bing & Grondahl, All God's Children, Jan Hagara, Maud Humphrey, Little Cheesers, Tom Clark, Laura's Attic, Cherished Teddies, Dreamsicles, David Winter, Possible Dreams, Lizzie High, Marty Bell, Fontanini, Bradford, Ashton-Drake, Reco, Dept. 56 (full-line), Emmett Kelly, Midwest Importer Santas and Nutcrackers, Schmid, Rockwell, J.H. Boone, Goebel, Old World, Sarah's Attic, B. Potter, WACO musicals and a large selection of cards and gifts.

GCC and Bradford Dealer. Layaway and shipping. Club Redemptions. Credit cards.

GRANDMA'S HOUSE

1211 4th. St., N.W.
Austin, MN 55912

PHONE: (507)433-9621

Monday-Saturday: 9:00-5:00
Nov. 1-Jan. 1: Sunday: 12:00-4:00
Holidays: 12:00-4:00

Sarah's Attic, Cat's Meow, Attic Babies, Snowbabies, All Through The House, Memories of Yesterday, Gail Laura, Treasured Memories, VickiLane, Copper, Heritage Lace, pottery, specialty foods, prints from Paragon, Malornis, Glynda Turley, Wood Master's Bowl Collection, Overly-Raker Inc., Town & Country Lighting, Tiffany Lamps, Mother Goose Originals, clocks especially for you, afghans, pillows, potpourri, Heart of the Woods, and North Shore Wood products.

Visa and Mastercard accepted. Layaways and shipping available. Free gift bags. Redemption Center for Cat's Meow and Sarah's Attic.

MINNESOTA

BLOOMINGTON DRUG & GIFT

509 W. 98th St.
Bloomington, MN 55420
PHONE: (612)884-7528

Monday-Friday: 8:30-9:30
Saturday & Sunday: 8:30-9:00

Hallmark Plus Store including Hallmark Ornaments, Precious Moments, Dept. 56 Showcase Dealer, Enesco: Enesco Musicals, Cherished Teddies, Calico Kittens, Sisters & Best Friends. Fenton Art Glass, Cast Art Dreamsicles, Lee Bortin, Rawcliffe Pewter, Mary Engelbreit, Cat's Meow, Lucy & Me, Brinn Dolls, Reco, Roman, Summerhill, Sandicast and Mikasa crystal.

Next to Byerly's.

Club redemption center for Precious Moments and Hallmark. GCC Member. Major credit cards accepted. Free gift wrap.

COLLECTIBLES SHOWCASE MALL OF AMERICA

W326 West Market
Bloomington, MN 55425
PHONE: (612)854-1553
(800)723-4072 (ORDERS)
FAX: (612)854-1668

Mon.-Sat.: 10:00-9:30; Sun. 11:00-7:00

The largest collectibles store of its kind in America, located in the largest US retail/entertainment complex. 14,000 sq. ft. devoted to fine collectibles and gifts. Over 100 custom curio cabinets displaying 1/2 mile of collectibles.

One of the largest Precious Moments selections, including retired pieces. Also Armani, Hummel, Swarovski, Lilliput Lane, Tom Clark, Lladro, David Winter, Ron Lee, Krystonia, Cherished Teddies, MOY, Lowell Davis, Muffy VanderBear, LEGENDS, Sandicast, Maud Humphrey, and much more.

Phone orders welcome. Major credit cards.

THE FINISHING TOUCH GIFTS

East Brainerd Mall
Brainerd, MN 56401
PHONE: (218)828-2067
FAX: (218)828-9361

Monday-Friday: 10:00-9:00
Saturday: 10:00-5:00; Sunday: 12:00-5:00

Showcase Dealer for Dept. 56--all Villages, Snowbabies, Merry Makers, All Through the House, Precious Moments, All God's Children, Cherished Teddies, Jan Hagara, Lilliput Lane, Swarovski, M.I. Hummel, David Winter, Lladro's Golden Moments, Maud Humphrey, Dreamsicles, Maruri, J.H. Boone, Fenton Art Glass, United Design, Possible Dreams.

Year round Christmas Shop featuring Old World, Christopher Radko, Kurt S. Adler, Fontanini, Byers' Choice, House of Hatten.

Visa, Mastercard, and Discover accepted. Layaway and shipping available. Free gift wrapping: $50.00 minimum.

BOB EVANS GIFTS

8501 Wyoming Ave. North
Brooklyn Park, MN 55445
PHONE: (612)425-2214
FAX: (612)425-3687

Monday-Friday: 9:00-9:00
Saturday: 9:00-5:00; Sunday: 12:00-5:00

Bradford plates, Byers' Choice Ltd., Cat's Meow, Dept. 56: Villages, accessories and Snowbabies. Emmett Kelly Jr. (Flambro), Hudson Pewter, Laura's Attic, Lilliput Lane, Lladro, Memories of Yesterday, Precious Moments, Reco plates, Rick Cain, Fontanini, Iris Arc, Possible Dreams, Miss Martha, Cherished Teddies, and Byers' Choice Ltd.

One of the largest gift shops in the Minneapolis Metro area.

MINNESOTA

SILVER DAWN JEWELRY & GIFTS

Village North Shopping Center
7629 Brooklyn Blvd.
Brooklyn Park, MN 55443
PHONE: (612)560-1530
FAX: (612)420-3285

Monday-Friday: 10-9; Saturday: 10-6
Sunday: 12:00-5:00

Authorized Dealer for Krystonia, Bubble Fairies by Jessica De Stefano, Star Trek Glitter Domes by Willitts Designs, Star Trek Pewter ships and figurines, Star Trek Magic Mugs, Master Works Pewter (Fantasy, Wildlife, Native American), Rawcliffe, Boyd Perry and Fort Pewter, Artesania Rinconada, World of Turturi, Castagna, Dreamsicles, Clay Art masks, Norfin Trolls, United Design (Stone Critters and Ltd. Santas and Easter Bunnies), Navajo Made Dream Catchers, Mandela's.

Visa, Mastercard and Discover. Layaways. Shipping. Special Orders. MJA Member.

HELGA'S HALLMARK

152 North Buchanan
Cambridge, MN 55008
PHONE: (612)689-5000

Monday-Friday: 9:00-8:00
Saturday: 9:00-5:00
Sunday: 12:00-4:00

Helga's Hallmark's service reflects their 14 years in the collectible business. Lines include: Dept. 56 Showcase Dealer, Precious Moments, Hummel, Swarovski, Marty Bell, Bing & Grondahl, David Winter, Hallmark Galleries, Dreamsicles, Memories of Yesterday, Maud Humphrey, Miss Martha's, Snowbabies, Cherished Teddies, Little Cheesers, Pigsville, Cat's Meow, Lowell Davis, Lizzie High, Annette Himstedt, and Tom Clark Gnomes.

NALED member. All major credit cards accepted. Layaways and shipping available.

MAINSTREET

4433 E. Superior St.
Duluth, MN 55804
PHONE: (218)525-3755

Monday-Friday: 9:30-5:30
Saturday: 9:30-5:00

The area's largest selection of handcrafted items from local artists. Dept. 56, Heritage Village Collection, Snowbabies, Byers' Choice Ltd. Carolers, Steinbach Ltd. Edition Nutcrackers and Smokers, Nan's cornhusk dolls, Gnomes, Kaleidoscopes, Memories of Yesterday, Isadore Needle Art, Maud Humphrey Bogart, Cat's Meow, Crabtree and Evelyn and Scarborough toiletries, Pasta Mama's, exquisite Christmas collectibles, fine jewelry, blown glass, wall decorations and Minnesota products (northern grown wild rice), both contemporary and country pieces.

Visa/MC. Gift certificates, layaway, giftwrap, shipping. Redemption Center for Byers' Choice. It's Worth a Special Trip!!

PAPILLON LTD.

Fitgers on the Lake
600 E. Superior
Duluth, MN 55802
PHONE: (218)726-0308
(800)950-3297

Monday-Saturday: 10-9; Sunday: 11-5

Serving the collector since 1966. Located in N.E. Minnesota. Lines include: Bradford plates, ANRI figurines and dolls, Chilmark, Hudson, Hamilton plates, Perillo, Lowell Davis, Hummel, Tom Clark Gnomes, David Winter, Lilliput, Royal Doulton, Swarovski, Kaiser, Emmet Kelly Jr., PenDelfin, Ashton-Drake, Lexington Hall dolls, Wee Forest Folk, Bing & Grondahl dolls, plates and figurines, Royal Copenhagen plates and figurines, Maruri, Roman, NAO by Lladro, Sandicast dogs, and Disney.

Secondary Market service in plates and figurines. Layaway and shipping available. All major credit cards accepted. Redemption Center.

MINNESOTA

GORDY'S CARDS & GIFTS

12785 Lake Blvd. Box 502
Lindstrom, MN 55045

PHONE: (612)257-6163

Monday-Thursday: 9:00-5:30
Friday: 9:00-8:00; Saturday: 9:00-5:30

800 Collector plates on display. Authorized Bradford Dealer. Ashton-Drake, Reco, Hamilton, Hadley plates, M.I. Hummel, current and retired Precious Moments, Memories of Yesterday, Cherished Teddies, Tom Clark Gnomes, Calico Kittens, Lilliput Lane, Terry Redlin prints. Large selection of plate frames.

Visa, Mastercard, Discover, and American Express accepted. Layaway. Shipping. Free gift wrapping. Secondary Market plate dealer. Personalized, reliable service.

GUSTAF'S FINE GIFTS & WORLD OF CHRISTMAS

13045 Lake Blvd. Box 722
Lindstrom, MN 55045

PHONE: (800)831-8413

Monday-Saturday: 9:30-5:30
Friday: 9:30-8:30; Sunday: 12:00-5:00
Extended Holiday Hours

Dept. 56 Showcase Dealer, Schmid Disney, Hummels, Lowell Davis, Precious Moments, Goebel Miniatures, Swarovski, Iris Arc, Cherished Teddies, Steiff, Madame Alexander Dolls, Raikes, Emmett Kelly, Possible Dreams Santas, Byers' Choice Carolers, Annalee Dolls, Laura's Attic, Collector Cars, Steins, Nutcrackers, Terry Redlin prints, Lladro, Golden Memories, Lilliput Lane, David Winter, Christopher Radko, Coca-Cola Houses, Fitz & Floyd Holiday Hamlet.

NALED Member. Layaway. Some secondary service. Visa, Mastercard, American Express and Discover accepted.

ODYSSEY GIFTS

334 River Hills Mall
Mankato, MN 56001

PHONE: (507)388-2006

Monday-Saturday: 10:00-9:00
Sunday: 12:00-5:00

Specialists in collectibles with an outstanding display of collector plates, figurines, cottages, dolls, and crystal. An active Bradford Instaquote Trading Center, PM (DSR), and Dept. 56 Showcase Dealer. Also featuring David Winter, Lilliput, Cairn Gnomes, Krystonia, Snowbabies, Memories Of Yesterday, Cherished Teddies, Miss Martha's, All God's Children, Hummel, Lladro, Swarovski, Disney Classics Collection, and Ashton-Drake.

Club Redemptions. Major credit cards accepted. Layaway and shipping are available. NALED member.

Second Location: 701 Apache Mall, Rochester, MN 55902 (507)282-6629.

SOMEBODY CARES

2034 Maplewood Mall
Maplewood, MN 55109

PHONE: (612)773-0015

Monday-Friday: 10:00-9:00
Saturday: 9:30-6:00; Sunday: 11:00-5:00

They carry a wide variety of collectibles including Lladro, Swarovski, M.I. Hummel, Armani, Emmett Kelly Jr., Dept. 56, Precious Moments, Bradford, David Winter, Memories of Yesterday, Sarah's Attic, Enchantica, Krystonia, Tom Clark Gnomes, dolls by Madame Alexander, Gorham, Victoria Ashlea, Victoria Impex, Goetz, and Corolle.

All major credit cards accepted. Layaway program available. Redemption Center for most clubs. Shipping available.

Additional Location: Rosedale Center, 1595 W. Highway 36 Roseville, MN 55113 (612)633-6939.

MINNESOTA

BACHMAN'S

6010 Lyndale Ave. South
Minneapolis, MN 55419-2289

PHONE: (612)861-7600
FAX: (612)861-7752

Majority of the Year
Weekdays: 8:30-8:30; Saturday: 8:30-5:30
Sunday: 11:00-5:00
(Will Vary Seasonally)

Since 1885! Dept. 56 Original Snow Village, Heritage Village, Snowbabies and Dept. 56 seasonal lines. Lilliput Lane, David Winter, Swarovski, Walter Brockman, Enesco Musicals, Hummel, Andrea by Sadek, Vaillancourt, Mark Hopkins, Walt Disney Classics Collection. Seasonal lines include Fontanini Nativity and Enesco Treasury Ornaments, Christopher Radko and Possible Dreams.

All major credit cards honored.

BYERLY'S GIFT GALLERY

3777 Park Center Blvd.
Minneapolis, MN 55416

PHONE: (612)929-2491
(800)328-3975

Mon.,Tues.,Wed., Sat.: 10:00-6:00
Thursday and Friday: 10:00-9:00
Sunday: 12:00-6:00

Chilmark, David Winter, Goebel Miniatures, Hand and Hammer, Silversmith, Baccarat, Daum, Kosta Boda, Lalique, Mats Jonasson, Orrefors, Swarovski, Val St. Lambert, Waterford, Belleek, Bing & Grondahl, Boehm, Cybis, Gien, Granget Herend China, Kaiser, Lenox, Lladro, M.I. Hummel, Mottahedeh, Royal Copenhagen, Royal Doulton.

Shipping available. Club redemption center. Visa, Mastercard and American Express accepted. Complimentary gift wrapping and shipping available.

HUTCH AND MANTLE

7625 Lindale S.
Minneapolis, MN 55423

PHONE: (612)869-2461
(800)242-2461
FAX: (612)869-0999

Monday-Friday: 10:00-5:00
Tuesday and Thursday: 10:00-8:30

A small family owned business built on friendly, customer service. Lines include: Lladro, Swarovski, Hummel. Limited edition lithographs: Russ Docken, Mario Fernandez, Terry Redlin, PenniAnn Cross, Maija, Jim Meger, Bruce Miller, Robert Olson. Collector dolls: Ashton-Drake, Dolls by Jerri, Gorham, Yolanda Bello, ANRI, wooden dolls, Jan Nahrgang, Hamilton including Zolan.

Secondary Market for Bradford plates and various prints. Redemption Center. Visa/Mastercard accepted. Layaway. Free coffee and gift wrapping. Custom Printing.

SCHUMACHER GIFTS

212 West Main St.
New Prague, MN 56071

PHONE: (612)758-2133
FAX: (612)758-2400

Sunday-Thursday: 9:00-9:00
Friday-Saturday: 9:00-10:00

Old World Christmas, Christopher Radko, Rochard, Steinbach, Ulbricht, Erzgebirge, Vaillancourt, M.I. Hummel, and Central European Imports.

Located in the award winning Schumachers New Prague Hotel. All major credit cards accepted.

MINNESOTA

KOPPEN'S KOLLECTIBLES

870 6TH St. (Behind A & W)
Pine City, MN 55063

PHONE: (612)629-6708
FAX: (612)629-6709

Mon.-Fri.: 8:00-9:00; Sat.: 8:00-7:00
Sunday: 10:00-5:00

Dept. 56 Showcase (All Villages), Cherished Teddies, Dreamsicles, Precious Moments (DSR), Sarah's Attic, Miss Martha's, Bradford Dealer, Lladro (Golden Memories), Iris Arc Crystal, Fontanini, David Winter, Snowbabies, MOY, Fitz and Floyd, Ashton-Drake, Castagna, All God's Children, Hallmark, Jan Hagara, Lilliput, Maud Humphrey, Steinbach, B & G / RC, Zolan, Enesco Musicals, Possible Dreams, Terry Redlin, Novelino, Schmid, Sports Impressions, and Sandicast.

All Club Redemptions. NALED and GCC member. All credit cards accepted. Layaway. Shipping anywhere in the U.S. Secondary Market on all lines.

HUNT'S HALLMARK CARD & GIFTS

Miracle Mile Shopping Center
Rochester, MN 55901

PHONE: (507)289-5152
(800)544-7021

Monday-Friday: 9:30-9:00
Saturday: 9:30-6:00; Sunday: 12:00-5:00

Hallmark Collectibles, Precious Moments, Dept. 56, Hummel, Laura's Attic, David Winter, collector plates (Bradford Dealer), Madame Alexander and other dolls, Cherished Teddies, Enesco Musicals, Jan Hagara and Maud Humphrey.

Visa, Mastercard, American Express and Discover accepted. Bradford Exchange Dealer. NALED Member.

Call anytime. Will gladly send by mail or UPS.

SEEFELDT'S GALLERY

Crossroads Mall
1655 W. County Rd. B2
Roseville, MN 55113

PHONE: (612)631-1397

Monday-Friday: 10-9; Saturday: 10-6
Sunday: 12:00-5:00

Over 600 collector plates on display. Dept. 56 Showcase Dealer, Authorized Bradford Dealer, David Winter, Lilliput, Lladro, Cairn Gnomes, PM, Armani, Swarovski, Sarah's Attic, Maruri, DeGrazia, Marty Bell, Miss Martha's, Enesco ornaments and musicals, Krystonia, PenniBears, Snowbabies, Jan Hagara, Hummel, MOY, Thomas Kinkade, Maud Humphrey, Rockwell, Fontanini, Margaret Furlong, Hamilton and Ashton-Drake Dolls, Goebel miniatures, Victoria Ashley, Gorham, Disney Classics, Dreamsicles, Hibel, Cherished Teddies, WACO, Melody In Motion, and more! NALED member. Layaway. Special orders. Redemption Center. Major cards accepted.

SEASONS TIQUE

209 S. Main
Stillwater, MN 55082

PHONE: (612)430-1240

Monday-Saturday: 9:30-8:00
Sunday: 12:00 -5:00

Dept. 56 Showcase Dealer (Heritage Village, Snow Village, Snowbabies, General Store, and All Through the House), Precious Moments, Hummel, Duncan Royale, Possible Dreams, Kitty Cucumber, Lucy & Me, Cherished Teddies, Annalee, Calico Kittens, Gnomes by Flambro, Enesco Small World of Music, Christopher Radko, Old World, Fontanini, German Nutcrackers, Smokers and Pyramids (Ulbricht/Steinbach), WACO Melody in Motion, and Fort Pewter.

Housed in historical 100 year old building with "Old World" look with year round Christmas gifts and collectibles. Most major credit cards accepted. Layaway available. Tours offered for 1-50 people.

MINNESOTA/MISSISSIPPI

FRIENDSHIP HALLMARK SHOP

Miracle Mile Shopping Center
5111 Excelsior Blvd.
St. Louis Park, MN 55416

PHONE: (612)992-6332

Monday-Friday: 9:30-9:00
Saturday: 9:30-5:30; Sunday: 12:00 -5:00

Hallmark Gold Crown store with 25 years of service to the collector. Located off Hwy 100 on Excelsior Blvd. Lines include: Dept. 56 Showcase Dealer, Precious Moments, Memories of Yesterday, Enesco Musicals, Cherished Teddies, Calico Kittens, David Winter, Hummels, Possible Dreams, Hudson Pewter, Dreamsicles, Iris Arc, Hallmark Ornaments, Fontanini, Sandicast, Goebel Angels, Steinbach Nutcrackers, Margaret Furlong, United Design and Beatrix Potter.

Redemption Center. GCC Member. Layaway. All major credit cards accepted. Shipping available.

PARK GIFT CENTER

Hillcrest Center
1626 White Bear Ave.
St. Paul, MN 55106

PHONE: (612)774-0236

Monday-Friday: 9:30-9:00
Saturday: 9:30-5:30; Sunday: 12:00-5:00

In business for 28 years. Located in Hillcrest Center just 10 minutes off I-94 or 694. Over 7,000 square feet of collectibles and gifts to satisfy any collector. Showcase Dealer for Dept. 56, including all Villages, accessories, Snowbabies, Merry Makers and All Through the House. Also Precious Moments (DSR), David Winter, Maud Humphrey, Iris Arc, Tom Clark, Emmett Kelly Jr., Lladro, Cherished Teddies, Calico Kittens, Sadek Birds, Sandicast, John Perry, and Hudson Pewter.

Club Redemptions. GCC Member. Visa and Mastercard. Free shipping on phone orders of $100 or more. Free gift wrap.

POST'S

345 Main St.
Zumbrota, MN 55992

PHONE: (507)732-5617

Monday-Saturday: 9:00-5:30
Thursday: 9:00-9:00

Located 20 miles north of Rochester and 60 miles south of Minneapolis on Hwy 52. Dolls include Ashton-Drake, Bradley, Middleton and Dynasty. Chilmark Showcase Dealer. Additional lines include Sandicast, German collectibles, Santas, Terry Redlin prints, Maruri, Dept. 56 Village Houses and Snowbabies. An Authorized Bradford Dealer. Also featuring Yankee Candles.

Visa, Mastercard and Discover accepted. Layaway and shipping available.

M & L GIFTS

2650 Beach Blvd.
Biloxi, MS 39531

PHONE: (601)388-4607

Mon-Sat: 10:00-9:00; Sun: 12:00-6:00

Swarovski Crystal, Precious Moments, Andrea by Sadek, Hummel, Tom Clark Creations, Lladro, David Winter, Lilliput Lane, Michael Garman, LEGENDS, All God's Children, Royal Doulton, Wedgwood, Duncan Royale, Lowell Davis, Dept. 56 Snow Village and Snowbabies, Maud Humphrey, Sarah's Attic, Laura's Attic, Memories of Yesterday, Dreamsicles, coins for collectors, and many more.

All major credit cards accepted. Layaway and shipping available.

MISSISSIPPI/MISSOURI

PITTY-PATS

74 Crescent Dr. (P.O. Box 1411)
Columbus, MS 39701
PHONE: (601)327-3358
FAX: (601)327-3358

Monday-Saturday: 10:00-5:00

In business and serving the collector since 1979. David Winter, Byers' Choice, Swarovski, Dept. 56, All God's Children, Emmett Kelly Jr., M.I. Hummel, G. Armani, Duncan Royale, Edna Hibel, Maruri, Jan Hagara, Cast Art, Christopher Radko, Old World, and Anheuser-Busch.

Visa and Mastercard accepted. Ship anywhere in US. Gift wrapping available. 90-day layaway program.

DOLL FANTASY & COLLECTIBLES

6194 U.S. Hwy 49
Hattiesburg, MS 39401
PHONE: (800)722-3655
FAX: (601)584-8505

Monday-Saturday: 10:00-6:00

Bradford and NALED dealer, Dept. 56, Precious Moments, All God's Children, Miss Martha's Originals, Lladro, Swarovski, M.I. Hummel, Lilliput Lane, David Winter, Armani, Memories of Yesterday, Lowell Davis, Goebel Miniatures, Cherished Teddies, Walt Disney Classics, PenniBears, Tom Clark, Iris Arc, Krystonia, Ashton-Drake, Enesco Musicals, LEGENDS, United Design, Wendy Lawton, Madame Alexander, Annette Himstedt, Corolle, North American Bear and Raikes.

Major credit cards and layaway accepted. Redemption Center for most collector clubs. Secondary Market Service.

ST. NICK'S NOOK

15531 Manchester Rd.
Ballwin, MO 63011
PHONE: (314)391-8787

Mon.-Sat.: 9:00-5:00; Thurs.: 9:00-9:00
Holiday Hours:
Mon.-Fri.: 8-9; Sat.: 9-5; Sun.: 11-5

Primary lines include Christopher Radko and Old World Ornaments, Byers' Choice, Possible Dreams, Annalee, Dept. 56 Showcase Dealer featuring all Villages, Snowbabies, Merry Makers, All Through the House, and Winter Silhouette, Cherished Teddies, Dreamsicles, House of Hatten, Kurt S. Adler, Margaret Furlong Designs, Midwest Importers, United Design, Roman Inc., Fontanini, David Winter, Shoemaker's Dream, and Koestel German Angels.

Year around Christmas store.

Mastercard/Visa accepted. Layaways and UPS shipping available. Club redemptions.

SANTA'S OUTPOST

2505 W. 76th St.
P.O. Box 1583
Branson, MO 65616
PHONE: (417)334-3807

Open 7 Days A Week: 9:00-5:00
Memorial Day-Labor Day: 9:00-Midnight

Open 364 days a year. Located across from Andy Williams Theater. Lines include: Precious Moments, Memories Of Yesterday, Dept. 56 Villages, All Through the House and Merry Makers, Enesco Ornaments, Enesco Musicals Showcase, Snowbabies, United Design, Possible Dreams, Cherished Teddies, David Winter, Old World Christmas, Lefton Colonial Villages, Steinbach Nutcrackers. Also a large selection of handmade ornaments and personalized ornaments.

All major credit cards accepted. Shipping available. Access to secondary market for Dept. 56.

MISSOURI

CAPE ART MART

21 Plaza Way
Cape Girardeau, MO 63701

PHONE: (314)334-6523

Monday-Friday: 9:00-5:30
Saturday: 12:00-4:00

Original Cabbage Patch Kids--Official Adoption Center. Hobby supplies, including HO and N trains, R/C planes, plastic models (good selection of Star Trek and Star Wars), rockets and kites. Fine art supplies (Liquitex Premier Dealer) and ready-made and custom framing.

Mastercard and Visa accepted. Layaway. Special orders available for items that are not in stock. Secondary Market Dealer for Original Cabbage Patch.

TOBACCO LANE

265 West Park Mall
Cape Girardeau, MO 63701

PHONE: (314)651-3414

Monday-Saturday: 10:00-9:30
Sunday: 12:00-6:00

Hummel, Memories of Yesterday, David Winter, Emmett Kelly Jr., LEGENDS, Chilmark, Anheuser-Busch Steinware, Cairn Studios: Tom Clark Gnomes, Tim Wolfe: Tracks; Lee Sievers: The Good Life. Maruri, Armani. Plates: Sandra Kuck, Terry Redlin and Artaffects.

The largest selection of handcarved Meerschawm pipes in the state. Friendly staff to help with any of your collectible needs.

NALED Member. Mastercard, Visa and Discover accepted. Free layaway. Shipping anywhere. Secondary Market.

EMILY'S HALLMARK & COLLECTIBLES

14855 Clayton Rd.
Chesterfield, MO 63017

**PHONE: (314)391-8755
(800)726-0440**

Monday-Friday: 9:00-9:00
Saturday: 9:00-6:00; Sunday: 11:00-5:00

Walt Disney Classics Collection, David Winter, Lilliput Lane, Lladro, Swarovski Crystal, Memories of Yesterday, Precious Moments, Hallmark Galleries, Armani, Hummel, Cherished Teddies, Calico Kittens, Dept. 56 Showcase Dealer, Hallmark, Carlton, and Enesco Ornaments.

Large selection of retired collectibles. UPS shipping. Free shipping on orders over $100. Mastercard, Visa and Discover accepted.

GIFTS n' THINGS

112A Chesterfield Mall
Chesterfield, MO 63017

PHONE: (314)532-9532

Monday-Saturday: 10:00-9:30
Sunday: 12:00-6:00

Dept. 56 Showcase Dealer, DSR for Precious Moments, Tom Clark, Memories of Yesterday, Lilliput, David Winter, Armani, Lladro, Hummel, Wee Forest Folk, Jan Hagara, Sarah's Attic, Anheuser steins, Lowell Davis, Andrea, Emmett Kelly Jr., Maruri, Iris Arc, Enesco Musicals, Cherished Teddies, Calico Kittens, Byers' Choice, Possible Dreams and Dreamsicles.

Second Location: 215 Village Square Shopping Center, Hazelwood, MO 63042. Phone: (314)731-7099. Monday: 10:00-9:00; Tuesday: 10:00-5:00; Wednesday-Saturday: 10:00-9:00; Sunday: 12:00-5:00.

Specializing in Secondary Market collectibles: cottages, figurines and steins.

MISSOURI

ELLY'S

2nd St. P.O. Box 114
Kimmswick, MO 63053
PHONE: (800)451-6056

Tuesday-Friday: 10:00-4:00
Weekends: 10:00-5:00; Closed Mondays

Chilmark, Lilliput Lane, David Winter, "Mo" Wideman, Harbour Lights, Lowell Davis, Homestead Life by Imhoff, Creart, Crystal World, Duncan Royale, Prints by Redlin, Civil War Prints by Gallon, Kuntsler, and Ashton-Drake Dolls.

Bradford Dealer. NALED member. Visa, Mastercard and Discover accepted. Free shipping for purchases over $50. Layaway progam available.

OAK LEAF GIFTS

Main Street of Poverty Flats
Rt. 2 Box 2537
Osage Beach, MO 65065
**PHONE: (314)348-0190
(800)677-1824**

Open Daily: 9:00-8:00
During Winter Months Closed at 5:00

Lowell Davis, LEGENDS, Armani, Precious Moments, Zook, United Design, Jan Hagara, Maud Humphrey, Laura's Attic, All God's Children, music boxes, Cherished Teddies, Annalee Dolls, Michael Garman, Daniel Monfort, Rinconada, Maruri, Emmett Kelly Jr., David Winter, Snowbabies, Sports Impressions, Disney Classics Collection, and Bossons. Hamilton, Perillo, and Sandra Kuck plates.

All major credit cards accepted. NALED member. Layaway available. Secondary Market Service. Store is located next to Main Street Opera.

YE COBBLESTONE SHOPPE & GALLERY

510 Tanner St.
Sikeston, MO 63801
PHONE: (314)471-8683

Monday-Saturday: 10:00-5:00
Or By Appointment

All Dept. 56, Swarovski, Lenox, Gorham, Hummel, Dreamsicles, Precious Moments, Byers' Choice, Cherished Teddies, Enesco, Sports Impressions, Maud Humphrey, Schmid, Hudson Pewter, Lowell Davis, Emmett Kelly, David Winter, Bradford Exchange and Hamilton plates, Armani, Fitz & Floyd, DeGrazia, Perillo, Michael's Ltd., Roman, Norman Rockwell, Gone With the Wind collectibles.

NALED member. Layaway and shipping available. Free gift wrapping. Call or write to receive a holiday catalog.

GAMBLE'S

3250-D East Battlefield
Springfield, MO 65804
PHONE: (417)881-7555

Monday-Saturday: 10:00-6:00

Lladro, Dept. 56, All God's Children, Memories of Yesterday, David Winter, Baccarat and Lalique, Largo, Chilmark, Hummel, Maruri, Lowell Davis.

Most major credit cards accepted. Layaway and shipping available. Redemption Center for the above. Free gift wrapping with purchase over $25.00.

MISSOURI

UNIQUE GIFT SHOPPE

3303 S. Campbell
Springfield, MO 65807

PHONE: (417)887-5476

Monday-Saturday: 10:00-9:00

Precious Moments, plates and frames, Lowell Davis, Tom Clark, Sarah's Attic Black Heritage, David Winter, Memories of Yesterday, Hummels, Maud Humphrey, Enesco Corporation, Cherished Teddies, Dept. 56 Snowbabies, LEGENDS, Sports Impressions, WACO Melody In Motion, and Terry Redlin prints.

A Shoppers Paradise! Authorized Bradford Dealer. Layaway and shipping available.

THE TINDER BOX

412 N.W. Plaza
St. Anne, MO 63074

**PHONE: (314)298-7134
(800)382-4427**

Monday-Saturday: 10:00-9:30
Sunday: 12:00-6:00

Hummel, David Winter, Chilmark, Flambro Emmett Kelly Jr., Rockwell Figurines, Bradford Exchange plates, German and commercial steins, Bosson Heads, Sarah's Attic. Also Specializing in pipes, pipe tobacco and cigars.

Mastercard, Visa, Discover and American Express accepted. Layaway and shipping available. Redemption Center for David Winter, Hummel, Chilmark and Emmett Kelly.

DEBORAH'S GIFTS

3215 Summit Ave.
St. Joseph, MO 64506

PHONE: (816)279-6225

Monday-Saturday: 10:00-5:00
Or By Appointment

ANRI, Armani, Bessie Pease Gutmann, Byers' Choice, *Chilmark, D. Mortensen, Dept. 56, Dreamsicles, Duncan Royale, Flavia, Hudson, Imhoff, Fitz & Floyd, Iris Arc, Jan Hagara, John Hine Studio, Cornell Importers, Dave Grossman, Kate Greenaway Dolls, Kirk-Stieff, Lefton's Village, LEGENDS, Lilliput Lane, Marge Crunkleton, Mark Hopkins Bronze, Little Cheesers, Lowell Davis, Margaret Furlong, Maud Humphrey, Michael Garman, Rockwell, P. Buckley Moss, Possible Dreams, Raikes Bears, Ron Lee, Sandra Kuck, Sarah's Attic, WACO, and Waterford Crystal. MC, Visa, Discover and personal checks accepted. *Master Showcase Dealer for Chilmark. 190 pieces in stock.

RYAN'S WORLD, INC.

1311 N. Belt
St. Joseph, MO 64506

**PHONE: (800) 622-RYAN
(816)232-5255**

Monday-Saturday: 10:00-5:30

In business for 20 years, specializing in collectibles. Dept. 56 (Heritage Village, Snow Village, Snowbabies, Merry Makers, All Through the House), Swarovski America, David Winter, Lladro, M.I. Hummel, Maud Humphrey Bogart, Lowell Davis, Chilmark, Hudson Pewter, J.H. Boone, Cherished Teddies, Sugar Town, Caithness, Emmett Kelly, Jr., Walt Disney Classics Collection, Enesco Musical Showcase, Enesco Treasury Ornaments, Roman Fontanini, and collectible dolls.

Redemption center for most collector clubs. Major credit cards accepted. Layaway plan. Gift wrap and shipping available.

MISSOURI/MONTANA

JOHNNIE BROCK'S

#40 Hampton Village and
Mackenzie Pointe Plaza
St. Louis, MO 63109

PHONE: (314)481-8900
(314)481-5252
FAX: (314)481-1042

Monday-Saturday: 9-9; Sunday: 11-5

Serving the St. Louis area for over 63 years. Precious Moments, MOY, Dept. 56, Cherished Teddies, Calico Kittens, M. I. Hummel, Sarah's Attic, D. Winter, Maud Humphrey, Hudson, Emmett Kelly, Iris Arc, Crystal World, Rick Cain, United Design, Maruri and Sadek Porcelain, Annalee, Ron Wall, M. Garman, Miss Martha's, Lucy & Me, L. Davis, Rockwell, LEGENDS, Sports Impressions, Anheuser-Busch, Cornell Importers, Lilliput Lane, Dreamsicles, Hallmark and Enesco ornaments.

Mastercard and Visa accepted. Free layaway. NALED member. Redemption Center for most clubs.

THRIFTY DRUG STORE, INC.

201 East Park Ave.
Anaconda, MT 59711

PHONE: (406)563-8441

Monday-Friday: 9:00-6:00
Saturday: 9:00-5:00

Dept. 56, Dickens' Village, North Pole, New England, Christmas in the City. Sarah's Attic, Laura's Attic by Enesco, Lilliput Lane, Frumps, Elfin Glen, Treasured Memories by Enesco, Sisters and Best Friends, Snowbabies, Anheuser-Busch, Cast Art, Dreamsicles, Dynasty Doll, Enesco Corp., Fenton Art Glass, GADCO, Lilliput Lane, Red Mill Mfg., Roman Inc., Summerhill Crystal, and United Design.

Visa and Mastercard accepted. 90-day layaway plan with 20% down.

LE BOUTIQUE

Rimrock Mall
300 South 24th St. West
Billings, MT 59102

PHONE: (406)656-2815
FAX: (406)256-5542

Mon.-Sat.: 10:00-9:00; Sun.: 12:00-5:00

Disney Classics, PM, Hummel, ANRI, Miss Martha, All God's Children, Sarah's Attic, LEGENDS, Chilmark, David Winter, Dept. 56, Napoleon Capodimonte, Swarovski, Lladro, Armani, PenDelfin, Bosson Heads, L. Davis, Lefton Houses, Maruri, Lilliput Lane, The Herd, MOY, Laura's Attic, Dreamsicles, Krystonia, Harbour Lights, Emmett Kelly, Ron Lee, Little Cheesers, Hagara, Tom Clark, Golden Memories, John Perry, Mill Creek, Cherished Teddies, Hudson Pewter, Maud Humphrey, Snowbabies, plates, steins, miniatures, over 1,000 dolls and bears. Major credit cards accepted. Mailing. Events. Free gift wrap. Service Redemptions.

THE SHIP'S BELL

101 E. 6th Ave.
Helena, MT 59601

PHONE: (406)443-4470

Monday-Friday: 10:00-5:30
Saturday: 11:00-4:00

Established in 1973, The Ship's Bell is an Authorized Bradford Dealer and has over 1000 plates on hand. Collectible lines include, M.I. Hummel, Reco International, Hamilton, Bradford Plates, Ernst, Villeroy & Boch, Christian Bell, Lowell Davis, Ashton-Drake, Greg Perillo, Terry Redlin, Norman Rockwell, Winton-Roland and more.

Layaway available.

A Great Little Shop! Aim to please!

MONTANA/NEBRASKA

HIGGINS HALLMARK B-3

Southgate Mall
101 E. 6th Ave.
Missoula, MT 59801
PHONE: (406)721-5026
FAX: (406)728-6982

Monday-Friday: 10:00-9:00
Saturday: 10:00-7:00; Sunday: 11:00-6:00

Hallmark Gold Crown Store. Hallmark and Enesco Ornaments, Calico Kittens, Sports Impressions, Dreamsicles, Sandicast, David Winter, Precious Moments, Dept. 56, Snowbabies, Hummel, Enesco Musical Collection, Cherished Teddies, Lilliput Lane, WACO. Also featuring local artwork.

Most major credit cards accepted. Layaway and shipping available. Redemption Center for Precious Moments, Hummel, and Waco. Free gift wrapping.

TRADITIONS

Southgate Mall
Missoula, MT 59801
PHONE: (406)543-3177

Monday-Friday: 10:00-9:00
Saturday: 10:00-7:00; Sunday: 11:00-6:00

Lines: .Lladro, Armani, Swarovski, Hummel, Walt Disney, MOY, PM EKJ, Bossons, Tom Clark Gnomes, Jan Hagara, Maruri, David Winter, Ron Lee, Harbour Light Lighthouses, Russian Laquer boxes and nesting dolls, Enesco Musicals, Nutcrackers and Smokers, plates, Sarah's Attic, Miss Martha, Mats Jonasson Crystal, Lucy & Me Bears, Neil Rose, Rick Cain, Paul Carrica, Chilmark, L. Davis, Maud Humphrey, Laura's Attic, United Design and one-of-a-kind, made-to-order porcelain dolls. Redemption Center for most collector clubs. Shipping available. Free gift wrapping. All major credit cards accepted. NALED Member.

L & L GIFTS AND COLLECTIBLES

1720 N. Bell
Fremont, NE 68025
PHONE: (800)831-6603
(402)727-7275

Monday-Saturday: 9:30-5:30
Thursday: 9:30-8:00

Precious Moments, Hummel, Swarovski, Lowell Davis, Maud Humphrey, Memories of Yesterday, Cherished Teddies, Dept. 56, Walt Disney Classics Collection, David Winter, Jan Hagara, Sports Impressions, Bradford Dealer, Ashton-Drake, Barbie, Hamilton, Zook Dolls, Madame Alexander, Sarah's Attic, Sandra Kuck, Norman Rockwell, Krystonia, and Bing & Grondahl, Royal Copenhagen.

NALED member. All major credit cards accepted. Layaway available. Next day shipping. Secondary Market Service.

GENI'S HALLMARK

8044 S. 84th St.
LaVista, NE 68128
PHONE: (402)331-7151
FAX: (402)331-5718

Monday-Friday: 9:00-9:00
Saturday: 9:00-7:00; Sunday: 10:00-6:00

A very large supply of Precious Moments and a rapidly growing supply of Lilliput Lane. Other lines include Dept. 56, Hallmark Keepsake Ornaments, United Design, Ladie and Friends, Cat's Meow, Cherished Teddies, and Dreamsicles.

All major credit cards accepted. Layaway and shipping are available.

NEBRASKA

FOUR STAR DRUG

1340 N. 66th St.
Lincoln, NE 68505

PHONE: (402)434-7712
FAX: (402)434-7744

In business for 31 years. Four Star Drug has 4 locations with large inventories. Call one number and check stock at all stores. Lines include: Precious Moments (DSR), Memories of Yesterday Heritage Dealer, Enesco Treasury ornaments Preferred Dealer, Maud Humphrey Gallery Dealer, Lilliput Lane, Lowell Davis, Dept. 56 (Villages and Snowbabies), Melody In Motion, Enesco Musicals, Possible Dreams Santas, Cast Art Dreamsicles, Cherished Teddies, Beer Steins, Hallmark Ornaments, Margaret Furlong, Sports Impressions, Little Cheesers and Fontanini.

Layaway plan available. Visa, Mastercard and Discover accepted. UPS or Postal shipping, free insurance on all shipments. Members only redemptions on all lines.

ROLLING ACRES GIFTS

400 S. 134th St.
Lincoln, NE 68520

PHONE: (402)483-7001
(800)359-4469

Monday-Saturday: 9:00-5:00

Tom Clark Gnomes, Tim Wolfe Animals, Annalee Dolls, Country Cousins and other Enesco, United Designs, The Legends of Christmas, Lisi, MaMa Babies, Wild Bryde Jewelry, The Londonshire by Possible Dreams, gifts for pet lovers including Country Companions, Calico Kittens, Puppy Dog Tails, animal magnets and key chains.

Most major credit cards accepted. Layaway and shipping available (free shipping for purchases over $75). Secondary Market Dealer. Redemption Center. Free gift wrapping.

AUDREY'S GIFT SHOP

7834 Dodge St.
Omaha, NE 68114

PHONE: (402)393-2774

Monday-Saturday: 9:30-5:30
Thursday: 9:30-7:00

ANRI, Precious Moments, Bradford Dealer, Lladro, David Winter, LEGENDS, Swarovski, Armani, Dept. 56, Tom Clark, Byers' Choice, Rick Cain, Neil Rose, Memories of Yesterday, Laura's Attic, Cherished Teddies, Calico Kittens, Bing & Grondahl, Carriage House Studio, Cast Art, Emmett Kelly Jr., Goebel Miniatures, Harbour Lights, Hummel, Iris Arc Crystal, Maruri USA, Royal Copenhagen and many others!

All major credit cards accepted. Layaway welcome.

SHARRON SHOP

Suite 223 Crossroads
7330 Dodge St.
Omaha, NE 68114

PHONE: (402)393-8311

Monday-Saturday: 10:00-9:00
Sunday: 12:00-6:00

Walt Disney Classics Collection, M.I. Hummel, Hibel, Lowell Davis, Swarovski, Lladro, Enesco Musicals, Duncan Royale, Dept. 56: Villages, Snowbabies, Merry Makers and All Through The House; Raikes Bears, Beatrix Potter, Mark Hopkins, Cherished Teddies, Sabino, Goebel Miniatures, DeGrazia, Maud Humphrey, Calico Kittens, Fenton Art Glass, PenDelfin, David Winter, Lilliput Lane, Maruri, Dreamsicles, and Dale Tiffany lamps.

Visa, Mastercard, Discover, and American Express accepted. Shipping available.

NEBRASKA/NEVADA

HALL OF CARDS

544 Seward St.
Seward, NE 68434
PHONE: (402)643-6112

Monday-Friday: 9:00-5:30
Saturday: 9:00-5:00

Hallmark Gold Plus Store. Precious Moments (DSR), Dept. 56, Snowbabies, Lowell Davis, Cherished Teddies, Memories Of Yesterday, David Winter, All God's Children, Hummel, Jan Hagara, Enesco: Lucy & Me, Country Cousins, Calico Kittens, Maud Humphrey, Sisters and Best Friends, Growing Up Girls, Kinka; and Hallmark ornaments.

Club Redemption Center. Visa and Mastercard accepted. Layaway and shipping available. Free gift wrapping.

CARLAN'S FINE GIFTS

The Fashion Show Mall
3200 Las Vegas Blvd. South
Las Vegas, NV 89109
PHONE: (800)733-6003

Open 7 Days A Week

Caring for your collectibles since 1973. A Dept. 56 Showcase Dealer and Premier Dealer for Enesco's Treasury ornaments and Small World of Music. Carlan's carries the worlds finest collectibles including Lladro, Swarovski, Hummel, Lilliput Lane, David Winter, Lenox, All God's Children, Lowell Davis, DeGrazia, P. Buckley Moss, Ashton-Drake, Ardleigh and Elliott Musicals, Belleek, Waterford, Wedgwood, Wee Forest Folk, Perillo, Memories of Yesterday, Hibel, Walt Disney Classics, Jan Hagara, Goebel bronze miniatures, Cherished Teddies, Elvis, Marilyn, Dreamsicles, Sports Collectibles, Krystonia, Rockwell, Emmett Kelly Jr., PM, Beatrix Potter, Bradford Dealer.

ETNYRE JEWELERS INC.

119 N. Virginia St.
Reno, NV 89501
**PHONE: (702)329-6887
         (800)621-6039 (ORDERS)**

Monday-Saturday: 10:00-5:30

Downtown Reno since 1949. Walt Disney Classics Collection, Swarovski Silver Crystal, David Winter Cottages, G. Armani, Tom Clark Gnomes, Enchantica Dragons and Wizards, Ron Lee Clowns and Cartoons, Chilmark Western Pewter, Crystal World, Hummel, Bossons wall ornaments, Maruri Eagles, Elephants, etc., and Pipestone Cow Camp China.

Free shipping and easy layaway plan. No sales tax out of state. Visa, Mastercard, American Express, Discover, Diners and Carte Blanche accepted. Large inventory to choose from. Etnyre Jewelers participates in collectible promotions. Call to be put on mailing list.

JAN'S HALLMARK

Smithridge Plaza
5071 South McCarran
Reno, NV 89502
**PHONE: (702)825-2205
FAX: (702)825-2393**

A Gold Crown Store.

John Perry, Precious Moments, Coralei, Bossons, Little Cheesers, Miss Martha, Victoria Impex Dolls, Brambly Hedge, Hudson Pewter, Hallmark Galleries, Dolls by Pauline, United Design, Sandicast, Steinbach Crystal, Tom Clark Gnomes, Cherished Teddies, Maud Humphrey, Bradley Dolls, Artesania Rinconada, Spoontiques Pewter, Iris Arc Crystal, MOY, All God's Chilren, Maurice Wideman, Raikes Bears, Tim Wolfe Animals, Enesco Musicals, Treasured Memories, Artemis, Snowbabies, Gund Bears, Frumps, Goebel, Lilliput Lane, Kate Greeenaway Collection, Lincoln County Garden Club, and David Winter.

NEW HAMPSHIRE

THE GREAT AMERICAN COUNTRY GIFT STORE

Seacoast Village Mall
Rt. 1
North Hampton, NH 03862

PHONE: (603)964-9330
FAX: (603)964-9916

Monday-Saturday: 10:00-5:00
Sunday: 12:00-5:00

Cat's Meow Village, Lizzie High Dolls, June McKenna, Lilliput Lane, Judi Vaillancourt, Snowbabies, Possible Dreams, Hudson Pewter, Designs Americana, and Sarah's Attic.

Mastercard and Visa accepted. Drop shipping and free gift wrapping. Redemption Center for collector clubs. In-store Cat's Meow collectors club (buy 12 get 1 free).

ACCENTS GIFTS & COLLECTIBLES

The Mall at Rockingham Park
99 Rockingham Park Blvd.
Salem, NH 03079

PHONE: (603)890-6606

Monday-Saturday: 10:00-9:30
Sunday: 12:00-6:00

Hummel, Swarovski, Lladro, Armani, David Winter, Lilliput Lane, LEGENDS, Chilmark, Memories of Yesterday, Precious Moments, Hudson Pewter, Emmett Kelly Sr and Jr., Rockwell, All God's Children, Miss Martha's, Herd, Maruri USA, Walt Disney Classics, Tom Clark, Krystonia, Mayflower Glass, Enesco Musicals, Dedham Pottery, Edna Hibel, June McKenna, Lizzie High, Lowell Davis, PenDelfin, Possible Dreams, Sports Impressions, Goebel, Bossons, Nobodys Fool and more. Secondary and Primary Market service.

Free Shipping. All Credit Cards accepted.

MARIE'S CRYSTAL LOFT

341 South Broadway
Salem, NH 03079

PHONE: (603)893-3569
(800)543-4315

Open Daily: 10:00-5:00
Tues., Thurs., Fri.: Open Until 8:00

Precious Moments, Annalee, Disney Classics Collection, Snowbabies, Hummel, Swarovski, Lilliput Lane, Hibel, Emmett Kelly Jr. and Sr., Cherished Teddies, Maud Humphrey, Rockwell, Lucy & Me, MOY, Treasured Memories, Enesco Small Wonder Musicals, Enesco Treasury Ornaments, Laura's Attic, Miss Martha's Originals, Krystonia, Caithness, Sebastian, Sports Impressions, Margaret Furlong, Beatrix Potter, PenDelfin, Royal Doulton, Belleek and Waterford. Also the finest lines of crystal and china.

Most major credit cards accepted. Layaway available. Free shipping. Redemption Center for most collectibles.

THE STRAW CELLAR

11 Main St.
P.O. Box 960
Wolfeboro, NH 03894

PHONE: (603)569-1516

Open 7 Days A Week: 9:00-5:00
Evenings in July and August

Lilliput Lane, All God's Children, Maud Humphrey, Cairn Studios, Ladie & Friends, Art Marketing plates, United Design, Castagna, Cat's Meow and Mill Creek Studios.

Free gift wrapping. Layaway available. Member of NALED and GCC. Most major credit cards accepted. Club Redemption Center.

NEW JERSEY

MATAWAN CARDS & GIFTS

Rt. 34 & Lloyd Rd.
Aberdeen, NJ 07747

PHONE: (908)583-9449
FAX: (908)290-1482

Monday-Friday: 9:30-8:30
Saturday: 9:30-6:30; Sunday: 10:00-4:30

Hallmark Ornaments, Precious Moments, Cherished Teddies, Memories Of Yesterday, Maud Humphrey, Calico Kittens, Enesco Musicals, Lladro, Dept. 56: All Villages, Snowbabies; M.I. Hummel, Silver Deer, Summerhill, David Winter, Dreamsicles, Lenox, Precious Moments Dolls, Iris Arc, Rawcliffe, Annalee, Effanbee, Sarah's Attic, Roman, Edna Hibel plates. Also featuring Russell Stover candy, cards and gifts.

Mastercard, Visa, American Express and Discover accepted. Layaway and shipping available. Free gift wrapping.

U & I GIFT SHOP

150 Farnsworth Ave.
Bordentown, NJ 08505

PHONE: (609)298-3334

Tuesday-Friday: 10:00-6:00
and Friday: 7:00pm-8:00pm
Saturday: 9:00-4:00

Dept. 56 Snowbabies, Cat's Meow Houses, Possible Dreams, Londonshire Animals, Border Fine Arts, Beatrix Potter, Sarah's Attic Black Heritage, Michael's Ltd., Hanford Heirlooms Stamps, Bossons, Clay Art Masques, Mark Klaus, Spoontique Pewter, Stone Critters, Precious Moments Dolls, Duncan Royale, Glassmasters, Kinka, Summerhill Crystal, Shelia's, Goebel Miniatures, Cornell Importers, and Constance Collection.

All major credit cards accepted. Free layaway. Redemption Center. Private shopping parties. Shipping available.

COUNTRY GIFTS

2 Main St.
P.O. Box 466
Branchville, NJ 07826

PHONE: (201)948-4600

Monday-Friday: 9:00-6:00
Saturday: 9:00-5:00

Precious Moments, Dept. 56, Byers' Choice Ltd., Cherished Teddies, Bradford Exchange Dealer, Cat's Meow, Shelia's, Little Cheesers, Hummel, Ladie and Friends, Perillo, Snowbabies, Cairn Studios, David Winter Cottages, Maud Humphrey, Memories of Yesterday, Norman Rockwell, J.H. Boone, Sports Impressions, Andrea by Sadek, Beatrix Potter, Raikes Bears, Krystonia, and Dreamsicles.

Most major credit cards accepted. Layaway and shipping available. Redemption Center. Sponsor of local Precious Moments Collector Club.

WESTON'S LIMITED EDITIONS

Monmouth Mall
Eatontown, NJ 07724

PHONE: (908)542-3550
(800)526-2391
FAX: (908)935-0436

Monday-Saturday: 10-9:30; Sunday: 12-5

AGC, Amish Collection, C. Radko, Calico Kittens, Napoleon Capodimonte, CT, D. Royale, Dave Grossman, EKJ, J.H. Boone, Designs Americana, Dreamsicles, Enesco Musicals, Kurt Adler Nutcrackers, Little Cheesers, LEGENDS, Lighthouses, Maruri, Lilliput Lane, Michael's Ltd., Mill Creek, Miss Martha, Pocket Dragons, Star Trek Possible Dreams Santas, SI, Summerhill, United Design, R Cain,Tomorrow-Today, WFF, Willitts. Dolls: Annalee, Lawton Ashton-Drake, Barbie, Hamilton, GADCO, Georgetown, Good-Kruger, Himstedt, M. Alexander, S. Wakeen, Spanos. Graphics: V.F. Fine Arts, Thomas Kinkade.

NEW JERSEY

KOTLIAR'S CARDS & COLLECTIBLE GIFTS

339 Menlo Park Mall
Edison, NJ 08837

PHONE: (908)549-1221

Monday-Saturday: 10:00-9:30
Sunday: 11:00-6:00
Hours Vary Per Location

PM, Lladro, Hummel, Armani, Dept. 56, DW, Lenox, Austin, Andrea by Sadek, Michael's Ltd., Maruri, Krystonia, Fantasy & Gallo Pewter, United Design, Chokin, Dreamsicles, Mikasa, Justin's Vases, Treasure Masters, Roman, Flambro, Melody In Motion, Hopkins, Reco, and Enesco complete line.

Other Locations: Garden State Plaza, Rt. 4 & 17, Paramus, NJ 07652. (201)587-9002 & (201)845-5770. Ocean County Mall, 1210 Hooper Ave., Toms River, NJ 08753. (908)240-0400 and (908)341-5300. Freehold Raceway Mall, 3710 Rt. 9 & 33, Freehold, NJ 07728. (908)462-6899.

CHINA ROYALE

46 W. Palisade Ave.
Englewood, NJ 07631

**PHONE: (201)568-1005
(800)666-9885
FAX: (201)568-1046**

Monday-Saturday: 9:30-5:30

Established in 1985. Plates and figurines. Precious Moments, Memories of Yesterday, Duncan Royale, Miss Martha's, Goebel Miniatures, Royal Doulton, Lowell Davis, Lilliput Lane, Swarovski, ANRI, M.I. Hummel, Lladro, Armani, Hibel, David Winter, Rockwell, Emmett Kelly, Maud Humphrey, PenDelfin, Walt Disney Classics, Sports Impressions, and more.

Bradford/NALED Dealer. All club redemptions. Major credit cards accepted. Layaway available. Secondary Market Service.

TOWER JEWELERS

270 Main St.
Hackensack, NJ 07601

PHONE: (201)487-9092

Monday-Saturday: 9:45- 5:15

A family owned and operated business since 1947, Tower Jewelers offers quality service in fine jewelry and limited edition crystal. They carry Silver Deer and Swarovski, and are a redemption center for both lines. Valued customers are given notice of crystal piece availability and advance notice of retired items.

All major credit cards accepted. Tower Jewelers credit card available. Layaway. Secondary Market on Swarovski and Silver Deer.

YESTERDAY TODAY AND TOMORROW
HOME OF VISIONS OF CHRISTMAS

Box 23, Route 31
Hampton, NJ 08827

**PHONE: (908)537-6214
(908)806-4909**

The largest selection of dolls! Virginia & Judith Turner, Daddy's Long Legs, Vlasta, Fay Zah Spanos, Sabine Esche, Middleton, Oldenburg, Inge Enderle, Grossle-Schmid, GADCO, Australian doll orders, Gail Hoyt, Madame Alexander, Sonya Bryer, Heidi Ott, and many others. Christmas collectibles, United Design, Sarah's Attic, Krystonia, Duncan Royale, Tom Clark, Christopher Radko, Enesco, Silvestri, Dept. 56, Kurt S. Adler, Annalee, Byers' Choice, unique country and Victorian accessories.

Free gift wrapping. Three month layaway program. Most major credit cards accepted. Secondary Market Dealer. Redemption Center.

NEW JERSEY

KATHE LUCEY GIFTS & COLLECTIBLES

Kenvil Plaza- Rt. 46
Kenvil, NJ 07847

**PHONE: (800)453-4324
(201)584-3848**

Tuesday-Thursday: 10:00-6:00
Friday: 10:00-8:00; Saturday: 10:00-5:00

A most friendly collectible store! Always ready to help with questions about collectibles, insuring them, repairing them...or anything else.

Very large selection of Hummel (old mark also), Swarovski Crystal, David Winter, Lilliput Lane, Lladro, Precious Moments, Walt Disney Classics, Lowell Davis, Krystonia, Pocket Dragons, Memories of Yesterday, Emmett Kelly, Maruri, ANRI, Melody In Motion, Bradford and other plates. Club Redemption Center. All major credit cards. Layaway. Satisfaction assured. Complimentary shipping and insurance.

MAEGREEN'S GIFTS

200 Clifton Ave.
Lakewood, NJ 08701

PHONE: (908)363-1177

Monday-Saturday: 9:30-5:30

Lladro, Hummel, Harbour Lights, David Winter, Emmett Kelly Jr., Golden Memories, Precious Moments, Lenox, Miss Martha's, Armani, Swarovski, Cherished Teddies, Lilliput Lane, WACO Products, Royal Doulton, Reco International, Belleek, Enesco Corporation.

Computerized Bridal Registry with crystal, china, giftware, etc. UPS shipping available. Major credit cards accepted. Free gift wrapping.

CLASSIC COLLECTIONS

47 Livingston Mall
Livingston, NJ 07039

**PHONE: (201)992-8605
(800)982-5051
FAX: (201)731-7155**

Monday-Saturday: 10:00-9:30
Sunday: 11:00-5:00

Lladro, Swarovski, M.I. Hummel, Precious Moments, David Winter, Lilliput Lane, Dept. 56 Lighted Houses and Snowbabies, Bradford dolls and plates, Lowell Davis, Tom Clark, Armani, Goebel Miniatures, Emmett Kelly Jr., All God's Children, Sarah's Attic, Krystonia, Chilmark, LEGENDS, ANRI, Maud Humphrey, Memories Of Yesterday, Jan Hagara, June McKenna, Neil Rose, Rockwell, Royal Doulton, Thomas Kinkade, Jon Herbert, Maurice Wideman, Ray Day, Crystal Zoo, Silver Deer, Iris Arc, Disney Classics, Perillo, Golden Memories, Louis Icart, Sports Impressions. Secondary Market Service. Layaway available.

ZASLOW'S FINE COLLECTIBLES

Strathmore Shopping Center
Hwy 34
Matawan, NJ 07747

**PHONE: (908)583-1499
(800)526-2355
FAX: (908)583-0743**

Monday-Saturday: 10:00-6:00
Friday: 10:00-8:00; Sunday: 11:00-3:00

Complete collectibles shop. Hundreds of plates on display. Dept. 56 Showcase Dealer, PM (DSR), Hummels, Dolls, David Winter, Walt Disney, Lilliput Lane, B.P. Gutmann, Maud Humphrey, Armani, sports collectibles, Michael's Ltd., Cherished Teddies, Krystonia, and many other collectible lines.

Redemption Center for most clubs. Charter member of NALED. Special orders and layaways welcome. Specializing in service and knowledge.

NEW JERSEY

HERITAGE DOLL SHOP

6595 Harding Hwy.
Mays Landing, NJ 08330
PHONE: (609)625-3647

Tuesday-Sunday: 12:00-6:00

A full line of doll making supplies--wholesale/retail, doll patterns, doll clothing, custom dressing, doll-making classes. New Jersey distributor for Wee Three Wigs, Kempter and Real Eyes. Greenware for dolls, Ashton-Drake (old and new), Bradford Exchange, GADCO, Pauline, Berjusa, Goebel, Hamilton, Georgetown, Zook, Lee Middleton, Gorham, Seymour Mann, Precious Heirloom, Madame Alexander, Mattel, Himstedt, and Annalee.

Visa, Mastercard, and Discover accepted. Daily UPS shipping.

CARRIAGE HOUSE COLLECTION

23 S. Kinderkamack Rd.
Montvale, NJ 07645
PHONE: (201)391-4136

Monday-Friday: 10:00-6:00
Saturday: 10:00-5:00; Thursday: Until 8:00

Cat's Meow, Cherished Teddies, Maud Humphrey Bogart, Shelia's, Lincoln County Garden Club, Boyd's Teddies, Dreamsicles, Laura's Attic, Possible Dreams, United Design Stone Critters, Pine Baroness, Salmon Falls Stoneware, Clay Art Masks, Calico Kittens, Midwest Importers.

Located in a house built in 1815. Handcrafted items and giftware.

Visa and Mastercard accepted. Layaways and shipping available.

MEYER HOUSE GIFT SHOP

2950 Rt. 23
Newfoundland, NJ 07435
PHONE: (201)697-7122

Monday-Friday: 10:00-9:00
Saturday: 10:00-6:00; Sunday: 12:00-5:00

Dept. 56 Showcase Dealer, all villages, Merry Makers, All Through the House, Winter Silhouette, and Snowbabies. Precious Moments (DSR), Cherished Teddies, Tom Clark, Chilmark, David Winter, M.I. Hummel, Lowell Davis, Perillo, Sandicast, Swarovski, Maruri, Iris Arc, Memories of Yesterday, Krystonia, Armani, Fontanini, All God's Children, Disney Classics Collection, and Miss Martha's.

All major credit cards accepted. Free UPS shipping within the U.S. with orders over $75.00. Phone orders welcome. Free gift wrapping available.

THE GIFT CARAVAN

5 Ridge Rd.
North Arlington, NJ 07031
PHONE: (201)997-1055

Tuesday, Wednesday, Saturday: 10-6
Thursday and Friday: 10:00-8:00
Closed Sunday and Monday

Authorized Swarovski Dealer, Authorized Bradford Dealer, David Winter, Lilliput Lane, Krystonia, Maud Humphrey, PenDelfin, Norman Rockwell Gallery, Ashton-Drake dolls, Emmett Kelly Jr., Cherished Teddies, Sisters & Best Friends, LEGENDS, and Chilmark.

Visa and Mastercard accepted. NALED member.

NEW JERSEY

OAKLAND DRUGS INC.

373 Ramapo Valley Rd.
Oakland, NJ 07436

PHONE: (201)337-7300

Monday-Friday: 9:00am-10:00pm
Saturday: 9:00-6:00; Sunday: 9:00-1:00

Come stop by! You will be surprised to see thousands of collectibles and gifts before your eyes. Seasonal Dept. 56, Heritage Village, Snow Village, Snowbabies, Merry Makers, Silver Deer, Glass Art, Gorham Dolls, Andrea by Sadek, Napoleon Capodimonte, Bunnykins, Brambly Hedge, Royal Albert, Beatrix Potter, Schmid, Enesco, PM, Memories of Yesterday, Calico Kittens, Cherished Teddies, David Winter. Also the complete line of Este Lauder, Lancome and Elizabeth Arden cosmetics. Gold Crown Hallmark Store. All major credit cards. Layaway plan offered. Mail orders accepted. Free gift wrapping. Redemption center for DW, Silver Deer, Hallmark Keepsake, PM and MOY.

KAY JAY'S DOLL EMPORIUM & HOSPITAL

9th and Simpson St.
Ocean City, NJ 08226

PHONE: (609)399-5632
FAX: (609)398-2386

Monday-Saturday: 10:00-5:00

Antique-Collectible-Playable Dolls and Doll related items. Doll making classes year round with supplies by Seeley. Wigs, clothes and many antique parts available.

Headquarters for Alexander, Ashton-Drake, Hamilton and Georgetown Collections, Effanbee, Ginny, Middleton, Good-Kruger, The Collectables, Susan Wakeen, Zook, and many original artist dolls. Browse through a galaxy of dolls from the past to future heirlooms. Visa, Mastercard and American Express. Mail orders. Layaway. Special orders. Doll Reader Magazine: Retailer of Year 1991!

GIFT GALLERY

Bergan Mall
Paramus, NJ 07652

PHONE: (201)845-0940
FAX: (201)845-0414

Monday-Saturday: 10:00-9:30

Specializing in personal service for that special collector. Located 25 minutes from New York City. Precious Moments, Sports Impressions, M.I.Hummel, Disney, Swarovski Crystal and Jewelry, Armani, Lladro, Melody In Motion, Sandicast, Snowbabies, Dept. 56, David Winter, Bradford Plates, Dram Tree, Anheuser Tom Clark, Lilliput Lane, Enesco Musicals, Cherished Teddies, Calico Kittens, Laura's Attic, Norman Rockwell, Krystonia, Dragon Key, The Herd, Maruri, Barbie, Susan Wakeen, Lee Middleton, Dynasty, Mann, Ashton-Drake, MOY, and much more!

Redemption Center for all club pieces. NALED Member. Layaway and shipping available. Major credit cards accepted.

TENDER THOUGHTS GIFTS & COLLECTIBLES

Garden State Plaza
Rt. 4 & 17
Paramus, NJ 07652

PHONE: (201)845-8585

Monday-Saturday: 10:00-9:30
Sunday: 11:00-6:00
Hours Vary Per Store

Precious Moments, Lladro, Hummel, Armani, Dept. 56, David Winter, Lenox, Austin, Andrea by Sadek, Michael Ltd., Maruri, Krystonia, Fantasy and Gallo Pewter, United Design, Dreamsicles, Chokin, Mikasa, Justin's Vases, Treasure Masters, Roman, Flambro, Melody In Motion, Hopkins, Reco, and Enesco complete line.

Other Locations: Rockaway Town Square Mall, Rt. 80 & Mt. Hope Ave. Rockaway, NJ 07866. (201)989-5444. Freehold Raceway Mall, 3710 Rt. 9 & 33, Freehold, NJ 07728. (908)462-6411.

NEW JERSEY

LI'L BIT OF COUNTRY GIFT SHOP

P.O. Box 219 Route 609
Richwood, NJ 08074

PHONE: (609)256-0099
FAX: (609)256-0099

Tuesday-Saturday: 10:00-4:30
Thursday: Open Until 8:00

Walt Disney Classics, Dept. 56 Village, Snowbabies, PM, DW, Lilliput Lane, Goebel Miniatures, Hummel, LEGENDS, SI, Lowell Davis, Yankee Candle, Calico Kittens, CT, MOY, Sisters & Best Friends, Hidden Kingdom, Gail Laura, Annalee, Steinbach Nutcrackers, Steiff Bears, Rockwell, Possible Dreams, Shoemakers, Gaslight Village, Krystonia, Dreamsicles, EKJ, Melody in Motion, Bradford plates, Stone Critters, Legend of the Little People, PenniBears, Roosevelt Bears, lighthouses, Cat's Meow, Amish Collection by Willitts, All Through the House, Spoontiques, Pencil Santas, and Rowe Pottery.

RYAN TWIST GALLERY

430 Teaneck Rd.
Ridgefield Park, NJ 07660

PHONE: (201)440-8222

Tuesday-Friday: 12:00-5:30
Saturday: 11:00-5:00

A very large selection of limited edition plates, dolls, figurines and sports collectibles. Featuring Ashton-Drake, Hamilton, Gartlan USA, Bradford Exchange, Georgetown Collection, Annette Himstedt, Lowell Davis, Middleton Dolls, Gotz, Zook, Tom Clark, Dolls by Jerri, Artist Collectibles, Roman, Hadley House, and many more.

Please call or visit to see the complete selection of collectibles and decorative accessories.

All major credit cards. Layaway available. Shipping available anywhere. Located 15 minutes outside of Manhattan, New York City with free parking.

COLLECTOR'S EMPORIUM

600 Meadowland Parkway
Secaucus, NJ 07094

PHONE: (201)863-2977

Monday-Friday: 10:30-6:00
Saturday: 10:00-6:00; Sunday: 12:00-5:00
Sept.-Dec. Open Until 8:00 on Thursday

A Very Unique Store! Dept. 56 Showcase Dealer, 400 plus plates on display, current and back issues. Bradford, Hummels, PM, David Winter, Lilliput Lane Cottages, Swarovski, Armani, Sports, dolls, figurines, accessories, and giftware.

Redemption Center for most clubs. Catalog available for $1.00. Open house promotions with Dept. 56, Swarovski, Hummels, plus others. Come visit during collectible show in Spring of 1994.

Mastercard and Visa accepted. Also does extensive Secondary Market Service. Layaways available. Shipping all over the country.

EMJAY SHOP

95th St. at Second Ave.
Stone Harbor, NJ 08247

PHONE: (609)368-1227
FAX: (609)368-3447

Jan.-April: Weekends Only
May-Dec.: Open Daily 10:00-5:00
24 Hour Answering Machine

David Winter, Lilliput Lane, Swarovski, Dept. 56, Snowbabies, Hummel, Tom Clark Gnomes, Lladro, Krystonia, Memories of Yesterday, Miss Martha, Precious Moments, Lowell Davis, Duncan Royale, Cherished Teddies, Calico Cats, Cat's Meow, Shelia's, Disney Classics, Madame Alexander, The Collectables, Wendy Lawton, Elke Hutchins Dolls, B & G, Royal Copenhagen, Daddy's Long Legs, Ellenbrooke Dolls, Harbour Lights, Lenox, Waterford/Wedgwood, Willitts, J.H. Boone.

In business for 28 years. NALED member. Layaway. UPS shipping. Redemption Center. Free gift wrap. Major credit cards.

NEW JERSEY

JIANA INC.

Union Market
2445 Springfield Ave.
Union, NJ 07083

PHONE: (908)964-4600
(201)492-1728
FAX: (201)492-8069

Friday-Saturday: 11:00-9:00
Sunday: 11:00-6:00

Outstanding display of figurines, dolls, and plates. Armani, Lladro, Maruri, Dept. 56, Reco, Enesco, Possible Dreams, Annalee, Duncan Royale, Krystonia, Enchantica, Ron Lee, Emmett Kelly, Flambro, Rockwell, Lilliput Lane, Cherished Teddies, Crystal Figurines, Plates, Sarah's Attic, Miss Martha, Artaffects. Dolls: Ashton-Drake, Himstedt, Gunzel, Hamilton, etc. Many retired items also available.

Authorized Bradford Exchange Dealer. Redemption Center for most clubs. NALED Dealer. All major credit cards accepted. Layaways welcome.

MEMORY LANE

1350 Galloping Hill Rd.
Union, NJ 07083

PHONE: (908)687-2071

Monday-Friday: 9:30-9:00
Saturday: 9:00-6:00; Sunday: 9:30-5:00

Disney Classics Collection, Dept. 56, Snowbabies and Houses, Precious Moments, All God's Children, Sarah's Attic, Miss Martha's, Harbour Lights, David Winter and John Herbert, Krystonia, Pocket Dragons, Lilliput Lane, Byers' Choice, Lizzie High, Memories Of Yesterday, John Perry, Hummel, Little Cheesers, Golden Memories, Cat's Meow, Shelia's, Sports Impressions, J.H. Boone, Daddy's Long Legs, Dreamsicles, Cairn, and PenDelfin.

Most major credit cards accepted. Layaway and shipping available. Gold Crown Hallmark Store. Bradford Dealer. Redemption center for all of the above. Free gift wrapping.

THE CRAFT EMPORIUM

34 E. Prospect St.
Waldwick, NJ 07463

PHONE: (201)670-0022

Tuesday-Saturday: 10:00-5:30
Thursday: 10:00-8:00; Sunday: 1:00-5:00

Lines include: Cat's Meow, Lizzie High, All God's Children, Sarah's Attic, Annalee, David Winter, Snowbabies, Simple Wonders, Shelia's Houses, Cherished Teddies, Dreamsicles, David Winter, Jan Hagara, Enesco Musicals, Belsnickles, Calico Kittens, and United Design.

NALED member. Secondary Market Service for Cat's Meow and All God's Children. Orders over $100 ship free in the continental U.S. Out of state orders are tax free. Visa, Mastercard, money orders and personal checks accepted. Layaway plan is available. Redemption center for all lines carried with clubs.

LITTLE ELEGANCE

1214 Willowbrook Mall
Wayne, NJ 07470

PHONE: (201)256-8489
(800)955-4966
FAX: (201)402-7226

Tuesday-Saturday: 10:00-5:30
Thursday: 10:00-8:00; Sunday: 1:00-5:00

In business for 22 years, Little Elegance is the largest collectible store in the New York Metropolitan area and the biggest Enesco Dealer in the region with PM, Maud Humphrey, Sarah's Attic, Sports Impressions, Enesco World of Musicals, CT, Calico Kittens, and Treasury of Christmas Ornaments. Lines include Dept. 56 Villages and Snowbabies, Armani, Lladro, MOY, Military Collectibles, Studio 7, Gorham, Victora Impex, Applause, and PM dolls, Swarovski, and framed stamps.

Most major credit cards. Layaway and shipping available. Redemption center for all collectibles. GCC Member.

NEW JERSEY/NEW MEXICO

OMA'S DOLL SHOP

301 N. Broadway
West Cape May, NJ 08204
PHONE: (609)884-8882

Open Daily: 10:00-5:30

Engel Puppen, Middleton, Susan Wakeen, Dolls by Jerri, Jan Shackleford, Heidi Ott, Good-Kruger, Annette Himstedt, Sonja Hartman, Royal House of Dolls, Gambina, Victoria Ashlea by Goebel, Ginny, Kewpie, Horsman, Gorham, Furga, Jesmar, Effanbee Dolls.

Visa, Mastercard, American Express and Discover accepted. Shipping available.

STATION GIFT EMPORIUM

Station Center
Route 22 East
Whitehouse Station, NJ 08889
PHONE: (908)534-1212

Monday-Wednesday and Saturday: 10:00-6:00; Thursday and Friday: 10:00-9:00

Walt Disney Classics, PM, Hummels, Ron Lee, Cat's Meow, Krystonia, Sarah's Attic, Fontanini, Enesco Musicals, Memories of Yesterday, Miss Martha, United Design, Dreamsicles, Beatrix Potter, Goebel Miniatures, Maud Humphrey Bogart, Iris Arc, Snowbabies, Reco, Marc Klaus..4,000 sq. feet of incredible gifts and collectibles. Also PenniBears, Cherished Teddies, Muffy, Steiff, Boyd's and Gund.

NALED Member.

Layaway available.

Visa and Mastercard.

Shipping available.

CHEZEM'S

3620 Juan Tabo N.E.
Albuquerque, NM 87111
PHONE: (505)292-6258

Monday-Friday: 9:30-8:00
Saturday: 9:30-6:00; Sunday: 10:00-5:00

New Mexico's largest gift and collectible shop! Showcase Dealer for Department 56 and Chilmark. Lilliput Lane, David Winter, Precious Moments, Caithness, Hummel, Lladro, Iris Arc Crystal, Swarovski, All God's Children and Miss Martha's Originals, Duncan Royale Santas, DeGrazia, Harbour Lighthouses, local art prints. Tom Clark Gnome expert on staff. Animal section: Maruri, Marty Sculptures, Castagna, Deer division of Kaiser. Dragons: Krystonia and Pocket Dragons. Sports; Sports Impressions, Collectible Resource.

GCC Dealer. UPS shipping available. All major credit cards accepted. Out of state layaway available.

LORRIE'S COLLECTIBLES & LORRIE'S HOLIDAY SHOP

3107 Eubank N.E.
Albuquerque, NM 87111
**PHONE: (505)292-0020
(800)945-0020**

Monday-Saturday: 9:30-5:30

Precious Moments (DSR), David Winter, Cat's Meow, Lilliput Lane, Lowell Davis, Memories of Yesterday, Maud Humphrey, Cherished Teddies, Dept. 56 all cottages and accessories, Walt Disney Classics Collection, Cairn Gnomes, Enesco Musicals, Swarovski Crystal, Krystonia, Iris Arc Crystal, All God's Children, Caithness, and collector plates.

All Club Redemptions. All major credit cards accepted. Layaways welcome. Secondary Market search service. Member of NALED.

NEW MEXICO/NEW YORK

DON'S COLLECTIBLES

3020 E. Majestic Ridge
Las Cruces, NM 88001

PHONE: (505)522-3721
(800)827-3721
FAX: (505)522-7909

Store Hours By Appointment Only

Secondary Market lines include Bossons and Hummels. Don's buys, sells, trades and restores collectibles. Cash paid for discontinued Bosson/Fraser-Art, produced by the W.H. Bossons (Sales) Ltd., Congleton, Cheshire, England; and Crown, Full-Bee, and Stylized Bee markings of M.I. Hummel Artware, product of the W. Goebel Porzellanfabrik, Roedental, Germany.

Don's gives 100% guaranteed satisfaction for all sales and restoration work with sales quotations and work estimates provided free of charge.

EDITIONS

128 E. Marcy St.
Sante Fe, NM 87501

PHONE: (505)820-6148

Monday-Saturday: 10:00-6:00

Chilmark, Hummel, DeGrazia, Iris Arc Crystal, Lilliput Lane, Walt Disney Classics Collection, Kaiser Porcelain, Lowell Davis, Maud Humphrey, Enesco Music Boxes, Mill Creek Studios, Maruri, Laura's Attic, Cherished Teddies, Dynasty and original one-of-a-kind Navaho dolls, Raikes Bears, Glass Eye Studio, Rare Book, as well as original historical documents.

Most major credit cards accepted. Layaway available. Secondary Market Service. All club redempions.

COUNTRY SETTING

Rt. 7
Bainbridge, NY 13733

PHONE: (607)967-3030

Tuesday-Friday: 10:00-5:30
Saturday: 10:00-4:30; Sunday: 12:00-4:30

Located along the Susquehanna River. Lines include: All God's Children, Byers' Choice Carolers, Cat's Meow Village, Lizzie High Dolls, Zook Dolls, Good-Kruger, Jan Hagara, Sarah's Attic, and Attic Babies.

A country furniture and gift store. Free gift wrapping. Shipping, layaway and gift certificates available. Annual open house. Visa, Mastercard and Discover accepted.

GALLERY 247

814 Merrick Rd.
Baldwin, NY 11510

PHONE: (516)868-4800
FAX: (516)868-4899

Tuesday-Saturday: 10:00-5:00

Enchantica, Krystonia, Sarah's Attic, Bradford Exchange. Collector prints by Greenwich Workshop, Hadley House, Mill Pond Press, Somerset Publishing, and Stamp prints.

All major credit cards accepted. Three month free layaway program. Secondary Market on prints and collectibles.

NEW YORK

TINY TREASURES LTD.

South Shore Mall
Bay Shore, NY 11706

**PHONE: (516)665-7730
(800)344-7730
FAX: (516)665-3665**

Monday-Saturday: 9:30-9:30
Sunday: 10:00-5:00

Dept. 56, Precious Moments, David Winter, Lilliput Lane, Wee Forest Folk, Lladro, Hummel, Swarovski, Lenox, MOY, Sarah's Attic, Maruri, Andrea by Sadek, Krystonia, Windstone, Madame Alexander, Little Souls, Bradford, Emmett Kelly Jr., Cherished Teddies, Snowbabies, All God's Children, LEGENDS, Calico Kittens, Enesco Musicals, Treasured Memories, Miss Martha, Capodimonte, Disney, Rawcliffe Pewter, Enesco North Pole Village, Middleton, Annalee, Byers' Choice, Possible Dreams. Club redemption center.

All major credit cards accepted. Layaway available. Free gift wrapping.

COLLECTIBLES FOREVER

P.O. Box 127
Bohemia, NY 11716-0127

PHONE: (516)563-1534

Monday-Sunday: 9:00-6:00
By Appointment Only

Your primary and secondary collectible specialists for Limited Edition plates, figurines, lithographs, dolls, etc. Gartlan, Salvino, Sports Impressions, PM, Schmid, Enesco, Goebel, Willitts, Dave Grossman, Hamilton, Edna Hibel, Reco, Lenox, Royal Copenhagen, Wedgwood, American Artists, Lynette Decor, Perillo, Western Authentic, Roman, Victoriana, Wild Wings, B&G, Kaiser, Anheuser-Busch, Ernst, Armstrong, Hadley House, Marty Bell, Richard Zolan, Lladro, Bareuther, Art Marketing, High Bank Porcelain, Heinrich/Villeroy & Boch and many more.

Redemption Center for several collector's clubs. Layaway. Send self-addressed stamped envelope for price list.

THE INDIAN TEPEE GIFT SHOP

Main Street P.O. Box 90
Bolton Landing, NY 12814-0090

PHONE: (518)644-9672

Open 7 Days A Week: 9:00-5:30
Extended Summer Hours

32 years specializing in major collectible and Indian Artifacts and fine gifts. Showcase Dealer for Dept. 56 (all Villages, Snowbabies, All Thru the House, Merry Makers) LEGENDS, Perillo, Monfort Sculptures, J.H. Boone, Mill Creek, Andrea, Flambro Gnomes, Emmett Kelley Jr., Cherished Teddies, Calico Kittens, Precious Moments, Possible Dreams, KSA, Midwest Santas, Steinbach Nutcrackers, Leo R. Smith, Dreamsicles, Lizzie High, Stone Critters, Castagna, Lynn Haney, Jan Shackelford, Willow Creek Bears, Fontanini, Byers' Choice, Jan Hagara, Duncan Royale. Major charges. Layaway and shipping available.

PORTS OF THE ORIENT

McKinney Mall
Buffalo, NY 14219

PHONE: (716)823-4131

Monday-Saturday: 10:00-9:00
Sunday: 12:00-5:00

Dept. 56, Swarovski, David Winter, Hummel, Tom Clark Gnomes, Andrea by Sadek, Precious Moments, All God's Children Sarah's Attic, Harbour Lights Lighthouses, Annalee, Armani, Ashton-Drake, Cherished Teddies, Clay Art, Daddy's Long Legs, Dreamsicles, Edna Hibel, EKJ, music boxes, oriental figurines, collectible dolls, and pewter.

Secondary Market Dealer. Member of GCC and NALED. All major credit cards. Layaway. Shipping anywhere in the US.

Additional Locations: Rainbow Centre, Niagara Falls, NY 14303. (716)882-2240.

Mainplace Mall, Buffalo, NY 14202. (716)855-1700.

NEW YORK

MICHAEL'S GIFTS

Penn Can Mall
Cicero, NY 13039

PHONE: (315)458-1498

Monday-Saturday: 10:00-9:00
Sunday: 12:00-5:00

Plates from the Bradford Exchange, dolls from the Ashton-Drake Galleries, Norman Rockwell, Hawthorne Architectural Register, Ardleigh Elliott, doll and plate accessories from Van Hygan and Smythe, All God's Children, Miss Martha's Collection, Krystonia, Armani, Andrea by Sadek, Enchantica, Hummels, Precious Moments, MOY, Emmett Kelly Jr., Perillo, Hibel, Sports Impressions, Willitts and Cherished Teddies.

Michael's Gifts is an Authorized Bradford Dealer member. All major credit cards accepted.

ALBERT'S ATTIC LTD.

10768 Main St.
Clarence, NY 14031

PHONE: (716)759-2988

Monday-Friday: 9:00-5:00
Saturday: 9:00-4:00
Sunday: 1:00-5:00 (June-Dec. 23)

Lilliput Lane, Dept. 56 (Snow Village, Heritage Villages, Snowbabies), Lowell Davis, LEGENDS, Chilmark, Byers' Choice, Mark Hopkins, Duncan Royale, All God's Children, Fontanini, ANRI, Enesco, Designs Americana, Hibel, PenDelfin, Cat's Meow, Michael Garman, Harbour Lights, Kevin Francis, Daddy's Long Legs, Rick Cain Studios, Christopher Radko, Goebel Miniatures, U.S. Historical Society, Whitley Bay, Keane Eyes, Boehm and ANNA-PERENNA

NALED Member. All major credit cards accepted. Secondary Market. Redemption Center.

QUEEN'S CUPBOARD

10225 Main St.
Clarence, NY 14031

PHONE: (716)759-2665

Tuesday-Saturday: 10:00-5:00
Sunday: By Chance

June McKenna, Cat's Meow Village, Sarah's Attic, Bossons, Little Cheesers, Harbour Lights, Fenton Art Glass, John Hine Studios, LEGENDS, Jan Hagara, Cairn Studio, Goebel (including miniatures), Hudson Pewter (Lance), United Design, and Margaret Furlong- Carriage House Collectibles.

Collector Clubs Redemption Center. All major credit cards accepted. Layaway and Secondary Market service.

CLARENCE CENTER EMPORIUM INC.

6000 Goodrich Rd.
Clarence Center, NY 14032

PHONE: (716)741-9946

Monday-Saturday: 10:00-5:30
Sunday: 12:00-5:30
Holiday Hours:
Monday-Saturday: 10:00-9:00
Sunday: 12:00-5:30

Dept. 56 Heritage Village, Snowbabies and Winter Silhouette. Christopher Radko, Old World Christmas, June McKenna, Possible Dreams, Shadow Dancer, German Nutcrackers, Jan Hagara, ANNA-PERENNA, Rien Poortvliet Gnomes from Flambro, Hibel, Sarah's Attic, Kurt S. Adler, Midwest Importers, Beatrix Potter books and animals, plus many other items.

Mastercard and Visa accepted. Layaway plan.

NEW YORK

CLIFTON PARK COUNTRY STORE

Clifton Country Mall
Clifton Park, NY 12065

PHONE: (518)371-0585

Monday-Saturday: 10:00-9:30
Sunday: 12:00-5:00

Clifton Park Country Store carries a large variety of collectibles. Including Precious Moments, Memories of Yesterday, Hummel, Treasured Memories, Emmett Kelly Jr., Rockwell/Main St., Reco, David Winter, Lilliput Lane, Dept. 56 Cottages, Snowbabies, Miss Martha's, Laura's Attic, Possible Dreams, Cast Art, United Design, Bradford Exchange, Cherished Teddies, Kitty Cucumber, Gail Laura, VickiLane, PenDelfin, Lucy & Me, Attic Babies, Lowell Davis, Sports Impressions, Lizzie High Dolls, Raikes Bears and others.

CLASSIC COLLECTIONS, INC.

29 Lake Road West
Congers, NY 10920

PHONE: (800)598-0819
FAX: (914)268-0888

Monday-Friday: 12:00-7:00
Saturday: 11:00-6:00; Sunday: 1:00-5:00

Disney Classics, Hummel, Armani, ANRI, Dept. 56, Rick Cain Sculptures, Neil Rose Sculptures, Miss Martha's Originals, Cherished Teddies, Lilliput Lane, Fraser Creations, David Winter, Memory Lane, Irish Heritage Collection, Harbour Lights, Mo Wideman, Hopkins Shop, Land of Legend, Pocket Dragons, Krystonia, Enchantica, Goebel Inc., Flambro Gnomes, United Design, Silver Deer, Summerhill Crystal, Crystal World, Possible Dreams, North American Bear, Perth Pewter, and Kurt S. Adler.

Free shipping UPS Ground. Visa and Mastercard accepted. Layaway.

THE LIMITED COLLECTOR

88 E. Market St.
Corning, NY 14830

PHONE: (607)936-6195
FAX: (607)962-7740

Monday-Saturday: 10:00-8:00
Sunday: 12:00-5:00

Limited Edition Collector plates, over 1,000 different ones in stock. Bradford Dealer. Precious Moments (DSR), Memories of Yesterday, Cherished Teddies, Willitts Carousels, Miss Martha Originals, Maud Humphrey, Lowell Davis, Duncan Royale, Hummel, Norman Rockwell, Emmett Kelly Jr., Jan Hagara, Ashton-Drake and Good-Kruger dolls, Sports Impressions, Gartlan U.S.A., Maruri, Michael Garman, Anheuser-Busch, Artaffects, Bing & Grondahl, LEGENDS, and WACO.

All major credit cards accepted. Shipping available. Redemption Center for most collector clubs. NALED member.

H.N. VAN TASIA

10 Robinson Ave.
E. Patchogue, NY 11772

PHONE: (516)475-2149
FAX: (516)475-2133

Monday-Saturday: 9:00-5:00;
Wednesday: 9:00-9:00

Bradford, Waterford, Lladro, Swarovski, Hummel, Tom Clark Gnomes, ANRI, Ashton-Drake, Lenox, Lilliput Lane, Norman Rockwell, Walt Disney Classics Collection, Boehm, Jan Hagara, Beatrix Potter, Hibel, Byers' Choice, Armani, David Winter, Michael's Limited, Tim Wolfe, Royal Doulton, Bing & Grondahl, Royal Copenhagen, Anheuser-Busch, and Cornell Importers steins, silver, pewter, and other fine giftware.

UPS shipping service and layaway available. Telephone and special orders accepted. All major credit cards accepted. Free shipping.

NEW YORK

COUNTRY GALLERY

Rt. 9 Dutchess Mall
Fishkill, NY 12524

PHONE: (914)897-2008

Monday-Saturday: 10:00-9:00
Sunday: 12:00-5:00

Hummels, Lladro, Wee Forest Folk, June McKenna, Sarah's Attic, Chilmark, Enchantica, Tom Clark, Precious Moments, Byers' Choice, David Winter, Swarovski, Lilliput Lane, Dept. 56, Snowbabies, Walt Disney Classics Collection, Attic Babies, Annalee, Cat's Meow, All God's Children, Memories Of Yesterday, Emmett Kelly Jr., Little Souls, Lowell Davis, Armani, Anheuser-Busch, Cherished Teddies, Harbour Lights, Shelia's, Sports Impressions, North American Bear, Boyds, Designs Americana, Krystonia, Country Folk Art, limited edition prints, Willitts, PenDelfin, Santas, dolls, plates and much more.

NALED member.

WAYNE PHARMACY

17 S. 1st St.
Fulton, NY 13069

PHONE: (315)593-2158

Monday-Friday: 9:00-9:00
Saturday: 9:00-6:00

Precious Moments, Memories of Yesterday, Sports Impressions, Cherished Teddies, Calico Kittens, Miss Martha, Fenton Glass, Michael Garman, Maud Humphrey, Possible Dreams, United Design, Raikes Bears, Hallmark Keepsake Ornaments and Merry Miniatures. Also featuring 1928 jewelry, unique salt and pepper shakers, baby, wedding and religious gifts.

Visa, Mastercard, and Discover accepted. Layaway and shipping available. Redemption Center.

THE COUNTRY PEDDLER

2 Washington Square
Greenwich, NY 12834

PHONE: (518)692-9279

Monday-Saturday: 9:30-5:00
Friday: 9:30-8:00; Sunday: 12:00-5:00
Closed Monday January-June

Dept. 56: Heritage and Snow Villages, Snowbabies, All Through the House, Merry Makers, Winter Silhouette. Duncan Royale, Byers' Choice, Enesco Musicals, Enesco Treasury Ornaments, PM, CT, Sports Impressions, MOY, Maud Humphrey, Miss Martha, David Winter, M.I. Hummel, Cornell Importers, Fenton Art, Gail Laura, Goebel, Iris Arc, Middleton, WACO, Dreamsicles, Sarah's Attic, Lizzie High, United Design, Rowe Pottery, Possible Dreams, Overly-Raker. Also featuring country items, Pilgrim Glass, hand-crafted jewelry and a bountiful Christmas loft.

Mastercard and Visa accepted. Layaway. Shipping. Free gift wrap.

KD HALLMARK GALLERY

Fairview Plaza
Hudson, NY 12534

PHONE: (518)828-1234
FAX: (518)828-1480

Hallmark Galleries, Precious Moments, Memories of Yesterday, Dept. 56, Vaillancourt, David Winter, Lizzie High, Cat's Meow Village, Michael Garman, Mill Creek, Hummel, Cherished Teddies, North American Bear, Hallmark Ornaments, Sarah's Attic, Maud Humphrey, Miss Martha's Collection, and Anheuser-Busch Steins.

Mastercard, Visa, and Discover accepted. Gold Crown Card program. Mail orders. Free collectors newletter. Some Secondary Market lines.

NEW YORK

CORNER COLLECTIONS

P.O. Box 336 Main St.
Hunter, NY 12442

PHONE: (518)263-4141
FAX: (518)263-3704

Tuesday-Sunday: 10:00-5:00
Monday by Appointment

Lladro, Armani, Swarovski, Walt Disney Classics Collection, Dept. 56, Lowell Davis, M.I. Hummel, Goebel Miniatures, ANRI, Irish Dresden, Cherished Teddies, Enesco Musicals, Tom Clark Gnomes, Land of Legend, MOY, Kitty Cucumber, Beatrix Potter, Fontanini, DeGrazia, LEGENDS, Neil Rose, Steins, Steinbach Nutcrackers and Smokers, David Winter, Lilliput, Maruri, Perillo, Figurines and plates, M. Garman, Laura's Attic, Enesco Ornaments, Calico Kittens, Willitts, Snowbaby Miniatures. DOLLS: Goebel, Gorham, Annalee, Susan Wakeen, EKJ, Cuckoo Clocks.

Visa/MC/Discover. Layaway. Secondary Market Dealer. NALED member.

KOTLIAR'S CARD & COLLECTIBLE GIFTS

Smithhaven Mall Card Shop
Smith Haven Mall
Lake Grove, NY 11755

PHONE: (516)360-3330
(516)724-4585

Monday-Saturday: 10:00-9:30
Sunday: 11:00-6:00

PM, Lladro, Hummel, Armani, Dept. 56, David Winter, Lenox, Austin, Andrea by Sadek, Michael's Ltd., Maruri, Krystonia, Fantasy & Gallo Pewter, United Design, Chokin, Dreamsicles, Mikasa, Justin's Vases, Treasure Masters, Roman, Flambro, Melody In Motion, Hopkins, Reco, and Enesco complete line. Items not available in all stores.

Other Locations: Roosevelt Field Shopping Center, Garden City NY 11530. (516)294-4005. Carousel Center Mall, 330 West Hiawatha Blvd., Syracuse NY 13204. (315)466-4607.

LYN GIFT SHOP

11 Atlantic Ave.
Lynbrook (Long Island), NY 11563

PHONE: (516)593-6500
FAX: (516)599-0864

Monday-Saturday: 9:00-6:00
Extended Holiday Hours

Anheuser-Busch, Annalee, Armani, Christopher Radko, Dept. 56 (All Villages and Snowbabies), Walt Disney Classics Collection, Precious Moments (DSR), Lilliput Lane, Lladro, Maruri, Napoleon Capodimonte, Royal Doulton, Schmid, Swarovski, Waterford Wedgwood, Alexander Dolls, Annalee, Belleek, Cherished Teddies, Hallmark Keepsake Ornaments, Hamilton Gifts, Hummel, PenDelfin, United Design, WACO Products.

Visa, Mastercard, American Express and Discover accepted. Layaway and shipping available. Free gift wrapping.

FAMILY GIFTS, INC.

4869 Merrick Rd.
Massapequa Park, NY 11762

PHONE: (516)795-3829

Monday-Saturday: 9:00-6:00
Friday: 9:00-7:00; Sunday: 10:00-4:00

Lladro, Hummel, Precious Moments, Walt Disney Classics Collection, Lilliput Lane, David Winter, Swarovski, Cherished Teddies, Annalee Dolls, Dept. 56, Armani, Lowell Davis, All God's Children, Sarah's Attic, Memories Of Yesterday, Ashton-Drake Dolls, Collectible Plates, Lenox China, Krystonia, PenDelfin, Snowbabies, Bulova Clocks, Emmett Kelly Jr., Cast Art, Fitz & Floyd, LEGENDS, Possible Dreams, and Goebel Miniatures.

Layaway. Shipping daily. Mastercard, Visa, and Discover accepted. Official Redemption Center for collectible lines carried.

NEW YORK

PREMIO GIFTS

700 Sunrise Mall
Massapequa, NY 11758

PHONE: (800)32-PREMIO
(516)795-3050
FAX: (516)795-3530

Monday-Saturday: 10:00-9:30
Sunday: 11:00-6:00

The collectible specialists-figurines, plates, and dolls. Department 56 Showcase Dealer, Lladro Vanguard Dealer, Bradford, Swarovski, Precious Moments (DSR), Hummel, G. Armani, Caithness, Goebel Miniatures, Lilliput Lane, David Winter, Tom Clark, Krystonia, Memories of Yesterday, Sports Impressions, Hallmark Ornaments, EKJ and more...

Redemption center for all collector clubs. NALED dealer. Free shipping and layaway available. Apply for premio instant credit. All major credit cards accepted. Mention this ad for a free gift with your purchase.

MEDFORD DESIGNS

2510 Rt. 112
Medford, NY 11763

PHONE: (516)289-6358

Monday-Saturday: 9:00-6:00

Precious Moments, LEGENDS, Ron Lee, Krystonia, Lilliput Lane, Pocket Dragons, PenniBears, Hummel, Little People, Sports Impressions, Gartlan USA, Cherished Teddies, Laura's Attic, Maud Humphrey, Enesco Musicals, Memories Of Yesterday, Goebel Miniatures, Willitts, Middleton, Dolls by Pauline, Sam Butcher, Precious Moments Dolls, Iris Arc, and Raikes Bears.

Redemption Center. Layaway. All major credit cards accepted. Shipping and gift wrapping available.

AURELIA'S WORLD OF DOLLS PLUS

2025 Merrick Rd.
Merrick, NY 11566

PHONE: (516)378-3556

Monday-Saturday: 10:00-6:00
Evenings By Appointment

Alexander, Corolle, R. Woods, Goetz, Middleton, Good-Kruger, Jeckle-Jansen, Pauline, Dolls by Jerri, Gorham, Heidi-Ott, Gambina, Georgetown, Roche, Sabina Esche, Seymour Mann, Dynasty, Hagara, Hibel, Barbie, Shader, Heritage, Grandma's Darlings, Studio Server Concepts, Pat Thompson, Kingstate, Showstoppers, Himstedt, Royal, Wendy Lawton, Takara, P. Parkins, Faith Wick, Karin Heller, Lenci, World, Alice Darling, P. Heath, Steiff, Muffy. Also handcrafted dollhouses and unique miniatures.

All major credit cards accepted. Layaway and shipping available.

THE LIMITED EDITION

2170 Sunrise Highway
Merrick, NY 11566

PHONE: (800)645-2864
(516)623-4400
FAX: (516)867-3701

Monday-Saturday: 10-9; Friday til 9

Market leader in both the primary and secondary world of collectibles since 1975. PM (DSR), Dept. 56 Showcase Dealer, Lladro Vanguard Dealer, Authorized Bradford Dealer, Swarovski, David Winter, Krystonia, Disney Classics, Hummel, Chilmark, Annalee, Cherished Teddies, MOY, Emmett Kelly Jr., Willitts, LEGENDS, Maruri, Armani, Musicals, Dreamsicles, Miss Martha's Originals, Rockwell, Lowell Davis, Maud Humphrey, All God's Children, and Byers' Choice.

NALED member. Charter members of most Manufacturers Advisory Board. Club Redemptions. Major credit cards accepted. Free gift wrapping. Shipping available.

NEW YORK

THE MINIATURE MANOR

283 Willis Ave.
Mineola, NY 11501

PHONE: (516)294-3960

Monday-Saturday: 11:00-5:00
Sunday: 12:00-4:00 (please call)

Dolls: Goebel, Zook, Lee Middleton, Victoria Ashley, and Ginny. Doll house miniatures A variety of handcrafted miniatures. John Wright reproduction of mechanical banks, dollhouses, etc.

Visa and Mastercard accepted. Shipping and layaway available. Decorating services for doll houses available.

CAMARAYS GIFTS

Westchester Mall
Mohegan Lake, NY 10547

PHONE: (914)528-0676

Open Daily: 10:00-9:00

Precious Moments(DSR), Lladro, David Winter, Swarovski, Emmett Kelly, Raikes Bears, Wee Forest Folk, Lladro, David Winter, Swarovski, Emmett Kelly, Dept. 56 Villages and Snowbabies, Hummel, Lenox, Enchantica Wizard, The Collectables, Ellenbrook dolls, Dolls by Jerri, and Gorham dolls.

All major credit cards accepted. Layaways welcome. Free shipping and gift wrapping.

ANN'S HALLMARK

163 Newburgh Mall
1067 Union Ave.
Newburgh, NY 12550

PHONE: (914)564-5585
FAX: (914)562-0478

Monday-Saturday: 10:00-9:30
Sunday: 12:00-5:00

Department 56 Showcase Dealer, Hallmark Ornaments, Precious Moments, Memories of Yesterday, All God's Children, Miss Martha's Originals, Cherished Teddies, Calico Kittens, David Winter, M.I. Hummel, Krystonia, Lowell Davis, Sandicast, Walt Disney Classics Collection, Sports Impressions, and Dreamsicles.

NALED member.

Two other great locations: Mid Valley Mall in Newburgh (914) 562-3111 and in the Big V Plaza in Vail's Gate (914) 562-1711. Hours for both stores are Monday-Saturday: 10:00-9:00 and Sunday: 12:00-5:00.

CERAMICA GIFT GALLERY

1009 Sixth Ave.
(Between 37th & 38th St.)
New York, NY 10018

PHONE: (212)354-9216
(800)666-9956
FAX: (212)302-5398

Monday-Friday: 9:30-5:30
Sunday: 12:00-5:00

Established in 1976. Plates and figurines. Precious Moments, Dept. 56, Memories of Yesterday, Duncan Royale, Miss Martha's, Goebel Miniatures, Royal Doulton, Lowell Davis, Lilliput Lane, Swarovski, ANRI, M.I. Hummel, Lladro, Armani, Hibel, David Winter, Rockwell, Emmett Kelly, Maud Humphrey, PenDelfin and more!

Bradford and NALED dealer. All club redemptions. All major credit cards accepted. Layaway available. Secondary Market Service.

Specializing in Special Orders!

NEW YORK

COW HARBOR FINE GIFTS AND COLLECTIBLES

450 Fort Salonga Rd.
Northport, NY 11768

PHONE: (516)261-7907
FAX: (516)261-7907

Monday-Saturday: 9:00am-9:00pm
Sunday: 9:00-5:00

Anheuser-Busch, Annalee, ANRI, Armani, Ashton-Drake, Bradford Dealer, Byers' Choice, DW, Dept. 56, Dreamsicles, Duncan Royale, Fontanini, Goebel, Gund, Hummel, Iris Arc, J.H. Boone, Krystonia, Lladro's Golden Memories, Middleton Dolls, Lilliput Lane, Limoges, MOY Heritage Dealer, Muffy VanderBear, Maruri, PM and Enesco's Collectibles, Possible Dreams, Schmid, Sandicast, Susan Wakeen, Steinbach, Swarovski Savvy, United Design, and more. Redemption Center for collector clubs. Major credit cards. Shipping and layaways. Friendly, personal and knowledgeable service.

HARBOR TOWNE GIFTS

Ames Plaza and 43 W. Bridge St.
Oswego, NY 13126

PHONE: (315)342-5356

Monday-Friday: 10:00-9:00
Saturday: 10:00-6:00; Sunday: 12:00-5:00

Precious Moments, Memories of Yesterday, Cherished Teddies, Dept. 56 Heritage Villages and Snowbabies, Miss Martha's Originals, All God's Children, Byers' Choice Carolers, Possible Dreams Santas, Lladro Golden Memories, Hummels, David Winter Cottages, Jan Hagara, Artaffects Ltd., Cast Art Dreamsicles, Fenton Art Glass, Iris Arc Crystal, Emmett Kelly Clowns, Roman Inc, Fontanini, and Sports Impressions.

All major credit cards accepted. Layaways welcome.

STEPHEN'S A TOUCH OF CHIRTMAS

Plattsburgh Plaza
316 Cornelia St.
Plattsburgh, NY 12901

PHONE: (518)561-4180
(800)696-6262 (NY ONLY)

Monday-Saturday: 10:00-5:00
Wednesday & Friday: 10:00-9:00
Additional Seasonal Hours

Tom Clark, Annalee and June McKenna primary and secondary pieces from 1983. Perillo, Sarah's Attic, Cat's Meow, Dept. 56: All Villages, Snowbabies; Treasured Memories, MOY, Maruri, Krystonia, Lizzie High, Rowe Pottery, dolls by Middleton, Effanbee, Wakeen, and others, several original prints.

Visa, Mastercard and Discover accepted. Layaway. Shipping worldwide. Secondary Market Dealer. Redemption Center.

MARESA'S CANDLELIGHT GIFT SHOPPE

403 E. Main St.
Port Jefferson, NY 11777

PHONE: (516)331-6245

Tuesday-Saturday: 10:00-6:00
Thursday: Until 8:00; Sunday: 12:00-6:00

In historic Port Jefferson. LEGENDS, Chilmark, Hudson Pewter, Lilliput, Enesco-Small World of Music, MOY, Sports Impressions, North Pole Village, Miss Martha, Treasured Memories, Lucy & Me, Paddington Bear, Laura's Attic, WACO Melody In Motion, CT, Harbour Lights, PenDelfin, Jan Hagara, Rockwell, Emmett Kelly Jr., Raikes, Avanti, The Collectables, Georgetown, Gorham, Victoria Ashley, Seymour Mann, Bradley, Possible Dreams, Brambly Hedge, Adorables (ANNA-PERENNA), Whitley Bay Santas, Tilly bears and candles. All major credit cards. UPS. Free gift wrapping. NALED member. Layaway. Some Secondary Market.

NEW YORK

KIT 'N' KABOODLE

Potsdam-Canton Rd.
Potsdam, NY 13676
PHONE: (315)265-2410

Monday-Friday: 10:00-6:00
Saturday: 10:00-5:00; Sunday: 1:00-5:00

Housing a year round Christmas room and a small gallery (Terry Redlin, Clark, Hulings and local artists), Kit 'N' Kaboodle has much to offer the collector! Hummel, Fenton Glass Crystal, Cat's Meow, Sarah's Attic, Possible Dreams, Krystonia, and other fantasy figures. Enesco Musicals, Kewpies, Fontanini, Duncan Royale Santas, Lefton Colonial Village, B.P. Gutmann, Jan Hagara, Lissi Martin, Dreamsicles, Enesco, Schmid, Perillo plates, Maud Humphrey Bogart, teddy bears: North American Bear, Muffy VanderBears, Raikes, Applause. Dolls: Middleton, Dynasty, Kate Greenaway, Effanbee, Bradley and many more. Most major credit cards accepted. Secondary Market. Layaway.

THE CLOCK MAN'S COLLECTIBLES

Poughkeepsie Plaza-Route 9
Poughkeepsie, NY 12601
PHONE: (914)473-9055
FAX: (914)473-9056

Monday-Friday: 10:00-9:00
Saturday: 10:00-6:00; Sunday: 12:00-5:00

The largest selection in Hudson Valley. Clock specialists, offering repairs and sales. Bradford Exchange plates, Ashton-Drake dolls, Dept. 56 Showcase Dealer, D. Winter, Hummel, PM, Lladro, Lizzie High, AGC, Chilmark, Hudson, Southwest Indian Pottery, Neil Rose, Rick Cain, Wee Forest Folk, Emmett Kelly, Lladro, Disney Classics, music boxes, Mill Pond Press Art, custom framing, and curio cabinets by H. Miller (will ship). NALED and GCC. Layaway plan. Secondary Market. Visa and Mastercard accepted. Phone orders taken.

Also located at Rhinebeck, NY 12572. Phone: (914)876-7715.

SEAWAY COUNTRY CORNER

"At The Corner"
Pultneyville, NY 14538
PHONE: (315)589-9040
(716)671-8051
FAX: (716)787-0057

Open 7 Days A Week: 6:00am-9:00pm

Steinbach Nutcracker Dealer, Kurt S. Adler Dealer, santas by Midwest Importer's and Possible Dreams, Annalee Doll Shop, Anheuser-Bush Dealer, Silver Deer Dealer, Fontanini Guild Dealer, Roman Inc. Dealer for Angela Tripi, Dolfi and Cipolletti Gallery, PenDelfin Dealer, Enesco, Cairn Studio Ltd., Ertl Collectibles, Lefton, Willitts Designs, Hansford Heirlooms, Duncan Royale and Fort Pewter.

All major credit cards accepted. Layways available. Secondary Market Service when available.

Office located at: 603 Lake Rd. Webster, NY 14580-1519. Phone: (716)671-8051.

THE CANAL TOWN COUNTRY STORE

2213 Ridge Rd. West
Rochester, NY 14626
PHONE: (716)225-5070

Monday-Saturday: 10:00-9:30
Sunday: 12:00-5:00

Their three stores carry Swarovski, Precious Moments, Hummel, Royal Doulton, Tom Clark Gnomes and Tim Wolfe, Lladro, Norman Rockwell, Duncan Royale Santas, David Winter and Lilliput Lane Cottages, Dept. 56 Lighted Cottages, All God's Children, Wee Forest Folk, Emmett Kelly Jr. Clowns, Enesco Treasury Ornaments, Enesco Musicals, Cherished Teddies, Sports Impressions, Calico Kittens, Snowbabies, All Through the House, Krystonia, complete Roman line including Fontanini and Bridal line.

Locations also in the Marketplace Mall-- (716)424-4120 and the Irondequoit Mall-- (716)338-3670.

NEW YORK

LINEHAN HALLMARK

Marketplace Mall
Rochester, NY 14623
PHONE: (716)424-5690

Open Daily: 10:00-9:30
Sunday: 12:00-5:00

Dept. 56 Showcase Dealer, Heritage Village, Snow Village, Christmas in the City and Snowbabies, Precious Moments (DSR), Hummel, Krystonia, Cast Art Dreamsicles, David Winter Cottages, Cherished Teddies, Harbour Lights.

Seasonal collectibles include Possible Dreams Santas, Designs Americana Pencil Santas, Margaret Furlong, Christopher Radko.

All major credit cards accepted. Redemption Center for Precious Moments, Hummel, Krystonia, David Winter, and Cast Art.

ELLIE'S LIMITED EDITIONS & COLLECTIBLES

1070 Middle Country Rd.
Seldon, NY 11784
PHONE: (516)698-3467

Tuesday-Friday:10:00-7:00
Saturday: 10:00-6:00; Sunday: 12:00-5:00
Closed Sundays during summer.

Collectible specialists serving all your collecting needs! Extensive selection of Limited Edition Plates and accessories-- Bradford Member, PM (DSR), MOY Heritage Dealer, Maud Humphrey Gallery, Dept. 56, Crystal figurines, M.I. Hummel, Lowell Davis, Dolls, Krystonia, Enchantica, Pewter Fantasy figurines, LEGENDS, Musical Showcase Dealer, CT, Michaels Ltd., Armani, Miss Martha's Originals, Perillo, Star Trek collectibles, United Design, Sandicast and much more! NALED Member. Redemption Center for major clubs. Major credit cards welcome. Layaway and shipping available.

COLLECTIBLY YOURS

80 E. Route 59
Spring Valley, NY 10977
PHONE: (914)425-9244
(800)863-7227

Tuesday-Saturday: 10:00-5:30
Open Sunday By Chance

Dept. 56 Villages, Snowbabies, Merry Makers, and All Through the House, Bradford Exchange, Ashton-Drake, Precious Moments, Thomas Kinkade, Lladro, Swarovski, Wee Forest Folk, Miss Martha's, All God's Children, Hummels, Krystonia, Lilliput Lane, David Winter, Armani, Little Cheesers, Hamilton Collection, Rockwell, Walt Disney Classics Collection, collector plates, and major collector's dolls.

NALED member. GCC, and Secondary Market Service. Layaway plan available. Visa, Mastercard and Discover accepted.

ISLAND TREASURES

2845 Richmond Ave.
Staten Island, NY 10314
PHONE: (718)698-1234
FAX: (718)698-1888

Monday-Saturday: 10:00-6:00
Sunday: 12:00-4:00
Thursday and Friday: 10:00-9:00

Plates, Precious Moments, Hummels, Dept. 56, Lladro, Rockwell, Perillo, Swarovski, Armani, Chilmark, Emmett Kelly Jr., Krystonia, Sports Impressions, Memories of Yesterday, Authorized Bradford Dealer, Hamilton Dolls, Ashton-Drake Dolls, Madame Alexander, All God's Children, Cherished Teddies, David Winter, Lilliput Lane, Michael's Ltd., Walt Disney Classics Collection, Robert Olszewski, dolls, cottages, lithos, frames and accessories.

Redemption Center for all collectibles. All major credit cards. NALED member. Layaway and Secondary Market Service.

NEW YORK

ALISA'S DOLLS

3 Arapaho Ct.
Suffern, NY 10901

PHONE: (914)368-2509

Open Daily: 8:00-7:00
24-Hour Answering Service

Specializing in one of a kind and very limited edition artist and ethnic dolls in porcelain, wood, wax, cernit, fimol, cloth and mixed media.

Brahms, Creager, Deval, Groessle Schmidt, Gunnell, Hall, Hockh, Lackman, Mountain Babies, P. Middleton, Tonner, Walters, Vlasta and many more.

Satisfaction guarenteed. Specializing in personalized service. Layaways. Will ship anywhere. Extensive references available. No credit cards accepted.

VICTORIAN TREASURES

21 Main St.
Warwick, NY 10990

PHONE: (914)986-7616

Monday-Saturday: 10:00-6:00
Sunday: 11:00-4:00

"A Wonderfully Unique Shop in a Victorian Setting."

Collectibles--delightful to give or receive. Currently carry The Cat's Meow, including specially commissioned Warwick pieces, Sarah's Attic, Deja Vu and Micheal's Ltd., Jan Hagara, Shelia's, and Glynda Turley. Reproduction paper products including The Gifted Line, Winslow Papers, and Old Print Factory.

Club Redemption Center. All major credit cards accepted. Layaway and shipping available. Special orders welcome.

MAGGIE'S GIFT SHOP

528 19th St.
Watervliet, NY 12189

PHONE: (518)273-3522

Monday-Saturday: 10:00-5:30
Tuesday and Friday: 10:00-8:30

Lladro, MOY, Rockwell, Royal Doulton, Lilliput, Maruri, Silver Deer, M. Garman, German Beer Steins, Austin Sculptures, LEGENDS, Kaiser, Sandra Kuck, Hummels, Possible Dreams, Wedgwood Jasperware, Hibel, Lithographs and prints, Swarovski, Chilmark Pewter, Hudson Pewter, Roman Brides of the Century, Armani, Emmett Kelly, Jan Hagara, Belcari, Disney Classics Collection, Galway, Royal Crown Darby, Schmid, Golden Memories, Daum Crystal, Gorham and Turner Dolls, Kinkade, Reco, Enchantica, Snowbabies, Duncan Royale, Belleek, Possible Dreams, Sports Impressions, Sisters & Best Friends, Dreamsicles and PM. Visa, Mastercard and Discover. Layaway. Shipping.

CHINA CONNECTION

460 Hempstead Ave.
W. Hempstead, NY 11552

PHONE: (516)481-8050
FAX: (516)486-0460

Monday-Wednesday and Saturday: 10-6
Thursday: 10:00-8:00; Friday: 10:00-7:00

Your one stop collectible/giftware shop: Lladro Vanguard Dealer, Swarovski Crystal, Precious Moments, M.I. Hummel, Walt Disney Classics, Cherished Teddies, Snowbabies, Dept. 56, Miss Martha, Emmett Kelly Jr., and Lilliput Lane.

Redemption Center for collectors clubs. Major credit cards accepted. Layaways, phone orders and shipping available.

NEW YORK/NORTH CAROLINA

PANDORA'S BOX

200 Hamilton Ave.
White Plains, NY 10601

PHONE: (914)997-9160

Monday-Saturday: 10:00-5:30

Authorized Bradford Dealer, M.I. Hummel. Precious Moments, Norman Rockwell, Lladro, Lilliput Lane, Olszewski Miniatures, Perillo, Maruri, Bing & Grondahl, Royal Copenhagen, Edna Hibel, Iris Arc, and Hummel Miniatures.

NALED Member. Mastercard, Visa and American Express accepted. Secondary Market Service. All collector clubs. Special accomodations on collector club items.

FARRINGTON SQUARE

Jefferson Valley Mall
650 Lee Blvd.
Yorktown Heights, NY 10598

**PHONE: (914)962-5911
(800)229-6789
FAX: (914)962-5990**

Monday-Saturday: 10:00-9:30
Sunday: 12:00-5:00

Dept. 56, Snowbabies, Precious Moments, Hummels, Goebel Miniatures, Lowell Davis, Sports Impressions, Lionel, LGB, Memories of Yesterday, All Through the House, Winter Silhouette, Alexander Dolls, Gorham, Dolls by Jerri, Collectables, Ginny, Raikes Bears, Steiff, North American Bears, Sarah's Attic, Maud Humphrey, Maruri, Walt Disney Classics Collection, Cherished Teddies, and more.

All major credit cards accepted. Layaways welcome. Some retired pieces available.

DOLL BOUTIQUE

330 N. Second St.
Albemarle, NC 28001

PHONE: (704)983-4811

Tuesday-Friday: 10:00-5:30
Saturday: 10:00-4:00

Doll Boutique is a doll store and more! Artist dolls, Madame Alexander, Susan Wakeen, Dolls by Jerri, Seymour Mann. Precious Moments, Dept. 56, Heritage and Snow Village, Snowbabies, David Winter, Lilliput Lane, Tom Clark Gnomes, Lowell Davis, Hagara, MOY, Maud Humphrey, Constance Collection, Cat's Meow, Dreamsicles, EKJ, Harbour Lights, Kurt S. Adler, M. Garman, Midwest Importers, Roman, Sarah's Attic, Schmid, Shelia's.

A Christmas Shop year round! Visa and Mastercard accepted. Layaway and shipping available. Secondary Market Dealer. Redemption Center for the above lines. Free gift wrapping.

RENY'S ANY OLD THING?

Highway 130 Waccamaw River
Ash, NC 28420

**PHONE: (800)424-6286
(919)287-3182**

Monday-Friday: 9:30-5:30
Saturday: 9:00-6:00; Sunday: 1:00-6:00

Key dealer for Cairn Studios: Tom Clark Gnomes, Tim Wolfe, and Lee Sievers. All God's Children, Dept. 56 Villages, David Winter, Maud Humphrey, Cat's Meow, Sarah's Attic, Precious Moments, Lowell Davis, Jan Hagara, Memories of Yesterday, Snowbabies. Limited Edition Santas including Old World Santas and Kurt S. Adler. Antiques and a full Christmas Shop.

Servicing the Brunswick County and North Carolina Beaches and Myrtle Beach.

Secondary Market Service. Visa and Mastercard accepted. Layaway. Daily shipping.

NORTH CAROLINA

ANDY'S HALLMARK SHOP

South Tunnel Rd.
Asheville Mall
Asheville, NC 28805

PHONE: (704)298-3903
FAX: (704)252-0759

All God's Children, Cairn Studio, Tom Clark Gnomes, Dept. 56: Heritage Villages, Snow Village, and Snowbabies, Cast Art, Dreamsicles, Enesco: Precious Moments, Cherished Teddies, and Calico Kittens. Sports Impressions, John Hine Studio, David Winter Cottages, Hallmark Keepsake Ornaments, Willitts Designs, and Star Trek Limited Editions.

Visa, Mastercard and American Express accepted. Shipping available. GCC Member.

Other locations at 1022 Lenoir Mall, 1031 Morgantown Blvd. Lenoir, NC. 28645 Phone: (704)758-7524; East Towne Mall, Knoxville, TN (615)522-1948 and Foothills Mall, Marysville, TN (615)983-5384.

J & W COLLECTIBLES

40 Westgate Parkway
Westgate Mall Suite 40P
Asheville, NC 28806

PHONE: (704)252-0475

Monday-Saturday: 10:00-6:00

Largest doll shop in Western North Carolina. Featuring Ashton-Drake, Hamilton Heritage, Robin Woods, Goetz, Barbies, Artist Collectibles, Precious Heirlooms, Middleton, Georgetown Collection, Vicki Walker, Jan Nahrgang, Zook, Ellenbrooke, and Annette Himstedt. Specializes in Bradford Plates, Hudson Pewter, Cairn Studios, Cherished Teddies, Nascar Cars, Western Art: Perillo, Neil Rose and Mill Creek.

All major credit cards accepted. Layaway available. Redemption Center for Lilliput Lane and Sandicast. Fast and friendly service. "It's inviting...it's delightful."

OLDE WORLD CHRISTMAS SHOPPE

5 Boston Way
Asheville, NC 28803

PHONE: (704)274-4819

Monday-Saturday: 10:00-5:30
Open Sunday: 1:00-5:00 June-December

Snow Village, Snowbabies, All Thru the House, LEGENDS, Steinbach, Ulbricht Nutcrackers and Smokers, ANRI, Cherished Teddies, Vaillancourt Folk Art, Miss Martha's, Lilliput Lane, Maud Humphrey, Lowell Davis, Annalee Mobilitee, Duncan Royale, M.I. Hummel, Silver Deer, and Laura's Attic.

NALED member. Secondary Market Service. 90 day layaway terms. All major credit cards accepted.

SASSY CATS & FRIENDS

5 Hendersonville Rd.
Asheville, NC 28803

PHONE: (704)274-1701

Monday-Saturday: 9:30-5:30

"Unique Gift and collectible shop for everyone, especially Cat Lovers." Featuring Cat's Meow Village, Lowell Davis, Sarah's Attic, Adorables, Kitty Cucumber, Calico Kittens, Little Cheesers, Clay Art, Enesco, Kurt S. Adler, Midwest Importers, and Schmid.

All major credit cards accepted. Secondary Market Service. Layaway and shipping available.

NORTH CAROLINA

COUNTRY PINE NEWTIQUES

Box 1861 N. Main St.
Blowing Rock, NC 28605

PHONE: (704)295-3719
(800)633-7895

Monday-Saturday: 9:00-6:00
Monday-Saturday: 9:00-9:00 (July-Aug)

The largest secondary market dealer in the country for Tom Clark figurines. They also stock Tim Wolfe, Lee Sievers, Wee Forest Folk, Memories Of Yesterday by Enesco, All God's Children, All Villages by Dept. 56, Byers' Choice, Cat's Meow, Western Sculptures by Daniel Monfort and Michael Garman, and Santas by June McKenna and Duncan Royale.

All major credit cards accepted. Six month layaway plan and free shipping on collectibles.

CALLAHAN'S OF CALABASH

9937 Beach Rd.
Calabash, NC 28467

PHONE: (800)344-3816

Summer: Open 7 Days A Week: 9:00-10:00
Winter: Open 7 Days A Week: 9:00-9:00

20,000 square feet of shopping fun, featuring St. Nick Nacks Christmas shop with over sixty themed trees. In this magical store you'll find Annalee, Margaret Furlong Designs, Fitz & Floyd, Wee Forest Folk, Christopher Radko ornaments, Possible Dreams, Byers' Choice, Lilliput Lane, Tom Clark, LEGENDS, Enesco Treasury, United Design and Dept. 56 including all lighted villages, Winter Silhouette, Merry Makers, All Through the House, ornaments and decorative accessories. Visit the store where Santa shops!

National Secondary Market for Dept. 56. Monthly newsletter concentrating on Dept. 56 collectibles.

AUNT EDYE'S COLLECTIBLES

9832 Albemarle Rd.
Charlotte, NC 28227

PHONE: (704)545-2658

Monday-Friday: 8:00-5:30
Saturday: 9:00-1:00

Plates: Gone With The Wind, Rockwell, Ducks Unlimited, Jerner's Ducks, Donald Zolan, Sandra Kuck, P. Buckley Moss, and The Hamilton Collection.

Collectibles: Hamilton Heritage Dolls, Lefton Colonial Villages, Barbies, Music Boxes, Prints/Lithos by Thomas Kinkade, WACO Melody In Motion, Winston Roland Lithophanes, David Grossman figurines. Others: carolers, angels, santas and unusual gift items.

Visa and Mastercard accepted. Complimentary gift wrapping.

BUSH'S On E aST

Twin Oaks Shopping Center
1419 D. East Blvd.
Charlotte, NC 28203

PHONE: (704)333-GIFT
FAX: (704)333-4438

Monday-Friday: 10-6; Saturday: 10-5
Other Hours by Appointment

Dept. 56: All Villages except Alpine, Snowbabies. Byers' Choice, Precious Moments, Memories of Yesterday, Maud Humphrey, Cherished Teddies, B.P. Gutmann, Santa Classics, Calico Kittens, Harbour Lights, Old World Christmas, Possible Dreams, Dreamsicles, Attic Babies, Lizzie High, David Winter, Miss Martha's, Sarah's Attic, Boyd's Collection, June McKenna, EKJ, Enesco Treasury Ornaments, Beatrix Potter, Sugartown, Marge Crunkleton, Roosevelt Bears, Old World Nutcrackers, Designs Americana.

Visa/MC accepted. Layaway and shipping. Free gift wrapping: Minimum $25.00 order.

NORTH CAROLINA

TINDER BOX

4400 Sharon Rd.
South Park Mall
Charlotte, NC 28211

PHONE: (704)366-5164
FAX: (704)343-9039

Monday-Saturday: 10:00-9:00
Sunday: 12:30-5:30

Swarovski*, Hummel*, Chilmark*, Tom Clark Gnomes*, Precious Moments*, David Winter*, Disney Classics*, Lilliput Lane Cottages*, Miss Martha's*, Bradford Exchange, Cherished Teddies and Emmett Kelly Jr.*.

NALED member. Layaway and gift wrapping available. Free UPS shipping anywhere in the continental USA.

Additional locations in Charlotte: Eastland (704)568-8798; Carolina Place (704)542-6115.

* Designates collector's club.

CREATIVE EXPRESSIONS & GIFTS, LTD.

North Duke Mall
3600 N. Duke St.
Durham, NC 27704

PHONE: (919)471-8968

Monday-Saturday: 10:00-9:00
Sunday: 2:00-6:00

Daddy's Long Legs (Star Dealer), Sarah's Attic, Attic Babies and Blackberry Bonnet. Lines also include Storybook Collection, The Pig Lady, Folk Dolls and Friends, Arnett Dolls. Also featuring fresh flowers, balloon bouquets and baskets, and personalized wedding gifts.

Mastercard, Visa, and American Express accepted. Layaway and shipping available. Local delivery available.

MORGAN IMPORTS

113 S. Gregson St.
Durham, NC 27701

PHONE: (919)688-1150
FAX: (919)688-0072

Monday-Saturday: 10:00-9:00
Sunday: 1:00-6:00

Dept. 56 Showcase Dealer, Byers' Choice, All God's Children, Miss Martha's Originals, Daddy's Long Legs, Christopher Radko, Whitley Bay, Lowell Davis, Duncan Royale Christmas figurines, Russian Matryoshka Nested Art Dolls, Margaret Furlong, Kurt S. Adler, and other unique collectibles.

In business, serving collectors for 23 years with quality and special items. Secondary Market Service available as well as shipping. Layaway welcome. Major credit cards accepted.

FRAN'S GIFTS

8309 Emerald Dr.
Emerald Isle, NC 28594

PHONE: (919)354-3151

Summer- Open Daily: 10:00-9:00
Winter- Open Daily: 10:00-6:00

Precious Moments, Dept. 56: Snow Village, Christmas in the City, Dickens' Village, New England Village, Snowbabies. Tom Clark Gnomes, John Palmer, Lee Sievers, Tim Wolfe, Memories of Yesterday, Laura's Attic, Miss Martha, Cherished Teddies, Calico Kitttens, Treasury of Christmas Ornaments, Harbour Lights lighthouses, Simpich, Possible Dreams, Margaret Furlong, Dreamsicles, Rick Cain Sculptures, The Lincoln County Garden Club.

Mastercard and Visa accepted. Layaway. Shipping. Secondary Market for Tom Clark. Also located at Atlantic Station Mall, Atlantic Beach.

NORTH CAROLINA

SEASONS GREETINGS

511 State St.
Greensboro, NC 27405

**PHONE: (800)280-6922
(919)378-1571**

Mon.-Fri.: 10:00-5:30; Sat: 10:00-5:00
Extended Holiday Hours

In the elegantly restored State Street Station Village of 35 unique shops and restaurants. Year-round Christmas and Collectibles; Dept. 56 Showcase Dealer and Collectors' Club, Byers' Choice, David Winter, Swarovski, Walt Disney Classics, Harbour Lights, All God's Children, Margaret Furlong, Little Cheesers, Duncan Royale, Annalee, Enesco, Cat's Meow, Hand & Hammer, Sports Impressions, Christopher Radko, Old World, Fontanini, Kurt S. Adler, Midwest, Roman, Silvestri, Shelia's, Miss Martha's, Dreamsicles, Sarah's Attic and more.

Club Redemption Center. Visa, MC, Discover. Layaway--Shipping Nationwide.

THE TINDER BOX

221 Four Seasons Town Centre
Greensboro, NC 27407

PHONE: (919)855-1301

Monday-Saturday: 10:00-9:00
Sunday: 1:00-5:00

Serving collectors since 1974. Authorized Bradford Dealer member, Dept. 56 Showcase Dealer, Walt Disney Classics Collection, David Winter, Tom Clark Gnomes, Harbour Lights Lighthouses, M.I. Hummel, Jon Herbert Shoehouses, Mill Creek Indian Sculpture, Hudson Pewter, Anheuser-Busch Steins, Sandicast, Michael Garman Sculptures, Little Cheesers and Sports Impressions.

All major credit cards accepted. Layaway available.

JOHN'S FLOWERS & GIFTS

2221 Stantonsburg Rd.
Greenville, NC 27858

**PHONE: (800) 282-5646
(919)752-3311
FAX: (919)752-1177**

Monday-Friday: 8:00-7:00
Saturday: 8:00-6:00
Sunday: 1:00-5:00

M.I. Hummel, Flambro/Emmett Kelly Jr., Dept. 56 Snowbabies, Dickens plates and figurines; Enesco/Sports Impressions and Laura's Attic; Lefton Colonial Village, Dynasty and Studio Edition Dolls, Byer's Choice Ltd., Williamsburg Candles, Candy/The Chocolate Factory, and collectible steins, including Original Thewalt, and Saturday Evening Post. Year round Christmas shop with many collectible ornaments, including, Old World, Snowbabies, Enesco, etc.

Layaway plan. All major credit cards accepted. Will ship anywhere worldwide.

THE BAVARIA HAUS

4144 Haywood Rd.
Horse Shoe, NC 28742

**PHONE: (704)891-5544
FAX: (704)891-4305**

Monday-Saturday: 10:00-5:00

Located on Route 191 between Hendersonville and Ashville, NC. Serving the collectors market for 7 years. The largest selection of secondary and primary Hummels in the area, as well as a Club Redemption Center for Hummel. Lines also include ANRI woodcarvings, Lilliput Lane, Victoria Ashlea, Gotz, and antique dolls, Lowell Davis, Steinbach Nutcrackers, Erzgebirge Pyramids and Smokers, Black Forest Cuckoo Clocks, Lauscha blown glass, antique hand painted Bavarian wardrobes and Thielen pewters.

Layaway available year round. Visa and Mastercard accepted. Secondary Market Service. Shipping is available.

NORTH CAROLINA

ALADDIN'S LAMP INC.

232 Main
Mt. Airy, NC 27030

PHONE: (919)789-3700
FAX: (919)786-7546

Monday-Thursday and Saturday: 9:00-6:00
Friday: 9:00-8:00

In business since 1971. Tom Clark Gnomes, Dept. 56 Villages, Precious Moments, Memories of Yesterday, Cherished Teddies, Sports Impressions, Fenton Glass, Lenox, Dynasty Dolls, Kate Greenaway dolls, Effanbee dolls, Dakin animals, North American Bear, Willitts Carousels, Lefton, Ruff Trolls. The store now boasts three levels: a flower shop, bridal registry, and cards and collectibles shop.

All major credit cards accepted. Daily UPS shipping. Secondary Market on Tom Clark Gnomes. Layaway available.

CHALET GIFT SHOP

6406 Virginia Dare Trail
Nags Head, NC 27959

PHONE: (919)441-6402
(800)424-2538

Open Daily: 9:00-6:00

Duncan Royale, Iris Arc Crystal, LEGENDS, Lladro, Sports Impressions; Limited Edition Dolls including Madame Alexander, Dolls by Jerri, and Goetz; P.J.'s Carousels, Emmett Kelly, Rick Cain, Knot Knoggins, Neil Rose Ltd. Edition Sculptures, David Winter Cottages, Lilliput Lane, Possible Dreams, Krystonia, and Michael Garman.

Most major credit cards accepted. Layaway and shipping available. Redemption Center.

SEASIDE ART GALLERY

2716 Va. Dare Trail South
P.O. Box 1
Nags Head, NC 27959

PHONE: (800)828-2444
(919)441-5418
FAX: (919)441-8563

Open Daily at 10:00am

Hummel, Perillo, Disney Animation cels, Contemporary Art, Antiques, Sculptures, Tiffany and other art glass, Oriental paperweights, Mexican jewelry, original art by Audubon, T.H. Benton, Bernard Buffet, Alexander Calder, Mary Cassatt, Marc Chagall, Winslow Homer, Louis Icart, Currier and Ives, Joan Miro, Greg Perillo, Pablo Picasso, Frederic Remington, Renoir, Rembrandt, Soyer and Whistler.

All major credit cards accepted. Layaway. Secondary Market for Hummel cels, Royal Doulton, Madame Alexander, Perillo and Lenox.

SAMANTHA'S

Twin Rivers Mall
New Bern, NC 28560

PHONE: (919)636-1855

Monday-Saturday: 10-9; Sunday: 1-6

Swarovski, Selections by Swarovski, Lladro, Maruri, Maud Humphrey Bogart, Memories of Yesterday, Lilliput Lane, David Winter, Showmaker's Dream, M.I. Hummel, Chilmark, LEGENDS, Hudson Pewter, Precious Moments, Lowell Davis, Disney Classics Collection, Kitty Cucumber, Golden Memories, Armani, Beatrix Potter, Jan Hagara, Dept 56 Villages, Snowbabies, Merry Makers, All Through the House, Tom Clark Gnomes, Waterfowl by the Palmers, The Good Life by Lee Sievers, Tracks, Caithness Paperweights, Sports Impressions.

American Express, Visa, Mastercard and Discover accepted. Layaway and shipping available. Secondary Market for Tom Clark Gnomes. Redemption Center.

NORTH CAROLINA

DANIELLE'S HALLMARK

Stonehenge Market
7436 Creedmoor Rd.
Raleigh, NC 27613

PHONE: (919)848-9700

Monday-Friday: 10:00-9:00
Saturday: 10:00-6:00
Sunday: 1:00-6:00

Located 3 miles north on Creedmoor Rd. (Hwy 50). Lines include Precious Moments, Dept. 56 villages, Snowbabies, David Winter, Lizzie High dolls, Enesco Musical Society, Cherished Teddies, Treasured Memories, Laura's Attic, Sports Impressions, Miss Martha's Originals, Sarah's Attic, Maud Humphrey, Daddy's Long Legs, Cast Art Dreamsicles, Iris Arc Crystal, Margaret Furlong Designs, Middleton Dolls, Miss Muffy Collection, United Design.

Redemption Center. Mastercard, Visa, and American Express accepted. Layaway available. Shipping. Free gift wrapping.

THE GIFT ATTIC

Crabtree Valley Mall
4325 Glenwood Ave.
Raleigh, NC 27612

PHONE: (919)781-1822
FAX: (919)781-0090

Monday-Saturday: 10:00-9:30

South's leading resource-Dept. 56 Showcase Dealer with exciting in-store club, Swarovski, Tom Clark Key Dealer, David Winter, Byers' Choice, Lilliput Lane, Wee Forest Folk, Cherished Teddies, Cat's Meow, Little Cheesers, Cast Art, Iris Arc, Krystonia, ANRI, M.I. Hummel, Lladro, Lowell Davis, Duncan Royale, Chilmark, Krystonia, Enesco Ornaments, All God's Children, Bosson Heads, Maruri, Olszewski, Michael Garman, David Blackman's The Sierra Brook Houses, Swiss Army Knives, lots and lots of animals and so much more...

In-store D56 club...GCC Dealer...NALED... Ship anywhere UPS goes. Credit cards.

PERFECT HARMONY, INC.

6586 Glenwood Ave.
Raleigh, NC 27612

PHONE: (919)782-9400

Monday-Wednesday: 10:00-6:00
Thursday-Saturday: 10-9; Sunday: 1-5

Armani, Bouquet Enterprise, Cat's Meow, Colonial Cottages, Enesco Musical Society, Fontanini, Margaret Furlong, Michael Garman, Harbour Lights, Hummel, Maud Humphrey, Iris Arc, Kaiser, Emmett Kelly, Krystonia, Laura's Attic, LEGENDS Mixed Media, Lilliput Lane, Lladro, London By Gaslight, Maruri, Miss Martha's, Memories of Yesterday, Bessie Pease Gutmann, PenDelfin, Pocket Dragons, Sarah's Attic, Shelia's, Snowbabies, and Walt Disney Classics Collection.

Shipping anywhere in continental U.S. Sole importers of hand-painted silk shades and squares. Club redemptions. Major credit cards. Instant membership on Lladro, Lilliput Lane and Memories of Yesterday.

AMY'S HALLMARK

3623 Sunset Ave.
Rocky Mount, NC 27804

PHONE: (919)443-2203

Monday-Saturday: 10-9; Sunday: 1-6

Two great collectible stores serving the collectors since 1980. Both stores located off I-95.

Full line of Dept. 56, Tom Clark Gnomes Key Dealer, David Winter, Lilliput Lane, London by Gaslight, Enesco Musical Showcase Dealer, Laura's Attic, Sports Impressions, Calico Kittens, Cherished Teddies, Hallmark Galleries, Fontanini, Byers' Choice, Precious Moments, Duncan Royale Santas, Emmett Kelly Jr., Hudson Pewter and Hallmark Keepsake Ornaments.

Secondary Market Service in ornaments and figurines. Redemption Center for collectibles listed. Layaway. Mastercard and Visa accepted. Shipping.

Second location: Becker Village Mall, Roanoke, NC 27870 (919)537-7478.

NORTH CAROLINA

QUEENS GIFT SHOPPE

105 North Main St.
Salisbury, NC 28144

PHONE: (704)633-7988

Monday-Saturday: 10:00-5:00

Serving collectors since 1969. Lines include: Swarovski Silver Crystal, David Winter, Caithness, M.I. Hummel, Steinbach, WACO Musicals (Melody In Motion), Hudson Pewter, Cairn Studio (Tom Clark Gnomes, Tim Wolfe), Byers' Choice Carolers, Ron Lee Clowns, Duncan Royale, Old World Ornaments and Nutcrackers, French Limoges, Mill Creek Studios, Rick Cain Studios, Lladro, Dept. 56 Villages, Snowbabies and more! Redemption Center for collector clubs.

Visa and Mastercard accepted. Shipping available.

TOOL SHED

1103 N. Main St.
Waynesville, NC 28786

PHONE: (704)452-5720

Open Daily: 10:00-5:30

Complete line of Dept. 56, Byers' Choice Carolers, David Winter, Duncan Royale, Bradford Dealer, Tom Clark, Cat's Meow, M.I. Hummel, Cherished Teddies, Precious Moments, Malcolm Cooper Pubs, Sports Impressions, Krystonia, Beatrix Potter, Lizzie High, The Villagers, June McKenna, Enesco Music Boxes, Brian Baker's Deja Vu Collection, Laura's Attic, Michael Garman, Annalee, Dreamsicles, Fitz & Floyd, Harbour Lights, J.H. Boone, Midwest Importers, Possible Dreams, and Roman.

All major credit cards accepted. Layaway and shipping available.

THE CANVAS GOOSE

7976 Market St.
Wilmington, NC 28405

PHONE: (919)686-9162

Monday-Saturday: 10:00-5:30

Byers' Choice Carolers, Department 56 Showcase Dealer, includes Dickens Village, New England Village, Alpine Village, Christmas in the City, North Pole, Snowbabies, Merry Makers, and All Through the House, as well as David Winter Cottages, Caithness Paperweights, ANRI Nativities, and Christopher Radko ornaments, Casenovia Abroad, Margaret Furlong Designs and antique furniture and accessories.

Visa, Mastercard and American Express accepted. UPS shipping is available. The Fine Antique and Gifts store!

ST. NICK'S

200 Hanes Mall
3320 Silas Creek Parkway
Winston Salem, NC 27103

PHONE: (919)760-2233

Monday-Saturday: 10:00-9:00
Sunday: 1:00-6:00

Tom Clark Gnomes, Precious Moments, Dept. 56 including Dickens Village, North Pole, Snow Village, New England, Christmas In the City lighted houses and Snowbabies, Possible Dreams Santas, Enesco Treasury of Ornaments, Hummels, Cherished Teddies, Fontanini, Enesco Treasury of Music boxes, Lucy & Me, Kitty Cucumber, Memories of Yesterday, Maud Humphrey, Lee Sievers and Tim Wolfe figurines from Cairn Studio, Wee Forest Folk, and Bing & Grondahl/ Royal Copenhagen.

Collector Club Redemption Center for Precious Moments, Hummel, Tom Clark, Memories of Yesterday, and Fontanini.

NORTH CAROLINA/NORTH DAKOTA

LYNNE'S HALLMARK SHOP & TREASURE ROOM

103 Yaupon Dr.
Yaupon Beach, NC 28465

PHONE: (919)278-9352
FAX: (919)278-9352

Winter Hours:
Monday-Saturday: 10:00-6:00
Sunday: 1:00-5:00
Summer and Holiday Hours:
Monday-Sunday: 9:00-9:00

Hallmark Ornaments, Dept. 56, Midwest Importers, Lowell Davis, Wood World, Schmid, Beatrix Potter, Enesco, Lefton's Colonial Village, Cast Art Dreamsicles, Rick Cain, Coca-Cola Collectibles, Sports Impressions.

Visa, Mastercard, American Express and Discover accepted. Layaway and shipping available.

JUNIQUE'S

Gateway Mall
Bismark, ND 58501

PHONE: (701)258-3542

Monday-Friday: 10:00-9:00
Saturday: 10:00-6:00
Sunday: 12:00-5:00

Precious Moments, Memories Of Yesterday, Enesco Musicals, Cherished Teddies, Calico Kittens, PM Country Dolls, Maud Humphrey, Lucy & Me, Sisters and Best Friends, M.I. Hummel, Lladro, Armani, Kitty Cucumber, Little Cheesers, United Design, Andrea by Sadek, Maruri, Nutcrackers by Kurt S. Adler and Midwest Importers, Reco plates, Sandra Kuck dolls, Chilmark, Chokin plates, Belleek, Dreamsicles, David Winter, Dynasty Dolls, Applause Dolls, Fenton Glass, Glass House Angels, and Myth & Magic Pewter.

Mastercard and Visa accepted. Layaway. Shipping. Free gift wrapping.

HATCH'S COLLECTOR'S CENTERS

West Acres
Fargo, ND 58103

PHONE: (701)282-4457
FAX: (701)282-7175

Monday-Saturday: 10:00-9:00
Sunday: 12:00-5:00

Dept. 56, Snowbabies, David Winter, Lilliput Lane, Precious Moments, Memories of Yesterday, Raikes, Lowell Davis, Jan Hagara, Tom Clark, Emmett Kelly, Bossons, Hummel, Cherished Teddies, Lincoln County Garden Club, Perillo, Sandicast, Chilmark, Maud Humphrey Bogart, Bing & Grondahl/Royal Copenhagen, Hallmark Ornaments, Bradford and Ashton-Drake, prints by Corinne Layton, Meger, Marty Bell, Fernandez and others.

Mail and phone orders welcome.

Stores also in Bismark and Minot.

BJORNSON IMPORTS

2800 S. Columbia Rd. (Box 17)
Grand Forks, ND 58201

PHONE: (701)775-2618

Monday-Saturday: 10:00-9:00
Sunday: 12:00-6:00

Serving collectors since 1974. Dept. 56 Showcase Dealer, Precious Moments (DSR), David Winter, M.I. Hummel, Byers' Choice, Walt Disney Classics Collection, All God's Children, Bradford Exchange, Ashton-Drake Dolls, Madame Alexander Dolls, Armani, Jan Hagara, Caithness, Waterford, Lladro, Belleek, Iris Arc Crystal, Miss Martha's Originals, Maud Humphrey, Lilliput Lane, Memories of Yesterday, Cherished Teddies, Spode, Krystonia, Dreamsicles, WACO, Porsgrund, Fenton Art Glass, Maruri, Midwest Importers and Sports Impressions.

Redemption Center for most collector clubs. Major credit cards. Layaway, shipping and free gift wrapping available.

NORTH DAKOTA/OHIO

THE FRAME MAKER LTD.

1901 DeMers Ave.
Grand Forks, ND 58201

**PHONE: (701)775-9675
(800)289-7775
(701)775-2211**

Monday-Friday: 9-5:30; Saturday: 9-12

Specializing in all areas of collectibles. Dept. 56, Roman, Laura's Attic, Cherished Teddies, Sports Impressions, Glass Eye, Dreamsicles, Kurt Adler, Limited Edition Collector plates. Artwork by: S. Kuck, B. Doolittle, Steve Lyman, Rod Fredericks, Wysocki, Terpning, Gurney, Christensen, Breedon, Landry, Bama, Bateman, Mayol, Daly, S. Hanks, Redlin, Ozz Franca, C. Petersen, Julie Kramer-Cole, Diana Casey, Robert Olson and many more.

Secondary Market prints. Customizing in inlaid frames and unique framing. All major credit cards accepted.

Second Location: Minnesota Art Gallery, South Forks Plaza in Grand Forks, ND.

HIGHLAND SQUARE GIFTS & COLLECTIBLES

878 W. Market St.
Akron, OH 44303

**PHONE: (216)867-4412
FAX: (216)867-4413**

Monday-Friday: 9:00-5:00
Saturday: 10:00-4:00

Lilliput Lane, ANRI, Little Cheesers, Ganz, Pocket Dragons, Cherished Teddies, Calico Kittens, Fenton Art Glass, Dreamsicles, Sports Impressions, Lucy & Me, Laura's Attic, Crystal World, B.P. Gutmann, Napoleon, Designs Americana, Willitts Carousels and Star Trek, Michael Garman, Neil Rose, Marty Sculptures. Also specializing in Concord candles, glassware, plush, Via Vermont and animal giftware.

Visa and Mastercard accepted. Layaway and shipping available. Free gift wrapping.

NORTH HILL GIFT SHOP

255 E. Tallmadge Ave.
Akron, OH 44310

PHONE: (216)535-4811

Monday-Saturday: 10:00-5:00

Dept. 56, Precious Moments, Lladro, Swarovski, Hummel, David Winter, Lilliput Lane, Rockwell, Duncan Royale, Bradford Exchange, ANRI, Lowell Davis, Fenton, Belleek, Walt Disney Classics, P. Buckley Moss, Cairn Studios, Margaret Furlong Designs, Emmett Kelly Jr., Goebel Miniatures, Panton-Krystonia, Maruri, WACO, Willitts, and Edna Hibel and Ashton-Drake dolls.

NALED member. Visa and Mastercard accepted.

THE OAK AND BARN

1289 State Route 309
Alger, OH 45812

PHONE: (419)634-6213

Jan-March: Monday-Saturday: 10:00-5:00
April-Oct: Monday-Saturday: 10:00-7:00
Nov-Dec: Monday-Saturday: 10:00-9:00
Open Sunday All Year: 1:00-5:00

M.I. Hummel, Swarovski, David Winter, Krystonia, Precious Moments, Memories of Yesterday, Raikes Bears, Flavia, Enesco Musicals, Christopher Radko, Fontanini, Dept. 56, House of Hatten Santas, Duncan Royale, Fenton Glass, Cherished Teddies, Calico Kittens, and Dreamsicles.

Two large barns. One features Christmas, including 10 theme trees. The other barn is divided into theme rooms, including throw pillows, rugs, baskets, cards and gifts, and of course, collectibles.

Mastercard, Visa, and Discover. Layaway. Gift wrap on request. UPS Shipping.

OHIO

LAUBER'S GENERAL STORE

Sauder Village
P.O. Box 235 Rt. 2
Archbold, OH 43502

PHONE: (419)446-2541
FAX: (419)445-5251

Nov.-April/ Monday-Saturday: 10:00-5:00
May-Oct./Daily: 9:30-5:00

Country Collectible Shop! Dolls by Gorham, Zook, Good-Kruger, Seymour Mann, Lissi, Gotz, Himstedt, Dynasty, Ginny, Philip Heath, and Madame Alexander. P. Buckley Moss prints, sculptures and plates. Possible Dreams Santa figurines, Lledo custom trucks, Sarah's Attic, Willits Dealer, Midwest Importers, Jan Hagara figurines, prints and dolls.

Major credit cards accepted. Shipping available.

CHRISTMAS TREASURE CHEST

668 U.S. Hwy 250 E. & I-71
Ashland, OH 44805

PHONE: (419)289-2831

Monday-Saturday: 9:00-7:00
Sunday: 11:00-7:00

Dept. 56, Snow Village, Cherished Teddies, Duncan Royale, Memories of Yesterday, Napoleon Capodimonte, Fontanini Nativity, Maruri, WWF World Wildlife Fund, Willitts Carousels, Possible Dreams Santas, Heritage Santas, Stamps, Christopher Radko, Snowbabies, Enesco Treasury Ornaments, Sports Impressions, Steinbach and Ulbricht Nutcrackers and Smokers, Cast Art, Light Houses, Kurt S. Adler, Lilliput Lane, Midwest Importers and Sugar Town.

NALED member. Visa and Mastercard accepted. Secondary Market Service. Layaway plan. Open all year round.

COLONIAL HOUSE ANTIQUES & GIFTS

182 Front St.
Berea, OH 44017

PHONE: (800)344-9299
(216)826-4169
(216)826-0839

Monday-Saturday: 10:00-5:00

Specializing in current and discontinued items in all lines including: Royal Doulton, David Winter, Lilliput Lane, Duncan Royale, ANRI, Kevin Francis, Walt Disney, Dept. 56, Snowbabies, Hummel, Bossons, Wee Forest Folk, and Olszewski Minatures.

A year round Christmas Store with Christmas collectibles, United Design, Mark Klaus, ANRI, Goebel. Cash, checks and major credit cards accepted. Layaway available.

LITTLE RED GIFT HOUSE

State Route 113 P.O. Box 36
Birmingham, OH 44816

PHONE: (216)965-5420

Tuesday-Saturday: 10:00-6:00
Sunday: 12:00-5:00

Specializing in Norman Rockwell plates and figurines. Bradford Dealer, Hummel, Precious Moments, Memories of Yesterday, Snow Village, Lilliput Lane, Ray Day, Disney, Jan Hagara, Emmett Kelly, Snowbabies, Laura's Attic, Possible Dreams Santas, Miss Martha's Collection, Sports Impressions, Cherished Teddies, Bing & Grondahl, Royal Copenhagen, prints and plates by Thomas Kinkade, Lena Liu, Sandra Kuck, Treasured Memories. A large selection of plate frames, domes, and accessories. Hundreds of collector plates, figurines and fine gifts on display.

NALED member. Mastercard and Visa accepted. Collector club redemptions. Layaway available.

OHIO

HUSTON GIFTS & DOLLS

7960 US Route 23
Chillicothe, OH 45601

PHONE: (614)663-2881

Monday-Saturday: 9:00-5:30
Sunday: 12:00-5:30

All God's Children, Snowbabies, Maud Humphrey Bogart, Madame Alexander, Middleton, Spanos, Susan Wakeen, Virginia Turner, Zook, Val Shelton, Ashton-Drake, Perillo, Dreamsicles, Fenton Glass, Raikes Bears, Yankee Candles and many other porcelain dolls. Visit the porcelain doll factory that produces over 250 reproduction of antique to modern dolls. See the dolls being made, painted and dressed. Also available are doll kits and accessories.

All major credit cards accepted. UPS shipping available. Layaways welcome. Free gift wrapping.

NANCY'S HALLMARK SHOPS

Route 42 at I-275
Cincinnati (Sharonville),
OH 45241

PHONE: (513)563-9200
FAX: (513)563-9206

Mon-Fri: 9-9; Sat: 9-7; Sun: 11-5

Precious Moments (DSR), Dept. 56 Showcase Dealer, Cairn Studios: Tom Clark/Tim Wolfe, Bearly People, Calico Kittens, Cat's Meow, Cherished Teddies, Chilmark, Daddy's Long Legs, David Winter, Disney Porcelain, Enesco Small World of Music, Hallmark Galleries, Hallmark Keepsake Ornaments, Hummel, Iris Arc, large selection of framed collectible stamps, Lilliput, MOY, Sarah's Attic, Sisters and Best Friends, Sports Impression, Swarovski, WACO Musicals, Will Moses Ltd. Ed. Prints. Extensive selection of Fantasy Collectibles. Extensive selection of Santas: Possible Dreams, D. Calla, L. Haney, Santas by Donna, etc.

SAXONY IMPORTS

542 Race St.
Cincinnati, OH 45202

PHONE: (513)621-7800
(800)669-7906

Call For Hours

Swarovski, M.I. Hummel, David Winter, Walt Disney Classics Collection, Royal Doulton, Lladro, Tom Clark Gnomes, Duncan Royale, Wee Forest Folk, Precious Moments, Memories of Yesterday, Dept. 56 (Showcase Dealer), Armani, collector plates, including Royal Copenhagen and Bing & Grondahl, Goebel Miniatures, Melody in Motion, Steinbach Nutcrackers, Anheuser-Busch Steins, Lowell Davis, Belleek China, and Lilliput Lane.

Most credit cards accepted. Layaway/shipping available, redemption center. NALED member, secondary market service.

STORY BOOK KIDS

3011 Glendale-Milford Rd.
Cincinnati, OH 45241-3130

PHONE: (513)769-5437(KIDS)
FAX: (513)769-5441

Tuesday-Saturday: 10:00-6:00

Tom Clark Gnomes, Cat's Meow, P. M., All God's Children, Sarah's Attic, Snowbabies, Dept. 56, Emmett Kelly Jr., Maud Humphrey Bogart, Lilliput Lane, North American Bears, Byers' Choice Carolers, Cherished Teddies, C. Radko, J.H. Boone, Fitz & Floyd, Lizzie High Dolls, Krystonia, United Design, Daddy's Long Legs, WACO, Royal Doulton, and Melody In Motion.

All major credit cards accepted. No fee layaway. NALED member. Secondary Market Service available.

Second location: 2071 Florence Mall, Florence, KY 41042-1442.

Hours: Monday-Saturday: 10:00-9:00; Sunday: 12:00-6:00. Phone: (606)525-7743.

OHIO

WM. EFFLER JEWELERS

7618 Hamilton Ave.
Cincinnati, OH 45231

PHONE: (513)521-6654
FAX: (513)521-6656

Tuesday-Saturday: 9:30-5:00
Friday: 9:30-8:00

In business for 73 years. Kurt S. Adler, Annalee Mobilitee Dolls, Armani, Byers' Choice Ltd., Dept. 56, Dynasty Doll, Enesco, Gorham, Lladro, M.I. Hummel, Kaiser Porcelain, Lladro, Maruri, Midwest Importers, Possible Dreams, Roman, Royal Doulton, Schmid, Summerhill Crystal and Glass, United Design, Cybis, ANNA PERENNA, Bareuther, Waterford Crystal, ANRI woodcarvings, Dresden figures, and Limoges boxes.

Second location: 2714 Erie Ave. Cincinnati, OH 45208. (513)321-3099.

Major credit cards accepted. Club Redemption Center. Shipping and layaway available.

COLLECTOR'S OUTLET

4979 West 130th St.
Cleveland, OH 44135

PHONE: (216)433-0505 (SAT/SUN)

Saturday and Sunday: 10:30-6:00
Weekdays call: (216)257-1141

Located in the Bazaar. Serving the collector for 11 years. Lines include: Ashton-Drake, Norman Rockwell Gallery, Hawthorne Architectural Register, Ardleigh Elliott, Van Hygan & Smyth frames, Hamilton plates and dolls, Perillo, Georgetown dolls, Krystonia, United Design, Hagen-Renaker, Emmett Kelly Sr., Castagna, posters, Precious Heirloom dolls, Artist Collectibles dolls, and Elvis Memorabilia.

Major credit cards accepted. Layaway and shipping available. Secondary Market Service.

NALED Member/Bradford Dealer.

CROWN HALLMARK SHOP

3890 East Broad St.
Columbus, OH 43213

PHONE: (614)237-3105
FAX: (614)237-5002

Monday-Friday: 10:00-9:00
Sunday: 12:00-6:00

In the collectible business for over 25 years. Precious Moments (DSR), Department 56 Showcase Dealer, M.I. Hummel, Tom Clark, Lladro, Swarovski, David Winter, Cat's Meow, Emmett Kelly, Jr., Sarah's Attic, Miss Martha's Originals, Cherished Teddies and Hallmark Keepsake Ornaments.

All major credit cards accepted. Shipping available. Redemption center for all collector clubs!

BELLFAIR COUNTRY STORES

1490 N. Fairfield Rd.
Dayton, OH 45432

PHONE: (513)426-3921
FAX: (513)426-3974

Monday-Saturday: 10-9; Sunday: 12-8

Personal Service! All Dept. 56, Precious Moments, Cat's Meow, Sarah's Attic, Iris Arc, Lilliput Lane, David Winter, Christopher Radko, M.I. Hummel, Armani, Cairn Studio Creations, one of Ohio's largest collections of German Nutcrackers and Smokers, Santas by Possible Dreams, Lowell Davis, LEGENDS, Krystonia, Pocket Dragons, Hidden Kingdom, Cherished Teddies, Calico Kittens, Enesco Treasury Ornaments, Duncan Royale, Little Cheesers, Kurt S. Adler, United Design, Roman, MOY, Napoleon, Old World Glass, and Shoemaker's Dream.

Visa, Mastercard and American Express. NALED Member. Layaway and UPS shipping available.

OHIO

DECLARK'S

Town & Country Shopping Center
206 E. Stroop Rd.
Dayton, OH 45429

PHONE: (513)294-4741
FAX: (513)294-5927

Monday-Saturday: 10:00-9:00
Sunday: 12:00-5:00

Dept. 56 Showcase Dealer, Precious Moments (DSR), Lladro, Hummel, Swarovski, David Winter Cottages, Lilliput Lane, Cat's Meow, Cairn Studio, Wee Forest Folk, Disney, All God's Children, Sarah's Attic, sports collectibles including Sports Impressions and Gartlan, steins, including Anheuser-Busch and Dram Tree. Limited Edition Plates: Bradford, Reco and many others. Ashton-Drake Dolls, Madame Alexander dolls, Chilmark, LEGENDS, Hallmark Ornaments and Collectibles, Marty Bell Lithographs, plus many more!

Mail order welcome. We accept all major credit cards.

GUSTIN'S HALLMARK STORES

2048 Miamisburg-Centerville Rd.
Dayton, OH 45458

PHONE: (513)435-9030
FAX: (513)433-7442

Monday-Saturday: 10:00-9:00
Sunday: 12:00-5:00

Featuring Precious Moments (DSR), Dept. 56, Memories of Yesterday, All God's Children, Miss Martha Originals, Cherished Teddies, Lilliput Lane, David Winter, Sarah's Attic, Cat's Meow, Possible Dreams, Anheuser-Busch, Cast Art, United Design, Dreamsicles, Hallmark Keepsake Ornaments, and VickiLane Designs.

Other locations include: 1055 S. Main St., Centerville. Phone: (513)433-1203; Route 675 at Route 48, Centerville. Phone: (513)435-1144; 2104 E. Whipp Rd., Kettering. Phone: (513)435-5384.

On-site engraving. US Postal and UPS shipping.

THE LITTLE HOUSE

423 North Main St.
Downtown Piqua, OH 45356

PHONE: (513)773-3666

Monday-Thursday: 10:00-6:00
Friday: 10:00-8:00
Saturday: 10:00-5:00

Dept. 56, Fontanini, Cat's Meow, Byers' Choice, David Winter, Cairn Studio, Precious Moments, Chilmark and Hudson Pewter, All God's Children, Miss Martha's Originals, Sarah's Attic, Kurt S. Adler Santas, Possible Dreams, Anri, M.I. Hummel, DeGrazia, Perillo, Laura's Attic, Fenton, Cherished Teddies, Kitty Cucumber, Treasured Memories, Snowbabies and Shoemaker's Dreams.

Visa and Mastercard accepted. Layaway. UPS shipping. Club Redemptions.

JAMES LOCKE JEWELERS

215 East Fifth St.
East Liverpool, OH 43920

PHONE: (216)385-9404
FAX: (216)385-4758

Monday-Saturday: 9:00-5:00
Thursday: 9:00-8:00

Royal Doulton, Lilliput Lane, Precious Moments (DSR), Norman Rockwell, M.I. Hummel, Maud Humphrey Bogart, Memories of Yesterday (Heritage Dealer), Cherished Teddies, Willitts and Tobin Fraley Carousels, Calico Kittens, Musicals, Sandra Kuck, Lucy & Me (Collectors Club). Dolls, including Gorham, Royal Douton, and Precious Moments porcelain dolls, North Pole Village, Sports Impressions, and Sebastians.

Club Redemption Center. UPS shipping. Mastercard, Visa, and Discover accepted.

OHIO

MILLER'S HALLMARK & GIFT GALLERY

1322 N. Barron St.
Eaton, OH 45320

PHONE: (513)456-4151

Monday-Friday: 9:00-9:00
Saturday: 9:00-6:00; Sunday: 12:00-5:00

Hummels, Precious Moments, Swarovski Crystal, Cherished Teddies, Walt Disney Classics Collection, Lladro, Memories of Yesterday, Goebel Miniatures, Hallmark Ornaments, and Galleries, Miss Martha's, David Winter, Sports Impressions, Maud Humphrey and Caithness paperweights.

Full-service Hallmark and collectibles showcase gallery. Expert appraisal services. UPS insured shipping. Phone and mail orders are welcome.

TERRY'S HALLMARK SHOP

320 W. National Rd.
Englewood, OH 45322

PHONE: (513)836-4569

Open 7 Days A Week: 10:00-8:00

Dept. 56 Houses and Snowbabies, Jan Hagara, Cat's Meow, Cairn Gnomes, Maud Humphrey, Precious Moments, Hummel, Disney Collectibles, Garman Professionals, Dreamsicles, Cherished Teddies, J.H. Boone, Hallmark Ornaments and Lilliput Lane.

Terry's Hallmark Shop was founded in 1972. In business serving the collectors for 21 years.

THINGS 'N PILLS

Northview Plaza
2705 N. Main St.
Findlay, OH 45840

PHONE: (419)424-1321

Monday-Saturday: 9:00-9:00

Precious Moments (DSR), Maud Humphrey, Miss Martha, Memories of Yesterday, Cherished Teddies, Calico Kittens, Sisters and Best Friends, Enesco Musicals, M.I. Hummel, Jan Hagara, Hudson Pewter, Sarah's Attic, Emmett Kelly, Lenox Giftware, Gold Crown Hallmark Retailer, Lilliput Lane, Roman, Fontanini Creches, Rockwell figurines, Dave Grossman, Fenton Art, Dreamsicles, United Design, Kitty Cucumber, Hallmark Ornaments, Dept. 56 Villages, PMC Dolls.

Visa, Mastercard, Discover and American Express accepted. Layaway and shipping available. Free gift wrap.

COPPER CANOPY GIFTIBLES

555 Main St.
Groveport, OH 43125

PHONE: (614)836-2488

Monday-Saturday: 10:00-6:00

Lilliput Lane, Precious Moments, Sisters & Best Friends, Memories Of Yesterday, Small World of Music, Treasury Ornaments, Michael Garman Productions, Roman Inc., Fenton Art Glass, Lee Middleton Dolls, Dept. 56 Snowbabies, All Through the House, Merry Makers, Robert Raikes Collectibles and Heidi Hares.

Visa, Mastercard and Discover accepted. Layaway plan is available. Shipping available anywhere in the USA.

OHIO

PORCELLANA LIMITED

16 North D St.
Hamilton, OH 45013

PHONE: (513)868-1511

Monday-Saturday: 10:00-5:30

Dept. 56 Showcase Store, Precious Moments, Cherished Teddies, Lladro, Swarovski, All God's Children, David Winter, Lilliput Lane, Hummel, Enesco Musicals, Byers' Choice Carolers, Steinbach Nutcrackers, Snowbabies, Winter Silhouette, Christopther Radko ornaments, Lizzie High dolls, and Lowell Davis.

Visa and Mastercard accepted. NALED member. GCC Store. Layaway available.

HARTVILLE COLLECTIBLES

788 Edison St.
Hartville, OH 44632

PHONE: (216)877-2172
FAX: (216)877-2101

Monday: 10:00-6:00
Tuesday-Saturday: 11:00-8:00
Closed Wednesday and Sunday

Dept. 56, Precious Moments, Hummel, Lladro, Cairn Studio Gnomes, Swarovski, David Winter, Lilliput Lane, Wee Forest Folk, Fenton, Madame Alexander dolls, Gorham Dolls, Goebel, Lowell Davis, Jan Hagara, Norman Rockwell, Flambro, Snowbabies, and many more fine lines of collectibles and giftware.

Visa, Mastercard and Discover accepted. Layaway plan available. They ship anywhere.

PEEK IN THE ATTIC

119 Greene St.
Marietta, OH 45750

PHONE: (614)373-2575

Monday-Saturday: 10:00-5:00
Sunday: 12:00-4:00 (June-Dec.)

One of the finest selections of collectible giftware in the area. All God's Children, Miss Martha, Maud Humphrey Bogart, Memories of Yesterday, Laura's Attic, Cherished Teddies, Lilliput Lane, Cat's Meow, The Herd, Dreamsicles, many collectible Santas and Angels by United Design, Possible Dreams, Designs Americana, Creative Carvings, Margaret Furlong Angels.

Visa, Mastercard, and Discover accepted. Layaway and UPS shipping available. Redemption Center. Free gift wrapping.

COLLECTOR'S GALLERY

647 Delaware Ave.
Marion, OH 43302

PHONE: (614)387-0602

Complete Collectible and Gift Center. Over 1 million dollars in collectible merchandise. All Dept. 56 Houses and Snowbabies, DW, Lilliput, Swarovski, LEGENDS, Lladro, Armani, Krystonia, June McKenna, Enchantica, Christopher Radko, and more. Prints: Kinkade, Marty Bell, Redlin, Harvey, Frace, Kuck, Lena Liu, and more. 700 Dolls in-stock- Alexander, Alice Darling, Himstedt, Ashton-Drake, Annalee, Barbie, GADCO, Collectables, Daddy's Long Legs, Fay Spanos, Good-Kruger, Goetz, Gunzel, Hamilton, Heidi Ott, Jeckle-Jansen, Jerri, Lizzie High, Middleton, Mann, Wakeen, Turner, Zook--Bears.

Member Gift Creations and NALED. Product lists available--personal service. Club Redemptions. Mail and phone orders welcome. Layaway and shipping. Major credit cards accepted.

OHIO

SETTLER'S COLLECTIONS

At Settler's Farm
14279 Old State Rd. (Rt. 608)
Middlefield, OH 44062

PHONE: (216)632-1009

Monday-Saturday: 10:00-5:30

Located in the heart of Amish country for over 15 years, they are a NALED member specializing in Dept. 56 Villages and Snowbabies, Lilliput Lane, Swarovski, Walt Disney Classics Collection, M.I. Hummel, Precious Moments, All God's Children, P. Buckley Moss plates and figurines, Christopher Radko, Michael Garman, Possible Dreams, Cat's Meow, Emmett Kelly Jr., Maruri, Neil J. Rose sculptures, Daddy's Long Legs, Castagna, Sandicast, Lizzie High, Lowell Davis, Mill Creek, VickiLane, Dreamsicles, Cherished Teddies. Redemption Center for collector clubs.

Mastercard and Visa accepted. Layaways and shipping available.

HUMMEL GIFT SHOP

E. Garfield Rd.
New Springfield, OH 44443

**PHONE: (800)223-2602-OHIO
(800)354-5438-USA**

Monday-Saturday: 10:00-5:00
Sunday: 1:00-5:00 (June-December)

The Midwest's premier collectible store. With 30,000 sq. feet and over 1 million collectibles (current and retired pieces) in seven galleries. Dept. 56 Showcase Dealer, Walt Disney, Duncan Royale, Goebel, Hummel, Gorham, David Winter, Lilliput Lane, Lenox, LEGENDS, Lladro, June McKenna, Midwest, Possible Dreams, Royal Doulton, Schmid, United Design, Swarovski, Caithness, Rockwell, Maruri, Hand & Hammer Silversmiths, Steinbach, Cybis, Tom Clark Gnomes, Capodimonte, Cherished Teddies, Precious Moments, MOY, Steiff, L. Davis, Cat's Meow, Kaiser and more!

Mastercard, Visa and layaways welcome.

GIFTS & TREASURES

1664 N. Main St. Suite 12
North Canton, OH 44720

Phone: (216)494-5511

Monday-Friday: 10:00-8:00
Saturday: 10:00-5:00
Sunday: 12:00-5:00

Tom Clark Gnomes, Tim Wolfe, Precious Moments, Dept. 56, Miss Martha's, All God's Children, Possible Dreams, Kurt S. Adler, United Design Santas and Angels, Schmid, Cherished Teddies, Calico Kittens, Sports Impressions, Cast Art, David Winter, Lilliput Lane, Iris Arc Crystal, Enesco music boxes, Cat's Meow, Norman Rockwell, Harbour Light lighthouses, Nutcrackers, Smokers, German and Anheuser-Busch beer steins, and Duncan Royale.

All major credit cards accepted. NALED Member. Layaways and shipping available. Secondary Market for Tom Clark.

BEEHIVE GIFTS, CLEVELAND

150 Great Northern Mall
N. Olmstead, OH 44070

PHONE: (216)777-2600

Open Daily: 10:00-9:00
Sunday: 12:00-5:00

M.I. Hummel, Precious Moments, David Winter, Flambro, Royal Doulton, Lladro, United Design Animals, Sports Impressions, Enesco Musicals, Fenton Art Glass, Disney Classics, Dept. 56 Showcase Dealer, Star Trek Collectibles, Chilmark/Hudson Pewter, American Indian Art, Austrian Crystal.

NALED member. All major credit cards accepted. Free layaway. Free UPS shipping. Free gift wrapping.

OHIO

LOLA & DALE GIFTS & COLLECTIBLES

6877 W. 130th St
Parma Heights, OH 44130

PHONE: (216)885-0444
(800)432-2506 (ORDERS)

Monday-Friday: 10:00-8:00
Saturday: 10:00-5:00

Precious Moments, both new and retired, Memories of Yesterday, Dept. 56 Dickens Houses, Lilliput Lane, Sarah's Attic, Sports Impressions, Sandicast, collector plates, Raikes Bears, Iris Arc Crystal, Maud Humphrey, Snowbabies, Miss Martha's, Cherished Teddies, and Calico Kittens.

Collector dolls include Georgetown, Ashton-Drake, Hamilton, Barbie, Hibel, Pauline and Legacy.

Bradford Exchange member. Mastercard, Visa and Discover accepted. NALED member. Secondary Market on Precious Moments, Dept. 56 and plates. UPS shipping available.

HOUSE OF TRADITION

111 East Second St.
Perrysburg, OH 43551

PHONE: (419)874-1151

Monday-Friday: 10:00-6:00
Saturday: 10:00-5:00

Doll and collectible specialists. One of the largest and finest selections in Ohio. Bradford, Ashton-Drake, All Dept. 56 Villages, Snowbabies, Hummel, Armani, Maruri, Swarovski, Enesco Musicals, Lilliput Lane, David Winter, Jan Hagara, Duncan Royale, Ulbricht and Steinbach Nutcrackers and Smokers, Russian Original nesting dolls, Lowell Davis, Castagna, Laura's Attic, Maud Humphrey, Amish Heritage Collection, Lighthouses by Cheryl Collin. Thomas Kinkade and Marty Bell prints and plates.

Special events and guest appearances. Newsletter and catalog. All major credit cards accepted. NALED member.

CELLAR CACHE

P.O. Box 540
451 Catawba Ave.
Put-in-Bay, OH 43456

PHONE: (419)285-2738

Available Year Round
Daily: 10:00-9:00

Serving collectors since 1984. All God's Children, Byers' Choice, Cherished Teddies, Calico Kittens, Maud Humphrey, Emmett Kelly, Dept. 56, David Winter, LEGENDS, M.I. Hummel, Lladro, Swarovski, Lizzie High, Lynn Haney, Jan Hagara, Wee Forest Folk, Precious Moments, Perillo, Harbour Lights, Raikes, Anheuser-Busch, P. Buckley Moss plates, Miss Martha's Originals, Royal Doulton, Shelia's, ANNA-PERENNA, Cast Art, Possible Dreams.

NALED member. Redemption Center for most collector clubs. Layaway and shipping available. Major credit cards accepted. Select Secondary Market Items.

KIRBY'S

7336 E. Main St.
Reynoldsburg, OH 43068

PHONE: (614)868-5754
(800)622-6963

Budweiser Anheuser-Busch Beer Steins, Mugs, and Ceramarte Collectibles.

Mastercard, Visa and Discover accepted. Secondary Market Dealer. Buy-Sell-Trade.

OHIO

SCHUMM PHARMACY HALLMARK & GIFTS
504 S. Main
Rockford, OH 45882
PHONE: (419)363-3630
FAX: (419)363-2498

Monday-Friday: 9:00-8:00
Saturday: 9:00-5:00
Nov.-Dec. Open Sunday: 1:00-5:00

Precious Moments (DSR), Memories of Yesterday Heritage Dealer, Dept. 56, Marty Bell Fine Art, Thomas Kinkade, Cherished Teddies, David Winter, Bradford Exchange, Sports Collectibles: Gartlan, Sports Impressions, Salvino. Ashton-Drake, Cast Art Dreamsicles, Tom Clark, LEGENDS, Hummel, ANRI, Dolls, Flambro, Lowell Davis, Lilliput, Raikes Bears, Jan Hagara, Sarah's Attic, ANNA-PERENNA, Hallmark Keepsake Ornaments, Possible Dreams.

Mastercard, Visa and Discover accepted. UPS and layaway service. NALED and GCC member.

STRUBLES OF SHELBY
82 W. Main
Shelby, OH 44875
PHONE: (419)342-2136

Monday-Saturday: 9:00-6:00
Closed Sunday

Cherished Teddies, Memories of Yesterday, Maud Humphrey, Precious Moment Signature Store, Colonial Village Realtor, Dreamsicles, Harbour Lights, Lefton Lighthouses, Enesco Small World of Music, Treasured Memories, and Laura's Attic. Collectible dolls include Middleton, Jerri, Gorham, Precious Moments Preferred Dealer, Phyllis, Zook, Nahrgang, Susan Wakeen, Parkins, Meggan, Artist Collectibles, and Victoria.

NALED member. Visa and Mastercard accepted. Layaway available.

PAT'S CARD & GIFTS
Westgate Village
Tiffin, OH 44883
PHONE: (419)447-8081

Monday-Friday: 10:00-8:30
Saturday: 10:00-4:30

Hummel, Dept. 56, All God's Children, Sarah's Attic, Precious Moments, Cherished Teddies, Calico Kittens, Raikes Bears, Anheuser-Busch, Dreamsicles, Porcelain dolls, Complete line of Hallmark, including Ornaments, and Fenton Glassware. Suncatchers, brass crystal and other distinctive giftware.

All major credit cards accepted. Free gift wrapping. Layaway and shipping available.

ROCHELLE'S FINE GIFTS
344 Franklin Park Mall
Toledo, OH 43623
PHONE: (419)472-7673
(800)458-6585
FAX: (419)472-0447

Monday-Saturday: 10:00-9:00
Sunday: 12:00-6:00

Precious Moments, Dept. 56 Villages, Snowbabies, Memories of Yesterday, Iris Arc, Armani, Disney Classics Collection, Jan Hagara, plates, dolls, Hummels, Emmett Kelly, Rockwell, Ebony, David Winter, Lilliput Lane, Shoemaker's Dream, Cherished Teddies, Little Cheesers, Sarah's Attic, Miss Martha, Maud Humphrey, Maurice Wideman, PenniBears, Krystonia, Duncan Royale Santas, Bossons and so much more!

NALED member. Layaway. Special orders accepted. Free gift wrapping. Secondary Market Service. Mastercard, Visa and Discover accepted.

OHIO

THE TOY STORE

Franklin Park Mall
5001 Monroe St.
Toledo, OH 43623

PHONE: (800)862-TOYS
FAX: (419)473-3947

Monday-Saturday: 10:00-9:00
Sunday: 12:00-6:00

Authorized Steiff Dealer, Steiff Limited Edition made exclusively for The Toy Store (1500 pieces only), Merrythought, Beaver Valley, North American Bear, Gund, Canterbury Bears, Lawton, Madame Alexander, Good-Kruger, Kathe Kruse, Annalee, Nesting Dolls, Breyer Horses Britains Soldiers. The largest annual doll/bear show.

All major credit cards accepted. Layaway. Courtesy gift wrap. Worldwide shipping.

MASTROPOLO GALLERIES

P.O. Box 366
Vandalia, OH 45377

PHONE: (513)890-5570

Monday-Saturday: 10:00-10:00
Sunday: 12:00-5:00
By Appointment Only

Limited Edition Art. Red Skelton Authorized Gallery. Lithographs by Alan Maley, Thomas Kinkade and more. Hamilton Gifts, Maud Humphrey Bogart Gallery and Redemption Center. Donald Zolan Trading Center, Artaffects and Enesco. Dolls by Gorham, Ashton-Drake, Hamilton, Reco, and Seymour Mann. New and Secondary market plates. Celebrating 25 years in the collectibles business.

Free shipping within the continental USA. Layaway available. Buy and sell services.

MUSIK BOX DOLL HAUS-MUSIK BOX HAUS, INC.

5551 & 5541 Liberty Ave. (Rt. 6)
Vermilion, OH 44089

PHONE: (216)967-4744
(800)832-4744

May-Dec./Monday-Saturday: 10:00-6:00
Sunday: 12:30-5:00
Jan.-April/Tuesday-Saturday: 10:00-6:00

Maud Humphrey, Precious Moments, Jan Hagara, Hibel, Sorrento, Porter Music Box, Kimberly, Via Vermont, WACO, Reco, Steinbach and custom designs.

Dolls: Gorham, Seymour Mann, Nahrgang, Charades, Middleton, Zook, Dynasty, Faith Wick, Georgetown, and other artist originals.

Visa, Mastercard and Discover accepted. Layaway. Free gift wrapping. UPS shipping. NALED and Musical Box Society International.

BOOKS, BRASS & CANDLES

P.O. Box 70
1050 N. Shoop Ave.
Wauseon, OH 43567

PHONE: (419)335-3787
FAX: (419)335-3887

Monday-Friday: 10:00-6:00
Saturday: 10:00-3:00

Lilliput Lane, Dept. 56 (Snow Village), Memories of Yesterday, All God's Children, Lowell Davis, Emmett Kelly Clowns, Miss Martha's, All God's Children, Enesco Corp., Duncan Royale, Dave Grossman Creations, Lilliput Lane, Reco, Roman, United Design, WACO, Schmid and Cherished Teddies.

Visa, Mastercard and Discover accepted. Layaways welcome.

OHIO

GINGERBREAD HOUSE
109 S. Miami St. (Rt. 48)
West Milton, OH 45383
PHONE: (513)698-3477
FAX: (513)698-6820

Tuesday-Saturday: 10:30-5:00
Call for Holiday and Special Event Hours

Featuring Annalee, Cat's Meow, David Winter, Dept. 56: Heritage Village, Snow Village, Snowbabies and All Through The House; Lilliput Lane, Ray Day, Memories Of Yesterday, Jan Hagara, Precious Moments, Santas, including Possible Dreams, and Kurt Adler, Laura's Attic, Cherished Teddies, Enesco Treasury Ornaments, Sports Impressions, Ashton-Drake Dolls, Sarah's Attic, Dreamsicles, Lucy & Me, Bradford Exchange.

NALED member. Layaways. Redemption Center. Secondary Market.

GALES GARDEN CENTER
2730 Som Center Rd.
Willoughby Hills, OH 44094
PHONE: (216)944-6066
FAX: (216)944-4764

Open 7 Days A Week: 9:00-6:00

Lilliput Lane, Krystonia, Walt Disney Classics Collection, Cat's Meow, Precious Moments, Lucy & Me, Dept. 56, Royal Doulton, Lenox, Baldwin Brass, Hummel, Cast Art.

Visa, Mastercard and Discover accepted. Free layaway. Redemption Center for Hummel, Precious Moments, Lilliput Lane, Walt Disney and Krystonia. Many assorted gift items available.

G.M. RICE FURNITURE, INC.
38 S. Mulberry St.
P.O. Box 827
Wilmington, OH 45177-0827
PHONE: (513)382-0323
FAX: (513)383-2590

Mon.-Wed. and Saturday: 9:00-5:30
Thursday and Friday: 9:00-8:00

In business "since 1909!" Dept. 56 Heritage Village Collection of Dickens, New England and North Pole, plus Snowbabies; Lilliput Lane English Cottage, plus Ray Day's American Landmarks; Enesco's Memories of Yesterday; Flambro's Emmett Kelly, Jr. Limited Editions; Fenton Glassware, and Duncan Royale Santas. Only one very rare Colonial Clock Co., Jacob Ebby Tall Case floor clock.

Visa, Mastercard and Discover accepted.

LITTLE SHOP ON THE PORTAGE
P.O. Box 189
330 W. Main St.
Woodville, OH 43469-0189
PHONE: (419)849-3742

Mon.-Sat.: 10-9; Sunday: 1:30-5:30

Retired and current Dept. 56 (all Villages and Snowbabies), Precious Moments, Bradford and Hamilton plates, Sandra Kuck plates and graphics, MOY, Enesco's North Pole Village and Treasury Of Christmas ornaments. Also Cherished Teddies, Laura's Attic, Miss Martha's, Christopher Radko, Amish Heritage Collection, Star Trek globes, plus retired Maud Humphrey, Brambly Hedge, Kinka, Ferrandiz, DeGrazia and Frances Hook. A level of selection, service and staff knowledge beyond the ordinary. MC, VISA and Discover. UPS. Layaway. Christmas catalog. NALED. Located on Rts. 20 and 105, SE of Toledo.

OHIO/OKLAHOMA

BECKETT'S DOLL HOUSE

692 High St.
Worthington, OH 43085

PHONE: (614)848-9636
(800)527-8290 (ORDERS)

Monday-Friday: 10:00-6:00
Saturday: 10:00-5:00; Sunday: 12:00-5:00

The largest selection of collectible and play dolls and animals in Central Ohio. Located at the intersection of Rts. 23 and 161. Madame Alexander, Ashton-Drake, Hamilton, Georgetown, Seymour Mann, Himstedt, Good-Kruger, Lawton, Corolle, Dolls by Jerri, Effanbee Dolls, Ellenbrooke, Oldenburg Originals, Turner, Sarah's Attic, Jan Hagara, Annalee, GADCO, Zook, Ginny, Barbie, Middleton, Collectables, North American, Steiff, Hermann, Merry Thought, Bearly There, Gund, Raikes, artist dolls and bears, plus many more.

Visa, Mastercard and Discover accepted. Secondary Market. Layaway welcome.

CURIO CABINET/ CHRISTMAS VILLAGE

679 High St.
Worthington, OH 43085

PHONE: (614)885-1986
FAX: (614)885-2043

Monday-Saturday: 10:00-5:30
Extended Seasonal Hours

Wee Forest Folk, Olszewski Miniatures, Dept. 56, David Winter, Lilliput Lane, Cherished Teddies, Maud Humphrey, Royal Doulton, Snowbabies, Disney Classics, Lincoln County Garden Club, PenniBears, Hummels, All God's Children, Cat's Meow, Christopher Radko, Duncan Royale, Swarovski, Kevin Francis, June McKenna, Margaret Furlong, Possible Dreams, Sheila's, Dreamsicles plus many more.

NALED and GCC member. Visa, Mastercard accepted. Layaway welcome. Secondary Market Services.

SHIRLEY'S GIFTS INC.

1021 West Broadway
Ardmore, OK 73401

PHONE: (405)223-2116

Monday-Saturday: 10:00-6:00

Dept. 56, Snowbabies, Swarovski, Precious Moments, Cherished Teddies, Laura's Attic, Miss Martha's Originals, Armani, Lladro, David Winter, Colonial Village, Tom Clark Gnomes, Tim Wolfe, Chilmark, LEGENDS, Hummel, Emmett Kelly Jr., All God's Children, Andrea by Sadek, Enesco Musicals, Possible Dreams, Fontanini, Sabino, Dreamsicles, Walt Disney Classics Collection, Maud Humphrey, Enesco Ornaments, Madame Alexander dolls, Precious Moments Company dolls, Norfin Trolls.

Visa, Mastercard and American Express accepted. Free shipping and insurance. Redemption Center. Secondary Market Dealer. NALED member.

THOMPSON'S

117 S. Bickford
El Reno, OK 73036

PHONE: (405)262-3552

Monday-Saturday: 9:00-8:00

Dept. 56, David Winter, Lilliput Lane, Precious Moments, Armani, Jan Hagara, June McKenna, Leo Smith, PenniBears, Mark Hopkins, Hallmark, Mats Jonasson, Margaret Furlong, Sandicast, Byers' Choice, Christopher Radko, Fitz & Floyd, Iris Arc, Lenox Collection, Midwest Importers, Charles Martine Limoges Boxes, Legends of Santa and Nutcrackers.

Visa, Mastercard and Discover accepted. Layaway available. Secondary Market Service.

OKLAHOMA

DODY'S HALLMARK

Central Mall #72
Lawton, OK 73501

PHONE: (800)562-5868

Monday-Saturday: 9:00-9:00

Has been in the collectible business for 15 years. Club Redemption for most collectible lines. Emmett Kelly Sr. by Dave Grossman and Stanton Arts, Hallmark Gallery, All God's Children, Victoria Ashlea. Enesco (DSR), Precious Moments, Maud Humphrey, Cherished Teddies, Laura's Attic, Memories of Yesterday, Miss Martha's, Kurt S. Adler, Armani, Ashton-Drake dolls, Bradford Exchange, Dept. 56 Showcase Dealer, Walt Disney Classics Collection, Emmett Kelly Jr., Hummel, David Winter, Jon Herbert Shoes and Father Time Clockhouses, Lilliput Lane, Sarah's Attic, WACO Melody In Motion and Olszewski Miniatures.

Layaway and shipping available. Secondary Market. Artist appearances.

SUZANNE'S GALLERY

54400 East 130th Rd.
Miami, OK 74354

PHONE: (918)542-3808
(918)542-1400
FAX: (918)542-1480

Monday-Friday: 10:00-4:00
Saturday & Sunday: By Appointment

Greenwich Workshop Dealer, Bev Doolittle, James Bama, Howard Terpning, Frank Wooten, William Phillips and James Gurney, Frank McCarthy, Ron Frederick, Kelly Haney, Jerome Tiger, Irene Spencer, Penni Anne Cross, and Craig Kodra. A large selection of limited edition hard to find prints.

Secondary Market Service. UPS shipping and layaways available. Drive in or fly in on their own personal air strip.

KABET'S

1901 N.W. Expressway
#1030 Penn Square
Oklahoma City, OK 73118

PHONE: (405)842-2242
(800)4-KABETS

Monday-Saturday: 10:00-9:00
Sunday: 1:00-6:00

A bountiful and unique selection of high-end contemporary gifts and furniture. Lines include Duncan Royale, Precious Moments, and Vienna bronzes, Russian Lacquer.

All major credit cards accepted. Layaway available. Secondary Market on all above lines listed.

Oklahoma's first gift shop, in business for 40 years.

LANZER'S GIFTS

4813 N. May Ave.
Oklahoma City, OK 73112

PHONE: (405)947-0651

Monday-Friday: 8:30-6:00;
Saturday: 9:00-6:00
Extended Holiday Hours

Located in Mayfair Village Shopping Center at 50th and North May. Owner Steven Lanzer formerly of Langsam's Drug. Lines include: Dept. 56 Villages, Snowbabies, Merry Makers, All Thru the House and accessories, David Winter, Andrea by Sadek, Memories of Yesterday, Cherished Teddies, Calico Kittens, Hummel, Miss Martha's, Steinbach Nutcracker, Iris Arc, Enesco Treasury Ornaments, Fontanini, Krystonia, Emmett Kelly Jr., Maud Humphrey, and Dreamsicles.

Hallmark plus store. GCC Member. Secondary Market in cottages and figurines. Redemption Center. Major charges and shipping available.

OKLAHOMA

NORTH POLE CITY COLLECTIBLES

4201 S. I-44
Oklahoma City, OK 73119

PHONE: (405)685-6635
FAX: (405)685-8347

Monday-Saturday: 9:30-6:00

Armani (Headquarter Store), Dept. 56 (Showcase Dealer), Precious Moments (DSR), Memories of Yesterday (Heritage Dealer), Cairn Studios (Key Dealer), Disney Classics Collection, and Disneyanna Collectibles.

Other collectible lines include Wee Forest Folk, Snowbabies, Raikes Bears, Emmett Kelly Jr., Dave Grossman, Mark Klaus, Byers' Choice.

Call for artist signing schedule.

American Express, Visa and Mastercard accepted. Layaways welcome.

W D GIFTS

110 West Seventh St.
Okmulgee, OK 74447

PHONE: (800)886-2228
(918)756-2229

Monday-Saturday: 9:30-5:30

A large display of collector plates, figurines, dolls and villages. Maud Humphrey Bogart, Cherished Teddies, Lefton's Colonial Village, Jan Hagara, Flambro Gnomes, Emmett Kelly Jr., Ashton-Drake, Middleton, Dynasty, S. Mann, Hello Dolly, Norman Rockwell Gallery, Ardleigh Musicals, Hawthorne Architectural Register and Enesco Musicals.

Bradford Exchange Dealer. NALED member. Secondary Market Dealer. Layaway available. All major credit cards accepted.

MARGO'S GIFT SHOP

Utica Square
2058 Yorktown Alley
Tulsa, OK 74114

PHONE: (918)747-8780
(800)88M-ARGO
FAX: (918)747-5740

Open Daily: 10:00-6:00

Christopher Radko Christmas Ornaments, Arthur Court Gallery Program, Duncan Royale, Maud Humphrey, Vietri, WB Studios, Botanic Garden by Portmeirion, Dept. 56 Snow Village Houses, Old World Christmas, Annalee Dolls, and Crane's fine stationery.

All major credit cards accepted. Shipping available.

RATHBONE'S FLAIR

4734 S. Peoria
Tulsa, OK 74105

PHONE: (918)747-8491
(800)43-FLAIR

Open Daily: 9:30-5:30
Thursday: Until 8:00; Sunday: 1:00-5:00

The store for all seasons. Dept. 56 Showcase Dealer, Tom Clark Gnomes, DW, Lladro, PM, Swarovski, Sarah's Attic, All God's Children, Armani, EKJ, Lilliput Lane, MOY, Hummel, Goebel Miniatures, North American Bear, Gund, Madame Alexander, Gorham dolls, Thomas Kinkade, Bradford dealer, Enesco Treasury Ornaments, limited edition nutcrackers and smokers, Lowell Davis, Disney Classics Collection, Maud Humphrey, ANRI, and Sports Impressions. Major credit cards accepted. Secondary Market Service. Free shipping for orders over $50. Club memberships paid. Call for information on frequent buyers club. NALED and GCC member.

OREGON

LITA SALE IMPORT

15565 Eilers Rd.
Aurora, OR 97002

PHONE: (503)678-1622

Showroom Open By Appointment Only

Phone anytime during waking hours for an appointment. Come and visit the world of dolls and nutcrackers. All of the Annette Himstedt dolls beginning with the 1987-88 Barefoot Children through the current series of each year. All of Annette's creations are displayed for your enjoyment.

Also visit one of the largest displays of Nutcrackers available. Lita specializes in limited edition Steinbach and Ulbricht Nutcrackers. Along with the limited edition pieces, past and current Nutrcrackers always are available. Personalized service for the hard to find pieces.

Ships internationally. Layaways available. Secondary Market Service.

SUE'S CHRISTMAS HOUSE and "NOT JUST FOR CHRISTMAS"

1037 N.W. Brooks St.
Bend, OR 97701

PHONE: (503)389-4430

Monday-Friday: 10:00-5:30
Saturday: 10:00-5:00
Sundays: 12:30-4:30

Annalee Mobilitee, Bing & Grondahl/ Royal Copenhagen, Byers' Choice, Christopher Radko, Dept. 56 Inc., Margaret Furlong Designs, Midwest Importers, Possible Dreams Santas, Roman, and Schmid. Eastern Oregon's Showcase Dealer for Dept. 56 Inc. Seasonal and general gift items.

All major credit cards accepted. Giftwrap and shipping service available. Collectors inventory list. Dept 56 Annual Open House.

CHETCO REXALL DRUG, INC.

890 Chetco Ave. (P.O. Box 547)
Brookings, OR 97415

PHONE: (503)469-2616

Monday-Friday: 8:30-5:30
Saturday: 9:00-6:00; Sunday: 12:00-4:00

Dept. 56 Villages, Sarah's Attic, Little Cheesers, Michael's Limited, Rick Cain Sculptures, Michael Garman Sculptures, Mark Hopkins Bronze Sculptures, Leo R. Smith III Limited Editions, Lincoln County Garden Club Limited Edition Collectible figurines, and Melody In Motion by WACO.

Free gift wrapping. Visa and Mastercard accepted. Layaways welcome.

'TIS THE SEASON

P.O. Box 613
Cannon Beach, OR 97110

PHONE: (503)436-1400
(800)227-2587

Open Daily: 10:00-5:00 In Winter
Open Until 6:00 In Summer

Dept. 56 Villages and Snowbabies, Old World Christmas, Christopher Radko, Leo Smith Carvings, Margaret Furlong Angels, Vaillancourt, United Design, Possible Dreams, June McKenna, Denise Calla, ANRI, Annalee Mobilitee Dolls, Cairn Studio, Midwest Importers, Tom Browning's Santa's Timeoff, Block China's Poisettia and Whimsy, Roman, and Walt Disney Classics Collection.

Visa and Mastercard accepted. Daily UPS service.

OREGON

A JOY FOREVER

16144 S.E. 82nd Dr.
Clackamas, OR 97015

PHONE: (503)657-4408

Monday-Saturday: 10:00-6:00

Retail Doll and Teddy Bear store! Featuring Ashton-Drake, Hamilton, Georgetown, Good-Kruger, Madame Alexander, Barbie and many more!

Many original artist dolls such as Himstedt Porcelains, Roche, Linda Mason, Julia Rueger and Jeckle-Jansen. Also featuring Steiff Bears, North American Bears (Muffy) and Merry Thought Bears!

Automatic monthy payment plan available- enjoy your layaway at home. All major credit cards accepted.

Secondary Market for Ashton-Drake Dolls! Redemption Center for many collectibles. Frequent artist visits!

BJ'S GIFTS & CARDS

Tanasbourne Village
2227 N.W. 185th
Hillsboro, OR 97124

PHONE: (503)645-1249
FAX: (503)690-0438

Monday-Friday: 10:00-8:00
Saturday: 10:00-6:00; Sunday: 12:00-5:00

Your one stop collectible shop. David Winter Cottages, Dept. 56-Dickens Village and New England Cottages, PenniBears, Sarah's Attic, Shoemaker's Dream, Cat's Meow Village, Rinconada, Tom Clark Gnomes, Margaret Furlong Ornaments, Lilliput Lane, Raikes Bears, North American and Muffy Bears, United Design, Santas, WACO Musicals, and Cast Art.

Redemption Center for collector clubs. Major credit cards and layaways welcome. Shipping available.

LOOK & LISTEN

160 E. Calif. St. P.O. Box 59
Jacksonville, OR 97530

PHONE: (503)899-7673

Open 7 Days A Week: 10:00-5:00

Tom Clark Gnomes, Annalee Dolls, Walt Disney Classics Collection, M.I. Hummel, Jan Hagara, Laura's Attic, Lizzie High, Sarah's Attic, All God's Children, David Winter Cottages, Lilliput Lane, Little Cheesers, Enesco Musicals, Fontanini, Duncan Royale, United Design, Midwest, Kurt S. Adler, Possible Dreams, Margaret Furlong ornaments, Christopher Radko ornaments, Hamilton, Cherished Teddies, Muffy Bears, Raikes, Lucy & Me, Emmett Kelly Jr., Ron Lee, WACO, "Red" Skelton paintings, plates and figurines.

Free shipping. All major credit cards accepted. Layaway plan. No sales tax!!!

THE ALABASTER EGG

529 Medford Center
Medford, OR 97504

PHONE: (503)779-9641

Monday-Friday: 10:00-6:00
Saturday: 10:00-5:00; Sunday: 12:00-4:00

Dolls by Ashton-Drake, Hamilton Collection, Susan Wakeen, Zook, Gunzel and more. Premier Dealer for Thomas Kinkade, Marty Bell, Authorized Bradford Dealer, Dept. 56, LEGENDS, Lilliput Lane, Lowell Davis, Cherished Teddies, Melodies In Motion Musicals, Michael Garman Sculptures, Enesco Musicals, United Design PenniBears, and Dreamsicles.

All major credit cards accepted. Layaway program available.

OREGON

VAN DUYN'S-DEVENDER HOUSE GIFTS

1600 N. Riverside #2145
Medford, OR 97501

PHONE: (503)772-5668

Monday-Friday: 10:00-9:00
Saturday: 10:00-7:00; Sunday: 11:00-6:00

Master Showcase Dealer for Chilmark, David Winter, Hummel, Iris Arc, Ron Lee preferred Dealer, Mark Hopkins Bronzes, Krystonia, Rick Cain, Windstone Editions, Marty, Beasties of The Kingdom, Melody In Motion. Also featuring Indian made jewelry, Indian Art, extensive line of Western art, Navajo, Sioux, and Hopi pottery, Sandicast, Lomonosov Porcelain from Russia, Maruri, Italian inlay music boxes, Onyx from Pakistan, lead crystal, brass silver. Complete line of VanDuyn's Chocolates.

Most major credit cards accepted. Layaway and UPS shipping available. Redemption Center.

ACCENT ON COLLECTIBLES GIFTS & GALLERY

9738 S.E. Washington Suite S
Portland, OR 97216

**PHONE: (503)253-0841
(503)252-3712**

Monday-Friday: 10-6; Saturday: 10-5

Plates, lithos, and figurines. Hummel, Goebel Miniatures, ANRI, Armani, DW, Lilliput Lane, PM, MOY, Ron Lee, Chilmark Master Showcase Dealer, LEGENDS, Sarah's Attic, All God's Children, Jan Hagara, Lladro, Swarovski, Mark Hopkins, Lefton, Bradford Dealer, Hamilton plates, Perillo, Bergsma, ANNA-PERENNA, Marty Bell, Kinkade, Hadley House, Somerset, Penni Anne Cross, Little Cheesers, Disney Classics. Dolls: Ashton-Drake, Hollywood, Jerri, Victoria Ashlea and Hamilton.

Redemption Center. NALED member. Secondary Market service in plates, lithos, and figurines. Mastercard, Visa and Discover. Layaway and shipping.

CHRISTMAS AT THE ZOO

118 N.W. 23rd Ave.
Portland, OR 97210

PHONE: (503)223-4048

Monday-Saturday: 10:00-6:00
Sunday: 12:00-4:00

A Premier Plush Animal and Year-Round Christmas store. Featuring: Steiff, North American Bear, Cooperstown Bears, Christopher Radko, Old World Christmas, Italian Glass ornaments, Annalee, Roman Inc., Kurt S. Adler, Midwest Importers, and Artist Bears.

All major credit cards accepted. Layaway available. Ship gladly.

CROWN SHOWCASE

902 Lloyd Center
Portland, OR 97232

PHONE: (503)280-0669

Monday-Saturday: 10:00-9:00
Sunday: 11:00-6:00

All major collectibles, including Hummel, Lladro, Dept. 56, Goebel, Caithness, Flambro, Swarovski, Iris Arc, Armani, All God's Children, Sarah's Attic, Miss Martha, Royal Copenhagen, Royal Doulton, David Winter, Lilliput Lane, Bing & Grondahl, Cairn, Precious Moments, Thomas Kinkade, Marty Bell, Maud Humphrey Bogart, Ron Lee, Memories of Yesterday, Disney Classics, Krystonia, Cherished Teddies, etc.

Open 7 days a week. All major credit cards accepted. Daily UPS shipping.

OREGON

THE PRESENT PEDDLER
Washington Square
9532 S.W. Washington Sq. Rd.
Portland, OR 97223
PHONE: (503)639-2325
(800)288-2325

Monday-Saturday: 10:00-9:00
Sunday: 10:00-6:00

Fine gifts and collectibles.

Annalee, Showcase Dealer for Dept. 56 (All Villages, accessories, Snowbabies and All Thru the House), Hummel, Goebel Miniatures, Swarovski, Lladro, Bergsma prints, David Winter Cottages, Margaret Furlong Angels, Old World Christmas Ornaments, Byers' Choice Dolls, Lilliput Lane, All God's Children, Thomas Kinkade, Sarah's Attic, Walt Disney Classics Collection, Boehm and much more.

Services include gift wrapping, UPS shipping, special orders, and layaway. Club Redemption Center. NALED and GCC member.

TICKLED PINK GIFT SHOP
4905 S.W. Scholls Ferry Rd.
Portland, OR 97225
PHONE:(503)297-4102
(800)233-4905 (ORDERS)

Monday-Saturday: 10:30-5:30

Olszewski Miniatures, Walt Disney Classics Collection, Hummels, Lladro, Lowell Davis, ANRI, B&G/RC, Royal Doulton, Belleek, Boehm, DeGrazia, Margaret Furlong, Fitz and Floyd, PenniBears, Swarovski, Lalique, Waterford, Miller Rogaska, Old World, Steinbach, Ulbricht and Erzgebirge Nutcrackers and Smokers, Christmas Ornaments: Old World Christmas, Christopher Radko, Elke Hutchins, Annette Himstedt, Madame Alexander, special Barbies, Original Cabbage Patch Kids, Steiff, North American Bears, Raikes, Russian Eggs, Boxes, and Dolls.

Collector Club redemptions. Free shipping on orders over $100. No Sales Tax. VISA and Mastercard. Layaway available.

DAS HAUS-AM-BERG
1132 Edgewater St. N.W.
Salem, OR 97304
PHONE: (503)363-0669

Monday-Friday: 10:00-5:30
Saturday: 10:00-5:00

"Serving Collectors since 1965!" Bradford, All God's Children, Tom Clark, Wee Forest Folk, Lowell Davis, Hummel, Lladro, David Winter, Lilliput Lane, Duncan Royale, Precious Moments, Cherished Teddies, Swarovski, Dept. 56 (Heritage and Snow Villages, Snowbabies, All Through The House, Merry Makers), Enesco (Treasury Ornaments, Lucy & Me Bears), Byers' Choice, Nutcrackers (Steinbach, Ulbricht, Milford, Erzgebirge), Christopher Radko, Krystonia, Lincoln County Garden Club, DeGrazia, Perillo, Sandra Kuck, Shoemaker's Dream (John Hine), Beatrix Potter, Royal Doulton, Tobin Fraley Carousels, Rockwell and Ron Lee.

THE TUDOR ROSE TEAROOM
480 Liberty
Salem, OR 97301
PHONE: (503)588-2345
(503)363-1452 (EVES.)

Monday-Friday: 9-5:30; Saturday: 12-5
Sundays In December: 12-5

Located two blocks from the heart of Salem. A Premier Dealer for Thomas Kinkade, Lladro, M.I. Hummel figurines and plates, Victoria Ashlea, Duncan Royale, David Winter, Ian Fraser, Lilliput Lane, Precious Moments, Cherished Teddies, WACO Melody In Motion, and Britains Metal Soldiers, Royal Doulton, Goebel Miniatures. A fine selection of English candies and groceries. Fine china and Crab Tree & Evelyn toiletries. Buy and sell on the secondary market in cottages, figurines and lithographs. Appraisal service available. Foremost authority on David Winter and Lilliput Lane Cottages and Thomas Kinkade lithographs.

OREGON

THAYERS RARE DISCOVERY

21 N. Columbia-P.O. Box 182
Seaside, OR 97138

PHONE: (503)738-8122

Open 7 Days A Week: 10:00-5:00

Bradford Exchange plates, David Winter, Lilliput Lane, All God's Children, Swarovski Crystal, Elke's Original Dolls, Tom Clark Gnomes, Ron Lee Clowns, Armani, Maruri Porcelains, Lee Middleton Dolls, Krystonia, Duncan Royale, Pocket Dragons, Ashton-Drake Dolls, Hummels, Dynasty Dolls, Artaffects, Hamilton Collection, Reco, United Design, Crystallite Crystal, Summerhill Crystal, Silver Deer, Susan Wakeen Dolls.

Secondary Market Service. Layaway plan. All major credit cards accepted.

SLEIGHBELLS CHRISTMAS SHOP

23855 S.W. 195th Place
Sherwood, OR 97140

PHONE: (503)625-6052

June 1-December Open Daily: 10:00-5:00

Christopher Radko, Dept. 56, Old World Christmas, House of Hatten Inc., Possible Dreams, Kurt S. Adler, Byers' Choice, Silvestri, Margaret Furlong Carriage House Studios Inc., and unusual handcrafted ornaments and gifts by local artists.

Visa and Mastercard accepted. Layaway plan. A 50-acre Christmas tree farm including large Christmas shop in barn.

SMALL WORLD COLLECTIBLES

Sunriver Village Bldg 13B
P.O. Box 4819
Sunriver, OR 97707

**PHONE: (503)593-3263
(800)325-3225**

Monday-Saturday: 9:00-8:00
Sunday: 10:00-6:00

Don't miss this slice of heaven in a collector's "Small World". DW, Lilliput, Harbour Lights, John Hopkins, Tom Clark, Tim Wolfe, Legends of the Little People, Hudson Pewter, Silver Deer Crystal Zoo, Dreamsicles, Krystonia, Moda D' Oggi, Marty Sculptures, Mill Creek's Randy Reading, Goebel Miniatures, Armani, Lladro, Hummel, PM, CT, Calico Kittens, MOY, Enesco Musicals, B.P. Gutmann, Jodi Jensen, Walt Disney Classics Collection and more! Visa and Mastercard. UPS shipping and layaway. Free gift wrap. Secondary Market Service. Quality service.

SPECIAL OCCASIONS

19171 Willamette Dr.
West Linn, OR 97068

PHONE: (503)697-1765

Monday-Friday: 10:00-7:00
Saturday: 10:00-6:00; Sunday: 12:00-5:00

Christopher Radko, Dept. 56: Villages, Snowbabies, accessories, Merry Makers, All Through the House. Old World Christmas Ornaments, Byers' Choice Carolers, Margaret Furlong Designs, Lizzie High Dolls, Star Dealer for Daddy's Long Legs, Premier Dealer for Thomas Kinkade, Marty Bell, June McKenna, Shelia's, and Fitz & Floyd Holiday Hamlet.

Visa and Mastercard accepted. Layaway and shipping available. Redemption Center for collector clubs. Free gift wrapping.

PENNSYLVANIA

BOB LAMSONS BEER STEINS

509 N. 22nd St.
Allentown, PA 18104

PHONE: (215)435-8611

Monday-Friday: 9:00-9:00
Saturday: 10:00-4:00
Other Hours By Appointment

Anheuser-Busch, Michelob, Budweiser, Bud Light, etc. Coors, Strohs, Miller, Heineken, Hamm's, Pabst, Olympia Steins and related collectibles with other beer affiliations.

All major credit cards accepted. Layaway program. Secondary Market and referrals service.

FORGET ME NOT CARD & GIFT

1860 Catasauqua Rd.
Allentown, PA 18103

PHONE: (215)266-1532
FAX: (215)797-6478

Monday-Friday: 10:00-9:00
Saturday: 10:00-6:00; Sunday: 12:00-5:00

Precious Moments, Dept. 56 Heritage Village, Snowbabies, Cherished Teddies, Bradford Dealer, Hollywood Dealer, Hamilton plates, Ashton-Drake dolls, Hibel, Middleton dolls, Sarah's Attic, Maud Humphrey, Sports Impressions, Miss Martha, Laura's Attic, Jan Hagara, Raikes Bears, Cast Art Dreamsicles, Fenton Glass, June McKenna, Enesco Musicals.

All major credit cards accepted. Layaway. Forget Me Not Clubs. Secondary Market Service. Redemption Center. Mail orders. Shipping available.

SOMETHING SPECIAL

Greenwood Center
1550 E. Pleasant Valley Blvd.
Altoona, PA 16602

PHONE: (814)949-9313

Open 7 Days A Week: 10:00-6:00

Lilliput Lane, Old World Glass. Collectible dolls: GADCO, Good-Kruger, Turner, Precious Heirloom, European Artist Dolls, and many other collectible doll lines. Steinbach Nutcrackers, Midwest, Fontanini, Cherished Teddies, Calico Kittens, Designs Americana, Christopher Radko, Willitts, Dreamsicles, Boyds Bears, Dept. 56: Heritage Village, Snowbabies.

Mastercard and Visa. Shipping. Redemption Center for Christopher Radko, Old World and Lilliput Lane.

THE RED CARDINAL

1121 Horsham Rd.
Horsham Twp, Ambler, PA 19002

PHONE: (215)628-2524
(800)568-2524

Open 7 Days 10:00-5:00
Friday Until 8:00; Sunday: 12:00-5:00

In business for 14 years. Located in a 250-year-old-farmhouse. All Dept. 56, Byers' Choice, Tom Clark, Lilliput Lane, David Winter, June McKenna, Cat's Meow, Caithness, Swarovski, Precious Moments, MOY, Enesco ornaments and musicals, Hummel, Walt Disney Classics, Sarah's Attic, All God's Children, Old World Glass Ornaments, Lizzie High, Lowell Davis, Maruri, Miss Martha's, Cherished Teddies, C. Radko, Michael's Ltd., Possible Dreams.

Daily UPS shipping. All major credit cards accepted. NALED member. Layaways. Club Redemption for all lines carried. The Red Cardinal, "Where customers become friends."

PENNSYLVANIA

AMERICAN CANDLE

Route 611
Bartonsville, PA 18321
**PHONE: (717)629-3388
(717)620-0350**

Monday-Thursday: 9-8;
Friday & Saturday: 9-9; Sunday: 9:30-5:30

All God's Children, Anheuser-Busch, Annalee Dolls, Armani, Byers' Choice, Cat's Meow, Cherished Teddies, Chilmark, Tom Clark Gnomes, Michael Davis, Dept. 56 Heritage Village, Dynasty Dolls, Enesco Musical Showcase, Fenton Glass, Jan Hagara, Hudson Pewter, Hummel, Maud Humphrey Bogart, Iris Arc Crystal, Emmett Kelly Jr. & Sr., Krystonia, LEGENDS, Lilliput Lane, Lladro, Lucy & Me Bears, MOY, Maruri, Melody In Motion, Mill Creek Studios, Miss Martha's, Precious Moments, Raikes Bears, Rawcliffe Pewter, Salvino, Sports Impressions, Sarah's Attic, Shelia's, Snowbabies, Swarovski, Summerhill Crystal, David Winter, Walt Disney Classics, Dreamsicles.

SOMEONE SPECIAL

Street Road Plaza
2635 Street Rd.
Bensalem, PA 19020
**PHONE: (800)237-7656
FAX: (215)245-4864**

Monday-Saturday: 10-5; Friday: 10-8

Serving collectors for 17 years. Lladro, Lenox, Maruri, Swarovski, M.I. Hummel, David Winter, Lilliput Lane, Emmett Kelly Jr., Precious Moments, WACO, Chilmark and Hudson Pewter, Sports Impressions, Hibel, Goebel Miniatures, Duncan Royale, Sandra Kuck, Madame Alexander, Norman Rockwell, Lee Middleton dolls, Emmett Kelly, Seiko and Bulova Clocks, Krystonia, Morini, Daddy's Long Legs, and Shoemaker's Dream.

Member of NALED. Redemption Center. Visa, Mastercard and American Express.

Second Location: Berlin Circle Plaza, Rt. 73 & Walker Ave., West Berlin NJ 08091. (609)768-7171.

WORLDWIDE COLLECTIBLES & GIFTS

P.O. Box 158
2 Lakeside Ave.
Berwyn, PA 19312-0158
**PHONE: (215)644-2442
FAX: (215)889-9549**

Monday-Saturday: 10:00-5:00
Operator on Duty 24 Hours for Phone Orders

Worldwide Collectibles is a mail-order company established in 1975. Dealing in current and secondary market pieces. Worldwide has particular expertise in full lines of Swarovski, ANRI, Waterford, Royal Copenhagen, B&G, Lilliput Lane, Lenox, Maruri, Hummel, Steiff, David Winter, Duncan Royale, Lladro, Precious Moments collector plates, bells, club pieces and many others.

The company maintains large inventories on all lines carried, with a free mail-order catalog available.

FRAME IT OR LEAVE IT & FIOLI GALLERY

4705 Library Rd.
Bethel Park, PA 15102
PHONE: (412)854-4590

Mon., Wed., Fri., Sat.: 10:00-6:00
Tuesday and Thursday: 10:00-8:00

Full-service frameshop and gallery, serving print collectors since 1982. Specializing but not limited to wildlife art. Complete offerings from Mill Pond, Hadley House, Wild Wings and Somerset House. Many prints on display by Bateman, Brenders, Seerey-Lester, Harvey, and many others. Extensive offering of duck stamp prints, both framed and unframed.

Secondary Market Service. Layaway and shipping available. All major credit cards accepted.

PENNSYLVANIA

THE CHRISTMAS TROLLEY

80 Carlisle Plaza Mall
Carlisle, PA 17013
PHONE: (717)249-7931
FAX: (717)249-7931
(CALL FIRST)

Monday-Saturday: 10:00-9:00
Sunday: 12:00-5:00

Dept. 56-all lighted Villages including Dickens, New England, North Pole, Snow, Alpine, Christmas in the City, Snowbabies and miniature pewter Snowbabies, Merry Makers, Possible Dreams Clothtique Santas, Shelia's hand painted collectibles, John Hine Shoehouses by Jon Herbert.

All major credit cards accepted. Layaway and shipping available. Secondary Market newsletter available in April and October. Redemption Center for Possible Dreams and Shelia's. Member of the Santa Claus Networks and Shelia's Collectors Society.

VILLAGE OF COLONIAL PEDDLERS

100 Shady Lane
Carlisle, PA 17013
PHONE: (717)243-9970

Monday-Saturday: 10:00-5:00
Sunday: 12:00-5:00

Serving the collectors for 22 years. Precious Moments (DSR), Dept. 56 Showcase Dealer, Snowbabies, David Winter, Emmett Kelly, Hummels, Annalee, June McKenna, Raikes Bears, Memories of Yesterday, Miss Martha's Originals, Maud Humphrey, Enesco Musicals, Laura's Attic, Iris Arc Crystal, Possible Dreams Santas, Sports Impressions, Cherished Teddies, and Dreamsicles.

All club redemptions. Major credit cards, layaway and UPS shipments. "Personal service in collectibles."

YE OLDE HOMESTEAD

100 Shady Lane
Carlisle, PA 17013
PHONE: (717)258-5488

Monday-Saturday: 10:00-5:00
Sunday: 12:00-5:00

Tom Clark Gnomes and Tim Wolfe, Sarah's Attic, All God's Children, Cat's Meow Village, Lilliput Lane, Rowe Pottery, Lizzie High Dolls, Imhoff's Homestead Collection and Michael's Limited (Brian Baker's Deja Vu Collection), Ben Cordsen pewter, Cinnamon Girl, Pigs from The Pig Lady.

Elegant glassware from the 1920s, 1930s and 1940s, some depression.

Collector club redemption center. Layaway. Shipping. Visa, Master Card, Discover.

LIMITED PLATES

341 Main St.
Collegeville, PA 19426
PHONE: (215)489-7799

Tuesday-Friday: 10:00-5:00
Saturday: 10:00-2:00

Bradford plates, Ashton-Drake dolls, Hummel figurines and plates, David Winter Cottages, Dept. 56 Lighted Houses, Dickens, Christmas in the City, Snow Village, Snowbabies, New England, and all accessories, Enesco music boxes, Bradford music boxes, Sports figurines and plates, Gartlan and Sport Impressions, Possible Dreams Santa's, Hamilton Collection, frames, and glass enclosed frames.

Mastercard, Visa and Discover accepted. 60 day layaway plan. Secondary Market plates and David Winter cottages.

PENNSYLVANIA

WATERLOO GARDENS, INC

136 Lancaster Ave.
Devon, PA 19333-1549

PHONE: (215)293-0800
FAX: (215)971-9523

Monday-Saturday: 8:00-5:30
Sunday: 9:00-5:00

Dept. 56 Showcase Dealer, Herend, Boehm, Lladro, Swarovski, Waterford, Halcyon Days, Snowbabies, Cat's Meow, Memories of Yesterday, Cherished Teddies, Merry Makers, Limoges Porcelain Boxes, Precious Moments, Sierra Brook Studios, Byers' Choice, Shelia's, Precious Moments and Oldham Porcelain Studio.

All major credit cards accepted. Special orders welcome.

"A COUNTRY GIFT SHOPPE"

Rt. 313 Dublin Pike
Dublin, PA 18917

PHONE: (215)249-9877
FAX: (215)249-3678

Monday-Saturday: 10:00-5:00

Lizzie High Dolls, Lizzie High Museum Collection on display. Little Souls, Barbara Bourgeau Richards Country Watercolors, Monroe Pottery, Brandywine Woodcrafts, Shadowdancers, The Salem Collection, Mary Hughes Prints, Rowe Pottery, Detweiler Woodquilts and Goodwin Weavers. Byers' Choice Carolers available at Christmas.

Visa and Mastercard accepted. Shipping is presently unavailable.

PICCADILLY CENTRE

1409 3rd. Ave.
Duncansville, PA 16635

PHONE: (814)695-8383
(800)235-3655
FAX: (814)695-5697

Monday-Saturday: 10:00-5:00
Sunday: 12:00-4:00; Seasonal Hours

Hundreds of collectible artist dolls, Armani, Bradford plates, Ashton-Drake Dolls, Rockwell figurines, Hamilton plates and dolls, Laura's Attic, MOY, Tom Clark Gnomes, Enesco Musicals, Precious Moments, Georgetown Collection dolls, Cherished Teddies, Calico Kittens, Little Cheesers, David Winter Cottages, Jon Herbert's Shoehouses, Beatrix Potter, Dept. 56 Snowbabies and All Through the House, German Nutcrackers and Smokers, United Design Santas. Redemption Center.

All major credit cards. Free layaway and shipping. NALED member. Bradford Dealer.

COUNTRY HAUS

558 E. High St.
Elizabethtown, PA 17022

PHONE: (717)367-5639

(Sept-May)Monday-Saturday: 10:00-5:00
Thursday and Friday: 10:00-8:00
(June-Aug) Tues. and Wed.: 10:00-5:00
Thurs. and Fri.: 10:00-8:00
Saturday: 10:00-3:00

June McKenna, Lizzie High, Byers' Choice, Dept. 56 (Dickens, North Pole, New England), Cat's Meow, Vaillancourt, Lilliput Lane, a large selection of Yankee candles Baldwin Brass, and Rowe Pottery. Fine pewter, tinware, potpourri, and Claire Burke Fragrances.

Layaway. Mastercard and Visa accepted. UPS shipping within the continental USA. Free parking.

PENNSYLVANIA

COLLECTORS COTTAGE

6044 Peach St.
Erie, PA 16509

PHONE: (814)864-7473

Monday-Saturday: 10:00-6:00
Friday: 10:00-9:00; Sunday: 1:00-5:00

Collector plates, dolls and figurines. Bradford Dealer. Hamilton Collection dolls and plates, Perillo, Donald Zolan, Sandra Kuck, Redlin, Ashton-Drake, Wimbledon Collection, Susan Wakeen, Middleton, Ginny, Georgetown, Good-Kruger, Jeckle-Jansen, Ultimate Collection, Artist Collectibles, Kingstate, Lilliput Lane, Kitty Cucumber, Cherished Teddies, Calico Kittens, Maud Humphrey, Bessie Gutmann, Snowbabies, Treasury Ornaments, Homestead Life, Castagna figurines, Sports Impressions plates and figurines, Muffy and V.I.B. Bears and much more.

All major credit cards accepted. Special orders and layaways welcome. Shipping available. Secondary Market Service.

THE EMPORIUM

3358 West 26th St.
Erie, PA 16506

PHONE: (814)833-2895

Monday-Saturday: 10:00-5:00

Dept. 56: Heritage Villlage, Snow Village, Winter Silhouettes, All Thru The House, Merry Makers and Snowbabies. Armani, Lilliput Lane, Sarah's Attic, Lowell Davis, Krystonia, Beatrix Potter, Jan Hagara, Lynn Haney Santas, Leo Smith Santas, PJ's Carousel Horses, Miss Martha's, Memories of Yesterday, June McKenna Figurines, Sandra Kuck plates and dolls, Musicals, including Enesco, Dept. 56, Schmid, Beatrix Potter, Willitts, David Winter Cottages, Laura's Attic, Precious Moments, Artina Gnomes, Edna Hibel plates, Jody Bergsma prints and plates, Ron Lee Clowns, Cherished Teddies and Lincoln County Garden Club.

NALED member. Secondary Market Service.

HIDDEN TREASURES

Village West 13 3330 W. 26th. St.
Erie, PA 16506

PHONE: (814)838-7747

Monday-Wednesday: 10-6
Thursday and Friday :10-8; Saturday: 10-5

Northwestern Pennsylvania's specialty shop for toys, dolls, and bears. Bears include Steiff, Hermann, Canterbury, Gund, Bearly There, Mama's Babies, Bears of LaJolla, Terry McVicker, McB Bears, Heidi Steiner, Beaver Valley, Sersha by Serietta, Carol Black, Barbara Golden Bessos, Bearcraft, North American Bear, Joan Woessner, Grandpapa Jingles, Brent. DOLLS: Little Souls, Dolls by Jerri, Susan Wakeen, Heidi Ott, Julie Good-Kruger, Middleton, Let's Play, Mad. Alexander, Hildegard Gunzel, Carin Lossnitzer, Sabina Esche, Gotz, Ginni by Vogue, Dolls by Pauline, Spanos, Jeckle-Jansen, Cherished Teddies, Snowbabies, Old World Christmas Nutcrackers and much more.

WATERLOO GARDENS, INC.

200 N. Whitford Rd.
Exton, PA 19341-2099

PHONE: (215)293-0800
FAX: (215)363-6416

Monday-Saturday: 8:00-5:30
Sunday: 9:00-5:00

Dept. 56 Showcase Dealer, Herend, Boehm, Lladro, Swarovski, Waterford, Halcyon Days, Snowbabies, Cat's Meow, Memories of Yesterday, Christopher Radko, Steinbach Nutcrackers, Cherished Teddies, Merry Makers, Limoges Porcelain Boxes, Sierra Brook Studios, Byers' Choice, Shelia's, Oldham Porcelain Studio.

All major credit cards accepted. Special orders welcome.

PENNSYLVANIA

LIMITED EDITIONS GIFT SHOP

19 N. 4th St.
Harrisburg, PA 17101

PHONE: (717)233-6188
FAX: (717)233-3889

Monday-Friday: 10:00-5:30
Saturday By Appointment

One of the largest selections of mulit-cultural artwork in Central PA.

Figurines: Duncan Royale, Maruri, Armani, Silver Deer, Constance Collection, Sarah's Attic, Possible Dreams, retired All God's Children, Marty Sculptures, Blackberry Bonnet, June McKenna, Wood World, Positive Image, Midwest Importers, Miss Martha, Artaffects.

Dolls: Sarah's Attic, Georgetown, Annette Himstedt, Renate Hoeck, Linda Mason, Goetz, Bob Mackie Barbie, B.J. Sterling, Seymour Mann, Daddy's Long Legs, Good-Kruger, Perillo, Uta Brauser, Turner, Stephens, Marlena Nielsen, Yolanda Bello.

MAPLENUT CREATIONS

5 Briarcrest Square
Hershey, PA 17033

PHONE: (717)533-5689

Monday-Friday: 10:00-8:00
Saturday: 10:00-6:00

Disney Classics, Maud Humphrey Bogart, M.I. Hummel, Maurice Wideman, P. Buckley Moss plates and figurines, Cherished Teddies, Sports Impressions, Salvino, Ashton-Drake Dolls, Ardleigh-Elliott Music Boxes, Norman Rockwell Gallery, Hawthorne Architectural Register, Thomas Kinkade plates and lithos, Sandra Kuck lithos and plates, Marty Bell Plates and Lithos, Brandywine Woodcrafts, Lynn Haney Collection, Bradford Exchange Authorized Dealer.

All major credit cards. A frequent shopper plan. Club Redemptions.

CRAYON SOUP

King of Prussia Plaza
King of Prussia, PA 19406

PHONE: (215)265-2446
(215)265-0458
FAX: (215)265-2979

Monday-Saturday: 10:00-9:30
Sunday: 11:00-5:00

All God's Children, Armani, Walt Disney Classics Collection, Enesco Musicals, Maud Humphrey, Iris Arc, Emmett Kelly Jr. and Sr., Lladro, LEGENDS, Lilliput Lane, Melody In Motion, Memories of Yesterday Heritage Dealer, Steinbach Nutcrackers, PenDelfin, Possible Dreams, Precious Moments (DSR), Sarah's Attic, Swarovski, Sports Impressions, and David Winter.

Approximately 40 open houses and artist appearances throughout the year. Free shipping. Major credit cards accepted. Layaway available. Redemption Center for most collectible lines.

THE COLLECTOR

Peddler's Village
P.O. Box 102
Lahaska, PA 18931

PHONE: (215)794-5813

Monday-Thursday: 10:00-5:30
Friday: 10:00-9:00
Saturday: 10:00-6:00; Sunday: 12:00-5:30
Extended Holiday Hours

Cat's Meow Village (a huge selection), Cherished Teddies, Dreamsicles, Jan Hagara, Reuge Music Boxes, Knot Knoggins, Adorables, Aus-Ben Studios, large variety of oil lamps.

Fantasy figures, Krystonia, Enchantica, Windstone Editions, Hopkins castles, Pocket Dragons, Bubble Fairies, Spoontiques pewter, Shube's pewter figurines and silver jewelry.

Most major credit cards accepted. Layaway and shipping available. Redemption Center. Staff knowledgeable about all lines.

PENNSYLVANIA

THE DEN

Peddlers Village P.O. Box 394
Lahaska, PA 18931

PHONE: (215)794-8493

Monday-Thursday: 10:00-5:30
Friday: 10:00-9:00; Saturday: 10:00-6:00
Sunday: 12:00-5:30

They specialize in the following collectibles...Anheuser-Busch, Bossons, Cairn Studios Key Account (Tom Clark Gnomes, Tim Wolfe Animals) Rick Cain, Cornell Importers, Flambro, Emmett Kelly Jr., David Winter, John Hine Studios, Lance Corp. (Master Showcase Dealer Chilmark Hudson), Maruri U.S.A., Polland Studios, Gregory Perillo plates, Possible Dreams, Sarah's Attic, Shelia's Collectible Houses, J.H. Boone, Margaret Furlong, Michael Garman, and Sports Impressions.

Visa, Mastercard and American Express accepted. Layaway plan available. NALED member. Secondary Market Service. Many Collector clubs.

DUTCH INDOOR VILLAGE

2191 Lincoln Hwy. East
Rt. 30 East
Lancaster, PA 17602

PHONE: (717)299-2348

Monday-Sunday: 10:00-9:00

Dept. 56 Showcase Dealer, Precious Moments, Lladro, Hummel, Cherished Teddies, Lucy & Me, Muffy Bear, Sports Impressions, Chilmark, LEGENDS, Annalee, Ashton-Drake dolls, Cairn Studio, Clothtique by Possible Dreams, Fabrique by Kurt Adler, Walt Disney Classics, Sarah's Attic, Daddy's Long Legs, Steinbach Nutcrackers and Smokers, David Winter Cottages and Jon Herbert Shoehouses, Swarovski, Fontanini. A large collection of pottery and country ware.

Major credit cards accepted. GCC Member. Free layaway. Free shipping.

THE FAMILY STYLE GIFT SHOP

2323 Lincoln Hwy. East
Lancaster, PA 17602

PHONE: (717)299-7235

April-Dec./ Open 7 Days A Week: 8:00-7:30
Call for Winter Hours

Your one stop shopping headquarters for the collector. Dept. 56 Showcase Dealer, Possible Dreams Santas-your Santa Claus Network Dealer, Cat's Meow, F.J. Designs, Authorized Dealer-Shelia's Collectible Houses, and a large selection of Lizzie High, Anheuser-Busch, Clay Art, Kurt S. Adler, VickiLane Designs. Personal service for the serious collector. A large selection of handmade Heirloom Quality Quilts, wallhangings, and handcrafts typical of the Lancaster County Community.

Secondary Market in Dept. 56. All major credit cards accepted. Layaway. Shipping daily. Dept. 56 Newletter published at least 4 times a year. Best Selection!

SAM'S STEINS & COLLECTIBLES

2207 Lincoln Hwy East (Rt. 30)
Lancaster, PA 17602

PHONE: (717)394-6404

June-Sept./ Mon.Tues.Wed. Sat.: 10-6
Thurs. and Fri.: 10-8; Sunday: 12-5
Oct.-May/ Tues. Wed. Sat: 10-6
Thurs and Fri: 10-8

Beer Steins from all U.S. Breweries, Anheuser-Busch, Yuengling, Coors, Strohs, Miller, Pabst, Hamm's, Heileman, and Germany. Over 600 different steins for sale. Also a large selection of Brewery Advertising. Neons, clocks, tap markers, trays, mirrors, signs, etc. Jim Beam decanters, Ertl collector banks, Coca-Cola trays and clocks. 12-page mailing list available for beer steins. Please send a 29¢ stamp.

Visa and Mastercard. Member of ABA, NABA, Stein Collectors International and Penn. Dutch Country Visitors Bureau.

PENNSYLVANIA

COMMUNITY CREATIONS, INC.

2 East 28th Div. Highway
Lititz, PA 17543

PHONE: (717)627-2667

Monday-Saturday: 10:00-4:00

Cat's Meow, Shelia's, Byers' Choice, and Lizzie High.

Call about special Cat's Meow "Hersey's" Limited Edition sets, with brown cats instead of black (for serious collectors only).

Area's largest Cat's Meow Dealer. #1 Nationally for three years. Visa and Mastercard accepted.

LE COLLECTION

127 Speers St.
Lower Speers, PA 15012

PHONE: (412)483-5330

Tuesday-Saturday: 12:00-9:00
Sunday: 12:00-5:00

Armani, Maud Humphrey, Dreamsicles, Cherished Teddies, Calico Kittens, Sports Impressions, Possible Dreams, Dept. 56 Snowbabies, Shelia's, Fitz & Floyd Holiday Hamlet, Edna Hibel plates and lithos. Plates: Sandra Kuck, G. Perillo, B. Burke, Hamilton. Willitts Star Trek globes and carousels. Dolls: J. Nahrgang, B. Ball, K. Kennedy, Seymour Mann. Precious Moments accessories and music boxes. Ornaments: Margaret Furlong, Hibel porcelain. Also featuring antique furniture, glassware, dolls.

Visa, Mastercard and Discover accepted. Shipping. Free gift wrapping. Search service available.

GLEN CENTER GIFTS

1969 Norristown Rd.
Maple Glen, PA 19002

PHONE: (215)643-2880
FAX: (215)643-7544

Monday-Friday: 8:30am-10:00pm
Saturday: 9:00-9:00; Sunday: 9:00-6:00

Open 365 days a year! Precious Moments, Hummel, Maud Humphrey, Expressions of Youth, Snowbabies, Dept. 56, Crystal Zoo (Silver Deer), Golden Memories by Lladro, Walt Disney Classics Collection, Cherished Teddies, Calico Kittens, Sports Impressions, Lenox, Mikasa, Anheuser-Busch steins and plates, Midwest Importers steins, Hallmark, brass, and home decor prints. Showcase of homemade candies. Specialized candy trays.

All major credit cards available. Free gift wrapping. Shipping available.

ALSTON'S HALLMARK STORES

Granite Run Mall
Middletown Rd. (Rt 352 & Rt. 1)
Media, PA 19063

PHONE: (215)565-5278

Monday-Saturday: 10:00-9:30
Sunday: 11:00-5:00

Serving the collector for 25 years, specializing in Hallmark Ornaments, Enesco, Dept. 56, The Hamilton Collection, John Hine Studios, Midwest Imports, Precious Art/ Panton, Roman, All God's Children, United Design Cat's Meow, Sarah's Attic, Precious Moments, Willitts Designs and other collectibles.

Mastercard and Visa accepted. Redemption Center. Member of GCC. Located 25 miles outside of Philadelphia.

18 other locations, such as: Glen Eagle Square 501 Wilm W. Chester Pike (Rt. 202) Glen Mills, PA 19342 (215)558-3222.

PENNSYLVANIA

RHOAD'S PHARMACY

4 South Union St.
Middletown, PA 17057
PHONE: (717)944-1341
FAX: (717)944-4131

Monday-Friday: 9:00-8:00
Saturday: 9:00-5:00

Walt Disney figurines, Hummel, Dept. 56 Dickens Village, Enesco Birthday Dolls, Possible Dreams, Byers' Choice Carolers, Calico Kittens, Cape Craftsman Carousels, Thickets and Sweet Briar. Also featuring Yankee Candles, Russell Stover Candies, Lang Graphics.

Most major credit cards accepted. Layaway and shipping available. Redemption Center for Hummel and Walt Disney.

JOHNSON'S JEWELRY & GIFTS

261 Market St., P.O. Box 187
Millersburg, PA 17061-0187
PHONE: (717)692-2571

Monday-Thursday: 9:00-5:30
Friday: 9:00-8:00; Saturday: 9:00-4:00

Lines include: Byers' Choice Ltd., Enesco Corp., Goebel, Gorham, The Hamilton Collection, M.I. Hummel Club, Lance Corp. Chilmark, Possible Dreams, Royal Copenhagen, Bing & Grondahl, Royal Doulton, Schmid, ANRI, Swarovski America Ltd., Carriage House Studio, Cazenova Abroad, Emmett Kelley Jr., Fenton Art Glass, Flambro Imports, Dave Grossman, Kirk Stieff, Lefton Village, Lunt Silver, Pickard, Sebastian Studios, Towle Silversmiths and Wallace Silversmiths.

No Secondary Market Service. All direct merchandise from manufacturers and distributors.

COLLECTOR'S MARKETPLACE

RR 1, Box 213B
Montrose, PA 18801
PHONE: (800)755-3123
PHONE/FAX: (717)278-4094

Phone/Mail Only. 24 Hours.

One of the top National Secondary Markets, Collector's Marketplace also specializes in primary product for Dept. 56, David Winter, Shoemaker's Dream, Lilliput Lane, All God's Children, Jan Hagara, Cherished Teddies, June McKenna, Nutcrackers: Erzgebirge, Steinbach, Ulbricht, Designs by Milford, Annalee, Maud Humphrey, and Michael's Ltd .

All major credit cards accepted. Collector's Marketplace ships anywhere in the U.S. Layaway available on primary product. Member of NALED, Gift Association of America, and Pennsylvania Retailers Association.

MOORE COLLECTIBLES

Treasure Hill Antiques
W. Main St.
Morgantown, PA 19543
PHONE: (215)286-7119

Open Daily: 9:30-5:30
Closed Tuesday

John Hine Studios, Lilliput Lane, Kaiser Porcelain, PenniBears, United Design, and Maruri.

All major credit cards accepted. Layaways available. Secondary Market Service.

PENNSYLVANIA

DESIGNED TREASURES

Parkridge Shopping Center
Rt. 363 and Ridge Pike
Norristown, PA 19403

PHONE: (215)631-9781

Monday-Saturday: 10:00-5:00
Friday: 10:00-9:00; Sunday: 10:00-4:00

Snowbabies and Villages from Dept. 56, Byers' Choice, Lizzie High, Possible Dreams, Shelia's, Cat's Meow, Steinbach, Rowe Pottery, Little Souls, Lilliput Lane, June McKenna, and Duncan Royale.

Visa and Mastercard accepted.

Layaways welcome.

JANET'S DOLLS AND COLLECTABLES

3040 Lincoln Hwy. East (Rt. 30)
Paradise, PA 17562

PHONE: (717)687-9908
(800)368-3655 (ORDERS)

Monday-Saturday: 10:00-6:00
Sunday: 10:00-5:00

Specializing in Dolls by Jerri, Pauline, Wakeen, Zook, Nahrgang, Middleton, Jeckle-Jansen, Good-Kruger, GADCO, Himstedt, Gorham, Phyllis Parkins, Barbies, Artists Collectibles, Daddy's Long Legs, Annalee, Lizzie High, plus more. Also a full-line of Cat's Meow, Dept. 56, Perillo, Lowell Davis, PenDelfin, Cherished Teddies, Jan Hagara, Maud Humphrey, Krystonia, Enesco Musicals, Raikes Bears, and plates.

Major credit cards and layaways welcome. Shipping available.

MAYFAIR JEWELERS

7255 Frankfort Ave.
Philadelphia, PA 19135

PHONE: (215)338-2682
FAX: (215)338-2692

Monday-Thursday: 10:30-5:30
Friday: 10:30-8:00; Saturday: 10:30-5:00

Swarovski, Lladro, Reed & Barton, Gorham, and Belleek. A full line of jewelry, 14k gold, diamonds and art carved wedding rings in stock.

All credit cards accepted. Free layaway. A second location in the Village at Newtown in Newton, PA 19940.

ROBERT ANTHONY JEWELERS

920 Walnut St.
Philadelphia, PA 19107

PHONE: (215)627-2900

Tues., Thurs., Fri.: 9:30-5:30;
Wed.: 9:30-7:00; Sat.: 9:30-4:00
Call for Summer Hours

Anna's Dolls, Bears and Collectibles! Madame Alexander, Bradford Dealer, Ashton-Drake Dolls, Barbie, Annalee, Daddy's Long Legs, Ginny, All God's Children, Sarah's Attic, Ron Lee, Maud Humphrey, Hummels, Memories of Yesterday, Armani, Steinbach Nutcrackers, Sports Impressions, Muffy Bear, Cherished Teddies, Raikes Bears, etc. Authorized Seiko Dealer. Fine Jewelry.

Robert Anthony Jewelers looks expensive, but they are not!

Major credit cards accepted. Layaway available.

PENNSYLVANIA

COLLECTOR'S CHOICE

Ross Park Mall
McKnight Rd.
Pittsburgh, PA 15237

**PHONE: (412)366-4477
(800)722-5231
FAX: (412)369-9614**

Monday-Saturday: 10:00-9:30
Sunday: 11-6 (Extended Holiday Hours)

Swarovski, David Winter, Lilliput Lane, Tom Clark Gnomes, EKJ, Armani, Hudson Pewter, Sports figurines and memorabilia, Sports Impressions and Salvino, Dept. 56 including Snowbabies, Sarah's Attic, M.I. Hummel. Plates: P. Buckley Moss, Hibel, Kuck. Precious Moments, Cherished Teddies, MOY, Maud Humphrey, Calico Kittens, Enesco Musicals, LEGENDS, Dreamsicles, Possible Dreams, Kurt S. Adler, Napoleon Capodimonte, Maruri.

Major credit cards accepted. Shipping. Layaway. Gift wrapping. Secondary Market Dealer for Precious Moments.

EUROPEAN TREASURES

4205 Murray Ave.
Pittsburgh, PA 15217

PHONE: (412)421-8660

Monday-Saturday: 10:00-5:00
Thursday: 10:00-7:00

Precious Moments, John Hine Studios, Armani, Lilliput Lane, Swarovski, Maud Humphrey, Hummels, LEGENDS, Memories of Yesterday, Miss Martha, Marty Bell, Calico Kittens, Cherished Teddies, Dept. 56, Dreamsicles, Edna Hibel, Goebel Miniatures, Kevin Francis, Kurt Adler, Little Cheesers, Cast Art, Maruri, Napoleon, PenDelfin, Possible Dreams, Precious Art/Panton, Salvino, Krystonia, and PenniBears.

All major credit cards accepted. NALED Member. Layaways available.

SAVILLE'S LIMITED EDITIONS

10 McIntyre Square
Pittsburgh, PA 15237

**PHONE: (412)366-5458
(800)331-1375
FAX: (412)369-9524**

Monday-Saturday: 10:00-9:00
Sunday: 12:00-5:00

Personal Service. Dept. 56 Showcase Dealer, Disney Classics, Swarovski, Goebel Miniatures, Chilmark, ANRI, Lladro, David Winter, Lilliput Lane, Shoemaker's Dream, All God's Children, Miss Martha's, Cherished Teddies, Memories of Yesterday, Maud Humphrey, Precious Moments, Wee Forest Folk, Lowell Davis, Emmett Kelly Jr., Krystonia, Hibel, Ashton-Drake, Bradford, Jan Hagara, P. Buckley Moss, Perillo, DeGrazia, M. Alexander Dolls, Byers' Choice and Susan Wakeen.

NALED member. Mastercard, Visa, American Express and Discover. Shipping and layaway available. Redemption Center.

THE STRAWBERRY PATCH

5109 Boyertown Pike
Reading, PA 19606

PHONE: (215)779-7035

Wednesday-Friday: 10:00-5:00
Saturday: 10:00-4:00; Sunday: 12:00-4:00

Byers' Choice Carolers, Lizzie High Dolls, June McKenna Santas, Little Souls, Attic Babies, Yankee Candles, Irvings Tin, Gail Laura Collectibles.

Visa and Mastercard accepted. Layaways available.

PENNSYLVANIA

SOUDERSBURG GIFTS & COLLECTIBLES
2914 Lincoln Hwy East P.O. Box 8
Ronks, PA 17572
PHONE: (717)687-8945

Tuesday-Saturday: 10:00-7:00

In business 15 years specializing in Hummel and Beatrix Potter plates, bells, figurines, dolls and toys. Other lines include music boxes, dolls and ornaments by Schmid. Francis peace prayer collectibles and Russberries toys. A large selection of Jake and Amos Condiments and kitchen kettles.

Layaway welcome. Will ship anywhere in the U.S. Visa and Mastercard accepted. Redemption Center for Hummel.

SPECIAL ATTRACTIONS
220 Desmond St.
Sayre, PA 18840-0430
PHONE: (717)888-9433
FAX: (717)888-7124

Mon.-Wed. and Sat.: 9:30-6:00
Thursday-Friday: 9:30-8:00

A store run by collectors for collectors. Bradford Dealer. Many retired and Artist signed pieces. Dolls, Precious Moments, LEGENDS preferred plus, Lladro, ANRI, Swarovski, Chilmark, music boxes, David Winter, Lilliput Lane, Krystonia, PenDelfin, Annalee, Possible Dreams Clothtique, Mark Klaus, June McKenna, Sports Impressions, plates, Rockwell, Hagara, Maud Humphrey, Rick Cain, Miss Martha, Cherished Teddies, Calico Kittens, Raikes, Emmett Kelly, J.H. Boone, Dept. 56, Pewter and more. NALED Member. MC/Visa/Disc/AE, and personal checks. Easy and extended layaways welcome. Free shipping. Free Buyers Bonus--send for details.

HEARTSTRINGS
P.O. Box 132 Route 40
Scenery Hill, PA 15360
PHONE: (412)945-5262

Monday-Saturday: 10:00-5:00
Sunday: 12:00-5:00

In this quaint, historic village Heartstrings offers many fine gifts and collectibles: Dept. 56 Villages-Dickens, North Pole, and Christmas in the City; Tom Clark Gnomes, Lilliput Lane Cottages including Ray Day's Americana series (current & retired), Jan Hagara figurines and dolls, Miss Martha Originals--All God's Children, Imhoff's Homestead Life (finely detailed terra cotta figurines), Dreamsicles, Hanford Heirloom Stamps, Duncan Royale santas, Fenton Art Glass, and much more. Mail order accepted--Ship daily.

Mastercard, Visa and Discover accepted.

CARGO WEST CHRISTMAS BARN
RR 1 Box 590
Rt. 611 (Exit 44 off I-80 W)
Scotrun, PA 18355
PHONE: (717)629-3122
(717)629-3233

Monday-Saturday: 10-5; Sunday: 12-5

The Pocono Mountains most exciting Christmas shop! Dept. 56 Showcase dealer, Annalee, Nutcrackers, United Designs, Possible Dreams, Anheuser-Busch, Dram Tree, Collectibles Resources, Fontanini, June McKenna, David Winter, Lilliput Lane, All God's Children, Jan Hagara, Maud Humphrey, Cherished Teddies, Little Cheesers, Trolls, PenniBears, Shoemaker's Dream, Raikes Bears, Steiff, Harbour Lights, and more.

All major credit cards accepted. Layaway and shipping. NALED member, Gift Association of America, PA Retailers Assoc. and Pocono Mtn. Vacation Bureau.

PENNSYLVANIA

MARIE'S GIFT SHOP

Rt. 390 Box 1055 (Exit 7 off I-84)
Tafton, PA 18464

PHONE: (717)226-3345

Monday-Saturday: 10:00-5:00
Sunday: 11:00-4:00

Current and hard-to-find back issues. Authorized Bradford, Ashton-Drake, Precious Moments, hundreds of Hummels, Hadley plates and prints by Terry Redlin and Ozz Franca, David Winter and Dept. 56 Cottages, Sports Impressions, Perillo, Reco, Schmid, Rockwell, P. Buckley Moss, Maud Humphrey, Jan Hagara, Hibel and most artists.

Club Redemptions, major credit cards accepted. Same day UPS shipping.

Locator service available.

McGILL'S STATIONERS INC.

3500 Lincoln Hwy.
Thorndale, PA 19372

PHONE: (215)383-6555
FAX: (215)383-7880

Monday-Friday: 9:00-5:30
Saturday: 9:00-5:00

Dept. 56: Dickens Village and Snowbabies. Enesco: Musicals, Cherished Teddies, Miss Martha's Originals, Precious Moments, Sports Impressions, and Ornaments. Hallmark: All lines, Gold Crown Dealer.

Tom Clark Gnomes.

All major credit cards accepted.

McGill's also has a store at the Oxford Mall, in Oxford, PA 19363. Phone (215)932-4630.

LAUCHNOR'S GIFTS & COLLECTABLES

7150 Hamilton Blvd.
Trexlertown, PA 18087

PHONE: (215)398-3008

Tues., Wed., Sat.: 10-5; Thurs.-Fri.: 10-8
Sunday: 12-5; Closed Monday

Your complete collectibles store. Featuring Hummels, Lladro, Swarovski, Walt Disney Classics Collection, David Winter, Lilliput Lane, Lowell Davis, ANRI, Goebel Miniatures, Precious Moments, Dept. 56, Cherished Teddies, Maruri, Memories of Yesterday, P. Buckley Moss, Snowbabies, Mark Klaus, Laura's Attic, LEGENDS, Gartlan, Salvino and Sports Impressions, Hagara, Humphrey, Miss Martha's, Perillo, Ashton-Drake and Hamilton dolls, model airplanes, DeGrazia, Dreamsicles, over 1,000 plates and accessories.

Bradford Dealer. NALED member. Center for most collector clubs. Credit card, shipping and layaway accepted.

THE WILD GOOSE

1141 Pittsburgh Rd.
Valencia, PA 16059

PHONE: (412)898-3340

Tuesday-Saturday: 10:00-5:00
Sunday: 12:00-4:00

Located 7 miles North of PA Turnpike, Exit 4. Specializing in collectibles, fine gifts and folk art since 1983. Christopher Radko, Dept. 56 Dickens, New England, Christmas in the City, North Pole, Snowbabies, Lizzie High Dolls, Byers' Choice, Tom Clark Gnomes, Duncan Royale, Margaret Furlong Design Ornaments, Bethany Lowe one-of-a- kind Santas.

Gift registry. All major credit cards are accepted. Gift wrapping, layaway and shipping are all available.

PENNSYLVANIA/RHODE ISLAND

GIFT DESIGN GALLERIES

254 Lehigh Valley Mall
Whitehall, PA 18052

PHONE: (215)266-1266
FAX: (215)266-9593

Monday-Saturday: 10:00-9:30
Sunday: 11:00-6:00

Specializing in limited edition collectibles. Premier Dealer for Chilmark, LEGENDS, Swarovski, M.I. Hummel, David Winter, Lilliput Lane, Dept. 56 houses, Lladro, Armani, Tom Clark, Emmett Kelly Jr., Precious Moments figurines, Hibel, Krystonia, Thomas Kinkade, Duncan Royale, June McKenna, Lowell Davis, ANRI figurines, PenDelfin, Miss Martha's Originals.

NALED member. Bradford Dealer. All major credit cards accepted. Layaway and UPS shipping available.

PAST & PRESENTS

At the Winfield House
Route 15 South (RR 2 Box 82)
Winfield, PA 17889

PHONE: (717)524-7666

Daily: 10:00-5:00. Extended Winter Hours

Visit one of central PA's finest shops in the historic Winfield House built in 1854. Featuring Christmas year-round plus fine collectibles including David Winter Cottages, Cat's Meow, Hudson Villagers, LEGENDS fine mixed media sculptures, Imhoff's Homestead Life, Dreamsicles, Glass Eye, Steinbach Nutcrackers and Smokers, Enesco Musicals and Treasury Ornaments, Possible Dream Santas, June McKenna, Gail Laura, Miss Martha, Lucy & Me, Duncan Royale, Treasured Memories, Fontanini Nativities, Snowbabies, and others. Visa, Mastercard and Discover. Layaway. Will ship anywhere. Located 10 1/2 miles south of Rt I-80, exit 30.

CHRISTMAS TREE HILL

In the Mansion
2840 Whiteford Rd.
York, PA 17402

PHONE: (717)755-9290
FAX: (717)741-9477

Monday-Saturday: 9:30-9:00
Sunday: 12:00-5:00

Dept. 56: Villages, Snowbabies, Merry Makers, All Through the House, Byers' Choice, Cat's Meow, June McKenna, Kurt S. Adler, Midwest Importers, Possible Dreams, Roman, M.I. Hummel, Enesco Muscials, Dreamsicles, DW, Margaret Furlong Designs, SI, Wood World, Old World Christmas, Silvestri, Santas by Donna, Steinbach Nutcrackers and Smokers, Rick Cain, Shelia's, Neil Rose, J.H. Boone, Lizzie High, United Design, AGC, Daddy's Long Legs. All major credit cards accepted. Layaway. Shipping. Free gift wrapping. Six locations: 4 in York, 1 in Lancaster and 1 in Reheboth Beach, DE.

NUANCE

300 County Rd.
Barrington, RI 02806

PHONE: (401)245-5219
(800)435-2902
OUTSIDE R.I.
FAX: (401)245-0737

Monday-Saturday: 10:00-5:30
Friday: 10:00-8:30; Sunday: 12:00-4:30

Dept. 56 (Villages and Snowbabies), Byers' Choice Carolers, Kurt S. Adler, Lance Corp., Lilliput Lane, Midwest Importers, Possible Dreams "SCN", Roman Inc., United Design, Carriage House Studio, Margaret Furlong Designs, Cast Art Dreamsicles, Cat's Meow, Ladie and Friends, Midwest Importers, Willitts Design, and WACO products.

Visa, Mastercard, American Express, Discover and Carte Blanche accepted. Layaway and mail order available.

RHODE ISLAND/SOUTH CAROLINA

SHEILA'S OF BLOCK ISLAND

234 Dodge St.
Block Island, RI 02807

PHONE: (401)466-2377
FAX: (401)466-5286

Summer: Open Daily: 10:00-9:00

Located 12 miles off the coast of Rhode Island and Long Island, NY.

Lines include Byers' Choice, Dept. 56, Snowbabies, Possible Dreams, Lizzie High, House of Hatten, Harbour Lights, Margaret Furlong Designs, Roman Inc.

Most major credit cards accepted. Shipping throughout the U.S.

THE GIFT BARN, INC.

Corner Rt. 1 & 2 P.O. Box 840
Charlestown, RI 02813

PHONE: (401)364-5050

May-Dec/ Open Daily 10:00-5:00
Evenings by Appointment
Jan.-April/ Tuesday-Friday: 11:00-5:00
Weekends: 10:00-5:00

Kurt S. Adler, Santa's World, Dept. 56, The Walt Disney Company, Gorham, Lance Corp., Lightpost Publishing, Possible Dreams, Roman, Schmid, John Hine Studios, Susan Wakeen Doll Co., and United Design.

Visa, Mastercard and Discover accepted. Layaways welcome. Secondary Market Service. UPS shipping.

FINDER'S KEEPERS

920 Bay St.
Beaufort, SC 29902

PHONE: (803)525-9200
FAX: (803)524-5425

Monday-Friday: 10:00-5:30
Saturday: 10:00-4:00; Sunday: 12:00-4:00

Lilliput Lane, Cat's Meow, The Pig Lady, The Great American Collectibles, Summerhill, Spoontiques, and United Design. There is more than what you see. Built in 1859 this unique building has room upon room of collectible and unique items. Browse through the Christmas shop and select unique, one-of-a-kind collectibles created by both local and regional artists.

Mastercard and Visa accepted. Layaways. Ship anywhere. Secondary Market Service.

NOT JUST COUNTRY

99 S. Market St.
Charleston, SC 29401

PHONE: (803)723-1010
(800)950-2533

Open 7 Days A Week: 10:00-5:00

Dept. 56, Byers' Choice, Enesco, Carriage House Studio, Cherished Teddies, Miss Martha's Originals, and Possible Dreams.

Mastercard and Visa accepted. Shipping available. Newsletter upon request. Redemption Center for Byers' Choice.

SOUTH CAROLINA

PURPLE PLUM TOO

231 King St.
Charleston, SC 29401

PHONE: (803)577-6952

Monday-Saturday: 10:00-6:00

All God's Children, Boehm, Byers' Choice, Chilmark, Christopher Radko, David Winter, Dept. 56, Duncan Royale, Emmett Kelly Jr., Fontanini, Goebel Miniatures, Harbour Lights, House of Hatten, Hummel, Le Mans, Lladro, Lowell Davis, Mark Hopkins, Norma DeCamp, North Pole Village, Possible Dreams, Precious Moments, Sorrento, Snowbabies, Stadden, Swarovski.

Second Location:

Purple Plum Gift, 45 South Market St. Phone (805)577-7337.

Visa and Mastercard accepted. Layaway and shipping. Redemption Center for all the above.

PEDDLERS PORCH INC.

Brickyard Shopping Center
9940 Two Notch Rd.
Columbia, SC 29223

PHONE: (803)736-2067

Monday-Saturday: 10:00-6:00

Dept. 56 Snow Village, Snowbabies, and other Dept. 56 gifts, Hummel, Lilliput Lane, Byers' Choice Carolers, Lowell Davis, Possible Dreams Santas, Sarah's Attic, Cat's Meow, David Winter, and Shelia's Collectibles.

Redemption Center for collector clubs, Hummel, Lilliput Lane, Cat's Meow, Sarah's Attic, Lowell Davis, etc.

Mastercard and Visa accepted.

ABRAMS

318 Laurel St.
Conway, SC 29526

PHONE: (803)248-9198

Monday-Saturday: 9:00-6:00

Serving satisfied customers for three generations. Outstanding selection of dolls and collectibles. Madame Alexander, Gotz, Limited Edition Barbie, Mann, Ashton-Drake, Annette Himstedt, Dolls by Jerri, Lee Middleton, Jan Nahrgang, Heidi Ott, Pauline, Robin Woods, Zook, Wakeen, Gorham, Lilliput Lane, Tom Clark Gnomes, Dept. 56 (All Thru the House, Merry Makers, General Store, Winter Silhouette), Bradford Dealer, Norman Rockwell, Raikes Bears, and more!

Special orders upon request.

Free shipping.

Layaway available.

TASTE MAKERS

547 Hwy. 174 P.O. Box 454
Edisto Island, SC 29438

PHONE: (803)869-2302

Easter-Mid Jan.: Mon.-Sat.: 10:00-5:00
Winter Hours: Thurs.,Fri.,Sat.: 10:00-5:00

Edisto Island, located 50 miles from Charleston, Summerville, and Beaufort SC, is the site of antibellum plantations. Local artists portray low country life, both past and present. Original signed paintings, prints, hand screened items and stationary. Ravenel Gaillard with international exhibitions. Ancora Gallery, Germany and French cultural center. Virginia Guerard, a local artist. Amelia Whaley, Charleston flower women. Clare Whitaker's waterscapes. Gullah dialect from Virginia Geraty, with tapes (video and audio), poems and books. Beth Smoak and Rose Ann Muckenfuss, Gullah books.

SOUTH CAROLINA

EMILY AUSTIN INC.

August Commons
2222 Augusta St.
Greenville, SC 29605

PHONE: (803)235-8621

Monday-Saturday: 10:00-5:00

Department 56: Snow Village, New England, Dickens, Alpine, North Pole, Accessories, All Thru the House, Merry Makers, Snowbabies. Old World Christmas and Christopher Radko ornaments. Midwest Importers, Possible Dreams, Byers' Choice, Hanford Heirloom Stamps.

Visa and Mastercard accepted. Layaway and Shipping available.

BAILEY'S LTD.

147 D. Lighthouse Rd.
Hilton Head, SC 29928

PHONE: (803)671-4715

Monday-Saturday: 10:00-6:00

Lalique, Boehm, Limoges Boxes, Halcyon Days, Royal Crown Derby, Staffordshire Enamels, Chilmark, Mark Hopkins (Showcase), L.S. Collection, William C. Wood, Deborah Henderson Studio, Amaranth Productions and Lynn West Collections, Lucy Maxym Russian Collections, Lynn Chase Ltd., Caithness Glass, Annieglass Studio, Correia Studios, Designs by Milford, and Christopher Radko.

Mastercard, Visa and American Express accepted. Pleasing discerning shoppers for over 50 years. Phone orders welcome.

CHRISTMAS ELEGANCE

4301 N. Kings Hwy. (Hwy 17)
P.O. Box 2482
Myrtle Beach, SC 29577

PHONE: (803)626-3100
(803)626-7873

May-Oct./Daily: 9:00am-10:00pm
Nov.-April/Daily: 9:00am-5:00pm

Dept. 56 Showcase Dealer, EKJ Collector Center. Authorized Dealer for Alexander Doll Co., Annalee, Annette Himstedt, ANRI, Byers' Choice, Rick Cain, Carriage House Studio, Classic Children, Barbies, Duncan Royale, Dynasty Dolls, Effanbee, Enesco, Goetz Dolls, D. Grossman, Harbour Lights, M.I. Hummel, Kurt S. Adler, Lilliput Lane, Lladro, Seymour Mann, McGuffy, Precious Art, PM, Reco, Roman, Ron Lee, Jan Hagara, Schmid, Steinbach, Turner Dolls, Ulbricht Nutcrackers, and United Design.

All major credit cards accepted. Shipping available.

TINDER BOX

10177 N. Kings Hwy.
Mrytle Beach, SC 29577

PHONE: (803)272-2336
(800)638-8899

Monday-Saturday: 10:00-9:00
Sunday: 1:00-6:00

Tom Clark Gnomes, Swarovski Crystal, David Winter, Lilliput Lane, Hummel, Bradford Exchange, Emmett Kelly, Jr., Sports Impressions, Rawcliffe Pewter, Willitts, Enesco, Cherished Teddies, Calico Kittens, Miss Martha, Sisters and Best Friends, Bossons, Michael Garman, Dragon Keep, Windstone, Krystonia.

All major credit cards. Club Redemption Center. 60-day layaway. Shipping. Free gift wrapping.

SOUTH CAROLINA/SOUTH DAKOTA

GIFTS FOR ALL

At Barefoot Landing
4866 Hwy. 17 South
N. Mrytle Beach, SC 29582

PHONE: (803)272-1313

January-Febuary Open Daily: 10:00-6:00
March-May: 10:00-9:00
June-September: 10:00-11:00
October-December: 10:00-9:00

Shelia's, Emmett Kelly Jr. and Sr., Fenton Art, Brandywine, Budweiser mugs, David Winter, Jon Herbert's Shoehouses, Cornell Importers Mugs.

Visa, Mastercard, American Express. Shipping available. Club Redemption for Shelia's.

CHRISTMAS AT PAWLEY'S THE HAMMOCK SHOPS

P.O. Box 950
Pawley's Island, SC 29585

**PHONE: (803)237-8814
(800)533-3826**

Monday-Saturday: 10:00-6:00
Sunday: 1:00-5:00

Dept. 56 Showcase Dealer, Precious Moments, Byers' Choice Carolers, Duncan Royale, Miss Martha's, Cherished Teddies, Calico Kittens, Tom Clark Gnomes, Lee Sievers, M.A. Hadley Pottery, Christopher Radko, Tim Wolfe, Annalee Dolls, Cat's Meow, Shelia's House, Carriage House Studio, June McKenna, Fontanini.

Most major credit cards accepted. Will ship anywhere. Layaway plan available. Redemption Center.

COUNTRY JUNCTION

2104 Platt Springs Rd.
West Columbia, SC 29169

PHONE: (803)791-0483

Monday-Friday: 10:00-6:00
Saturday: 10:00-5:00

Your collectible source in current and secondary market: Tom Clark Gnomes, All God's Children, Byers' Choice, Shelia's Collectible Houses, Cat's Meow, David Winter, Emmett Kelly Jr., Snowbabies, Maud Humphrey, Dickens Village, North Pole Village, Annalee Dolls, Cherished Teddies, Dreamsicles, Lowell Davis, Sisters and Best Friends.

Layaway and shipping. Visa, Mastercard and personal checks accepted.

GIFT GALLERY

313 Main Ave.
Brookings, SD 57006

PHONE: (605)692-9405

Monday-Friday: 8:00-6:00
Thursday: 8:00-9:00
Saturday: 8:00-5:30; Sunday: 12:00-4:00

Area's principal collector center for Precious Moments (DSR), Dept. 56 (Houses and Snowbabies), M.I. Hummel, Memories of Yesterday, Miss Martha, Emmett Kelly Jr., Byers' Choice, Maud Humphrey, Cherished Teddies, Jan Hagara, All God's Children, Laura's Attic, Cast Art Dreamsicles, Fontanini, Annalee, Calico Kittens, Golden Memories by Lladro, Possible Dreams and Raikes Bears.

NALED Member. Layaway offered. Visa, Mastercard, American Express and Discover accepted. UPS shipping. Contact Helen Jones.

SOUTH DAKOTA

COUNTRY 'N CHRISTMAS IN "THE ATTIC"

505 Third St. - P.O. Box 489
Garretson, SD 57030

PHONE: (605)594-2225
FAX: (605)594-6776

Monday-Saturday: 9:00-6:00
Sunday: 1:00-6:00

Extensive selection of Frances Hook figurines and plates. Dept. 56: Snowbabies, All Through the House, Merry Makers, Winter Silhouette. Possible Dreams Santas, Designs Americana, Precious Moments, Laura's Attic, Roman/Ceramica Excelsis, and Fontanini, Fenton Art Glass, Old World Christmas. Also featuring country items, dried silk and floral arrangements, lace, candles, and brass. A Victorian tea room and old fashioned ice cream soda fountain!

Visa and Mastercard accepted. Layaway and shipping available. Free gift wrapping.

DAKOTA SUE

521 North Main St.
Mitchell, SD 57301

PHONE: (605)996-9125

Summer Hours
Monday-Friday: 8:00-8:00
Saturday: 8:00-5:00; Sunday: 1:00-5:00
Winter Hours
Monday-Saturday: 9:30-5:30

Attic Babies, Cherished Teddies, Dept. 56 Heritage Village Collection and All Through The House, Lizzie High Dolls, and Jan Hagara Dolls.

The store is located half a block south of the Corn Palace, a tourist attraction.

Visa and Mastercard accepted.

THE GIFT TREE OF RAPID CITY

625 Mt. Rushmore Rd.
Rapid City, SD 57701

PHONE: (800)858-9801

Monday-Saturday: 9:00-5:30

Tom Clark Gnomes, Sarah's Attic, Lilliput Lane, Beasties of the Kingdom, WACO music boxes, Emmett Kelly, Enchantica, Krystonia, Sandicast, Windstone, Carousel Horses, All God's Children, Magic Mushroom Lamps and Land of Legends Pocket Dragons, and Trolls.

All major credit cards accepted. Secondary Market Service available. No shipping on orders over $50.00. Layaways welcome.

AKERS GIFTS & COLLECTIBLES

1825 S. Minnesota Ave.
Sioux Falls, SD 57105

PHONE: (605)339-1325
(800)865-1325
FAX: (605)339-2205

Monday-Saturday: 9:30-5:30

Swarovski, Lladro, David Winter, Hummel, Jan Hagara, Dept. 56 Showcase, Precious Moments (DSR), Emmett Kelly Jr. and Sr., Memories of Yesterday Heritage, Lilliput Lane, Belleek, Anri, Cherished Teddies, Maud Humphrey, Marty Bell, Tom Clark, Walt Disney Classics Collection, Bradford Exchange, Christopher Radko, Maruri USA, Reco International, Possible Dreams, United Design, Old World, Annalee, and June McKenna.

NALED Member. All major credit cards accepted. Shipping and layaway available. Club membership redemption.

SOUTH DAKOTA/TENNESSEE

COUNTRY 'N MORE TWO

The Empire Mall
4001 W. 41st St.
Sioux Falls, SD 57116

PHONE: (605)361-9797
FAX: (605)361-0302

Monday-Saturday: 10-9; Sunday: 12-6

All Dept. 56 Villages, Snowbabies and All Through the House, Communicor International, Memories of Yesterday, All God's Children, Miss Martha's Originals, Jan Hagara, David Winter, Maud Humphrey, Calico Kittens, Sisters & Best Friends, Willitts Carousels, P. Buckley Moss plates and sculptures, Richard Zolan plates and miniature pictures, Raikes, Amish Heritage Collection, Fontanini, Possible Dreams, Kurt Adler Santas, Enesco Treasury of Christmas Ornaments. Always adding new collectibles.

Visa, Mastercard and Discover accepted. Shipping and layaway available. Redemption Center. All calls welcome!

BLACK HILLS ARTCRAFT & LANGERS

603 Main St.
Spearfish, SD 57783

PHONE: (605)642-3752

Open 7 Days A Week
Summer: 8:00-8:00; Winter: 8:00-5:30

Kurt S. Adler, Armani, Dept. 56, Walt Disney, Duncan Royale, Precious Moments and other lines by Enesco (Laura's Attic, MOY, Cherished Teddies, etc.), Emmett Kelly Jr., Gartlan, Goebel, Goebel Miniatures, Gorham, Hamilton, John Hine, Hummel, Kaiser Porcelain, Lilliput Lane, Lladro, Maruri, Possible Dreams, Krystonia, Enchantica, Roman, Schmid (Lowell Davis, Yamada), Sarah's Attic, Swarovski, United Design, WACO, Cairn Studios, Cast Art Dreamsicles, Fenton Art Glass, J.H. Boone, Iris Arc and Jan Hagara.

All major credit cards accepted. Layaway and shipping available.

FLOWERS & GIFTS BY FRANK GRAY

6240 Stage Plaza East
Bartlett, TN 38134

PHONE: (901)382-0100
(800)982-7112

Monday-Saturday: 8:30-5:00

Swarovski Crystal, United Design: Angels Collection, The Legend of Santa Claus, Winterlight, Lion and Lamb, Natures Gallery, Waterwonders, Itty Bitty, Stonecritters, Victorian Angels, Jolly Old Elf. National Heritage Gallery Ltd. Edition "Gone With the Wind" prints.

A full-service florist. Most major credit cards accepted. Layaway and shipping available. Free gift wrapping.

LAURA'S LOFT

4198 Highway 96
(at I-40 West Exit 182)
Burns, TN 37029

PHONE: (615)446-2470

Monday-Saturday: 10:00-6:00
Sunday: 1:00-5:00

All God's Children, Miss Martha's Collection, Sarah's Attic, Lilliput Lane, Maud Humphrey Bogart, June McKenna Collectibles, Memories Of Yesterday, Lefton's Colonial Village, Cat's Meow Village, Johanna Zook Dolls, Cherished Teddies, Jan Hagara, Calico Kittens, Dave Grossman's Gone With the Wind, Neil Rose Indian Sculptures, Raikes Bears, Enesco Corporation, Hamilton Gifts, Willitts Designs Co., Coca-Cola Collection, and Precious Moments dolls.

Layaway available. Mastercard, Visa, and Discover accepted. Secondary Market. Major Club Redemption Center.

TENNESSEE

HI HAT COLLECTIBLES

East Town Antique Mall
6503 Slater Rd.
Chattanooga, TN 37412

PHONE: (615)899-5498
FAX: (615)855-1826

Open Daily 10:00-6:00

Disney Classics, Department 56, David Winter, Hummel, Cherished Teddies, Calico Kittens, Harbour Lights, Anheuser Steins, Belleek, Wedgwood, Beatrix Potter, Royal Doulton, Annalee Mobilitee Dolls, Miss Martha's, Laura's Attic, Maud Humphrey, Lilliput Lane, Sisters and Best Friends, Enesco Musicals and Ornaments, Jon Herbert Shoehouses, Raikes, Lowell Davis, Michael Garman, Jan Hagara, Armani, John Sandridge Prints/Figurines.

Secondary Market for figurines, cottages, steins, ornaments and plates. Club Redemption Center. Layaway and shipping available. Major credit cards accepted.

HILLTOP HOUSE

2675 Lake Rd.
Dyersburg, TN 38024

PHONE: (901)285-6810

Monday-Friday: 9:00-6:30
Saturday: 9:00-8:00

Dept. 56, Swarovski, David Winter, Hummel, Lilliput Lane, Emmett Kelly Jr., Melody In Motion, Cherished Teddies, Dreamsicles, Precious Moments, Bradford Dealer, and Sports Impressions.

Visa and Mastercard accepted. Shipping in USA. Layaway available. Free gift wrapping.

BARBARA'S GATLINBURG SHOPS

Three Locations on the Parkway
963, 716, 511 Parkway
Gatlinburg, TN 37738

PHONE: (800)433-1132
(615)436-3454
FAX: (615)436-3219

Open Daily: 9:00-9:00

Collectible lines, including secondary market: Chilmark, Hudson, Swarovski, LEGENDS, Tom Clark Gnomes, Sandicast, Cades Cove by National Heritage Gallery, Snow Village, Snowbabies, David Winter, Lilliput Lane, Wee Forest Folk, Lladro, Mark Hopkins Bronze, John Cody Prints, Cherished Teddies, Krystonia, Maud Humphrey, AGC, Byers' Choice, Dreamsicles, The Gatlinburg Puzzle, Gatlinburg Black Bears, Books, and Videos.

Visa, Mastercard, and American Express accepted. Redemption Center. NALED Member. Shipping available.

THE BUCKBOARD

Downtown Traders Mall
805 Parkway Suite 8
Gatlinburg, TN 37738

PHONE: (615)436-4692

Open Year Round

Coca-Cola Collectibles, Anheuser-Busch Steins, Tom Clark Gnomes and Woodspirits, The Herd by Marty, The McSwine collection by Flambro, Jan Hagara, CUI Steins, Winston Cup Champions Steins, Nostalgia gifts, old and reproduction signs and ads, collector's tins, commemorative softdrink bottles and cans.

All major credit cards accepted. Phone and mail orders welcome. Secondary Market for steins and Tom Clark. Answering machine always on!

Located at traffic light #7 in the heart of Gatlinburg.

TENNESSEE

THE LEMON TREE

636 Parkway
Gatlinburg, TN 37738
PHONE: (800)598-0908
(615)436-4602

Open Daily: 9:00-9:00 April-December
Open Daily: 10:00-6:00 January-March

Your premier collectible showcase for over 20 years. Dept. 56, PM, Lladro, Armani, Hummel, LEGENDS, Disney Classics, Calico Kittens, Kewpie Collections, Indian Territory, Stanton Arts, Merry Makers, Snowbabies, Treasury ornaments, Krystonia, MOY, Goebel Miniatures, EKJ, Lowell Davis, Lilliput, Maruri, Lefton, Miss Martha's, Maud Humphrey, David Winter, Small World of Music, Cabbage Patch, Michael Garman, Duncan Royale, Fontanini, Cain Studios, Laura's Attic, Perillo, Sports Impressions, Daddy's Long Legs, Cherished Teddies. Secondary Market. Redemption Center. Layaway, newsletter and shipping available.

MOUNTAIN LEATHER

Downtown Trader's Mall
805 Parkway #9
Gatlinburg, TN 37738
PHONE: (615)436-4801

Fine handcrafted, snake and leather goods, Austrian and Natural Crystal, Hand Blown Glass, and Rawcliffe Pewter. Also featuring Gatlinburg's largest Tom Clark and Tim Wolfe Collections.

Visa, Mastercard and American Express as well as personal checks accepted. Phone and mail orders welcome. Located on the corner of stop light #7, next to Midtown Lodge, on the "Parkway."

THE VILLAGE SHOPS

Hwy. 25 East
Harrogate, TN 37752
PHONE: (615)869-4708
(615)869-5597

Monday-Saturday: 9:00-7:00
Sunday: 1:00-5:00

Located at Cumberland Gap, 60 miles north of Knoxville on the KY/VA border. Serving the collector for 10 years. Lines include: Precious Moments Signature Dealer and soft sculptured dolls, Cherished Teddies, Maud Humphrey, Enesco Musicals, Kurt Adler Santas and Steinbach Nutcrackers, Dept. 56 (Villages, accessories, All Thru the House), Sports Impressions, Hamilton dolls and plates, Seymour Mann dolls, Shelia's, Fitz & Floyd, Dave Grossman, Lee Middleton, and Zook dolls.

Layaway and shipping available. Visa and Mastercard accepted.

JAN'S HALLMARK

207 W. Main St.
Hendersonville, TN 37075
PHONE: (615)822-1147

Monday-Saturday: 9:00-8:00
Sunday: 12:00-5:00

A full-line Hallmark and bookstore with Hallmark Keepsake ornaments, Enesco ornaments, Precious Moments, Possible Dreams, Cherished Teddies, Dreamsicles, David Winter Cottages, All God's Children, Snowbabies, Annalee Dolls, Iris Arc Crystal, Laura's Attic, Russ Berrie Trolls, Hallmark miniatures, Texas Stamps, Cast Art, Department 56, Flambro Imports, Little Cheesers and Nutcrackers.

Layaways available. Hallmark Gold Crown Card. All major credit cards accepted.

TENNESSEE

THE OLD COUNTRY STORE

Casey Jones Village
Jackson, TN 38305

PHONE: (800)748-9588

Open Daily 6:00am-10:00pm

Tom Clark Gnomes, Precious Moments, All God's Children, Lefton Colonial Village, Sports Impressions, David Winter, Bradford Exchange, Hummel, Emmett Kelly Jr., WACO Musicals, Iris Arc, Laura's Attic, Cherished Teddies, Monfort, Maurice Wideman, and Walt Disney Classics Collection.

All major credit cards accepted. NALED member. Layaway available.

FLOWERAMA

The Mall in Johnson City
2011 N. Roan St.
Johnson City, TN 37601

**PHONE: (615)282-4644
(800)786-4644**

Monday-Saturday: 10:00-9:00
Sunday: 1:00-6:00

Tom Clark Gnomes, Chilmark, Dept. 56, Snow Village, Snowbabies, Sports Impressions, Cherished Teddies, Calico Kittens, Emmett Kelly, Margaret Furlong, Austrian Crystal, Maruri Birds, PenDelfin, Sarah's Attic, Hummels, Lowell Davis, Lladro, Sandicast, Natures Window Decoys, Dreamsicles, Willitts Carousels, The Good Life, David Winter Cottages, Raikes Bears.

All major credit cards accepted. Shipping available. Layaways welcome. Secondary Market Dealer. Redemption Center.

GIFTS & COLLECTIBLES

Colonial Heights Pharmacy
4221 Fort Henry Dr.
Kingsport, TN 37663

**PHONE: (615)239-5935
(800)541-6862
FAX: (615)239-6136**

Monday-Saturday: 9-8; Sunday: 1-6

Hummel, Precious Moments, Swarovski, Armani, Lladro, Walt Disney Classics Collection, Dept. 56 (Heritage Village, Snow Village, Snowbabies), Fontanini, Goebel Miniatures, Duncan Royale, Daddy's Long Legs, Sports Impressions, Jan Hagara, Sarah's Attic, All God's Children, Miss Martha, Lilliput Lane, PenDelfin, Cherished Teddies, Bergsma, Rick Cain, David Winter, Mark Hopkins, LEGENDS, Lowell Davis, Tom Clark, Byers' Choice, Lee Bortin, Neil Rose, Frumps, Krystonia, Enchantica, and Laura's Attic. All major credit cards accepted. GCC member. Layaway and UPS shipping available.

ANDY'S HALLMARK SHOP

East Towne Mall
3010 Mall Rd.
Knoxville, TN 37924

**PHONE: (615)522-1948
FAX: (704)252-0759**

All God's Children, Cairn Studio, Tom Clark Gnomes, Dept. 56: Heritage Villages, Snow Village, and Snowbabies. Cast Art Dreamsicles, Enesco: Precious Moments, Cherished Teddies, Calico Kittens and Sports Impressions. John Hine Studios, David Winter Cottages, Hallmark Keepsake Ornaments, Willitts Designs, and Star Trek Limited Editions.

Visa, Mastercard and American Express accepted. Shipping available. GCC Member.

Other locations at 181 Foothills Mall, Maryville, TN 37801, Phone: (615) 983-5384; Lenoir Mall, Lenoir, NC (704)758-7524; and Asheville Mall, Asheville, NC (704)298-3903.

TENNESSEE

COBWEB CORNER

4438 Western Ave. 640 Plaza
Knoxville, TN 37921

PHONE: (615)637-4078
FAX: (615)544-1995

Monday-Saturday: 10:00-9:00
Sunday: 1:00-6:00

A collectors paradise! Dept. 56, Lefton, Lilliput Lane, Jan Hagara, Memories of Yesterday, Precious Moments, Enesco musicals and ornaments, Walt Disney, Kitty Cucumber, Emmett Kelly, Gone With The Wind, Possible Dreams Clothtique, All God's Children, Miss Martha's Originals, Cades Cove Series, Lucy & Me Bears, Muffy Bears, Tom Clark Gnomes, Lowell Davis, PenniBears, Little Cheesers, Cherished Teddies, Hallmark Ornaments, past and present.

Layaway and shipping available.

COUNTRY SUNSHINE

620 Campbell Station Rd.
Knoxville, TN 37922

PHONE: (615)966-6508

Monday-Saturday: 10:00-5:30

In the collectible business for 10 years. Located in Station West Complex right off interstate I-40 and I-75. Inventory includes collectibles and upscale home decorative accessories and gifts. David Winter, Lilliput Lane, Jan Hagara, Maud Humphrey, Enesco Calico Kittens, Cherished Teddies, Miss Martha Collection, All God's Children, Lizzie High, and VickiLane.

Club Redemption Center for all of the above collectibles. Layaway. American Express, Visa and Mastercard accepted. Shipping available. Christmas open house in November.

THE ORANGE BLOSSOM

231 N. Lindell
Martin, TN 38237

PHONE: (800)826-3629
(901)587-5091

Monday-Friday: 9:00-5:00
Saturday: 10:00-4:00

All God's Children, Cherished Teddies, Daddy's Long Legs, Dept. 56, David Winter, Good-Kruger Dolls, Laura's Attic, Miss Martha's Originals, Possible Dreams Santas, Snowbabies, Lilliput Lane, Ashton-Drake, Vaillancourt Folk Art, Rowe Pottery, and Walt Disney Classics Collection.

All major credit cards accepted. Layaway and shipping available. NALED member. Authorized Bradford Dealer.

PATTY'S HALLMARK

1644 Memorial Blvd.
Murfreesboro, TN 37129

PHONE: (615)890-8310

Monday-Friday: 9:00-7:00
Saturday: 10:00-6:00; Sunday: 1:00-5:00

LEGENDS (Preferred Dealer), All God's Children, Precious Moments, David Winter Cottages, Lilliput Lane Cottages, Duncan Royale, M.I. Hummel, Memories of Yesterday, Maud Humphrey, Iris Arc, Golden Memories, Jan Hagara, Emmett Kelly Jr., Ron Lee Clowns, Willitts, Hallmark Keepsake Ornaments, Cherished Teddies, Dreamsicles, Fenton Art Glass, Iris Arc Crystal, Little Cheesers, Michael Garman Productions, Roman, Sports Impressions, United Design.

NALED member. All major credit cards accepted.

TENNESSEE

BARBARA MANDRELL COUNTRY

1510 Division St.
Nashville, TN 37203
PHONE: (615)242-7800
FAX: (615)726-3315

Open Daily: 9:00-5:00

Award winning Christmas and gift shop features a wide variety of theme trees, decorations, gifts and collectibles such as: Dept. 56, Precious Moments, Enesco Deluxe Music Boxes and Treasury Ornaments, Annalee, Byers' Choice, Possible Dreams, KSA Fabriche, United Design, Cherished Teddies, Fontanini Nativities, Sports Impressions, Emmett Kelly, Jr., Steinbachs, Midwest Importers, Coca-Cola, Dreamsicles, World Doll and Red Mill. Constantly adding new lines.

All major credit cards accepted. Gladly ship within the USA. Special Orders. Layaway and buyers club.

KATY'S

4502 Harding Rd.
Nashville, TN 37205
PHONE: (800)829-1422
(615)383-1422
FAX: (615)383-9138

Monday-Saturday: 9:00-6:00

Walt Disney Classics Collection, Hallmark Ornaments and Collectibles, Swarovski Crystal, Byers' Choice, Duncan Royale, Margaret Furlong, Hummel, David Winter, Lilliput Lane, Jan Hagara, Sandra Kuck, Dept. 56 (Snow Village), Possible Dreams, Armani, ANRI, and Steinbach Crystal.

Free Shipping on orders over $100.

Visa and Mastercard accepted.

ROYAL DUTCH

4009 Hillsboro Park
Nashville, TN 37215
PHONE: (800)972-3394
(615)297-6020

Monday-Saturday: 10:00-5:00

Dept. 56 Showcase Dealer, Swarovski, Hummel, Chilmark, ANRI, Precious Moments, Wee Forest Folk, Lladro, Lowell Davis, David Winter, Lilliput Lane, Royal Doulton, Halcyon Days, enamel boxes, Christopher Radko, Olszewski, Emmett Kelly, Steinbach and C. Ulbricht Nutcrackers, and Walt Disney Classics Collection.

Most major credit cards. Layaway and shipping available. Secondary market dealer. Redemption Center for most major clubs.

PIGEON FORGE DOLLS & BEARS INC.

4030 Parkway
Pigeon Forge, TN 37863
PHONE: (615)453-9741
(800)344-9032 (Orders)
FAX: (615)428-8721

June 1- Nov 1: Open 7 Days: 9:00-9:00
Off Season: Open 7 Days: 9:00-6:00

Dolls: Madame Alexander, Ginny, Turner, Himstedt, Wakeen, Spanos, Artist Collectibles, Phyllis Parkins, Dolls by Jerri, Effanbee, Gunzel, Nahrgang, GADCO, Karen Henderson, Good-Kruger, World Dolls. Teddy Bears: Muffy VanderBear, Steiff, Herman, Merry Thoughts, Barbara's Originals, B-2 Bears, Barbara Bessos, Orzek. Others: Annalee, doll furniture, tea sets and display cases.

Most major credit cards accepted. UPS shipping. Layaway. Collectors club.

TENNESSEE/TEXAS

THE LEMON TREE

870 Winfield Dunn Pkwy Hwy 66
Sevierville, TN 37862

PHONE: (800)598-0908
(615)436-4602

Open Daily: 9:00-9:00 April-December
Open Daily: 10:00-6:00 January-March

Your premier collectible showcase for over 20 years. Dept 56, Precious Moments, Lladro, Armani, Hummel, LEGENDS, Disney Classics Collection, Calico Kittens, Kewpie Collections, Indian Territory, Stanton Arts, Merry Makers, Snowbabies, Treasury Ornaments, Krystonia, MOY, Goebel, EKJ., Lowell Davis, Lilliput, Maruri, Lefton, Miss Martha's, Maud Humphrey, David Winter, Small World of Music, Cabbage Patch, Michael Garman, Duncan Royale, Fontanini, Cain Studios, Laura's Attic, Perillo, Sports Impressions, Daddy's Long Legs, Cherished Teddies. Secondary Market. Redemption Center. Layaway, newsletters and shipping available.

SWEETWATER FLOWER SHOP
GIFTS AND COLLECTIBLES

118 W. North St.
P.O. Box 67
Sweetwater, TN 37874

PHONE: (615)337-6623

Mon.-Tues. and Thurs.-Sat.: 9:00-5:00
Closed Wednesday and Sunday

Dept. 56: Dickens, North Pole, Snow and New England Villages, Snowbabies, All Through The House. All God's Children, PM, David Winter, Lilliput, Hagara, MOY, CT, Calico Kittens, Sports Impressions, Dreamsicles, Swarovski, Possible Dreams, Alex Haley, Raikes, Cairn, Hummel, J.H. Boone, Ladie & Friends, Krystonia, Sarah's Attic, Willitts, Miss Martha's, Maruri. Dolls: Gorham, Dynasty, Middleton.

Visa, Mastercard and American Express accepted. Shipping. Free gift wrapping. Many retired items available.

HAPPINESS HALLMARK

202 Lincoln Square
Arlington, TX 76011

PHONE: (817)277-8341

Monday-Saturday: 10:00-8:00
Sunday: 12:00-5:00

Family owned and serving the metroplex for 18 year! Your one stop shop for Precious Moments (DSR), Dept. 56, Hallmark Galleries, Cherished Teddies, Calico Kittens, MOY, Sports Impressions, Miss Martha, David Winter Cottages, Emmett Kelly Jr., M.I. Hummel, Gnomes, Sarah's Attic, Maud Humphrey, Chilmark, Norman Rockwell, Sebastian Figurines, Lilliput Lane, Whimsical World of Pocket Dragons, Andrea by Sadek, Maruri Birds, Enesco Musicals, Thomas Kinkade Pictures, Fenton, The Legend of Santa Claus, Hallmark Ornaments, Precious Moments Country (dolls), Cast Art.

Happiness Hallmark & Holly's Hallmark 11 Stores serving the Metroplex.

PIPE WORLD, INC.

2160 Highland Mall
Austin, TX 78752

PHONE: (800)880-4438
(512)451-3713

Monday-Saturday: 10-9; Sunday: 12-6

Tom Clark Gnomes, All God's Children, Sarah's Attic, Krystonia, Ron Lee, LEGENDS, Chilmark, Daniel Montfort, Terrance Patterson, Sinapau Studio, Creart, Rick Cain, Neil Rose, Gary Rose, Paul Carrico, Mayflower Glass, Aus-Ben Studios, David Winter, Sandicast, Castagna, Bossons, Red Mill, Westland Carousel Horses, Second Nature, Budweiser Steins, Madison, Marty Bear Foot, Purrfect Pets, Dragon Keep, The Herd, Little Cheesers, Tim Wolfe, Lee Sievers, Willitts Designs, Hanford Heirlooms.

Mastercard, Visa, and Discover accepted. Layaway. Secondary Market. Redemption Center.

TEXAS

MR 'C' COLLECTIBLES

1014 South Broadway #102
Carrollton, TX 75006-7287

**PHONE: (800)221-4057
(214)242-5100**

Tuesday-Saturday: 10:00-5:30

Hummel, Hibel, All God's Children, Miss Martha's Creations (Enesco), Memories of Yesterday, Precious Moments, Bing & Grondahl, Holiday Hamlet, Dynasty dolls, Kuck, Perillo, Donald Zolan, Rockwell, Stone, Xaras, bells, frames, eggs, music boxes, and Little Cheesers.

Large Secondary Market for Limited Edition Plates, Figurines, and Lithos. Major credit cards and layaway available. NALED member. UPS shipping daily. Personal service.

MY FAVORITE THINGS

208 Houston St.
Cedar Hill, TX 75104

PHONE: (214)299-6900

Tuesday-Friday: 10:00-5:30
Saturday: 10:00-5:00

A shoppe of fine gifts and collectibles in the South Dallas Suburbs. Bradford Dealer, Ashton-Drake, Madame Alexander, All God's Children, Cat's Meow Village, Jan Hagara, P. Buckley Moss, stained glass, Possible Dreams, Sabino, Lefton Colonial Village, art gallery, Thomas Kindade and Lena Liu prints and plates. Fine gifts for your home and gift giving pleasure.

All major credit cards accepted. Layaway available.

D'S PIPES ETC.

200 N. 15th St.
Corsicana, TX 75110

PHONE: (800)522-9953

Open Daily: 10:00-5:30

Lilliput Lane, Hummels, All God's Children, Sarah's Attic, Precious Moments, Memories of Yesterday, Sports Impressions, Golden Memories, Duncan Royale, Laura's Attic, Jan Hagara, Little Cheesers, Cherished Teddies, Calico Cats, and David Winter.

Secondary Market Service for All God's Children and Sarah's Attic. All major credit cards accepted.

THE DOLL COLLECTION

6959 W. Arapaho #509
Dallas, TX 75248

**PHONE: (214)458-7823
(800)899-5823 (ORDERS)**

Monday-Friday: 10-5:30; Saturday: 10-5

Alexander, Wendy Lawton, Paul Crees, H. Gunzel, Annette Himstedt, Dolls by Jerri, Daddy's Long Legs, Bunnies by the Bay, Robert Tonner, S. Krey, Patricia Rose, R.J. Wright, S. Esche, Blythe & Snodgrass, Good-Kruger, A. Darling, H. Ott, Parkins, Deval, Monika, Roche, Linda Mason, Heidi Pluzoch, Elke Hutchens, Lenci, Helen Kish, Robin Woods, Kathe Kruse, Edna Dali, J&J, Effanbee, Barbie, Muffy Vanderbear, Gotz, Corolle, American Beauty, Anja, S. Hartmann, Gail Hoyt, Dee Ann Duttrey, Dolls by Pauline, Lee Middleton, Linda Steele, Beaver Valley, Maggie Iacono, Sylvia Natterer, Steiff, Precious Babies. Plus many artist bears and bunnies!

Major credit cards accepted. Free layaway.

TEXAS

LADYBUG LANE

Olla Podrida Collectible Mall
12215 Coit Rd. #112
Dallas, TX 75251

PHONE: (214)661-3692

Monday-Saturday: 10:00-6:00
Thursday: 10:00-9:00; Sunday: 12:00-6:00

A unique shoppe in one of-a-kind-mall. Madame Alexander, Wakeen, Middleton, Swarovski, Tom Clark, LEGENDS Mixed Media Preferred Dealer, Lilliput Lane, Laura's Attic, Castagna, United Design, Miss Martha's Originals, All God's Children, Precious Moments, Cherished Teddies, Shoemaker's Dream, Armani, Dept. 56, Walberg, Monfort, Rawcliffe pewter, Emmett Kelly, Perillo, DeGrazia, David Winter, Krystonia, Pocket Dragons, Fontanini, Ron Lee and Leo Smith.

Major credit cards accepted. Layaway and shipping available. NALED member. All redemptions honored. Family operated.

THE OLD WORLD

Ste 2480 13350 Dallas Pkwy.
Dallas, TX 75240

PHONE: (214)385-8919
(800)767-8919

Monday-Saturday: 10:00-9:00
Sunday: 12:00-6:00

Established since 1966. Lines include David Winter, Wee Forest Folk, Hummels, Lladro, Boehm porcelains, Maruri porcelains, Russian Icons, Halycon Days Enamel boxes, Swarovski, Chilmark, LEGENDS, Vanderveen Bronze, Lowell Davis, and Sabino crystal.

Headquarters for all collector society redemptions.

All major credit cards accepted.

SERENDIPITY

1203 Old Town
Dallas, TX 75206

PHONE: (214)692-0249
(800)767-4027
FAX: (214)692-5773

Monday-Saturday: 10:00-6:00

Imagine 10,000 square feet of collectibles and you've seen Serendipity, one of the largest collectibles retailers in the country. ANRI, Andrea, Hummel, Bing & Grondahl, Royal Copenhagen, Lalique, Kaiser, Marty, Dresden, Swarovski, Mats Jonasson, Hibel, Lowell Davis, Chilmark, Royal Doulton, Duncan Royale, Lladro, Sabino, Steinbach Nutcracker, David Winter, Olszewski, Mark Hopkins, Rosenthal, Herend, Maruri, Polland Studios, Whitley Bay and Russian Boxes.

Club Redemptions. Secondary Market Service. Layaways and shipping available. Specializing in service and special orders. All major credit cards accepted.

SUGAR & SPICE GIFT SHOP

910 S. Cockrell Hill Rd.
Duncanville, TX 75137

PHONE: (214)780-5977

Monday-Saturday: 10:00-6:00

All God's Children and Miss Martha Originals. Cairn Studio's Tom Clark, Tim Wolfe and Lee Sievers. Sarah's Attic, Maud Humphrey Bogart, Little Cheesers, Cat's Meow, Byers' Choice Carolers, Tuf Times, Daddy's Long Legs Dolls, Laura's Attic, Annalee Dolls, and Cherished Teddies.

Layaway. Visa and Mastercard accepted. Secondary Market on all lines.

TEXAS

COLLECTIBLES

1530 Lomaland
El Paso, TX 79935

PHONE: (915)594-0162

Monday-Saturday: 10:00-6:00

Dept. 56 Showcase Dealer: All Villages, Snowbabies, All Thru the House, Merry Makers, Winter Silhouettes. Sarah's Attic, Cat's Meow, North American Bear, personalized gift baskets, greeting cards, Yankee Candles, Crabtree & Evelyn, Enesco Music Boxes, and seasonal collectibles.

Dept. 56 Showcase. All major credit cards accepted. Layaway available.

"Collectibles" offers two store locations in El Paso. Second location: 4700 N. Mesa, 79912 (915) 534-4243.

COUNTRY COTTAGE

Trawood at Lomaland
2050 Trawood Suite 4
El Paso, TX 79935

PHONE: (915)593-2008

Monday-Saturday: 10:00-6:00

Your one stop Country gift store in El Paso featuring Daddy's Long Legs, Lizzie High, Byers' Choice, All God's Children, June McKenna, Attic Babies, Sternsy Bears, Lang Graphics Collection, Yankee Candles, Matthews Wire, lamps, dried flowers, New Canaan jams and jellys, Fredricksburg fudge, Marshall pottery.

Visa and Mastercard accepted. Layaway and shipping available.

COLLECTIBLE HEIRLOOMS

1140 Baybrook Mall
Friendswood, TX 77546

PHONE: (713)486-5023

Monday-Saturday: 10:00-9:00
Saturday: 12:00-6:00

Serving the Lladro, Armani, David Winter, Emmett Kelly Jr., All God's Children, Swarovski, Sports Impressions, Austin, Miller Import, Hummel, and Dept. 56 Collector.

All major credit cards accepted. NALED member. Free shipping on orders over $200. Layaway welcome. Welcome the opportunity to serve you. Thirty minutes from Houston.

COLLECTORS CHOICE

4529 Stonewall
Greenville, TX 75401

PHONE: (903)455-5017
FAX: (903)454-9412

Monday-Friday: 8:30-5:30
Saturday: 9:00-12:00

All's God's Children, ANRI, Armani, David Winter, Duncan Royale, Emmett Kelly Jr., Gartlan, Hummels, Jan Hagara, Kaiser, Lefton, Lilliput Lane, Lowell Davis, Lee Middleton, Maruri, WACO Melody In Motion, and Silver Deer.

All major credit cards accepted. Layaway and shipping available.

TEXAS

GIFTS & WRAPS

618 W. Main St.
Gun Barrel City, TX 75147

PHONE: (903)887-2316
FAX: (903)887-6748

Monday-Friday: 10:00-5:00
Saturday: 9:00-5:00

Located one hour S.E. of Dallas, on Cedar Creek Lake. Specializing in Cat's Meow, Maud Humphrey, Memories of Yesterday, Sandicast, Laura's Attic, Cherished Teddies, Calico Cats, United Design, Ron Lee Clowns and Looney Tunes, Sports Impressions, Miller Imports Crystals, Enesco Musicals and Ornaments, Raikes Bears, Seymour Mann, Largo Western Art, Possible Dreams, Collectible Resource sports collectibles, Little Cheesers, and Silver Deer.

Redemption Center. 90 day layaway plan. All major credit cards accepted. Both UPS and Post Office shipping available.

THE ANTIQUE IMAGE

2121 W. San Houston Pkwy N.
Houston, TX 77043

PHONE: (713)461-9531

Hours: 10:00-6:00

David Winter Cottages, Lilliput Lane, Lefton Colonial Village, Snowbabies, Royal Doulton, Byers' Choice, Miss Martha's Collection, Memories of Yesterday, Lowell Davis, Thomas Kinkade, Shoemaker's Dream Houses, Clock Houses, Kitty Cucumber, Possible Dreams, United Design Santas, Maruri, Pocket Dragons, Plates, Pulaski collector cabinets, and much more!

All major credit cards accepted.

ASHLEY AVERY'S COLLECTABLES

1218 Willowbrook Mall
Houston, TX 77070

PHONE: (713)894-5449
FAX: (713)955-1490

Monday-Saturday: 10:00-9:00
Sunday: 12:00-6:00

Swarovski, Armani, Lladro, David Winter, All God's Children, Hummel, Sabino, Walt Disney Collection, Napoleon Capodimonte, Dept. 56, Chilmark, Maruri, Precious Moments, Austin, Andrea by Sadek, Cast Art, John Perry.

All credit cards accepted. Layaway and shipping available. Secondary Market Dealer. Redemption Center.

CHERISHED ENCHANTMENTS

10910 Old Katy Rd.
Houston, TX 77043

PHONE: (800)435-6521 (ORDERS)
(713)827-7352

Monday-Thursday: By Appointment
Friday-Saturday: 10:00-6:00
Sunday: 11:00-6:00

Wee Forest Folk, David Winter, Lilliput Lane, Thomas Kinkade, Marty Bell, Bradford Exchange Dealer, Snowbabies, Chilmark, LEGENDS, Ashton-Drake dolls, Robin Woods, Enchantica, Krystonia, Pocket Dragons, and Cherished Teddies.

All major credit cards. Layaway. Free shipping. Redemption for all of the above.

TEXAS

SPENCER'S CHINA & GALLERY

3772 Richmond Ave.
Houston, TX 77027

**PHONE: (713)871-8900
(800)742-7766
FAX: (713)871-1140**

Monday-Friday: 9:00-5:00
Saturday: 10:00-5:00

Disney Classics Collection, LEGENDS, David Winter, Lilliput Lane, Lladro, Dennis Lewan canvas art and plates, G. Harvey Western art, Waterford Crystal, Lenox China, Christian Dior, Noritake, Mikasa, Royal Worcester, Spode, Wedgwood, Johnson Brothers, Cuthbertson, Arthur Court, Portmeirion, and Nanbe.

All major credit cards accepted. Layaway. Secondary Market Dealer. Full Bridal Registry. Major lines of china available.

TRUDY'S HALLMARK

4348 Highway 6 North
Houston, TX 77084

PHONE: (713)859-2077

Monday-Saturday: 9:30-7:00
Sunday: 12:00-5:00

Precious Moments, Memories of Yesterday, Hummel, All God's Children, Cherished Teddies, Lowell Davis, Tom Clark Gnomes, Snowbabies, Dept. 56, Hallmark Ornaments and collectibles, Maud Humphrey, Pocket Dragons, Krystonia, David Winter, Lilliput Lane.

Most major credit cards accepted. Layaway and shipping available. GCC Member. Redemption Center.

Second Location: 7059 Highway 6 North, Houston, TX 77095. Phone: (713)463-0593. Hours: Monday-Friday: 10:00-8:00; Saturday: 9:30-7:00; Sunday: 12:00-5:00.

HOLIDAY HOUSE

237 Ave. Q
Huntsville, TX 77340

PHONE: (409)295-7338

Open Daily: 9:30-5:30

Dept. 56 Villages, Precious Moments, All God's Children, Cairn Gnomes, Cat's Meow, Hummel, Old World Christmas, David Winter, Lilliput Lane, Enesco Treasury Ornaments, Hibel, Maud Humphrey, Dreamsicles, Willitts Designs, Fontanini, and Cherished Teddies.

NALED member. All major credit cards are accepted. Secondary Market available. Layaways welcome.

GIFTS CARTOONS & COLLECTIBLES

1101 Melbourne
Hurst, TX 76053

PHONE: (817)590-0324

Monday-Saturday: 10:00-9:00
Sunday: 12:00-6:00

Swarovski, Hummel, Rockwell (Grossman and Norman Rockwell Gallery). Plates: Bradford, Kuck, Reco, Hibel. PM, MOY, CT, Calico Kittens, Laura's Attic, Enesco Musicals, Edna Hibel plates, prints, jewelry boxes. Maruri, full-line of North American Bear: VIB and Muffy. Andrea by Sadek, Lilliput Lane, Dept. 56 Villages, Snowbabies, All Through the House, Merry Makers. Sports Impressions, Gartlan USA and other sports items. Also featuring specialty gift items including porcelain flowers, animal figurines, music boxes, crystal wedding gifts, men's line. In-store club membership--call for details.

Layaway. Shipping. Special Orders.

TEXAS

MERRY'S CHRISTMAS AND CLOWNS

113 N. MacArthur
Irving, TX 75061

PHONE: (214)259-9876
FAX: (214)259-3528

Monday-Friday: 9:00-5:00
Saturday: 10:00-6:00

Red Skelton paintings and plates, Jim Howle Paintings, Emmett Kelly Jr., Ron Lee, Dreamsicles, Cherished Teddies, United Design Santas, Possible Dreams Santas, Dept. 56., Steinbach Nutcrackers, Coca-Cola Collectibles.

Mastercard, Visa and Discover accepted. Shipping and layaway available. Secondary market dealer and redemption center for Emmett Kelly, Ron Lee, Red Skelton and Jim Howle. Texas' only clown shop.

YESTERYEAR NICK NACKS

102 S. Polk St.
Jefferson, TX 75657

PHONE: (903)665-8692
(800)460-8692

Open 7 Days A Week: 10:00-5:00

Located in the fifth oldest town in Texas, 150 miles east of Dallas.

All God's Children, Emmett Kelly, Tom Clark Gnomes, Dept. 56 lighted houses, Snowbabies, Fenton glassware, Authentic Model nesting dolls, J.B. Bean Bears, Mann porcelain dolls, United Design, The Herd Elephants, Angela Tripi figurines, Fontanini Signature Collection, Old World Christmas Ornaments, House of Hatten, Collectible Santas and Angels, Constance Collection, Daddy's Long Legs, Dreamsicles, Midwest Importers, Possible Dreams. Baseball plaques and figurines.

Most major credit cards accepted. Layaway and shipping available. Redemption Center.

ELOISE'S COLLECTIBLES II

948A S. Fry Rd.
(1 Mile South of I-10)
Katy, TX 77450

PHONE: (713)578-6655

Monday-Friday: 10:00-6:00
Saturday: 10:00-5:00

Collectibles specialist. Bradford Dealer, Lladro, M.I. Hummel, Precious Moments (DSR), Wee Forest Folk, Ashton-Drake, Dept. 56 Showcase Dealer, Swarovski, Armani, Hibel, Krystonia, Memories of Yesterday, Sarah's Attic, Lilliput Lane, David Winter, Kinkade prints, Lowell Davis, Cherished Teddies, Sports Collectibles, Iris Arc, plate frames, domes and cases and many more lines.

Redemption Center for most clubs. Layaway and shipping available. NALED member. All major credit cards accepted.

LA TRADITIONAL-ANRI WOODCARVED FIGURINES

924 Riviera
Mansfield, TX 76063

PHONE: (817)473-0339

Mail Appointment Only/
Call for an Appointment

Specializing in Anri Woodcarved figurines only. Many out of issue pieces as well as new ones. Club Anri members receive discount on all purchases. Write for inventory sheet and price list. In business since 1974. Registered with Better Business Bureau.

TEXAS

COLLECTOR SHOP, INC.

1220 N. Town East Blvd.
Suite 220
Mesquite, TX 75150

PHONE: (214)613-2051

Open Daily: 10:00-6:00

Precious Moments, Tom Clark Gnomes, Sarah's Attic, Dept. 56, Melody In Motion, Maud Humphrey, David Winter, Lilliput Lane, Memories of Yesterday, Flambro Imports, Lowell Davis, Gorham, Goebel, Schmid, Chilmark, Reco, LEGENDS, Lionel Trains, Precious Art/Panton, Maruri USA, Norman Rockwell Gallery, Sports Impressions, Cherished Teddies, Effanbee Dolls, Emmett Kelly Jr., Hummels, Jan Hagara, Little Cheesers, Michael Garman, Stanton Art, Wee Forest Folk, Cairn, Stanton Art, VickiLane Designs, Dept. 56, Enesco, and Miss Martha's Originals.

All major credit cards accepted. Layaway program. Secondary Market Service on Precious Moments and Tom Clark.

OPA'S HAUS & OHI EXCHANGE

1600 River Rd.
New Braunfels, TX 78132

**PHONE: (210)629-1191
(800)627-1600 (Orders)
FAX: (512)629-0153**

Open Daily

One of the Southwest's major collectibles retailers. Geared well for mail order, the firm is a leader in the marketing of old TM/retired M.I. Hummel figurines, plus Steins of all types. Also a redemption center for David Winter, Swarovski, Lilliput, Krystonia, Enesco etc., Dept. 56. The OHI Exchange division is the original secondary market exchange. It features numerous buyer/seller safeguards and offers almost every retired item in almost every category of collectible figurines! Great shipping facilities.

Major credit cards accepted.

FRONTIER GALLERIES

1926 E. 8th St.
Odessa, TX 79761

PHONE: (915)333-3000

Monday-Saturday: 10:00-6:00

Lines include: All God's Children, Precious Moments, Andrea by Sadek, Swarovski, Enesco Musicals, Cherished Teddies, Calico Kittens, Lowell Davis, Laura's Attic, Hummels, Maud Humphrey, Edna Hibel, Sarah's Attic, Miss Martha's, David Winter Cottages, Norman Rockwell, Sandra Kuck plates, The North Pole Village, Louis Icart, DeGrazia, Enesco Treasury Ornaments, Royal Doulton, Emmett Kelly, Adorables, Sabino, Lee Sievers, Melody In Motion, Miniature Limoge, Gnomes.

Mastercard, Visa, Discover, American Express accepted. Layaway. Secondary Market. ISA appraiser on staff.

EVALENE'S IMPORTS

1401 S. Columbia
Plainview, TX 79072

PHONE: (806)296-9393

Monday-Saturday: 9:00-6:00

Precious Moments, Sarah's Attic, WACO/Melody In Motion, Laura's Attic, Jan Hagara, Miss Martha Originals, Lefton Village, Anri, Largo, Fenton Glass, Pilgrim glass.

16,000 square feet also featuring: antiques, artwork, furniture, housewares, pottery, garden center, straw market, party goods, Pfaltzgraff dinnerware, fireplace equipment, candles and silk flowers and arrangements.

Visa, Mastercard and Discover accepted. Layaway. Free gift wrapping. Shipping available.

Evalene McDonald, owner and manager.

TEXAS

THE BLUE GOOSE

1029 E. 15th St.
Plano, TX 75074

PHONE: (214)881-9295
FAX: (214)881-1898

Open 7 Days A Week: 10:00-6:00

Lizzie High, Byers' Choice, Annalee Mobilitee Dolls, Possible Dreams, Dept. 56 Heritage Villages, Jan Hagara, Snowbabies, Cat's Meow, Cast Art, Cherished Teddies, Dreamsicles, Enesco, United Design, North American Bears, Muffy Collection, Hansford Collection, and Lincoln County Garden Club.

Visa, Mastercard, and American Express accepted. Layaway and shipping available.

HELENE'S FINE ARTS AND FRAMING

2001 Coit Rd. Suite 305
Plano, TX 75075

PHONE: (214)867-1733
(214)985-1021

Monday-Saturday: 10:00-6:00
Sunday: 1:00-5:00

Figurines by Walt Disney Classics Collection, Armani, Chilmark, Mark Hopkins Bronzes, Joseph Boffil. P. Buckley Moss plates. Duck Stamp prints, all states and federal limited edition prints by Charles Frace, King, Erte, Hallam, Tarkay, Mike Akinson, G. Harvey, Robert Summers, Larry Dyke, Phillip Crowe, original art by many artists.

Most major credit cards accepted. Shipping available. Secondary Market Dealer. Redemption Center for Armani and Walt Disney. Custom framing.

JOAN'S HALLMARK SHOPS

2070 Spring Creek Pkwy.
Plano, TX 75023

PHONE: (214)517-4835
FAX: (214)517-9577

Monday-Saturday: 9:00-8:00
Sunday: 12:00-5:00

Precious Moments, David Winter, London By Gaslignt, Lilliput Lane, Madame Alexander, Dept. 56, Heritage Village, Snowbabies, Roosevelt Bears, Hallmark Ornaments, Merry Miniatures, etc, M.I. Hummel, Dreamsicles, Cherished Teddies, Calico Kittens, Lucy & Me, Muffy VanderBear.

Most major credit cards accepted. Layaway. Shipping. Redemption Center.

Other Locations:

1900 Preston Rd., Plano, TX 75093. Phone (214)867-1135.

1705 W. University Dr. McKinney, TX 75069. Phone (214)548-2664.

ELOISE'S GIFTS & ANTIQUES

722 S. Goliad
Rockwall, TX 75087

PHONE: (214)771-6371
FAX: (214)771-6371

Monday-Saturday: 10:00-6:00
Sunday: 12:00-6:00

Tom Clark, All God's Children, Armani, Emmett Kelly Jr., David Winter, Maud Humphrey, Hibel, Enesco, Hagara, Lowell Davis, Lladro, Sarah's Attic, Wee Forest Folk, Windy Meadows, R. Olszewski, Lilliput Lane, Swarovski, United Design, Sandicast, Byers' Choice, Lizzie High, Dreamsicles, Cat's Meow, Dept. 56, Cherished Teddies, Duncan Royale, Maruri, Lightpost, Michael Garman, Possible Dreams, WACO, Willitts, Ron Lee and Frumps.

Major credit cards accepted. 90 day layaway program. NALED member. Bradford Exchange Dealer member.

TEXAS

ROBERTSON'S HAMS/ D & D GIFTS

P.O. Box 176
Royse City, TX 75189
**PHONE: (214)636-9402
(214)771-1532**

Tuesday-Saturday: 9:00-6:00

The largest Norman Rockwell collection in U.S. LEGENDS, Chilmark, Largo, Monfort, Sarah's Attic, Marie's Collectibles, All God's Children, John Perry, Lowell Davis, Walt Disney, Hummel, Maruri, Gorham Birds, carousel horses, Perillo, Valencia, Fontanini, Melody In Motion, Jan Hagara, Emmett Kelly, Precious Moments, cottages, steins, Glassmasters, and the largest G. Harvey Dealer in the North Texas area (prints and bronzes). Extensive artworks. Custom Framing. Robertson's Hams also have a large selection of meats that are sugar cured, hickory smoked and no water added. They also have real beef jerky.

AMANDA'S FINE GIFTS

279 Central Park Mall
San Antonio, TX 78216-5506
**PHONE: (210)525-0412
(800)441-4458**

Monday-Saturday: 10:00-9:00
Sunday: 12:00-6:00

The largest Lladro dealer in the Southwest. Swarovski, M.I. Hummel, Miss Martha's, Originals, Tom Clark Gnomes, Ron Lee, Armani, Chilmark, Sarah's Attic, Duncan Royale, Lowell Davis, Bossons, Walt Disney Classics, and Lalique.

All major credit cards accepted. 9-month layaway plan with no interest. Shipping available.

COLLECTOR'S GALLERY

2211 N.W. Military Hwy.
San Antonio, TX 78213
PHONE: (210)341-7222

Monday-Saturday: 10:00-6:00

Dept. 56, Hummels, Precious Moments, Byers' Choice, Lladro, Swarovski, Lowell Davis, Lilliput Lane, David Winter, Enchantica, Krystonia, Chilmark, LEGENDS, Goebel minis, Snowbabies, Wee Forest Folk, Cat's Meow, Shelia's, Disney Classics, Cherished Teddies, MOY, Maud Humphrey, Emmett Kelly, Sarah's Attic, Sports Impressions, Michael's Ltd., Cybis, Caithness, Orient & Flume, M. Furlong, Enesco Treasury Ornaments, J. McKenna, B&G/ RC, Old World Christmas, Christopher Radko, Daddy's Long Legs. Lithos by Redlin, Sandra Kuck, Thomas Kinkade, Lena Liu, Hibel, Stone, and Bell.

Visa, Mastercard and American Express. Layaway available. UPS shipping. Secondary Market.

THE SHEPHERD'S SHOPPE

431 McCarty
San Antonio, TX 78216
**PHONE: (210)342-4811
(800)332-7330
FAX: (210)342-5176**

Monday-Saturday: 10:00-9:00

Lladro, Hummel, Lilliput Lane, Dept. 56, Maud Humphrey Bogart, Miss Martha, Jan Hagara, Memories of Yesterday, Sarah's Attic, Sports Impressions, Precious Moments, Swarovski, Iris Arc, Cherished Teddies, Beatrix Potter, Thomas Kinkade, Lowell Davis, and Little Cheesers.

NALED member. Layaway available. Major credit cards accepted. UPS shipping.

TEXAS

SPRING GREEN

319 Gentry
Spring, TX 77373

PHONE: (713)288-9181
FAX: (713)288-9181

Tuesday-Saturday: 10:00-5:00
Sunday: 12:00-5:00

Thomas Kinkade, Marty Bell, Alan Maley (all canvas on all of the above), and Bradford.

Located just north of Houston in a resort community of Old Town Spring. Spring Green concentrates on fine art and gifts that fairly match their value.

Secondary Market Service on art. All major credit cards are accepted. Layaway available.

ANTIQUE HAVEN

Route 1 Box 60
Stanton, TX 79782

PHONE: (800)299-3480

Monday-Saturday: 10:00-5:30

Located 12 miles east of Midland on North Service Rd. off Interstate Highway 20. Our Lines include: All God's Children, Tom Clark Gnomes, Tim Wolfe's "Tracks", Lee Sievers Creations, Cherished Teddies, Little Cheesers, LEGENDS, Armani, Hummels, Maud Humphrey, Miss Martha's Collection by Enesco, Cast Art Dreamsicles, Lowell Davis, Yankee Candles, Laura's Attic, Possible Dreams, Cat's Meow, The Herd, and Growing Up Girls.

Mastercard, Visa and Discover accepted. A 10-month layaway plan. Free shipping. Secondary Market Dealer.

TILLIE'S

918 Coronado Blvd.
Universal City, TX 78148

PHONE: (210)658-1444

Monday-Saturday: 10:00-5:30

Annalee, Attic Babies, Daddy's Long Legs, Lizzie High, Original Cabbage Patch, All God's Children, ANRI, Bossons, Byer's Choice, Christopher Radko, Lowell Davis, Sarah's Attic, Lynn West and Vaillancourt Santas, Beaver Valley, Bear Brown Collectibles, Cherished Teddies, Gund, Muffy's, Steiff, Wendy Brent, Wee Forest Folk, Barbie, The Collectables, Dolls by Jerri, GADCO, Himstedt, Johannes Zook, Goebel Miniatures, Middleton Dolls, Sports Impressions, Susan Wakeen, Memories of Yesterday, and Mc B. Bears.

6 month layaway plan available.

GIFT CREATIONS

568 El Dorado Blvd.
Webster, TX 77598

PHONE: (713)280-8766
FAX: (713)280-8079

Monday-Friday: 10:00-8:00
Saturday: 9:00-7:00; Sunday: 12:00-6:00

Tom Clark Gnomes, All God's Children, Miss Martha's Collection, Dreamsicles, Sandicast, Emmett Kelly Jr., Napoleon Capodimonte, Enesco Musicals, Dept. 56: All Villages, Snowbabies, All Through the House; David Winter, Shoemaker's Dream, Possible Dreams Santas, Iris Arc, Roman Fontanini, Krystonia, Pocket Dragons, Windstone Edition, Little Cheesers, Maud Humphrey, Andrea by Sadek, PM, MOY, Cherished Teddies, Calico Kittens, Kitty Cucumber, Sisters & Best Friends. Enesco Treasury and Carlton Ornaments.

All major credit cards accepted. Layaway. Shipping. Redemption Center and instant gratification kits for most collectibles.

TEXAS/UTAH

FINISHING TOUCH

4020 Rhea Rd.
Wichita Falls, TX 76308
PHONE: (800)877-0070
FAX: (817)696-0611

Monday-Saturday: 9:30-6:30

Tom Clark Gnomes, Walt Disney Classics, Precious Moments, Miss Martha's Collection, All God's Children, Lilliput Lane, Sarah's Attic, Lladro, Hummel, Armani, Snowbabies, Swarovski Crystal, Cherished Teddies, Wee Forest Folk, Memories of Yesterday, Emmett Kelly Jr. and Sr., Duncan Royale, WACO Musicals, Ron Lee, LEGENDS, Chilmark, Pocket Dragons--just too many to list! Visit their 10,000 square feet of fantastic shopping.

All major credit cards accepted. Shipping anywhere.

COLLECTIBLES ELITE
LIMITED EDITIONS

648 East State Rd.
American Fork, UT 84003
PHONE: (801)756-8777

Monday-Saturday: 10:00-6:00

Your one stop collectibles shop. Dealership for Walt Disney Classics Collection, Bradford Exchange, Precious Moments, MOY, Ashton-Drake, Maud Humphrey, Jan Hagara, Krystonia, Miss Martha Originals, All God's Children, Lilliput Lane, and Thomas Kinkade. Also carry Donald Zolan, Artaffects, North Pole Village, Cherished Teddies, Small World of Music, Roger Davis's "Flight of the Phoenix", Elegance in Marble, dolls, bells, thimbles, carousels, jewelry boxes, music boxes, lithographs, pottery, pewter, plates, frames, racks, hangers and more.

Visa, Discover, Mastercard. Layaway. Gift certificates and free gift wrapping.

LARSEN HALLMARK & GIFTS

2340 A Ogden City Mall
Ogden, UT 84401
PHONE: (801)392-5011

Monday-Friday: 10:00-9:00
Saturday: 10:00-7:00; Sunday: 12:00-5:00

Bradford Dealer, Armani, Lladro, Dept. 56, David Winter, Lilliput Lane, Cairn Studios-Tom Clark and Tim Wolfe, Precious Moments, Cherished Teddies, Memories of Yesterday, Shoemaker's Dream, Pocket Dragons, Krystonia, Hallmark Ornaments, Frumps, Raikes, Snowbabies, Designs Americana, Cast Art-Dreamsicles, Sandicast, Artesania Rinconada, Castagna, Little Cheesers, Reco, Sandra Kuck, Red Mill Mfg. Roman, Willitts Designs.

Redemption Center for most collector clubs. All major credit cards accepted. Layaway and shipping available.

LARSEN HALLMARK

University Mall
Orem, UT 84058
PHONE: (801)224-2066
(801)224-2552

Monday-Saturday: 10:00-9:00

Dept. 56, Precious Moments, David Winter, Lilliput Lane, Cairn Studios: Tom Clark, Tim Wolfe, Lee Sievers. Cherished Teddies, Krystonia, Memories of Yesterday, Shoemaker's Dream, Pocket Dragons, Frumps, Hallmark Ornaments, Raikes, Snowbabies, Designs Americana, Cast Art, Sandicast, Artesania Rinconada, Castagna, Little Cheesers, Lucy & Me, Sisters, Treasured Memories, Jan Hagara, Roman, Willitts Designs.

Redemption Center for most collector clubs. All major credit cards accepted. Layaway and shipping available.

UTAH/VERMONT

TOMMY KNOCKERS

537 Main St.
P.O. Box 753
Park City, UT 84060

PHONE: (801)649-8482

Open Daily: 10:00
December-April: 10:00-10:00

Located in the historic mining town of Park City, in the Park City ski resort.

Lladro, Chilmark Showcase Dealer, Remington Bronzes, Lilliput Lane, Showcase Dealer for Enesco Musicals, Mark Hopkins Showcase Dealer.

Club Redemption Center. Layaway. Discover, Visa, Mastercard and American Express accepted. Shipping available. Free gift wrapping.

PEWTER & THINGS

Green Mountain Village Shops
Manchester Ctr., VT 05255

PHONE: (802)362-3673

Open 7 Days A Week: 9:30-6:00

LEGENDS, Lilliput Lane Cottages Ltd., Bubble Fairies, Brian Baker's Deja Vu, Lance Corp., Superior Models, Perth Pewter, Chilmark, Hudson's Villagers, Partha Pewter, A Childs Memory Collection, W.T. Wilson for Pewter Port, Mats Jonasson/Sweden, Cain Studios, Kirk Stieff, Meadow Mountain Desk Jewelry by Charles Hill, Michael's Ltd., Pewter Nativity Sets, Pewter Christmas ornaments, items from all major pewterers, and La Leonessa Pewter.

Major credit cards accepted.

DANFORTH PEWTERERS

P.O. Box 828
Middlebury, VT

PHONE: (802)388-0098
FAX: (802)388-0099

Open Monday-Saturday: 10:00-5:00
Sundays (June-Dec.): 11:00-4:00

Specializing in handcrafted lead-free pewterware all made in Vermont. Elegant plates, bowls, oil lamps and candlesticks plus handcast buttons, ornaments and figurines. Owner designers Fred and Judi Danforth have been in business for 20 years, continuing the family tradition which began with the well known colonial pewtersmith Thomas Danforth II in 1703.

For a catalog send $1.00 to the address above. Mastercard and Visa accepted. Parking and shipping available.

THE CHRISTMAS LOFT

Route 7
Shelburne, VT 05482

PHONE: (802)985-4166

Open Daily: 9:30-5:00
Expanded Hours July-December

Decorative Christmas accessories and collectibles. Dept. 56 Showcase Dealer (Villages, Snowbabies, all Department 56 collectibles), Christopher Radko glass, David Winter, Steinbach Nutcrackers and Smokers, Byers' Choice, Vaillancourt, Lynn Haney and June McKenna Santas, Tom Clark Gnomes, Miss Martha, Precious Moments, Cherished Teddies, Fontanini, Disney, Enesco music boxes and Treasury ornaments, and Laura's Attic.

Secondary Market Service in Dept. 56.

Second location: Route 3, Meredith, NH 03253 (603)279-5711. For orders call toll free at 1-800-962-6180.

VIRGINIA

THE CHRISTMAS ATTIC INC.

125 S. Union
Alexandria, VA 22314

PHONE: (703)548-2829

Open Every Day

Dept. 56 Showcase Dealer, Tom Clark Gnomes, Annalee, Byers' Choice, German Nutcrackers, Christopher Radko, Precious Moments, Lilliput Lane, Wee Forest Folk, Miss Martha, Krystonia, Lee Middleton dolls, Snowbabies, United Design Angels.

Visa and Mastercard accepted. Layaway and shipping available. Redemption Center.

Other Locations: 201 King St., Alexandria, VA 22314 (703)548-4267.

301 20th St, Virginia Beach, VA 23451 (804)425-7624.

333 Waterside Dr., Norfolk, VA 23510. Phone (804)625-2551.

LA MAISONETTE

13938 Lee Jackson Hwy.
Chantilly, VA 22021

**PHONE: (800)995-7259
(703)378-5522**

Monday-Friday: 10:00-8:00
Saturday: 10:00-6:00; Sunday: 12:00-5:00

Anheuser-Busch, Inc., The Cat's Meow, Dept. 56 Snowbabies, Enesco, Precious Moments, John Hine Studios-David Winter, Maruri USA, Lance Corp.-Chilmark and Hudson, Summerhill Crystal, and United Design.

Mastercard, Visa and Discover accepted. Secondary Market Service available for Precious Moments and Cat's Meow (custom service). Redemption forms. Shipping service.

CILLA'S HALLMARK SHOP

1735 Parkview Dr.
Chesapeake, VA 23320

**PHONE: (804)424-2551
FAX: (804)424-5765**

Monday-Saturday: 9:00-9:00
Sunday: 12:30-5:00

All God's Children, Precious Moments, Cat's Meow, Shelia's, Sports Impressions, Hallmark Gallery, Tom Clark Gnomes, Attic Babies, David Winter, Lilliput Lane, Maud Humphrey, Memories Of Yesterday, Cherished Teddies, Calico Kittens, Sarah's Attic, Enesco Small World of Music, Lizzie High, Jan Hagara, Laura's Attic, Miss Martha's, B.P.Gutmann, Little Cheesers, Golden Memories, United Design, Fenton Art Glass, Texas Stamps, LEGENDS, Goebel U.S., F.O.R.T.

Visa, Mastercard, and American Express accepted. Layaway available. Redemption Center.

SCOTSWORLD LTD.

P.O. Box 434
Fairfax Station, VA 22039

**PHONE: (800)423-6556
(703)690-2212**

Monday-Friday: 9:00-5:00

Lilliput Lane Collectibles from England, Scotland, Wales, Ireland, Germany, France, Netherlands and American Landmarks. Land of Legend Pocket Dragons, Stadden Figures, Nutcrackers, Dram Glasses, Toby Mugs and teapots.

Lilliput Lane catalog--$5.00. Land of Legend Catalog--$1.00. Catalog cost refundable with first order. Visa and Mastercard accepted.

VIRGINIA

MICHELLE'S GIFT & GALLERY

Hwy. 52 North/ P.O. Box 277
Fancy Gap, VA 24328

PHONE: (703)728-5043

Monday-Friday: 10-5; Saturday: 10-6
Sunday: 1-5; Closed Tuesday

P.J.'s Carousel Horses, Maud Humphrey, Knot Knoggins, Reco Plates, Pewter Collectibles, United Design, Guidhall, Fenton, sculptures by artist Michelle Phelps, many collectible doll lines, Kurt S. Adler nutcrackers and smokers, Limited Edition prints including Chuck Wrenn, David Wright, and Larry Zabel. Additional items include Southwest jewelry, quilts, powderhorns, music boxes, santas, handmade baskets, pottery, unique hand-forged iron work, Civil War portraits, plus a Victorian room full of Victorian Treasures.

Visa, Mastercard and Discover accepted. Layaway and shipping available.

CHRISTMAS PAST & PRESENTS GIFT SHOP

Historic District
712 Caroline St.
Fredericksburg, VA 22401

PHONE: (703)899-XMAS

Maud Humphrey Bogart, Dept. 56, Snowbabies, Heritage Village, Snow Village, Christmas in the City, North Pole, Emmett Kelly Jr., Kurt S. Adler, Marina's Russian Collection, Midwest Importers, Old World Glass, Fontanini Nativities, Dolfi Dolls, Nutcrackers and Smokers, Collectors Thimbles, Possible Dreams Santas, Lil' Dolls by United Design, Margaret Furlong Angels, Kneeling Santa by Roman, Jan Hagara, and Santas of the Nation.

Redemption Center for lines listed with clubs. UPS shipping. Layaway plan is available.

THE CHRISTMAS GALLERY

P.O. Box 410 14110 Lee Hwy.
Gainesville, VA 22065

PHONE: (703)754-9872
FAX: (703)754-2422

Open Daily: 9:00-5:00

Radko, Annalee Dolls, June McKenna, Dept. 56 Showcase Dealer, KSA Collectibles, Steinbach Nutcrackers, Enesco Cherished Teddies, Collectible Christmas ornaments, Music Box Society, Fontanini, Byers' Choice, Old World Glass Collectibles, Possible Dreams, Miss Martha's Collection, and Leo Smith III Collection.

Secondary Market on Dept. 56 Village House series. Major credit cards accepted. Layaway plan available.

Second Location: 304C Mill St., Occoquan, VA. Phone (703)494-4937.

DOR-DONN COLLECTIBLES

RT. 17 Box 685
Gloucester, VA 23061

PHONE: (804)693-4258

Monday-Saturday: 9:00-5:00
Sunday By Appointment Only

Authorized Bradford and Ashton Drake Dealer. Collector plates, figurines, and music boxes. Plates by L. Liu, C. Frace, E. Hibel, F. Hook, C. Layton, L. Kaatz, T. Kinkade and K. Daniel. Dolls by: Y. Bello, K. Hippensteel, C. McClure, J. McClelland, J. Good-Kruger, S. Kuck. Most artists represented.

Visa and Mastercard accepted. Mail and phone orders available.

VIRGINIA

HARROGATE'S LTD.

120 West Queen's Way
Hampton, VA 23669

PHONE: (804)723-3163

Monday-Saturday: 9:30-5:30

China: Ceralene, Wedgwood, Lynn Chase, Bernardaud, Mottahedeh, Royal Worcester, Spode, Royal Doulton, Royal Crown Derby, Herend, Rosenthal.

Collectibles: Christopher Radko, Enesco Music boxes, Herend figurines, Lladro Collectors Society, June McKenna Santas, Royal Crown Derby paperweights, Russian Lacquer boxes.

Crystal: Baccarat, Orrefors, Wedgwood, Miller Rogaska, Kosta Boda.

Various other types of gifts for all occasions. Specializing in the unusual or hard to find gift for that hard to buy for person.

KAROLSON'S TREASURES

312 E. Market St.
Leesburg, VA 22075

PHONE: (703)771-1776

Tuesday-Saturday: 10:00-6:00
Sunday: 12:00-5:00

Tom Clark, David Winter, Lilliput Lane, Krystonia, Cat's Meow, Hudson-Lance, Duncan Royale, John Perry, Mill Creek-Knot Knoggins, Dreamsicles, Designs Americana, Jon Herbert's Shoehouses, Castagna of Italy, and Clare Craft of England.

Mastercard, Visa, and Discover accepted. 60 day layaway plan. Shipping available. Secondary Market for Tom Clark, David Winter and Lilliput Lane.

THE ENGLISH COTTAGE

8679 Sudley Rd.
Manassas, VA 22110

PHONE: (703)361-4571
FAX: (703)338-3662

Monday-Saturday: 10:00-7:00
Sunday: 12:00-5:00

Current and Secondary Market pieces for David Winter, Dept. 56: Dicken's Village, Snowbabies and North Pole; Byers' Choice Carolers, Marty Bell Fine Art, Angela Tripi figures and much more.

All major credit cards accepted. Layaway available. Secondary Market Service.

GAZEBO GIFTS

293 Newmarket Square
Newport News, VA 23605

PHONE: (804)826-5748
(800)800-MISY

Monday-Saturday: 10:00-6:00
Sunday: 12:30-5:30

Primary and Secondary Market. Virginia's collectible source since 1970! Bradford plate dealer, Dept. 56, David Winter, Lilliput Lane, Disney Classics, Hummels, Ashton-Drake and Madame Alexander dolls, All God's Children, Miss Martha's, Sarah's Attic, Precious Moments, Memories of Yesterday, Cherished Teddies, Emmett Kelly, Lladro, Swarovski, Lowell Davis, P. Buckley Moss, and Jan Hagara.

Major credit cards accepted. Layaway and shipping available. NALED member.

VIRGINIA

FOX RUN, INC.

203 Washington St.
Occoquan, VA 22125

PHONE: (703)494-4321

Monday-Saturday: 11:00-5:00
Sunday: 12:00-5:00

Specializing in something for everyone! All God's Children, Crunkleton Santas, Cherished Teddies, Laura's Attic, Enesco Musicals, Fenton Glass, Sarah's Attic, Lefton Lighthouses, Harbour Lights, Lilliput Lane, Collectible Bears, Folk Art, Bessie Pease Gutmann, Anheuser-Busch steins, Sports Impressions, Rockdale Pottery, Lincoln County Garden Club and antiques.

Visa, Mastercard and Discover accepted. Layaway available. Daily UPS shipping. Free shipment for orders over $50.00.

THE GOLDEN GOOSE

404 Mill St.
Occoquan, VA 22125

PHONE: (703)494-4964

Open Daily: 11:00-4:00

Dept. 56: Dickens Village, North Pole, Christmas in the City, Snow Village, Merry Makers, Winter Silhouettes, Snowbabies. Byers' Choice, Possible Dreams, Old World Ornaments, Fontanini, and Steinbach Nutcrackers and Smokers.

Visa and Mastercard accepted. Phone and mail orders welcome.

BIGGS LIMITED EDITIONS

5517 Lakeside Ave.
Richmond, VA 23228

PHONE: (804)266-7744
(800)637-0704

Monday-Saturday: 9:00-5:00

Current doll lines: Annette Himstedt, Paul Creese, Elke Hutchens, Madame Alexander and many others. Other lines include: Boehm, Chilmark, David Winter, Hummel, Lladro, LEGENDS, Steinbach, Swarovski, Disney and many others.

Buy and sell many of the retired pieces in the lines mentioned above, as well as others. Call for more information. Ship worldwide, including APO's. During the holidays they run a seasonal Christmas shop with lines such as Fontanini, Kurt Adler, Erzgebirge, Disney, Silvestri and many others.

Second location is at: 1601 Willow Lawn Dr. Richmond, VA 23230. Phone (804)282-0282.

C & W ENTERPRISES

P.O. Box 610
Salem, VA 24153

PHONE: (703)389-9384
FAX: (703)389-2832

Mon., Fri., Sat.:10-5; Sun.: 12-5

Enesco Christmas Ornaments, MOY (Redemption Center), Kewpie, Music Boxes(Redemption Center), North Pole Village, Laura's Attic, Pine Hollow, Lucy & Me, Seasonal Artplas Miniatures; Midwest-Leo Smith. Dolls: Mde. Alex., Gunzel, Effanbee, Himstedt, Vogue, Ginny, Lewis Carroll's Alice in Wonderland by Faith Wick. Steiff-Bears, Animals, Limited Editions. Hantel-Victorian Miniatures (Redemption Center) Victorian Reproduction Paper, Original & reproduction paper dolls, Shackman items. Primarily mail order. MC/Visa; Layaway; Secondary Market: Lines above, plus Hallmark, Carlton, Barbies, Sasha, Rockwell, Suzanne Gibson, Abigail Brahms, Cabbage Patch, Heidi Ott, Coleco.

VIRGINIA

"APPLE BARN"

1124 Apple Orchard Lane
Troutville, VA 24175

PHONE: (703)992-3551

Monday-Saturday: 10:00-6:00
Sunday: 1:00-5:00; August-December
Closed January

North of Roanoke, VA Exit 150 on I-81. Cat's Meow (#1 Dealer in VA), All God's Children, Miss Martha's Collection, Byers' Choice, Possible Dreams, VickiLane, Precious Moments (Preferred Doll Dealer), Lizzie High Dolls, Dept. 56: Snowbabies, Dickens Village; Gail Laura Calender Rabbits, Enesco Birthday Dolls, and Cherished Teddies.

Redemption Center for all collector clubs. Shipping. Visa, Mastercard and Discover accepted.

A TOUCH OF LOVE

416 W. Main St.
Waynesboro, VA 22980

PHONE: (703)942-3844
(800)433-3844

Monday-Saturday: 9:00-5:00

The largest doll shop in the Shenandoah Valley, specializing in a doll collector's dream. Alexander, Gotz, Good-Kruger, Bolden, Middleton, Hamilton, Heidi Ott, Julie Rueger, Wakeen, Lissi, Treffeisen, Berjusa, Jeckle-Jansen, Turner, The Collectables, Autumn, Hartmann, Spanos, Frederica, Zook, Jerri, GADCO, World Dolls, Effanbee, Georgetown, Seymour Mann, Dynasty, Kolesar, Ness, Mason, Mattel, Himstedt, Artists Collectibles, European Artist, Lawton, Grossle, Hardgrave.

Layaway. Free shipping. Most major credit cards accepted.

CREEKSIDE COLLECTIBLES & GIFTS

150 Creekside Lane
Creekside Village
Winchester, VA 22602

PHONE: (703)662-0270

Monday-Saturday: 10:00-5:00
Sunday: 12:00-4:00

Lilliput Lane, Lowell Davis, Tom Clark, Chilmark, Jan Hagara, Cat's Meow, Hummels, LEGENDS, June McKenna, Lladro, Snowbabies, Byers' Choice Carolers, Walt Disney Collection, David Winter, Annalee, Memories of Yesterday, Goebel Miniatures, Michael Garman, Fontanini, Hudson Villagers, Cherished Teddies, nesting dolls, limited edition and artist dolls including Good-Kruger, Dolls by Jerri, Turner, Himstedt, Lawton, The Collectables, Ashton-Drake and more.

Major credit cards accepted. Layaway available.

CHRISTMAS ACORN

Rt. 2 Box 206
Wytheville, VA 24382

PHONE: (703)637-6635

Open 7 Days A Week: 10:00-7:00

Department 56 both current and retired pieces: All Villages, Snowbabies, All Thru the House, Merry Makers, Accessories. Steinbach Nutcrackers, P.J. Carousel Horses and a full line of Christmas decor including Kurt S. Adler and Midwest Importers.

Come enjoy the country setting and ride the world's only Christmas Carousel.

Visa and Mastercard. Shipping available. Redemption Center for PJ's Carousel.

WASHINGTON

THE GIFT HAUS

601 West Wishkah
Aberdeen, WA 98520
PHONE: (206)532-8261

Monday-Saturday: 9:30-5:30

Dept. 56 Showcase Dealer, Snowbabies, Precious Moments (DSR), Memories of Yesterday, Cherished Teddies, All God's Children, Swarovski, David Winter, Sarah's Attic, Miss Martha, Hummel figurines and plates, Dreamsicles, and ANRI figurines.

UPS shipping nationwide. Visa, Mastercard and American Express accepted.

FACET COLLECTOR'S SHOWCASE

262 Bellevue Square
Bellevue, WA 98004
**PHONE: (206)451-3580
(800)285-9876**

Daily: 9:30-9:30; Sunday: 10:00-6:00

Lladro, Swarovski, LEGENDS, Lilliput Lane, All God's Children, Armani, Caithness, Chilmark, Tom Clark Gnomes and Tim Wolfe, Emmett Kelly Jr., Gartlan USA, Olszewski, Ron Lee, Royal Doulton, and Royal Copenhagen, M.I. Hummel, Lenox, ANRI, Walt Disney Classics Collection, Bing & Grondahl.

Visa, Mastercard and Discover accepted. Layaway plan. No sales tax if shipped out of state. Gift wrappping. A Secondary Market Dealer. Facet Collector's Showcase has 80 showcases of collectibles to choose from. It is one of the most beautiful stores on the West Coast.

THE MOLE HOLE

152 Bellevue Square
Bellevue, WA 98004
PHONE: (206)453-9353

Monday-Saturday: 9:30-9:30
Sunday: 11:00-6:00

Wee Forest Folk, David Winter, Harbour Lights, Shoemaker's Dream, Hummel, All God's Children, Tom Clark, Jan Hagara, Golden Memories, Ron Lee, Emmett Kelly Jr., United Design, Dept. 56 Cottages, Krystonia, Possible Dreams, North American Bear Co., Willitts Carousels, Madame Alexander, Hamilton and Seymour Mann dolls, Hamilton and Reco plates and more.

Major credit cards accepted. Shipping anywhere in the U.S.

BELLE PROVENCE

23730-F Bothell Evt Hwy.
(In Country Village)
Bothell, WA 98021
PHONE: (206)483-4696

Open Daily: 10:00-5:00
Sunday: 12:00-4:00

Beatrix Potter, you will find the largest selection of Peter Rabbit and His Friends. Brambly Hedge, Jill Barklem's enchanting field mice. Bunnykins, Royal Doulton's beloved little bunnies. Christopher Radko, the collectible Christmas ornaments that need no introduction. Wee Forest Folk. Portmeirion and Limoges China, Crummles, Limoges, Ronald Smith Enamels, and Salamander Bells. Art tiles by "Tales in Tiles."

Shipping anywhere in the continental US via UPS. Visa, Mastercard and American Express accepted.

WASHINGTON

THE STENCILED GOOSE

1714 Canyon Rd.
P.O. Box 1510
Ellensburg, WA 98926

PHONE: (509)925-9494
FLORAL: (509)925-4149

Open Daily Hours: 8:00-8:00

The most unique gift and espresso shop on the West Coast featuring Ellensburg's own "Majestic Coffee." Offering a full service floral shop specializing in "English Garden" arrangements. Featuring specialty items produced in the Pacific Northwest. Plan a visit the first week in November for an "Elegant Christmas Open House" featuring: Cat's Meow Houses, Lizzie High Dolls, Muffybears, Attic Babies, Daddy's Long Legs and Thomas Kinkade graphics.

All major credit cards accepted. Layaways and shipping available. Free gift wrapping.

Located in the center of the state of Washington, exit 109 off Interstate 90.

THE VILLAGE SHOPPE

1444 Cole St.
Enumclaw, WA 98022

PHONE: (206)825-6481

Monday-Saturday: 10:00-5:30

Tom Clark Gnomes, Lilliput Lane, Dept. 56, ANRI, Lucy & Me, Sarah's Attic, Deja Vu, Cherished Teddies, Maud Humphrey Bogart, Laura's Attic, Imhoff's Homestead Life, Largo, Mill Creek, Seagull Pewter, Duncan Royale, Royal Copenhagen, Bing & Grondahl, Crystal Fantasy, Thimbles, German Nutcrackers and Beer Steins, Goebel's Rockwell and Crystal, Bear Creek, Designs Americana, Margaret Furlong Designs, Napoleon, Roman, Inc., Fontanini, Spode, Royal Worcester, and United Design.

Visa, Mastercard, American Express accepted. Layaways welcome. Phone and mail orders accepted. Some Redemption Certificates honored.

ANDERSEN'S CHINA, CRYSTAL, SILVER

1480 Northwest Gilman Blvd.
Issaquah, WA 98027

PHONE: (206)392-4462
(800)541-1241

Monday-Saturday: 10:00-6:00
Sunday: 12:00-5:00

Representing all major china, silver, crystal and collectors plates. Plates include M.I. Hummel, Goebel Miniatures, Royal Doulton, Royal Copenhagen, Bing & Grondahl, Spode, Belleek, Villeroy & Boch, Lenox, Lalique, Wedgwood, Fitz & Floyd, Gorham, Schmid, Haviland, International Silver, Pickard, Reed & Barton, Rosenthal, Royal Worcester.

All major credit cards accepted. Layaway and shipping available. Secondary Market Dealer. Redemption Center.

TANNENBAUM SHOPPE

217 8th St., P.O. Box 129
Leavenworth, WA 98826

PHONE: (509)548-7014

Open Daily Summer Hours: 9:00-5:00
Winter Hours: 11:00-4:00

Dept. 56, John Hine, Wee Forest Folk, Tom Clark, Precious Moments, Hummel, Lladro, Swarovski, Olszewski Miniatures, Cat's Meow, Maud Humphrey, Cherished Teddies, ANRI, Authorized Bradford Dealer Member, Walt Disney Classics Collection.

Leavenworth's Showcase of Fine Collectibles. Christmas all year round!

Visa and Mastercard accepted. NALED and GCC member.

WASHINGTON

JANSEN FLOWERS & GIFT GALLERY

1052 Washington Way
Longview, WA 98632

PHONE: (206)423-0450
FAX: (206)425-4271

Monday-Friday: 8:00-7:00
Saturday: 8:00-6:00; Sunday: 12:00-5:00

Collector plates: Bradford, Reco, Artaffects and Hamilton. Dept. 56 Showcase Dealer, All God's Children, Miss Martha's Originals, Lilliput Lane, David Winter, M.I. Hummel, Krystonia, Memories of Yesterday, Maud Humphrey, Swarovski, and Precious Moments.

Major credit cards accepted. NALED member. Layaway available. Club Redemptions.

COUNTRY TYME GIFTS

316 S. Main
Montesano, WA 98563

PHONE: (206)249-5588

Monday-Saturday: 10:00-6:00
Sunday: 12:00-4:00

Dept. 56, Maud Humphrey, Snowbabies, Cherished Teddies, Calico Kittens, Glynda Turley Prints, Precious Moments accessories, Enesco Treasury of Christmas Ornaments, Little Cheesers, Lincoln County Garden Club, Miss Martha's, and Sports Impressions.

Visa and Mastercard accepted. Layaway and shipping available. Free coffee. Gift wrapping available.

ACCENTS

222 Capital Way N.
Olympia, WA 98501

PHONE: (206)352-9951

Monday-Friday: 10:00-6:00
Saturday: 10:00-5:00; Sunday: 12:00-4:00

Lilliput Lane, Armani, Tom Clark Gnomes, Cairn Studios, Sarah's Attic, Flambro, Mark Hopkins Bronzes, and Fenton.

Doll Lines include: Goetz, Middleton and Dynasty.

Visa and Mastercard accepted. Layaway and shipping available. Redemption Center for Armani, Lilliput Lane, Tom Clark Gnomes and Sarah's Attic. Homemade fudge, espresso and deli bar.

ANDRE'S FINE GIFTS

228 W. First St. Suite P
Port Angeles, WA 98362

PHONE: (800)525-2429
FAX: (206)457-3647

Open Daily: 10:00-5:30

Cairn, Carriage House, David Winter, Fenton, Goebel, Harbour Lights, Hudson Pewter, Chilmark, Lladro, Maruri, Krystonia, M.I. Hummel, Sandicast, Swarovski, WACO, and Windstone.

Daily UPS shipping. Discover, Visa, Mastercard, and American Express accepted on phone orders.

Thank You--Orders are appreciated!

WASHINGTON

SLUYS GIFTS

18924 Front St. NE
Poulsbo, WA 98370

PHONE: (206)779-7171
FAX: (206)779-8204

Daily: 9:00-6:00; Sunday: 11:00-5:00

Hummels, Goebel Miniatures, ANRI, DeGrazia, Hudson, Maruri, Harbour Lights, Maud Humphrey, David Winter, Jon Herbert, Chilmark, Miss Martha, North American Bears, Raikes, Breyer, Roman, Ron Lee, Steinbach, C. Ulbricht and Erzgebirge Nutcrackers, Gorham, Victoria Impex, Lee Middleton and Zook Dolls, Emmett Kelly Sr./Grossman, Beatrix Potter, German steins, Matryoshkas, Toys, and Hand & Hammer.

A fun store to shop located on the shores of Liberty Bay in Downtown Poulsbo. Come listen to their glorious Porter music box.

SERENDIPITY GIFTS & COLLECTIBLES

South Hill Mall
3500 S. Meridian #830
Puyallup, WA 98373

PHONE: (206)770-1990

Monday-Friday: 10:00-9:00
Saturday: 10:00-7:00; Sunday: 11:00-6:00

Personal service in collectibles! Authorized Bradford Dealer, Swarovski, Lladro, Hummel, Chilmark, Lilliput Lane, David Winter, All God's Children, Sarah's Attic, Lee Middleton and Ashton-Drake dolls, Walt Disney Classics Collection, Rick Cain sculptures, Thomas Kinkade prints, Tom Clark Gnomes, Tim Wolfe "Tracks," Armani, Pocket Dragons, and Dept. 56.

Visa, Mastercard and Discover. Layaway. Shipping anywhere in the continental U.S. Redemption Center for most of the above lines.

THE PLATE HUTCH

15001 Military Rd. South
Seattle, WA 98188

PHONE: (206)241-8114
(206)833-4922

Thursday-Sunday: 12:00-6:00

ANNA-PERENNA, Goebel, Bradford, Hamilton, Bing & Grondahl, Royal Copenhagen, Reco, Pemberton & Oakes, Jan Hagara, Royal Doulton, Edna Hibel, Artaffects, Ebeling & Reuss, Schmid, Enesco, Roman, American Artists, Artists of the World, Kaiser, Bossons, Bareuther, Porsgrund, Henrikson, Arabia, Lenox, Pickard, Ron Lee, Dave Grossman, Duncan Royale, Hadley Company, Tri-Par, Willitts, and Miss Martha Originals. Also decorative display items such as hangers, frames and doll cases from Bard's and Lynette Decor.

Visa and Mastercard accepted. Layaway and shipping available. In business since 1977. Will do seek-and-search for retired pieces. Redemption Center.

WATERFRONT LANDMARK

1101 Alaskan Way-Pier 55
Seattle, WA 98101

PHONE: (206)622-3939

Open 7 Days A Week

Located on Seattle's Central Waterfront. LEGENDS fine art sculpture, Ron Lee Clowns, Hebron Metal Sculptures, Rick Cain Studios, Dept. 56, Cairn Studios, Sandicast, Vera Russell Pottery, Iris Arc, Summerhill Crystal, Silver Deer, Cast Art, J.H. Boone, Crystalite, Northwest Indian Carvings, Mayflower Glass, Big Sky Carvers, Sue Coleman, specimen sea shells, Mt. Saint Helens Art Glass.

All major credit cards accepted. Shipping and layaway available.

WASHINGTON

YE OLDE CURIOSITY SHOP

1001 Alaskan Way-Pier 54
Seattle, WA 98104-1028

PHONE: (206)682-5844
FAX: (206)682-4656

Open 7 Days A Week
Extended Summer Hours

Four generations of one family since 1899! Chilmark Showcase Dealer, Mark Hopkins Bronze Sculptures, C. Alan Johnson Eskimo figurines, Bossons Artware, Hopkins Shop Castles, Kachinas, Icons, Krystonia, Lomonosov Porcelain, Russian Matreshka Dolls and Lacquer Boxes, music boxes, Russian Fairy Tale Plates, one of a kind Northwestern Indian Masks, Totem poles and plaques, Alaskan and Northwestern Indian Baskets.

All major credit cards accepted. Layaway. Shipping.

CAROLS & CAROUSELS

West 621 Mallon
Spokane, WA 99201

PHONE: (509)326-6099

Monday-Saturday: 10:00-6:00
Friday: 10:00-9:00; Sunday: 12:00-5:00

Washington state's largest Dept. 56 Showcase Dealer: All Villages, Merry Makers, Snowbabies, and All Through the House. Also featuring M.I. Hummel, Possible Dreams Santas, Walt Disney Classics Collection, Byers' Choice, Swarovski, Iris Arc, Goebel Miniatures, Lilliput Lane, Steinbach and Christian Ulbricht Nutcrackers, Rinconada, Hidden Kingdom, Roosevelt Bears, Lee Middleton Dolls, Willitts Carousel Horses, Belsnickle, Lizzie High Dolls.

Visa, Mastercard, American Express and Discover accepted. Shipping and layaway available. Secondary Market Advisory.

Second Location: 2814 E 29th. Phone: (509)535-1364. 10-6 Monday-Saturday.

HALPIN'S

E. 11406 Sprague
Spokane, WA 99206

PHONE: (509)928-9500

9:00-10:00 Daily

Precious Moments (DSR), Hummels, Krystonia, Chilmark, Memories of Yesterday, Jan Hagara, Cherished Teddies, Laura's Attic, Calico Kittens, Snow Village, Snowbabies, Hallmark Keepsake Ornaments, Enesco Treasury of Christmas Ornaments, Possible Dreams Clothtique, Duncan Royale Santas, Ron Lee Clowns, Enesco Small World of Music, All God's Children, Walt Disney Classics Collection, Dreamsicles, North Pole Village, Maud Humphrey, Sports Impressions, Sisters & Best Friends, Maruri Eagles, Iris Arc Crystal Figurines, Raikes Bears, Sarah's Attic and Lizzie High Dolls.

THE CHALET COLLECTORS GALLERY

7024 27th St. West
Tacoma, WA 98466-5215

PHONE: (206)564-0326

Monday-Saturday: 10:00-6:00

This NALED Dealer specializes in plates, figurines, dolls and lithographs. Dept. 56 Villages, Snowbabies, Merry Makers. Enesco PM, MOY, Miss Martha's, Musicals. Large inventory of plates: Bradford, Hamilton, Reco, Danish Blue, American Artists, Artaffects, Hadley House, Moss, Gartlan, Hagara. David Winter, Lilliput Lane, M.I. Hummel, DeGrazia, Bergsma, Sarah's Attic, All God's Children, Tom Clark. Hudson Pewter, Nutcrackers. Display accessories. Dolls by Ashton-Drake and Hamilton Collection.

Visa and MC accepted. Layaway and shipping. GCC Member. Customer appreciation program.

WASHINGTON

THE CONNOISSEUR SHOP

8 Tacoma Ave. North
Tacoma, WA 98403

PHONE: (206)272-8282

Monday-Saturday: 10:00-5:30
Extended Holiday Hours

Armani, Designs Americana, Whitley Bay, Pocket Dragons, Snowbabies, Dept. 56 Villages, Merry Makers, dinnerware and collector plates, Muffy Bears.

Also featuring Firelight Glass Candles, Root Beeswax Candles, Blenko Glass Cosmetics and extensive greeting card collection. Come visit the shop that "warms your heart."

Visa, Mastercard and American Express accepted. Layaway and shipping available. Free gift wrapping.

THE GOLD SHOPPE'S COLLECTORS GALLERY

4020 South Steele St. Suite #103
Tacoma, WA 98409

PHONE: (800)457-8476
FAX: (206)473-9285

Monday-Friday: 10-7; Saturday: 10-5

Walt Disney Classics, Department 56: Dickens, North Pole, New England, Christmas In The City. Lilliput Lane Cottages, M.I. Hummel, Lladro, David Winter Cottages, Bradford Exchange, Enesco Treasury Ornaments, Annalee, and Precious Moments. Also featuring Animation Art from Warner Bros., Hanna-Barbera, Don Bluth, Walter Lantz, Toon Art, etc. Lithographs by Sandra Kuck, Terry Redlin, Donald Zolan, Ray Day, all Wild Wings, etc..

Specializing in custom framing.

Secondary Market Dealer. Visa, Mastercard, and American Express. NALED Dealer Member.

JOANS RAINBOW DOLLS

5428 S. Tacoma Way
Tacoma, WA 98409

PHONE: (800)582-3655
(206)474-9505
FAX: (206)474-7611

Wednesday-Friday: 9:30-5:00
Saturday: 10:00-4:00

Dolls: Barbie, Madame Alexander, and Ginnys Dolls, Dolls by Pauline, Kewpies, Ethnic Dolls, Annette Himstedt, Heartline, Shirley Temple, Raggedy Ann and Andy, Muffy VanderBears. Hallmark ornaments and other fine collectibles. The largest doll shop in the NW. We have 5,000 square feet of dolls.

All major credit cards accepted. Both layaway and shipping are available.

NATALIA'S COLLECTIBLES

19949 130th N.E.
Woodinville, WA 98072

PHONE: (206)481-4575

Tuesday-Saturday: 10:00-7:00

Primary Lines include: Ashton-Drake, Hamilton, Gorham, Georgetown and Paradise Gallery Dolls. Knowles, Hamilton, W.S. George, Perillo, Reco, and all other lines of limited edition plates. Thomas Kinkade, Redlin, Donald Zolan, Sandra Kuck, and Hibel limited prints. Sarah's Attic, Maud Humphrey, Jan Hagara, Rockwell and Cherished Teddies figurines.

NALED member. Layaway program. Secondary Market on all lines carried and full line Bradford Exchange Dealer.

WASHINGTON/WEST VIRGINIA

STEFAN'S EUROPEAN GIFTS

Track 29, 1 West Yakima Ave.
Yakima, WA 98902

PHONE: (509)457-5503

Monday-Saturday: 10:00-6:00
Sunday: 12:00-5:00

All God's Children, M.I. Hummel, Bradford plates, Ashton-Drake, Fontanini, Lilliput Lane, Old World Christmas, Steinbach, Ulbricht, and Erzgebirge Nutcrackers. Extensive German and Russian Collectibles.

NALED member. Visa and Mastercard accepted. Layaways. Free shipping. Secondary Market on plates.

ADAMS FINE GIFTS & COLLECTIBLES

Huntington Mall
Barboursville, WV 25504

PHONE: (304)733-0719
(800)926-0719

Monday-Saturday: 10:00-9:00
Sunday: 12:00-6:00

Cat's Meow Villages, Tom Clark Gnomes, Bradford Exchange, All God's Children, Disney Collection, Shelia's, Gartlan, Salvino, Sports Impressions, Chilmark, Hallmark Ornaments, Precious Moments, Lilliput Lane, David Winter, Harbour Lights, P. Buckley Moss plates and ornaments, Wee Forest Folk, Snowbabies, North Pole Village by Enesco, Lizzie High, Memories of Yesterday, Cherished Teddies, Miss Martha's, Swarovski, Dept. 56 Villages, and Hummel.

Free UPS shipping on orders over $30.00.

*TIS THE SEASONS

213 South St.
Bluefield, WV 24701

PHONE: (304)325-8360

Monday-Friday: 9:00-5:30
Saturday: 10:00-4:00

Whatever the reason it is the season for that special collectible from *Tis The Seasons. Featuring Ashton-Drake dolls, Annalee Mobilitee, Cat's Meow Village, Cherished Teddies, Gail Laura, Ladie and Friends, Middleton Dolls and Playmobile toys.

Secondary Market Service. All major credit cards welcome. Layaway and shipping available.

ADAMS FINE GIFTS & COLLECTIBLES

1046 Charleston Town Center
Charleston, WV 25389

PHONE: (304)345-7017
(800)765-4623

Monday-Saturday: 10:00-9:00
Sunday: 12:30-5:30

Cat's Meow Villages, Shelia's, Tom Clark Gnomes, Swarovski, Hummel, Precious Moments, Lilliput Lane, David Winter, Harbour Lights, Annalee, Memories of Yesterday, P. Buckley Moss plates and ornaments, Wee Forest Folk, Snowbabies, North Pole Village by Enesco, Possible Dreams, Chilmark, Gartlan, Salvino, Sports Impressions, Hudson, Lizzie High, Miss Martha's, Disney Classics Collection, Bradford Exchange, and Cherished Teddies.

Free UPS shipping on orders over $30.00.

WEST VIRGINIA

REFLECTIONS OF JUDY
2825 Main St.
Hurricane, WV 25526
PHONE: (304)562-1027

Monday-Friday: 10-6; Thursday: 10-8
Saturday: 10-4

Located in a 115 year old house, featuring Maud Humphrey, Shelia's, Tom Clark Gnomes, Little Cheesers, Calico Kittens, Cherished Teddies, a large selection of rubber stamps and accessories, Yankee Candles, Ann Taylor graphics, Glynda Turley graphics, Dreamsicles, custom designed dried and silk flowers, handmade baskets, pottery, miniature flowers, fruits and vegetables, Mulberry Potpourri, and gift baskets.

Major credit cards accepted. Layaway. Shipping. Limited Secondary Market. Gift wrapping.

FIVE SISTERS GIFTS
315 W. Stephen St.
Martinsburg, WV 25401
PHONE: (304)263-0804

Monday-Wednesday: 10-6
Thursday-Saturday: 10-9; Sunday: 11-6

Collectibles: Cherished Teddies, Melody In Motion, Chilmark, Lilliput Lane, Pocket Dragons, Iris Arc, Beatrix Potter, Precious Moments, Snowbabies, Walt Disney Classics Collection, M.I. Hummel, David Winter, Lowell Davis, Victoria Ashlea, Kitty Cucumber, Daddy's Long Legs.

Also featuring custom gift baskets, fine crystal giftware, Seiko clocks, Linden clocks and greeting cards.

Visa, Mastercard, Discover and American Express. Layaway. Ship UPS daily. Secondary market dealer.

Specializing in personal service!

SHARON'S DOLLS
Rt. 1 Box 235 R
Martinsburg, WV 25401
PHONE: (304)267-4882

Tuesday-Saturday: 11:00-7:00

Located off Interstate 81, take exit 12 to Rt. 45, 2 miles west, Doll Cottage on right side. In business for 10 years, specializing in top original artist dolls and bears. Thousands to choose from: Himstedt, Barbies, GADCO, Turner, Linda Steele, Georgetown, Alexander, Linda Mason, Gorham, Good-Kruger, Wendy Lawton, Jerri, American Beauty, Goetz, Susan Wakeen, Middleton, Seymour Mann, Corolle, Robin Woods, Cindy McClure, Karen Heller, Terry Die, Yolanda Bello, Zook, Effanbee, Mattel, Ellenbrooke, World Doll, Gunzel, Janet Ness, Roche, Raikes, Steiff, Gorham and Wendy Brent Bears.

All major credit cards accepted. UPS shipping daily. Layaway plan available.

LITTLE PORTION TREASURES & BOOKS
1061 Market St.
Wheeling, WV 26003
PHONE: (304)233-5782

Monday-Saturday: 10:00-5:00

Little Portion, in business for 19 years, specializes in unique Nativity sets and religious art. Collectibles: Hummel, Olszewski, DeGrazia, Dept. 56, Amish Heritage, Roman, Duncan Royale, Miss Martha, Hagara, Humphrey, Hibel, Harbour Lights, Lilliput, and Precious Moments. Plates: Bradford, Hamilton, Reco. Dolls: Ashton-Drake, Georgetown, Hamilton. Fenton, Marty, Sandicast, Perillo, and wildlife art including Mill Creek, Neil Rose, Castagna.

Collectible redemptions. Secondary market for Bradford and Precious Moments. UPS. Free gift wrapping. Layaway. Visa/MC/Discover.

WISCONSIN

MAXINE'S CARDS & GIFTS

101 Front St.
Beaver Dam, WI 53916

PHONE: (414)887-7330

Monday-Saturday: 9:00-5:00
Friday: 9:00-8:00

Their specialty is collectibles. Bradford plates and dolls, M.I. Hummel, Precious Moments, Swarovski Crystal, Dept. 56 Villages and Snowbabies, Laura's Attic, David Winter Cottages, Sports Impressions, Neil Rose Indian items, beer steins, Cherished Teddies and many other collectibles.

Redemption Center for clubs. Mastercard, Visa and Discover accepted. NALED member. Layaway and shipping available.

COLLECTIBLES ETC., INC.

8362 N. 49th St.
Brown Deer, WI 53223-3696

**PHONE: (414)355-4545
(800)558-5594**

Monday-Saturday: Open at 10:00

All older and current: Precious Moments, collector plates, Ashton-Drake dolls, Hamilton dolls, Zolan, P. Buckley Moss, Terry Redlin, Maruri USA. Other lines include: ANRI, B & G/ RC, Danbury Mint, Schmid, VF Fine Arts, Walt Disney Classics Collection, PenDelfin, Jan Hagara, Incolay, M.I. Hummel, Hibel, Goebel, Hutschenreuther, Dave Grossman Creations, and many other artists and collectible items too numerous to mention.

NALED dealer and Bradford Exchange member. Visa, Mastercard and Discover accepted. Layaway Available. Ship Worldwide.

Call before visiting. They expect to be moving to a new location.

COUNTRY TREASURES

216 N. Bridge St.
Chippewa Falls, WI 54729

**PHONE: (715)723-8883
FAX: (715)723-4574**

Mon., Tues., Wed., Fri.: 9:00-5:30
Thursday: 9:00-8:30
Saturday: 9:00-5:00; Sunday: 12:00-4:30

Dept. 56 Showcase Dealer, Precious Moments (DSR), Cairn Studios, David Winter Cottages, Sarah's Attic, Cherished Teddies, Laura's Attic, Maud Humphrey Bogart, Raikes Bears, Byers' Choice, Muffy VanderBear, Snowbabies, Winter Silhouette, All Thru the House, Dickens plates, Merry Makers, Sandicast, Dreamsicles, United Design, Hallmark, Enesco ornaments and musicals, Possible Dreams Santas, Cat's Meow, Sports Impressions, Middleton Dolls, and Daddy's Long Legs.

Mastercard, Visa and American Express accepted.

THE CHRISTMAS HOUSE

519 E. Wall St./P.O. Box 1267
Eagle River, WI 54521

PHONE: (715)479-4944

Monday-Saturday: 10-5; Sunday: 11-3

Byers' Choice, Dept. 56: Snow, Dickens', New England, and Christmas in the City Village, Merry Makers, All Through the House, Snowbabies, Fontanini, Duncan Royale, United Design, Annalee, RC/ B & G plates, Hummel, Kitty Cucumber, Beatrix Potter, Lynn Haney and Possible Dreams Santas, C. Radko, Old World Christmas, Goebel Miniatures, MOY, P. Buckley Moss, Enesco Treasury Ornaments, PM, KSA, Midwest, Roman, and Dreamsicles.

Visit The Wood Shed next door featuring collectibles and unique decorative items: WACO, Lizzie High, LEGENDS, Michael Garman, Tom Clark Gnomes, Tom Tabor decoys, T. Redlin, S. Zoellick, D. Koetzke.

Visa, Mastercard and Discover accepted. Free gift wrapping. Shipping available.

WISCONSIN

KRISTMAS KRINGLE SHOPPE

15-17 Court St.
Fond du Lac, WI 54935
PHONE: (414)923-8210
FAX: (414)923-8207

Mon., Wed., .Fri.: 8:00-9:00
Tues., Thurs., Sat.: 8:00-5:00

Showcase dealer for all Dept 56, Snowbabies, Hummel, Swarovski, David Winter, Lilliput Lane, Byers' Choice, Annalee, Wee Forest Folk, Fontanini, Steinbach, Schmid Disney, United Design Santas, Memories of Yesterday, Krystonia, and Christopher Radko, Cherished Teddies, Cat's Meow, Enesco Musicals, Little Cheesers, and Possible Dreams Santas.

All major credit cards accepted. Layaway available. Open all year round!

KRIDER PHARMACY & GIFTS

Marquette Center
1119 W. Mason St.
Green Bay, WI 54303
PHONE: (414)499-1381

Monday-Friday: 9:00-8:00
Saturday: 9:00-5:00

Dept. 56 Houses, Snowbabies, All Thru the House. Collector plates including Reco Bradford and Hollywood. Dolls including Ashton-Drake and Lexington. Precious Moments, Hummel, Swarovski, Cherished Teddies, Rockwell, Emmett Kelly, Tom Clark Gnomes, Fenton Glassware, David Winter Cottages, Maud Humphrey, Music Boxes, Gund Bears, decorative glassware and accessories. Nice giftware in all price ranges.

Visa and Mastercard accepted. Shipping available. 30/60 day layaway plan. Redemption Center for Swarovski and Precious Moments.

Something for everyone!

P.J.'S COLLECTIBLES
AND CHRISTMAS TOO!

B2225 Port Plaza Mall
Green Bay, WI 54301
PHONE: (414)437-3443

Monday-Friday: 10:00-9:00
Saturday: 10:00-6:00; Sunday: 11:00-5:00

Green Bays's premier collectible store. Dept. 56 Showcase Dealer, ANRI, Walt Disney Classics Collection, Lladro, Bradford Exchange, Precious Moments, Swarovski, Iris Arc, M.I. Hummel, Gartlan, MOY, Maud Humphrey, Lilliput Lane, Chilmark, Cherished Teddies, David Winter, Lowell Davis, Duncan Royale, All God's Children, EKJ, Krystonia, LEGENDS, Sports Impressions, Calico Kittens, Ashton-Drake, Rockwell, Malcolm Cooper, Snowbabies, Thomas Kinkade, Old World Christmas, Christopher Radko, Tom Clark, Nutcrackers, plates, dolls, figurines and more. Redemption Center. Layaway and shipping. Major credit cards accepted.

SOUKUP ENTERPRISES

2181 S. Oneida
Green Bay, WI 54304
PHONE: (414)498-3655

Monday-Friday: 9:00-5:00
Wednesday: 9:00-8:00
Saturday: 9:00-2:00

Green Bay's Most Unique Gift Shop Handling: Dept. 56, Duncan Royale, Precious Moments, Goebel Inc., M.I. Hummel, Lilliput Lane, Lladro, Possible Dreams, Charles Sadek, ANRI, Lissi, Raikes, Steinbach, Lowell Davis, Beatrix Potter, Effanbee, Maud Humphrey Bogart, Nahrgang Collection, Schmid, Dynasty Dolls, plus many other unique dolls. Gund and other plush animals, women's and children's apparel, silk floral, 14k jewelry, and unique lines of collectible santas.

WISCONSIN

XMAS PAST

7287 Hwy. 51
Hazelhurst, WI 54531

PHONE: (715)356-4553

Monday-Saturday: 9:00-5:00
Sunday: 9:00-4:00

Xmas Past carries many collectible lines and also a complete line of Christmas decorations, Christopher Radko, Possible Dreams, Old World Christmas, Byers' Choice, Steinbach, Snowbabies by Dept. 56. Midwest Importers Santas, Nutcrackers and Smokers. Flambro Clowns/Emmett Kelly Jr. and Wisconsin's largest display of Dept. 56 Heritage and Snow Village Houses.

Mastercard, Visa, Discover and American Express accepted. Secondary Market Service.

LASTING IMPRESSIONS

1127 Cass St.
La Crosse, WI 54601

**PHONE: (800)658-9089
(608)784-7201
FAX: (608)785-0004**

Monday-Friday: 10:00-5:00
Saturday: 10:00-4:00
Extended Holiday Hours

Dept. 56 Villages, Snowbabies, Swarovski, Lladro, David Winter, Maud Humphrey, Cherished Teddies, Calico Kittens, Emmett Kelly, Precious Moments, Goebel Olszewski Miniatures, ANRI, Hummel, Lowell Davis, DeGrazia, Duncan Royale, Bradford Dealer, and much more.

Mastercard, Visa and Discover accepted. Free UPS shipping for orders over $100.

ARTISAN GIFT SHOPPE, LTD.

4116 Monona Dr.
Madison, WI 53716

PHONE: (608)221-3200

Monday-Friday: 9:30-8:30
Saturday: 9:30-5:00

Authorized Bradford dealer, Hollywood Dealer, Hamilton, Reco, Terry Redlin, Sandra Kuck and Perillo plates, David Winter and Lilliput Cottages, Dept. 56: Snow Village, Dickens, New England, Alpine, Christmas in the City and Snowbabies. Madame Alexander and Pauline Dolls, Tom Clark Gnomes, Precious Moments, Hummel, Lladro, Golden Memories, Byers' Choice, Possible Dreams, Maruri Birds and Eagles, and Disney Collectibles.

Collector's Club Membership. All credit cards accepted.

DON'S HALLMARK SHOPS

3009 Perry St.
Madison, WI 53713

PHONE: (608)274-3595

Hallmark Galleries, Dept. 56, Precious Moments, David Winter, Hummels, Lilliput Lane, Enchantica, Sadek Birds, Disney Classics, Maruri, Sandicast, Lladro, Memories of Yesterday, Enesco musicals, Dickens Village, Christmas in the City, New England Village, Alpine Village, Snow Village, North Pole Collection and Snowbabies.

Mastercard, Visa and Discover accepted. Free gift wrapping. UPS shipping available.

WISCONSIN

GREEN TREE GIFTS & COLLECTABLES

831 South 8th St.
Manitowoc, WI 54220
PHONE: (414)684-4300

Monday & Friday: 9:00-8:00
Tues., Wed., Thurs.: 9:00-5:00
Saturday: 9:00-4:00; Sunday: 12:00-4:00

Bradford Exchange plates, Precious Moments, Memories of Yesterday, Hummel, Rockwell, Ashton-Drake dolls, Terry Redlin, Dept. 56 (Dickens, North Pole, Snowbabies), Country Cousins, Miss Martha's Originals, Cherished Teddies, and Krystonia.

Collector Club Redemption Center for Hummel, Memories of Yesterday, Precious Moments, and Krystonia. NALED member. Visa and Mastercard accepted. Free layaway. Secondary Market "on most lines."

RUSTIC TOUCH

Shopko Plaza
3315 Calumet Ave.
Manitowoc, WI 54220
PHONE: (414)684-0889

Monday-Friday: 10:00-9:00
Saturday: 10:00-5:00; Sunday: 12:00-5:00

All Dept. 56 lines, Precious Moments, Memories of Yesterday, Hummel, David Winter, Lilliput Lane, Swarovski, Krystonia, Little Cheesers, Christopher Radko, Chilmark, Enesco Musicals, Cherished Teddies, Middleton dolls, Dreamsicles, Denise Calla, Byers' Choice, Anheuser-Busch, Band Creations, Cat's Meow, Clay Art, Duncan Royale, Emmett Kelly Jr., J.H. Boone, Margaret Furlong Designs, Maruri USA, Old World, Roman Inc., Sports Impressions, plates, extensive giftware selection, crystal, and frames.

Major credit cards accepted. GCC Member. Shipping and layaway available.

BEAUCHENE'S LIMITED EDITIONS

400 N. Main St. P.O. Box 461
Mequon-Thiensville, WI 53092
PHONE: (414)242-0170
FAX: (414)242-7399

Monday-Saturday: 10-6; Sunday: 12-4

Bradford Exchange, Ashton-Drake and all other dolls, Lowell Davis, Maud Humphrey, Lilliput Lane, Snow Village, Dept. 56 Heritage Villages, Snowbabies, Precious Moments, Hummels, Sarah's Attic, Miss Martha's Collection, Enesco and C. Radko Ornaments, United Design, Cherished Teddies, PenniBears, Swarovski Crystal, Jan Hagara, Enchantica, MOY, Sports Impressions, Thomas Kinkade prints, Terry Redlin, Marty Bell, Edna Hibel, LEGENDS, Walt Disney Classics Collection, Armani, Calico Cats, Laura's Attic.

Visa, Mastercard and Discover accepted. NALED member. Layaway, mail order specialty, gift wrap. Club Redemptions.

A COUNTRY MOUSE GIFTS & COLLECTIBLES

7940 W. Layton Ave.
Milwaukee, WI 53220
PHONE: (414)281-4210

Monday-Friday: 10:00-7:00
Saturday: 10:00-5:00

Southwest side, just off I-894, where collectors get service. Precious Moments (DSR), Bradford plate dealer, Dept. 56. Villages and Snowbabies, Lizzie High wood dolls, Cat's Meow, Memories of Yesterday, Cherished Teddies, Calico Kitty, David Winter, Lilliput Lane, Pocket Dragons, Iris Arc, Armani, M.I. Hummel, Byer's Choice, Ashton-Drake dolls, Chilmark, Emmett Kelly Jr., Enesco ornaments, and Krystonia.

Redemption Center for most collector clubs. Mastercard and Visa accepted.

WISCONSIN

MADER'S TOWER GALLERY

1041 N. Old World 3rd St.
Milwaukee, WI 53203

**PHONE: (414)271-1911
(800)558-7171**

Open 7 Days A Week: 11:00-9:00

Mader's has been serving the collectors since the early 1970's. Lines include: Lladro Vanguard Dealer, Lowell Davis, Maruri, LEGENDS Heritage Dealer, Enesco music boxes, M.I. Hummel plates and figurines, Swarovski Crystal, Armani, Bing & Grondahl, Royal Copenhagen, Limited Edition prints such as Robert Bateman, Carl Brenders, Bradley Parrish, Paul Calle, Owen Gromme, Terry Redlin, Thomas Kinkade and others.

Secondary Market service in figurines, graphics and plates. Club Redemption Center. Financing available. Major credit cards accepted. Shipping in U.S.

MRS. LACKOVICH'S CHRISTMAS HOUSE

P.O. Box 610
600 1st Street
Newglarus, WI 53574

PHONE: (608)527-5106

Open 7 Days A Week: 9:00-5:00

Dept. 56 Villages, Snowbabies, All Thru the House, Merry Makers; Lilliput Lane, Byers' Choice, Disney, All God's Children, Miss Martha's, Maud Humphrey, Cherished Teddies, Duncan Royale, Christopher Radko, David Winter, Dreamsicles, Gorham, Midwest, Old World, Possible Dreams, Roman, Kurt Adler.

GCC Member. Mastercard and Visa accepted.

PINE CREEK COLLECTIBLES

110 W. Wisconsin Ave.
Oconomowoc, WI 53066

PHONE: (414)567-9766

Tuesday-Friday: 10:00-5:00
Saturday: 10:00-4:00; Sunday: 12:00-4:00

Located 30 miles West of Milwaukee. Dept. 56: Snow Village, Merry Makers, Winter Silhouette, All Through the House; Thomas Kinkade, Wee Forest Folk, Lilliput Lane, Sarah's Attic, Christopher Radko Ornaments, Lowell Davis, Harbour Lights, Cherished Teddies, Calico Kittens, Memories of Yesterday, Laura's Attic, Possible Dreams, Fenton Glass, Maruri, Hidden Kingdom, Old World Ornaments, Emmett Kelly, Jr., Shelia's.

Mastercard and Visa accepted. Shipping available. Layaway. Redemption Center.

KIE'S PHARMACY AND GIFTS

1210 N. Green Bay Rd.
Racine, WI 53406

**PHONE: (414)886-8160
FAX: (414)886-8160**

Monday-Friday: 8:30-9:00
Saturday: 8:30-6:00; Sunday: 9:00-5:00

M.I. Hummel, Jan Hagara, Precious Moments, Memories of Yesterday, Snowbabies, Snow Village, Bradford, Krystonia, Sarah's Attic, Miss Martha's, Lilliput Lane, David Winter, Armani, Maruri, Edna Hibel, Sandra Kuck, Hudson, Chilmark, Golden Memories, All God's Children, Sports Impressions, Cherished Teddies. Bradford Dealer Member.

NALED Member. Mastercard and Visa accepted.

WISCONSIN

MILAEGER'S

4838 Douglas Ave.
Racine, WI 53402

PHONE: (414)639-2040
(800)669-1229
FAX: (414)639-1855

Monday-Friday: 9:00-8:00
Saturday: 9:00-5:00; Sunday: 9:30-5:00

A unique gift store featuring an outstanding assortment of collectibles. Dept. 56 Showcase Dealer (All Villages, Snowbabies, Merry Makers, All Thru the House, Winter Silhouettes), Byers' Choice Carolers, Steinbach Nutcrackers, House of Hatten: Denise Calla Collection. The most outstanding collection of Santas anywhere. Also Precious Moments, MOY, Cast Art Dreamsicles, Ladie and Friends, Lizzie High, Maruri, Fontanini, Castagna, Harbour Lights and Fraser Creations.

Redemption Center. Free shipping. Special orders welcome. Mastercard, Visa and Discover.

TANNENBAUM HOLIDAY SHOP

11054 Hwy. 42
Sister Bay, WI 54234

PHONE: (414)854-5004
FAX: (414)854-9285

Open Daily: 10:00-5:00

Dept. 56, Byers' Choice Carolers, Beatrix Potter, Steinbach, Christian Ulbricht, Old World Christmas, Denise Calla, Fontanini, Margaret Furlong, Cat's Meow, Christopher Radko, Dreamsicles, Kurt S. Adler, Midwest Importers, Possible Dreams, Roman Inc., Schmid, Silver Deer, United Design, Vaillancourt Folk Art.

Housed in a 100-year-old church in beautiful Door County. With 3,500 square feet displaying over 40 themed trees.

All major credit cards accepted. Layaways welcome.

RED CROSS GIFTS

122 Walnut St.
Spooner, WI 54801

PHONE: (715)635-2117
(800)344-9958
FAX: (715)635-8135

Monday-Saturday: 9:00-5:00

Dept. 56, Mark Klaus, Lladro, Hummel, ANRI, LEGENDS, Chilmark, Precious Moments, Maud Humphrey, DeGrazia, Swarovski, Ashton-Drake, MOY, Lowell Davis, Anheuser-Busch, ANNA-PERENNA, Artaffects, Artists of the World, Band Creations, Belleek, B & G, Bradford Exchange, Cairn Studio, Carlton, Cherished Teddies, Dreamsicles, Duncan Royale, Emmett Kelly Jr., Flambro, Gartlan USA, Dave Grossman Creations, Hallmark Keepsake Ornaments, John Hine Studios, Iris Arc Crystal, Jan Hagara, Land of Legend, Lilliput Lane, Maruri, Napoleon, Reco, Roman, RC, Sports Impressions, Walt Disney. Over 1,500 plates in stock!

THE GIFT TREE

2441 8th St. South
Wisconsin Rapids, WI 54494

PHONE: (715)424-2441

Mon., Tue., Wed., Sat.: 9:30-5:00
Thursday-Friday: 9:30-8:00
Sunday: 12:00-4:00

Bradford Exchange Dealer, Department 56 Showcase Dealer, Snowbabies and Winter Silhouette figurines, Lladro, Golden Memories, Swarovski, Waterford, Walt Disney Classics Collection, M.I. Hummel, Lowell Davis, Maruri, David Winter, Terry Redlin prints and plates, Lilliput Lane, Byers' Choice, Andrea by Sadek, De Grazia, Lena Liu plates and prints, Rick Cain Sculptures, Fontanini by Roman, Gorham Dolls, Victoria Impex, Gund, Steiff, Castagna figurines. B & G / Royal Copenhagen, Midwest Importers, Artists of the World and Dreamsicles.

Serving the collector for 20 years. Visa and Mastercard accepted. Layaway.

WYOMING/CANADA

LOVE'S GIFTS & OTHER THINGS

1402 Sheridan Ave.
Cody, WY 82414

PHONE: (307)587-2214

Monday-Saturday: 9:00-6:00
Summer Hours: Mon.-Sat. : 9:00-9:00

Precious Moments, Tom Clark, David Winter Cottages, Shoemaker's Houses, Cherished Teddies, Cairn Studio, Carlton, Cast Art, Clay Art, Fenton Art Glass, Hamilton Gifts, John Hine Studios, Lefton Village, Napoleon, Red Mill Mfg., Roman, United Design and Laura's Attic.

Visa, Mastercard and Discover accepted. UPS shipping. Secondary Market Service.

PAT'S HALLMARK SHOP

200 S. Gillette Ave.
Gillette, WY 82716

PHONE: (307)686-1296

Monday-Saturday: 8:30-5:30

Primary lines; Specializing in David Winter, Lilliput Lane, Precious Moments, Hummels, Jan Hagara, Memories of Yesterday, Sarah's Attic, LEGENDS, Chilmark, Hallmark Keepsake Ornaments, Cherished Teddies, Madame Alexander dolls, Jan Shackleford dolls and Dept. 56.

In business, serving the collector for 16 years! All major credit cards accepted. Redemption Center.

COLLECTORS TREASURE HOUSE LTD.

340-9737 MacLeod Trail South
Calgary, AB T2J 0P6

PHONE: (403)253-9586

Monday-Friday: 10:00-6:00
Saturday: 10:00-5:00

Bradford Exchange Dealer. Limited Edition Plates, Ashton-Drake Dolls, Maud Humphrey Bogart figurines, Cherished Teddies, and Trisha Romance figurines.

Visa and Mastercard accepted. Collectors Treasure House Ltd. has good luck finding Secondary Market plates.

THE COUNTRY SAMPLER

#173, 4211-106 St.
Edmonton, AB T6J 6L7

PHONE: (403)435-2013
FAX: (403)463-8829

Monday-Saturday: 10:00-6:00
Friday: 10:00-9:00; Sunday: 12:00-5:00

Golden Heart Store for Sarah's Attic, Star Dealer for Daddy's Long Legs, Cat's Meow Village, Byers' Choice Carolers, Dept. 56, Frumps, and Designs Americana. Also featuring country decorating accessories and pine furniture. Catalogs and price lists available for Sarah's Attic, Cat's Meow, and Daddy's Long Legs.

American Express, Mastercard and Visa accepted. Layaway and shipping available. Redemption Center for Sarah's Attic, Cat's Meow and Daddy's Long Legs.

CANADA

TOMORROW'S TREASURES

2 Main St.
Bobcaygeon, ONT K0M 1A0
PHONE: (705)738-2147

Summer Hours:
Monday-Saturday: 10:00-5:30
Sunday: 12:00-4:00
Winter Hours:
Same as Summer Hours; Closed Wednesdays and Month of February

"The Plate and Doll Place"

Authorized Bradford Exchange Dealer. Ashton-Drake dolls, Sandra Kuck, Terry Redlin, and Lena Liu lithos.

The largest dealer in Kawartha area. All major artists and suppliers available. Visa and Mastercard accepted. NALED Member. Secondary Market service on plates.

BRANDY TREE

White Oaks Mall
1105 Wellington Rd. S (Hwy. 401)
London, ONT N6E 1V4
PHONE: (519)681-3241 (STORE)
(519)652-6931 (OFFICE)
FAX: (519)652-6547 (OFFICE)

Monday-Saturday: 10-9:30; Sunday: 12-5

The largest Precious Moments dealer in Western Ontario and usually have in excess of 300 different Precious Moments figurines in stock. Other collectible lines include Cherished Teddies, Memories of Yesterday, Miss Martha's, Laura's Attic, Sports Impression, PenDelfin, Krystonia, Lilliput Lane, Dept. 56 (Heritage Village and Snowbabies), Myth and Magic, Bossons, Little Cheesers, Sandicast and Country Artists.

Visa, Mastercard, and American Express accepted. Secondary Market for PM and PenDelfin. PM special events on Mother's Day weekend.

OVER THE RAINBOW GALLERY OF COLLECTABLES

188 Queen St. South
Mississauga, ONT L5M 1L3
PHONE: (416)821-2131
FAX: (416)321-8449

Monday-Friday: 10-6; Saturday: 10-5
Sunday By Appointment Only

Plates: Reco, Winston Roland, Hamilton, Artaffects, Pemberton & Oakes, Hadley House, Kaiser, E. Hibel, Terry Redlin, Greg Perillo, Sandra Kuck, D. Zolan, Sherwood, F. Stone, Nori Peters, and S. DeVille. Figurines: MOY, PM, CT, SI, Gartlan USA, Bossons, Maud Humphrey, Treasured Memories, Jody Bergsma, DW, Myths & Magic Pewter by Tudor Mint, Michael's Ltd., Spode. Dolls: Dynasty, Ashton-Drake. Prints: T. Redlin, V.F. Fine Arts, Jody Bergsma. Also notecards by collectible artists.

Visa/MC/AE accepted. Layaway and shipping. NALED member.

CHORNYJS'-HADKE

884 Queen E.
Sault Ste. Marie, ONT P6A 2B4
PHONE: (705)253-0315
FAX: (705)949-6451

Monday-Saturday: 10:00-5:00
Friday: 10:00-7:30

Primary and Secondary collector plates, 1,500 on display; Dept. 56 including Snowbabies, Hummel, Precious Moments, Treasured Memories, Memories of Yesterday, Ashton-Drake dolls, Mats Jonasson, Emmett Kelly Jr., Country Artists. Limited Edition Lithos; Stone, Kuck etc. Plates: Bradford Exchange, Reco, Artaffects and Pemberton & Oakes. Wedgwood. Decorated eggs: Ukraine and Faberge styles.

Visa and Mastercard accepted. NALED member. Layaway. Secondary Market Dealer.

CANADA

SHANFIELDS-MEYERS JEWELLERY & CHINA

188 Ouellette Ave.
Windsor, ONT N9A 1A4

PHONE: (313)961-8435
FAX: (519)253-3355

Monday-Wednesday: 9-6
Thursday and Friday: 9-9; Sunday: 10-6

Tremendous selection of current and discontinued collector plates and figurines by Royal Doulton, Hummel, Precious Moments, ANRI, Beswick Crystal, Swarovski, Waterford, Lalique, Baccarat, Atlantis, and Gorham. Sterling, Silverplate, Stainless, and Flatware Silver and Tea Services. Best brands of dinnerware with over 2,000 patterns. Current and discontinued dolls, paperweights, thimbles, and Christmas ornaments. Reasonable Secondary Market prices.

Visa, Mastercard, and Am. Express accepted. Layaways and shipping. Bridal registry. Secondary Market Service.

YORKTON PLATE GALLERY

316 Broadway West
Yorkton, SASK S3N 0N6

PHONE: (306)783-2171
FAX: (306)786-7723

Daily: 10:00-6:00; Thursday: 10:00-9:00

Collectibles of all kinds! Plates from the Bradford Exchange, D.H. Ussher, Prairie Images, Frederick Dickson, Buckhorn, Hadley House, Hamilton, dolls, original paintings, lithos, figurines, coins, frames, and sport collectibles.

Active secondary market. Major credit cards accepted. Layaway plan. Mail order service

Index

HOW TO USE THIS INDEX WITH KEY TO STATES

Sample: ❶   ❷

All God's Children, 11, 54, 62, 69, 73, 79, 108, 114, 152, 169, 214, 221

❶ Manufacturer / Collectible Line / Artist
❷ Page: See "Key To States" (below)
(Page 11 indicates a retailer in California, Page 54 indicates a retailer in Florida, etc.)

—A—

A Childs Memory Collection, 238
Accessories, 10-12, 25, 27, 32-33, 36, 38-39, 45, 48-49, 61, 63, 67, 74, 80-82, 84, 88, 96, 100, 106, 113, 119, 129, 131, 134, 135, 137, 153, 157, 162, 170, 179, 182-183, 213, 224, 248, 251, 253, 258
Adagio, 45
Adams, Herman, 70
Adler, Kurt S., 11, 14-15, 23, 30, 41-42, 44, 57, 87, 89, 91-92, 96, 102-103, 105, 111, 113, 119-121, 132, 137, 143, 152, 153, 161-163, 169, 172-173, 175-176, 180-182, 184-185, 188, 192, 194, 197, 198, 200, 207, 211, 214-215, 217, 220, 222, 225, 240, 242-243, 252, 256-257; See also Collectible Santas, Nutcrackers
Adorables, 13, 104, 168, 173, 206, 233
Akinson, Mike, 234
Albee, Rick, 26

All God's Children, 1-3, 7-8, 10-12, 14, 16-18, 21-29, 32-40, 42, 44-47, 49-52, 54-56, 59-69, 71-77, 79, 85, 87-90, 92, 96, 98-100, 102-103, 106-108, 110, 112-116, 119, 126, 130, 136-137, 139, 141-143, 145, 147, 150-152, 154-155, 158-162, 164-170, 172-176, 178, 180, 183, 185, 187-191, 193-195, 197-203, 206, 208-212, 214, 216, 218-224, 226-237, 239, 241-244, 246-248, 250, 253, 256; See also Miss Martha's Originals
All That Jazz and On Cue, 79, 109
Alva Museum Replicas, 96
Amaranth Productions, 217
American Artists, 45, 53, 58, 127, 161, 247-248
American Bear Co., 1, 53-55, 80, 132, 136, 172, 183, 197, 199, 234, 244, 247
American Beauty, 227, 251
American Greetings, 83, 101

KEY TO STATES

AL: 1-3	**DE:** 46	**IA:** 95-98	**MN:** 136-142	**NM:** 159-160	**RI:** 214-215	**VA:** 239-243
AK: 3	**FL:** 47-61	**KS:** 98-100	**MS:** 142-143	**NY:** 160-172	**SC:** 215-218	**WA:** 244-250
AZ: 4-7	**GA:** 61-70	**KY:** 100-101	**MO:** 143-147	**NC:** 172-180	**SD:** 218-220	**WV:** 250-251
AR: 7-8	**HA:** 70	**LA:** 101-104	**MT:** 147-148	**ND:** 180-181	**TN:** 220-226	**WI:** 252-257
CA: 8-37	**ID:** 70-71	**ME:** 104-105	**NE:** 148-150	**OH:** 181-193	**TX:** 226-237	**WY:** 258
CO: 37-39	**IL:** 71-85	**MD:** 106-110	**NV:** 150	**OK:** 193-195	**UT:** 237-238	**CANADA:**
CT: 40-46	**IN:** 86-95	**MA:** 111-115	**NH:** 151	**OR:** 196-200	**VT:** 238	258-260
		MI: 115-135	**NJ:** 152-159	**PA:** 201-214		

American Indian Art, 22, 188
Amish Heritage Collection, 7, 39, 88, 96, 152, 157, 189, 192, 220
Andrea by Sadek, 1, 5, 7, 9, 12, 22, 26, 31, 37-38, 59-60, 70, 78, 81, 97, 106, 121, 134-135, 140, 142, 152-153, 156, 161-162, 165, 180, 193-194, 226, 230-231, 233, 236, 253, 257; See also Sadek
Angel Babies, 62
Angels, 12, 52, 65-66, 93, 104, 118, 123, 125, 142-143, 174, 180, 187-188, 196, 199, 220, 232, 239-240
Anheuser-Busch, 1, 7, 13, 15, 43-44, 48, 54-55, 57, 63, 65, 70-72, 81, 83, 87, 89, 91, 93, 97, 101, 106-107, 109, 124, 126, 143-144, 147, 156, 161, 163-165, 168, 176, 183, 185, 188-190, 201-202, 207, 208, 212, 221, 226, 239, 242, 255, 257
Animal Antics, 121
Animation Art from Warner Bros., 249
ANNA-PERENNA, 16, 54, 88, 162, 168, 184, 189-190, 198, 247, 257; See also P. Buckley Moss
Annalee Mobilitee Dolls, 2, 6, 8, 14-15, 17, 20-23, 26, 28 29, 32-33, 35, 41-42, 44-47, 49-55, 57, 61-62, 67-68, 71, 73, 77-81, 85, 87, 98-101, 105, 108-109, 111-115, 118, 120-121, 124, 126, 131-132, 139, 141, 143, 145, 147, 149, 151-153, 155, 157-158, 161, 164-166, 168-169, 173-174, 176, 179, 184, 187, 191-193, 195-199, 202-203, 207, 209-210, 212, 217-219, 221-222, 225, 228, 234, 236, 239-240, 243, 249-250, 252-253
ANRI, 2, 6-7, 16, 18, 28, 30, 33, 37, 40, 43, 45, 47, 53-55, 58, 61, 74, 76-79, 82-83, 87-88, 91-98, 100, 102, 112, 115, 119-120, 134, 136, 138, 140, 146-147, 149, 153-154, 162-163, 165, 167-168, 173, 176, 178-179, 181-182, 184-185, 190, 195-196, 198-199, 202, 209, 211-214, 217, 219, 225, 228-229, 232-233, 236, 244-245, 247, 252-254, 257, 260
Antiques, 29, 43, 88, 118, 176

Applause, 169, 180
Archer, Linda, 13
Ardleigh & Elliott Musicals, 9, 48, 58, 82, 85, 101, 110, 129, 133, 150, 162, 184, 195, 206
Armani, 2-7, 9-12, 14-17, 21-23, 27-33, 35, 37-39, 41-42, 44, 46-53, 55-56, 64, 69-70, 72, 78-81, 84, 88, 92, 95, 97-99, 101-103, 105-108, 110-111, 113, 115, 118-119, 121, 126, 134-135, 137, 139, 141, 143-151, 153-158, 161-168, 170-171, 177-178, 180, 183-184, 187, 189-190, 193-195, 198, 200, 202, 204-206, 208, 210-211, 214, 220-223, 225-226, 228-230, 232, 234-237, 244, 246-247, 249, 255-256
Armstrong's, 34, 53, 161
Arnett Dolls, 175
Artaffects Ltd., 14-15, 45, 56, 58, 69, 71, 76, 79, 83, 85-86, 98, 101, 111, 130, 135, 144, 158, 163, 168, 191, 200, 206, 237, 246-248, 257, 259; See also Greg Perillo, Carol Roeda, Simple Wonders
Artemis, 150
Artesania Rinconada, 26, 47, 69, 81, 123, 138, 145, 150, 197, 237, 248
Artina Gnomes, 71, 205
Artist Collectibles, 22, 43, 66, 94, 135, 157, 173, 184, 190, 205, 225
Artline, 120
Artply, 67
Ashton-Drake, 1-2, 6, 8-16, 18, 20-22, 26-27, 30, 32, 34-37, 39, 42-43, 46, 48, 50, 53, 55-58, 60, 62-63, 66, 69, 71-75, 77, 79-84, 86-87, 91-92, 94-95, 98-99, 101, 105-106, 108, 110, 112-115, 119, 122, 125-127, 129-130, 133-134, 136, 138-143, 145, 147-148, 150, 152, 155-158, 161-163, 165, 168-170, 173, 180-181, 183-185, 187, 189-195, 197-198, 200-201, 203-207, 210-211, 213, 224, 227, 230, 232, 237, 240-241, 243, 247-253, 255, 257-259
Attic Babies, 8, 13, 16, 19, 22, 28, 32, 51, 56, 70, 76, 80, 104, 136, 160, 163-164, 174-175, 211, 219, 229, 236, 239, 245
Atwell, Lucie, 34

Aus-Ben Studios, 56, 206, 226
Austin Sculptures, 24, 67, 97, 171
Austrian Crystal, 188, 223
Avonlea Traditions, 16

—B—

B-2 Bears, 225
Baccarat Crystal, 24, 26, 31, 35, 42, 57, 110, 125, 140, 145, 241, 260
Baker, Brian, 13, 48, 61, 79-80, 100, 107, 179, 203, 238; See also Michael's Ltd.
Baldwin Brass, 9, 88, 109-110, 117, 119, 123, 126, 130, 135, 160, 192, 204
Ball, Bette, 208
Bama, James, 181, 194
Band Creations, 124, 255, 257
Bannister, Patti, 26, 36, 102
Barbie Dolls, 1, 3, 13, 18, 53-54, 62, 67, 86, 92, 106, 117, 123, 148, 152, 156, 166, 187, 189, 193, 197, 206, 210, 216, 227, 236, 249
Barbour, Joyce, 18
Bard's, 12, 247
Barefoot Children, 196
Bareuther, 161, 184, 247
Barklem, Jill, 244
Barnes, Jesse, 84
Barton, Donna, 1, 10, 22, 44, 84, 100, 110, 125, 210, 245
Basement Babies, 76
Bateman, Robert, 17, 19, 26, 181, 202, 256
Bearcraft, 129, 205
Bearly People, 14, 51, 53, 118, 120, 123, 127, 183, 193, 205
Bearly There, 123, 193, 205
Beasties of The Kingdom, 47, 198, 219

Beatrix Potter, 3-4, 6, 8-10, 16, 20, 23-24, 35-36, 40-41, 44-45, 53, 56-57, 62, 64, 66, 72, 76-77, 83, 88, 97, 100, 107, 110, 124-125, 127, 136, 142, 149-152, 156, 159, 162-163, 165, 174, 177, 179-180, 199, 204-205, 212, 221, 235, 244, 247, 251-253, 257; See also Royal Doulton
Beer Steins, 3, 10, 14-15, 19, 54, 72, 106, 108, 149, 171, 188-189, 201, 207, 245, 252
Belcari, 76, 171
Bell, Marty, 6-11, 13, 16-18, 20-24, 26-32, 34-35, 37, 39, 48, 64, 66, 69, 74, 86, 98, 102, 107, 117, 130-131, 134, 136, 138, 141, 147-148, 161, 180, 185, 187, 189-190, 197-198, 200, 206, 211, 219, 230, 235-236, 241, 255
Belle, Debbie, 244
Belleek China, 7, 9, 40, 77, 79, 108, 119-120, 130, 140, 150-151, 154, 165, 171, 180-181, 183, 199, 210, 219, 221, 245, 257
Bello, Yolanda, 66, 77, 86, 123, 129, 140, 206, 240, 251
Bells, 7, 38, 82-83, 91, 119, 202, 212, 227, 237, 244
Belsnickle, 41, 80, 105, 125, 158, 248
Benton, T.H., 177
Bergsma, Jody, 10, 12, 28, 47, 53, 64, 67, 73, 85, 97, 104, 130, 132, 136, 198-199, 205, 223, 248, 259; See also Reco Intl.
Berjusa, 53, 67, 86, 123, 155, 243
Bessos, Barbara, 205, 225
Beswick Crystal, 260
Bing & Grondahl, 6-7, 21, 38-39, 43, 48-50, 57, 65, 76-78, 80, 82, 88, 94-95, 97-101, 106, 112, 114, 119, 129, 136, 138, 140, 141, 148-149, 157, 163, 172, 179-180, 182-183, 196, 198,

KEY TO STATES							
AL: 1-3	DE: 46	IA: 95-98	MN: 136-142	NM: 159-160	RI: 214-215	VA: 239-243
AK: 3	FL: 47-61	KS: 98-100	MS: 142-143	NY: 160-172	SC: 215-218	WA: 244-250
AZ: 4-7	GA: 61-70	KY: 100-101	MO: 143-147	NC: 172-180	SD: 218-220	WV: 250-251
AR: 7-8	HA: 70	LA: 101-104	MT: 147-148	ND: 180-181	TN: 220-226	WI: 252-257
CA: 8-37	ID: 70-71	ME: 104-105	NE: 148-150	OH: 181-193	TX: 226-237	WY: 258
CO: 37-39	IL: 71-85	MD: 106-110	NV: 150	OK: 193-195	UT: 237-238	CANADA:
CT: 40-46	IN: 86-95	MA: 111-115	NH: 151	OR: 196-200	VT: 238	258-260
		MI: 115-135	NJ: 152-159	PA: 201-214		

209, 227-228, 244-245, 247, 251, 252, 256, 257
Birds of Song, 31
Black, Leroy, 50
Black, Carol, 205
Black Desire Series, 109
Black Forest Cuckoo Clocks, 65, 176
Black Heritage, 80, 146, 152
Black Hills Gold, 65
Blackberry Bonnet Collection, 40, 69, 109, 175, 206
Blackman, David, 178
Blackshear, Thomas, 77; See also Hamilton Collection
Blenko Glass, 249
Bloom, Isabel, 96-97
Bluth, Don, 249
Boehm, 2, 5, 8, 16, 26, 33, 53, 55, 77, 140, 162-163, 199, 204-205, 216-217, 228, 242
Boffil, Joseph, 234
Bogart, Maud Humphrey, 1-9, 11-12, 14-15, 17-18, 20-21, 23-28, 30-38, 40-47, 49, 52-53, 55-57, 59-66, 68-73, 75-81, 83-91, 94-98, 100-110, 112-121, 125, 128-130, 132-138, 141-142, 145-155, 158-160, 163-164, 166-167, 169-170, 172-174, 177-180, 183, 185-187, 189-195, 198, 201-203, 205-206, 208-213, 218-222, 224, 226, 228, 230-231, 233-237, 239-240, 245-249, 251-259
Bolden, Marilyn, 50, 129, 243
Bonita Bears, 69, 88, 118
Border Fine Arts, 152
Bortin, Lee, 137, 223
Bossons, 1, 6, 14-15, 18, 27-28, 37, 39, 52, 57, 74, 76, 99, 103-104, 112, 115, 126, 128, 145-148, 150-152, 160, 162, 178, 180, 182, 190, 207, 217, 226, 235-236, 247-248, 259
Bourke Leather, 42
Bovano of Cheshire, 38, 47, 76
Bowls, 136
Boyd's Bears, 1, 20, 36, 50, 54, 86, 100, 104, 155, 159, 164, 174, 201

Bradford, 1-3, 6-9, 11-15, 17-18, 20, 22, 24-28, 30-35, 37, 39, 43, 46, 50, 55, 58, 62-63, 66, 72-82, 84-85, 87, 90-95, 98, 101-102, 106, 108, 113-114, 118, 122, 125-126, 129, 133-142, 145-150, 155-158, 162-163, 166, 168-170, 172-173, 176, 179, 182, 184, 195, 197-198, 200-201, 203-206, 210, 212-214, 216, 221, 224, 227, 232, 237, 240-241, 245, 247, 250, 252, 254-256, 259
Bradley Dolls, 12, 20, 22, 25, 39, 88, 97, 101, 105, 118, 122, 142, 150, 168-169, 256
Brahms, Abigail, 88, 171, 242
Brambly Hedge, 6, 36, 42, 77, 133, 150, 156, 168, 192, 244
Brandywine Woodcrafts, 204, 206, 218
Brauser, Uta, 129, 206
Breedon, Christensen, 181
Brenders, Carl, 202, 256
Brent, Wendy, 32, 86, 90, 205, 236, 251
Brewery Advertising, 54
Breyer Horses, 153
Brinn Dolls, 137
Britains, 50, 191, 199
Bronson, 7
Browning, Tom, Santa's Timeoff, 196
Brush Strokes, 94, 116
Bryer Horses, 50, 123, 153
Bubble Fairies, 16, 47, 88, 104, 138, 206, 238
Buccellati, 10
Bunnykins, 36, 88, 107, 156, 244
Burgues, 77
Burke, Brenda, 12, 33, 102, 204, 208; See also H & G Studios
Burns, 12, 220
Butcher, Sam, 166
Byers' Choice, 1-3, 5, 7, 12, 14-15, 17, 19-21, 26, 28, 30, 32-37, 40-42, 44-47, 49, 51-57, 59, 61-70, 72, 74-76, 79-80, 82, 84-85, 88-94, 96-100, 103-105, 108-113, 115, 119-122, 124-126, 131, 135, 137-139, 143-146, 149, 152-153, 158, 160-164, 166, 168, 174-176,

178-180, 183-185, 187, 189, 193, 195-196, 199-202, 204-205, 208-211, 213-218, 221, 223, 225, 228-230, 234-235, 238-243, 248, 252-258

—C—

Cabbage Patch Kids, 3, 55, 67, 104, 144, 199, 222, 226, 236, 242; See also Original Appalachian Artwork
Cabinets, 36, 137, 169, 230
Cades Cove Series, 221, 224
Cain, Rick, 6, 9, 11, 18, 23, 26, 36, 39, 51, 53, 69-70, 82, 90, 93, 99, 104, 106, 125-126, 128, 131, 137, 147-149, 152, 162-163, 169, 175, 177, 179-180, 196, 198, 207, 212, 214, 217, 222-223, 226, 238, 247, 257
Cairn Studio, 1, 3, 6-7, 17, 30, 39, 58, 81-82, 100, 124, 139, 141, 144, 151-152, 159, 172-173, 181, 183, 186-187, 195, 207, 220, 231, 237, 246-247, 252; See also Tom Clark
Caithness Paperweights, 3, 5, 7, 9, 11, 23, 27, 30, 41-42, 48-49, 51-53, 69, 74, 146, 151, 159, 166, 177, 179-180, 186, 188, 198, 201, 217, 235, 244
Calder, Alexander, 177
Calico Kittens, 1, 5, 10-11, 14-15, 21-22, 33, 35-37, 41, 43, 45-48, 50-54, 56-57, 60, 62, 64-65, 68, 71, 73, 75-76, 78-79, 81-83, 85-86, 88-91, 93-94, 96-98, 101, 103, 106-107, 109, 111-112, 114-115, 117, 122, 124, 127, 130-131, 133-135, 137, 139, 141-142, 144, 147-150, 152, 155-158, 161, 164-165, 167, 169, 173-174, 178, 180-181, 183-186, 188-190, 194, 200-201, 204-205, 208-209, 211-212, 217-218, 220-224, 226-227, 230-231, 233-234, 236, 239, 246, 248, 251, 253-256
Calla, Denise, 183, 196, 255, 257
Calle, Paul, 256
Campbell Kids, 58, 146, 224
Canadian Plates, 96
Canter, Gary, 70
Canterbury Bears, 191
Capodimonte, 29, 31, 35, 37, 39, 55, 76, 78, 83-84, 91, 96-97, 101-102, 121-122, 135, 147, 152, 156, 161, 165, 181-182, 184, 188, 211, 230, 236, 245, 257-258
Carlton Ornaments, 10, 37, 73, 78-79, 85, 133, 144, 236, 242, 257-258
Carousel Horses, 9, 12, 28, 47-48, 56, 64, 71, 74, 86, 96, 116, 134, 163, 177, 181-182, 185, 199, 205, 208-209, 219-220, 223, 226, 235, 237, 240, 243-244, 248
Carrey, Martha, 39, 124, 224
Carriage House Studios Inc., 49, 56-57, 68, 149, 155, 200, 209, 214-215, 217-218, 246; See also Margaret Furlong
Carrico, Paul, 148
Casey, Diana, 181, 223
Caspari, 57
Cassatt, Mary, 177
Cast Art, 9, 13, 15, 23-24, 36, 39-41, 46, 48, 50-51, 53, 56, 60, 62, 66, 71, 81, 83, 89, 98, 102, 105, 117, 122, 127-128, 131-132, 136-137, 143, 147, 149, 163, 165, 168, 170, 173, 178, 180, 182, 185, 188-190, 192, 197, 201, 211, 214, 218, 220, 222-223, 226, 230, 234, 236-237, 247, 257-258; See also Dreamsicles
Castagna, 8, 15, 21, 43, 46-47, 61, 65, 87, 92, 110, 119, 122, 128, 131, 138, 141,

---

KEY TO STATES

AL: 1-3	**DE:** 46	**IA:** 95-98	**MN:** 136-142	**NM:** 159-160	**RI:** 214-215	**VA:** 239-243
AK: 3	**FL:** 47-61	**KS:** 98-100	**MS:** 142-143	**NY:** 160-172	**SC:** 215-218	**WA:** 244-250
AZ: 4-7	**GA:** 61-70	**KY:** 100-101	**MO:** 143-147	**NC:** 172-180	**SD:** 218-220	**WV:** 250-251
AR: 7-8	**HA:** 70	**LA:** 101-104	**MT:** 147-148	**ND:** 180-181	**TN:** 220-226	**WI:** 252-257
CA: 8-37	**ID:** 70-71	**ME:** 104-105	**NE:** 148-150	**OH:** 181-193	**TX:** 226-237	**WY:** 258
CO: 37-39	**IL:** 71-85	**MD:** 106-110	**NV:** 150	**OK:** 193-195	**UT:** 237-238	**CANADA:**
CT: 40-46	**IN:** 86-95	**MA:** 111-115	**NH:** 151	**OR:** 196-200	**VT:** 238	258-260
		MI: 115-135	**NJ:** 152-159	**PA:** 201-214		

151, 159, 161, 184, 188-189, 205, 226, 228, 237, 241, 251, 257
Cat Collectibles, 2, 36, 46, 52, 62, 70, 73, 81, 85, 157, 173, 208, 227, 230, 255
Cat's Meow, 1-2, 6-7, 11, 19, 21, 23, 29, 32, 35, 40-41, 44-46, 49, 51-52, 54-56, 60-61, 63-64, 66-67, 71-75, 79-80, 82, 85-86, 89, 97, 101, 103-105, 107-111, 113-118, 123-125, 129, 131-132, 136-138, 148, 151-152, 155, 157-160, 162, 164, 168-169, 171-174, 176, 178-179, 183-188, 192-193, 197, 201-208, 210, 214-216, 218, 220, 227-231, 234-236, 239, 241, 243, 245, 250, 252-253, 255, 257-258
Cazenovia Abroad, 57, 179, 209
Celebration Quilts, 51, 94
Ceralene, 241
Ceramica Excelsis, 219
Chase, Lynn, 125, 217, 241
Cherished Teddies, 1-15, 18, 20-24, 26-27, 29, 32-69, 71-103, 105-112, 114-120, 122-128, 130-139, 141-152, 154-175, 177-195, 197-213, 215, 217-228, 230-246, 248-259
Chilmark, 2-6, 8, 11-12, 15-16, 18, 22, 27-29, 31, 33, 37-40, 43, 45, 49, 51, 53, 55, 57-58, 61, 65, 68-71, 79, 81, 83, 88, 90, 92-93, 97, 99-100, 102-103, 106, 108, 110, 112-113, 115, 121-122, 126-127, 130-131, 134, 138, 140, 142, 144-148, 150-151, 154-155, 159-160, 162, 164, 166, 168-171, 175, 177-178, 180, 183, 185, 188, 193, 198, 202, 207, 209, 211-212, 214, 216-217, 221, 223, 225-226, 228, 230, 233-235, 237-238, 242-244, 246-248, 250-251, 253, 255-258; See also Hudson, Lance
Chokin, 111, 153, 156, 165, 180
Christiansen, James, 19
Christmas Giftware, 19, 79, 131, 240, 244
Christmas Ornaments, 1, 5, 8-11, 15, 17, 19-20, 23-25, 27, 31-32, 35-37, 39-44, 46, 48-51, 54-57, 59-61, 64, 67-69, 71-74, 76-79, 81-85, 87, 89, 91, 93-94, 96-97, 99-100, 104, 106-109, 111, 114-117, 120, 122-129, 131-133,

135-137, 140-144, 146-152, 158, 164-167, 169, 173-176, 178-180, 182-187, 190, 192-195, 197-201, 205, 208, 212-214, 217, 220-226, 230-238, 240, 242, 244, 246, 248-250, 252, 255-258, 260
Christopher Radko, 1, 10, 12, 14, 19-20, 22, 24, 30, 41, 44, 46-47, 52-54, 57, 61, 64, 66, 68-69, 72, 74, 79, 87, 89, 93, 97, 104, 109, 113, 125, 131-132, 137, 139-141, 143, 152-153, 162, 165, 170, 174-176, 179, 181-184, 187-188, 192-193, 195-201, 205, 213, 216-219, 225, 235-236, 238-241, 244, 252-257
Civil War, 79, 145, 240
Claire Craft, 1, 104, 241
Clark, Tom, 1-11, 14-15, 17-18, 20-23, 25-28, 30, 32, 35, 37-40, 42, 45-46, 48-49, 52-53, 55-66, 68-72, 74-75, 78-79, 81, 85, 87-90, 93-101, 103-105, 107, 112-116, 119, 122, 125-126, 128, 130-139, 142-144, 146-151, 153-157, 159, 161, 163-166, 168-169, 172-180, 183-184, 188, 190, 193, 195, 197, 199-204, 207, 211-214, 216-219, 221-224, 226, 228, 231-239, 241, 243-248, 250-254, 258; See also Cairn Studios
Classic Children, 217
Classical Creamware, 41
Clay Art, 22, 30, 99, 105, 122-123, 138, 152, 155, 161, 173, 207, 255, 258
Clocks, 11, 28, 36, 48, 65, 72, 84, 134, 136, 165, 176, 202, 207, 251
Cloisonne, 55
Clothtique, 77, 91, 109, 203, 207, 212, 224, 248
Clowns, 5, 19, 28, 31, 35, 39-40, 47, 49, 58, 62, 64, 87, 96, 101, 110, 112, 118, 131, 150, 168-169, 179, 191, 200, 205, 224, 230, 232, 247-248, 254
Co-Boys, 40
Coca-Cola Collectibles, 19, 34, 68, 89, 91, 96, 126, 139, 180, 207, 220-221, 225, 232
Cody, John, 221, 258
Cole, J. Kramer, 12, 26, 181

Cole Fine Art, 127
Collectables, 1-2, 6, 11, 14-15, 20, 22, 33, 66-67, 83, 86, 88, 94, 97, 114, 118, 123, 129-130, 132, 134, 156-157, 167-168, 172, 177, 187, 193, 210, 213, 230, 236, 243, 255, 259; See also Phyllis Parkins
Collectible Santas, 2-3, 7, 12, 17, 20, 23-24, 31-32, 36, 40-41, 47, 49, 52, 54-55, 59, 63, 65-69, 73, 76-77, 80, 85, 87, 89-93, 96-98, 100, 102, 104-105, 109, 111, 113-114, 119-120, 122, 124, 125, 129, 131-133, 136, 138-139, 142, 149, 152, 157, 159, 161, 164, 168-170, 172, 174, 178-179, 181-185, 187-188, 190, 192, 196-197, 203-205, 211-214, 216, 219-220, 222, 224, 230, 232, 236, 238, 240-242, 248, 252-254, 257
Colibri, 28
Collectible Bears, 1, 3-5, 9-10, 18-23, 26, 30, 32-33, 37-38, 50, 53-55, 58, 60, 66-67, 69, 71-74, 78, 80-81, 83, 86-90, 92-94, 97-98, 100, 104-105, 110, 114, 116, 118, 120, 123-127, 129, 131-134, 136, 146-150, 152, 157, 160-161, 163-164, 166-169, 172, 174, 181, 183, 189-191, 193, 195, 197-199, 201-203, 205, 210, 212, 216, 218, 220-221, 223-225, 227, 229-230, 232, 234, 236, 242, 247-249, 251-253
Collectible Creches, 38, 186
Collectible Houses, 15, 25, 28, 46-47, 49-52, 64, 66-67, 73, 85, 97-98, 112-114, 131, 139, 142, 147, 152, 154, 158, 167, 178-179, 182, 186-187, 189, 195, 203, 206-207, 214, 218, 230, 232, 245, 253-254, 258
Collectors Cars, 120, 139
Collectors Thimbles, 13, 17, 82, 131, 237, 240, 245, 260

Collin, Cheryl, 111, 189
Colonial Casting, 45
Colonial Village Collection, 7-8, 14, 21, 23, 30, 50, 62-63, 69, 72, 80, 83, 85, 91, 101-102, 110, 132, 169, 176, 178, 180, 190, 193, 195, 220, 223, 227, 230; See also Lefton
Communicorp International, 91, 96, 220
Comoys of London, 28
Connecticut House, 43
Connoisseur, 5, 55, 249
Constance Collection, 44-45, 61, 68, 82, 94, 109, 132, 152, 172, 206, 232
Cookie Cutters, 73
Cooper, Malcolm, 40, 179, 253
Cooperstown Bears, 83, 88, 198
Corcilius, Cat, 12
Cornell Importers, 14, 65, 87, 126, 146-147, 152, 163-164, 207, 218
Cornhusk Dolls, 97, 138
Corolle, 5, 43, 53, 86, 90, 139, 143, 166, 193, 227, 251; See also Mattel
Correia Studios, 217
Costanza, A., 76
Cottage Prints, 2, 8, 25, 32, 34, 36, 38, 53, 66, 68, 86, 101-102, 124, 192, 205, 229, 241, 251
Cottontale Lane, 12
Country Companions, 149
Country Cousins, 123, 149-150, 255
Court, Arthur, 97, 195, 231, 253
Craft, Clare, 104, 241
Cranberry Glass, 43
Creart, 101, 145, 226
Creative Carvings, 86, 187
Crees, Paul, 117, 227, 242
Cross Gallery, 6

KEY TO STATES

AL: 1-3	DE: 46	IA: 95-98	MN: 136-142	NM: 159-160	RI: 214-215	VA: 239-243
AK: 3	FL: 47-61	KS: 98-100	MS: 142-143	NY: 160-172	SC: 215-218	WA: 244-250
AZ: 4-7	GA: 61-70	KY: 100-101	MO: 143-147	NC: 172-180	SD: 218-220	WV: 250-251
AR: 7-8	HA: 70	LA: 101-104	MT: 147-148	ND: 180-181	TN: 220-226	WI: 252-257
CA: 8-37	ID: 70-71	ME: 104-105	NE: 148-150	OH: 181-193	TX: 226-237	WY: 258
CO: 37-39	IL: 71-85	MD: 106-110	NV: 150	OK: 193-195	UT: 237-238	CANADA:
CT: 40-46	IN: 86-95	MA: 111-115	NH: 151	OR: 196-200	VT: 238	258-260
		MI: 115-135	NJ: 152-159	PA: 201-214		

Crowe, Phillip, 234
Crummels, 41, 88, 110, 244
Crunkleton, Marge, 146, 174, 242
Crystal By Happy World, 16
Crystal Fantasy, 245
Crystal Figurines, 22, 158, 170, 248
Crystal Jewelry, 76
Crystal Palace, 16
Crystal World, 18, 26, 118-119, 121, 145, 147, 150, 163, 181
Crystal Zoo, 154, 200, 208
Crystallite Crystal, 200
Cuckoo Clocks, 11, 65, 134, 165, 176
CUI, 54, 65, 126, 221
Cuthbertson, 231
Cybis, 2, 5, 7, 9, 16, 26, 30, 53, 55, 77, 140, 184, 188, 235

—D—

D'Oggi, Moda, 200
Daddy's Long Legs, 7-8, 15, 19, 22-23, 28, 31-32, 40, 46, 53, 67, 69-71, 74, 94, 98, 108, 110, 117, 124, 126, 132, 153, 157-158, 161-162, 175, 178, 183, 187-188, 200, 202, 206-207, 210, 214, 222-224, 226-229, 232, 235-236, 245, 251-252, 258
Dakin, 67, 86, 123, 177
Dali, Edna, 33, 90, 117, 227
Daly, 181
Danbury Mint, 252
Danforth, Judi, 238
Daniel, K., 240
Darling, Alice, 3, 50, 166, 187, 227
Darlings, 166
Daum, 16, 140, 171
Davis, Lowell, 1-4, 6-11, 13, 16-18, 20-21, 25-26, 29-30, 32-34, 37-40, 43-47, 49-55, 57-58, 61-62, 64-66, 68-69, 71-79, 81-82, 85-88, 90-106, 108, 112-116, 118, 120, 124-126, 128-129, 132, 134, 136-139, 142-151, 153-155, 157, 159-160, 162-167, 170, 172-173, 175-178, 180-181, 183-184, 187-191, 195, 197, 199, 201, 205, 210-211, 213-214, 216, 218, 220-226, 228-236, 241, 243, 251, 253-257
Davis, Michael, 202
Davis, Roger, 237
Day, Ray, 12, 37, 66, 70, 92-93, 96, 154, 182, 192, 212, 249
De Grazia, 4-7, 9, 18, 20-21, 25-27, 33-34, 36, 38-39, 43, 45, 57-58, 62, 72, 74, 77-78, 80, 82, 84-85, 87-88, 95, 97-98, 105, 113, 120, 126, 130, 132-133, 136, 141, 145, 149-150, 159-160, 165, 185, 192, 199, 211, 213, 228, 233, 247-248, 251, 254, 257
De Stefano, Jessica, 138
Deborah Henderson Studio, 217
Decoy Ducks, 65, 83, 174, 223
Dedham Pottery, 112, 131, 151
Delphi, 96
Dept. 56 *Villages*, 1-17, 20-27, 29-38, 40-57, 59-72, 74-82, 85, 87-106, 108-120, 122, 124-126, 128-150, 152-159, 161-205, 207-226, 228-259
Accessories, 15, 23, 30, 46, 57, 72, 91, 94, 97, 102, 104, 115, 117, 122, 124, 126, 130, 131, 142, 159, 174, 194, 199-200, 203, 208, 217, 222, 238, 243, 246
Alpine Village, 20, 179, 254
All Through the House, 1, 13, 15, 20, 24, 30, 44, 46-47, 51-52, 56, 59, 63, 67-68, 72, 90, 94, 96-97, 101-102, 104, 108-109, 113, 115, 117, 120, 122, 124-126, 130-132, 135-137, 141-143, 146, 149, 155, 157, 161, 164, 169-170, 172-174, 177, 179, 186, 192, 194, 199-200, 204-205, 214, 216-217, 219-220, 222, 226, 229, 231, 236, 243, 248, 252-253, 256-257
Christmas In The City, 7, 12, 20, 24, 30-31, 35, 41, 47-49, 51-52, 56, 59-60, 76, 102, 111, 113, 122, 147, 170, 175, 179, 203, 212-213, 240, 242, 249, 252, 254
Dickens' Village, 7, 12, 20, 24, 30, 31, 35, 47, 48, 49, 51, 52, 56, 59, 60, 65, 68, 76, 95, 97, 99, 102, 103, 111, 113, 122, 132, 147, 175, 179, 189, 192, 203, 204,

209, 212, 213, 217, 226, 241-242, 249, 252, 255
Heritage Village Collection, 17, 21, 24, 32, 34, 39, 41, 57, 75, 88-89, 91, 93, 96, 104-105, 111, 117, 120, 138, 140-141, 146, 156, 162-163, 168, 170, 173, 189, 192, 201-202, 212, 219-220, 223, 234, 240, 255, 259
Little Town of Bethlehem, 20, 24
Merry Makers, 1, 13, 20, 24, 46, 51, 56, 67-68, 90, 94, 97, 101-102, 104, 109, 113, 115, 122, 124-126, 130, 132, 137, 142-143, 146, 149, 155-156, 161, 164, 170, 174, 177, 179, 186, 194, 199-200, 203-205, 214, 216-217, 219, 222, 226, 229, 231, 242-243, 248-249, 252, 256-257
New England Village, 20, 35, 65, 111, 175, 179, 226, 254
North Pole Village, 24, 47, 49, 57, 59, 97, 254
Snowbabies, 1-3, 5-6, 8-13, 15-17, 20-21, 23-25, 27, 30-33, 35, 37-57, 59-69, 71-72, 74-83, 85, 87, 89-109, 111-115, 117-119, 122-143, 145-152, 154-159, 161-165, 167-180, 182-183, 185-190, 192-196, 199-205, 208, 210-211, 213-224, 226, 229-232, 234-244, 246, 248-257, 259
Snow Village, 1, 5, 7, 12, 20-21, 24, 30, 41, 46, 48, 51-52, 56-57, 64, 75-76, 89, 91, 93, 95, 102-104, 111, 113, 117, 120, 122, 140-142, 146, 156, 162, 164, 170, 172-173, 175, 179, 182, 191-192, 195, 199, 203, 205, 216-217, 221, 223, 225, 240, 242, 248, 254-256
Winter Silhouette, 1, 15, 20, 24, 38, 56, 63, 83, 92, 97, 102, 104, 124, 131, 143, 155, 162, 164, 172, 174, 187, 205, 216,

219, 229, 242, 252, 256-257
Designs Americana, 20, 24, 41, 65, 90, 104, 127, 151-152, 162, 164, 170, 174, 181, 187, 201, 219, 237, 241, 245, 249, 258
Designs Americana Santas / Pencil Santas, 20, 24, 41, 90, 157, 170
Detweiler Woodquilts, 204
Deval, 90, 129, 171, 227
Die, Terry, 251
Dolfi Dolls, 48, 169, 240
Doll Repairs, 3
Dolls by Jerri, 2
Dolls by Pauline, 5, 14, 73, 88, 118, 150, 166, 205, 227, 249, 254
Dolls, 93, 105, 132, 176-177
Dolphi, 97
Doolittle, Bev, 19, 181, 194
Dooney & Bourke Leather, 42
Dragon Keep, 3, 15, 17, 22, 28, 33, 37, 39, 45, 47, 69, 71-72, 79, 85, 104, 107-108, 113, 136, 150, 152, 154, 156, 158-159, 163, 166, 178, 181, 184, 200, 206, 217, 219, 226, 228, 230-231, 236-237, 239, 247, 249, 251, 255
Dram Tree, 43, 54, 63, 156, 185, 212
Dreamsicles, 1-3, 5, 8, 10-13, 17, 20-21, 23-24, 26, 29, 35-37, 39-41, 44, 46, 48-49, 51-56, 61-62, 64-68, 71-76, 78-80, 82-85, 87, 89-91, 95-98, 100-102, 104-105, 107, 109-111, 114-117, 121-128, 131-138, 141-150, 152-153, 155-159, 161, 164-176, 178-181, 183, 185-188, 190, 192-194, 197, 200-203, 206, 208, 211-214, 218, 220-226, 231-232, 234, 236-237, 241, 244, 248, 251-252, 255-257; See also Cast Art
Dresden, 2, 55, 165, 184, 228

KEY TO STATES

AL: 1-3	**DE:** 46	**IA:** 95-98	**MN:** 136-142	**NM:** 159-160	**RI:** 214-215	**VA:** 239-243
AK: 3	**FL:** 47-61	**KS:** 98-100	**MS:** 142-143	**NY:** 160-172	**SC:** 215-218	**WA:** 244-250
AZ: 4-7	**GA:** 61-70	**KY:** 100-101	**MO:** 143-147	**NC:** 172-180	**SD:** 218-220	**WV:** 250-251
AR: 7-8	**HA:** 70	**LA:** 101-104	**MT:** 147-148	**ND:** 180-181	**TN:** 220-226	**WI:** 252-257
CA: 8-37	**ID:** 70-71	**ME:** 104-105	**NE:** 148-150	**OH:** 181-193	**TX:** 226-237	**WY:** 258
CO: 37-39	**IL:** 71-85	**MD:** 106-110	**NV:** 150	**OK:** 193-195	**UT:** 237-238	**CANADA:**
CT: 40-46	**IN:** 86-95	**MA:** 111-115	**NH:** 151	**OR:** 196-200	**VT:** 238	258-260
		MI: 115-135	**NJ:** 152-159	**PA:** 201-214		

Duck House, 29
Duck Stamp, 202, 234
Ducks Unlimited, 83, 174
Duncan Royale, 2-4, 6-7, 9, 11, 18, 23, 25-26, 31-34, 36-37, 40, 42, 45-47, 49, 53, 57-59, 61-65, 67-70, 79-80, 83, 87-88, 92-93, 97-105, 109-111, 114, 116, 121-122, 125-126, 128, 131-132, 134-136, 141-143, 145-146, 149, 152-153, 157-159, 161-164, 167-169, 171, 173-179, 181-184, 188-195, 197, 199-200, 202, 206, 210, 212-214, 216-218, 220, 222-229, 234-235, 237, 241, 245, 247-248, 251-257
DuPont, 28
DuraCraft, 67
Dyke, Larry, 131, 133-134, 234
Dynasty Dolls, 86, 92, 147, 177, 180, 184, 200, 202, 217, 227, 253

— E —

Easter Bunnies, 138
Ebony Collections, 31-32, 40, 62, 110
Effanbee Dolls, 1, 159, 177, 193, 233
Egg Fantasies, 2
Eggs, 97
Elizabeth Exclusive, 50
Elke Hutchins Originals, 66, 157, 199-200, 227, 242
Ellenbrooke Dolls, 22, 66, 92, 157, 167, 173, 193, 251
Elvis Memorabilia, 96, 150, 184
Enchanted Kingdom, 28
Enchantica, 2, 6, 12, 16-17, 28, 36-37, 41, 48, 51, 70, 76, 117, 127, 130, 134, 139, 150, 158, 160, 162-164, 167, 170-171, 187, 206, 219-220, 223, 230, 235, 254-255
Enderle, Inge, 153
Enesco Corp., 10, 127, 136, 146-147, 154, 158, 191, 209, 220, 243; See also Cherished Kittens, Growing Up Girls, B. P. Gutmann, Maud Humphrey, Sisters & Best Friends, Sports Impressions
Enesco Musicals, 1, 5, 7-14, 17, 20, 23, 26-27, 30, 34-38, 44, 46-48, 50, 55-56, 61-62, 64, 70-75, 77-79, 81-83, 85, 90-94, 97-99, 103, 105-108, 110-111, 115, 117, 119, 122, 126-128, 130-132, 137, 140-144, 146, 148-152, 156, 158-161, 164-166, 168-169, 178-181, 183, 186-190, 193, 195, 197, 200-204, 206, 210-211, 213-214, 221-222, 224, 226, 229-231, 233, 236-239, 241-242, 248, 253-256
Enesco North Pole Village, 62, 68, 77, 79, 108, 161
Enesco Treasury of Christmas Ornaments, 9-11, 17, 20, 23-24, 27, 32, 36-37, 39, 42-43, 56, 73, 78-79, 81, 91, 93, 96-97, 99, 106, 108, 114, 120, 122, 127, 132, 140, 146, 149-151, 164, 169, 174, 179, 182, 184, 186, 192, 194-195, 199, 205, 214, 220, 222, 225-226, 231, 233, 235-236, 238, 242, 246, 248-249, 252
Engel Puppen, 159
Ernst, 147, 161
Erte, 234
Ertl, 19, 169, 207
Erzgebirge Nutcrackers, 10, 132, 140, 176, 199, 209, 242, 247, 250
Esche, Sabine, 38, 53, 90, 129, 134, 153, 166, 205, 227
European Artist, 5, 117, 201, 243
Expressions of Youth, 57, 208

— F —

F. J. Designs, 207
F.O.R.T., 39, 43, 78, 88, 104, 121, 130, 138, 141, 168-169, 223, 239
Fairies, 16, 22, 47, 68, 88, 104, 114, 138, 206, 238
Fanikins, 76
Fantasy Collectibles, 27, 39, 111, 131, 138, 143, 153, 156, 165, 169-170, 183, 206, 245
Father Time Clock, 47, 121, 194
Fenton Art Glass, 1-3, 7, 10-11, 16, 21, 34, 45, 49, 55, 62, 71, 74, 78-79, 89, 96-99, 101, 104-106, 108-109, 119,

121-122, 125, 127, 131, 135, 137, 147, 149, 162, 164, 168-169, 177, 180-181, 183, 185-188, 190, 192, 201-202, 209, 212, 218-220, 224, 226, 232-233, 239-240, 242, 246-247, 251, 253, 256, 258

Fernandez, 12, 18, 140, 180

Ferrandiz, 43, 115, 192; See also ANRI

Fiba, 29

Firelight Glass Candles, 134, 249

Fitz & Floyd, 8-9, 14, 19, 26, 34, 36, 46, 48, 52, 88, 97, 100, 110, 125, 139, 141, 145-146, 165, 174, 179, 183, 193, 199-200, 208, 222, 245; See also Holiday Hamlet

Flambro Imports, 14, 27, 51, 58, 62, 81-83, 87, 89, 97-99, 104, 111, 113, 116, 137, 141, 146, 153, 156, 158, 161-163, 165, 176, 187-188, 190, 192, 195, 198, 207, 209, 221-222, 233, 246, 254, 257

Flavia, 83, 146, 181

Folk Art, 12, 32, 44, 47, 59, 63, 81, 86, 100, 120, 164, 173, 175, 213, 224, 242, 257

Fontanini, 1-6, 15, 20, 24, 29, 38, 40, 44, 52, 54, 56-57, 60-61, 64, 68, 70, 76, 78, 81, 84, 88, 91, 96-97, 100-101, 103-105, 108-109, 111, 113-114, 116-118, 120, 122-123, 126, 129, 131-134, 136-137, 140-143, 146, 149, 155, 159, 161-162, 165, 168-169, 176, 178-179, 181-182, 185-186, 193-194, 197, 201, 207, 212, 214, 216, 218-220, 222-223, 225-226, 228, 231-232, 235-236, 238, 240, 242-243, 245, 250, 252-253, 257; See also Roman, Inc.

Frace, Charles, 12, 19, 26, 187, 234, 240

Frames, 6, 10, 18, 21, 24-25, 27, 36, 45, 58, 72, 82, 84, 95, 101, 113, 121-122, 127, 129, 133-134, 139, 146, 170, 181-182, 184, 203, 227, 232, 237, 247, 255, 260; See also Accessories

Franca, Ozz, 24, 26, 36, 84, 130, 181, 213

Francis, Kevin, 65, 69, 162, 182, 193, 211

Fraser, Ian, 199

Fraser Creations, 15, 26, 37, 68-69, 101, 163, 199, 257

Frederica, 53, 243

Frederick Dickson, 260

Fredericks, Rod, 19, 181

Freske, Judy, 88

Frumps, 1, 3, 26, 37, 86, 98, 104, 147, 150, 223, 234, 237, 258

Furlong, Margaret, 2, 6, 32, 41, 45, 56-57, 64, 67-69, 83, 85, 113, 116, 123-124, 126, 129, 136, 141-143, 146, 149, 151, 170, 174-176, 178-179, 181, 187, 193, 196-197, 199-200, 207-208, 213-215, 223, 225, 235, 240, 245, 255, 257

—G—

GADCO, 3, 17, 22, 34, 50, 53, 66, 88, 92, 105, 117, 123, 147, 152-153, 155, 187, 193, 201, 210, 225, 236, 243, 251

Gail Laura, 19, 46, 91, 109, 123, 136, 157, 163-164, 211, 214, 243, 250

Gaillard, Ravenel, 216

Gallo Pewter, 7, 12, 54, 104, 111, 153, 156, 165

Gallway Crystal, 35

Gambina, 159, 166

Ganz, 80, 181

Garman, Michael, 1, 7, 14-15, 18, 21, 34, 47, 53, 55, 62, 64-65, 68-70, 84, 89-90, 99-100, 103-104, 119, 130, 135, 142, 145-146, 162-164, 174, 176-179, 181,

KEY TO STATES								
AL: 1-3	**DE:** 46	**IA:** 95-98	**MN:** 136-142	**NM:** 159-160	**RI:** 214-215	**VA:** 239-243		
AK: 3	**FL:** 47-61	**KS:** 98-100	**MS:** 142-143	**NY:** 160-172	**SC:** 215-218	**WA:** 244-250		
AZ: 4-7	**GA:** 61-70	**KY:** 100-101	**MO:** 143-147	**NC:** 172-180	**SD:** 218-220	**WV:** 250-251		
AR: 7-8	**HA:** 70	**LA:** 101-104	**MT:** 147-148	**ND:** 180-181	**TN:** 220-226	**WI:** 252-257		
CA: 8-37	**ID:** 70-71	**ME:** 104-105	**NE:** 148-150	**OH:** 181-193	**TX:** 226-237	**WY:** 258		
CO: 37-39	**IL:** 71-85	**MD:** 106-110	**NV:** 150	**OK:** 193-195	**UT:** 237-238	**CANADA:**		
CT: 40-46	**IN:** 86-95	**MA:** 111-115	**NH:** 151	**OR:** 196-200	**VT:** 238	258-260		
		MI: 115-135	**NJ:** 152-159	**PA:** 201-214				

186, 188, 196-197, 207, 217, 221-222, 224, 226, 233-234, 243, 252
Gartlan USA, 6, 8, 13, 15-17, 21, 23, 27, 30, 34, 43, 79, 98, 102, 112-113, 115, 117, 119, 127, 133, 157, 161, 163, 166, 185, 190, 203, 213, 220, 229, 231, 244, 248, 250, 253, 257, 259
GATCO, 130
Georgetown Collection, 3, 5, 13, 15, 18, 22, 50, 53, 58, 66, 74, 81, 86-87, 92, 105, 108, 114, 117-118, 123, 126, 130, 132, 152, 155-157, 166, 168, 173, 184, 189, 191, 193, 197, 204-206, 243, 249, 251
Geraty, Virginia, 216
German Steins, 3, 7, 10, 14, 87, 90, 106, 121, 171, 247
Gertz, 124
Gibson, Suzanne, 36, 242
Gift Link, 113; See also Lilliput Lane
Ginny Dolls, 3, 29-30, 50, 54, 67, 86, 88, 94, 105, 107, 123-124, 156, 159, 167, 172, 182, 193, 205, 210, 225, 242, 249
Glass Baron, 47, 103, 110, 121
Glass Eye Crystal, 35, 45, 47, 83, 160, 181, 214
Glassmasters, 65, 69, 152, 235
Gnomes, 1-4, 6-7, 11, 14-15, 17, 20-21, 23, 25-26, 28, 30, 32, 37-40, 42, 46, 48-49, 52-53, 59, 61-63, 66, 69, 71-72, 74-75, 78, 81-82, 85, 87, 89, 93, 97-101, 104-105, 107, 113-114, 116, 122, 125, 128, 131-132, 138-139, 141, 144, 148-150, 157, 159, 161-163, 165, 169, 172-173, 175-179, 183, 186-188, 193, 195, 197, 200, 202-205, 207, 211-213, 216-219, 221, 223-224, 226, 231-233, 235-239, 244-247, 250-254
Goebel Bells, 7
Goebel Dolls, 135
Goebel Inc, 14, 163, 239, 253
Goebel Miniatures, 6-7, 9-11, 13-14, 26, 33-34, 43-44, 47, 51-53, 57, 62, 70, 79, 83-85, 88, 92, 98, 101, 110, 112-113, 116, 128, 134, 139-141, 143, 149, 152-154, 157, 159, 162, 165-167, 172, 181, 183, 186, 195, 198-200, 202, 211,

213, 216, 220, 222-223, 235-236, 243, 245, 247-248, 252, 254
Goetz / Gotz Dolls, 3, 5, 22, 86, 88, 94, 98, 123, 130, 157, 176, 182, 205, 216-217, 227, 243
Golden Moments, 129, 137
Gone With The Wind, 20, 53, 61-62, 64, 66, 145, 174, 220, 224
Good-Kruger Dolls, 15, 22, 33-34, 50, 53, 66, 74, 86, 94-95, 105, 117-118, 123, 129-130, 152, 156, 159-160, 163, 166, 182, 187, 191, 193, 197, 201, 205-206, 210, 224-225, 227, 240, 243, 251
Goodwin Weavers, 110, 204
Gorham, Inc., 1
Gorham Birds, 235
Gorham Crystal, 96-97
Gorham Dolls, 1, 16-17, 93, 101, 156, 167, 172, 187, 195, 257
Goyesca, 27
Grandma's Darlings, 166
Grandpapa Jingles, 205
Granget, 6, 53, 140
Green, Donna, 104
Greenaway Dolls, 146, 169, 177
Greenleaf, 67
Greenware, 155
Greenwich Workshop, 3, 71, 102, 114, 160, 164, 194
Grizzly, 124
Groessle Schmidt, 171
Gromme, Owen, 256
Grossman, David, 2-3, 13, 20, 22, 56, 61, 64, 68, 70, 82, 91, 97, 100-101, 111, 129, 146, 152, 161, 174, 186, 191, 194-195, 209, 217, 220, 222, 231, 247, 252, 257; See also Emmett Kelly, Sr., Norman Rockwell
Growing Up Girls, 76, 79, 107, 150, 236
Guerard, Virginia, 216
Guildhall, 106, 240
Gund Bears, 32, 55, 67, 88, 90, 94, 105, 114, 123-124, 150, 159, 168, 191, 193, 195, 205, 236, 253, 257
Gunzel, Hildegard, 50, 53, 86, 92, 94, 105, 123-124, 129, 134, 158, 187, 197,

205, 225, 227, 242, 251
Gurney, James, 19, 181, 194
Gutmann, Bessie Pease, 10, 14, 16, 57, 77, 79, 81, 86, 91, 97, 100, 109, 130, 133, 146, 154, 169, 174, 178, 181, 200, 205, 239, 242

—H—

H & G Studios, 13, 34, 58
Hackett American, 34
Hadden, Mary Ellen, 120
Hadley House, 3, 10, 13, 15, 22, 34, 56, 58, 70-71, 73, 84-86, 93-94, 102, 106, 116, 127, 131, 139, 157, 160-161, 198, 202, 213, 218, 247-248, 259-260; See also Franca, Ozz, Hanks, Steve; Redlin, Terry
Hadley Pottery, 131, 218
Hagara, Jan, 1, 3-4, 6-7, 9, 11-14, 17-18, 20-21, 23-27, 31-36, 41, 43, 45-47, 53, 55, 58, 61-62, 64-66, 68-70, 72-73, 75, 77-84, 86-89, 92-94, 96-98, 100-106, 110, 112-114, 116-117, 119, 123, 125-128, 130, 133-134, 136-137, 141, 143-148, 150, 154, 158, 160-163, 166, 168-169, 171-172, 177, 180, 182, 186-187, 189-193, 195, 197-198, 201-202, 205-206, 209-213, 217-221, 223-227, 229, 233-235, 237, 239-241, 243-244, 247-249, 251-252, 255-258
Hagen-Renaker, 26, 41, 184
Halcyon Days, 42, 204-205, 217, 225
Haley, Alex, 226
Hall, Kristy, 88
Hallmark Galleries, 23, 31, 40, 42, 60, 64, 81-82, 85, 91, 99, 117, 133, 138, 144, 150, 164, 178, 183, 194, 226, 239, 254
Hallmark, Gold Crown, 25, 27, 31, 41-42, 71, 83, 101, 117, 135-136, 142, 148, 150, 156, 158, 164, 186, 213, 222
Hallmark Ornaments, 1, 5, 23, 25, 27, 31, 36, 43-44, 48-49, 51, 54-56, 59, 64, 67, 69, 71, 81-83, 89, 91, 94, 97, 99-100, 104, 107, 115-117, 124, 126, 128, 135-137, 142, 148-150, 152, 156, 164-167, 173, 178, 180, 183-186, 190, 208, 222-226, 231, 234, 237, 248-250, 257-258
Hamilton Collection, 1, 5, 7, 11-16, 18, 20, 22-23, 27, 29, 34, 45, 49-51, 53, 56-58, 62-63, 66, 69, 72-74, 76, 79, 81-87, 89, 93-95, 98, 101-102, 105-106, 108-109, 111-112, 114, 117, 119, 125-127, 129-130, 132-134, 138-141, 145, 147-148, 152, 155-158, 161, 165, 170, 172-174, 184, 187, 189, 191-193, 197-198, 200-201, 203-205, 208-209, 213, 220, 222, 243-244, 246-249, 251-252, 254, 258-260
Hamilton Gifts, 14, 72, 86, 89, 93, 106, 109, 165, 191, 220, 258
Hamilton Heritage Dolls, 13-14, 22, 27, 63, 66, 74, 79, 82-83, 125, 127, 129, 133, 170, 174, 213, 222, 252, 260
Hamilton Plates, 14, 16, 20, 22-23, 66, 76, 84, 111, 138, 145, 184, 192, 198, 201, 204
Hand & Hammer, 1, 10, 57, 140, 176, 188, 247
Hand-Cut Crystal, 55
Haney, Lynn, 19, 40, 65, 76, 104, 131, 161, 183, 189, 205-206, 238, 252
Hanford Heirloom Stamps, 48, 51, 65, 68, 135, 152, 169, 212, 217, 222, 226, 234, 239
Hanks, Steve, 26, 71, 84, 181
Hanna-Barbera, 249

KEY TO STATES

AL: 1-3	DE: 46	IA: 95-98	MN: 136-142	NM: 159-160	RI: 214-215	VA: 239-243
AK: 3	FL: 47-61	KS: 98-100	MS: 142-143	NY: 160-172	SC: 215-218	WA: 244-250
AZ: 4-7	GA: 61-70	KY: 100-101	MO: 143-147	NC: 172-180	SD: 218-220	WV: 250-251
AR: 7-8	HA: 70	LA: 101-104	MT: 147-148	ND: 180-181	TN: 220-226	WI: 252-257
CA: 8-37	ID: 70-71	ME: 104-105	NE: 148-150	OH: 181-193	TX: 226-237	WY: 258
CO: 37-39	IL: 71-85	MD: 106-110	NV: 150	OK: 193-195	UT: 237-238	CANADA:
CT: 40-46	IN: 86-95	MA: 111-115	NH: 151	OR: 196-200	VT: 238	258-260
		MI: 115-135	NJ: 152-159	PA: 201-214		

Harbour Lights, 6, 8-9, 26, 28, 31, 34, 37, 39-41, 44, 46-47, 52, 54, 61, 68-70, 77, 79, 89-90, 97, 99, 106, 110-111, 113-114, 116, 118, 124, 132, 135, 145, 147-149, 152, 154, 157-159, 161-164, 168, 170, 172, 174-176, 178-179, 188-190, 200, 212, 215-217, 221, 242, 244, 246-247, 250-251, 256-257

Hartmann, Sonja, 53, 88, 124, 129, 227, 243

Haut Papier Paper, 57

Haviland, 245

Hawthorne Architectural Register, 14, 33, 66, 85, 101, 110, 129, 162, 184, 195, 206

Heath, Philip, 166, 182

Heath-Orange, Christine, 129

Hebron Metal Sculptures, 247

Heidi Hares, 186

Heileman, 207

Heirloom Quality Quilts, 207

Heller, Karen, 251

Heller, Karin, 166

Hello Dolly, 195

Henderson, Karen, 100, 217, 225

Henrikson, 247

Herbert, Jon Shoehouses, 5, 15, 26, 35-36, 47, 54, 62, 70, 154, 158, 176, 194, 203-204, 207, 218, 221, 241, 247

Herd by Marty Sculptures, 39, 47, 53, 57, 65, 90-91, 104, 116, 128, 147, 151, 156, 187, 221, 226, 232, 236

Herend, 42, 106, 110, 125, 140, 204-205, 228, 241

Heritage Lace, 24, 136

Heritage Santa Collection, 76, 108, 120, 182

Herman Bears, 23, 43, 70, 94, 123, 225

Hermann, 124-125, 129, 193, 205

Hibel, Edna, 5-7, 9, 14, 16-18, 20-21, 26-27, 36, 41, 43, 45, 47-48, 50, 52, 55-58, 60, 62, 78, 84-85, 92, 94, 102, 104, 108, 112-115, 118, 122, 125, 127, 130-132, 134, 141, 143, 149-153, 161-163, 166-167, 171-172, 181, 189, 191, 201-202, 205, 208, 211, 213-214,

227-228, 231-235, 240, 247, 249, 251-252, 255-256, 259

Hidden Kingdom, 1, 3-4, 23, 33, 51, 54, 68, 105, 125, 127, 132, 157, 184, 248, 256

Hill, Charles, 238

Himstedt, Annette, 3, 17-18, 20, 22, 38, 50, 53-54, 70, 74, 84, 86, 88, 90, 92, 94, 105, 114, 117, 123, 129, 132, 134, 138, 143, 152, 155, 157-159, 166, 173, 182, 187, 193, 196-197, 199, 206, 210, 216-217, 225, 227, 236, 242-243, 249, 251; See also Mattel

Hippensteel Dolls, 79, 240

Hoeck, Renate, 206

Holcombe, Martha, 25; See also All Gods Children, Miss Martha's Originals

Holiday Hamlet, 19, 48, 52, 139, 200, 208, 227; See also Fitz & Floyd

Holly Hobbie, 83

Hollywood Limited Editions, 7, 22, 26, 29, 34, 49, 51, 76, 96, 102, 119, 198, 201, 253-254

Homestead Country Folks, 103

Homestead Life, 68, 145, 205, 212, 214, 245

Hook, Francis, 19, 53, 58, 83, 97, 112, 115, 192, 219, 240

Hootchoo Collection, 7

Hopkins, John, 47, 82, 200

Hopkins, Mark, 12, 15, 27, 29, 48, 70, 88, 101, 106, 140, 146, 149, 162, 193, 196, 198, 216-217, 221, 223, 228, 234, 238, 246, 248

Hopkins Shop, 30-31, 34, 39, 163, 248

House of Angels, 180

House of Hatten, 20, 24, 68, 76, 137, 143, 181, 200, 215-216, 232, 257

Houses; See also Collectible Houses

Howard Miller, 55, 134

Howle, Jim, 232

Hoya, 125

Hoyt, Gail, 153, 227

Hudson Pewter, 3, 13, 15, 37, 39, 42, 45, 47, 65, 69-70, 72, 77-78, 83, 101, 104,

108, 110, 112, 118, 126, 132, 134, 136-137, 142, 145-147, 150-151, 162, 168, 171, 173, 176-179, 185-186, 188, 200, 202, 211, 214, 241, 243, 246, 248; See also Chilmark, Lance

Hughes Positive Images, 69

Hummel, M.I., 1-9, 11-18, 20-23, 25-46, 48-50, 52, 54-58, 62-66, 68, 70-74, 76-84, 86, 88-93, 95-97, 99-106, 108-116, 119-123, 125-126, 128-130, 132, 134-161, 163-173, 175-190, 192-195, 197-203, 206-209, 211-212, 214, 216-235, 237, 242, 244-257, 259-260

Hummingbirds, 31

Humphrey Bogart, Maud, 1-9, 11-12, 14-15, 17-18, 20-21, 23-28, 30-38, 40-47, 49, 52-53, 55-57, 59-66, 68-73, 75-81, 83-91, 94-98, 100-110, 112-121, 125, 128-130, 132-138, 141-142, 145-155, 158-160, 163-164, 166-167, 169-170, 172-174, 177-180, 183, 185-187, 189-195, 198, 201-203, 205-206, 208-213, 218-222, 224, 226, 228, 230-231, 233-237, 239-240, 245-249, 251-259

Hutschenreuther, 252

—I—

Icart, Louis, 14, 26, 52, 79, 106, 154, 177, 233

Imhoff's Homestead Life, 26, 68, 73, 145-146, 203, 212, 214, 245

Incolay Studio, 28-29, 33, 58, 130, 252

Indian Art, 5, 8, 18-19, 22, 43, 45, 52, 68, 104, 127, 161, 169, 176, 188, 198, 220, 222, 226, 247-248, 252

Indian Territory, 68, 222, 226

International Silver, 245

Iris Arc, 2, 4-5, 15, 22-23, 26, 33, 40, 47-48, 51, 53-54, 60, 66, 70-72, 77, 81, 85-86, 88, 90, 99-101, 108, 112, 119-120, 122, 126-127, 129, 134, 136-137, 139, 141-144, 146-147, 149-150, 152, 154-155, 159-160, 164, 166, 168, 172, 177-178, 180, 183-184, 188-190, 193-194, 198, 202-203, 206, 220, 222-224, 232, 235-236, 247-248, 251, 253, 255, 257

Irish Dresden, 165

Irish Heritage Collection, 163

Irvings Tin, 211

Isadore Needle Art, 138

Ispanky, 2, 77, 91, 116

Itty Bitty, 220

—J—

J. B. Bean Bears, 232

J. H. Boone, 4, 7, 12-15, 23, 43, 46, 48, 51, 56, 58, 64-65, 69-70, 73, 81-82, 85, 87, 89, 91, 93, 98, 100, 114-115, 124, 128, 136-137, 146, 152, 157-158, 161, 168, 179, 183, 186, 207, 212, 214, 220, 226, 247, 255

Jacobson, Donna, 70, 125

Jarrett Studios, 67

Jeckle-Jansen, 38, 53, 57, 77, 90, 92, 117, 166, 187, 197, 200, 205, 210, 243

Jennie, 53

Jerner's Ducks, 174

Jerome, Francis, 33

John Hine Studios, 1-2, 28, 34, 46, 48, 51, 58, 64, 76, 86, 89, 96, 101, 105-106, 114, 118, 122, 125, 127, 129, 133, 146, 162, 173, 199, 203, 207-209, 211, 215, 220, 223, 239, 245, 257-258

KEY TO STATES

AL: 1-3	**DE:** 46	**IA:** 95-98	**MN:** 136-142	**NM:** 159-160	**RI:** 214-215	**VA:** 239-243
AK: 3	**FL:** 47-61	**KS:** 98-100	**MS:** 142-143	**NY:** 160-172	**SC:** 215-218	**WA:** 244-250
AZ: 4-7	**GA:** 61-70	**KY:** 100-101	**MO:** 143-147	**NC:** 172-180	**SD:** 218-220	**WV:** 250-251
AR: 7-8	**HA:** 70	**LA:** 101-104	**MT:** 147-148	**ND:** 180-181	**TN:** 220-226	**WI:** 252-257
CA: 8-37	**ID:** 70-71	**ME:** 104-105	**NE:** 148-150	**OH:** 181-193	**TX:** 226-237	**WY:** 258
CO: 37-39	**IL:** 71-85	**MD:** 106-110	**NV:** 150	**OK:** 193-195	**UT:** 237-238	**CANADA:**
CT: 40-46	**IN:** 86-95	**MA:** 111-115	**NH:** 151	**OR:** 196-200	**VT:** 238	258-260
		MI: 115-135	**NJ:** 152-159	**PA:** 201-214		

Johnson, Johnny, 3
Johnson Brothers, 231
Jolly Old Elf, 220
Jonasson, Mats, 5, 35, 38, 41, 47-48, 140, 148, 193, 228, 238, 259
Jones, Julie, 123
Josef, Don, 62, 66, 76, 79, 89, 123, 132

—K—

Kaatz, Lynn, 77, 240
Kachina Dolls, 45, 248
Kaiser, 2, 8, 18, 47, 49-50, 53, 62, 65, 69-70, 79, 121, 129-130, 132, 134, 138, 140, 159-161, 171, 178, 184, 188, 209, 220, 228-229, 247, 259
Kaleidescopes, 26, 138
Kate Greenaway Dolls, 146, 169, 177
Kay, Sarah, 43, 53, 156
Kazmar, 77
Keane Eyes, 162
Keep The Herd, 39, 226
Kelly, Jr. Emmett, 1-3, 6-9, 14, 16, 18, 23, 31, 39-40, 44-53, 55-56, 58, 61, 63-66, 68, 70, 74, 76, 78, 80-85, 87-91, 95-103, 106, 108-116, 118-122, 125-130, 133-139, 142-147, 149-151, 153-155, 158, 161-171, 175-178, 180-184, 186, 188-195, 197, 202-203, 206-207, 209, 211-212, 214, 216-221, 223-226, 228-229, 232-237, 240-241, 244, 247, 253-257, 259; See also Flambro Imports
Kelly, Sr. Emmett, 23, 53, 56, 58, 62, 66, 69, 121, 151, 184, 194, 247
Kennedy, Karen, 135, 208
Kewpie Dolls, 18, 22, 29, 74, 94, 159, 169, 222, 226, 242, 249
Kiddie Car Classics, 42
King, 206, 216, 234, 239
Kingdom of Knoch, 3-4, 23, 28, 33, 47, 51, 54, 68, 105, 121, 125, 127, 132, 157, 184, 198, 219, 248, 256
Kingstate, 53, 58, 86, 118, 134, 166, 205
Kinka, 21, 27, 129, 150, 152, 192
Kinkade, Thomas, 5-8, 10-13, 16-22, 24-27, 29-35, 37-39, 45-46, 64, 66, 69, 73-74, 84-85, 88, 92-93, 101-102, 108-109, 112, 115, 117, 121, 123-124, 127, 129-130, 132, 134, 141, 152, 154, 170-171, 174, 182, 187, 189-191, 195, 197-200, 206, 214, 226, 230, 232, 235-237, 240, 245, 247, 249, 253, 255-256
Kirk-Stieff, 1, 14, 45, 84, 110, 125, 146, 191, 209, 238
Kish, Helen, 50, 53, 123, 227
Kitty Cucumber, 3, 26, 53, 68-70, 73, 89, 91, 97, 115, 123, 125, 141, 163, 165, 173, 177, 179-180, 185-186, 205, 224, 230, 236, 251-252
Klaus, Mark, 19, 23, 112, 152, 159, 182, 195, 212-213, 257
Knock On Wood, 105
Knot Knoggins, 20, 73, 101, 177, 206, 240-241
Knowles, Edwin M., 22, 58, 101, 114, 249
Kodra, Craig, 194
Koestel German Angels, 143
Koetzke, D, 252
Kolesar, 243
Kosta Boda, 16, 140, 241
Krey, Susan, 123, 129, 227
Kruse, Kathe, 88, 129, 191, 227
Krystonia, 2-4, 6, 8-9, 11-12, 14-18, 20-24, 27-28, 30-31, 33, 35, 37, 39, 41-49, 52-54, 56, 62-63, 66, 68-69, 71-72, 75-76, 79, 81-82, 84-85, 88, 91, 93, 95-100, 102, 104, 106, 108-109, 111-116, 119-120, 126-128, 130-131, 133-134, 136-139, 141, 143, 147-148, 150-170, 177-181, 183-184, 187, 190, 192, 194, 198-200, 202, 205-206, 210-212, 214, 217, 219-223, 226, 228, 230-233, 235-237, 239, 241, 244, 246, 248, 253, 255-256, 259; See also Precious Art / Panton
Kuntsler, 145
Kurz, 12

—L—

L.S. Collection, 135, 217
La Leonessa Pewter, 238

Lackey, Gail, 88
Ladie & Friends, 1, 17, 19, 32, 46-47, 49, 54, 74, 80, 89, 105, 124, 135, 148, 151-152, 214, 226, 250, 257; See also Lizzie High Dolls
Lalique, 1, 5, 9, 16, 24, 26, 31, 35, 55, 88, 97, 125, 140, 145, 199, 217, 228, 235, 245, 260
Lance, 5, 41, 44, 48, 53, 72, 89, 106, 110, 134-136, 162, 207, 209, 214-215, 238-239; See also Chilmark, Hudson Pewter
Land of Legends, 5, 58, 62, 136, 163, 165, 219, 239, 257
Landry, 181
Landstrom's Black Hills Gold, 65
Lang Graphics Collection, 209, 229
Lantz, Walter, 249
Largo Western Art, 1, 50, 69-70, 145, 230, 233, 235, 245
Lasher, Kimberly, 88
Laura's Attic, 1-4, 6-7, 9, 14, 17-18, 20-21, 23, 26-27, 33, 36-37, 39, 43, 45-48, 51-57, 61-62, 64-65, 71, 73-75, 78-79, 82-84, 86-87, 89-91, 93-94, 98-99, 102-103, 108-109, 111-112, 115-116, 120, 127-128, 130-131, 133-134, 136-137, 139, 141-142, 145, 147-149, 151, 155-156, 160, 163, 165-166, 168, 173, 175-176, 178-179, 181-182, 185, 187, 189-190, 192-194, 197, 201, 203-205, 213, 218-224, 226-228, 230-231, 233, 236, 238-239, 242, 245, 248, 252, 255-256, 258-259
Lauscha Blown Glass, 176
Lawton, Wendy, 1, 17, 20, 32-34, 50, 74, 86, 88, 90, 94, 105-106, 118, 123-124, 130, 134, 143, 152, 157, 166, 191, 193-194, 227, 243, 251

Layton, Corrine, 8, 14, 16, 18, 24, 32-33, 86, 102, 132, 180, 240, 255
Le Fever's World of Sinterklaas, 12
Lefton Company, Geo. Zoltan, 27, 30, 36, 62-63, 77, 80, 83, 91, 93, 100-101, 104, 110, 116, 143, 146-147, 169, 174, 176-177, 180, 190, 195, 198, 209, 220, 222-224, 226-227, 229-230, 233, 242, 258; See also Colonial Village
Legacy Dolls, 10, 58, 121, 189
LEGENDS, 2, 4-8, 12, 16-18, 22-23, 26-31, 38-39, 45, 47-49, 51-53, 55, 57, 61, 63-65, 68-71, 74, 79, 87-88, 93, 96, 98-99, 103, 105-106, 108, 111, 117, 119, 121, 124, 128, 130-131, 134-137, 142-147, 149, 151-152, 154-155, 157, 161-163, 165-166, 168, 170-171, 173-174, 177-178, 184-185, 187-190, 193, 197-198, 200, 202, 206-207, 211-214, 219, 221-224, 226, 228, 230-231, 233, 235-239, 242-244, 247, 252-253, 255-258
Legends of Little People, 58, 62, 104, 157, 163, 165, 220, 226, 239, 257
Legends of Santa, 38-39, 193
Leiber, Judith Purses, 31
Lenci, 29, 43, 90, 166, 227
Lenox, 7-9, 23-24, 26, 40, 43, 79, 110-111, 125, 134, 140, 145, 150, 152-154, 156-157, 161, 163, 165, 167, 177, 186, 188, 192-193, 202, 208, 231, 244-245, 247
Lesher, K., 90
Lester, Alice, 50
Lewan, Dennis Patrick, 8, 11, 19-20, 22, 26, 31-34, 36, 231; See also H & G Studios
Lexington, 5, 14, 16, 101, 106, 116, 125, 134, 138, 253

```
                        KEY TO STATES
   AL: 1-3      DE: 46       IA: 95-98      MN: 136-142    NM: 159-160   RI: 214-215   VA: 239-243
   AK: 3        FL: 47-61    KS: 98-100     MS: 142-143    NY: 160-172   SC: 215-218   WA: 244-250
   AZ: 4-7      GA: 61-70    KY: 100-101    MO: 143-147    NC: 172-180   SD: 218-220   WV: 250-251
   AR: 7-8      HA: 70       LA: 101-104    MT: 147-148    ND: 180-181   TN: 220-226   WI: 252-257
   CA: 8-37     ID: 70-71    ME: 104-105    NE: 148-150    OH: 181-193   TX: 226-237   WY: 258
   CO: 37-39    IL: 71-85    MD: 106-110    NV: 150        OK: 193-195   UT: 237-238   CANADA:
   CT: 40-46    IN: 86-95    MA: 111-115    NH: 151        OR: 196-200   VT: 238         258-260
                             MI: 115-135    NJ: 152-159    PA: 201-214
```

LGB, 172
Lightpost Publishing, 7, 215, 234;
  See also Kinkade, Thomas
Lilliput Lane, 1-18, 20-28, 30-52, 54-66, 68-72, 74-83, 85, 87, 89-93, 95, 97-99, 101-104, 106-119, 122, 124-130, 132-178, 180-195, 197-206, 209-217, 219-235, 237-239, 241-251, 253-259
Limoges, 30, 33, 35, 100, 103, 110, 179, 184, 193, 204-205, 217, 233
Lincoln County Garden Club, 56, 67-68, 92, 110, 150, 155, 175, 180, 193, 196, 199, 205, 234, 242, 246
Linden Clocks, 28, 251
Lionel Ornaments, 108, 172, 233
Lissi, 5, 29, 66-67, 97, 149, 169, 182, 243, 253
Lithographs, 6, 18-19, 21-22, 24, 28, 34, 36, 41, 45, 58, 72, 74-75, 81, 85, 93-96, 111, 113-115, 117, 122, 130-131, 140, 161, 170-171, 174, 185, 191, 198-199, 206, 208, 227, 235, 237, 248-249, 259-260
Little Cheesers, 4, 13-17, 20, 22-23, 26-29, 33, 35-37, 44, 46-47, 55-56, 60-62, 65-66, 69-70, 73, 77, 80, 85, 104, 113, 118, 127, 136, 138, 146-147, 149-150, 152, 158, 162, 170, 173, 176, 178, 180-181, 184, 190, 196-198, 204, 211-212, 222, 224, 226-228, 230, 233, 235-237, 239, 246, 251, 253, 255, 259
Little Folk Dolls, 120
Little Havens, 68
Little People, 7, 62, 104, 111, 157, 166, 200
Little Souls, 13, 205
Liu, Lena, 8, 18, 22, 33-34, 72, 77, 111, 182, 187, 227, 235, 257, 259
Lizzie High, 8, 16, 21, 26, 28, 35, 39-40, 44, 47, 51, 56, 59-60, 62, 64, 66-67, 70, 75-76, 79-80, 82-83, 85, 90, 93, 100, 103-105, 109, 111, 115, 121-122, 124, 136, 138, 151, 158, 160-161, 163-164, 168-169, 174, 178-179, 183, 187-189, 197, 200-201, 203-204, 207-208, 210-211, 213-215, 219, 224, 229, 234, 236, 239, 243, 245, 248, 250, 252, 255, 257; See also Ladie & Friends
Lladro, 1-11, 14-18, 20-21, 23-24, 26-38, 40-42, 44-55, 58-62, 64-66, 68-72, 74-83, 88, 91-100, 103, 106-108, 110-113, 115-116, 118-120, 123, 125-130, 134-154, 156-159, 161, 163-172, 177-181, 183-189, 193, 195, 198-200, 202, 204-208, 210-214, 216-223, 225-226, 228-232, 234-235, 237-238, 241-247, 249, 253-254, 256-257
Lledo, 182
Lomonosov Russian Porcelain, 38, 198, 248
London By Gaslight, 64, 69-70, 178, 234
Londonshire Animals, 152
Longaberger Baskets, 94, 116
Looney Tunes, 14, 121, 230
Lossnitzer, Carin, 88, 205
Lowe, Bethany, 213
Lucy & Me, 1, 21, 23, 57, 71, 75, 77, 83, 107, 115, 120, 123, 137, 141, 147-148, 150-151, 163, 168, 179-181, 185, 192, 197, 199, 202, 207, 214, 217, 224, 234, 237, 242, 245
Lucy Maxym Russian Collections, 217
Lundberg, 42
Lunt, 84, 110, 125, 209
Luvlife Collectibles, 69, 109
Lyman, Steve, 19, 181
Lynette Decor, 12, 34, 101, 161, 247; See also Accessories, Frames

—M—

Madame Alexander, 2-4, 21, 24, 29-30, 32-35, 42, 44, 52-53, 55, 58, 64, 66-67, 81, 83-84, 86, 90, 94-95, 98, 105-106, 108, 110, 117-119, 124, 130, 132, 139, 141, 143, 148, 152-153, 155, 157, 161, 165, 170, 172, 177, 180, 182-183, 185, 187, 191, 193, 195, 197, 199, 202, 210-211, 216-217, 225, 227-228, 234, 241-242, 244, 249, 254, 258
Maggy Maid, 53
Mago, 111
Maija, 18, 36, 140
Maley, Alan, 8, 17, 24, 26, 33-34, 191, 236

Malornis, 136
Mama's Babies, 149
Marina's Russian Collection, 120, 240
Marseille, Armand, 29
Martinez, Martin, 21
Martinsburg, R., 251
Marty Bear Foot, 226
Marty Sculptures, 7, 21, 47, 82, 159, 181, 200, 206
Maruri, 1-2, 4-7, 9, 11, 14, 16, 21, 23-24, 26-27, 31, 33, 35, 37, 41-42, 45, 47-48, 52-53, 55-56, 58, 60, 62, 65, 68, 70, 72, 74, 78-79, 84, 88, 90, 95, 97, 102, 106, 111, 113, 118-119, 121-122, 127-128, 130-133, 135-138, 141-145, 147-156, 158-161, 163, 165-166, 168, 171-172, 177-178, 180-182, 184, 188-189, 198, 200-202, 206-207, 209, 211, 213, 219-220, 222-223, 226, 228-231, 233-235, 239, 246-248, 252, 254-257
Mason, Linda, 92, 197, 206, 227, 243, 251, 253
Master Works Pewter, 138
Mattel, 5, 22, 34, 54, 92, 105, 117-118, 132, 155, 243, 251; See also Corolle, Annette Himstedt
Mayflower Glass, 7, 88, 151, 226, 247
McB Bears, 205, 236
McCarthy, Frank, 19, 194
McClelland, John, 77, 92, 111, 240; See also Reco Intl.
McClure, Cindy, 240, 251
McCormick, 19
McGill, 213
McGuffy, 66, 217
McHugh, 82
McKee, Kay, 53
McKenna, June, 8, 32, 34, 42, 44-47, 55-56, 59, 63, 68-69, 87, 97, 104-105, 109-111, 114-115, 124, 129, 131, 135, 151, 154, 162, 164, 168, 174, 179, 187-188, 193, 196, 200-201, 203-206, 209-212, 214, 218-220, 229, 235, 238, 240-241, 243
McPherson, 98
McVicker, Terry, 205
Meger, Jim, 140, 180
Meggan, 190
Meissen, 2, 55
Melody in Motion, 1-2, 6, 8, 17, 23, 28, 34, 36-37, 39, 42, 44, 67, 78, 82, 89, 91, 93, 104, 107-108, 111-112, 114, 121, 126, 141, 146, 149, 153-154, 156-157, 165, 168, 174, 179, 183, 194, 196-199, 202, 206, 221, 229, 233, 235, 251
Memories of Yesterday, 1, 4-7, 9-12, 14-15, 17-18, 20-23, 25-27, 30, 35-36, 38-39, 41, 43-57, 59-65, 69-85, 87-93, 95-108, 111-120, 125-130, 132-139, 141-159, 161-168, 170-172, 174-175, 177-192, 194-195, 198, 200-206, 210-211, 213, 218-220, 222, 224, 226-227, 230-233, 235-237, 239, 241-244, 246, 248, 250, 252-259
Merry Thought, 83, 88, 123, 125, 191, 193, 197
Merry Tymes, 76
Meyer, Mary, 118, 155
Michael's Ltd., 13, 48, 54, 61, 65, 72-73, 80, 85, 100, 107, 110-111, 121, 145, 152-154, 156, 165, 170-171, 179, 201, 203, 209, 235, 238, 245, 259; See also Brian Baker
Middleton Dolls, 28, 42, 46, 53, 56, 73, 85, 89, 98, 127, 135, 157, 166, 168, 178, 186, 200-202, 236, 239, 248, 250, 252, 255

KEY TO STATES

AL: 1-3	**DE:** 46	**IA:** 95-98	**MN:** 136-142	**NM:** 159-160	**RI:** 214-215	**VA:** 239-243
AK: 3	**FL:** 47-61	**KS:** 98-100	**MS:** 142-143	**NY:** 160-172	**SC:** 215-218	**WA:** 244-250
AZ: 4-7	**GA:** 61-70	**KY:** 100-101	**MO:** 143-147	**NC:** 172-180	**SD:** 218-220	**WV:** 250-251
AR: 7-8	**HA:** 70	**LA:** 101-104	**MT:** 147-148	**ND:** 180-181	**TN:** 220-226	**WI:** 252-257
CA: 8-37	**ID:** 70-71	**ME:** 104-105	**NE:** 148-150	**OH:** 181-193	**TX:** 226-237	**WY:** 258
CO: 37-39	**IL:** 71-85	**MD:** 106-110	**NV:** 150	**OK:** 193-195	**UT:** 237-238	**CANADA:**
CT: 40-46	**IN:** 86-95	**MA:** 111-115	**NH:** 151	**OR:** 196-200	**VT:** 238	258-260
		MI: 115-135	**NJ:** 152-159	**PA:** 201-214		

Midwest Importers, 10, 12-13, 16, 22, 32, 35-36, 41-42, 44, 46, 56-57, 68, 70-71, 73, 75-76, 85, 87-89, 97, 103, 105, 108-109, 111, 113, 119-120, 123-124, 131-132, 135-136, 143, 155, 161-162, 169, 172-173, 176, 179-180, 182, 184, 188, 193, 196-198, 201, 206, 208, 214, 217, 225, 232, 240, 243, 252, 254, 256-257; See also Leo R. Smith, Nutcrackers, Santas

Mikasa, 111, 134, 137, 153, 156, 165, 208, 231

Milford Nutcrackers, 19, 37, 67-68, 199, 209, 217

Mill Creek, 4, 7, 12, 38, 45, 68-69, 87, 101, 104, 113, 121, 123, 127, 135-136, 147, 151-152, 160-161, 164, 173, 176, 179, 188, 200, 202, 245, 251

Mill Pond, 71, 102, 160, 169, 202

Miller Imports, 229

Miniature Limoge, 233

Miro, Joan, 177

Miss Martha Originals, 34, 63, 97, 114, 124, 163, 185, 224, 228, 233, 237, 247; See also All God's Children

Mixed Blessings / Linda Archer, 13

MJC International, 67

Monika, 88, 117, 227

Monroe Pottery, 204

Mont Blanc, 44

Montfort, Daniel, 1, 14, 64, 69, 101, 128, 145, 161, 174, 223, 226, 228, 235

Moran, Malcolm, 77

Morgan, Doris, 82, 90, 129, 175

Mortensen, D., 114, 146

Moses, Erlene, 33, 111, 183

Moss, P. Buckley, 4, 6-7, 11, 16-17, 19, 21-22, 27-29, 32-33, 38, 42-43, 46, 48, 50, 57, 62-63, 69, 77-78, 87, 92, 95-98, 101, 112-113, 122, 132, 136, 146, 150, 174, 181-182, 188-189, 206, 211, 213, 220, 227, 234, 241, 248, 250, 252; See also ANNA-PERENNA

Mother Goose Originals, 136

Mottahedeh, 125, 140, 241

Mountain Babies, 171

Moussali, 97

Mt. Saint Helens Art Glass, 247

Muckenfuss, Rose Ann, 216

Muffy Vanderbears, 3, 17, 26, 29, 32-33, 35-36, 49, 51-52, 60, 66-67, 74, 80, 83, 88, 90, 94, 97-98, 100, 102, 120, 124, 132, 134, 137, 168-169, 197, 207, 210, 224-225, 227, 234, 245, 249, 252

Munro, 51

Murano Clowns, 35

Murray, Allan, 24, 33-34, 211

Music Boxes, 20, 30, 41, 44, 46, 51, 55, 57-58, 62, 66, 74, 81-82, 85, 91, 96, 98, 101, 103-104, 108, 113, 116, 129, 133, 145, 160-161, 169, 174, 179, 188, 198, 203, 206, 208, 212, 219, 225, 227, 229, 231, 237-238, 240-242, 248, 253, 256

—N—

Naber Kids, 29, 67, 92, 123

Nahrgang, Jan, 66, 70, 88, 129, 135, 140, 173, 190-191, 208, 210, 216, 225, 253

Nan, 97, 138

Nanbe, 231

NAO / Lladro, 7, 27, 138

National Heritage Gallery, 220-221

Native American, 48, 51, 111, 138

Nativity Sets, 20, 24, 52, 57, 61, 93, 104, 109, 140, 179, 182, 214, 225, 238, 240, 251

Natures Gallery, 220

Ness, Janet, 33, 50, 129, 243, 251

Nesting Dolls, 90, 109, 125, 148, 189, 191, 232, 243, 247-248

Norfin Trolls, 138, 193

Noritake, 65, 110, 231

North American Bears, 1, 53-55, 80, 123, 132, 136, 172, 183, 197, 199, 234, 247

Nova, 45

Novelino, 21, 89, 141

Nutcrackers, 3, 5, 10-12, 30, 37, 40-41, 44, 46, 53, 67-68, 70, 72, 74, 77, 81, 87, 89-93, 97, 101, 103-104, 108-109, 112-115, 120-121, 131-132, 136, 138-139, 141-143, 148, 152, 157, 161-162, 165, 173-174, 176, 179-180,

182-184, 187-189, 193, 195-196, 199, 201, 204-207, 209-210, 212, 214, 217, 222, 225, 232, 238-240, 242-243, 245, 247-248, 250, 253-254, 257

—O—

Old World Christmas, 12, 14, 20, 22, 24, 30, 35, 40, 52, 54, 57, 68, 72, 81, 93, 97, 104, 109, 113, 120, 122-125, 131-132, 135-137, 140-141, 143, 162, 172-174, 176, 179, 184, 195-196, 198-201, 205, 214, 217, 219, 228, 231-232, 235, 240, 242, 250, 252-257

Oldenburg Originals, 106, 123, 153, 193

Oldham Porcelain Studio, 204-205

Olson, Robert, 140, 181

Olszewski, 1-2, 6, 17-18, 30, 33, 37, 43, 48, 53, 55, 69, 126, 130, 170, 172, 178, 182, 193-194, 199, 225, 228, 234, 244-245, 251, 254

Olympia Steins, 201

Omnibus, 36

Original Appalachian Artwork, 3, 62, 67, 88, 144, 199-200, 236; See also Cabbage Patch Kids

Orrefors, 26, 35, 125, 140, 241

Orzeck, 225

Otagiri Portmeirion, 110

Ott, Heidi, 3, 50, 88, 153, 159, 187, 205, 216, 227, 242-243

Overly-Raker Santa, 108, 136, 164

—P—

P.A. Cross, 26, 34, 37, 81, 140, 194, 198

Paddington Bears, 32, 168

Palmer, John, 175

Panton Art, 70, 208, 211, 233; See also Krystonia

Paperweights, 22, 38, 41-42, 57, 69, 74, 76, 177, 179, 186, 241, 260

Paradise Gallery, 3-5, 17, 106, 114, 125, 146, 210, 224, 249

Paragon Pictures, 106

Parkins, Phyllis dolls, 47, 53, 58, 86, 117, 124, 166, 190, 210, 225, 227; See also Collectables, The

Parks, Don, 86

Partha Pewter, 238

Partners in Crime, 60, 73, 89, 91, 97

Past Impressions, 10

Patterson, Terrance, 226

Paul, Barbara, 19-20

Pemberton & Oakes, 45, 49, 84, 101, 247, 259; See also Donald Zolan

PenDelfin, 1, 15, 36, 42, 44-46, 53-54, 61-62, 64-65, 69, 98, 101-102, 109, 112-113, 115-116, 122, 138, 147, 149, 151, 153, 155, 158, 162-165, 167-169, 178, 206, 210-212, 214, 223, 252, 259

PenniBears, 4, 7, 15, 17, 21, 23, 26, 28, 33, 35-36, 39, 49, 54-55, 61-63, 69-70, 73, 77, 81, 85, 87, 94, 103, 115, 128, 135, 141, 143, 157, 159, 166, 190, 193, 197, 199, 209, 211-212, 224, 255

Perillo, Greg, 4, 6-7, 9-10, 14, 17-18, 20-21, 26-27, 33-40, 43, 45, 48, 50, 53, 56-58, 60, 62, 70, 77, 80, 82, 85-86, 88, 92, 95, 106, 111-113, 122, 126, 132-134, 136, 138, 145, 147, 150, 152, 154-155, 161-162, 165, 168-170, 172-173, 177, 180, 183-185, 189, 198-199, 205-208, 210-211, 213, 222, 226-228, 235, 249, 251, 254, 259

KEY TO STATES

AL: 1-3	**DE:** 46	**IA:** 95-98	**MN:** 136-142	**NM:** 159-160	**RI:** 214-215	**VA:** 239-243
AK: 3	**FL:** 47-61	**KS:** 98-100	**MS:** 142-143	**NY:** 160-172	**SC:** 215-218	**WA:** 244-250
AZ: 4-7	**GA:** 61-70	**KY:** 100-101	**MO:** 143-147	**NC:** 172-180	**SD:** 218-220	**WV:** 250-251
AR: 7-8	**HA:** 70	**LA:** 101-104	**MT:** 147-148	**ND:** 180-181	**TN:** 220-226	**WI:** 252-257
CA: 8-37	**ID:** 70-71	**ME:** 104-105	**NE:** 148-150	**OH:** 181-193	**TX:** 226-237	**WY:** 258
CO: 37-39	**IL:** 71-85	**MD:** 106-110	**NV:** 150	**OK:** 193-195	**UT:** 237-238	**CANADA:**
CT: 40-46	**IN:** 86-95	**MA:** 111-115	**NH:** 151	**OR:** 196-200	**VT:** 238	258-260
		MI: 115-135	**NJ:** 152-159	**PA:** 201-214		

Perry, John, 69, 142, 147, 150, 158, 230, 235, 241
Perth Pewter, 12, 22, 39, 45, 104, 113, 115, 163, 238
Perthshire, 42
Peterson, Charles, 84
Pewter, 3-5, 7, 12-13, 15, 18, 21-22, 28, 32, 37-39, 42-45, 47-48, 53-54, 61, 65, 69-70, 72, 77-78, 83, 87, 90, 96, 101, 104, 106, 108, 110-113, 118, 121-122, 126, 131-132, 134-138, 141-142, 145-147, 150-153, 156, 161-163, 165, 168-171, 173, 176-180, 185-186, 188, 200, 202-204, 206, 211-212, 217, 222, 228, 237-238, 240, 245-246, 248, 259
Pfaltzgraff, 233
Phyllis Parkins, 47, 53, 58, 86, 117, 124, 210, 225
Picasso, 177
Pickard, 209, 245, 247
Pig Lady, 110, 175, 203, 215
Pigsville, 138
Pilgrim Glass, 164, 233
Pine Baroness, 155
Pine Hollow, 242
PJ's Carousels, 9, 56, 64, 177, 240, 243, 253
Plates, 1, 4, 7, 11, 13, 15-16, 18, 20-21, 25, 30, 36-37, 51, 54, 58, 63, 71, 75, 77, 80-82, 92, 95-96, 98, 119, 127, 129, 133-134, 139, 141, 157, 159, 161, 163, 165, 170, 181-183, 185, 189, 195, 202, 205, 227, 240, 246, 249, 252-253, 258-260
Pluzoch, H, 227
PM Country Dolls, 180, 186
Pocket Dragons, 15, 17, 22, 33, 37, 39, 45, 47, 69, 71-72, 79, 85, 104, 107-108, 113, 136, 152, 154, 158-159, 163, 166, 178, 181, 184, 200, 206, 219, 226, 228, 230-231, 236-237, 239, 247, 249, 251, 255
Polland, Don, 14, 38, 53, 58, 70, 207, 228
Poortvliet, Rien, 62, 162
Porsgrund, 97, 180, 247
Port Meirion, 41, 110, 195, 231, 244

Porter Music Boxes, 191, 247
Positive Image, 1, 62, 67, 69, 109, 206
Possible Dreams, 2, 20, 24, 41, 59, 73, 77, 85, 90, 93, 96-97, 100, 105, 109, 114, 120, 124, 133, 139, 149, 152, 168, 170, 179, 182, 196, 203, 207, 212, 214, 216, 219, 224, 232, 236, 240, 248, 252-253
Precious Art / Panton, 51, 58, 70, 113, 208, 211, 217, 233; See also Krystonia
Precious Heirlooms, 22, 66, 155, 173, 184, 201
Precious Moments, 1-15, 17, 20-21, 23-37, 39-52, 54-60, 62-66, 68-85, 87-120, 122-130, 132-139, 141-159, 161-175, 177-195, 198-208, 211-214, 216-228, 230-239, 241, 243-246, 248-260
Precious Moments Dolls, 5, 21, 77, 83, 91, 109, 152, 166, 220
Precious Moments Gold Cards, 96
Preisner Pewter, 43, 45
Princeton Galleries, 36, 132
Pro-Sport Creations, 34, 102
Purrfect Pets, 47, 226

—R—

Raggedy Ann, 13, 249
Raikes Bears, 1, 3-6, 10, 14, 21-23, 26, 30, 32-38, 53-55, 58, 60, 62, 66-67, 69, 71-73, 81, 83, 87-89, 92-93, 95-98, 104-105, 110, 114, 116, 118, 123, 126-127, 132-134, 139, 143, 146, 149-150, 152, 160, 163-164, 166-169, 172, 180-181, 183, 186, 189-190, 193, 195, 197, 199, 201-203, 210, 212, 216, 218, 220-221, 223, 226, 230, 237, 247-248, 251-253
Rawcliffe Pewter, 12, 21, 45, 48, 54, 83, 106, 114, 121, 137-138, 152, 161, 202, 217, 222, 228
Reading, Randy, 200, 211
Reco International, 7, 16-17, 22, 36, 40, 45, 47-48, 51, 58, 66, 83-84, 86, 89, 94, 96-98, 101-102, 111, 114, 116, 119, 128, 130, 133, 136-137, 139, 147, 153-154, 156, 158-159, 161, 163, 165, 171, 180,

185, 191, 200, 213, 217, 219, 231, 233, 237, 240, 244, 246-249, 251, 253-254, 257, 259; See also Bergsma, Jody; Kuck, Sandra; McClelland, John
Red Mill Mfg., 7, 30, 46, 62, 83, 101, 147, 225-226, 237, 258
Redlin, Terry, 12, 17-18, 24, 26, 36, 38, 64, 71, 75, 77, 81-82, 84-85, 87, 92, 94-95, 116, 121, 125, 139-142, 144-147, 169, 181, 187, 205, 213, 235, 249, 252, 254-257, 259
Reed & Barton, 1, 10, 44, 84, 100, 110, 125, 210, 245
Remington, Frederic, 177, 238
Renoir, 177
Resch, Thelma, 66, 88
Reuge Music Boxes, 74, 206
Rhodes Studios, 82
Richards, Barbara Bourgeau, 32, 204
Robart's Mice, 104
Roberts, Xavier, 67
Roche, Lynn & Michale, 117, 123, 129, 166, 197, 227, 251
Rock Santas, 97
Rockdale Pottery, 242
Rockwell, Norman, 8, 18, 36, 38, 40, 43, 45, 49, 52-53, 56, 64-65, 72, 76, 82-83, 85, 87, 90, 96-98, 102, 106, 108, 111-112, 122, 125, 127, 129-130, 133-134, 145-148, 152, 155-156, 162-163, 169, 172, 182, 184-188, 195, 202, 204, 206, 216, 226, 231, 233, 235
Roeda, Carol, 111
Rogaska, Miller, 199, 241
Rohn Sculptures, 2
Roland Lithophanes, 174
Roman, Inc., 1, 15, 22, 27, 29-30, 35, 42, 44, 47-48, 53-54, 56-58, 61-62, 65, 71-73, 76, 83-85, 89, 91, 93, 97, 99, 101-102, 104-106, 108, 111, 118-119, 122, 126-127, 130-134, 136-138, 143, 145-147, 152-153, 156-157, 161, 165, 168-169, 171-172, 176, 179, 181, 184, 186, 191, 196, 198, 208, 214-215, 217, 219-220, 224, 236-237, 240, 245, 247, 251-252, 255-258
Roman Classic Bride, 93, 171
Ron Lee, 1, 5-9, 11, 14, 16-18, 21, 23, 26, 28-29, 31, 35, 39-40, 45, 47, 49, 51, 53, 62, 64, 74, 79, 101-102, 104, 112, 114-115, 118-119, 131, 134, 137, 146-148, 150, 158-159, 166, 179, 197-200, 205, 210, 217, 224, 226, 228, 230, 232, 234-235, 237, 244, 247-248
Ron Wall Miniatures, 70, 103, 147
Roosevelt Bears, 22, 98, 124, 157, 165, 174, 234, 248
Root Beeswax Candles, 249
Rose, Neil, 21, 39, 73, 85, 104, 163, 177, 188, 220, 252
Rosenthal, 228, 241, 245
Roth Trefferson, 117
Rowe Pottery, 29, 100, 107, 110-111, 129, 157, 164, 168, 203-204, 210, 224
Royal Albert, 36, 121, 156
Royal Copenhagen, 6-7, 10, 20-21, 34, 39-40, 43, 48-50, 57-58, 62, 72, 77-78, 80, 82, 88, 97, 99, 106, 109-110, 112, 119, 125, 136, 138, 140-141, 148-149, 157, 161, 163, 172, 179-180, 182-183, 196, 198-199, 202, 209, 228, 235, 244-245, 247, 252, 256-257
Royal Crown Derby, 57, 77, 217, 241
Royal Crystal Rock, 44
Royal Doulton, 2, 5-6, 8-11, 26, 34, 36, 43, 45, 50, 54-55, 57, 62, 70, 72, 74, 76, 79-81, 88, 106, 110, 112-113, 119, 125,

KEY TO STATES

AL: 1-3	**DE:** 46	**IA:** 95-98	**MN:** 136-142	**NM:** 159-160	**RI:** 214-215	**VA:** 239-243
AK: 3	**FL:** 47-61	**KS:** 98-100	**MS:** 142-143	**NY:** 160-172	**SC:** 215-218	**WA:** 244-250
AZ: 4-7	**GA:** 61-70	**KY:** 100-101	**MO:** 143-147	**NC:** 172-180	**SD:** 218-220	**WV:** 250-251
AR: 7-8	**HA:** 70	**LA:** 101-104	**MT:** 147-148	**ND:** 180-181	**TN:** 220-226	**WI:** 252-257
CA: 8-37	**ID:** 70-71	**ME:** 104-105	**NE:** 148-150	**OH:** 181-193	**TX:** 226-237	**WY:** 258
CO: 37-39	**IL:** 71-85	**MD:** 106-110	**NV:** 150	**OK:** 193-195	**UT:** 237-238	**CANADA:**
CT: 40-46	**IN:** 86-95	**MA:** 111-115	**NH:** 151	**OR:** 196-200	**VT:** 238	258-260
		MI: 115-135	**NJ:** 152-159	**PA:** 201-214		

130, 134, 138, 140, 142, 151, 153-154, 163, 165, 167, 169, 171, 177, 182-185, 188-189, 192-193, 198-199, 209, 221, 225, 228, 230, 233, 241, 244-245, 247, 260
Royal Worcester, 231, 241, 245
Rubel, Tom Santas, 41
Rueger, Julia, 123, 129, 197, 243
Russ Berrie Trolls, 177, 222
Russian Alexander Nevesky Collection, 19
Russian Boxes, 51, 228
Russian Collectibles, 120, 129, 240, 250
Russian Eggs, 199
Russian Icons, 228
Russian Lacquer, 148, 194, 241
Russian Nesting Dolls, 67, 90, 109, 175
Russian Plates, 13, 248
Rust, Don, 121

—S—

Sabino Glass, 7, 22, 48, 99, 101, 149, 193, 227-228, 230, 233
Sadek, 1, 4-5, 7, 9, 12, 22, 24, 37, 59-60, 70, 78, 81, 97, 100, 106, 110-111, 118, 121, 134-135, 140, 142, 147, 152-153, 156, 161-162, 165, 180, 193-194, 226, 230-231, 233, 236, 253-254, 257; See also Andrea by Sadek
Sadler Teapots, 76
Salmon Falls Stoneware, 155
Salvino, 34, 88, 117, 161, 190, 202, 206, 211, 213, 250
Sandicast, 5, 8-10, 20-21, 28, 35, 39, 41-43, 47, 50, 53, 59-60, 62, 65, 69, 76, 79-81, 96, 98-99, 101-102, 104, 110, 114, 118, 123, 127, 131, 134, 136-138, 141-142, 148, 150, 155-156, 167-168, 170, 173, 176, 180, 188-189, 193, 198, 219, 221, 223, 226, 230, 234, 236-237, 246-247, 251-252, 254, 259
Sandridge, John, 69, 221
Santas; See Collectible Santas
Sarah's Attic, 1-10, 14-15, 17, 19-23, 26-28, 32-35, 37, 39-40, 43-45, 47, 49-50, 53-54, 56, 58-60, 62, 64-67,
69-74, 77-78, 80, 85-88, 90, 92-93, 95, 97-108, 110-113, 115-116, 118-119, 121-124, 126-131, 133, 136, 139, 141-142, 144, 146-148, 151-154, 158-162, 164-165, 168-169, 171-176, 178, 182-186, 189-190, 192-199, 201-203, 205-208, 210-211, 216, 219-220, 223, 226-229, 232-237, 239, 241-242, 244-249, 252, 255-256, 258
Savvy (Swarovski), 76, 121, 168
Schaefer, Ed, 84
Schmeling, Karin, 88
Schmid Disney, 2, 85, 127, 139, 253
Schmid, 1-2, 8, 14, 16, 22, 32, 36, 40-42, 44-45, 48, 51, 56-58, 62, 70, 72, 77-78, 82-83, 85, 89, 102, 105-106, 109, 127, 136, 139, 141, 145, 156, 161, 165, 168-169, 171-173, 180, 184, 188, 191, 196, 205, 209, 212-213, 215, 217, 220, 233, 245, 247, 252-253, 257
Schrott, Rotraut, 28, 66, 90
Seagull Pewter, 45, 48, 54, 121, 135, 245
Seasonal Artplas Miniatures, 242
Sebastian Miniatures, 40, 43, 45, 75, 79, 83, 91, 97, 102-103, 106, 111, 113, 130, 151, 209, 226
Second Nature Wildlife Sculptures, 70, 226
Seiko clocks, 118, 202, 210, 251
Seivers, Lee, 69, 128, 236
Sersha by Serietta, 205
Seymour Mann, 5, 7, 16, 19-20, 22, 29, 46, 53, 58, 66-67, 71, 74, 86-87, 92-94, 118, 132, 134, 155-156, 166, 168, 172, 182, 187, 191, 193, 195, 206, 208, 216-217, 222, 230, 232, 243-244, 251
Shackleford, Jan, 15, 90, 127, 159, 258
Shackman, 242
Shader, 166
Shadow Dancer, 162, 204
Shelia's Houses, 1-3, 15, 19, 46, 48, 54-55, 61, 63-64, 66-68, 74, 85, 87, 89, 91, 98, 101, 104, 109-111, 114, 121, 124, 152, 155, 157-158, 164, 171-172, 176, 178, 189, 200, 202-205, 207-208, 210, 214, 216, 218, 222, 235, 239, 250-251, 256
Shelton, Val, 94, 123, 183

Shoehouses, 26, 70, 125, 127, 176, 203-204, 207, 218, 221, 241
Shoemaker's Dream, 4, 39, 43, 45-47, 50, 53, 55, 68, 101-102, 104, 109, 122, 143, 184-185, 190, 197, 199, 202, 209, 211-212, 228, 230, 236-237, 244, 258
Shube's Pewter, 206
Sierra Brook Studios, 6, 29, 64, 178, 204-205
Silver Deer, 37, 39, 42, 45, 47-48, 58, 61, 73-74, 79, 85, 92, 105, 116-117, 128, 130-131, 134, 152-154, 156, 163, 169, 171, 173, 200, 206, 208, 229-230, 247, 257
Silvestri, 30, 42, 57, 87, 108, 131, 135, 153, 176, 200, 214, 242
Simpich, 44, 104, 175
Simpkins, Lee woodcarvings, 67
Simple Wonders, 6, 158
Sissel, Robert, 84
Sisters & Best Friends, 36-37, 41, 46, 51, 57, 62, 72-73, 76, 79, 81-82, 89, 94, 96-97, 106, 110-111, 135, 137, 147, 150, 155, 157, 171, 180, 183, 186, 217-218, 220-221, 236-237, 248, 251
Skelton, Red, 17-18, 23, 43, 53, 62, 95, 134, 191, 197, 232
Sloan, Richard, 84
Smith, Leo R III, 8, 13, 49, 68, 76, 100, 120, 124, 131, 135, 161, 193, 196, 205, 228, 240; See also Midwest Importers
Smith, Ronald, 244
Smith Santas, 49, 205
Smoak, Beth, 216
Smokers, 11, 14, 40, 68, 87, 90, 92, 103, 109, 115, 131, 138, 141, 148, 165, 173, 176, 182, 184, 188-189, 195, 199, 204, 207, 214, 238, 240, 242, 254

Somerset House, 160, 198, 202
Southern Heritage, 59, 67-68
Spain, Nancy, 129
Spangler's Realm, 69
Spanos Dolls, 22, 53, 66, 125, 152-153, 183, 187, 205, 225, 243
Spencer, Irene, 53, 194
Spencer Light Houses, 113
Spiegal-Lohr, Linda, 129
Spode, 100, 180, 231, 241, 245, 259
Spoontiques, 38, 45, 91, 103, 122, 131, 134, 150, 152, 157, 206, 215
Sports Collectibles, 8-9, 28, 48, 60, 65, 71-72, 75, 125, 150, 154, 157, 185, 190, 230, 232
Sports Impressions, 2-3, 5-9, 11, 13-16, 20-23, 26-27, 30, 33-34, 36-38, 40-41, 43-45, 47, 49-53, 55-60, 62, 64-65, 69, 71, 73-74, 77-79, 82-83, 85-89, 91, 94-95, 98, 101-102, 104, 106, 108, 111-120, 127-128, 130, 132-134, 136, 141, 145-149, 151-154, 156-159, 161-164, 166-173, 176-183, 185-186, 188-190, 192, 195, 201-203, 205-208, 210-214, 217, 221-227, 229-231, 233, 235-236, 239, 242, 246, 248, 250, 252-253, 255-257, 259
Stadden Figures, 216, 239
Staffordshire, 88, 116, 217
Stamps, 62, 65, 68, 83, 90, 123, 135, 152, 158, 182-183, 212, 217, 222, 239, 251
Stanton Arts, 51, 54, 91, 99, 127, 131, 194, 222, 226, 233, 236; See also Emmett Kelly, Sr.
Star Collection, 35
Star Trek, 36, 48, 51, 55, 89-90, 106, 138, 144, 152, 170, 173, 181, 188, 192, 208, 223

```
                        KEY TO STATES
  AL: 1-3      DE: 46       IA: 95-98     MN: 136-142   NM: 159-160   RI: 214-215   VA: 239-243
  AK: 3        FL: 47-61    KS: 98-100    MS: 142-143   NY: 160-172   SC: 215-218   WA: 244-250
  AZ: 4-7      GA: 61-70    KY: 100-101   MO: 143-147   NC: 172-180   SD: 218-220   WV: 250-251
  AR: 7-8      HA: 70       LA: 101-104   MT: 147-148   ND: 180-181   TN: 220-226   WI: 252-257
  CA: 8-37     ID: 70-71    ME: 104-105   NE: 148-150   OH: 181-193   TX: 226-237   WY: 258
  CO: 37-39    IL: 71-85    MD: 106-110   NV: 150       OK: 193-195   UT: 237-238   CANADA:
  CT: 40-46    IN: 86-95    MA: 111-115   NH: 151       OR: 196-200   VT: 238          258-260
                            MI: 115-135   NJ: 152-159   PA: 201-214
```

Steele, Linda, 227, 249, 251
Steiff Bears, 32, 51, 58, 60, 64, 67, 76, 79, 86, 88, 90, 94, 99, 105, 114, 116, 123-125, 129, 139, 157, 159, 166, 172, 188, 191, 193, 197-199, 202, 205, 212, 225, 227, 236, 251, 257
Steinbach Crystal, 14, 48, 101, 150, 225
Steinbach Nutcrackers, 10, 37, 46, 53, 70, 72, 74, 81, 90, 92, 101, 103-104, 108-109, 112, 115, 120, 132, 138, 142-143, 157, 161, 165, 169, 176, 183, 187, 189, 194, 201, 205-207, 210, 214, 222, 225, 228, 232, 238, 240, 242-243, 247-248, 257
Steinbach Steins, 101
Steiner, Heidi, 96, 205
Sternsy Bears, 229
Stobart, John, 102
Stone, Fred, 6, 11-12, 18-19, 26, 32, 36, 49, 58, 62, 82, 94, 101-102, 113, 115, 126, 259
Stone Critters, 47, 73, 123, 132, 138, 152, 155, 157, 161
Storybook Collection, 1, 62, 77, 104, 175
Studio Edition Dolls, 132, 176
Sugartown, 15, 78-79, 106, 146, 174, 182
Summer Breeze, 61, 65, 74
Summerhill Crystal, 38, 41, 44, 72, 76, 99, 137, 147, 152, 163, 184, 200, 202, 215, 239, 247
Summers, Robert, 234
Superman, 14
Swarovski America Ltd., 1-12, 14-18, 20-21, 23-24, 26-28, 30-38, 40-56, 59, 61, 63-64, 66, 68-71, 75-76, 78-82, 84-85, 88, 91-92, 95-96, 98-99, 106-108, 110-115, 117, 119, 121, 123, 125-126, 128, 130, 134-151, 153-159, 161, 163-171, 175-179, 181, 183-189, 193, 195, 198-202, 204-207, 209-214, 216-217, 219-221, 223, 225-226, 228-235, 237, 241-242, 244-248, 250, 252-257, 260
Swarovski Classics, 53
Swarovski Selection, 2, 6, 42, 47
Swiss Army Knives, 178

—T—

Tabor, Tom, 28, 252
Takahashi, 109
Tank, Thomas Collectibles, 120
Tattered Rabbit, 32
Teacups and Saucers, 7
Teddy Bears, 4, 9, 55, 74, 88, 169, 197, 225; See also Collectible Bears
Temple, Shirley, 65, 249
Tender Touches, 42, 83, 117
Terpning, Howard, 19, 181, 194
Terrones, Marie, 33
The Legend of Santa Claus, 220, 226
The Pig Lady, 110, 175, 203, 215
The Ultimate Collection, 66, 86
The Villagers, 104, 179, 214, 238, 243
Thewalt, 176
Thimbles, 13, 17, 82, 131, 237, 240, 245, 260
Thompson, Pat, 53, 86, 88, 166, 193
Thumb Print Teddies, 13, 19, 67
Tide-Rider, 94
Tierney, Louise, 53
Tiffany, 29, 136, 149, 177
Timeless Creations, 5
Tin Toys, 50
Tobin Fraley, 10, 23, 35, 43, 71, 82, 86, 116, 185, 199
Toby Jugs, 69, 90, 239
Tomorrow-Today, 108, 152
Tonner, Robert, 50, 129, 171, 227
Toon Art, 249
Top Cats, 2
Towle Silversmiths, 10, 84, 110, 125, 209
Town Square Collection, 64, 116, 156
Toys, 30, 50, 54, 67, 105, 205, 212, 247, 250
Treasure Masters, 111, 153, 156, 165
Treffeisen, Ruth, 33
Tripi, Angela, 62, 76, 104, 169, 232, 241
Trobe, Carol, 88
Tuf Times, 228
Turley, Glynda, 7, 22, 32, 65, 73, 86, 102, 105, 111, 123, 136, 171, 246, 251
Turner Dolls, 17, 22, 53, 86, 88, 118, 123,

129-130, 153, 171, 183, 187, 193, 201, 206, 217, 225, 243, 251

— U —

Ulbricht, Christian, 2, 10, 40, 68, 77, 90, 103, 108, 120, 131, 140-141, 173, 182, 189, 196, 199, 209, 217, 225, 247-248, 250, 257

Ultimate Collection, 66, 86, 205

United Design, 2, 4, 7-8, 10, 14, 16-17, 21-22, 26, 29, 31, 38, 40, 43-44, 46-47, 49, 53-54, 56, 59, 62, 64-65, 68-72, 74, 76, 78-79, 84, 87, 89, 91-93, 95, 98-99, 101-105, 109, 111, 114-115, 117, 119, 121-123, 127-128, 131-133, 135-138, 142-143, 145, 147-148, 150-153, 155-156, 158-159, 162-165, 168, 170, 174, 178, 180, 182-188, 191, 196-197, 200, 204, 208-209, 214-215, 217, 219-220, 224-225, 228, 230, 232, 234, 239-240, 244-245, 252-253, 255, 257-258

United Design Little People, 7

United Design PenniBears, 4, 7, 15, 17, 21, 23, 26, 28, 33, 35-36, 39, 49, 54-55, 61-63, 69-70, 73, 77, 81, 85, 87, 94, 103, 115, 128, 135, 141, 143, 157, 159, 166, 190, 193, 197, 199, 209, 211-212, 224, 255

United Design Santas, 7, 17, 54, 65, 93, 188, 197, 204, 230, 232, 253

United Design Stone Critters, 132, 138, 155, 188, 208

United Design, 27, 38-39, 85, 89, 103, 149, 212

Ussher, D.H., 117, 260

— V —

V.F. Fine Arts, 10, 48, 84, 91, 101, 152, 252, 259

Vaillancourt, 12, 44, 47, 59, 63, 68, 100, 125, 173, 224, 236, 257

Van-Hygen & Smythe, 12, 101, 129, 162, 184

Vanderbilt, Gloria, 84

Vandermark Merrit Glass, 53

Vanderveen Bronze, 228

Varga Calendars, 57

Via Vermont, 62, 181, 191

VIB Bears, 83, 90, 120, 205

VickiLane, 14, 35, 51, 56, 73, 85, 101, 136, 163, 185, 188, 207, 224, 233, 243

Victoria Ashlea, 18, 54, 76, 88, 135, 139, 141, 159, 167-168, 176, 194, 198-199, 251

Victoria Impex, 15, 134, 139, 150, 158, 247, 257

Victoriana, 161

Vietri, 195

Viking Import House, 49

Villeroy & Boch, 13, 58, 147, 161, 245

Virginia Metal Crafters, 70, 96, 109-110

Vitro Disney, 121

Vlasta, 117, 124, 153, 171

Vogue, 205, 242

— W —

W.S. George, 101, 249

WACO, 4, 23, 34, 36-37, 39, 41, 52-53, 64, 70, 79, 87, 97, 104, 114, 121-122, 128, 136, 141, 146, 148, 154, 163-165, 168, 174, 179-181, 183, 191, 194, 196-197, 199, 202, 214, 219-220, 223, 229, 233-234, 237, 246, 252; See also

KEY TO STATES

AL: 1-3	**DE:** 46	**IA:** 95-98	**MN:** 136-142	**NM:** 159-160	**RI:** 214-215	**VA:** 239-243
AK: 3	**FL:** 47-61	**KS:** 98-100	**MS:** 142-143	**NY:** 160-172	**SC:** 215-218	**WA:** 244-250
AZ: 4-7	**GA:** 61-70	**KY:** 100-101	**MO:** 143-147	**NC:** 172-180	**SD:** 218-220	**WV:** 250-251
AR: 7-8	**HA:** 70	**LA:** 101-104	**MT:** 147-148	**ND:** 180-181	**TN:** 220-226	**WI:** 252-257
CA: 8-37	**ID:** 70-71	**ME:** 104-105	**NE:** 148-150	**OH:** 181-193	**TX:** 226-237	**WY:** 258
CO: 37-39	**IL:** 71-85	**MD:** 106-110	**NV:** 150	**OK:** 193-195	**UT:** 237-238	**CANADA:**
CT: 40-46	**IN:** 86-95	**MA:** 111-115	**NH:** 151	**OR:** 196-200	**VT:** 238	258-260
		MI: 115-135	**NJ:** 152-159	**PA:** 201-214		

Melody in Motion
Wakeen, Susan Dolls, 2-3, 5, 47, 50, 53, 67, 74, 91-92, 117, 122-124, 134, 152, 156, 159, 165, 168, 172, 183, 187, 190, 197, 200, 205, 210-211, 215-216, 225, 228, 236, 243, 251
Walberg, 228
Walker, Vickie, 58, 86, 173
Wall, Ron, 28, 39, 70, 83, 98, 103, 138, 147, 150, 252
Wallace, 2, 67, 84, 110, 125, 209
Walmer, 67
Walt Disney, 1-12, 16-21, 23, 25-28, 30-31, 33-34, 36-39, 42, 44, 47-50, 52-57, 61-64, 66, 68-72, 76-79, 81-82, 85, 87-90, 92-93, 95, 98-100, 102-108, 110, 112-116, 119-121, 123-124, 126-130, 134-135, 138-141, 143-151, 153-161, 163-167, 169-172, 175-178, 180-183, 185-186, 188, 190, 192-202, 206-209, 211, 213, 215, 219-226, 230-231, 234-235, 237-238, 241-245, 247-257
Walt Disney Classics Collection, 1-12, 16-21, 23, 25-28, 30-31, 33-34, 36-39, 42, 44, 47-50, 52-57, 61-64, 66, 68-72, 76-79, 81-82, 85, 87-90, 92-93, 95, 98-100, 102-108, 110, 112-116, 119-121, 123-124, 126-130, 134-135, 138-141, 143-151, 153-161, 163-167, 169-172, 175-178, 180-183, 185-186, 188, 190, 192-202, 206-209, 211, 213, 215, 219-226, 230-231, 234-235, 237-238, 241-245, 247-257
Ward, Michael, 26, 70
Warner Bros., 11, 249
Waterford, 1, 9, 16, 24, 26, 31, 35, 47, 49, 78, 93, 100, 110, 112, 118, 123, 125, 134, 140, 146, 150-151, 157, 163, 165, 180, 184, 199, 202, 204-205, 231, 257, 260
Waterglobes, 91, 129
Waterwonders, 220
Wedgwood, 171
Wee Forest Folk, 4, 7-10, 14-15, 18, 21, 24, 26, 28, 30, 32-34, 36-39, 41-42, 46-47, 54-55, 59, 61-64, 66, 68-69, 71-72, 74, 79, 81, 94, 103, 112-116, 119, 126-127, 130-131, 134, 138, 144, 150, 152, 161, 164, 167, 169-170, 174, 178-179, 182-183, 185, 187, 189, 193, 195, 199, 211, 221, 225, 228, 230, 232-237, 239, 244-245, 250, 253, 256
Weil, Raymond, 31
West, Doug, 117
West, Lynn, 19, 68, 217, 236
Wester, G., 17, 26, 231, 234-235
Western Art, 17, 55, 161, 173-174, 198, 230-231
Westland Carousel Horses, 22, 47, 51, 134, 226
Westminister Graphics, 121
Westmoreland, 83
Whaley, Amelia, 77, 216
Whetherbee Studios, 47
Whiskers, 47
Whitaker, Clare, 216
Whitehurst, 30
Whitley Bay, 68, 79, 162, 168, 175, 228, 249
Wick, Faith, 86, 166, 191, 242
Wideman, Maurice, 6, 11, 54, 57, 68, 70, 79, 88, 101-102, 110, 121, 125, 145, 150, 154, 163, 190, 206, 223
Wieghorst, Olaf, 6, 17
Wild Wings, 96, 161, 202, 249
Wildlife Art, 3, 19, 30, 36, 65, 70, 125, 138, 182, 202, 251
Williamsburg Candles, 176
Willitts, 7, 12, 14, 27, 31, 36, 39, 46, 48, 86, 96, 101, 106, 114, 125, 138, 163, 169, 173, 177, 181-182, 208, 214, 220, 223, 226, 231, 237, 244, 248
Willowcreek Bears, 161
Wilson, W.T., 238
Wimbleton, 205
Windstone, 28, 34, 69, 113, 161, 198, 206, 217, 219, 236, 246
Windy Meadows, 4, 19, 37, 47, 54, 70, 128, 234
Winston Cup Champions Steins, 221
Winston Roland, 15, 80, 134, 147, 174, 259

Winter, David, 1-12, 14-18, 21-28, 30-66, 68-76, 78-85, 87-119, 121-122, 124-131, 133-159, 161, 163-170, 172-190, 192-195, 197-207, 209, 211-214, 216-239, 241-244, 246-259; See also John Hine Studios
Winterlight, 220
Woessner, Joan, 205
Wolfe, Tim, 1, 3-5, 14-15, 22-23, 26-28, 30, 38, 55, 69, 71, 98, 103-104, 115, 128, 133, 144, 149-150, 163, 169, 172, 174-175, 179, 183, 188, 193, 200, 203, 207, 218, 222, 226, 228, 236-237, 244, 247
Wolff, Gretchen and Gustave, 14, 38
Wolford, 130
Wood, William C., 217
Wood Carvings, 67
Wood World, 76, 180, 206, 214
Woodbury, 43, 45, 135
Woods, Robin Dolls, 29, 43, 50, 67, 92, 94, 101, 123-124, 136, 166, 173, 216, 227, 230, 251
Woodspirits, 69, 87, 221
Woodstock Chimes, 96
World Doll, 3, 61, 225, 251
World of Turturi, 138
World Wildlife Fund, 182
Wright, David, 240
Wright, John, 90, 129, 167, 227
Wysocki, 181

—X—

Xaras, 227

—Y—

Yankee Candles, 32, 68, 92, 101, 105, 107, 111, 123, 132, 142, 157, 183, 204, 209, 211, 229, 236, 251
Yuengling, 207

—Z—

Zabel, Larry, 240
Zambelli, 53
Zanini, 53
Zippo, 28
Zoellick, S., 252
Zolan, Donald plates, 122
Zolan, Donald, 6, 9, 11-13, 17-18, 20, 24, 26-27, 32, 36, 45, 56, 62, 71, 77, 82, 85-86, 95-96, 111, 117, 122, 124-125, 129, 140-141, 161, 174, 191, 205, 220, 227, 237, 249, 252, 259; See also Pemberton & Oakes
Zolan, Richard, 96, 161, 220
Zook, Johannes Originals, 3, 17, 20, 22, 50, 53, 67, 80-81, 84, 86-87, 94, 117-118, 122, 124, 130, 134, 145, 148, 155-157, 160, 167, 173, 182-183, 190-191, 193, 197, 210, 216, 220, 222, 236, 243, 247, 251
Zuber, 2, 77, 121

KEY TO STATES

AL: 1-3	DE: 46	IA: 95-98	MN: 136-142	NM: 159-160	RI: 214-215	VA: 239-243
AK: 3	FL: 47-61	KS: 98-100	MS: 142-143	NY: 160-172	SC: 215-218	WA: 244-250
AZ: 4-7	GA: 61-70	KY: 100-101	MO: 143-147	NC: 172-180	SD: 218-220	WV: 250-251
AR: 7-8	HA: 70	LA: 101-104	MT: 147-148	ND: 180-181	TN: 220-226	WI: 252-257
CA: 8-37	ID: 70-71	ME: 104-105	NE: 148-150	OH: 181-193	TX: 226-237	WY: 258
CO: 37-39	IL: 71-85	MD: 106-110	NV: 150	OK: 193-195	UT: 237-238	CANADA:
CT: 40-46	IN: 86-95	MA: 111-115	NH: 151	OR: 196-200	VT: 238	258-260
		MI: 115-135	NJ: 152-159	PA: 201-214		

Collectors' Information Bureau
presents Photo Contest:

Shoot 'N Smile
Collector Style!

HONORING THE PREMIER EDITION OF THE *DIRECTORY TO LIMITED EDITION COLLECTIBLE STORES*

Grand Prize
COLLECT-A-PHOTO: TRAVEL AMERICA

Trip for 2 to the July 1995 South Bend Collectibles Exposition
- 2 Airline tickets to South Bend, Indiana
- 2 tickets to the 2-day Exposition, sponsored by McRand, International
- 3 nights lodging in South Bend
- Breakfast with a collectibles artist
- 2 tickets to the Memories banquet hosted by McRand, International

Awarded to the individual who visits and photographs the most stores featured in the *DIRECTORY TO LIMITED EDITION COLLECTIBLE STORES*.

Plus 25 randomly drawn consolation prizes: Win CIB books and collectibles collectively worth thousands of dollars!

PLUS 4 FIRST PRIZE CATEGORIES!

CONTEST RULES AND REGULATIONS

Grand Prize: COLLECT-A-PHOTO: TRAVEL AMERICA

- ☐ All photographs must be labeled on the back with entrant's name and address, and store name and location.
- ☐ Entrant and store name must be clearly visible in the photograph.
- ☐ All photographs must be mailed in one envelope with the official entry form (no facsimiles, please).
- ☐ Entries must be received no later than April 1, 1995.

4 Additional $1000 Prizes:
COLLECTIBLES FROM WELL-KNOWN ARTISTS AND MANUFACTURERS

Categories Include:
1) Most Humorous
2) Most Original
3) Greatest Distance from Home
   (approximate mileage must be specified on back of photo / we will verify)
4) Most Creative Use of CIB book(s) in Photo

- ☐ Photograph must be labeled on the back with entrant's name and address, and store name and location.
- ☐ Entrant and store name must be clearly visible in the photograph.
- ☐ Photograph must be mailed with the official entry form (no facsimiles, please).
- ☐ Entry must be received no later than April 1, 1995.

Additional Rules and Regulations: Must be 18 years or older to be eligible. Only one entrant per family per category. CIB employees, members, and their families, as well as featured collectible store owners, employees, and their families not eligible. All photographs become the property of the Collectors' Information Bureau. Winners will be notified by May 1, 1995. No substitutions on awards. Not valid where void or prohibited.

Collect-A-Photo: Travel America
Official Entry Form

NAME _____

ADDRESS _____

PHONE _____

CATEGORY: Please check appropriate box(es)

☐ GRAND PRIZE   ☐ MOST HUMOROUS   ☐ MOST ORIGINAL
☐ FARTHEST FROM HOME   ☐ MOST CREATIVE WITH CIB BOOK(S)

Entries must be received by April 1, 1995.

MAIL TO: Collectors' Information Bureau, Shoot 'N Smile: Collector Style!, 2420 Burton S.E., Grand Rapids, MI 49546

(Mechanical Reproductions of this entry form will be considered ineligible)

Four Great Collectibles Offers!

COMPLIMENTARY COPY
"The C.I.B. Report"
Published three times annually
Contains the latest collectibles news:
- Recent product introductions
- New collector clubs
- Convention News
- 40 Page Color Newsletter
- Artist Open Houses, Demonstrations
- Retirement Announcements
- $4.00 Value

Read Our Books!

Four Great Collectibles Offers!

☐ **Yes!**

Please send me a *complimentary* copy of the "C.I.B. Report" newsletter, highlighting the latest collectible news when available.

☐ **Yes!**

Please send me brochures for the following books:

☐ Collectibles Market Guide & Price Index
☐ Collectibles Price Guide
☐ Directory to Secondary Market Retailers

Name _____
Address _____
City _____ State _____ Zip _____
I purchased this book from _____
I am a collector of ☐ Plates ☐ Figurines ☐ Bells ☐ Graphics ☐ Christmas Ornaments ☐ Dolls ☐ Steins ☐ Other _____
Your comments on this book will be appreciated. _____

Mail to:
Collectors' Information Bureau
2420 Burton S.E.
Grand Rapids, MI 49546
Phone (616) 942-6898
Fax (616) 942-8594